ST. MARY'S COLLEGE
LIBRARY

Date Due	Date Due	Date Due
16.21.	27.11.	ba.

ENCYCLOPEDIA OF SAINTS

CLEMENS JÖCKLE

PARKGATE
BOOKS

Jacket illustrations:
St George, St Francis of Assisi,
St Agnes and St Martin

Translated by
the German Translation Center

Published in 1997 for:

Parkgate Books Ltd
London House
Great Eastern Wharf
Parkgate Road
London SW11 4NQ
Great Britain

9 8 7 6 5 4 3 2 1

© 1997 by I.P. Verlagsgesellschaft
International Publishing GmbH, München

ISBN: 1-85585-520-8

Reprographics by Fotolito Longo, Frangart
Typeset by Satz & Repro Grieb, München
Printed and bound in Spain

Foreword

At the very heart of the Church, however many sinners it may embrace, stands sainthood. The whole community of baptised Christians is, in the words of the First Epistle of St Peter, "a chosen generation, a royal priesthood, an holy nation." For this reason the early Church did not elevate individual members. Yet the hallowed custom grew up, by which a feast was held in honour of a saint on the anniversary of his or her death or burial, because – and this first comes down to us in the writings of the Christians of Smyrna about the death of their bishop, Polycarp – the anniversary feast became important for the whole community. Underlying this was the notion that martyrs had the power of intercession.

From its earliest origins the saint's day is considered a celebration of Christ. It does not glorify the deceased, but rather Jesus Christ, who has accomplished his Resurrection in the struggle of every saint; this becomes clear when we note that, at the centre of the liturgy of the saint's day is not a reading of the acts of the martyrs, nor the *vitae sanctorum*, nor legends – the saint is scarcely addressed during the liturgy, other than in the church prayer – but the preaching of the Word of God.

The sanctity of all Christians is important to their congregation and to the entire church, when the pattern of their life in Christ takes on dimensions beyond the usual. This first occurred with the martyrs bearing witness with their own blood, when they proclaimed their faith to the last, and continued in the confessorship. In this way the image of the saint became as colourful and varied as human life itself. It remains evident that sanctity is a gift of God and the veneration of saints leads ultimately to praise of the grace of God.

This encyclopedia lists a selection of saints including all those contained in the Roman-Catholic General Calendar published on 21st March 1969, at the behest of Pope Paul VI, in his *Motu proprio, "Mysterii Paschalis"*. This forms part of the "Basic ordinance of the ecclesiastical year and calendar". A number other saints have been taken from the separate calendars of regional churches. Those selected enjoy a particular traditional veneration, have a rich iconography or are remarkable for some other reason. In a few rare cases saints are included, even though they have been removed from the official calendars. An example is the entry on St Christopher, who is greatly venerated as a helper in time of need.

The author is especially grateful to Dr Lothar Altmann, of I. P. Verlag, Munich, for suggesting the book and seeing it through to publication. Thanks also go to the translators of the foreign language editions.

Clemens Jöckle,
Speyer, Germany, on the Feast of St Stephen, King of Hungary

c.	=	circa
14C	=	14th century
esp.	=	especially
fig.	=	figure
form.	=	formerly
nr	=	near
OFM	=	Ordo Fratrum Minorum (Franciscan Order)
OP	=	Ordo Praedicatorum (Dominican Order)
orig.	=	originally
OST	=	Ordo Sanctissimae Trinitatis (Trinitarian Order)
S or St	=	saint
SJ	=	Societas Jesu (Jesuit Order)
SS	=	saints
var.	=	variant
Mk.	=	St Mark
Mt.	=	St Matthew
Jo.	=	St John
Lk.	=	St Luke
Cor.	=	Corinthians
Rev.	=	Book of Revelation
*	=	born
†	=	died

Achatius

(Acacius, Akakios, Agatus) and the 10,000 martyrs of Armenia,
martyr, saint

Feast-day: 22nd June

Legend: originated in the 12C on the model of the Theban Legion, to encourage crusaders, 1343 translated into German by Giselher von Slatheim: the pagan prince A. with his 9,000 soldiers is recruited by the Roman emperors Hadrian and Antoninus for a campaign in Asia Minor. – Angels promise A. victory if he prays to Christ. – After the victory, A. and his troops are conducted to Mount Ararat (Armenia) for instruction in the faith, where they live for 30 days on heavenly food and abjure paganism. – A. and his 10,000 men are baptised. – The mountain opens up, and A. and his troops see a vision of their martyrdom. – Hadrian and Antoninus recruit seven oriental kings against the renegades. – A. and his troops refuse to make pagan sacrifices and worship graven images. – The mob throw stones at A., which bounce off. – A. and his troops are beaten with cudgels, at which the earth begins to shake. – Fire sears the hands of their torturers. – Another 1,000 people are converted to Christianity. – The emperor makes A. and his 10,000 companions walk on nails (var: traps) but angels carry them over. – A. and his companions are scourged and crowned with thorns. The hands of the thugs wither as this happens. A. and his companions are crucified on Mount Ararat, whereupon the sun darkens and and the moon turns blood-red, and / or (var.) they are spiked on thorn-bushes. – Meanwhile, A. is blinded with an auger.

Patronage: invoked against the fear of death, strong religious doubts, terminal diseases. One of the 14 Holy Helpers.

Veneration and cult sites: under Pope Gregory XIII (1572–1585), admitted to the Martyrologium Romanum. Relics in Rome, Bologna, Avignon, Cologne, Berne, Engelberg (Switzerland) (12C) and Halle (Halle Heiltum, fol. 276v).

Superstitions: in the monastery of Engelberg, Switzerland, the relic of St A. was held up towards fires to put them out.

Representations in Art: *Apparel:* as a negro (Reisbach, Lower Bavaria, painting by the Danube School, c. 1520); knight (Strasbourg Cathedral, stained glass c. 1250), crusader nobleman with ducal hat or biretta (monastery of Nonnberg nr Salzburg, painting c. 1460); as venerable patriarch (Oberstadion, painting c. 1458); in a loincloth spiked on a thorn bush (St Stephan, Wiener Neustadt, painting from 2nd half of 15C). Depictions as a bishop result from confusion with A. of Malitene († 499) who spoke out against the

Nestorians at the Council of Ephesus in 431 (Dominican church, Maastricht, fresco 1337). *Attributes:* thorn bush, withered branch (St Stephan, Vienna, tomb of Friedrich c. 1500); thorn (Wallraf-Richartz Museum, Cologne, Holy Family altar c. 1500); crowned with thorns (Paris, Anne of Brittany's book of hours, early 15C); flag, spear (St Jakob, Bolzano, fig. c. 1500); sword (Cade, Saxony, wing of retable, c. 1500/10); battleaxe (Baar, Switzerland, charnel house of St Anna, 16C fig.); crusader banner (Pogstall, Austria, painting c. 1500); palm tree (Georgianum, Munich, Ambrase Collection, Innsbruck, painting 1515); cross, crucifix (Graphische Sammlung, Munich, 18C drawing by C. D. Asam). *Martyrdom:* Germ. Nationalmuseum, Nuremberg, predella of St Augustine altar, c. 1480; monastery church of Marienstern, Panschwitz-Kuckau, Saxony, wing of Magdalene altar c. 1525. *Cycles:* St Severin, Boppard, late 13C mural; Berne Cathedral, choir window by Nikolaus Magerfritz and Bernhard 1447; Kunsthalle, Hamburg, painting by Pontormo 1528/29.

Adalbert of Prague

(Vojtech) Bishop, martyr, saint

Feast-day: 23rd Apr (day of his martyrdom)
Life: * c. 956 in Libice, son of Prince Slavnik, educated in Magdeburg, 982 consecrated by Archbishop Willigis of Mainz as second bishop of Prague. A. twice left his diocese in protest against heathen practices, and lived as a Benedictine monk in Rome. 996 after the murder of his family by Vrsovecs, he returned to Poland and worked with the mission to East Prussia, where he was murdered by pagan Prussians on 23rd April. Duke Boleslav the Bold had A. buried in Gniezno Cathedral, where A. had been ordained. In 1000, Emperor Otto III went on a pilgrimage to A.'s tomb. In 1039, his relics were transferred to Prague as war booty and buried in St Vitus's Cathedral.

Legends: historical legends: A.'s election as bishop is announced by a demoniac who forces his way into the cathedral in Prague, after which the devil exits via the demoniac's mouth. – A. baptises King Stephen of Hungary. – 993 A. founds the monastery at Brevnov monastery. – A. blesses Bohemia.

Legends of miracles: during a drought, A. prays for rain for the land. – Through Duke Boleslav, A. frees two Christian boys. – A. protects an adulteress. – In Wielun, A. steps on the head of a serpent, and all serpents within one mile lose their heads and are turned to stone. – A. forbids frogs to stop croaking and disturbing his prayers.

Legends of martyrdom and death: A. is skewered on spits by Prussians in Kaliningrad / Königsberg (East Prussia) and beaten to death with an oar. – After the beheading, A.'s head is stuck on a pole. – Poland redeems his body from the pagans. – Pending the transfer to Gniezno, A.'s body is watched over by an eagle.

Legends after his death: A. and Jan Hus celebrate a mass (cf. painting in the castle gallery at Nelahozeves, Vltava, originally from Vlneves, c. 1520).

Patronage: patron saint of Bohemia, together with Prokop and Vaclav (Wenceslas).

Veneration and cult sites: tomb in St Vitus's Cathedral, Prague; relic of pyxis in Gniezno Cathedral. Main cult locations: Prague, Gniezno, Wroclaw, Bohemia, Silesia, Poland, Hungary, Germany and Italy.

Superstitions: particularly in Silesia, St A.'s Day is regarded as a day for a change in the weather: frogs stop croaking for as many days after the feast-day as they croaked before it. –

Water taken from wells located in the immediate vicinity of churches dedicated to St A. has special healing powers.

Representations in Art: *Apparel:* As a bishop in vestments with crosier and mitre (National Museum, Prague, votive picture of Ocko of Vlasim, c. 1370); as an archbishop with pallium (S Bartolomeo all' Isola Tiberina, Rome, 11C); as a monk in Benedictine habit (Karlstein castle, fresco 1357); bearded (since the 16C). *Attributes:* severed head (Gniezno Cathedral, reliquary 1494); oar (Corpus Christi church, Wroclaw, painting 1497); spits (Hrncir, Bohemia, 18C painting); banner (Schedel's World Chronicle, woodcut 1493); devil with cloven hoof under A.'s feet (St Adalbert, Aachen, fig. from 2nd half of 14C). *Cycles:* Gniezno, 18 reliefs on bronze doors of Cathedral, 1175. St Vitus, Prague, 10 reliefs on silver sarcophagus by Peter of Rennen, 1662.

Adrian of Nicomedeia

Roman officer, martyr, saint

Feast-day: 8th Sept (Martyriologium Hieronymianum 4th March, eastern Church 26th Aug)

Life: an officer in Nicomedeia under Emperor Galerius (305–311) and his co-ruler Maximian (285–305), he was martyred during the persecution of the Christians. His remains were transferred to Constantinople and (in 7C) to Rome.

Legends: A. persecutes 23 Christians, whose steadfastness converts him. – He refuses, in the face of Emperor Galerius, to sacrifice to the gods, is put in chains and imprisoned. – His wife Natalia, disguised in men's clothes as a secret Christian, takes care of her husband and fellow-believers in prison. – A.'s legs are smashed on an anvil and his arms chopped off with an axe, whereupon he dies. – Natalia secretly purloins one of A.'s arms. – Emperor Galerius tries to have the mortal remains of A. and his fellow-believers burnt, but heavenly rain extinguishes the fire. – Their bodies are taken to Constantinople. – Bearing A.'s arm, Natalia flees on a ship belonging to a tribune who lusts after her, and is protected on her journey by A., who makes the wind blow in the wrong direction, forcing the tribune's ship to return and driving away the devil who is trying to lead Natalia in the wrong direction to perdition. – Natalia attaches the arm to the body perserved in Constantinople, and thereupon dies.

Patronage: patron of Grammont nr Ghent and Lisbon, of soldiers, prison warders, executioners, smiths and messengers, in cases of sudden death and plague.

Veneration and cult sites: Byzantium (from 4C), Rome (since 7C), Grammont nr Ghent, Lisbon, the Netherlands (12C), France (12C).

Superstitions: on 3rd April (the original feast-day), St Adrian cakes (pancakes) should be eaten – presumably a Christian version of the antique custom of a procession in honour of the earth goddess on the same day, when people ate hot and greasy food.

Representations in Art: *Apparel:* in tunic and coat (11C Ellenhard sacramentary, Bamberg; Capella Palatina, Palermo, 12C); as a young warrior in armour (common in the Netherlands); in bourgeois clothes (Marienkirche, Lübeck, late 15C painting). *Attributes:* anvil (hospital of St John, wing of altar by Hans Memling, late 15C); sword (Sint-Lenaarts / St Leonard, stained glass 1544); axe (Landesmuseum, Hanover, wing of altar 1525); flag / banner with cross (library of S Marco, Venice, Grimani breviary, illumination 1475); severed hand (Marienkirche, Lübeck, late 15C painting); lion (Nellesen Collection, Aachen, late 15C altar painting); on a ram (Museum für Kunst u. Kunstgeschichte, Dortmund, 16C Lower Rhine fig.). *Martyrdom:* Stuttgart Passional, 1130; Landesbibliothek, Stuttgart, 12C Zwiefalten Martyrdom. *Cycles:* Institute of Art, Chicago, early 12C reliquary; National Library, Vienna, legend of St A. by the Mary of Burgundy miniaturist, 1483.

Aegidius

(Giles, Gilg, Gilles, Till) Hermit, abbot, saint
Feast-day: 1st Sept
Life: hermit in Provence, first abbot of the monastery of St-Gilles later named after him. † 720. Pilgrimages to his tomb since the 11C.
Legend: * in Athens to a royal house and had a good education, particularly of the scriptures. – On his way to church, A. gives his coat to a sick person. – A. drives out the demon from a demoniac screaming in church. – A. rescues a ship in distress, which in return takes him to Rome. In Arles, A. cures a women of fever. – A. withdraws to solitude in Vredemius in Provence. – A. withdraws completely from mankind to a secluded cave with a well. – A. lives on milk from a hind. – The animal is pursued by a hunting party of the Visigothic king Flavius Wamba and seeks protection with A. The dogs of the hunting party are unable to get near the cave.

A thoughtless huntsman injures A. with an arrow. The king and the bishop of Nîmes discover the wounded A. and found a monastery, where A. becomes abbot. – A. intercedes for Charles (originally Charles Martel, later transferred to Charlemagne) for his unshriven sins. An angel places Charles's receipted confession on the altar when A. reads mass. – In Nîmes, A. brings the son of the prince back to life. – Together with privileges for his monastery, A. receives from Pope Gregory two door-panels with apostle sculptures, which he throws into the Tiber and commends to God. The doors float by themselves to the port of St-Gilles, France, where he finds them on his return. – When another monk doubts the virginity of Mary and writes three questions in the sand, three white lilies spring up from barren soil as A.'s answer.
Patronage: patron saint of Carinthia and Styria; patron of the cities of Toulouse, Edinburgh, Osnabrück, Nuremberg, Brunswick; of archers, horse-dealers, shipwrecked people and nursing mothers. One of the 14 Holy Helpers (since 15C), invoked against infertility, leprosy, epilepsy, for good confessions and (in Alsace) against ear-ache.
Veneration and cult sites: tomb in St-Gilles, relics in St Sernin, Toulouse. In the Middle Ages, particularly venerated in politically disputed areas, e.g. Aachen (at Charlemagne's shrine), Chartres (stained glass), Edinburgh, Burgundy, Poland, Vienna (St John's coat of the Order of the Golden Fleece), as the patron saint of hospitals, and venerated all over Europe as a popular saint.
Superstition: an important day for changes of weather. A. creates the autumn, deciding its length, quality and wind direction. – A. keeps the weather steady for four weeks. On 1st September, in Spain a special blessing is read over fennel as a remedy for animals. In the diocese of Cologne, children who cry a lot are called "mewling Giles".

Representations in Art: *Apparel:* as a Benedictine abbot in a fleece coat (Parnkofen / Lower Bavaria, fig. c. 1510); with alb and chasuble (S Clemente, Rome, 11C fresco in lower church); in pluvial (Paul Arbaud Museum, Aix-en-Provence, painting c. 1450); in pontifical robes (National Museum, Copenhagen, mid–15C sculptural retable from Preetz). *Attributes:* abbot's crosier, rule book (gallery at Staatl. Museen, Berlin, altar painting besides a crucifixion scene, c. 1220); biretta (Hohenstadt, Lower Bavaria, fig. c. 1480); sometimes portrayed with mitre (Heiligenblut, Carinthia, early 16C fig.); pontificals (Lengmoos, Upper Bavaria, early 15C fig.); arrow, hind (Narodni Galeri, Prague, Wittingau altar c. 1380); A.'s breast pierced by an arrow (Esztergom Museum, painting by Thomas of Kolosvar 1427); A.'s hand and hind pierced by arrow (National Gallery, Washington, painting by St-Gilles Master). *Cycles:* Austrian National Library, mid–14C Krummau illuminated codex; scenes in voussoirs of south doorway of Chartres Cathedral, c. 1200; Victoria & Albert Museum, London, outer side of right wing of Apocalypse altar from the workshop of Master Bertram.

Afra of Augsburg
Martyr, saint
Feast-day: 7th Aug
Life: suffered martyrdom c. 304 during persecutions under Diocletian. Buried nr St Ulrich, Augsburg area, orig. in a tomb.
Legend: * the daughter of the king of Cyprus. – A. dreams that she will become the queen of Augsburg, and moves to Augsburg with her mother. – A. runs a brothel. – Bishop Narcissus of Gerona, reaching Augsburg during the persecution of Christians, innocently lodges in with A., who is converted by the grace at mealtimes. – A. hides St Narcissus from pursuers under a bundle of flax. – A.

is baptised and becomes a Christian. – A. refuses to worship graven images. – A. suffers martyrdom by fire, bound to a tree by the River Lech. – A.'s mother Hilaria builds a chapel for the tomb of her daughter. – After their conversion, Hilaria and her maids (Eunomia, Eutropia and Digna) are burned alive in their house (private chapel in bishop's palace, Eichstätt, painting by Holbein the Elder 1490). – In a dream, A. leads St Ulrich to a synod on the banks of the R. Lech convened by St Peter against Duke Arnulf the Wicked. – Mosquitoes defend the tomb of St Narcissus in Gerona when troops fighting Pedro III of Aragon, try to plunder it.
Patronage: prostitutes, penitents, lost souls, medicinal herbs, fire.
Veneration and cult sites: buried since the 8C in St A., Augsburg. Cult and pilgrimage historically recorded since 565. 1012 Benedictine monastery of St Ulrich & St Afra, where 1064 her sarcophagus was allegedly found again. Dedications at numerous churches and chapels, incl. Le Mans, Neresheim Abbey, Maidbronn nr Würzburg, Speyer Cathedral.
Superstition: herbs stored in St Afra's Tower, Augsburg are protected against vermin. – In Anhalt, the magic spell "Afra nostra" makes shotguns malfunction (presumably more an onomatopeic than a real connection with St Afra).
Representations in Art: *Apparel:* dressed as a contemporary lady of rank. *Attributes:* head covering as a sign of penitence (Landesmuseum, Stuttgart, Zwiefalten Martyrium c. 1147); the crown of a king's daughter (Victoria & Albert Museum, London, dedication page in Augsburg psaltery by Georg Beck, 1495); palm tree, ointment container in allusion to the attributes of the penitent Mary Magdalene (Freiburg Minster, 13C stained glass; pyre, pile of burning wood (Nonnberg Monastery, Salzburg, painting c. 1500); tree (Rechbergreuthen, fig, c. 1490); pillar to

S, AFRA M.

which A. is tied (Schedel's World Chronicle, woodcut 1493); burning pile of wood (Frankfurt Cathedral, Striegel altar, 1505); withered brushwood (St Stephan, Vienna, ducal chapel, mid–15C fig.); rope as sign of fetters (Ulm Cathedral, choir stalls, relief 1474); bundle of flax (Wallraf-Richartz Museum, Cologne, 15C wing of St Thomas retable by the Master of the Bartholomy Altar); arolla pine nut as sign of the saint's origin, taken from the Augsburg coat of arms. *Cycles:* Landesbibliothek, Stuttgart, Stuttgart Passional c. 1130; St Jakob, Straubing, 15C reliefs; Valencia Cathedral, painting c. 1500 (in connection with St Narcissus).

Agatha of Catania

Martyr, saint

Feast-day: 5th Feb (other feast-days, 5th, 12th, 25th July / 5th Oct / 6th Dec).

Life: A. came from a noble Sicilian family and suffered martyrdom during the persecution of Christians by the emperor Decius.

Legend: A. refuses a proposal of marriage by the city prefect Quintian. – A. is handed over to a procuress, who gives her an aphrodisiac, but she succeeds in preserving her chastity. – A. does not renounce her Christian faith and so is tortured. – Her breasts are cut off, whereupon St Peter appears and heals her. – A. is rolled naked over hot coals mixed with sharp splinters of glass, and dies. – During A's funeral a youth appears, who places a marble tablet in the coffin bearing the inscription "Mentem sanctam, spontaneam, honorem Deo et patriae liberationem". A is crowned in heaven. – Quintian is thrown into the river by his own horse. – When Etna erupts on the anniversary of A.'s death, the stream of lava is stopped when A.'s veil is carried up to the lava (Ingstetten, fresco by K. Huber, 1791). A. cures the sick mother of St Lucy.

Patronage: patron saint of Catania. Invoked against volcanic eruptions, fire, earthquakes. Patron saint of bellfounders, goldcasters, goldsmiths, blast-furnace workers and miners, weavers, nursemaids, the hungry, invoked against diseases of the breast and inflammations.

Veneration and cult sites: buried in Catania. Relic of veil in Florence Cathedral.

Superstition: St A. candles protect household goods from fire. Bread blessed in the bakery on the eve of St A. (4th Feb) protects newly bought animals in the stalls and all animals on their first visit to the pasture, and also makes calving easier. – On the River Isar, people with diseases of the breast are given St A. bread. – St A. bread protects the land from disease and vermin. – St A. bread helps the farmer to assess the future yield of a newly sown crop. – St A. bread in a butter churn speeds up the churning process. – If St A. bread is goes mouldy, somebody in the house will die. – St A. bread thrown into water shows where somebody has drowned. – St A. bread im relieves homesickness. – St A. bread provides protection on a dangerous journey. – St A. bread keeps servants chaste. – St A. bread protects against evil spirits and witches. – St A. bread is a protection against fire, and burns if thrown into the fire. – Special blessing spells (St A. notes) are thrown into the fire to put it out. – In Weizen, Baden, infertile women go on a pilgrimage on St A.'s Day. – Anyone drinking holy water on St A.'s Day will not be bitten by a snake. – In the Czech Republic, geese are kept in on St A.'s Day to stop them running into other stalls.

Representations in Art: *Apparel:* with long, belted robe and coat in the antique manner (S Apollinare in Classe, Ravenna, 6C mosaic) or according to contemporary fashion, sometimes with veil or half-naked (Palazzo Pitti, Florence, painting by Sebastino del Piombo 1520). *Attributes:* pincers as instrument of torture (Wiesenkirche, Soest, St Aldegrave altar, 16C fig.); crown in covered hands (catacomb of S Gennaro, Naples, fresco post–763); palm tree (Wallraf-Richartz Museum, Cologne, 15C painting); torch (St Stephan, Vienna, bishops' gate, end of 14C); Tortsche = spiral-shaped candle (Landesmuseum, Darmstadt, painting from 1st half of 15C); bread (St Lorenz Chapel, Rottweil, fig. c. 1510); severed breasts on a cord (Archbishop's Palace, Fermo, 15C painting); breasts lying on a book (Schnutgen Museum, Cologne, late 14C relief); breasts in a bowl (Musée Fabre, Montpellier, painting by F. Zurbaran 1630/32); breast wounds (Pinacoteca, Naples, 17C painting by Massimo Stanzione); one of the undamaged breasts placed on a plate (Valladolid Cathedral, 18C fig.). *Martyrdom:* Landesmuseum, Stuttgart,

Stuttgart Passional c. 1130. *Cycles:* St A., Castoreale, predella c. 1420; St A. Chapel, Disentis, mural 1430/40; St A., Cremona, altar retable c. 1400, 16C frescoes; St A., Florence, 16C frescoes by Giovanni Bizelli; Agatharied (Upper Bavaria), late 15C triptych; Clermont-Ferrand Cathedral, 13C stained glass.

Agnes of Rome
Virgin, martyr, saint

Feast-day: 21st Jan (date of burial), 28th Jan (vision of Agnes with the lamb). In the Eastern Church 5th July.

Life: A. came from a noble Roman family and suffered martyrdom as a young woman, either under Emperor Diocletian (304) or even earlier, under Valerian (258/59).

Legends: the 13-year-old A. refuses the courtship of a city prefect's son. – A. is betrothed to Christ with a golden ring. – A. is recognized as a Christian and brought to court. – A. is brought naked to a brothel but long hair covers her body like a coat. – An angel clothes A. in a robe of light, which illuminates the brothel. – The city prefect's lovesick son touches A.'s body and dies (var. is strangled by an evil spirit). – A. asks God to bring the prefect's son back to life, which comes to pass. – A. is thrown by another judge into the fire, which goes out. – A. suffers martyrdom by a having a sword thrust through her body (var.: throat). – Pagans molest the Christians during A.'s funeral by throwing stones. – A.'s adopted sister Emerentiana, a catechumen, is stoned by pagans as she watches over A.'s grave. – The pagans are killed by an earthquake, accompanied by thunder and lightning. – After eight days a virgin's wreath appears on A.'s grave, and below it, Agnes with a lamb. – At A.'s grave, Constantia, the daughter of Empress Helena, is cured of leprosy. – In Rome, Constantia founds the church of S Agnese fuori le mura, built over A.'s grave. – A. appears to St Martin of Tours with SS Thecla, Peter and Paul. – By order of the pope, Paulinus, the priest of S Agnese, tormented by strong unchaste temptations, marries the portrait of St A. by exchanging rings to ensure that sinful temptation is removed from him.

Patronage: Order of the Holy Trinity, virgins, children, engaged couples, hostels for female workers, gardeners.

Veneration and cult sites: S Agnese fuori le mura, Rome (the church over the grave was founded in the 4C by Constantia, rebuilt 624–638); S Agnese in Agone, Rome (location of her martyrdom), built 8C, rebuilt 1652 by Borromini; 966 transfer of the relics to Utrecht; 1048 by order of Pope Damasus II, transfer to Brixen, the Netherlands and Germany.

Superstitions: St A.'s Day is an important day, heralding the first spring larks and swarming bees. – During the night before her feast-day, A. shows young women their future husbands in their dreams, if they have fasted previously. – Chickens lay well if they receive the first small cake from a pan on A.'s feast-day.

Representations in Art: *Apparel:* robed in the antique manner (Cimitero de Panfilo, Rome, 4C gilt glass); in a long, belted robe and cloak wrapped loosely around her body, partly in contemporary fashion (Ulm Minster, early 16C retable fig.); her body covered by her hair (Gemäldegalerie Alter Meister, Dresden, painting by J. de Ribera, 1641). *Attributes:* a martyr's crown on her head (S Maria Antiqua, Rome, mural 817–824); a martyr's crown on a cloth (S Prassede, Rome, early 9C mosaic); a martyr's crown, held by God the Father over her head, a scroll, sword, fire at her feet (S Agnese fuori le mura, Rome, 7C mosaic); a peacock feather (Wallraf-Richartz Museum, Cologne, 15C painting by the master of the Ursula Legend); palm tree (St Dionysius, Esslingen, late 13C

The Virgin Mary and the archangels

1   *All Saints, by Albrecht Dürer, Vienna, Kunsthistorisches Museum*

2   *Archangel Michael, by Hubert Gerhard, Munich, St Michael's church*

3   *Archangel Gabriel, mosaic, Istanbul, Hagia Sophia*

4   *Annunciation of the Virgin, by Simone Martini, Florence, Uffizi*

5   *Birth of the Virgin, by Albrecht Altdorfer, Munich, Alte Pinakothek*

6   *Adoration of the Kings, door relief, Cologne, Sta Maria im Kapitol*

7   *Holy Family, by Martin Schongauer, Vienna, Kunsthistorisches Museum*

8   *Immaculata Virgin, by Giambattista Tiepolo, Madrid, Prado*

1

2

3

4

5

6

stained glass); a lily and a burning lamp as embodiment of the wise virgin (Oratorium S Silvestio at S Martino ai monti, Rome, early 13C mosaic; a lamb (S Apollinare Nuovo, Ravenna, 6C mosaic); a lamb with crusader flag (Cathedral Museum, Siena, Maesta by Duccio 1311); raised bridal ring (Cathedral Treasury, Münster, fig. c. 1520). *Special scenes:* mystic betrothal of St Agnes with the Christ-child (Kereszteny Muzeum, Esztergom (Hungary), painting from 2nd half of 15C); mystic engagement with lamb representing Christ (Sinzenich, fig. c. 1500). *Martyrdom:* by stabbing (Lateran church, chapel of S Lorenzo, fresco 1277–1280); by beheading (Passau Cathedral, painting by J. M. Rottmayr 1694). *Cycles:* S Maria di Donna, Naples, mid–14C fresco; S Teodoro, Pavia, 16C fresco; British Museum, London, gold chalice for Charles V of France, 1381.

Albertus Magnus

OP, bishop, Doctor of the Church, saint
Feast-day: 15th Nov (date of death)
Life: * before 1200 in Lauingen, the son of a knight of the house of Bollstatt. 1223 entered the Dominican order in Padua, moved to Cologne, 1228 began teaching in Hildesheim, Freiburg im Breisgau, Regensburg and Strasbourg. 1243–1244 magister at the theological faculty in Paris, 1248–1254 in Cologne, 1254 Dominican Provincial of Germany, 1260–1262 bishop of Regensburg, 1264–1266 in Würzburg, 1268 in Strasbourg, from 1270 in Cologne. † 15th Nov, 1280. An important writer and preacher for the crusades, teacher of St Thomas Aquinas and Ulrich of Strasbourg. Buried in St Andreas, Cologne. Beatified in 1622, canonized 1931. 1954 remains transferred from a Gothic to a Roman stone sarcophagus.
Legends: A., who is a bad pupil, receives wisdom in a vision of the mother of God. – A. predicts the greatness of his pupil St Thom-

as Aquinas. – With his knowledge of magic, A. helps to abduct a king's daughter from France. – A. climbs up on a ball thrown in the air. – A. has a magic cup (var.: magic sack), with which he cures the sick. – A. rides to Rome on the the Devil's back. – In St Peter's, A. conjures up serpents. – During a visit by King William of Holland, A. makes flowers bloom in the middle of winter. – Shortly before his death, his knowledge deserts him, making him realise that it too is a divine gift. – In his later years, A. lives as an hermit. – St A.'s body is blessed by Bishop Siegfried of Westerburg. – Gottfried of Duisburg appears over St A.'s grave.
Patronage: miners, naturalists (since 1941).
Veneration and cult sites: St Andreas, Cologne, pilgrimages beginning shortly after his death; relics in Lauingen (top of head) and Regensburg (shoulderblade); Dominican Order; patron saint of Cologne University. In Westphalia and in the former diocese of Salzburg there are 'Alberti panels', whose

nine double paintings illustrate examples and counterparts of A.'s doctrine of virtue based on good deeds pleasing to God.

Superstition: many magic books are wrongly connected with A., e.g. "Egyptian Mysteries for Humans and Animals".

Representations in Art: *Apparel:* in Dominican habit with cassock tunic, scapular and open cap with hood (Dominican church, Wimpfen, fig. 1737); scapular, pluvial and mitre (Cologne, woodcut in Rudolfus de Noviomagio, Legenda Litteralis, 1480); in pontifical vestments (St Andreas, Cologne, tomb fig. 1671); as a scholar (Cologne University, fig. by G. Marcks 1956); sitting at a writing desk (chapter house, Treviso, painting by Tomaso da Modena 1352); as a preacher (Cologne Town Hall, 19C tower by A. Iven). *Attributes:* mitre, book, crosier (Kelheim parish church, fig. c. 1460); rejecting the mitre (Friesach, early 18C painting); pointing to a Dominican monastery (St Andreas, Cologne, painting by J. Hulsmann); quill (Collegiate Library, Klosterneuburg, the initial U in A.'s commentary on 14C Gospel of St Luke, MS 35 fol. 1); putto with quill (Dominican Church, Landshut, fig. at the high altar, 1760). *Cycles:* Cologne, Legenda litteralis, woodcuts 1480; Uffizi, Florence, painting by Fra Angelico (school); castle chapel, Racconigi, 19C stained glass; Alberti chapel, Regensburg, 19C painting by Altheimer.

Alexis of Edessa
Confessor, saint

Feast-day: 17th July (eastern Church 17th March, Syrian Monophysites 12th March)

Life: the Syrian vita was written between 450 and 475. According to this, * the son of wealthy Roman parents and, after a long discussion with his bride, left her on their wedding night to go on a pilgrimage to the Holy Land. † as a hermit in Edessa.

Legends: in Edessa, A. is venerated as a saint during his lifetime, after the sexton of the church has a vision of the holiness of the beggar. – A. flees on a ship. – Contrary winds blow the ship to Rome. – His father, the Roman senator Euphemius, fails to recognize him and gives him shelter as a beggar. – Unrecognized, A. lives beneath the cellar stairs in his father's house. – His father's servants bring him food. – A maid empties washing-up water over A. – During mass, a voice and peal of bells call on the congregation to search for a saint in the city. – After A.'s death, a letter he has left is deciphered by the Pope, revealing the origin of the beggar (var.: at the news of his imminent demise, the Pope finds a letter to his father in the hands of the dying A., in which he makes himself known). – A servant with a torch finds A.'s body. – Several people are healed by touching A's body. – A. is buried in the church of St Boniface (418–422).

Patronage: Alexians, Brotherhood for the Care of Sick and Mentally Disturbed Persons (based in Aachen), Beghards, Beguines, pilgrims, beggars, vagabonds (Lower Austria), the sick, girdlers; invoked against earthquakes, lightning and bad weather (Augsburg), epidemics (Paderborn) and plague (Bad Hall salt-water spa).

Veneration and cult sites: tomb in SS Bonifacio e Alessio, Rome; relics brought by St Adalbert of Prague to Brevnov, Prague; relics in S Niccolo presso Olitono, Rome; Polling nr Weilheim. Patron of Alexian Order; 2nd patron of city of Innsbruck. In the late Middle Ages, the patron of numerous leprosy chapels, e.g. in Freising. Side chapels under galleries as in Prien (Chiemsee), Prüfening. Altar dedications formerly in Tegernsee (1324), Beguine hermitage, Speyer (1377), Waldsassen, St Peter (Munich), Scheyern, Heiligkreuz nr Vienna. St Alexis staircases in many convents, e.g. St Walburg (Eichstätt), Säben, Landshut, Seligenthal, Maria

Medingen, Bad Wörishofen, Ursuline convent (Vienna).

Superstition: On St Alexis's Day, corn ears open when it rains.

Representations in Art: *Apparel:* in hermit clothes (Monreale Cathedral, 12C mosaic); as a naked ascetic (Recklinghausen Icon Museum, 17C Russian icon); dressed as a pilgrim (Breisach Cathedral, 15C stone fig. at Lettner). *Attributes:* book (Oberbiberg, Upper Bavaria, late 17C fig.); pilgrim's staff (Kriebstein – Saxony, 16C painting); alms basket (Carmelite Church, Boppard, late 15C mural); bowl with spoon (Brandenburg Cathedral, high altar retable, c. 1400); staircase, asleep underneath (Stadtpfarrkirche, Donauwörth, fig. by Gregor Erhart 1503); stairs with maid pouring water from a slop bucket (pulpit in Strasbourg Cathedral, late 15C fig.); stairs held in the hand (Bad Oberdorf, altar painting c. 1490); Brevnov Monastery, Prague, fig. by J. J. Steinfels c. 1690); letter (Kriebstein, Saxony, 16C painting); scroll (Wallraf-Richartz Museum, Cologne, altar retable, 2nd half of 15C). *Cycles:* S Godehard, Hildesheim, 11C book illumination; S Clemente, Rome, lower church, 11C fresco; Frauenkirche, Esslingen, fresco c. 1340.

Aloysius Gonzaga

SJ, saint

Feast-day: 21st June (translation day 25th June).

Life: * 1568 in Castiglione delle Stiviere, the eldest son of Ferdinand Gonzaga, marquis of Mantua-Castiglione; 1581–1583 page at the court of Philip II of Spain. Devotion and penance induced him to reject his inheritance. 1581 admitted to the Society of Jesus, noviciate in Rome. † 1591 aged 23 years after catching an infection caring for plague victims. Buried in S Ignazio, Rome, canonized in 1726.

Legends: A. receives first holy communion from S Carlo Borromeo. – A. flees from court after refusing an order to kiss a girl's shadow. – A. learns in a vision that he will die within a year after a strict penance. – A. and St Antony of Padua are shown the way to heaven by the Archangel Gabriel.

Patronage: Mantua, county of Castiglione, young students (since 1729), invoked against the plague and diseases of the eye.

Veneration and cult sites: tomb in S Ignazio, Rome, head relic in Castiglione. Patron saint of numerous seminaries and youth congregations.

Superstitions: protective prayers for horses at St-Alar in Lower Brittany; in Bavaria, often confused with St Eloi because of the dialect pronunciation of both names as "Loisl".

Representations in Art: *Apparel:* in princely raiment with prince's hat (Heiligenkreuz church, Landsberg (Lech), painting by C. T. Scheffler 1754); dressed as a Jesuit novice with cassock and super-pelliceum. *Attributes*: lily, scourge, skull, crucifix (City Museum, Mannheim, fig. by Paul Egell 1750); with the Christ-child in his arms (Prague, fig. by Matthias Braun); in the angelic gloria (S Ignazio, Rome, relief by Pierre Legros II 1698/99). *Cycles*: Augsburg, mid–18C sequence of copper engravings by Göz-Klauber; otherwise individual scenes.

Alphege of Canterbury

(Aelfheah, Elphege, Elphegus) archbishop, martyr, saint

Feast-day: 19th April

Life: Born in 953; monk in Deerhurst, diocese of Worcester; founded the abbey of Bath and was appointed abbot; in 984, A. became bishop of Winchester, in 1006 archbishop of Canterbury. During the Danish invasion, A. suffered his martyrdom in 1012.

Veneration and cult sites: Buried in St Paul's Cathedral, London; translated to Canterbury in 1023; relics in Bath, Glastonbury, Ramsey, Reading, Durham, York Minster, Westminster Abbey.

Representation in Art: *Apparel*: as bishop in pontifical vestments with mitre (Oxford, New College, ante-chapel, stained glass, circa 1380/86); dressed as Benedictine monk (Oxford, Bodleian Library Tanner MS 17, book illumination, early 15th century). *Attributes*: palm branch, crosier (Private Collection, portable shrine, relief, circa 1200); stone (Wells Cathedral, figure, 13th century); axe, stones (Oxford, Bodleian Library Tanner MS 17, book illumination, early 15th century). *Martyrdom*: A. naked on a beach before a ship, murdered (copperplate engraving by J. J. Ebersbach, in: J. Giulini, Daily Edification of a true Christian, Augsburg, 1754, 323); A's beheading (Paris, Bibliothèque Nationale MS lat.17294, book illumination, circa 1424/1435). *Cycles*: Canterbury Cathedral, stained glass, circa 1200.

Alphonsus Liguori

Bishop, Redemptorist, Doctor of the Church

Feast-day: 2nd Aug

Life: * 1696 in Marianelle nr Naples, 1713 graduated in both branches of the law, worked as a lawyer, 1724 gave up his work to become a monk, 1726 ordained, forerunner of modern lay apostolate, 1730/31 co-founder of the Order of the Holy Redeemer in Scala nr Amalfi, 1732 foundation of the Congregation of the Holy Redeemer (Bohemia), 1749 papal approval of Order, which devoted itself to popular evangelism, 1762 Bishop of S Agata de' Goti nr Naples, 1766 foundation of an institution for nuns, 1775 relinquished his see to write on theological matters. † 1787 in the monastery of Pagani nr Naples, where he is buried. 1838 beatified, 1871 elevated to Doctor of the Church for his writings on moral theology.

Patronage: lay apostolate.

Veneration and cult sites: Redemptorists, Pagani nr Naples, S Agata de' Goti.

Representations in Art: *Apparel*: as a young priest in a cassock (Pagani, painting 1768); in Redemptorist dress, bent double because of gout (devotional picture, Czech Republic). *Attributes*: Cross.

Amand of Maastricht

Bishop, Benedictine, saint

Life: * c. 594 in the Nantes area, Benedictine monk, hermit nr Bourges, bishop of Maastricht 647–649; at times with the mission in Tyrol and Salzburg, founder of numerous abbeys and churches in Flanders all dedicated to St Peter. † 679 or 684 in Elno.

Legends: in A.'s legend vita written by his pupil Baudemundus, A. is originally a monk on the island of Ogia near La Rochelle, where he chases away an exceptionally large snake with the sign of the cross. – For 15 years, A. lives as a hermit on water and barley bread. – On a journey to Rome, A. has a vision in which St Peter issues the order to begin a mission to Gaul. – A. brings back an executed man to life to prove that God is more gracious than a worldly judge. – A. frees prisoners. – A. escapes attempts on his life by enemies who lure him to a mountain to kill him, whereupon God sends a storm over them. – A. introduces St Bavo into the monastery. – A. charges King Dagobert with misdeeds, is banished by him, but is soon recalled. – He baptises Sigisbert, son of Dagobert. – The baby Sigisbert answers St A. during baptism with 'amen'. – A. minstrel who mocks A. is possessed by an evil spirit and dies miserably. – St Adelgundis of Maubeuge sees St A. ascend to heaven.

Patronage: apostle of Belgium, patron saint of Flanders, Maastricht, Utrecht, Salzburg and wine dealers.

Veneration and cult sites: buried in St Peter, Salzburg (transferred in the 8C by St Rupert); Belgium, Worms.

Representations in Art: *Apparel:* as a bishop in vestments mostly with mitre and/or crosier (St Peter, Salzburg, shrine fig. 1446); as a preacher (St Paul, Antwerp, outer section of the Raising of the Cross by P. P. Rubens). *Attributes:* snake (St Peter, Salzburg, silver statuette c. 1750); model of a church (Lille Museum, 16C seated fig.). *Cycles:* Bibliothèque Municipale, Valenciennes, MS 501 c. 1175; London Victoria and Albert Museum, late 13C reliefs on reliquary by Hugo of Oignes. *Special scenes:* baptism of Sigisbert (St Niklaas, Ghent, 16C painting by Jan van Cleve; transfer of relics (St Peter, Salzburg, ceiling painting by F. X. König 1757).

Ambrose of Milan

Bishop, confessor, one of four great western Doctors of the Church, saint
Feast-day: 7th Dec (day of his baptism)
Life: * 333/34 or 339/40 in Trier, the son of the praefectus praetoris Galliarum, after the death of his father returned with his mother to Rome, where he was educated in rhetoric and law. By 370, A. was Consularis Liguriae et Aemiliae in Milan. 374 in the dispute between Catholics and Arians over the election of bishops, A., catechumen at the time, wanted by virtue of his office to restore order and was the surprise choice of both parties as bishop of Milan. 382 at A.'s instigation, the statue of Victoria, removed under Gratian from the debating chamber of the Roman senate, was not put back again despite the pagan majority in the senate led by Rhetor Symmachus. A. prevented the attempts of the Arian emperor's mother Justina to give Arianism more prestige by assigning a Milan church. In the synods at Aquileia (381) and Rome (382), A. ensured that Arianism was pushed back into Illyria. A. enforced the Church's demand that Emperor Theodosius do penance after the emperor ordered the death of 7000 people following a rebellion in Thessaloniki. Amongst his writings written for pastoral purposes, there are exegeses, homilies and catechisms, and a work on Christian ethics. A. distinguished himself through his courageous and aggressive defence of the freedom of the Church against every attempt by the state to interfere. He wrote polemical treatises against Arianism, Sabelius and Eunomius. In addition, A. wrote and composed many hymns, such as "Aeterne rerum conditor". † 4th April, 397, buried in S Ambrogio, Milan.

Legends: A. swarm of bees settle in the mouth of the newborn A. – During the election of the bishop, a child calls out his name. – A. flees, to try to avoid being elected bishop. – A. castigates the Arians. – A. refuses Emperor Theodosius entry to the church and gives him absolution only after he does penance. – Completely lost in reverie, A. celebrates the funeral mass of St Martin. – A. finds the bodies of SS Gervase and Protase and consecrates the relics. – A. leads Dona-

tor to the Christ-child. – A. crowns Bishop Angilbert II of Milan. – A. revives the child Pansophius. – A. saves a house from flooding. – A. cures a demoniac. – An Arian heretic sees an angel whisper in A.'s ear during a sermon. – At the dwelling of a wealthy Tuscan, Ambrose flees from the sins of the house, and a little later the wealthy man is swallowed up by the earth. – During a mass, A. cures St Nicetas. – A. disputes with St Augustine, and converts and baptises him along with his son Adeodat. – An angel predicts A.'s death to Bishop Honoratus of Vercellae. – A. brandishes a whip during a battle of the Milanese against Emperor Ludwig of Bavaria.

Patronage: patron saint of Milan and Bologna, candlemakers, bee-keepers, gingerbread makers and stonemasons.

Veneration and cult sites: 789 Benedictine abbey erected over his grave in Milan. The anniversary of his death (4th April) is called Brosia Day, when in academic schools in Italy a school bishop is elected by the children and a children's festival is held.

Superstitions: A.'s hymn "Obduxere polum nubila coeli" is sung during drought or constant rain to pray for better weather.

Representations in Art: *Apparel:* long tunic and simple cloak, with a cross at the breast (S Ambrogio, Milan, chapel of S Vittore); as a bishop with pluvial (St Peter, Salzburg, late 15C painting); as a bishop in the scriptorium (Eremitani, Padua, 15C fresco by Niccolo Pizzolo); as a teacher and Doctor of the Church (S Maria Antiqua, Rome, mural); as a bystanding figure of authority during the birth of Jesus in questions of the Immaculate Conception (Gemäldegalerie, Dresden, 17C painting by Dosso Dossi) and in the Mariology (Catholic Academy, Trier, stained glass by H. Dieckmann, 1933); in portrayals of theological disputes, as an advocate of divine revelation and the Eucharist (Vatican, Rome, Stanza Disputa by Raphael 1508). *Attrib-*

utes: cross (Bibliotheca Ambrosiana, Milan, cod. graec. 89); book, crosier, whip (Wallraf-Richartz Museum, Cologne, painting in the St Thomas altar 1499); a quill and dove as a sign of divine inspiration (Milan, S Ambrogio ciborium, 12C tympanon sculpture); model of a church (Sacristia de Santiago, Bilbao, fig. 1545); child in the cradle (Alte Pinakothek, Munich, Elders of the Church retable by Michael Pacher 1483); thrusting his crosier into the mouth of a chieftain kneeling at his feet (Chartres, south doorway, left hand figs. c. 1215/20); beehive (monastery church at Waldsassen, fig. c. 1700). *Cycles:* S Ambrogio, Milan, 9C wrought Paliotto reliefs); 12C apsidal mosaic in S Ambrogio, Milan; St Catherine chapel in upper church of S Clemente, Rome, by Masolino, pre–1431.

Andrew

Apostle, martyr, saint

Feast-day: 30th Nov, 9th May (translation day)

Life: * in Bethesda, the son of a fisherman called Jonas. A. lived in Capernaeum and was a follower of John the Baptist before being called by Christ as his first disciple (synoptic gospels). Along with Peter, James the Elder and St John, he is one of the first four disciples of Christ. He is mentioned by name in the Feeding of the 5,000 (Jo. 6, 8–9), in Christ's resurrection speech (Mk. 13,3), when Jesus foretells His death (Jo. 12, 20–22) and when the Holy Spirit descends (Acts). Early Christian writers such as Gregory of Nazianzus, Theodoret, Nicephorus, Origen and Jerome mention Pontus, Bithynia, the Balkans, Thrace, Greece, Epirus and Achaea as particular sites of A.'s missionary and preaching career. † 60/62 martyred on the cross, presumably in Patras under Governor Aegeas.

Legends: A. preaches to the Scythians. – An angel leads A. to a ship, which brings him to St Matthew in Murgundia (var.: Mirmidonia). – A. finds the prison door open and heals the disfigured face (var.: blindness) of St Matthew. – The people of Murgundia drag the bound A. through their town. – A. converts them and goes to Antioch. – The parents of a young nobleman who follows A. against their wishes set fire to A.'s house, but thanks to A.'s help the youth is able to put out the fire with a glass of water. – When they try to enter the house with a ladder, the young man's parents are blinded and die five days later. – A. converts and rescues the pregnant wife of a murderer who cannot give birth and has called on the goddess Diana. – A. drives away the sins of a lustful man called Nicolas by fasting for five days, which the sinner has to maintain for six months. – A beautiful young man requests A.'s assistance in combating the incestuous approaches of his mother and her unjust accusations before a judge. – The judge orders the young man to be put into a sack with tar and to be thrown it into the river. When A. intercedes, he is thrown into prison. – After A.'s prayer, an earth tremor throws everyone to the ground, lightning strikes and burns the evil woman to death. The judge is converted. – In Nicaea, A. drives out seven demons and revives a young man killed by the demons after they were driven out of town in the shape of dogs. – A. brings forty shipwrecked people back to life. – In Constantinople, A. as the "founder of Byzantium" appoints Stachys as the first patriarch at the Church of St Mary on the Acropolis. – A. builds churches in Achaea. – A. baptises Maximila, the wife of Aegeas, governor of Patras. In a dispute with learned men, A. remains steady in his faith. – Aegeas has A. scourged (by 21 soldiers) and tied to a slow death on a saltire cross.- Hanging on the cross, A. preaches for two days to the people. – When soldiers go to torment A.'s body on the cross, their arms are suddenly paralysed. – A divine light shrouds the dying A. – When Aegeas mocks A., he is struck by madness and dies on his way home. – Maximila buries A. honourably. – Manna flows from A.'s grave. – Disguised as a pilgrim, A. rescues the bishop from the lures of the Devil disguised as a woman. – A. helps a bishop whose church has had property taken from it unjustly, by inflicting illness and sudden death on the usurper.

Patronage: Order of the Golden Fleece (founded 1429 by Philip the Good), the Scottish King James's Order of St Andrew (instituted 1540), Order of St Andrew of Czar Peter I (founded 1698), Russia, Greece, Burgundy, Spain, Scotland, Sicily, Lower Austria; Naples, Ravenna, Brescia, Amalfi, Mantua, Manila, Bruges, Bordeaux, Patras. Patron saint of fishermen, fishmongers, ropemakers, butchers, watercarriers, spinsters, mines, weddings; invoked against gout, sore throats, matrimonial infertility.

Veneration and cult sites: feast day since the 4C; 357 relics transferred to Church of the Apostles, Constantinople, 1208 relics in Ravenna (since 6C), Milan, Brescia, Nola, Amalfi (1208 by Cardinal Peter of Capua), sandal of St A. in Trier (by Bishop Egbert, end of 10C), right hand in Moscow (13C), Siegburg, Servatius treasure, St Andrew's Chest (early 13C), Patras, head relic, 1462 transferred to Rome by Pius II, 1964 returned by Paul VI, another head relic in Pienza. Tooth relic in Namur. Relics of St A.'s cross in Beaune nr Marseille, Abbey of St Victor, and Palace Chapel, Brussels; early dedications in 5C archbishop's chapel, Ravenna, St Andrew's Monastery, Rome c. 600 (on Coelius Hill). Particularly venerated in Austria, Spain, Würzburg (cathedral previously dedicated to A.).

Superstitions: Eve of St Andrew's is a fateful day for young women eager to marry because their future husband will appear to them if

they pray and do various things (depending on region and usually completely naked), e.g. if they sweep their rooms with a new broom while naked, if they step on a piece of silver on the floor of in their room while naked, if they look up the chimney naked etc. But if, on St A.'s Day, a young man or woman sees a coffin behind a tree, she/he remains single. – Children suffering from a cough embrace the saint's statue on St A.'s Day. – On St A.'s Eve, hidden treasures can be found more easily.

Representations in Art: *Apparel:* long, belted tunic and pallium, reinterpreted from the Middle Ages as a close-fitting cloak drawn tight at the throat, barefooted; in the Eastern Church, wearing sandals and with hair on end (archbishop's chapel, Ravenna, mosaic c. 1500); as fisherman with short tunic, in martyrdom with a loincloth. *Attributes:*

scroll (S Lorenzo fuori le mura, Rome, 8C painting); open book (St Sebald, Nuremberg, fig. by Veit Stoss c. 1506); book (Atri Cathedral, 13/14C fresco); Latin cross (Aachen Cathedral, shrine of St Mary, relief c. 1230); saltire cross, St Andrew's cross (Diocesan Museum, Freising, painting by the Master of the Polling Panels, c. 1460); cross with two crossbars (Erfurt Cathedral, fig. on tower, c. 1350); fish (S Agostino, S Gimigniano, retable by P. F. Fiorentino 1449); fishing net (Musées Royaux des Beaux-Arts, Brussels, 17C painting by J. Ribera); two fishes (copper engraving by J. Callot, 1631/32); rope (Staatsgalerie, Stuttgart, Graphic Collection, chalk drawing by D. Tiepolo, 1751/53). *Martyrdom:* common, e.g. Städel, Frankfurt, painting by the Lochner workshop; Seville Museum, painting by J. de las Roselas, 1609/12. *Cycles:* British Museum, London, antependium from Solsona, c. 1200; Chartres Cathedral, stained glass; Metropolitan Museum, New York, 15C painting by L. Borrassa; S Andrea della Valle, Rome, apse calotte by Domenichino, 1624–1628; St Andreas, Heinrichshofen, ceiling fresco by F. M. Kuen, 1753. *Special scenes:* miracle of the bread (National Gallery, Melbourne, painting by the master of the 15C Catherine Legend); A. being called (Sistine Chapel, Rome, painting by D. Ghirlandaio 1586); head of St Andrew carried by two angels (S Andrea della Valle, Rome, fresco 1660).

Angela Merici of Brescia

Founder of order, saint

Feast-day: 27th Jan (day of death), 21st Feb (Martyriologium Romanum), 31st May (Translation feast for Capuchins)

Life: * 1474 in Desenzano on Lake Garda, grew up as an orphan in the house of her uncle; from 1516 in Brescia, 1525 pilgrimage to Palestine with periodic loss of sight, 25th Nov 1535 founded the "Co-operative of St Ursula" with twelve colleagues, first Mother Superior of the order. Originally, the members were supposed to live with their families without any distinctive dress, observe evangelical advice and busy themselves with the education of girls, particularly from the lower social classes. † 27th Jan, 1540. Buried in S Afra, Brescia, papal approval of foundation in 1544. 1768 beatified, 1807 canonized.

Patronage: Ursulines, young girls at school, young people.

Veneration and cult sites: Brescia and in the branches of the Order of St Ursula.

Representations in Art: *Apparel:* dressed as an Ursuline nun (S Afra, Brescia, sacristy painting 1550); as pilgrim (19C steel engraving by G. M. Tagliaferri). *Attributes:* table with cross and book (Coll. Casati, Milan,

18C painting); lilies, rosary, rule-book (art trade, painting by A. Steiner of Felsburg). *Cycle:* St Ursula, Chiari nr Brescia, 16C painting).

Anne

Mother of Mary, saint

Feast-day: 26th July (instituted 1481 in the Roman calendar by Pope Sixtus IV, 1584 universally by Pope Gregory XIII), eastern Church 25th July (Joachim and Anne 9th Sept, St Anne's conception 9th Dec).

Legends: the life of St Anne in apocryphal gospels, esp. the proto-gospel of St James, on the model of Hannah in the Old Testament, mother of Samuel (1 Sam. 1 – 2.11). * the daughter of Emerentia (var.: Susanna). – A. is supposed to come from the Levite tribe. – A. chooses from her suitors. – A. distributes her wealth among the poor. – As wife of Joachim, A. is childless until old age. – In the temple at Jerusalem, a priest refuses Joachim's sacrifice – he is accursed by law on account of his childlessness. – Joachim flees from Anne. – A. laments and is mocked by her maid Euthina (var: Judith). An angel foretells to Joachim, who is living among herdsmen, the birth of Mary – The same angel tells A., who is looking at a bird's nest, to go to the golden gate to meet her husband. – The three-year-old Mary is brought into the Temple by Joachim and A. bearing the customary offering at the end of weaning period. – Without help, Mary climbs the 15 steps to the altar for burnt offerings. – After the blessing by the high priest, Mary is caressed by A. (kolakeia). – A. teaches the young Mary to read. – Mary says goodbye to A. and Joachim to go to Jerusalem as a temple virgin. – On the way to the temple, the ancestors step from their sarcophaguses in expectation of their forthcoming redemption. – Mary is accepted among the throng of temple virgins in Jerusalem, where A. and Joachim try to visit her but are turned away by Mary. – After Joachim's death, A. remarries twice. With one of her husbands, Stolanus, she has two daughters named Mary. – A. dies at the age of 72 in Jerusalem. – A.'s grave is identified with a sheep-pond, near the Sheep's Gate in Jerusalem.

Patronage: brotherhoods in numerous places (Steinerberg, Switzerland, 1609, Goslar 1622, Vienna 1668, St A. brotherhood of intellectual workers, Koblenz.

Patronage: widows, pregnant women, childless women, plague victims, nursemaids, bridal couples, household goods, housewives, home helps, tailors, grocers, millers, ropemakers, lace makers, male servants, weavers, cabinet-makers, boatmen on the River Elbe, miners, the dying; invoked in Brittany for green grass and a good hay harvest; patron saint of Florence (because the tyrant Walter of Brienne was successfully driven out on St A.'s Day), Naples, Innsbruck (because the Bavarians left Wilten on St A.'s Day), patron of Como hospital 1468, Rozsnyo / Roznava (now Slovakia).

Veneration and cult sites: relics (fakes): Maphorion of St Anne, Constantinople; Apt Cathedral, body (9C); St Stephan, Vienna, hand relic; Annaberg (Saxony), cranium; Annaberg (Silesia), thumb relic; further relics in S Angelo, Peschiera (Lake Garda) (9C), Weingarten (1182), Bremen (1199), Chartres (1204), Lützel (Switzerland) (1205), Mainz (1212), Düren (1501), Baupré (1688), Montreal (1841), Paderborn, Minden, Regensburg, Salamanca, Genoa. Pilgrimage destinations include Anne d'Auray (Brittany), Nantes, Annaberg (Lower Austria), Annaberg (Saxony), Burrweiler (Pfalz), Rosenberg nr Wroclaw, Niederschlettenbach (Pfalz); Altwasser (Czech Republic), Fujieda (Japan), Las Palmas. Tuesday is dedicated to St A. – Franciscans, Benedictines, Augustinian canons, Carmelites, German orders, Burgundy, England, Church of St Anne at the Sheep's

Pool, Jerusalem, Trier Collegiate Foundation (promoted by Johannes Trithemius).

Superstitions: pregnant women carry a St A. note in their bosom. – St A.'s water serves as a remedy for physical ailments such as fever, headache, chest and stomach pains and afflictions of the eye. – Gout can be cured by a quotation in which A. takes on the personified pains and sends them on the Wild Hunt.

Representations in Art: *Apparel:* as a matron in a green coat and red shirt, headscarf, in the given style of the time (Landesmuseum, Münster, painting by the Liesborn master c. 1480); cap (Collegiate Church, Wimpfen, fig. c. 1500). *Attributes:* finger to lips, to indicate the Immaculate Conception (National Museum, Warsaw, mural from Faras, Nubia, 2nd half of 8C); book (Bürgersaal, Munich, fig. 1710); stem of lily (Chartres Cathedral, rose window in N. transept, 13C stained glass); clothed infant Mary with small crown on the arm (Liebfrauen church, Worms, south door c. 1300); A. pregnant with infant Mary in a mandorla on her lap (S Marco library, Venice, book illumination by

S Bening in Grimani breviary, c. 1510); Mary and Christ as infants, arranged in formation on A.'s lap and arm – the 'Selbdritt' of St A. (Paderborn Cathedral, treasury, fig. c. 1520); with infants Mary and Christ seated opposite each other on her lap (St Gallen Abbey Library, early coloured print, 15C); A. with Mary on a bench, between them the young Jesus (Dahlem, Berlin, fig. by Gerhaert of Leyden, pre–1463); A. and Mary standing, the naked infant Jesus between them treading on a serpent (Galleria Borghese, Rome, painting by Caravaggio 1605). *Cycles:* Chora church, Constantinople, 14C mosaic; S Marco, Venice, rear of 13C tabernacle pillar); Olinda, Brazil, 18C Franciscan church. *Special scenes:* Emerentiana root (Museo Lazaro Galdiano, Madrid, Flemish painting c. 1500); theological dispute about the Immaculate Conception (Historisches Museum, Frankfurt, Flemish painting c. 1490).

Anselm of Canterbury

Archbishop, Benedictine, Doctor of the Church, saint

Feast-day: 21st Apr

Life: * c. 1033/34 in Aosta, Piedmont, 1060 entered Benedictine monastery of Le Bec nr Rouen, 1073 became abbot, 1093 appointed archbishop of Canterbury by William the Conqueror. A. fought for the freedom of the Church and was therefore exiled in 1097, reinstated by Henry I. 1103 exiled again, but 1106 was able to return to England. Important theological writings on the proof of God and the Immaculate Conception. † 1109 in Canterbury and buried there (his shrine was

destroyed during the Reformation). 1494 canonised, 1720 named as Doctor of the Church.

Legends: the Mother of God appears in A.'s study. – Mary appears to A. and Martin, as conqueror of the heretics, between God the Father and Jesus. – A. rescues the Benedictine abbot Elphin from shipwreck.

Veneration and cult sites: Canterbury, Aosta, Turin, Le Bec.

Representations in Art: *Apparel:* in episcopal vestment with chasuble (Admont Collegiate Library, MS 289 fol., third quarter of 12C); with pluvial (Jerusalem Church / Bruges, late 16C stained glass); as an abbot (S Francesco / S Miniato al tedesco, 14C fresco). *Attributes:* presenting book to Mathilda of Tuscany (Bodleian Library, Oxford, MS. Auct. D 26 fol. 156, c. 1150); book (Diocesan Museum, Münster, early 16C stone relief from Vinnenberg); writing desk (Busseto Abbey, Parma painting by M. Anselmi, 1st half of 16C); quill (Antwerp, 19C painting by Th. Boejeramus); banner with the text "Non puto esse verum amatorem virginis, qui celebrare respuit festum suae conceptiones" (Pinacoteca, Lucca, painting c. 1477). *Special scenes:* in connection with the Immaculate Conception (S Francesco, Fiesole, late 15C painting by Piero di Cosimo); A. in the theological dispute over the Immaculate Conception with Eve and the serpent (Gemäldegalerie, Berlin, painting by Girolamo Genga c. 1515).

Ansgar of Hamburg

(Anskar) Bishop, saint

Feast-day: 3rd Feb

Life: * 801 nr Corbie (Picardy), entered the monastery there, 823 teacher at the monastery school in Corvey (Westphalia), 826–828 commissioned by the emperor Ludwig to do missionary work in Denmark and Sweden. 831 ordained bishop of the newly founded

diocese of Hamburg by Drogo of Metz in the presence of the bishops of Mainz, Reims, Trier, Bremen and Verden. 832 appointed by Pope Gregory IV as legate of the northern nations, 845 bishop of Bremen, 852 second missionary journey to Sweden. † 865 in Bremen.

Legends: A. enters monastery of Corbie at the age of 5, after the death of his mother. – A. knots fishing nets. – A. ransoms prisoners. – A. founds St Petri, Hamburg. – A. is granted several visions.

Patronage: see of Hamburg, Bremen.

Veneration and cult sites: north-west Germany, Scandinavia.

Representations in Art: *Apparel:* as bishop with crosier, mitre and pallium (Borby nr Eckenforde, tympanon relief, 2nd half of 12C); as Benedictine monk and messenger of faith (abbey church, Muri, fresco by F. Giorgioli, 1696/97). *Attributes:* model of church (St Petri, Hamburg, fig. by Bernd Notke 1480/90); Bremen council key (collegiate church, Ramelsloh, late 15C stained glass). *Cycles:* St Ansgar, Bremen, 15C murals).

Antony of Egypt

Hermit, saint

Feast-day: 17th Jan

Life: * shortly after 250, c. 271 visited Alexandria as a monk and attracted a large crowd of people because everybody wanted to see the man of God; he lived on Mt Colcim, not far from the Red Sea, at the foot of which a colony of hermits was established. Aged 90, A. visited Paul of Thebes. † 356 aged 105. Amongst his writings are 7 letters in Latin, including introductory lessons for novice monks.

Legends: the vita was written by Athanasius of Alexandria. It shows the ongoing fight of the victorious man of God against demons, with the characteristics of a miracle-worker: A. studies holy scripture. – A. distributes his possessions among the poor, in radical adherence to Christ's words: "Go and sell all thou hast and give to the poor" (Mt. 19, 21). – A. delivers his sister to a community of virgins. – A. drives out demons from a girl. – A. lives in a rock tomb. – The devil appears to A. disguised as a black boy. – A. is beaten and pushed about in his cave by a huge host of evil spirits so badly that a servant (var.: another hermit) thinks he is dead and carries him off on his shoulder to be buried, but A. regions consciousness during the night. – On his way into the desert, A. sees a silver bowl on the ground but recognizes it as a diabolic mirage and leaves it untouched. The bowl disappears in a puff of smoke. – When A. sees the world covered with a tangle of loops, a vision explains to him that the world can only be freed from entanglement by humility. – Angels lift A. into heaven, the devils being unable to prevent it because as a monk in the desert he is without sin. – An archer who takes objection to the happiness of the hermits, is repeatedly told by A. to draw his bow until finally he refuses to do so for fear of breaking his bow. A. interprets this to him as an image of life with God: "If we drew beyond our stature, we would soon break." – An angel is sent to A. when he is bored and lonely, to encourage him through work and prayer. – In a vision, A. sees horses destroying God's altar and interprets this as danger for the Christian faith. Two years later, the Arian dispute breaks out. – To the Egyptian prince Bellachius, who, as a supporter of Arius, has had faithful nuns stripped and scourged, A. writes a letter threatening him with God's wrath. – Five days later, Bellachius is trampled to death by his own horse. – A. goes to look for the hermit Paul of Thebes, whereupon a satyr, centaur and wolf show him the way. – A raven which brings Paul of Thebes his daily meal, gets two loaves on the day of A.'s visit. – In a vision, A. learns of the death of Paul of Thebes, whose soul is carried into heaven by angels.

– Two lions dig Paul of Thebes's grave. – When A. feels that his death is near, he asks his colleagues to bring back after his death the coat given to him by Athanasius. – In accordance with his wishes, A. is buried at a secret location, which is why his body was only discovered in 561 and brought to Alexandria. Posthumous legends: A. cures the son of a nobleman of St Antony's Fire.

Patronage: Order of St Antony (founded 1059 in St Didier-de-la-Motte), St Antony's canons (founded 1217 for the care of the sick), Order of the Knights of St Antony (founded 1382 by Adalbert of Bavaria); patron saint of the poor, the sick, domestic animals, pigs, swineherds, butchers, brush makers, knightly orders. Invoked against St A.'s Fire and plague.

Veneration and cult sites: Constantinople (body rescued from Saracens in 635); relics in Freckenhorst (since 865), Ospidale di S Maria della Scala, Siena (15C), Burgundy.

Superstitions: St A.'s water is used against St A.'s Fire, which can be imposed by A. as a penalty as well as removed by him as protector. – In Silesia, St A.'s Fire is cured if a male strikes sparks from a female's skin three times with a flint. – St A. pigs, identified by bells around their necks, got their name from the privilege granted to the Order of St Antony to let their pigs graze freely, in return for the Order's charitable services. They are maintained by the community, and at Christmas (var.: New Year's Eve) crowned with a wreath of ivy against quinsy and witchcraft and delivered to the butcher. The meat is distributed in church to the poor. – At Graveson on the Rhône estuary, on 27th April they dip a statue of A. into a stream three times to ensure a good harvest, protection from epidemics and the safe delivery of babies. – St A.'s bread does not go mouldy. – In the Allgäu, rooms should not be swept on St A.'s day to ensure that they are spared bugs.

Representations in Art: *Apparel:* as hermit in a narrow, full-length, woven tunic with wide sleeves (St Kunibert, Cologne, mural c. 1250); as a grey-haired monk in a belted hairshirt with black cloak, in the habit of the Order of St Antony, a gathered, belted robe with medium-width sleeves, a small scapular with hood and cap, often with a small tau (T-Shaped) cross sewn on it as a sign of the Order of St Antony, and a biretta (Polytechnic College, Zürich, cornpaper from Cologne, c. 1470/80). *Attributes:* walking stick (Alte Pinakothek, Munich, painting by Stephan Lochner); Tau crook (Unterlinden Museum, Colmar, painting from Isenheim Virgin altar by Martin Schongauer, c. 1470); abbot's crook (Landesmuseum, Münster, fig. from early 16C retable at Marienfeld Monastery); crosier with a ball-like knob (St Jakob, Rothenburg, high altar fig. by Tilman Riemenschneider); crosier (Enkhausen nr Arnsberg, early 16C fig.); hand-sized Tau cross (Gallmannsweil nr Stockach, late 15C fig.); hand cross to ward off demons successfully

(Marienstein Church, Eichstätt, painting c. 1500); cross with two crossbars (old parish church, Garmisch, stained glass c. 1440), rosary (Marienkirche, Rostock, early 16C fig. on St Roch altar); rule-book of Order (Unterlinden Museum, Colmar, fig. on Isenheim altar by Hans Hagenauer); small bell, symbolising the Order of St Antony's right to collect alms for their hospitals (Marienkirche, Lübeck, fig. on choir screen 1518); walking stick with small bell (Gehmen, Westphalia, late 15C fig.); Tau staff with small bell (Zoschau, Saxony, early 16C retable painting); two small bells fixed to crosspieces of tau cross (Reisbach, Lower Bavaria, fig. c. 1510); small bell on a torch (Münster, Westphalia, former choir screen fig. c. 1545); small bell around the neck of a piglet (St Nikolai, Rostock, painting c. 1450); torch (Laer, Westphalia, fig. c. 1450); container with fire (Zulpich, retable fig. c. 1500); standing in flames (Mesum, Westphalia, fig. c. 1500); sitting above flames in allusion to the fight against St Antony's Fire (Graphische Sammlung, woodcut c. 1450); piglet (Altenbeken, Westphalia, fig. c. 1500); piglet beneath cap (Fehmarn Castle, 15C fig.); piglet eating (Stadtkirche, Besigheim, relief c. 1520); devil under the foot of St Antony (Havixbeck, late 15C fig.); two devils (Enkhausen, 15C fig.); three devils (Studienbibliothek, Linz, anonymous 15C copper engraving); devil with ornate goblet (Annenmuseum, Lübeck, retable fig. from the St Antony reredos, 1522); grotesque (Herford Cathedral, late 15C fig.); three horned grotesques (Cappenberg, late 15C fig.). *Special scenes:* visit of A. to Paul of Thebes (Prado, Madrid, painting by Velasquez); temptation of A. (Unterlinden Museum, Colmar, wing of Isenheim altar by Master MGN; Duisburg Museum, painting by Max Ernst, 1945; Bremen Art Hall, triptych by Max Beckmann, 1936/37; temptation of A. by the Devil in the form of a woman with claws (Prado, Madrid, painting by Johann Patinir). *Cycles:* Chartres Cathedral, 13C stained glass on S side of choir); Salem (museum in form. monastery, Salem altar by M. Schaffner, 1517); Munich (Alte Pinakothek, painting from Cologne c. 1500).

Antony Maria Claret

Archbishop, Claretian, saint
Feast-day: 23rd Oct.
Life: * in 1807 in Sallent / Spain, the son of a weaver, 1835 ordained, unable to become a Jesuit because of poor health, missionary preacher in Catalonia, 1849 founded the congregation of the "Sons of the Immaculate Heart of Mary" (Claretian monks), 1855 founded the "Apostolic Training Institute of the Immaculate Conception" (Claretian nuns), 1850–1857 archbishop of Santiago de Cuba, 1857 confessor to Isabella II, 1869/70 participant at First Vatican Council, † 24th Oct 1870 at the Cistercian monastery of Fontfroide (Southern France).
Representations in Art: *Apparel:* as archbishop in a soutane, rochet and cappa magna (Cura Generalizia dei P. P. Claretani, Rome, 19C painting by Federico Barrio). *Attribute:* radiant medallion around his neck, above the cross on his chest.

Antony Maria Zaccaria of Cremona

Barnabite, saint.
Feast-day: 5th July
Life: * 1502 in Cremona, worked as a doctor, 1528 ordained, 1530 co-founder of the regular order of St Paul (Barnabites, called after St Barnabas monastery, Milan, which they occupied in 1538) and the 'English Sisters of St Paul' (Anglicans). He popularised the forty-hour prayer, promoted the cult of the altar sacraments and introduced Friday bell ringing as a Church custom. † 1539.
Representations in Art: *Apparel:* in Barnabite habit (copper engraving in Weigel, Co-

lumnae militantis ecclesiae, Nuremberg, 1725, no. 64). *Attributes:* lily, chalice, host (Biblioteca Ambrosiana, Milan, 17C painting by V. Santagostini).

Antony of Padua

Franziscan, saint
Feast-day: 13th June
Life: * 1195 in Lisbon as Fernando Martin de Bulhom, 1212 entered the Order of Austin Canons in Coimbra, studied theology, 1220 went over to the Franciscan monastery in Coimbra, prompted by the arrival of the relics of 5 Franciscan martyrs from Morocco. Selection of name of Order. In the same year, A. went as a missionary to Morocco, where illness stopped him preaching. On his return, A. ended up in Sicily. 1221 participated in the General Chapter of the order in Assisi, where he was admitted to the province of Romagna, withdrew to the isolated hermitage of Monte Paolo nr Forli. 1222–1224 worked as an itinerant preacher attacking the Cathars, taught in the Franciscan monastery of Bologna and introduced the theology of St Augustine to his order. 1224–1227 preached in France against the Albigenses, was guardian in Puy, 1226 custos in Limoges, 1227 provincial of Romagna, 1230 released from office to dedicate himself entirely to preaching in Padua. In his speeches, A. criticised political and social conditions, and demanded the release of debtors from prison, for the last year of his life lived in a walnut tree in Camposampiero, † 1231 on his way to Padua. 1232 canonized, 1263 relics translated to S Antonio. 1946 named Doctor of the Church.
Legends: as a preacher: A. preaches to fish because they gather round him while people do not. – A. preaches in the rain without his audience getting wet. – The tyrant Ezzelin is so moved by A.'s sermon that he puts a rope around his neck and admits his sins. – At a

And. Matth. Wolffgang Sculps.

funeral, A. preaches on Lk. 12, 34: "Where your treasure is, there will your heart be also". The relatives of a deceased miser later find his heart in his money chest. – A. shows the sacrament to a donkey that has starved for three days, at which the donkey kneels and refuses his fodder. A heretic is converted thereby. – Acting on the words of Mt. 5, 29, a young man cuts off his leg in remorse at maltreating his mother with it. – At the mother's request, A. restores the leg. – A. gets a baby to testify to the adultery of his mother. – A. revives his nephew, who drowned the day before. – A. brings back to life a baby which has fallen into boiling water. – A. brings a young man back to life so that he can testify to the innocence of his father (var.: his parents), who is accused of murdering him. – A demoniac, around whose neck A. has hung a piece of paper bearing the antiphon "Ecce crucem" while he is asleep, is freed from demons. – Thanks to A., a glass goblet thrown to the ground does not shatter. – A. rescues a woman wounded by her husband. – The Christ-child appears to A. in a nimbus. – A further 47 posthumous legends are known, including: A. rescues a ship from foundering. – A. frees Alicante from the control of the Bey of Algiers. – A. helps at the capture of Oran in 1732.

Patronage: patron saint of Padua, Lisbon, Split, Paderborn, Hildesheim; of lovers, married couples, women, children, travellers, horses, donkeys, miners, faience manufacturers. Invoked against infertility, fever, demons, shipwreck, war, plague and for the retrieval of lost articles.

Veneration and cult sites: relics in S Antonio, Padua, translocated in the presence of St Bonaventure. Venerated universally, particularly among Franciscans and in Il Santo, Padua.

Superstitions: St Antony's blessing against evil spirits, also banishment of evil spirits in searching for treasure.

Representations in Art: as a young, beardless Franciscan (Accademia, Florence, 13C diptych by Berlingheri); as a bearded Franciscan (S Francesco / Assisi, upper church, 13C fresco); as an Austin canon (18C copper engraving by J. B. Jezl); as a scholar (Accademia, Bergamo, painting by Sebastiano del Piombo); as an admiral in uniform (St Anton nr Riez, 18C fig.). *Attributes:* book (Wallraf-Richartz Museum, Cologne, painting, 1st half of 15C); flame (S Croce, Florence, fresco by A. Gaddi, c. 1394); burning heart (Aracoeli, Rome, 15C painting by Benozzo Gozzoli); lily (Il Santo, Padua, fig. by Donatello, 1448); baby Jesus standing or sitting (Kunsthistorisches Museum, Vienna, painting by G. David c. 1500); the baby Jesus in a mandorla on his chest (Badajoz Cathedral, wooden carving in choir stalls 1555); the infant Jesus in a prayer-nut lying on an open book (Prado, Madrid, painting by El Greco c. 1600); fish, paper with cross (Kunsthistorisches Museum, Vienna, antependium c. 1502); donkey, monstrance and host (Creisfeld, Saxony, predella c. 1500). *Special scenes:* as preacher in a walnut tree (Accademia, Venice, 17C painting by Sebastiani); sermon to the fish (Gal. Borghese, Rome, 16C painting by Veronese); the miracle of the Host (Esztergom Kereszteny Muzeum, painting, 1st half of 18C); vision of the Christ-child (Hermitage, St Petersburg, painting by Murillo). *Cycles:* S Francesco, Assisi, upr church, stained glass c. 1300); S Antonio, Padua, high altar sculptures by Donatello and his workshop; St Anton, Partenkirchen, fresco by Joh. Ev. Holzer 1736.

Apollinaris of Ravenna

Bishop, martyr, saint

Feast-day: 23rd July (day of death)

Life: first bishop of Ravenna, † c. 75 in Classis nr Ravenna or alternatively c. 200, martyrdom doubtful. Buried in Classis, 856 translation of relics to the church S Martino al cielo d'oro in Ravenna, since renamed S Apollinare Nuovo.

Legends: A. accompanies the apostle St Peter from Antioch to Rome as a disciple. – A. works as a missionary in Ravenna. – A. cures the blind son of the soldier Irenaeus. – A. is anointed as bishop by St Peter. – A. has to defend himself before the Ravenna tribunal. – A. cures the wife of the tribune Thecla. – A. raises from the dead the daughter of the city prefect, Rufus. – A. is thrown into prison and is fed by angels. – A. demolishes the Temple of Apollo in Ravenna with prayers. – After being roughed up, A. escapes on a ship. – A. preaches in Dalmatia. On his return to Ravenna, A. is clubbed to death. – A. appears to Romuald, founder of the Camaldoli.

Patronage: Classis, Ravenna, Burtscheid, Aachen, St A. monasteries, Remagen, Düsseldorf, needle-workers; invoked against gout, gallstones, epilepsy and diseases of the sexual organs.

Veneration and cult sites: relics in S Apollinare Nuovo, Ravenna, Rheims, St Benigne, Dijon, Apollinarisberg nr Remagen (head relic since 1394, pilgrimage since the 14C), St Lamberti, Düsseldorf, Siegburg Parish Church (St A. shrine since 1446), Gorkum nr Utrecht (arm relic), Obermichelbach nr Mulhouse (Alsace), St A. monastery in Burtscheid, Aachen (founded by Otto III).

Superstitions: anyone sacrificing his own weight in corn to A. on the Apollinarisberg will be cured of epilepsy.

Representations in Art: *Apparel:* as bishop of the Byzantine rite in dalmatic, planeta and pallium (S Apollinare in Classe, 6C mosaic); as a bishop of the Latin rite, with crosier and mitre (Pinacoteca, Spoleto, painting by L. di Tomme c. 1370). *Attributes:* crown (S Apollinare Nuovo / Ravenna, nave mosaic 3rd qtr of 6C); club (woodcut from "Vita Sanctorum", 1498). *Cycles:* Chartres Cathedral, 13C stained glass; S Apollinare, Rome, fresco as extant in 16C engravings by Pomarancio; Apollinarisberg nr Remagen, mural by A. Müller 1856.

Apollonia of Alexandria

Virgin, martyr, saint

Feast-day: 9th Feb

Life: A. suffered martyrdom in Alexandria in 249, as an aged Christian.

Legends: the daughter of a king, A. possesses immense wealth and is served in a tower by twelve virgins. – A. gives away her jewels, a gift from her favourite brother. – A. refuses an arranged marriage. – A. is led by an angel to a hermit, where she is baptised. – A. is told by angels to preach in Alexandria. – A. experiences the hate of a sorcerer, who rouses the mob against her, so that she and other Christian women are dragged into the street and martyred. – The princess suffers martyrdom at her father's orders. (Var: A., the sister of Laurence, goes to Egypt where she suffers martyrdom under Emperor Decius). – A.'s eyes are gouged out but angels heal them. – A.'s ears are filled with lead. – A. is flayed with a knife. – A.'s jaw is shattered to knock out all her teeth (var.: all are extracted with pliers). – A. leaps voluntarily into a fire, to avoid being pushed into it (var: A. is beheaded).

Patronage: dentists, invoked against toothache.

Veneration and cult sites: cult spread from the east all over Europe, esp. in the Rhine area in Germany and the Netherlands. Pilgrimage to the "Löffelkapili" in Staufen (Black Forest).

Superstition: anyone rinsing their mouths with water from St A.'s well on the Kapellenberg in Saxony will never have toothache again. – In Staufen (Black Forest), people with toothache lay their spoons at the feet of a statue of A. in the "Löffelkapili", and the pain is eased. – In the same place, women hang the shirts of children with teething problems on the statue of A. – In Bavaria, St A. roots remove maggots from teeth.

Representations in Art: *Apparel:* as a virgin in contemporary dress (Musées Royaux des Beaux-Arts, Brussels, late 15C painting by the master of the St Lucy Legend); with head covering (Museo Civico, Pisa, 14C painting by S Martini); as a princess (National Gallery, Prague, painting on frame of the Schwanberg Visitation, c. 1450); as a court lady (Louvre, Paris, painting by F. Zurbaran 1636); as a hermit (copper engraving by J. Sadeler based on M. de Vos, 1600). *Attributes:* palm tree (Museo del Castelvecchio, Verona, 16C painting by Martino da Verona); pliers with tooth (Old Chapel, Regensburg, mid–18C fig.); closed book (Poldi-Pezzoli Collection, Milan, 15C painting); open book (City Art Museum, St Louis, 15C painting); book pouch (numerous early woodcuts); chisel (Bergheim, high altar, fig. 1707); chisel and claw hammer as dentist's equipment (Villingen Museum, late 15C tapestry); crown, sceptre (National Gallery, Prague, painting on frame of Schwanberg Visitation, c. 1450); auger to gouge out eyes, flaying knife and pliers (Kunstgewerbe Museum, Cologne, wall hanging from Neuburg-on-Danube, c. 1425). *Martyrdom:* extraction of teeth (Regional Museum, Brno, painting c. 1430); on the rack (Musée Condée, Chantilly, Etienne Chevalier's Book of Hours, illumination c. 1450); death by fire (copper engraving by J. Sadeler based on M. de Vos, 1600). *Cycles:* Accademia, Florence, 16C predella by F. Granacci).

Athanasius the Great of Alexandria

Bishop, Doctor of the Church, saint
Feast-day: 2nd May
Life: * c. 296 in Alexandria, took part in Council of Nicea in 325 as deacon and secretary to bishop Alexander, first disputes with the Arians there, 328 consecrated as bishop of Alexandria. Following his refusal to readmit Arius to the community of the faithful, A. was deposed on the strength of false accusations from the Synod of Tyre and exiled by Emperor Constantine to Trier. 337 returned after the death of Constantine, 339 deposed again at the Synod of Antioch, and fled to Pope Julian I in Rome. 346 Emperor Constantius permitted his return after the death of his anti-bishop Gregory in 345, on the basis of an application made in 343 by the Synod of Sardica. 355 deposed again by the Council of Milan, so he took himself off to the monks in the Egyptian desert. His anti-bishop George was murdered in 361. Recalled in 362 by Emperor Julian, he was driven out by pagan reaction for the fourth time as a "trouble-maker and enemy of the gods". Banished for the fifth time under Emperor Valens. When his diocesans turned nasty, he was soon recalled again. † in 373 in office. His most important writings include three orations against the Arians in which he defended the Nicene doctrine of the infinite origin of the Son from the Father and the unity of the Son with the Father. C. 357 A. wrote the vita of St Antony whom he had met personally in his youth.

Veneration and cult sites: venerated as a Doctor of the Church in the Latin Church and all Eastern Churches.

Representations in Art: *Apparel:* as a bishop in the rite of the Eastern Church, with stoicharion, epitrachelion, epigonation, phelonion, omophorion and gospels (Capella Palatina, Palermo, post 1130); as bishop of the Latin rite (Valladolid Cathedral, late 15C painting by the master of S Ildefonso); as a cardinal (Gotha Museum, sketch by P. P. Rubens 1620); as a monk writing (Landesmuseum, Stuttgart, Stuttgart Passional, 12C illumination). *Attribute:* scroll (13C mosaic in S Marco / Venice). *Special scenes:* wis-

dom inspires A. (copper engraving in Giulini, devotional book, Augsburg 1754).

Augustine of Canterbury

Bishop, Apostle of England, saint
Feast-day: 28th May, 26th May (in England, Martyrologium Romanum, Benedictine Order).
Life: as prior of the Benedictine monastery of St Andrew in Rome, sent by Pope Gregory the Great with c. 40 companions on a mission to England. The Frankish princess Bertha helped to ensure the success of the mission. A. sought a compromise between old British, Saxon and Roman rites and gradually helped to reduce mistrust. A. was appointed archbishop of Canterbury and 601 Primate of England. † 26th May 604/605. Buried in the monastery church of St Peter and Paul in Canterbury.
Legends: A. is discouraged by reports of the savagery of the Anglo-Saxons and returns to Rome. – The pope sends him off a second time. – A. converts King Ethelbert of Kent.
Representations in Art: *Apparel:* as a bishop in vestments (Canterbury Cathedral, stained glass c. 1470); as a Benedictine missionary (Muri monastery church, fresco by F. A. Giorgioli, 1696/97). *Special scenes:* A.'s arrival in England (S Giorgio, Rome, Capelle del Triclino, fresco by Viviano da Urbino).

Augustine of Hippo

Bishop, one of the four western Fathers of the Church, Doctor of the Church, saint
Feast-day: 28th Aug
Life: * 354 in Thagaste. Originally intended by his father as a rhetorician, A. studied in Thagaste and Madaura. 371 moved to Carthage and until c. 384 led a dissipated life in a concubinage that produced a son Adeodatus († 390). Although his mother Monica was a Christian, she was led by her ambition for a glorious career for her son. As A. read the set text of Cicero's "Hortensius", his longing for philosophical wisdom was awakened. A. adopted the doctrine of Manichaeism, which unlike Christianity seemed to him an enlightened, less authoritative religion. 374/75 became a teacher of the liberal arts in Thagaste, but his mother banned him from the parental home because of his apostasy. His scepticism of Manichaeism was increased by a discussion with the Manichaean bishop Faustus of Mileve, whose educational defects were transparent to A. 383 moved to Rome against the wishes of his mother, 384 with the assistance of the city prefect, Quintus Aurelius Symmachus, became a teacher of rhetoric in Milan. Listening to the sermons of Bishop Ambrose of Milan, who was in the habit of explaining the Old Testament allegorically, A. found it possible to postulate God as pure spirit, the intellectuality of the soul and the freedom of will despite certain statements in the Old Testament. 386 study of the writings of Plotinus, during which the Neo-Platonist presbyter Simplicianus showed A. how the logos theology of the St John prologue rounded off Plotinus's nous doctrine. Through philosophy, A. gained access to faith in God. A. also had a direct conversion experience: lying under a fig tree, he heard a childish voice addressing him several times: rush about, lie down, take and read. He opened the letters of Paul, found Romans 13, 13, and all the darkness of doubt disappeared. In autumn 386 he resigned his teaching post and moved to the country estate of a friend in Cassiacum, to prepare for baptism at the beginning of the next Lent. In his Confessions, A. describes how he planned to renounce marriage and live abstemiously, devoting himself entirely to the search for truth. 387 baptised together with his son by Bishop Ambrose on Easter Saturday. A.'s mother Monica died in Ostia before A. returned to Africa. A. lived in mo-

nastic seclusion in Thagaste. 391 Bishop Valerius of Hippo wanted him to become his presbyter. 395 consecrated as coadjutor-bishop of Hippo, and after the death of Valerius, A. became bishop of Hippo. Principally his influence is characterised by the disputes with Manichaeism and treatises against the heresies of the North African Donatists. 411 disputation in Carthage with 286 Catholic and 279 Donatist bishops. After 412 disputations with and refutations of Pelagianism. † 28th Aug 430 in Hippo. In his writings, which made him one of the most important philosophers and theologians of the Early Church, he christianized Neo-Platonism. In his studies, A. dealt with many subjects, for instance, proof of the existence of God, the Trinity, original sin and grace or the sacraments, but he also took a view on ethical and social issues.

Legends: as a child, A. believes that fig trees cry if the fruit is picked. – A.'s mother Monica dreams of a wooden gate at which she meets a young man who predicts that, wherever she is, so will he be. – A. escapes secretly from Thagaste to Carthage. – Suffering toothache, A. reads the opinion of the philosopher Cornelius that it is the ultimate blessing for the body to feel no pain, meanwhile A. is going hoarse with pain. Only after he writes on wax plates that Christians should pray for him, does he feels healthy again. – At A.'s baptism, the Te Deum is created as a dialogue between Ambrose and A. – A. eradicates the Anabaptists, Donatists and Manichaeists. – A. exorcizes the devil from a Hippene woman with his tears, which drop into an oil vessel. – With his prayers but without his personal presence, A. drives out the devil from a young man. – A. washes the feet of a pilgrim and recognizes Christ. – A. heals a sick man before a dangerous operation. – Whilst thinking about the Trinity, A. meets a boy who wants to scoop the ocean into a hollow in the sand

with a ladle, and he thus receives an answer to his doubts: it is easier to do this than to grasp the nature of God. – A. is permitted to examine the record of sins which the devil has drawn up for mankind and discovers under his own entry the sin of forgetting compline. After he has remedied the deficiency, the entry disappears, much to the fury of the Devil. -

Patronage: Augustine canons, Augustine hermits, Carthage, theologians.

Veneration and cult sites: c. 700 body brought from Sardinia to S Pietro in Ciel d'Oro, Pavia; 1695 rediscovery of the crypt where he was hidden in the 12C in the confusion of war. In the 18C in Pavia Cathedral, 1900 taken back. Carthage (since the 10C), Trier (10C), Spain (1677, by request of Charles II of Spain, church festival).

Superstitions: guardian of the hour between 12 and 1; people who die in this hour can request the special intercession of A.

Representations in Art: *Apparel:* in a toga as a Roman author's portrait (Lateran, Rome, old library under the Capella Sancta Sanctorum, late 6C fresco); as a bishop in chasuble with pallium (Nonnberg monastery, Salzburg, mid–12C mural); as a bishop in pluvial (Landesmuseum, Münster, 18C fig.); as a bishop in cassock and cappa magna (Ognisanti, Florence, fresco by S Botticelli); as a scholar (Ognisanti, Florence, fresco by S Botticelli); as an Augustine canon (Heiligenkreuz, Augsburg, painting by Josef Magges, 1767); as an Augustine hermit (S Agostino, Rimini, 14C fresco). *Attributes:* angel whispering into his ear (Bibliothèque Nationale, Paris, 11C book illumination in Cod. Par. lat. 1987 fol. 143); dove of the Spirit (Alte Pinakothek, Munich, altar of the Doctors of Church from Neustift, Brixen by M. Pacher, 1483); eagle (Kupferstichkabinett, Berlin, 15C engraving by the master of the Berlin Passion); writer (Orleans Library, 10C book illumination MS 46 fol. 1); group of pupils (Florence, 12C English book illumination in MS Pluto 12.17 fol. 3v); individual pupil (Engelberg, 12C book illumination in Cod. 15 fol. 125); quill and inkwell in his hand (Ognisanti Church, Florence, fresco by S Botticelli); quill held up by a putto (Heiligenkreuz, Augsburg, painting by Josef Magges, 1767); spectacles (St Lorenz, Nuremberg, painting 1477); child with spoon as allusion to the legend (Diocesan Museum, Eichstätt, left wing of the Rosary Altar c. 1500); heart in the hand, pierced by two arrows as symbol of the love for God and one's brother (Landesmuseum, Münster, 15C painting by the master of the Schopping retable); burning heart (Landesmuseum, Bonn, early 15C triptych); a wreath of lilies held up by putti, lily, reins, Cupid with arrow as indication of the excesses of youth and conversion (St A., Mainz, fresco by Joh. Bapt. Enderle, 1771/72. *Special scenes:* A. between Christ pointing at his wounded side and the mother of God, pressing milk from her breast (Academia S Fernando, Madrid, painting by P. P. Rubens); motif of the 'rush about / lie down' legend (Louvre, Paris, drawing by Charles le Brun); presentation of the St A. Rule (Accademia, Venice, painting by Carlo Calieri). *Cycles:* St A., Erfurt, stained glass, 1st qtr of 14C; S Pietro in Ciel d'Oro, Pavia, reliefs by Giovanni Balduccio 1362; St A., S Gimignano, fresco by Benozzo Gozzoli and Giusto d'Andrea, 1465; Neustift nr Brixen, altar painting by the Uttenheim master 1460/70; Augustine Canons, Rottenbuch, frescoes by M. Günther 1742; St A., Mainz, frescoes by Joh. Bapt. Enderle, 1771/72.

B

Barbara

Virgin, martyr, Holy Helper, saint

Feast-day: 4th Dec

Legends: according to the Dicta Originis de Beata Barbara, the 9C vita and passion by Simeon Metaphrastes, and an extended legend by Johann of Wackerzeele written in the 2nd half of the 15C, * in the 3C in Nicodemia (var: in Heliopolis or Catania) as the beautiful, clever daughter of the pagan Dioscurus. – B. sends a letter with questions to Origen, a Doctor of the Church, who sends an answer via the priest Valentinus. – B. calls Valentinus a doctor and gains access this way. – Valentinus baptizes B. (var.: B. is enlightened by the Holy Spirit, climbs into a pagan well and is baptised by John the Baptist in a vision). – B. opposes her father's marriage plans for her, is converted to Christianity and orders, as a symbol, that a third window be let into the bathing house attached to the tower (var: that three crosses be chiselled into the stone) (var: her father imprisons her in the tower to see if solitude will help her find pleasure in the prospect of marriage). – B. receives an ostrich feather from the infant Jesus as a symbol of virginity. – B. explains to her father the meaning of the third window, whereupon he has her condemned. – When she flees, a rock opens and hides B. in a wondrous way (var: B. is dragged by her hair before the prefect Marcianus, who has her chased naked through the streets and caned). – Variant not written down: the canes turn into ostrich feathers, at which B. escapes and hides in the rock-face. – A shepherd betrays B. – Thereupon the shepherd's sheep are turned into locusts. – B. is imprisoned, caned, clubbed (var: her breasts are cut off) and burnt with torches. – B. is to be flogged naked on the market place but angels cover her with a snow-white robe. – B. is beheaded by her father (var: B. is cared for at night by angels or Christ to give her strength to endure the tortures of the following day). – Before she dies, B. prays for all those who remember her suffering and intercedes to save them from plague, death and God's Judgement. – After the deed is done, B.'s father is struck by lightning. – Posthumous legends: B. rescues a Premonstratensian monk from drowning. – B. protects a farmer from the blow of a soldier's sword. – B. cures cripples and poor people who pray by her body.

Patronage: patron saint of Edessa and Cairo, of architects, construction workers, miners (particularly in Saxony, Silesia, Bohemia, South Tyrol, Lorraine and – since the 19C – in the Ruhr district), tilers, prisoners, casters, bell-ringers, hatters, chefs, bricklayers, young girls, butchers, stonemasons, grave-

diggers, carpenters and artillerymen; patron saint of towers and fortifications, firemen, the army and invoked for a favourable hour of death.

Veneration and cult sites: relics c. 1000 in S Marco, Venice, later S Giovanni Evangelista, Torcello.

Superstitions: St B.'s Day is a momentous day for the coming year. On St B.'s Day no needlework must be done or the hens will not lay for a whole year. – In Hungary, buried treasures should be dug up on St B.'s Eve. – On St B.'s Eve, miners put food and drink on the dining room table to feed the "Miner". Anyone lighting a candle to the saint on St B.'s Day will die a natural death. – St B. bells are rung during violent storms. – Cherry boughs put in a vase on St B.'s Day bloom on Christmas Eve. – In Lower Austria, one bough is put into a vase for every member of the family. The one whose branch blooms first is lucky in the coming year.

Representations in Art: *Apparel:* in tunic and pallium (S Maria Antiqua, Rome, fresco 705/706); in a long belted robe with mantle (Bavarian National Museum, Munich, Pahler altar, painting c. 1400/10); in contemporary upper-class dress with mob cap (Wallraf-Richartz Museum, Cologne, painting by the Master of the Holy Family c. 1514/15); in contemporary dress with crown (Ehrenfriedersdorf, Saxony, fig. 1512); in protective cloak (St Sebastian, Kallwang, Styria, fig. 1692). *Attributes:* cross (S Maria Antiqua, Rome, fresco 705/706); book (Stadtmuseum, Leipzig, painting c. 1500); square tower in landscape (Annaberg-Buchholz, Munzer altar, painting 1521/22); round tower in landscape (Wallraf-Richartz Museum, Cologne, painting by the Master of the Holy Family c. 1514/15); round tower on the ground (Wallraf-Richartz Museum, Cologne, painting by the Master of the Kirchsahrer altar, 1425/30); hexagonal tower on the ground (Wallraf-Richartz Museum, Cologne, painting by the Master of the Gregory Legend, c. 1460); square tower on the ground (Oberstadion, Württemberg, painting 1458); hexagonal tower in her hand (Wallraf-Richartz Museum, Cologne, painting c. 1370/80); round tower in her hand (Wallraf-Richartz Museum, Cologne, painting c. 1330); round tower with hexagonal first floor in her hand (Wallraf-Richartz Museum, Cologne, painting by the Master of the Assumption, c. 1470); square tower in her hand (Wallraf-Richartz Museum, Cologne, painting by Stephan Lochner, 1445/59); round tower with chalice and host in her hand (Wallraf-Richartz Museum, Cologne, painting by the St Severin Master c. 1505/10); round tower with chalice and host on the upper thigh (Wallraf-Richartz Museum, Cologne, painting by the Master of the St Ursula Legend, c. 1485); square tower with chalice and host on the ground (Kupferstichkabinett, Berlin, cornpaper c. 1470/80); chalice with host in tower niche (Donzdorf, late 15C painting); chalice with host but no tower (Alte Pinakothek, Munich, painting by H. Holbein the Elder, 1516); chalice without host (Oberbobritzsch, Saxony, altar fig. 1512); torch, two swords at her feet (Kunstgewerbemuseum, Cologne, weaving c. 1525); ostrich feather (Kaiser-Friedrich Museum, Berlin, 16C stained glass by H. Baldung-Grien); figure of the defeated pagan (Dioscurus ?) at her feet (St Stephan, Vienna, bridal gate fig. c. 1370); gun-barrel (Brera, Milan, 17C painting by G. B. Morini); palm tree (Lübeck Cathedral, 15C dorsal relief); sword (Ipthausen / Lower Franconia, fig. c. 1760). *Special scenes:* B.'s escape from her torturers (Dulwich College Gallery, London, painting by P. P. Rubens, c. 1620); B. has a window cut into the tower (Pinacoteca, Città del Vaticano, painting by the S Miniato master, c. 1660/80); B. rescues a Premonstratensian monk and a farmer from the sword (Musée des Arts Décoratifs, Paris, 15/16C painting); B. appears in the clouds to the dying (Untermieming, Tyrol, 18C rectory painting by J. E. Holzer); B. as church patron invites the faithful to a Lutheran (!) Communion (Holzkirch nr Ulm, mid–18C painting. *Martyrdom:* B.'s beheading (Oberbobritzsch, Saxony, painting 1521). *Cycles:* numerous. Following Simeon Metaphrastes: Helsinki, National Museum, painting by Master Francke, 1st half of 15C;

following Dicta Originis: Neustift nr Brixen, painting by F. Pacher c. 1475/80; Wackerzeele version: Musées Royaux du Cinquantenaire, Brussels, 16C carved altar.

Barnabas

Companion of St Paul the Apostle, martyr, saint

Feast-day: 11th June, in Eastern Church rites 11th Apr

Life: mentioned in Acts 14, 14 as an apostle in the wider sense. B. (i.e. 'the son of consolation') is the name given to him by the Apostles. His real name was Joses Justus, a Levite from Cyprus, according to Acts 4, 36. B. was well-known in the Early Church for his generosity and charity. He sold a plot of land and laid the money at the feet of the Apostles (Acts 4, 36). B. introduced Saul to the Apostles (Acts 9, 27), preached with St Paul in Antioch (Acts 9, 27) and brought the money they collected there to Jerusalem (Acts 11, 22ff.). 45–48 B. accompanied St Paul on his first missionary journey (Acts 13 – 14) and took part in the meeting of the apostles in Jerusalem (Acts 15, 2ff.). On St Paul's second missionary journey, B. went off separately with his cousin John Mark to Cyprus (Acts 15, 36–39; Colossians 4, 10). According to 1 Cor. 9, 6, B. worked again with St Paul in Corinth. According to Tertullian, B. was the author of the epistle to the Hebrews.

Legends: B. goes as a missionary to Alexandria, Macedonia, Rome and Milan. – B. is the first bishop of Milan. – B. goes as a missionary to Cyprus, taking with him St Matthew's Gospel. – He cures the sick by blessing them with the scriptures. – He cures Timon by laying on his hands. – The sorcerer Elymas, whom Paul deprives of his sight for a time, refuses B. access to Paphos. – When B. sees men and women running naked into the pagan temple, he demolishes it with prayer. –

In Salamis, B. is caught by Jews, stoned and burned alive. – His disciples secretly steal the container with his body, which was supposed to be thrown into the sea, and bury it in a cave.

Patronage: patron saint of Milan and Florence because of victories attributed to B. against Siena on St B.'s Day 1269 at Colle Val d'Elsa and in 1289 against Arezzo near Campaldino; of the Barnabite Order for educating young people and for missionary work, founded by A. M. Zaccaria in 1530; of weavers and coopers; invoked against sorrow, quarrels and hailstorms.

Veneration and cult sites: 485/486 discovery of the grave; the emperor Zeno orders the relics, together with a manuscript of the Gospel according to St Matthew, to be removed to St B., Constantinople; St B.'s ashes in Milan since the 5C, head since the 6C. Relics in Edenna nr Bergamo, Pavia, Genoa, Cremona, Bologna, Naples, Prague, Cologne, Andechs, Toulouse, Tournai, Namur, Florence (since 1311).

Superstitions: rain on B.'s day damages the grape harvest.

Representations in Art: *Apparel:* in episcopal vestments (St Mary's Chapel, St-Junien, mid–13C fresco); as a cardinal (Accademia, Carrara, 15C painting by A. Vivarini); in loincloth and coat (Bergamo Cathedral, 18C (?) painting by A Boselli); in bourgeois dress (Accademia, Venice, 16C painting by P. Veronese). *Attributes:* Gospel scroll (Lucca Chapter Library, Passional C, book illumination c. 1125); Gospel (Zafra, painting by F. Zurbaran, 1643/44); olive branch (Ospedale della Misericordia, Prado, 14C painting by G. da Milano); model of a church (Milan Cathedral, 18C fig.); halberd (Bibliothèque Nationale, Paris, lat. 10532, 16C book illumination); scissors, beggar at his feet (Accademia, Venice, 16C painting by P. Veronese). *Special scenes:* B.'s election as apostle by the Holy Spirit (Antwerp Museum, painting by A. Francken the Elder c. 1600); popular pagan sacrifice to St Paul and B. in Lystra (Städel, Frankfurt, painting by A. Elsheimer c. 1600); B. cures the sick by laying on the Gospel (S Giorgio in Braida / Verona, painting by P. Veronese c. 1560); B. parts company from St Paul (S Barnaba / Milan, painting by S Peterzano c. 1573/92). *Martyrdom:* Bibliothèque Nationale, Paris, lat. 1023, late 13C book illumination. *Cycles:* very rare. Examples include Pinacoteca, Città del Vaticano, painting by a 14C (?) master of the Orcagna school; New York, art trade, painting by M. di Bartolommeo, c. 1500.

Bartholomew
Apostle, martyr, saint

Feast-day: 24th Aug (translation feast 4th Dec), in the Greek rites 11th Aug

Life: in the New Testament, mentioned only in the Synoptic Gospels and is regarded, along with Andrew, as the first convert. Identified in the 11C by Rupert of Deutz with Nathanael, whom Jesus describes as "a true Israelite, in whom there is nothing false". If one accepts this interpretation, Nathanael would be the proper name and "Bar Tolomai (= son of Tolomai) a cognomen like Bar Jona in the case of Simon.

Legends: legends from his childhood: the Devil exchanges the baby with a changeling after his mother has given herself to the Devil. – As an adult, B. returns home and cures the crippled hand of his mother after receiving baptism. – According to the apocryphal Gospel according to B: B. asks Jesus numerous questions, e.g. about the descent to the underworld and the release of Adam, all patriarchs, Abraham, Isaac and Jacob. – B. questions the mother of God about the incarnation of the Son of God. – In a kind of apocalyptic spectacle, Jesus shows B. the adversary of mankind.

According to various traditions: B. questions and conjures an idol in Astaroth, India, the destination of his first missionary journey (Golden Legend). – According to Rhabanus Maurus, B. converts Polymios, the brother of King Astyages, later consecrated as bishop. B. drives out a demon from the sleepwalking daughter of Polymios. – B. has a graven image chained by angels which nonetheless refuses to accept the sacrifices of a pagan priest. – B. dedicates the pagan temple to the True God. – On B.'s orders, angels construct the church tower of the new house of God – Astyages and his pagan priests are possessed and die soon later. – According to an Armenian homily, B. travels to Adana in Turkey, to the Medes and Persians, to Bostra, Germania, the Parthians and Elamites and to Golthon (var: according to St John Chrysostom,

B. makes a missionary journey to Lycaonia (now Konya), Mesopotamia and the Parthians). According to Coptic tradition, B. is the companion of Andrew (var: of Matthew or Philip). – B. suffers martyrdom by stoning and subsequently the stake (var: B. is crucified). – B. is crucified upside down. – B. is flayed and then crucified. – B. is flayed, then cast into the sea. – B. is flayed and beaten to death. – B. is flayed and crucified. – B. is thrown into the sea by the wife of King Astyages in a sack weighed down with sand.

Patronage: apostle of Greater Armenia, patron saint of the see of Liège, the towns of Altenburg, Béthune, Curzola, Frankfurt am Main, Fermo, Plzen, Maastricht, of bakers, miners, bookbinders, tanners, glove makers, shepherds, country folk, leather workers, butchers, millers, tailors, shoemakers, wine growers, of Florentine oil, salt and cheese merchants.

Veneration and cult sites: body allegedly in monastery of Bachkale in Armenia, translocated c. 410 to Nephergerd by Bishop Maruta, 507 to Daras, Mesopotamia by Emperor Anastasius I, 983 to the island of Tiber by Emperor Otto II, the cranium since 1283 in Frankfurt, Main; relics in Lipari, Sicily from 580, 883 moved to Benevento for protection from the Saracens. Arm relic brought to Canterbury by King Edward the Confessor.

Superstitions: a day of change for the autumn weather. – On St B.'s Day, blacksmiths hammer on cold anvils to tighten the Devil's chains. – Butter made on St B.'s Day without salt possesses special healing powers. – St B.'s Day has numerous weird characteristics, is regarded as a day for witches' to revel.

Representations in Art: *Apparel:* as an apostle in a long, belted tunic and pallium (St Ursula, Cologne, painting c. 1275); musclebound with anatomical precision (Milan Cathedral, fig. by Marco d'Agrate, c. 1552/62); as a naked cephalophore (National Gallery, Perugia, 14C fresco). *Attributes:* scroll

(Monreale Cathedral, 12C mosaic); book (Vatican caves, Città del Vaticano, 15C fig. by M. del Pollaiuolo); knife (Alte Pinakothek, Munich, painting by the Bartholomew Master, c. 1500); vanquished King Astyages at his feet (Naumburg Cathedral, stained glass c. 1250); chained Satan (Vich Cathedral, fig. by P. Oller c. 1425); flayed skin in hand (Epiphany shrine, fig. by Nicholas of Verdun c. 1220); skin hanging over left arm (Frankfurt Cathedral, choir stall relief 1352); skin carried on a stick resting on shoulder (National Library, Ljubljana, Glagolitic breviary, 15C book illumination); skin hanging from the shoulder (National Gallery, Perugia, 14C fresco); presenting skin with both hands (Silesia Museum, Wroclaw, fig. by Th. Weissfeld 1705); tree (Certosa di Pavia, mid–16C painting attrib. to G. B. da Sesto); banner (Uffizi, Florence, 14C painting by J. di Landino). *Special scenes:* changeling child after the birth (Museo Civico, San Gimignano, painting by L. di Nicolò di Pietro Gerini, 1401). *Martyrdom:* flaying B. on a knacker's bench (Museo Civico, Siena, painting by associate of G. da Siena, c. 1270); tied to a pole, B. is tortured as in the Marsyas Iconography (S Staé, Venice, painting by G. B. Tiepolo, 1722/23); B. raised on a beam to be flayed (Prado, Madrid, painting by J. de Ribera, 1630); B. being flayed standing tied to a tree (Pardubice parish church, 17C painting by M. L. Willmann); B. crucified upright (Kupferstichkabinett, Berlin, woodcut by L. Cranach the Elder, 1510/15); B. crucified upside down (rare portrayal in an anonymous copper engraving, c. 1500); B. being beheaded (Museo Civico, San Gimignano, painting by L. di Nicolo di Gerini, 1401). *Cycles:* Dominican church, Colmar, 13C stained glass; S Bartolomeo del Fossato,0 Genoa, 14C painting by B. di Modena.

Basil the Great

Archbishop, Doctor of the Church, saint

Feast-day: 2nd Jan (14th June anniversary of his consecration as bishop, in the Greek rites on 1st Jan, 30th Jan with St John Chrysostom and St Gregory of Nazianzus).

Life: * about 330 in Caesarea, Cappadocia, the son of a rhetorician from a high-ranking family, studied rhetoric in Caesarea, Constantinople and Athens, was a friend of Gregory of Nazianzus, 356 baptised. Visited the best-known ascetics in Syria, Palestine, Egypt and Mesopotamia. B. decided to live as hermit with like-minded people nr Neo-Caesarea, Pontus. 358 visited by his friend Gregory, B. and Gregory together wrote the Philocalia and drew up two monastic rules. 364 presbyter in Caesarea, with Eusebius's help, 370 bishop of Caesarea, metropolitan of Cappadocia and exarch of the diocese of Pontus. Standing firm on doctrines laid down by the Council of Nicaea, B. fought Arianism, which was v. influential under Emperor Valens. 371 to reduce B.'s influence, Valens divided the diocese into two. – B.'s extensive writings show a strong change of direction towards the ethical and practical problems of community theology and are not limited to pure speculation. In the liturgical field, B. regulated the order of the service and published an anaphora, but the canon occasionally used in Greek rites known as the St B. Liturgy is a much modified affair. Amongst his dogmatic writings, B. dealt in 375 with the divinity of the Holy Spirit, which B. saw as emanating from the Father via the Son; but the Holy Spirit possesses not only the spirit of the Son but also part of the father's, using the Nazianzan formulation expressis verbis, because B., as Gregory of Nazianzus notes, saw the foundation of salvation not in the expression but in the thing itself. 364 in three books written in response to Eunomius, who maintained that people could comprehend the essence of God, B. dealt with ac-

cess to the knowledge of God and reached the conclusion that people could only know as much about God as was expressed in His works. Because God has invested all his power in his works, we can indeed experience God's omnipotence but not his essence. According to B., God's characteristics are derived by human reasons through the things of the senses and are therefore subjective, but there is reality even in this. B. rejected the primacy of the papacy, viewing the bishop of Rome as the leader of the western bishops, but granted him an authoritative role in issues of dogma. For B., unity and agreement could only be achieved through constant correspondence and communication with like-minded bishops of the community. In the field of ethics, B. was strongly influenced by Neo-Platonism. B. emphasized reason and free will and posited as important rules for attaining perfection in life "recognize yourself" and "watch yourself". At the same time, he overcame the disturbing one-sidednesses of asceticism, such as the rejection of marriage or property. † 1st Jan 379 in Caesarea.

Legends: according to the Golden Legend: the hermit Ephraim sees a column of fire reaching to heaven as a symbol of B.'s greatness. – Ephraim sees the flaming tongue in B.'s mouth. – B. miraculously makes Ephraim speak Greek. – Emperor Valens attempts, through his head cook Demosthenes, to force B. to become Arian, but is unsuccessful even with the threat of torture. – When Emperor Valens tries to issue the order to exile B., the quill breaks and he abandons his plan. – B. cures a young man who has given himself to the Devil to force the love of a woman. – B. converts a Jewish doctor. – A woman's sin over a letter of debt is wiped out when she throws herself on B.'s coffin in despair.

Patronage: Order of St Basil.

Mariolatry and the Holy Family

9 *Coronation ot the Virgin Mary, by Fra Angelico, Florence, Uffizi*

10 *Shrine of the Virgin, Fatima, Portugal*

11 *Shrine of the Virgin, Lourdes, France*

12 *Shrine of the Virgin, Czestochowa, Poland*

13 *Anne, Mary and Christ-Child, by Masaccio/Masolino, Florence, Uffizi*

14 *Holy Family, by Geertgen tot Sint Jans, Amsterdam, Rijksmuseum*

15 *John baptising Christ, by Perugino, Vienna, Kunsthistorisches Museum*

16 *Christ with Mary and Martha, by Jacopo Tintoretto, Munich, Alte Pinakothek*

17 *Mary Magdalene, by Georges de la Tour, Paris, Louvre*

9

10

11

13

14

15

17

Veneration and cult sites: body buried in Caesarea.

Representations in Art: *Apparel:* as a bishop of the Orthodox rite in stoicharion, phelonion and omophorion (Capella Palatina, Palermo, 12C mosaic); as a bishop in an invented pseudo-Greek vestment (Louvre, Paris, 17C painting by F. Herrera); as a bishop of the Latin rite (Baptistry, Florence, early 14C mosaic); in a communion chasuble with pallium (Prado, Madrid, 17C painting from El Greco school); as a monk of the Order of St Basil (Palazzo Communale, Massa Maritima, 14C painting by A. Lorenzetti); as a Benedictine monk in cuculla (Malaga Cathedral, 17C (?) fig. by P. des Menas); as a hermit (Linz Library, etching by M. Renz / J. de Monatlegre, 1758). *Attributes:* Gospels (S Maria Antiqua, Rome, 8C mural); founder at his feet (Meissen Cathedral, mid–14C choir screen fig.); model of a church (Malaga Cathedral, 17C (?) fig. by P de Menas); books, skull (Antwerp, copper engraving by B. Bolswert, 1619); with dove over his head (Louvre, Paris, 17C painting by F. Herrera). *Special scenes:* B. pulls a sinner from the devil's claws (Landesmuseum, Stuttgart, passional illumination, c. 1120); B. as the father of Coenobite monasticism (Louvre, Paris, 17C painting by F. Herrera); St B. conducts mass in the presence of Emperor Valens (S Maria degli Angeli, Rome, painting by P. Subleyras, 1747).

Bede, The Venerable
Benedictine, Doctor of the Church, saint
Feast-day: 25th May (before calender reform 27th May)
Life: * 672/73 in England, at seven an oblate at the monastery of Monkwearmouth nr Sunderland, later a Benedictine monk in Jarrow. B.'s writings treat all known fields of knowledge of the time such as grammar, prosody, rhetoric, mathematics, natural science, meteorology, astronomy, music and poetry. Wrote a martyrologium based on historical sources and the first western history of monasteries and monks. His letters contain theological ideas which were widely disseminated and taken up by scholasticism. † 735. 1899 Leo XIII proclaimed him a Doctor of the Church.
Legends: a companion mockingly tells the now-blind B. that many people await to hear his sermon. In reality, he stands alone in the countryside, but the stones loudly say 'amen'.
Veneration and cult sites: body buried in Durham.
Superstitions: a list of 42 unlucky days in the year originates from B. It was widely copied. B. took it from "De ostentis" by John Laurentius Lydos (490–565 AD.).
Representations in Art: very rare. *Apparel:* as Benedictine (Viterbo Cathedral, 15/16C fresco by L. de Viterbo). *Attribute:* book (Benedictine Monastery, Münster, 18C relic). The attributes mentioned in literature – quill, ruler and a book – derive only from uncertain representations attributed to B.

Benedict of Nursia
Founder of order, saint
Feast-day: 11th July (original 8C translation feast, prior to calendar reform the feast-day was on the day of his death, 21st March)
Life: * 480 in Nursia (Norica), Umbria, the son of a noble family. Studied in Rome, but fled to a community of ascetics in Affile because of the immoral behaviour of his fellow students, later spent three years as a hermit in Aniotal's cave nr Subiaco in the Sabines. Elected abbot of Vicovaro monastery, he implemented reforms for a strict monastic life; after a monk tried to poison him, returned to Subiaco and was re-elected abbot. 529 moved the monastery to Monte Cassino. Drew up a rule and popularised the Order

based on it, such that it became the basis of western monasticism. 543 visit by King Totila. 547 twelve monasteries already established, with 150 monks in Monte Cassino. † 21st March 547. B. s rule is distinguished by restraint and adaptability. B. unified several ascetic traditions of eastern monasticism such as Pachomius, Basil, Makarios with the southern Gallic monasticism centred on Lérins. Important sources were the papers of John Cassian and the Rule of the Master. B. regulated the life of a monastic community both internally and externally under the headings of stabilitas loci (attachment to location), conversatio morum suorum (moral change) and oboedientia (obedience). Core principles of his rule are the rule of prayer, work and the performance of Divine Office, which takes precedence over everything. With this rule, the Benedictine monasteries made their most important creative contribution to western culture.

Legends: according to Gregory the Great: through prayer, B. repairs a vessel accidentally broken by his nurse. – The monk Romanus gives ascetic clothes to B. and at a bell signal lowers some bread to B. on a rope from his cave. – The devil destroys the bell. – God sends a priest with paschal food to B. – B. fights the temptation of woman by rolling naked in thorns (var: acc. to Golden Legend: when B. leaves his cave, three ravens follow him and two angels show him the way to his new place of work). – During his time as abbot of a monastery, monks try to poison him but when B. blesses the poisoned chalice, the glass is shattered. – B. leaves the place and returns to his cave. – B. drives away the Devil with a cane, but the Devil, disguised as a black boy, distracts a monk in prayer so that he wanders off. – B. marks an important well on a mountainside. – B. causes the blade of a sickle dropped into a lake to rise to the surface again by dipping the shaft in the water. – On B.'s instructions, his pupil Maurus

walks – without being aware of it – on the water to rescue a drowning pupil, Placidus. – B. has the poisoned bread sent by the envious presbyter, Florentius, carried away by a raven. – Florentius is killed by a falling balcony after getting seven girls to dance a roundelay naked in the monastery garden. – B. imposes a penance on the messenger who brings news of Florentius's death because he is delighted about the death. – B. transforms a sanctuary of Apollo into a church. – During the construction of a church, B. drives the devil out of a block of stone which cannot be moved. – B. extinguishes the glow of a fire the Devil has conjured up in an overturned idol. – Through prayer, B. revives a young monk killed by a falling wall. – Despite their denials, B. sees through monks who have consumed forbidden food and drink outside the monastery, at the house of a pious woman. – B. reproaches a monk who was persuaded by his companion to eat and drink on a journey. – B. recognizes Riggo, the sword bearer of King Totila, although at the command of his master he is supposed to appear before B. disguised in royal clothes and acting the king. – B. predicts to King Totila a nine-year reign in Rome and death in the tenth year. – B. frees a cleric from an evil spirit, and orders him to abstain from eating meat and to renounce higher office; in old age, the cleric forgets the order and the evil spirit returns immediately. – B. cries over the forthcoming destruction of his monastery. – B. sees in his mind that a monk has secretly hidden a cask of wine and warns him later not to drink it; the monk later finds a snake in a bottle. – B. sees a monk secretly accepting small cloths as gifts, hiding them under his robe. – B. recognizes the secret pride of a monk who has to hold the candle for him during meals and dislikes serving. – During famine, B. predicts that 300 sacks of flour will be at the door the following day. – In a dream, B. orders the abbot and prior of the monastery nr Terracina to build a new monastery. – Two high-ranking, God-fearing women threatened with excommunication die and, as seen by their nurse in a vision, have to leave the service after the deacon's extra omnes; at B.'s request, the punishment is revoked. – A young monk who has left the monastery without a blessing for his journey, dies on his way to his parents but the earth refuses to keep him, whereupon B. buries him with the Eucharist at his breast. – A dragon prevents an inconstant monk from leaving his monastery. – B. cures a leper. – A debtor in trouble is helped when the sum owed is found in a grain chest, thanks to B.'s prayers. – B. cures a young man's skin disease caused by poisoning. – After a monk refuses B.'s instruction to give a sub-deacon the oil remaining in the store-room, in a rage B. orders the bottle to be thrown out of the store to ensure that nothing remains in the monastery as a result of disobedience; the bottle does not break, and so can be given to the petitioner. – As B. prays, an empty barrel slowly fills itself with oil. – With a slap on the face, B. drives out a devil that is tormenting a monk. – With a glimpse from his book, B. strikes off the chains of a farmer tortured from greed by the Arian Goth, Zalla, and tames the wildness of the Goth. – B. revives a dead child. – B. sees the soul of his sister Scholastica ascending to heaven. – In Bishop German of Auxerre's hour of death, B. sees the world unified in a ray of sunlight and the angels carrying the soul of the bishop in a fireball to heaven. – B. predicts his death. – B. dies standing upright, supported by his two brothers. – After B.'s death, a mentally deranged woman is cured in his cave nr Subiaco. – For further legends, see under "Scholastica".

Patronage: Benedictines, Europe (declared Father of Europe by Pius XII, and patron saint of the West by Paul VI, 1964), of the Capetians, France, speleologists (since 1957),

coppersmiths, teachers, schoolchildren, the dying, miners; invoked against poisoning, inflammation, gallstones, fever, magic and in battles.

Veneration and cult sites: body in Monte Cassino, 637 moved to Fleury, under Pope Zacharias (741–752) returned to Monte Cassino, grave discovered in 1945 during reconstruction work after war damage; relics in Einsiedeln, Metten, Benediktbeuern (with lead bull from Pope Hadrian I, 772–795). Benedictines driven out by Lombard incursions c. 580/590 founded SS Andrea e Gregorio in Rome; St Augustine in Canterbury, the first Benedictine monastery in England; 816 Charlemagne imposed the Rule of St B. on all monasteries in the empire.

Superstitions: guardian of the hour of death between 9 and 10; St B. peals are rung to keep evil spirits away from the dying. – St B.

medallions or St B. pennies serve as charms to cure people and animals. – St B. herb and St B. roots are medicinal plants and help the retrieval of stolen timber. – B.'s blessing protects against witches and the Devil.

Representations in Art: *Apparel:* in long, belted tunic, scapular with hood (Rome, coemeterium by S Ermete, 9C fresco); in white / yellow-checked tunic (Stift Nonnberg, Salzburg, fresco c. 1140); in cuculla or fleece, since 1550 only in black on the order of Pope Paul III (Fürstenfeld, early 16C fig.); in the habit of a Benedictine monk with biretta (Vornbach, late 15C fig.); as an Olivetan in a white habit (S Miniato / Florence, fresco by S Aretino, 1387); as an abbot in pontifical mass vestments (Cismar monastery church, relief c. 1310/20); as an abbot in pluvial with mitre and crosier (Museo Civico, Messina, 15C painting by A. da Messina. *Attributes:* closed book (Stadtbibliothek, Bamberg, Ms. Ed. II 11, book illumination, c. 990); with the open rule-book at his chest (Alzenau, Lower Franconia, fig. c. 1760); inspirational angel (Fontana Maggiore, Perugia, fig. by G. Pisano, 1287/95); feather (Winchester Cathedral, 13C fresco); mitre (castle church, Chemnitz, fig. 1525); mitre at his feet (St Emmeram, Regensburg, shrine of St Dionysius, relief c. 1440); amphora-like bottle with dark liquid (Prüfening Monastery, 12C mural); broken goblet on a book (Blaubeuren Monastery, 16C fig. by G. Erhart); broken embossed goblet with snake (Kunsthistorisches Museum, Vienna, 16C relief by A. Lackner); goblet with snake (St Panthaleon, Cologne, stained glass 1622); angel holding book and chalice (Neresheim Abbey Church, 18C fresco by M. Knoller); cane (Museo di S Marco, Florence, 15C painting from Fra Angelico school); simple crosier (Blaubeuren Monastery Church, 16C fig. by G. Erhart); T-shaped crosier (Palazzo Communale, Borgo S Sepolcro, 15C painting by P. della Francesca); abbot's crosier (Museo Poldi Pezzoli, Milan,

15C painting by G. Padovano); broken sieve on the floor (Musées Royaux des Beaux-Arts, Brussels, 16C painting by J. van Coninxloo); corn sieve (St Panthaleon, Cologne, stained glass, 1622); raven (monastery church of Seitenstetten, Lower Austria, relief by T. Stammel c. 1750); basket (Sacro Speco, Subiaco, Chiesa Inferiore, 18C fig. by A. Raggi; ladder of humility (Seligenthal Monastery, late 15C mural); ball of fire (Collegiate Church, Gottweig, painting by J. M. Schmidt 1773); ball of fire, host (Benedictine monastery of Bourgeuil, 18C painting by J. Restout II). *Special scenes:* the young B. kills desire in a thorn bush (Wolfegg Castle, painting by J. C. Storer 1661); seated under a palm tree, B. draws up the Benedictine Rule (Wiblingen, choir-stall relief by F. J. Christian, 1777); B. discusses the Rule with Church representatives (Alte Pinakothek, Munich, late 15C painting by J. Polack); B. expounds the Rule to monks kneeling in front of him (Regia Galleria, Parma, 14C painting by S Aretino); B. sees the Holy Trinity enveloped in fire (Prado, Madrid, 17C painting by A. Cano); death of B. (Ochsenhausen, fig. by E. Verhelst 1741); B. in triumphal chariot (Melk Abbey, prelature fresco by P. Troger, 1739); B. appears to Emperor Henry II, who is suffering from gallstones, and removes his doubt over the authenticity of the relics (Bamberg Cathedral, emperor's tomb, relief by T. Riemenschneider, 1499). *Cycles:* numerous, e.g. S Miniato, Florence, frescoes by S Aretino, 1387; Badia cloister, Florence, frescoes by G. di Consalvo, 1435/49; Albertina, Vienna, e.g. cartoons for stained glass by A. Dürer, 1496; Monte Oliveto Maggiore, frescoes by L. Signorelli, 1497; St Peter, Black Forest, cloister, 18C painting.

Bernard of Clairvaux

Cistercian, abbot, Doctor of the Church, saint

Feast-day: 20th Aug

Life: * in 1090 in the castle of Fontaines-les-Dijon, the son of Tescelin de Saur and Aleth de Montbard, studied in Châtillon-sur-Seine. 1112 admitted with thirty other young people to the reformed monastery of Citeaux, 1113 professed, 1115 sent as abbot with twelve monks to found a monastery at Clairvaux; 1118 first daughter foundation at Trois-Fontaines, which was followed in B.'s lifetime by 67 further new foundations. B. reformed the religious life of his time, was an adviser to the Pope and at the behest of Pope Eugene III raised forces in France, Flanders and the Rhineland for a Second Crusade (1147–49), which turned into a fiasco. The failure bore heavily on B. With unjust harshness, B. had the teachings of Abelard, representative of a dialetical, rational theology, condemned as heresies. After the concordat of Worms in 1122 B. developed a mystic piety in his writings, which became the basis of later mysticism in the west. † 20th Aug 1153 in Clairvaux. Canonised 1173.

Legends: acc. to the Golden Legend: B. is dedicated to God as a child by his mother. – In a dream, B.'s mother sees herself with a white dog with red stripes on its body. The dream is interpreted to her as meaning that the boy will bark violently against the opponents of the Church. – B. chases away a sorceress who wants to cure his headache, at which the pain disappears. – During the shepherd's mass on Christmas morning, B. is granted a vision of the Christ-child. – B. is led into temptation by a woman; to cool his ardour, he throws himself into ice-cold water. – B. resists the lures of a prostitute who lies down naked next to him as he sleeps, whereupon she flees because of his virtue. – In an inn, B. is tempted by the landlady. He drives her away by crying three times "robbers, thieves". – B. forewarns his brother Gerard of an enemy's spear thrust. – B.'s brother is indeed injured and taken prisoner, but B.'s call in the night removes his chains, the prison doors open by themselves and Gerard escapes. He and his brother enter a Cistercian monastery. – His youngest brother, Nivardus, later yearns to put on the habit of the Order, too. – When robbers steal from a courier the sum of 600 marks of silver intended for B., B. thanks God that this burden has been taken from him. – B. refuses to retaliate after a canon slaps his face. – B. refuses to admit his haughty sister Humbeline to the convent, but she thinks things over and lives an unconsummated marriage. – During an illness, B. sees the punishment of God and proves the Devil wrong with argument. – B. rides to the Carthusian monastery on a magnificently saddled horse and realises it only after the Carthusians reprimand him. – Lost in thought, B. looks out over Lake Geneva and asks his companion where the water is. – B. gives money to a monk addicted to gambling, and sends him out into the world; the monk gambles everything away, but B. admits him again to the monastery to prove that one may not lose both. – B. loses the monk Rupert to Cluny; when he wants to recall him by a letter, it rains, but the writer is able to finish because the power of B.'s love keeps the rain off the paper. – B. bets a farmer his horse that the farmer cannot speak the Lord's Prayer reverently and wins because during the prayer, the farmer thinks about a magnificent saddle. – B. banishes flies tormenting the monks, and they are found dead next morning. – B. heals a woman possessed by an evil spirit. – B. cures a women of unspeakable lust by giving her his crosier to put into bed beside her. – B. converts the excommunicated Prince of Aquitaine and prepares him for penitance as he is brought face to face with the body of Christ. – During the Sacrament, B. recogniz-

es the holiness of the dead Bishop Malachy of Hibernia. – More detailed legends from William of Thierry, Ernald of Boneval and Gaufried of Auxerre, amongst others: B. gets the Devil to hold together the broken wheel of a loaded grain cart. – In Speyer, B. completes the Salve Regina with the final verse "O clemens, o pia". – In Speyer, King Conrad III brings sick children to B. – After the sermon on Midsummer Day, B. is carried out of Speyer Cathedral by the king on a wave of popular enthusiasm for his sermon. – At B.'s demand "Monstra te esse matrem" (= show that you are a mother), the mother of God sprays his cheek with milk from her breast. – B. is embraced by the crucified Christ in a vision.

Patronage: Cistercians, Burgundy, Gibraltar, Liguria, patron saint of Genoa, 3rd patron saint of Speyer Cathedral, of bees, bee-keepers, candlemakers, climbers in distress; against children's diseases, possession, animal epidemics, storms; and during the hour of death.

Veneration and cult sites: buried in Clairvaux; after the monastery was abolished in 1790, transferred to the church of Ville-sous-la-Ferte; head in Troyes Cathedral.

Superstitions: in Vyssi Brod, Bohemia, special blessing formulas for women giving birth. – B.'s name is used in incantations against demons.

Representations in Art: *Apparel:* as a Cistercian in white cuculla (Marienfeld / Westphalia, early 17C fig.); in black cuculla (Alte Pinakothek, Munich, 15C painting from the Heisterbach altar); in a chasuble (Pinacoteca, Sanginesio, painting by S Folchetti 1492); in alb and hooded cloak (Freiburg Cathedral, fig. c. 1300); in protective cloak (Altenberg, early 16C stained glass by the St Severin Master and A. Woensam). *Attributes:* paring knife (Musée Dobrée Cod. V, Nantes, 12/13C book illumination; scroll (Poblet, cod. 3, 13C book illumination); book, abbot's crosier (Chéramy Collection, Paris, painting by El Greco, 1577/79); open book (S Placido Convent, Madrid, 17C fig.); mitre lying on a book (Museo de Bellas Artes, Zaragoza, late 17C painting by V. Verdusan); mitre (Clairvaux Abbey, 17C fig.); mitre at his feet (Museo de Santa Cruz, Toledo, 17C fig.); chained devil (Maria Maggiore, Rome, 17C fig.); crucifix (Cistercian abbey / Schontal, 18C relief); tools of torture (Cistercian abbey, Stams, 18C painting by F. Wergant); rosary (S Giovenale, Orvieto, 14C fresco); beehive (St Andreas, Antwerp, 17C fig. by A. Quellinus); wheel with devil (Wallraf-Richartz Museum, Cologne, 15C painting by the master of the Golden Panel); radiant nimbus with Mary's monogram (Neumünster Collegiate Church / Würzburg, fig. 1742); little white dog (Hummelshain, 14C fig.); reliquary (Bar-sur-Aube, 14C fig.); ladder of humility (Seligenthal Monastery Library, late 15C mural). *Special scenes:* B. seated at a desk, writing (Dijon Museum, painting by Ph. Quentin, c. 1600); Mary's appearance to B., in the 'Doctrina' (Alte Pinakothek, Munich, painting by P. Perugino, c. 1500); Mary's appearance to B. with bared breast and without lactation (Wallraf-Richartz Museum, Cologne, painting by the Life of Mary master, 2nd half of 15C); lactation of B. by Mary (Metropolitan Museum of Art, New York, painting by J. Bellegambe, c. 1510); B. embraced by Christ bending down from the cross – the 'Amplexus' (Prado, Madrid, painting by F. Ribalta, 1582). *Cycles:* numerous, e.g. Cistercian monastery, Heilbronn, stained glass, 2nd half of 15C; Cologne and Shrewsbury, cathedral sacristies; Gondorf, St Matthew chapel; Schnutgen Museum, Cologne, early 16C stained glass from Altenberg by A. Woensam and the St Severin master; Chiaravalle, reliefs by C. Garavaglia, 1645.

Bernardino of Siena
(Bernardino degli Albizechi)
Franciscan friar, saint
Feast-day: 20th May
Life: * 8th Sept, 1330 in Massima Marittima SW of Florence, the scion of the distinguished Albizechi family. 1402 entered the Franciscan order, 1404 ordained. B. joined the Observants in Colomaio. 1417 began his career as populist preacher in central and northern Italy, campaigning to improve public manners and morals. Together with John of

Capistrano (q.v.), propounded the Holy Name of Jesus; within the Order, he was a reformer within the Observant movement. 1433 accompanied King Sigismond to Rome for imperial coronation, 1439 active at the Council of Florence for the union of the Greek Orthodox and Latin churches; 1438–42 Vicar General of the Observants. He refused the bishoprics of Siena, Ferrara and Urbino offered to him. † 20th May, 1444 in L'Aquila nr Rome. Canonisation 1450.

Legends: B. gets an 8-month-old child to prove the innocence of its mother. – B. cures the blind and wounded. – B. resurrects a dead man. – Numerous posthumous miracles at his grave.

Patronage: Observants, patron saint of Massima Marittima, of wool weavers, against hoarseness, chest complaints, bleeding.

Veneration and cult sites: body in S Francesco, L'Aquila. Relics in Osservanza, Siena; pilgrimage to S Maria in Aracoeli, Rome, Siena, Massima Marittima, Perugia.

Superstitions: In his writings "De idolatriae cultu", B. attacks superstition, but passes on many of the usual abuses of the late Middle Ages.

Representations in Art: *Apparel:* as a Franciscan in a long habit with knitted cingulum and cowl (Museo del Greco, Toledo, painting by El Greco c. 1600). *Attributes:* open book with biblical text (Annenmuseum, Lübeck, 15C painting); IHS monogram in round disc surrounded by rays (Wallraf-Richartz Museum, Cologne, painting by the Master of the Glorification of the Virgin, 3rd qtr of 15C); IHS monogram in round disc, from which crucifix projects (Annenmuseum, Lübeck, 15C painting); IHS monogram on rectangular panel surrounded by rays (Palazzo Publico, Siena, fresco by S di Pietro 1450); crucifix (chapter house of Siena Cathedral, fresco by S di Pietro 1427); crucifix with IHS monogram (Pinacoteca Nazionale, Siena, mid–15C painting); three mitres (Kirch-Ro-

sin, Mecklenburg, retable fig. c. 1500); three mitres, three bishop's crooks (Kirchlinde, Westfalen, retable fig. c. 1500); dove prompting at left ear (Ospedale, Siena, 15C painting). *Special scenes:* Elevation of B. by angels (chapter house of Siena Cathedral, 15C fresco); B. preaches to crowd in Piazza del Campo (chapter house of Siena Cathedral, fresco by S di Pietro 1427). *Cycles:* S Maria in Aracoeli, Rome, frescoes by Pinturicchio 1485/86; Galleria Nazionale, Perugia, painting by F. di Lorenzo c. 1500; S Francesco, Lodi, fresco attr. to Giacomo da Lodi.

Birgitta of Sweden

Wife, pilgrim, founder of Order, saint

Feast-day: 23rd July (prior to calendar reform, 8th Oct, in Sweden 7th Oct.).

Life: * 1302/3 in Finstad/Upland, of a distinguished family related to the royal family. Receiving a pious education, she had visions from an early age. 1316 happily married to Ulf Gudmarsson, and subsequently gave birth to eight children. 1335 lady-in-waiting at royal court; 1342 pilgrimage with her husband to Santiago de Compostela. After their return, Ulf Gudmarsson retired to the Cistercian monastery of Alvastra nr Linköping, where † on 12th Feb, 1344. The death of her husband changed B.'s life. 1344 settled in Alvastra monastery, where she had her famous vision of being God's bride and mediator. Founded an order, a site for which was provided by King Magnus Erikson at Vadstena by Lake Vätter. 1349 journey to Rome; 1370 papal consent to a joint monastery for monks and nuns (annulled 1442) on the model of the rule for Fontefrault conceived by Urban V; 1372/3 pilgrimage to Holy Land; lived a further 24 years in Italy. There B. had great influence on both spiritual and temporal leaders for the moral renewal of her time. † 23rd July, 1372 in Rome. Beatification 1391 on

the basis of a deposition by the emperor Charles IV in 1377. The visions of B. are composed in Swedish and and were translated into Latin by Petrus Olavi of Alvastra and Magister Matthias of Linköping. The visions – above all, the setting of the birth in Bethlehem – influenced the iconography of the Christmas scene: B. saw a white-clothed Mary praying before the enhaloed naked infant. Motifs such as the rainbow in the Madonna by the MGN Master in Stuppach can be traced back to B.'s vision, esp. as (acc. to B.) Mary hovers over the world in constant prayer like a rainbow.

Patronage: pilgrims, a favourable hour of death.

Veneration and cult sites: 1374 body transported by her daughter Katharina to Vad-

stena. Arm relic in Rome, relic in Legden (Westphalia) . Sweden, Scandinavia.

Superstitions: collection of 15 'prayers' by B. on the subject of Jesus's Passion. They enumerate the precise number of lashes of the whip, blows and torments and could be worn as a charm (condemned by the Church, but still found today).

Representations in Art: *Apparel:* as a nun in the apparel of the Brigettine Order, in a long robe with folds and white sleeves, on the head over the veil the leather snood of the choral singer's headgear and two side pieces crossed over at right angles (Metropolitan Museum, New York, fig. c. 1500); as a widow with a white scarf (Historiska Museet, Stockholm, 15C painting by H. Rode [?]). *Attributes:* abbess's staff (Legden, 15C fig.); open book (Vadstena, fig. c. 1440); book with B. writing in it with a quill (Germ. Nationalmuseum, Nuremberg, painting c. 1500); with quill in her right hand (Heilig-Geist-Spital, Lübeck, late 15C retable fig.); inkwell, quill, book (Metropolitan Museum, New York, fig. c. 1500); inkwell, quill container (Historiska Museet, 15C painting by H. Rode [?]); crown, heraldic lion (Bibliotheca Metropolitana, Prague, 15C woodcut); pilgrim's hat (choir stalls in St Stephan, Vienna, 15C fig.); bag, pilgrim's crown hanging from pilgrim's staff (Germ. Nationalmuseum, Nuremberg, painting c. 1500); heart and cross (Malchin, Mecklenberg, 15C painting). *Special scenes:* an angel dictating to B. the rule of her Order (Historisches Museum, Frankfurt, 15C painting by Brussels Master); B. distributes her rule (S Maria Novella, Florence, early 16C painting by Fra Bartolommeo); B. receives the heavenly vision from Mary who is giving birth on her knees (S Maria Novella, Florence, late 14C fresco); B. receives the vision from Christ on the pillar (National Gallery, London, 17C painting by D. Velasquez); riding a white horse into Vadstena and receiving a scroll from an angel (Bibl. Nazionale, Turin, MS I.III.23, illumination, 1st half of 14C).

Blaise of Sebaste

Bishop, Holy Helper, saint

Feast-day: 3rd Feb (until 11C 15th Feb, in Greek rite 11th Feb).

Life: B. was bishop of Sebaste (modern Sivas, Anatolia), and was martyred c. 316.

Legends: acc. to the Golden Legend, B. is elected bishop by the populace because of his outstanding gentleness and his saintly way of life. – During the persecution of the Christians under Diocletian, B. escapes to a cave and ekes out a hermit's life. – Birds bring B. food in his cave. – B. blesses wild animals. – B. lays hands on sick animals and heals them. – B. saves the animals gathered around him from hunters. – B. heals the son of a widow who gets a fishbone stuck in his gullet. – B. causes a wolf to return unharmed a pig stolen from a widow. – B. is thrown into prison by the ruler of a town. – At the interrogation, B. calls the pagan gods devils. – The widow whose pig was rescued by B. brings the pig's head, bread and a candle to B. in prison. – B. instructs the widow to sacrifice a candle every year in memory of B., which will bring great blessing. – The pagan ruler has B. strung from a wooden beam and his flesh torn off by iron hatchets. – Seven women collect B.'s blood at the martyrdom spot, are themselves interrogated, cunningly declare their readiness to sacrifice to the idols if the latter are washed beforehand in a pool, but instead of sacrificing to them, they throw the statues into the water. – The women are martyred as B. was, but are given strenght by an angel. – The fire in the furnace into which they are to be thrown goes out. – The ruler has the women beheaded; B. is thrown in the pool, but does not drown because the water dries up at the sign of the cross. – B. is beheaded.

Patronage: patron saint of the Guelphs and the city of Dubrovnik; of doctors, building workers. wind musicians, tanners, plasterers, pets, hatmakers, bricklayers, tailors, shoemakers, soap-boilers, stone-carvers, hosiery workers, weavers, chandlers, windmill owners, wool dealers, cattle; against neck complaints.

Veneration and cult sites: relics in Brunswick, Constantinople, Cologne, Lübeck, Milan, the seminary at Mainz, Montpellier, Naples, Paray-le-Monial, Dubrovnik, Rome, St Blasien, Tarranto, Trier.

Superstitions: the weather in early spring changes on St B.'s Day. – Since the early 6th cent, there has been an incantation in B.'s name to remove bones from the gullet. – St B. water is given to young chicks to stop the fox getting them. – On St B.'s Day, horses are blessed. – St B.'s bread cures neckache. – On St B.'s Day no spinning may be done or the roof will be blown off.

Representations in Art: *Apparel:* as a bishop in pontifical robes with chasuble (Monreale Cathedral, 12C mosaic); as a bishop in pluvial with mitre and crook (Frauenkirche, Mengen, late 15C). *Attributes:* book (S Maria Antiqua, Rome, 10C fresco); cattle at his feet (Morpeth, Northumberland, stained glass c. 1400); wolf and pig at his feet (Guelph Treasury, Berlin, assembly room of Otto the Mild, 11C book cover relief); pig's head in his hand (Hautzenberg, painting c. 1490); horn (Neusitz, retable fig. 1515); heckle (Leitmeritz, painting c. 1460); boy (St B., Krombeke, 18C medallion); candle burning in his left hand (Lübeck Cathedral, Geveraden altar, fig. 1492); targe (Kunsthistorisches Museum, Vienna, fig. by A. Lackner 1518); candle woven out of three thin wax fillets (cemetery chapel, Risstissen, fig. 1483); two crossed candles (altar of grace, Vierzehnheiligen, by J. M. Feichtmayr 1784); wax taper (Aachen Cathedral treasury, late 5C painting); candlestick with candle

(Fehmarn Castle, late 15C fig.). *Special scenes:* B. pulls a fishbone out of a boy's throat (Lorca/Spain, 18C painting by Salzillo); the miracle with the wolf and the pig (St Thomas, Strasbourg, pre–1277 relief); B. heals sick animals (St B.'s Chapel, Kaufbeuren, woven tapestry c. 1578); B. in solitude on Mt Argaeus (Augsburg Library, copper engraving from J. Guilini, Tägliche Erbauung eines Wahren Christen, 1753). *Martyrdom:* martyrdom with the flaying and decapitation (Erzbischöfliches Diözesanmuseum, Abdinghof portable altar, early 12C inlay work by Roger of Helmarshausen; south doorway of Chartres Cathedral, fig. c. 1225). *Cycles:* lower church of S Clemente, Rome, mosaic c. 1100; St Paul im Lavanttal, pluvial embroidery 1225/30; St B.'s Chapel, Kaufbeuren, painting c. 1485; St B.'s church, Ehingen, frescoes 1738.

Bonaventure of Bagnoreggio

(John Fidanza) Franciscan friar, bishop, Doctor of the Church, saint

Feast-day: 15th July

Life: * 1217 or 1221 in Civita di Bagnoreggio, son of the doctor Giovanni di Fidanza and Maria di Ritello. When he fell gravely ill at the age of 7, his mother promised him to St Francis of Assisi. 1236–42 in Paris to study the liberal arts under Alexander of Hales; 1243 joined the Franciscan order. 1253 completion of novitiate and biblical/theological studies, became magister. On 2nd Feb, 1257, following the forced resignation of John of Parma, elected Minister General of Order, directing it energetically and with pragmatism from Paris until 20th May, 1274. On 12th Aug, 1257 admitted to the college of professors, on 28th May, 1273 called to Rome by Pope Gregory X for appointment as cardinal-bishop of Albano and the preparations for the 2nd Council of Lyons. B. took part in the negotiations for a union with the Greek Orthodox church, in which the political crisis affecting the Emperor Michael VIII Palaeologus was exploited. B. preached at the completion of the short-lived union. † 15th July, 1274. Canonisation on 15th July, 1274. Appointed Doctor of the Church by Pope Sixtus V in 1588. – In his numerous writings such as the commentary on Peter the Lombard's Sentences, a commentary on the scriptures and many others, B. constructs a speculative train of theological argument based on neo-Platonic and Augustinian thought, in contrast to St Thomas Aquinas, who helped the philosophy of Aristotle to a breakthrough. For B., the concept of "world" in the Exemplarist sense means the image and likeness of God. The human spirit can reach God if his religious devotion has enabled him to overcome the appearance of things. Umbrae (shadows), Vestigia (traces) and Imagines (images) allow the believer to recognise God's image and in these traces

attain an experience of God akin to the love of God. – As Minister General, B. mediated between the strict and liberal factions in the mendicant dispute, while insisting on the existing rule of the Order, and created the Legenda major as the official Vita of St Francis of Assisi. Earlier versions of his life were destroyed.

Legends: the newborn infant is blessed by Francis of Assisi. – As a 7-yr-old boy, B. is healed by St Francis. – In gratitude, the mother takes him to St Francis again, who exclaims "O buona ventura" (O happy future). – B. raises a stillborn child from the dead. – B. shows St Thomas of Aquinas a crucifix as the source of his wisdom. – An angel announces to B. that Gregory X is ot be the new pope. – The papal delegation with the decree of B.'s appointment as cardinal-bishop rea-

ches B. while he is washing up in the kitchen. – Not wanting to interrupt his work, B. tells the commission to hang the cardinal's hat on a tree for the time being. – B. considers himself unworthy of communion until an angel brings over to him part of a priest's wafer. – The last communion pierces B.'s heart through his chest.

Patronage: Franciscans, theologians, workers, children, load-bearers, silk manufacturers.

Veneration and cult sites: body interred in the sacristy of the Franciscan monastery in Lyons, c. 1450 transferred to the church of St Francis in Lyons; 1562 during the Huguenot persecutions the body was burned; the head was saved, but vanished in 1807. Arm relic in Bagnoreggio, as gift of Charles VIII of France.

Representations in Art: *Apparel:* as a Franciscan with a habit gathered with a cord (Pinacoteca, Carrara, 16C painting by Bronzino); as a Franciscan with a strapped book pouch (Kunsthistorisches Museum, Vienna, antependium 1502); as a bishop with pluvial over the Franciscan habit (St-Nicolas, Troyes, fig. by F. Gentil c. 1510); in Capuchin habit with pluvial and bishop's crosier (Provincial Museum, Seville, 17C painting by B. E. Murillo); as a cardinal in cappa magna (Lille Museum, painting by P. P. Rubens c. 1600); as a theologian at his desk (Bergamo Cathedral, 18C painting by Morelli). *Attributes:* cardinal's hat hanging on a tree (Wallraf-Richartz-Museum, Cologne, painting by the Master of the Glorification of the Virgin c. 1480); cardinal's hat at his feet (Louvre, Paris, 16C fig. from della Robbia workshop); cardinal's hat suspended above heraldic arms (Wallraf-Richartz-Museum, Cologne, painting by St Severin Master c. 1500); cardinal's hat suspended over mitre (Aquila, 16C painting by Cola dell'Amatrice); cardinal's hat hanging on the wall (Museo Francescano, Rome, 17C painting); cardinal's hat on bookstand (Kirchliner, fig. c. 1500); cardinal's hat in hand (Gransee, early 16C painting); angel bearing mitre (Provincial Museum, Sevilla, 17C painting by B. E. Murillo); cardinal's hat at his neck (Kunsthistorisches Museum, Vienna, antependium 1502); angel's head on pluvial (Corciano, painting by B. Bonfigli 1472); book (Wroclaw Museum, early 16C painting); crucifix in hand (Bayerisches Nationalmuseum, Munich, early 16C painting); crucifix with branches and leaves sprouting at sides (Kunsthistorisches Museum, antependium 1502); crucifix with ribbon inscriptions from B.'s tracts (Corciano, painting by B. Bonfigli 1472); tree of the Cross as an allusion to B.'s tract "Ecce lignum Vitae" (Dahlem Gallery, Berlin, 15C painting by C. Crivelli); tree of the cross with pelican (Accademia, Florence, painting attrib. to Pacino da Buonaguida 1347). *Special scenes:* B. as witness of the Immaculate Conception (Douai Museum, early 16C painting by J. Bellegambe); B. in tree listening to St Anthony of Padua (Accademia, Venice, 15C painting by L. Bastiani); B. writing his tracts (S Croce, Florence, painting by T. Gaddi 1330/40); B. raises a stillborn child from the dead (Pinacoteca Naz., Bologna, painting by F. Gessi post 1600); B. shows St Thomas the sources of his writings (formerly Kaiser-Friedrich-Museum, Berlin, painting by F. Zurbarán 1629). *Cycles:* formerly St B.'s church, Seville, painting by F. Zurbarán 1629; formerly Chateau Vilandry, painting by B. Herrera the Elder 1627.

Boniface

(Winfrith) Benedictine monk, bishop, martyr, apostle of the Germans, saint

Feast-day: 5th June (celebration of consecration as bishop on 1st Dec).

Life: * 672/75 in Wessex as Winfrith, scion of a noble Anglo-Saxon family. Educated as a boy in the Benedictine monastery of Exeter and Nursling (Hants); entered the Order and became head of the monastic school in Nursling. Author of a grammar and a book of prosody. 716 mission to Friesia failed because of B.'s unrealistic expectations. Despite his election as abbot, he asked Pope Gregory to be sent as a missionary, who on 15th May, 719 added the epithet Bonifatius to his given name. Mission in Thuringia, and jointly with Willibrord in Friesia; after 721 in Hessen, where he founded the monastery of Amoeneburg; 722 consecrated bishop during his second trip to Rome. At Geismar, cut down the pagans' sacred donary oak; in conflict with Frankish clergy; 732 third trip to Rome, appointed by Gregory III archbishop and papal vicar of the missionary territory. B. organised the Church in Bavaria, Alemannia, Hessen, Thüringen; 744 founded monastery of Fulda, legate of the west Frankish Church. B. set up dioceses in Germany with fixed frontiers, thus creating a firm ecclesiastical organisation based on centres in Passau, Salzburg, Freising and Regensburg, to which Würzburg, Buraburg, Erfurt (741) and Eichstätt were later added. 748 diocese of Mainz as personal missionary diocese. After the ousting of the household steward Carloman, B. lost his leading position at the Frankish court. 753/4 renewed his mission to Friesia. Along with 52 companions, B. suffered a martyr's death on 5th June, 754 near Dokkum, beside the River Borne. In a solemn translation procession, the body of B. was brought via Mainz to Fulda.

Legends: B.'s father refuses to let the boy devote himself to God and is therefore struck down with illness. – B. absolves the household steward Carloman from the sin of stealing church property. – B. builds a chapel from the wood of the felled donary oak. – B. anoints Pippin king of the Franks. – B. hands over to his successor Gregory the keys of the cathedral church of Utrecht. – B. destroys an idol. – B. receives a fish from a dove, as food for him and his companions Adalar and Eoban. – B. curses the gold of the Thuringians into stone, at which every penny turns into a stone lentil. – A spring surges up at the spot of B.'s martyrdom.

Patronage: Apostle of the Germans, Boniface missions for Christians in the diaspora, the diocese of Fulda, brewers, tailors.

Veneration and cult sites: tomb in Fulda, blood relic in Utrecht, relics in Mainz Cathedral, Freckenhorst Abbey (since 851), Notre-Dame Bruges (since 1124). Venerated in the dioceses of Mainz, Fulda, Berlin, Eichstätt, Görlitz, Dresden-Meissen, Freising (Munich), Osnabrück. Pilgrimages in Dokkum and Hulfensberg (Eichsfeld). Former pilgrimage-type traditions in Freckenhorst Abbey, Hamlin, Langensalza, St Salvator Utrecht.

Superstitions: B. rides as a good spirit at the side of wild huntsmen and warns them to turn back. – On St B.'s day, beans must be set if they are to thrive.

Representations in Art: *Apparel:* as a bishop in missal chasuble, with pallium, mitre, crook (Petersberg, Fulda, 12C relief); as a bishop in pluvial (Mainz Cathedral, fig. on Gemmingen tomb by H. Backoffen post 1514); as a monk (S Severino, Perugia, late 15C painting by Perugino); as a monk (S Severino, late 15C painting by Perugino); as a monk with flock gown and pallium (abbey of Isny, 18C fresco); as a Benedictine monk in habit (abbey of Ottobeuren, 18C fresco); as a Benedictine abbot with flock gown, infula, crook (former Egmond, St Adalbert Abbey, painting by J. van Scorel 1525). *Attributes:* dagger with pierced book (font at Schlitz, relief 1487); dagger spearing book from below (Epiphany altar, Fulda Cathedral, fig. c. 1700); book with dagger thrust from above (market fountain sculpture, Mainz 1528); book struck at edge (Eisenach Museum, fig. c. 1500); dagger without book (Eichenzell rectory, relief c. 1500); crosier with double bars as symbol of papal legate (Geisa, relief c. 1500); hand crucifix with double bars (Dietges, wood fig. c. 1780); archepiscopal crosier with single bar (seminary library, Mainz, copper engraving in Serarius, Mainzergeschichte 1604); penitent's whip (chasuble, Amersfoort, embroidery c. 1520); spring (copper engraving by C. Bloemaert after a painting by A. Bloemaert c. 1630); well (Antwerp, woodcut from Ribadeneira-Roswey-de's Legend of the Saints 1629); bottle jug (St Maria Minor, Utrecht, 18C fig.). *Special scenes:* B. preaching to pagans (St Frans Xavier, Amsterdam, painting by J. Collaert 1620); B. blesses Sturm before dispatching him to Fulda (Fulda Seminary, painting by A. Herrlein c. 1792); B. receives the donatory document from Carloman (Fulda Seminary, painting by A. Herrlein c. 1792); B. strikes a

S. BONIFACIVS ARCHIÉP. MOGVNTINVS. M.

spring (Propsteischloss, Sannerz, painting post 1778); felling of the donary oak (formerly St B.'s church, Munich, 19C mural by J. Schraudolph); B. with Willibrord at prayer before Deus patiens (Assumption of the Virgin, Huissen, painting by J. Bijlert c. 1650). *Martyrdom:* Mainz Cathedral, Liebenstein epitaph, relief c. 1508; abbey of Muri, mural by F. A. Giorgioli 1696–7. *Cycles:* Erfurt Cathedral, stained glass c. 1410; Sturm altar, Fulda Cathedral, 18C relief; St B. coffin in Notre-Dame, Bruges, relief by M. Blootacker 1624; St Bonifaz, Munich, 19C mural by M. Hess and J. Schraudolph; Gemäldegalerie, Berlin, 19C painting by A. Rethel.

Brigid of Ireland

(Brigit, Bridget, Bride) abbess of Kildare, saint
Feast-day: 1st February (Diocese of Cologne: 14th July)
Life: Born circa 453 in Fochart in Northern Ireland (today Faugher) as the illegitimate daughter of King Dubtach of Ireland; B. grew up on a farm, became a nun in 467 and founded the double monastery of Kildare (a wooden church) west of Dublin. B. was known for her hospitality and compassion and care for the poor. D. 525.
Legends: Numerous Lives in prose and verse form in Old Irish, Middle English, Middle High German and Italian: On the farm, B. distributes butter to the poor, which is returned to her by an angel. – As evidence of her virginity, a branch at the altar is in leaf during B's vocation. – This branch heals the sick. – B. heals a severed hand.
Patronage: In Ireland: livestock.
Veneration and cult sites: Buried in Kildare, relics in Bruges, Honau (Alsace), Strasbourg, Belém near Lisbon, Lumiar; her cult extended by Scottish Monks to France, the Netherlands, Rhineland and southern Germany, and northern Italy.

Representation in Art: *Apparel:* as matron in long, girded robe, overmantle and head veil (Stuttgart, Landesbibliothek, Stuttgart Passional, book illumination, 12th century); as virgin (Copenhagen, National Museum, Lisbjerg altar, relief, circa 1140); as abbess (SS Dredenaux, figure, early 16th century); as herdswoman (Antwerp, Folklore Museum, devotional graphic, 18th century). *Attributes:* Branch (Copenhagen, National Museum, Lisbjerg Altar, relief, circa 1140); wreath around the veil (Strasbourg Cathedral, stained glass, circa 1245); palm branch, large-format open book (Cologne, Wallraf-Richartz Museum, painting by the Master of the Glorification of the Virgin Mary, circa 1470); abbesses' staff (SS Dredenaux, figure, early 16th century); cow lying at feet (Cologne, Wallraf-Richartz Museum, painting by the Master of St Severin, circa 1505–10); goose lying at feet (Augsburg, church of the Holy Cross, drawing (copy) of a lost silver figure, 1625); *Special scenes:* B. heals the sick (woodcut from the Saints of the Family, Friends and Relatives of Emperor Maximilian I, 1516); B. is carried by angels across the sea to the birth of Christ (Edinburgh, National Gallery, painting by J. Duncan, circa 1900); *Cycles:* Paris, Bibliothèque Nationale MS lat.17294, book illumination, 1433).

Bruno the Carthusian

Confessor, founder of order, saint
Feast-day: 6th Oct
Life: * c. 1030/35 in Cologne to the Hartefaust family. Ordained after studying in Rheims and Cologne, where he became a canon at St Kunibert's. 1057 head of the cathedral school at Reims; his pupils included Odo of Chatillon, later Pope Urban II; 1075 chancellor in Reims. After quarrelling with the archbishop Manasse, who had fallen out with Pope Gregory VII, B. had to leave

Reims in a hurry, but returned in 1080 after Manasse was deposed. 1081 became archbishop elect, but was forced to withdraw in the face of a candidate put up by king Herlinand of Laon. 1083 admitted by Robert de Molesme as a Benedictine monk, B. gained permission to set up a hermits' settlement in Seche-Fontaine, in the diocese of Langres. 1084 to Bishop Hugo of Grenoble with six companions, who granted them the mountainous region of Chartreuse. An oratory developed, surrounded by individual cells. 1090 called by Urban II to Rome, 1081 established a charterhouse at La Torre in Calabria. † there on 6th Oct, 1101. No official canonisation; 1514 and 1623 confirmation of the cult.

Legends: B. receives the rule of the Order from the Virgin and Child. – B. is converted by his dead teacher Raymond Diocres, who announces his own damnation from his bier. – B. rejects the bishopric of Reggio di Calabria. – A sick man is healed with water from B.'s tomb.

Patronage: Carthusians.

Veneration and cult sites: body in the church of S Stefano de Bosco.

Representations in Art: *Apparel:* in the garb of the Order, i.e. white habit, cowl (Wallraf-Richartz Museum, painting by Master of the Holy Family, 1515). *Attributes:* olive branch (Wallraf-Richartz Museum, Cologne, painting by A. Woensam 1535); index finger to lips (Cadiz Cathedral, 17C fig. by M. Montanez); star on his chest, globe, sceptre (Museo S Carlos, Valencia, 17C painting by F. Ribalta); cross, globe, skull (former Charterhouse, Hildesheim, late 17C fig.); cross in front of face, mitre and staff at his feet (Monasterio

del Paular, 17th cent fig. by G. Fernandez);
lily (art trade, 17C copper engraving by G.
Rousselet). *Special scenes:* Mary appearing
to B. (Palazzo Reale, Naples, 17C painting by
J. Ribera); B. receives the rule of the Order
from Mary (Louvre, Paris, 17C painting by Le
Sueur); B. and the speaking corpse of his
teacher (Wallraf-Richartz Museum, painting
by Master of the Bruno Legend 1488/89).
Cycles: Margaretental charterhouse, Basle,
mural by Lawelin c. 1440; S Martino charterhouse, Naples, painting by M. Stanzione
1635; Louvre, Paris, 17C painting by E. Le
Sueur; Lyons charterhouse, painting by F.
Perrier 1630; Bayerisches Nationalmuseum,
Munich, 19C stained glass by H. Schaper.

C

Cajetan of Thiene

(Kajetan, Gaetano) Theatine, saint

Feast-day: 7th August

Life: born in October 1480 in Vicenza, son of Gasparo of Thiene. In Padua he studied law and completed his studies with a doctorate. He became the secretary of Pope Julian II and papal protonotary; 1516 ordained as priest and member of the Brotherhood (Oratory) of Divine Love. Together with Ignatius of Loyola and Charles Borromeo he was regarded as representative of the church reforms of the 16th century. In 1519, he joined the Vicenza Brotherhood of St Jerome, founded by Bernardin of Flètre, caring for the poor and infirm. In 1524, together with Giovanni Pietro Caraffa, archbishop of Theate (later Pope Paul IV), Paolo Consigliari and Bonifacio de'-Colli, he founded a congregation bound by vow (Theatines). In 1527 he was driven out of Rome and worked alternately in Venice and Naples. Characteristic of him was his poverty, trusting to divine providence. – he died on 7th August 1548 in Naples. Beatified 1629, canonized 1671.

Legends: C.'s mother sacrifices her child to the mother of God. – At Christmas 1517, Mary presents her child to C. in a vision at S Maria Maggiore. – The mother of God moistens C.'s cheek with milk from her breast. –

C. cures N. Caffarelli. – C. proves to be incorruptible. – C. helps the people in Naples stricken with the plague. – C. intercedes for Christ, stopping lightning by throwing himself between the lightning and Christ, requesting that the anger be directed at himself. – C. prays for the successor of Adelheid of Savoy.

Patronage: Kaufbeuern since 1672; patron of the Theatine Order; domestic animals in Bavaria; invoked against the plague. Reverence and cultic sites: mortal remains in Naples, S Paolo Maggiore; Munich, Theatine Church.

Representation in Art: *Apparel:* in habit of the Order with soutane, white socks, belt, biretta and rosary (Munich, St Kajetan, fig. by R. Boos, 2nd half of the 18th century); in chorroc and stole (Barcelona, Cathedral, fig., 18th century). *Attributes:* Order cross (Naples, S Paolo Maggiore, painting, 16th century); winged, burning heart (Prague, Charles' Bridge, fig. by F. M. Brokoff, 1709); rulebook (Vicenza, S Giuliano, fig. by Marinaldi, 17th century); open gospel with the inscription of Mt 6. 24–33 (Milan, S Antonio Abbas, painting by G. B. Crespi, circa 1700); lily, birds (Naples, Monastero de la Sapienza, painting of the Vaccaro school, 17th century); grain sheaves and cornucopia with flow-

ers and fruit (attribute of the Providentia Dei) (Modena, S Vicente, painting by Fra F. Caselli, 17th century); Christ-child on his arm (Reisach at the Inn, Monastery Church, fig., 1751); skull (Venice, S Nicola da Tolentino, painting by Palma il Giovanne, circa 1600); heretic under his feet (Barcelona, Museum, fig. attributed to M. Sala, 2nd half of the 17th century); model of a church (Rampazzo, Parish Church, painting by Tiepolo, 1757); protecting livestock (Munich, Bavarian State Library, copperplate engraving by J. A. Lidl, 18th century). *Special scenes:* Mary's presentation of the child to C. (Ferrara, Sacristy of the Theatine Church, painting by F. Galetti, 17th century); C.'s lactatio (Überlingen, Cathedral, relief at the C. altar, 17th century); the confirmation of foundation of C.'s Order by Pope Clement VII (Vicenza, S Stefano, painting by Maganza, 17th century); C. caring for the infirm (Milan, Brera, painting by S. Ricci, late 17th/early 18th century); plague in Naples (Munich, S Kajetan, painting by J. Sandrat, 1672); C. throws himself between lightning and Christ (Vicenza, S Stefano, painting by Maffei, 17th century); C. prays before the crucified (Ferrara, S Maria dei Teatini, painting by A. Rivarolo, 17th century). *Cycles:* Naples, S Paolo Maggiore, reliefs by D. A. Vaccaro, 17th century; Ferrara, S Maria della Piet, frescoes by C. Maiola, 17th century; Salzburg, St Kajetan, reliefs, 18th century.

Callistus I

(Kallistus, Kalixtus, Calixtus) Pope, Martyr, saint

Feast-day: 14th October (day of burial)

Life: the former slave of the Christian Carpophorus, who gave him his freedom, C. became the first deacon of Pope Zephyrinus and was responsible for the administration of the parish cemetery, now the Callistus catacomb on the Appian Way. During his pontificate (217–222) he fought against heretics, particularly against Sabelius's Monarchians who denied the Holy Trinity. In this dispute he was accused of a dishonest past and of laxity by the antipope Hippolytus because C. permitted adulators into the community of the Church and accepted marriages between noble women and slaves (further information under Hippolytus). C. introduced the art of mural painting to the churches. He was buried in the Roman Coemeterium of the Calepodius.

Legends: according to the legend, written in the 7th century, C. is thrown out of a window and drowned in a well, a rock around his neck.

Veneration and cult sites: Pope Gregory III translated his mortal remains to S Maria in Trastevere, Rome. Relics are in the Cysoing abbey near Tournai (since 854); Fulda; Reims; Naples, S Maria Maggiore.

Representation in Art: *Apparel:* as priest in chasuble (Rome, S Maria in Trastevere, mosaic, 12th century); as pope with conical tiara and rational (Reims, vertical northern house, fig., 1225/30; as pope in pluvial with tiara (Pienza, Cathedral, painting by Vecciet-ta, 1461/62). *Attributes:* cross staff, book (Mailing, C. Chapel, fig., circa 1480); stone on a book (Vienna, St Stephan, choir-stalls, fig., circa 1487); surrounds of a well at his feet (Nuremberg, Germanic National Museum, painting, circa 1500). *Martyrdom:* Stuttgart, Regional Library, Stuttgart Passionale, book illustration, circa 1130.

Camillus of Lellis

(Kamillus, Camillo) Camillian, Founder of an Order, saint

Feast-day: 14th July (before the reformation of the calendar: 18th July)

Life: born on 25th May 1550 in Bucchianico near Chieti, son of an officer, serving Charles V. He was orphaned at an early age. Between 1559 and 1574 he participated in Venice's war against the Turks. At home again, he gambled away all his belongings. In 1575, he worked as a building labourer at the Capuchin monastery at Manfredonia, was converted and joined the Capuchins but had to leave because of a bad foot complaint. He was cured in the San Giacomo Hospital in Rome where he worked as male nurse and hospital director. In 1582, in association with his adviser, Philip Neri, he founded an order for the care of the sick (Compagnieri dei Ministri degli Infermi). In 1584 he was ordained as a priest. In 1591, the Order was unified with the Order of Regular Clerks serving the infirm, also called Fathers of a Good Death, led by C. In 1607 he retired as head of the Order. Within the care of the infirm it stood for the reformation of hospitals. He died on 14th July 1614 in Rome. Canonized 1746.

Patronage: Camillians, hospitals, male nurses, the sick and dying.

Veneration and cult sites: his mortal remains were buried in Rome, S Maddalena.

Representation in Art: *Apparel:* as member of the Order with red cross on his soutane or coat (Rome, S Maddalena, fig. by P. Campana, 1735). *Attributes:* crucifix, book, angel, skull (Rome, S Camilli, relief, early 19th century); rosary (Rome, St Peter, fig. by P. Pacelli, 1735). *Special scenes:* in discussion with an aristocrat (Rome, S Maddalena, painting by G. Panozza, 18th century); C. as male nurse (Rome, S Maria in Trivio, painting by A. Gherardi, 17th century); C. rescues the infirm of the hospital from the 1598 flood of the Tiber (Rome, Museo di Roma, painting by P. Subleyras, 1746); C.'s Amplexus by Christ (Bologna, S Gregorio, painting by F. Torelli, 1743).

Casimir of Poland

Prince, saint

Feast-day: 4th March

Life: born on 5th October 1458, the third child of the Jagellon Casimir IV and Elizabeth of Hapsburg, daughter of Emperor Albrecht. In 1471 elected as king of Hungary but renounced his right to the throne in favour of Matthias Corvinus. He was briefly the Polish regent whilst his father was in Lithuania. C. distinguished himself through devotion and veneration of the mother of God. He died on 4th March 1484 in Grodno of consumption. Beatified in 1521, canonized 1602.

Legends: C. composes the hymn "Omne die dic Maria". – C. is crowned by the mother of God with her child. – C. revives a boy. – C. intervenes in a miraculous way in the Battles of Polock, in 1518 and 1654, against the Russians.

Patronage: Knights of St John; youth of Poland and Lithuania; national literary hero; invoked against enemies of religion and the fatherland.

Veneration and cult sites: mortal remains in Vilna, Cathedral.

Representation in Art: *Apparel:* as king in coat with the coat of arms of Poland and Lithuania (Vilna, Cathedral, painting, before 1594); as Mary's knight (Florence, Palazzo Pitti, painting by C. Dolci, 17th century). *Attributes:* Palm tree (Crosno, Poland, Parish Church, painting, 16th century); lily, cross (Munich, Bavarian National Museum, ivory relief, circa 1700). *Special scenes:* C.'s coronation by the mother of God (Palermo, Museo Nazionale, painting by P. Novelli, called Monrealese, circa 1629); revival of a boy (Vil-

na, Cathedral, C. Chapel, frescoes by G. Campana, 1636); C. helps the Lithuanian's against the Russians (Vilna, St Peter and Paul, relief, late 17th century). *Cycles:* copperplate engravings according to Ilarione de S Antonio, Il breve Compendio della vita, morte e miracoli del principe Casimiro by N. Perrey, 1626; currently strong demand in Lithuania for C. portraits.

Catherine of Alexandria

(Katharina) Virgin, Martyr, saint

Feast-day: 25th November

Legends: legend motifs from C.'s childhood: her childless parents take advice from an astrologer. – An artist has, as God of all Gods, created a crucifix and all pagan paintings in the temple fall to the floor. – The parents pray for a child to this God in the temple. – C. is born. – Legends according to the Passion, written in the 6/7th century and translated into Latin in the 8th century: born as daughter of King Costus, C. is well educated in the liberal arts. – After the death of her parents, C. is wealthy and has numerous servants. – Out of pride, C. refuses all suitors because none seems good enough for her. – A hermit reveals Christ to her as the real bridegroom. – In 307, at the age of 18, C., in a dispute about the truth of Christianity, wins over 50 pagan philosophers and converts them, who were allegedly nominated by Emperor Maxentius. – On the emperor's orders, those 50 philosophers are burned. – C. firmly refuses to sacrifice to the pagan idols. – C. is beaten with sticks and thrown into prison where she is fed and cared for by angels (var: Christ sends a white dove with divine food). The empress releases C. but the emperor sentences her to death tied to a wheel. – An angel destroyed the torture wheel. – The empress and the gaolers are then converted. – All are tortured and beheaded. – C.'s body releases blood and milk.

– Angels carry C.'s body to Mount Sinai where she is buried.

Patronage: 2nd patron saint of Valais and the diocese of Sitten; Paris University; libraries; hospitals; young girls; virgins; married women; pupils; teachers; theologians; philosophers; rhetoricians; solicitors; notaries; universities; book printers; wagon-makers; potters; millers; bakers; sinners; milliners of Parisian haute couture (so-called Catherinettes), rope makers; boatmen; tanners; shoemakers; barbers; invoked against diseases of the head and tongue; for nursing mothers suffering from lack of milk; for assistance in searching for drowned people; arable crops.

Veneration and cult sites: tumulus cult at Mount Sinai; Catherine monasteries; relics in Rouen, Cologne, Grevenrode, Nuremberg. Venerated in France since the 11th century, in Germany since the 12th century. Early patronage of Werden (1059), Zwickau (1125), Xanten (1128).

Superstition: significant annual day for the weather of the forthcoming winter. – Due to the closeness to Advent, C. day was the last day of revelry, therefore the custom of C. dance. – Patron for the early morning hour between 4 and 5. – In Tyrol, C. oil was regarded as a remedy against the plague, gout, cold, breathing difficulties, intestinal worms, pains of the womb etc. – In Styria, a child's navel of children is rubbed with C. oil to protect against worms. – A. fig, cooked in C. oil, protects against angina. – In Hungary, if a man washes his face with a woman's shirt, he sees his future wife in his dream.

Representation in Art: *Apparel:* as virginal princess with crown (Aschaffenburg, Parish Church of the Mother of God, fig., late 12th century); as virgin with bonnet (Landershofen, fig., circa 1500); as virgin with veil (Munich, Bavarian National Museum, fig, circa 1420); as cephalophore (Siena, S Agostino, painting by A. Lorenzetti, 1st half of the 14th century). *Attributes:* cross (Monreale, Cathedral, mosaic, 12th century); crown in hand (Naples, catacomb of S Gennaro, mural painting, after 763); palm tree (Siena, Pinacoteca Nazionale, painting by P. Lorenzetti, circa 1330); book (Gelnhausen, St Mary's Church, relief, circa 1225); small wheel (Strasbourg, Cathedral, Catherine Chapel, fig., circa 1330); broken wheel (Perugia, Galleria Nazionale, painting by Fra Angelico, 1st half of the 15th century); sword (Freiburg, Cathedral, St Mary's Church, mural painting, circa 1330); sword (Lugano, Thyssen Collection, painting by Caravaggio, early 17th century); three wheels (Atri, Cathedral, mural painting, 15th century); lily and plate with scientific names (Palermo, painting, 14th century); emperor at her feet (Paderborn, portal of the Cathedral, fig., middle of the 13th century); *Special scenes:* mystic wedding of St C. with the Christ-child (Brussels, Musées Royaux des Beaux-Arts, painting by M. Coffermans, 2nd half of the 16th century); C.'s wedding with her bridegroom, Christ (Allentown, USA, Museum, painting by G. del Biondo, 17th century); C.'s wedding with the Christ-child, Mary absent (San Severino, Pinacoteca Communale, painting by L. Salimbeni, circa 1400); a hermit shows C. the Madonna (Esztergom, Christian Museum, painting, 15th century); C. discusses with pagan philosophers (Rotterdam, Boymans-van Boyningen Museum, painting by J. Provost, 1515/25); Empress Faustina visits C. in prison (Nuremberg, Germanic National Museum, painting by the master of the HG, 1st half of the 16th century); C. in paradise (Verona, Museum, painting by S. da Zevio, 15th century). *Martyrdom:* C.'s martyrdom (Dresden, Painting Gallery of Old Masters, painting by L. Cranach the Elder, 1506); angels destroy C. wheel by lightning (Madrid, Prado, painting by the master of Sigüenza, 15th century); angels bury C.'s body on Mount Sinai (Milan, Brera, mural painting by B. Luini, 16th century); angels carry C.'s soul into heaven (Brussels, Musées Royaux des Beaux-Arts, painting by G. de Crayer, 17th century). *Cycles:* including childhood Legends: Nuremberg, St Sebald, dorsal, embroidery, circa 1440/50; numerous according to the Passional, amongst others: Cologne, St Maria Lyskirchen, mural painting, late 13th century; Angers, Cathedral, stained glass, circa 1160/77; Soest, St Maria zur Höhe, mural painting, circa 1250/60; Alsenborn, Pfalz, mural painting, 13th century; Münster, stained glass, circa 1320; Rome, S Clemente, mural painting, circa 1425; Immenhausen near Hofgeismar, mural painting, 1483.

Catherine of Siena

(Caterina Benincasa)

Member of the Dominican Third Order, Doctor of the Church (since 1970), saint

Feast-day: 29th April (before the calendar reform: 30th April)

Life: born about 1347 in Siena, the 25th child of a wool dyer; should have married at the age of 12 but C. refused. In 1365 she joined the Third Order of St Dominic; 1374 she cared for those stricken by the plague. – C. was appreciated as adviser to several princes. – In 1374, due to her mystic inclination, she had to answer to the General Chapter of the Dominicans in Florence. – In 1376, C. persuaded Pope Gregory XI to return from Avignon to Rome. – In 1377 she founded the Belvaro convent. – During the Great Schism of 1378, when French cardinals refused Pope Urban VI and nominated the antipope, Clement VII, C. tried to convince numerous clerical dignitaries with her letters to accept

Urban VI. In 1378, at the request of Pope Urban, she moved to Rome. Stigmatized on 1st April 1375. C.'s book *Libro della divina providenza* dealt with the issue of the cognition of God and Providence and has a high literary standing, ranking with Petrarch and Dante. She died on 29th April 1380 in Rome. Canonized 1461.

Legends: C. receives the habit of the order from Dominic – C. gives her habit to a beggar and receives a divine habit from Christ. – In a mystic vision, C. marries Christ. – C. exchanges her heart with that of Jesus. – Christ gives C. wisdom and powerful eloquence to enable her to preach His Gospel to the Church leaders. – Instead of a golden engagement ring, C. selects Christ's crown of thorns. – C. receives holy communion from Christ. – For her parents, C. begs for deliverance from purgatory by taking on their pains of sin. – C.'s prayer converts highwaymen. – The dead Agnes of Montepulciano raises her foot to enable C. to kiss it. – During an increase in prices, C. bakes good bread from spoiled flour. – C. fights for Palmerina's soul. – C. accompanies the young aristocrat Andrea dei Tuldo, who deserted the Church, and conveys to him a new approach to faith in face of death. – C. exorcises several devils. – C. cures the head of Siena hospital of the plague. – At C.'s mortal remains, several disabled people are healed.

Patronage: Third Order of St Dominic; 2nd patron saint of Rome (since 1866); main patron saint of Italy since 18th June 1939; of the dying; for the receipt of the last rites at the hour of death, of laundrywomen, invoked against headaches and the plague.

Veneration and cult sites: her mortal remains are in Rome, S Maria sopra Minerva; relics are in Siena, S Domenico (head); Venice, S Giovanni e Paolo (foot); pilgrimage to her birthplace in Siena.

Superstition: During the C.'s night the Catherine flower blooms. Witches' processions on C.'s night are more connected with the old feast-day (30th April) and less with the meaning of the feast.

Representation in Art: *Apparel:* in habit of the Order with girdled dress, medium-wide sleeves, scapular, coat, flag, consecration staff and white head veil (Rome, S Maria sopra Minerva, fig. by Isaia da Pisa, 1450); with dark veil (Diessen, Bavaria, Dominican Convent, painting, 18th century); as nurse (Antwerp, Musée des Beaux-Arts, painting, circa 1470/80); in protective coat (Siena, Oratorio S Caterina della Notte, painting by M. Balducci, 16th century). *Attributes:* stigmata, in 1475 forbidden by Pope Sixtus IV, approved again by Pope Urban VIII (Cambridge, Mass. Fogg Art Museum Harvard University, painting by G. die Paolo, 15th century); lilies in the stigmata (Barcelona, Museum, painting, 15th century); crown of thorns (Perugia, Galleria Nazionale, painting by Fra Angelico, circa 1437); heart (Florence, S Marco, painting by Fra Angelico, 1425/35); crucifix (Munich, Alte Pinakothek, painting by D. Ghirlandaio, 1490); skull (Siena, Accademia delle Belle Arti, painting by Sodoma, early 16th century); rosary (Valencia, Colegio del Patriarca, painting, early 16th century); devil at her feet (Rieti, Museo Civico, fresco by Antoniazzi Romano, late 15th century); tiara in her hand (Rome, S Lorenzo, grave of Pius IX, mosaic by L. Seitz, late 19th century); people stricken by the plague (Diessen, Bavaria, Dominican Convent, painting, early 18th century). *Special scenes:* C. receives the habit of the Order from Dominic (Setignano, Berendson Collection, painting by Neroccio, 2nd half of the 15th century); C.'s wedding with Christ (Pisa, Museo Civico, painting, circa 1385); C.'s wedding with the Christchild (London, National Gallery, painting by L. da Sanseverino, late 15th century); stigmatization (Siena, Accademia, painting by D. Beccafumi, early 16th century); C.'s confirmation of the stigmatization by Pope Pius II (Siena, Biccherna, painting, 1499; presentation of the crown of thorns (Venice, Accademia, painting by F. Bissolo, 16th century); exchange of hearts (Milan, Museo Poldi Pezzoli, painting by G. Ferrari, 1st half of the 16th century); C. drinks at Christ's side wound (Rome, Monumento commemorativo at the Via del Papa, relief by F. Messina, 1962); presentation of the rules for the second and third Dominican Orders (Edinburgh, National Gallery of Scotland, painting by C. Rosselli, circa 1480); canonisation by Pope Pius II (Siena, Libreria Piccolomini, fresco by Pinturicchio, circa 1506). *Cycles:* not standardized, few motifs: amongst others, Siena, Casa S Caterina, frescoes by G. del Pacchia, after 1418; Cleveland, Museum of Art; New York, Heinemann Collection; Lugano, Thyssen Collection; New York, Metropolitan Museum; Minneapolis, Institute of Arts, painting by Giovanni di Paolo, 1st half of the 15th century.

Cecilia

Virgin, martyr, saint

Feast-day: 22nd Nov. (in Greek rite 24th Nov.)

Ecclesiastical historical background: A church in Rome founded in the 5C is supposed to stand on the site of the house of the Roman patrician Valerian. The feast-day of the saint is possibly the day the church was consecrated, its original dedication not having been handed down. However, the name probably derives from the old Roman family name of the Caecilians. The church was renovated during the rule of Pope Paschal I (817–24).

Legends: acc. to the late 5C Passion and the Golden Legend, C. comes from a noble Roman family and asks God to preserve her virginal purity. – C. marries the young Valerian, and on her wedding night wears a hairshirt under her golden robes. – C. explains to her husband on their wedding night that she has an angel from heaven as a lover, who is watching over her body. – Valerian wants to see the angel and is sent by C. to see Pope Urban, who lives in exile. Beggars show Valerian the way to Pope Urban. – There, an old man in gleaming robes appears to Valerian, carrying the book of faith. – Pope Urban baptises Valerian. – On his return, he sees C. in conversation with the angel. – The angel gives C. a wreath of roses from Paradise and Valerian a wreath of lilies from there. – Valerian's brother Tiburtius notice the scent of the heavenly flowers and is converted to Christianity by C. and baptised. – Tiburtius and Valerian secretly bury martyrs during the persecution of Christians and give alms.

– The pagan prefect Alimachus has them beaten and hands them over to Maximum for safe keeping, along with C. – Maximus is converted and baptised in the house of C. – C. comforts Valerian and Tiburtius in prison. When they are beheaded, Maximus sees their souls entering heaven. – Maximus is martyred by being clubbed to death with lumps of lead. – C. buries Maximus. – C. preaches on a block of stone outside her house and Urban baptises the converted. – In front of a judge, C. refuses to sacrifice to idols. – C. is put into boiling water in the caldarium of her own house, but remains unharmed. (Variant: C. is put fully clothed in a cauldron containing boiling water.) – C. is supposed to be beheaded in the bath, but even after three blow the executioner is incapable of severing her head. – The half-dead C. bequeaths her possessions to the church (variant: to the poor) and endows her building as a church. (Variant: C. is thereupon beheaded in the bath.) – C. is beheaded with a sword in the open air.

Patronage: St Cecilia societies and confraternities of St Cecilia founded in the 18C to cultivate the church music of Palestrina; church music, choral singers, poets, musicians, singers, instrument makers, (in Bavaria) luthiers; organ-builders as a result of a misapprehension arising during the 15C/16C from the sentence "cantantibus organis C. virgo in corde suo soli Domino decantabat" (i.e. while the instruments resounded, the virgin C. sang in her heart only to the Lord) at the depiction of marriage in the legend to the effect that it had entered the festival antiphon in the 8C.

Veneration and cult sites: canonical saint since the mid–5th cent; translation of the bones (probably of a member of the Caecilians buried there) from the Catacombs of Callixtus to Trastevere by Pope Paschal I; 1599 at the opening of the coffin, the body is said to have been found undecayed. Relics in Albi, Hildesheim, St C. in Trastevere, Rome.

Representations in Art: *Apparel:* in Byzantine court apparel (S Marco, Venice, 11C mosaic); in a long, belted robe (St Kunibert, Cologne, early 13C stained glass); in contemporary fashionable women's clothing (Wallraf-Richartz Museum, Cologne, early 18C painting); with crown cap (doorway of St C.'s church, Cologne, relief c. 1200); with veil beneath a coronet (Pinocateca, Siena, painting by P. Lorenzetti 1332); as prostrate figure after the discovery of the body (S C. in Trastevere, Rome, fig. by Maderna 1599/1600). *Attributes:* crown in veiled hands (S Apollinare Nuovo, 6C mosaic); palm bough (Uffizzi, Florence, early 14C painting by C Master); ostrich feather (Goudstikker Collection, Amsterdam, painting by Frankfurt Master c. 1505); sword (St Kunibert, Cologne, reliquary chest, painting c. 1400); book (S Salvatore al Monte, Florence, early 15C painting by G. del Ponte); wreath of roses and lilies (Albi Cathedral, 16C fig.); wreath of white and red roses (Metropolitan Museum, New York, painting by Raphael 1505); two wreaths (Wallraf-Richartz Museum, Cologne, painting 1st half of 15C); three wreaths (Schlossmuseum, Berlin, painting c. 1420); angel (Museo Capodimonte, painting by B. Cavallino 1645); a single rose (Wallraf-Richartz Museum, Cologne, painting by St Severin Master c. 1500); putti with palm bough, crown and wreath (episcopal curia, Poznan, 17C painting by Fiasella da Sarzana); musical instruments as decoration around her neck (Rijksmuseum, Amsterdam, Master of the Virgo inter virgines c. 1480); organ played by angels (St Andreas, Cologne, St Severin Master c. 1500); lute played by angels (Palermo Cathedral, painting by R. Quartararo c. 1500); playing the organ (S Clemente, Brescia, painting by Moretto c. 1530); angels treading bellows (Wallraf-Richartz Museum, Cologne,

Master of the Bartholomew Altar 1500); holding an organ (Pinacoteca, Bologna, painting by Raphael 1515); sitting at an upright organ (Galerie der alten Meister, Dresden, painting by C Dolci c. 1671); playing a zither (Städel, Frankfurt, painting by Master of Garden of Paradise c. 1420); playing a cello (Louvre, Paris, 17C painting by Domenichino); harp (Louvre, Paris, painting by P. Mignard, 2nd half of 17C); three neck wounds (Accademia di S Luca, Rome, late 17C painting by A. Pozzi); belt (Pinacoteca, Bologna, painting by Raphael 1515); lily sceptre (Güstrow Cathedral, fig. c. 1490); lily (Galerie alter Meister, Dresden, painting by C Dolci c. 1871); wise virgin with lamp (altar ciborium, S Cecilia, Rome, fig. by A. di Cambio 1293); lamp in hand (oratory of S Silvestro, Rome, early 13C fresco); little dog (Wallraf-Richartz Museum, Cologne, early 16C painting by A. Woensam); falcon (Leiden Museum, 15C painting by C Engelbrechtsz). *Special scenes:* C. receives wreath and crown from infant Jesus (Veidelek Collection, Prague, late 15C painting by C Engelbrechtsz); C. as muse crowning the artist with wreath (Albertina, Vienna, 19C drawing by Scheffer von Leonhardshoff); angel crowning C. with wreath (S C. in Trastevere, Rome, 17C painting by G. Reni); angel crowns C. and Tiburtius with wreaths (Brera, Milan, painting by O. Gentileschi 1620); Christ crowns C. (S C. in Trastevere, Rome, fresco by S. Conca 1725); burial of C. (Musée du Luxembourg, Paris, painting by A. W. Bouguerau, 2nd half of 19C). *Martyrdom:* C. kneeling to await the sword (S C. in Trastevere, Rome, 17C painting by G. Reni); C. lying wounded on the ground (Montpellier Museum, painting by N. Poussin, 1st half of 17C). *Cycles:* (examples) S Urbano alla Caffarella, Rome, 11C mosaics); S C. in Trastevere, Rome, late 11C frescoes; S Maria in Carmine, Florence, late 14C frescoes; S Giacomo Maggiore, Bologna, mid–15C frescoes.

Charlemagne
Emperor, beatified

Feast-day: 28th January (translation feasts: 27th January in Aachen, 30th July in Paris)

Life: born around 742, son of Pepin the Short. In 768 he became, together with his brother Carloman, king of the Franks and conquered Aquitaine in 769. In 771 he became sole ruler and, following a cry for help from Pope Hadrian I, went to Italy to depose King Desiderius of Lombardy and assumed the crown himself. He renewed the union with the Church, concluded by his father. He took over the protectorate of the Church state. In 788 he deposed Prince Thassilo of Bavaria. In 800 he was crowned as emperor by Pope Leo III in Rome. In 804 he ended the war against Saxony, leading to the final subjugation of Saxony. At his court, C. founded a school with the best-known western scholars. Moreover, he founded new dioceses and interfered in internal ecclesiastical matters. Due to the unclear decisions of the Council of Nicaea regarding the Franconian theological worship of paintings, C. criticised Pope Hadrian I. At the 794 Frankfurt Synod, C. represented Adoptianism, a variation of Arianism, declaring that Christ was a human being, blessed by God. During his reign, C.'s ideal was the creation of a theocracy. In the Middle Ages, C. was regarded as the model of a wise, just and noble-minded ruler. This picture was clouded by certain personal weaknesses. He died on 28th January 814.

Legends: from the Compostela legend of the 11th century, attributed to the surroundings of Bishop Turpin of Reims: James appears to C. to reveal his grave to him. – C. receives absolution from his sins through a banner presented by an angel. – C.'s sins are forgiven by the hermit Giles. – C. prays at Pamplona. – C. destroys Mohammed's idols. – A selection of individual legends from the Legenda aurea: an angel presents relics of Jesus to C., including the prepuce from circumci-

S. CAROLVS MAGNVS.

sion, the umbilical cord and his children's sandals. After his coronation in Rome, C. orders that his son Pepin should receive the tonsure and join a monastery because of a conspiracy against his father. – C. can bend four horseshoes straight in at once and split a knight on horseback with one blow of his sword. – Further important elements of C. legends were handed down in the *Chanson de Roland* of the 12th century; in the emperor's chronicle (after 1147); in "Charles" by Stricker (circa 1230/50); in the *Karlmeinet* (14th century) and also by Einhard; sometimes the narrations fall between heroic saga and Christian legend but mostly within the limits of the former.

Patronage: Brotherhood of the Artist's Faculty of Arts of French and German Nations at the Sorbonne, Paris.

Veneration and cult sites: his mortal remains are in Aachen, Pfalz Chapel. Relics are, amongst other locations, in Aachen, Charlemagne's shrine; canonized in 1165 on the order of Emperor Frederic Barbarossa by Archbishop Reinald of Dassel, recognized by the antipope Paschalis III but not by Pope Alexander III. Aachen and Osnabrück later received permission to venerate C. The cult linked with his pilgrimage to Compostela was revived in the 11th century. Locations in which C. had allegedly established monasteries or dioceses began in the 13th century with the veneration, for instance, in Bremen, Brixen, Feuchtwangen, Frankfurt, Fulda, Halberstadt, Hersfeld, Münster, Seligenstadt, Sitten, Zürich and Verden. Emperor Charles VI introduced the cult of C. to Prague and Nuremberg and the French King Charles V to Paris and the dioceses of Reims, Rouen, St Quentin.

Representation in Art: *Apparel:* as Franconian commander (Rome, S Susanna, circa 800); as dying commander in coronation robes (Nuremberg, Germanic National Museum, painting by A. Dürer, 1512); as com-

mander standing in full armour with crown, imperial orb, sceptre (Alzenau, St Justinus, fig, circa 1758); with the French imperial coat of arms on his patterned clothes (Aachen, Cathedral Treasury, relic bust, circa 1350); kneeling as founder of a church (Aachen, Charles's seal, relief, circa 1328); in protective coat (Vienna, Austrian National Library, Hagiologium Brabantinum, book illustration, 1476/84); as Gospel preacher – deacon function of the German kings (Aachen, coronation Gospel, book cover by Hans of Reutlingen). *Attributes:* model of a church (Aachen, Cathedral, fig., circa 1430); sword (Vienna, Austrian National Library Cod. 1859, Charles VI's prayer-book, book illustration, 1516–1519). *Cycles:* Rome, S Maria in Cosmedin, mural painting, before 1124; Charlemagne's shrine, relief, 1215; St Gallen, Collegiate Library, Stricker's "Karl", book illustration, circa 1300; Aachen, Town Hall, mural painting by A. Rethel, 19th century.

Charles Borromeo

Cardinal, Archbishop, saint

Feast-day: 4th November

Life: born on 2nd October 1538 in the castle of Arona on Lake Maggiore, the son of an aristocratic family. At the age of twelve he received the clerical tonsure and robe. Through the commendatory abbacy of the Arona Benedictine Order he received the corresponding revenues without being obliged to administer the church by himself, a deplorable state, which originated from the Carolingians, an d was opposed by C. later. At Pavia university he studied law and obtained a doctorate in civil and canon law in 1559. He became the administrator of the large properties owned by his family. Through his uncle, Cardinal Gian Angelo Medici, later Pope Pius IV, he was appointed as secretary; in 1560 to cardinal deacon and administrator of Milan. In 1562, after the death of his brother, Federigo, he turned to the ascetic life, was ordained as a priest in 1563 and a short time later as bishop. He energetically supported Church reform and the implementation of the decisions of the Tridentine Council, founded two priest seminaries and one for missionaries who were to have been sent to Switzerland, which turned protestant, because three Grisons valleys belonged to Milan. He promoted the Brotherhoods of the Holy Altar Sacrament, founded in 1535, and founded the Borromaeum for poor students. Despite vigorous opposition, C. fought clerical concubinage, superstition, misuse and ignorance of the people and increased the general standards and discipline within the clergy. In 1576, after the plague broke out in Milan, C. organised aid; on Passion Sunday 1584 he took stock for the last time on Monte di Varallo. He died on 3rd November 1584 in Milan. C. was the embodiment of the ideal bishop of Tridentine reform. Beatified in 1602, canonized in 1610).

Legends: C. predicts the end of the plague because following his prayer he has a vision of an angel inserting his sword into its scabbard.

Patronage: Borromeons (Congregation of Nursing); the diocese of Lugano and Basle; Borromeo societies; public libraries; pastoral workers; priest seminaries and boarding schools; Salzburg University; invoked against the plague.

Veneration and cult sites: the cult spread quickly throughout Europe; patron saint of numerous churches, amongst others, the Vienna Karlskirche.

Representation in Art: *Apparel:* as cardinal in choir clothes (Rome, S Carlo ai Catinari, painting by G. Reni, 17th century); in chasuble or pluvial (Milan, Brera, anonymous drawings, 17th century); in rochet, mozetta and biretta (Waidhofen on the Thaya, fig., 1721). *Attributes:* cardinal's hat (Seville,

The Apostles

18   *The Veil of Veronica, by the Munich Master of St Veronica, Munich, Alte Pinakothek*

19   *Crucifixion of St Peter, by Michelangelo Caravaggio, Rome, S. Maria del Popolo*

20   *St Peter's church in Rome, after a painting by Giovanni Paolo Pannini*

21   *The apostle Andrew and Francis of Assisi, by El Greco, Madrid, Prado*

22/23 *The "Four Apostles": on the left, John and Peter, on the right Paul and Mark, by Albrecht Dürer, Munich, Alte Pinakothek*

24   *St James the Great, 18th century figure, Unterpfaffenhofen, Germany, church of St Jakob*

25   *Santiago de Compostela, Spain*

26   *Doubting Thomas, painting in a Gospel Lectionary, Munich, Bayerische Staatsbibliothek*

21

22

23

Museum, fig., 18th century); crucifix (Münster, Cathedral, fig., 1737); nail relic (Bilbao, Collection Valds, painting by Zurbaràn, 17th century); skull, whip (Unlingen, fig. by Christian the Elder, 1722); plague arrows, rope around his neck (Straubing, Ursula Church, fig. by E. Q. Asam, 1738); relic of S Chiodo in his hand (Cellio, Parish Church, painting by T. da Varallo, 1st quarter of the 17th century); dove (Milan, S Gottardo i Corte, painting by D. Crespi, circa 1610). *Special scenes:* C. offers the Eucharist to the sick (Ghent, Museum, painting by T. Boyermans, 17th century); C. visits the sick (Rome, S Adriano, painting by O. Borgianini, 17th century); penitent's procession in Milan (Rome S Carlo ai Catinari, painting by P. da Cortona, 1667); banquet with C. (Milan, S Maria della Passione, painting by Crespi, early 17th century); C. predicts the end of the plague (Antwerp, St Jacob, painting by J.

Jordaens, 17th century). *Cycles:* Milan, Cathedral, painting, 1602/10; Milan, Cathedral Crypt, reliefs, 17th century; Vienna, Karlskirche, reliefs by Ch. Mader, 1730; Volders, frescoes by M. Knoller, 1776.

Charles Lwanga and companions
Martyrs of Uganda, saint
Feast-day: 3rd June
Life: born in 1865 in Bulimu, Uganda. Baptised in 1885. During the persecution of the Christians by King Mwanga, C. and his twelve companions, pages at the imperial court, were burned alive. Beatified in 1920, canonized in 1964 during the 3rd session of the 2nd Vatican Council.
Patronage: African youth (since 1934).
No representations in art.

Chilian with Colonat and Totnan
of Würzburg
(Kilian, Killena, Kyllena) Itinerant bishop, Priest and Deacon, Martyr, saint
Feast-day: 8th July
Life: C. originated from Ireland and came to Würzburg as an itinerant bishop where he worked with his companions for several years. – He had a dispute with the family of a Thuringian prince because he forbade the marriage of Prince Gozbert to his sister-in law, Gailana. On Gailana's orders, C. and his companions were murdered in about 689.
Legends: according to the Passio, circa 840: from the pope, C. receives the missionary order to go to Franconia and is ordained as bishop. – C. converts Prince Gozbert and his people to Christianity. – The mortal remains are buried in a stable. – After the murder, the murderers and Gailana become insane and commit suicide. – The devil abducts Gailana. – The mortal remains of the martyrs are found by Atalongus.

Patronage: Franconia; diocese of Würzburg; decorators; protection against eye diseases; gout and rheumatism. Due to the song of Victor of Scheffel, wrongly named as patron saint of wine growers.

Veneration and cult sites: on 8th July 752 the mortal remains were translated to the church on the Marienberg by Bishop Burchard; in 788, in the presence of Charlemagne, translated to the Salvator Cathedral (now Neumünster) by Bishop Berowelf. Pilgrimage in Würzburg; Lower Franconia; diocese of Paderborn; Bamberg; Lambach, Upper Austria.

Superstition: eyes, moistened with water from the Würzburg (Neumünster) C. vault, are protected against disease. – Turnips, planted on C. day grow particularly large. – If one sees on C.'s night, a glowing fern and takes it, one can be invisible.

Representation in Art: *Apparel:* C. in mass chasuble with crosier and book (Paderborn, Cathedral, fig., 14th century); in pluvial (Langenleiten, Parish Church, fig., 16th century); Colonat as priest in mass chasuble, Totnan in dalmatic (Hassfurt, Parish Church, fig., circa 1500); Colonat and Totnan in dal-matic (Würzburg, Neumünster, fig. as copies according to T. Riemenschneider, 1510). *Attributes:* sword (Würzburg, Main-Franconian Museum, flag embroidery, 1266). *Martyrdom:* C.'s beheading with the sword (Unteraufsee, Castle Chapel, painting, 1515); C. clubbed to death (Heidelberg, University Library, Legenda aurea Pal. germ. 144, book illustration, 1419); pierced with sword and lance (Oberwang, Parish Church, fig. by M. Guggenbichler, 1708). *Cycles:* Münnerstadt. C. window, stained glass, circa 1430; Würzburg, Main-Franconian Museum (formerly Lorenz Church, Nuremberg), painting, circa 1475; Münnerstadt, reliefs by Veit Stoss, 1503; Würzburg, Cathedral, so-called C. tapestry, circa 1688.

Christopher

Martyr, Holy Helper, saint

Feast-day: 24th July (prior to calendar reform 25th July)

Legends: A Passion has developed in Chalcedon since the 5C around the figure of the man-eating cynocephalus, which by a wondrous blessing is given baptism, a human countenance, the capacity to speak and the name of C. In later versions of the legend, C. is a soldier in an imperial army and acquires the ability to speak by enjoying the fruits of paradise. During persecutions by one King Dagnus (= Decius?), C. suffers martyrdom. In later versions, the legend is incremented with features of the ideal image of chivalry; the by now non-bestial appearance of the "C. canineus" rests on the interpretation of the name by Walther von Speyer as "a man from Canaan etc.". Some episodes acc. to the Golden Legend: * as a man-eating reprobus among the cynocephalus populace, the ambition of C. – a giant some 12 miles long – is to serve the greatest king. – C. notices that the said king crosses himself whenever the Devil is mentioned, and he therefore takes service with the Devil because the latter must be greater than the king. – When the Devil turns tail before a wayside Cross, C. learns that Christ is mightier than the Devil, and so he quits the latter's service. – C. seeks Christ and finds a hermit, who instructs C. to carry pilgrims over the river. – A child asks C. to carry him over the river, but C. is scarcely able to sustain the burden of the boy across the river. – The boy reveals himself as Christ and announces that, as a sign of the truth, C.'s staff will turn green next morning. – Christ baptises C. as they cross the river. – C. comes to Samos, where, amazed by the sign of the burgeoning staff, 8,000 people are converted. – The king has C. taken captive after C. converts a few of his mercenaries. – The mercenaries are beheaded. – The king sends two trollopes, Nicaea and Aquilina, to C. in prison to change his mind, but they too declare themselves for Christianity. – Using their girdles, the wenches tear down the idols from their plinths. – Nicaea is hanged and Aquilina burned at the stake and beheaded. C. is thrashed with an iron rod. – A glowing helmet is put on C.'s head and he is tied to an iron stool, under which a fire with pitch is lit, but the stool melts and leaves C. unharmed. – C. is tied to a post and used by archers for target practice, but the arrows get suspended in the air. – When the king mocks the miracle, one of the arrows drops out of the air and hits him in the eye, blinding him. – C. tells the king, after he has beheaded him, to dab C.'s blood on the eye. – C. is beheaded (variant: drowned in a well). – The king's eye is healed, at which the king becomes a believer.

Patronage: patron of America, motor travel, Christian youth, fortresses, sailors, porters, carters, athletes, gardeners, fruiterers, miners, treasure-seekers, milliners, dyers, bookbinders, the Cruciferi and Cavalieri dell'Al-

topascio, pilgrims, travellers, doctors; against accidents, plague, eye complaints, drought, hail, tempest, all dangers, mortal danger (C. confraternities since the 1C against a sudden and uncontrite death).

Veneration and cult sites: relics in St Peter's, Rome, St-Denis nr Paris; an impression of C.'s footprint in S Trinita della Cava nr Sorrento. Cult of C. along the mediaeval pilgrim routes and hospices, e.g. in St C. in Arlberg (since 1386, burnt down in 1957). Pilgrimages in St-Christophe-le-Jajolet and St-Christophe-de-Rocquigny.

Superstitions: the sight of a picture of St C. gives protection against sudden death on this day without the last rites. (This notion was strongly criticised by Erasmus of Rotterdam and other humanists.) – St C. prayers for attaining prosperity and success in treasure-hunting. – St C. ducats are worn as amulets and fixed to the dashboard of cars.

Representations in Art: *Apparel:* as a young martyr (S Maria Antiqua, Rome, 10C mural); as a full-face giant carrying the infant Jesus in ornate ceremonial dress, with a long, richly patterned robe, belt with ribbon-style ornamentation and a long, often ermine-lined cloak (St Cyriakus, Niedermendig, 13C mural); as a giant with a lion's head (Martyrologium Usuardi in Landesbibliothek, Stuttgart, illumination c. 1140); as 12-mile giant (S Vincenzo di Galliano, Como, early 11C mural); as a giant in a knee-length or gathered robe and mantle (Königsfelden, stained glass c. 1330); as a walking giant (Alte Pinakothek, Munich, painting by Master of the Pearls of Brabant c. 1485); as a ferryman with headband (Cologne Cathedral, fig. c. 1470); in ducal apparel (Lilienfeld, HS 151, mid 14C pen-and-ink drawing); in belted pilgrim's cloak (mercy altar, Vierzehnheiligen, fig. by J. M. Feichtmayr 1764); as a bearded old man (Frauenkirche, Munich, fig. by Rasso Master c. 1530); as a youthful bearer of Christ (S Clemente, Rome, fresco by Masaccio 1427);

as a cynocephalus (only eastern churches); as a Christ-like figure with the infant Jesus (St Elisabeth, Marburg, 13C mural); as Atlas with the globe (Germanisches Nationalmuseum, Nuremberg, drawing by F. A. Maulpertsch 1762); as an athlete (Prado, Madrid, painting by J. Ribera 1637); C. on horseback (16C woodcut by I. A. M. Master of Zwolle); C. with breastplate (Linz Museum, early 16C painting by the monogrammist S W); knight with Christ child at the crossroads (Amsterdam museum, 16C painting by J. de Cock). *Attributes:* book (S Maria Antiqua, Rome, 10C mural); stone with which C. is supposed to have been drowned (St Barbara, Soghale, 11C mural); staff beating leaves (mural in St Junien, end 11C/early 12C); palm tree (S Cristoforo, Siena, painting by Sano di Pietro 1444); martyr's palm (late 12C mural in Irschen); pilgrim's staff with leaves (St Andreas, Cologne, 13C mural); staff ending in pinnacle (Germ. Nationalmuseum, Nuremberg, painting by S Lochner c. 1445); wasted tree trunk (Cologne Cathedral, fig. c. 1470); palm trunk (Parque de Automovilismo de Ejecito, Madrid, early 20C fig.); the Christ child riding piggyback on C. (Tour Ferrande, Pernes, mural c. 1275); clothed infant Jesus with book (Regensburg Cathedral, fig. c. 1325); naked infant Jesus (mercy altar, Vierzehnheiligen, fig. by J. M. Feichmayr 1764); benedictory infant Christ (Bruges Museum, 15C painting by H. Memling); clinging child (St Sebald, Nuremberg, 15C fig.); child with orb and cross – pennant (chapel, Chemille, early 16C mural); child enthroned on globe (Bissing Collection, Munich, painting by J. de Cock c. 1520); calm waters (Kunstmuseum, Basle, painting by K. Witz c. 1430); oars (Cod. Lambeth MS. 209, British Museum, London, illumination, 2nd half of 13C); stormy waters (Kunstmuseum, Basle, 15C painting by W. Huber); hermit with lamp (Alte Pinakothek, 17C painting by J. Mandyn); water full of monsters (Wienhau-

sen, 14C mural); globe (S Maria della Grazie, Offida, 14C mural by A. Nuzi or follower); glass ball (Escorial, painting by J. de Patinir c. 1521); wreath of roses (St Jakob/S Tyrol, 15C mural); globe (Kunstmuseum, Basle, mid–16C painting by Messkirch Master); fish (Boymans van Beuningen Museum, Rotterdam, painting by H. Bosch c. 1500); pouch with bread (Zagreb Museum, painting c. 1522); pilgrim's pouch worn at belt (S Juliano, Seville, mural by J. Sanchez de Castro 1484). *Special scenes:* C. as allegory of Protestant Communion doctrine (Alte Pinakothek, Munich, 17C painting by J. Mandyn). *Cycles:* S Vicenzo di Galliano, 11C mural; Bayerische Staatsbibliothek, Munich, illustrations to the Vita of C. by Walter von Speyer, illumination 1170/80; Dominican church at Bolzano, mural c. 1370; Eremitani, Padua, frescoes by Asuino da Forli, Bono da Ferrara and A. Mantegna c. 1450; St Christophe, Paris, frescoes by J. Martin-Ferriére 1933.

Clare of Assisi

Foundress of the Poor Clares (2nd Order) of St Francis, saint

Feast-day: 11th August (before the calendar reform: 12th August)

Life: born in 1194 at Assisi of the influential Offreduccio Favarone family. C. was the first disciple of St Francis of Assisi and received her habit in 1212 in Portiuncula from Francis. Together with her mother, Ortolana, and her sisters, Agnes and Beatrice, she founded branches in Damiano near Assisi. Pope Innocent III granted C. the privilege of poverty. At the age of 30 she became ill and confined to bed. In 1253, Pope Innocent IV acknowledged the Order. She died on 11th August 1253. Her body is still not decomposed. Canonized on 15th August 1255.

Legends: attributed to Thomas of Celano and written in 1255/56; other papers including 26 legends were written before 1492 by Magdalena Staimerin: after a sermon by St Francis on Palm Sunday 1212, C. with the agreement of Bishop Guido of Assisi, who presents her with a palm branch secretly leaves her parents' home. – Her relatives try to abduct C. from the convent. – For the community of 50 sisters, C. multiplies a loaf of bread to ensure that all have enough to eat. – During the pope's visit, C. blesses the bread which divides itself into four portions. – During the Saracen attack of 1240, the convent is endangered but C.drives the enemy away, the Ciborium in her hand. – Saracens who try to climb the wall of the convent fall blinded into the depths. – During her prayers in the church, the Christ-child appears to C., above the Ciborium. – Her sister, Agnes, at C.'s death-bed sees virgins with white clothes and golden crowns. The most beautiful of them kisses C. – On her death-bed, C. has a vision of the Christmas mass in S Francesco (reason for the patronage of television!).

Patronage: Poor Clares; patron saint of Assisi; of the blind; laundry-women; embroiderers; gilders; glaziers; glass painters, television.

Veneration and cult sites: her mortal remains were buried in S Giorgio; in 1260 translated to the newly built Assisi S Chiara church; her body can be seen in a glass shrine.

Superstition: French C. springs are good for the eyes. – In Catalonia, C. drives away clouds. – In Brittany, St Elmo's fire is called "Feu Ste-Claire"; if this disease occurs they appeal to her.

Representation in Art: *Apparel:* in dark habit of the Order with veil, white headband and a collar, girdled with a rope (Assisi, S Francesco lower church, fresco by A. Lorenzetti, 14th century); with white veil (Assisi, S Francesco, fresco by S. Martini, 14th century). *Attributes:* monstrance (Cologne, Wall-

raf-Richartz Museum, painting, early 15th century); crucifix (Erfurt, Barfüsser Church, painting, 15th century); book (Freiburg, Switzerland, Franciscan Church, painting, 1480); palm branch (Messina, Museum, painting, 15th century); lily (Florence, S Croce, Bardi Chapel, fresco by Giotto, 1325/29); abbess' crosier (Moosbach, Wiesenkirche, fig, 1757); prayer-cord (Dresden, Painting Gallery of Old Masters, painting Sienese school, early 15th century); burning lamp (Regensburg, Cathedral Treasury, silk embroidery, circa 1300); burning horn (Washington, Kress Foundation, painting by U. Lorenzetti, 14th century); flaming vase (Siena, Pinacoteca Nazionale, painting by G. di Paolo, 15th century). *Special scenes:* C.'s hair is cut by St Francis (Königsfelden (Aarau), stained glass, 14th century); C. drives away the Saracens with prayers (Naples, S Chiara, painting by F. de Mura, 18th century, destroyed); C.'s vision of the Christ-child (St Petersburg, Hermitage, painting by Guercino, 17th century); St C.'s death (Dresden, Painting Gallery of Old Masters, painting by Murillo, 17th century); confirmation of the Order rules (Lisbon, Madre de Reus, painting attributed to C. Lopez, 1530/40). *Cycles:* numerous, amongst others in Karlsruhe, Bibl. HS. Thennenbach 4, book illustration, 15th century; Assisi, S Chiara, frescoes of the Giotto school, 14th century; Königsfelden (Aarau), stained glass, 14th century; Nuremberg, St Jacob, altar painting, 14th century; Trescorre, Oratorio Suardi, mural painting by L. Lotto, 1524.

Clement Romanus

(Klemens, Clemens) Pope, Martyr, saint
Feast-day: 23rd November
Life: C. was identified by Origen and Eusebius as the companion of Paul the apostle, mentioned in Phil. 4.3 and, after Irenaeus, the third successor of Peter in Rome and, according to Tertullian, ordained by Peter. His letter to the Corinthians (circa 96), after the turmoil in their Christian community, following the revolt of younger members against the presbyters, successfully driving them away, became famous. The letter was in the form of a *nouthesy* (admonition) and demanded, by explaining the structure of an army, the subordination of members to those ecclesiastical leaders, nominated by the apostles or their successors. They could be removed because they did not get their authority from the community but directly from the apostles as Christ's envoys.

Legends: C. is born the son of Faustinianus and Macidania. – In the presence of Linus and Cletus, Peter ordains C. as his successor. – Despite his ordination by Peter, C. gives priority to his election as pope to prevent the custom of the predecessor nominating his successor. – C. is therefore elected after Cletus. – C. converts Flavia Domitilla to Christianity, the niece of Emperor Domitian. – C. converts Theodora, Sisinnius's wife. Sisinnius, who spies on his wife is suddenly blinded and rendered deaf in a church. – C. cures Sisinnius from his affliction but Sisinnius believes himself to be the victim of magic and orders C.'s arrest. However, the torturers chain the pillars instead of C. because they too are blinded. – Peter appears to Sisinnius, he is converted and baptised. – Prefect Mamertinus banishes C. to the Chersones peninsula because C. refuses to sacrifice to the idols. – C. works in a marble quarry and prays for spring water because water has to be carried long distances. C. sees a lamb raise its right leg to show the spring to the bishop. – On the peninsula, C. converts numerous people. – During the persecution of the Christians under Emperor Trajan, C. is thrown into the sea with an anchor around his neck. – C.'s body is found on the seabed in a chapel built by angels. – On the anniversary of his martyrdom, the water retreats to open the way to the chapel for the faithful. – In the 9th century, Cyrillus and Methodius translate the body to Rome.

Patronage: patron saint of the Crimean peninsula; patron saint of Aarhus; Compiègne; Velletri; Seville; of children; stonemasons; marble workers; sailors; hatters; invoked against disaster at sea, storms and lightning.

Veneration and cult sites: canon saint; grave on the Crimean peninsula at Chersonese; in 868, the body was allegedly translated to Rome and buried in S Clemente; at the old Roman Titulus Clementis, a three-naved basilica was built in the 4th century but destroyed in 1084 by the Normans; today it is the lower church of S Clemente. Relics are in Pescara. Particular veneration in the diocese of Cologne (7th century) and Westphalia.

Superstition: C.'s day was regarded as the beginning of winter. – On C.' day all ships must sail into ports. – C.' day is at the end of the church year and the last day of 'fun' before Advent for children and young people.

Representation in Art: *Apparel:* in tunica (Rome, S Maria Antiqua, mural painting, 705/706); as orant with pallium (Venice, S Marco, southern dome, mosaic, after 1200); as pope with pallium, tiara with one crown and mass chasuble (Strasbourg, Cathedral, stained glass, 13th century); as pope with pluvial and tiara with three crowns (Cologne, St Kunibert, relic shrine, painting, circa 1400); as bishop with mitre (perhaps confused with Willibrord who received the name Clement as bishop) (Lügum, Parish Church, painting, 14th century); crown (Ravenna, S Apollinare Nuovo, mosaic, 6th century); book (Rome, S Clemente, fresco, 9th century); small cross (Poggibonsi, S Michele in Padule, painting, middle of the 15th century); cross crosier (Breslau, Corpus Christi Church, painting, 1497; anchor (Linz, Parish Church, painting by the master of the Lysberg passion, 1460/70); triere at his feet (Rome, S Clemente, triumphal arch, mosaic, 13th century); chapel in the sea (Chartres, Cathedral, southern portal, 1215); lamb, well (Aschaffenburg, Castle Library, Halle heiltum, book illustration, 16th century); tiara (Florence, Uffizi, painting by Ghirlandaio, 15th century). *Special scenes:* C. receives the key from Peter (Münster, Regional Museum, painting, 15th century); on a mission (Borgo Velino, SS Dionisio, Rustico e Eleuterio, fresco, 15th century); C. prays to the Holy Trinity (Munich, Alte Pinakothek, painting by G. B. Tiepolo, 18th century). *Martyrdom:* drowning into the sea with millstone around his neck (Stuttgart, Regional Library, Zwiefalten Martyrologium, book illustration, 1st third of the 12th century); drowning in the sea with anchor around his neck (Città del Vaticano, Sala Clementina, painting by P. Brill, 1602). *Cycles:* Rome, S Clemente, lower Church, mural painting, late 11th century; Rome, S Clemente upper Church, frescoes by P. Pietri, Conco and Odazzi, 18th century; Cologne, St Kunibert, stained glass, early 13th century; Liebenburg near Hanover, Castle Chapel, frescoes by J. G. Wink, 18th century.

Colman of Melk

Pilgrim, Martyr, saint
Feast-day: 13th October
Life: of Irish origin. During his 1012 pilgrimage to the Holy Land he was arrested and hanged from a tree as an alleged Hungarian spy. His body did not decompose for two years.

Patronage: patron saint of Austria, 1663 replaced by Leopold; of livestock, of people sentenced to be hanged; invoked against headaches; the plague; for rain and a good marriage.

Veneration and cult sites: mortal remains translated to Melk, where his grave is, by margrave Henry II. Particular veneration in

Austria, Hungary, Tyrol and Bavaria as popular patron saint of farmers; feast in his own name in the dioceses of Vienna; St Pölten and Eisenstadt. Numerous chapels and local pilgrimages with Colomani riding, for instance, in Taugl near Salzburg and Thalgau.

Superstition: those who tug the bell-pull in Thalgau arouse C.'s attention and the request is heard. – As popular custom in Aigen, a heavy iron statue of C. is lifted and thrown, head first, to the ground (so-called Kolmännl). The Colmanni book, small in size, is regarded as an amulet against danger and harm, against thieves, lightning, bullets, witches, fire, epilepsy; the Colmani blessing protects livestock.

Representation in Art: *Apparel:* in pilgrims' clothes with trousers, shoes, girdled skirt, coat and pilgrims' hat (Passau, Cathedral, Trennbach Chapel, fig. early 16th century). *Attributes:* pilgrims' flask (St C. near Tengling, fig., 1515); rope in his hand (Vienna, St Stephan, Emperor Frederic's grave, fig. early 16th century); rope around his neck (Vienna, Stephan Cathedral, pulpit, fig., early 16th century); lance-head (Munich-Perlach, relief, early 16th century); pliers, canes, stones (Vienna, Albertina, woodcut, c. 1515). *Martyrdom:* at the gallows, a henchman removes C.'s skin (Stift Heiligenkreuz, painting by Jrg Breu the Elder, c. 1505). *Cycle:* Haslach/Upper Bavaria, painting, 18th century.

Columbanus

(Kolumban, Columban) Abbot, Saint
Feast-day: 23rd November; in Feldkirch, St Gallen and Chur 27th November
Life: born about 543 in Leinster (Central Ireland) About 560 he joined the Bangor monastery (near Belfast) as a monk. In 591 he travelled with twelve companions, amongst them St Gallus, to England and Burgundy or Austrasia. He founded numerous monasteries, amongst them Luxeuil near Belfort. C. wrote a *Regula coenobalis* and two penitential books. C.'s rules for monks were very strict and inspired by his Irish spirit but were later replaced by the more lenient rules of Benedict. In conflict over the date of Easter he wanted to hold back Gallic customs and turned with this dispute directly to the Pope. C. challenged King Theoderic for an explanation of his immorality and was banished in 612 from Burgundy, lived for two years at Lake Zürich and Bregenz and then moved to Upper Italy where he founded the Bobbio abbey near Piacenza. He died on 23rd November 615.

S. COLVMBANVS
Abbas.

Legends: at C.'s birth, his mother dreams that she has given birth to the sun. – A dove delivers the word of God to C. – C. cures several possessed people. – In a bear's cave, C. makes a spring flow. – Pope Gregory gives C. an alabaster goblet from the wedding of Cana.

Patronage: Ireland, Bobbio; invoked against floods and mental illness.

Veneration and cult sites: mortal remains in Bobbio; Italy; France; Switzerland.

Representation in Art: *Apparel:* as abbot with crosier (Stuttgart, Regional Library, Zwiefalten Martyrdom, book illustration, 12th century); as monk (Borgo, S Colombano, fresco by B. Lanzani, 15/16th century). *Attributes:* pilgrim at his feet (Città del Vaticano, Bibliotheca Vaticana, fig., 20th century); for the attribute of a bear and sun, often mentioned in literature (confused with Columba or Gallus?), all proof is missing. *Special scenes:* C. and Gallus cross Lake Constance (St Gallen, Collegiate Library, Cod. 602, book illustration, 1452). *Cycle:* Bobbio, Treasury, relic shrine, relief by G. de Patriarchi, 1482.

Conrad of Parzham

Capuchin lay brother, saint

Feast-day: 21st April

Life: born on 2nd December 1818 in Parzham, Bavaria, the son of Johann Ev. Birndorfer. He lived on the parental farm. In 1849 he joined the Altötting Capuchin monastery as a lay brother, took his vows on 4th October 1852 and worked as a door-keeper for 41 years. He died on 21st April 1894. Beatified in 1930, canonized in 1934. He was well known for his helpfulness to the poor, pilgrims, children and journeymen.

Patronage: Hungarian and Bavarian Capuchin Order Province; Catholic journeymen associations; Seraphim love matters; rural Catholic youth of the diocese of Würzburg; door-keepers; porters; invoked as helper in all emergencies.

Veneration and cult sites: buried in the Altötting Capuchin Church; participated in the Altötting painting of Mary.

Representation in Art: *Apparel:* in brown Capuchin habit (Altötting, St Anna, death cell, painting, 20th century). *Attributes:* cross (Altötting, St Anna, shrine fig. 20th century); beggar and bread basket (Parzham, Venus farm, fig., 20th century); jug (Altötting, fig. at the well, 20th century). All portraits of C. are of a low artistic value.

Corbinian of Freising

Bishop, saint

Feast-day: 8th September; diocese of Munich-Freising 20th November; diocese of Bolzano-Brixen 9th September.

Life: born about 680, probably in Castrus (Aparjon) near Melun-sur-Seine, the son of the Frank Waltekis and Keltin (Irin) Corbiniana. He built a cell at the German Chapel, located near his home town, where he lived for 14 years as a hermit. In 709/10 he made a pilgrimage to Rome and founded a small monastery in Keins (near Meran/Merano) with its own rules. After 714 he lived in Rome, was ordained as bishop and sent to France. At the request of Prince Grimoald, he made Freising his bishopric seat. – C. was hated by Grimoald's concubine, Piltrud, because he condemned the unlawful relationship. – C. fled to Keins until he was called back by Grimoald's successor, Prince Hugibert. He died on 8th September 720/30.

Legends: During his pilgrimage to Rome, C. loads a bear with the burden from the mule he has eaten. – When C. feels that his end is near, he summons his brothers, celebrates the Eucharist and dies in their midst.

Patronage: diocese of Freising, now archdiocese of Munich-Freising.

S. CORBINIANVS EPISCOPVS FRISINGENSIS.

C. loads the luggage on the bear (Munich, Alte Pinakothek, painting by J. Polack, 1483); C.'s death (Munich, Alte Pinakothek, painting by J. Polack, 1483); C.'s apotheosis (Freising, Cathedral, fresco by C. D. Asam, 1723/24). *Cycles:* St Korbinian in the Puster valley, painting by F. Pacher, c.1470; Freising, Cathedral, parapet under the gallery, fresco by C. D. Asam, 1723/24.

Cornelius

Pope, Martyr, saint

Feast-day: 16th September

Life: in June 251, after 15 months with no-one in post and after the Christian persecution under Emperor Decius, C. was elected by majority vote as pope. In 251, during his Pontificate (until 253), he was in dispute with the antipope Novatian over the issue of practical penitence, particularly regarding the re-admission of Christians, apostatized during persecution. Whilst Novatian had a strict point of view, C.'s opinion was more moderate and he re-admitted apostate Christians after penitence and absolution. C. was supported by Bishop Cyprian of Carthage and a Roman synod excommunicated Novatian. In a letter to Bishop Fabius of Antioch, C. supplied important information about the organisation of the Roman congregation, amongst others, seven degrees of ordination are mentioned for the Roman cleric. Emperor Gallus banished C. to Centumdellae (now Civitavecchia, west of Rome). He died there on 14th September 253 (no martyrdom).

Legends: Emperor Decius recalls him from exile and orders him to be hit with blocks of lead. – C. is ordered to make a sacrifice to Mars in the temple but he refuses. – On his way to the temple, C. cures the paralysed Salustia, wife of a Roman officer, who is converted, together with 20 soldiers. – To-

Veneration and cult sites: his mortal remains were buried at Zeno Castle near Meran/Merano; translated in 765/68 to Freising by Bishop Arbeo; numerous relics in Bavarian churches.

Superstition: At the C. spring in Weihenstephan, eye diseases are washed away.

Representation in Art: *Apparel:* as priest (Bamberg, Governmental Library, Sacramentarium Gregorianum, book illustration, 1052/78); as bishop in Pontifical clothes (Augsburg, Cathedral, choir-stalls, relief by U. Glurer, 1486/88); as bishop in pluvial (Rott am Inn, former Benedictine Monastery, fig. by I. Günther, 1760/62). *Attributes:* book (Munich, Main Governmental Archive, seal of the Cathedral Chapter, Freising, 1267); with Church model (Freising, Bishops Gallery in the Prince's Cloister, painting by J. Lederer, c. 1700); bear (Munich-Thalkirchen, fig., late 15th century). *Special scenes:*

gether with the newly converted, C. is tortured.

Patronage: livestock with horns; invoked against epilepsy (also called Cornel disease) and nervous disorders.

Veneration and cult sites: canon saint; his mortal remains were buried in the Lucina crypt of the Callixtus Chapel in Rome; Relics in Kornelimünster near Aachen (head, arm, so-called reliquiar in form of a horn as a synonym for Cornu-Cornelius); Cologne, St Severin, St-Corneille-de-Compiège; pilgrimage to Kornelimünster; veneration in Germany; England and the Netherlands. In Cologne, St Severin, a "Höönches mass" took place every Monday by presenting the horn relic.

Superstition: in Wörresbach, C. is called upon in a 'worm blessing'. – In Kornelimünster, epileptics drink blessed water from the C. horn.

Representation in Art: *Apparel:* in phelonion and tunica (Rome, S Paolo fuori le Mura, mural painting, 6th century); as pope with conical tiara and Cappa magna (Munich, Alte Pinakothek, painting by S. Lochner, circa 1440); as pope with pallium (Ahrweiler, Parish Church, mural painting, circa 1450). *Attributes:* crown in hand (Ravenna, S Apollinare Nuovo, mosaic, 6th century); sword (Vaduz, Collection of Liechtenstein Castle, painting by the master of Messkirch, 16th century); palm tree (Kornelimünster, fig. circa 1470); Tiara, cross crosier (Antwerp, Cathedral, stained glass, early 16th century); horn (Cologne, St Severin, painting, circa 1520); cows (Carnac, St-Cornély, fig., 1639). *Special scenes:* C. 's admission into heaven (Kornelimünster, painting, 18th century). *Martyrdom:* Palencia, S Cebrin, painting by J. Valmareda, circa 1530.

Cosmas and Damian

Doctors, Martyrs, saints

Feast-day: 26th September; in the rites of the Eastern Church on 17th October, 1st November or 1st July.

Legends: C. and D. are twin-brothers of Aegna who study medicine and treat people free of charge. – In this way, C. and D. convert many people to Christianity. – C. and D., like Christ, cure the paralysed and the blind, exorcise devils and revive the dead. – C. and D. cure animals, for instance, a camel. – After she has been cured, Palladia forces an egg on D. as payment. After D.'s death, C. refuses therefore to be buried next to D. – Christ appears to C. and excuses D. – C. and D. are brought to governor Lysias and interrogated. – After C. and D. refuse to make a sacrifice to the idol, they are chained and drowned in the sea but rescued by an angel and brought again before the judge. – Two devils maltreat the judge who associates the rescue by the angels with magic. – Lysias orders C. and D. to be thrown into the fire but they remain unharmed whilst the flames spread and burn many pagans. – C. and D. are tortured but the angels make the torturers weary. – C. and D. are crucified and stoned by the people but the stones bounce back and injure those who throw them. – Arrows shot at C. and D, also bounce back. – Finally C. and D. are beheaded. – Many posthumous healings take place at C. and D.'s tomb. – A farmer is cured after a snake bites him in the belly as he sleeps. – The wife of Malbo is rescued when two demons want to throw her into the abyss. – C. and D. transplant the leg of a dead Moor on to the sexton of SS Cosma e Damiano, Rome, who has a diseased leg.

Patronage: patron saints of Florence; Jesuits, the Confrèrie St-Côme des Chirurgiens de Paris; since 1533 Collège de Chirurgie; Confrèrie of Luzarches; nurses; doctors; pharmacists; surgeons; the infirm; medical faculties at universities; chemists; hairdressers; grocers; physicists, dentists and confectioners.

Veneration and cult sites: C. and D. graves are in Kyrrhos, Syria; pilgrims' destination in the 6th century and replaced under Justinian with a larger church; relics are in Tours (since the 6th century); Centula (since the 9th century), Prüm, Essen, Hildesheim, Bremen (since the 16th century in Munich, St Michael); since the 4th century Roman canon saints, the first saints originating from the Orient. Patron saint of Aleppo, Edessa, Aegae, Jerusalem, Amida, Constantinople, Blachern quarter with hospital and pharmacy; Rome, SS Cosma e Damiano (built in 526–530 by Pope Felix IV); Liège (since 560), Vzelise, Lorraine, Brageac (Bas-Limousin), Florence, Bad Cannstadt (since 1170), Gutenzell, Kaufbeuren; veneration between River Weser and Elbe in the Rhineland, Swabia, Southern Tyrol, Piedmont, Sicily, Spain.

Superstition: CD. ointment, according to the Liber Ordinum mixed from the contents of silos, drives disease, the plague and all other evils away. – In France, CD. ointment helps against headaches and in Italy against gout. – In Upper Bavaria, before Lent begins one must pray to C. and D. to ensure that Lent also benefits the health.

Representation in Art: *Apparel:* in planeta (Parenzo, Euphrasiana basilica, mosaic, 16th century); in narrow trousers, short, girdled skirt, open at the front and closed coat thrown over the shoulder (Essen Cathedral Treasury, book cover of the Theophanus gospel, relief, 11th century); with spiral-like scholar's coat with wide sleeves or splits, covered by upper cloth with shoulder collar and biretta (Nuremberg, Germanic National Museum, painting of the M. Wohlgemut Studio, circa 1500); as doctors and surgeons, mainly differentiated in the northern Alps (Maikammer, Alsterweiler Chapel, painting, 1445); as Orientals (Arget, St Michael, fig.

by I. Günther, circa 1770). *Attributes:* crown in hand, doctor's bag at the belt (Rome, SS Cosma e Damiano, mosaic, 526/530); scrolls (Berlin, Early Christian and Byzantine Collection, mosaic from Ravenna, 6th century); palm tree (Hilperting, Upper Bavaria, fig., circa 1500); sword, all medical instruments and instruments of torture, amongst others, scissors (Gutenzell, procession flag, embroidery, after 1755); axe (Wechterswinkel, fig., 1680); cross and stone (León, Cathedral, painting by the master of Palanquinos, 15th century); ointment containers, ointment spatula (Hildesheim, Cathedral, Epiphanius Shrine, relief, 12th century); medicine container, surgical instrument, so-called spatula forceps, instrument-bag of the surgeon (Berlin, Emperor Frederic Museum, painting by D. Veneziano, 15th century); spatula forceps, ointment container, medicine box with different compartments (Florence, Uffizi, painting by Bicci di Lorenzo, 1429); C. as academic doctor with urine glass, D. as surgeon doctor with ointment container, ointment spatula (Frankfurt, Städel, painting by R. van der Weyden, before 1450); urine glass, ointment container, book (Munich-Pipping, stained glass, 1479); pharmacist's container, spoon, retort (Zürich, University, Historical Medical Collection, fig., 18th century); with medicine container with compartments as medicine cabinet (Kaufbeuren, fig., 15th century); with prescription and writing quill (Passau, Hofapotheke, painting, 17th century); book and quill (S Miniato, S Domenico, painting by Giusto d'Andrea, 15th century); Lance with lonche (orthodox liturgical instrument to cut bread) (Venice, Tesoro di S Marco, relief, 12th century). *Special scenes:* healing of eyes in a pharmacy (Kaufbeuren, S Kosmas and Damian, fresco, 1743); angels mix C. and D.'s ointments and pills (Basle, Collection of Historical Pharmaceutical Objects, painting, 18th century); curing of a camel (Bremen, Cathedral, relief, 14th century); transplant of a Moor's leg (Stuttgart, Regional Württemberg Museum, painting, 2nd half of the 15th century); C. and D. cure a farmer, bitten in the belly by a snake (Munich, St Michael, reliquary, painting, circa 1400); C. and D. rescue Malbo's wife, on horseback, from demons (New Haven, Jarves Collection, painting by M. di Nardo, 17th century); C. and D. as assistants of a surgeon professor during his lecture (unknown location, painting by J. Anwander. *Martyrdom:* C. and D. are thrown into the sea and rescued; Lysias is tortured by demons and released (Munich, Alte Pinakothek, painting by Fra Angelico, 1440); C.'s and D.'s crucifixion (Venice, S Giorgio Maggiore, painting by Tintoretto, 16th century); C.'s and D.'s beheading (Stuttgart, Regional Library, Zwiefalten martyrdom, book illustration, 13th century). *Cycles:* Goslar, Market Church, stained glass, 13th century; Washington; Munich, Dublin, Paris, Florence, S Marco, painting by Fra Angelico, 1440; Caluire near Lyon, St-Côme-et-St-Damien, stained glass by Abbé Louis Ribes, 1962; Florence, Museo di S Marco, painting from the Annalena Monastery by Fra Angelico, 15th century.

Crispin and Crispinian

(Crispinus and Crispinianus, Krispinus and Krispianus) Martyrs, saints
Feast-day: 25th October, translation feast 20th June
Legends: C. and C. are brothers and originate from a noble Roman family. – C. and C. flee during the Diocletianic persecution of the Christians to Soissons where they learn the art of shoemaking, make shoes for the poor free of charge and in this way contribute to the spread of Christianity. – C. and C. are tempted by the devil, impersonating a cripple with a wooden leg. – C. and C.

distribute their belongings to the poor. – C. and C. rescue a drowned child. – As Christians, C. and C. are arrested in their workshop. – C. and C. are interrogated by the judge Rictiovarus who orders their beating. – His torturers drive awls under their fingernails and toenails. – Strips are cut from their skin and the awl springs back against the torturers. – C. and C. are thrown into the frozen Aisne, a millstone around their necks. – The water of the Aisne warms itself miraculously and carries C. and C. to the banks. – The judge orders the saints to be put into a container with liquid lead; a drop of the lead blinds the judge. – Lead is poured over C. and C. and they are cooked in oil but the angels comfort them. – C. and C. are supposed to burn at the stake but they remain unharmed. – The judge goes mad and throws himself into the flames of the stake. – Even wild animals refuse to touch C. and C.'s mortal remains. Christians bury C. and C. secretly on the other side of the river.
Patronage: patron saint of the diocese of Osnabrück, patron saint of Soissons, Osnabrück, of tanners, saddlers, shoemakers and weavers.
Veneration and cult sites: the relics are in Soissons and Osnabrück, venerated throughout Europe.
Superstition: on C. and C. night, the Scalaer spirits meet and ride on fire-breathing horses down the River Rhine.
Representation in Art: *Apparel:* in long robe, to the feet, with coat, open at the front, fixed at the breast by a clasp (Osnabrück, Cathedral Treasury, C. and C. shrine, relief, 13th century); in civilian clothes according to contemporary fashion (Eichstätt, Cathedral, guild pole of the shoemakers, fig., circa 1723); in craftsmen's clothes (Constance, Holy Trinity Church, fig., circa 1650); with apron (Paris, Homberg Collection, fig., late 15th century); as bishop with mitre and cro-

sier (Münster, Regional Museum, relief, 1663); naked in a tub of lead and at the stake (Beaujeu, stained glass, 15th century). *Attributes:* palm tree (Borgao, Finland, chalice, relief, 13th century); book (Salzburg, Nonnberg, painting, late 15th century); cross (Palermo, Confrateria dei SS Crispo e Crispiniano, painting by P. Ruzzolone, late 15th century); millstone (Erkelenz, fig., circa 1500); knife (Naples, SS Crispo e Crispiniano, painting, 15/16th century); sword (Kalkar, fig., early 16th century); awl under the nails (Bourg, Notre-Dame, choir-stalls, relief, 16th century); tub with lead, stake (Beaujeu, stained glass, 15th century); shoe (Schwabach, St John's Church, fig., 15th century); shoemaker's knife (Turin, Cathedral, painting by D. Ferrari, 16th century); hammer, pliers,

awl, wire (Horst, fig., 16th century); cutting leather (Paris, Garnier collection, fig., middle of the 15th century); skins, processing with scissors (Gouda, Museum, painting by P. Pourbus, middle of the 16th century). *Special scenes:* C. and C. in their workshop, gifts to the poor (Vienna, Austrian Gallery in the Belvedere, painting, circa 1520); Dionysius of Paris welcomes C. and C. (Gosors, St Gervais, stained glass, 1531); C. and C. as preachers (Brussels, Palais Egmont, drawing by R. Strebelle, 1935); C. and C. on their journey to Soissons (Epinal, Museum, woodcut, circa 1825); rescue of the drowned child (Soissons, Washington, stained glass, 13th century); arrest of C. and C. in their workshop (Troyes, St Pantaleon, fig., 2nd half of the 16th century). *Martyrdom:* torturers drive awls under the fingernails (Zürich, Regional Swiss Museum, painting, circa 1500); all motifs of torture (Warsaw, Museum, altar, painting, circa 1500; Herenthals, painting by P. Bormann, late 15th century). *Cycles:* Brienne-le Château, stained glass, 16th century; Turin, Cathedral, painting by G. M. Spanozzi, early 16th century; Bourg-en-Bresse, stained glass, 16th century.

Cuthbert of Lindisfarne

Bishop, saint

Feast-day: 20th March.

Life: Born circa 634 of an Anglo-Saxon family, C. became a monk at Melrose in 651 and prior in 661. After the Synod of Whitby C. adopted Roman customs. In 676 he lived on Inner Farne as a hermit; in 685 he became the bishop of Lindisfarne. D. 20th March 687.

Legends: C's horse finds a loaf of bread in a thatched roof. – An angel heals C's knee with a poultice. – C. preaches in Lindisfarne. – C. miraculously extinguishes a fire.

Veneration and cult sites: The discovery of the incorruption of his body interred in Lindisfarne increased his cult; after the Danish invasion in 793, the canons left the island with C's shrine, travelled round northern England and Scotland, before settling in Chester-le-Street; translation to Durham in 999; translation to the new Norman Cathedral in 1104. In 1828, secondary relics were taken from C's shrine. Durham is the centre of C's cult; in England, 83 churches are dedicated to Cuthbert.

Representation in Art: *Apparel:* as bishop in pontifical vestments with chasuble and mitre (Carlisle Cathedral, figure, 10th-11th century); *Attributes:* crosier, book (York Minster, stained glass, 14th century); head of St Oswald (Durham Cathedral, figure, circa 1320); *Cycles:* Oxford, University College

Library MS 165, book illumination, late 11th/early 12th century; London, British Museum Cod.Add. 39, 913, book illumination, late 12th century; York Minster, stained glass, circa 1450; Carlisle Cathedral, painting, end 15th century; Pittington, St Laurentius, wall-painting, 12th century.

Cyprian of Carthage

(Kyprianos, Thascius Caecilius Cyprianus)

Bishop, Martyr, Doctor of the Church, saint

Feast-day: 16th September (in Russian rites 31st August)

Life: reliable information from C.'s papers "Ad Donatium" and "Acta proconsularia": born circa 200/210 in Carthage, the son of wealthy, pagan parents; educated as rhetorician; circa 246 converted as Christianity and baptized by the priest Caecilianus; 248/249 ordained to bishop of Carthage. During the persecution of the Christians under Emperor Decius (circa 250), he lived in seclusion. After the persecution the dispute began over the re-admission of those who had deserted the faith; Deacon Felicissimus held strict views. At the Carthage Synod of 251, C. excommunicated the leaders of the opposition party and declared that Church officials should be strictly penitent but could, following further persecution and before the penitence was complete, receive the Eucharist again. In 255, C. had a dispute with Pope Stephan I about the validity of baptism by heretics and regarded it as temporarily invalid for Asia Minor and did not fall in with Rome's stance. On 14th September 254, during the persecution of the Christians under Valerius he was beheaded. – After Augustine, C. is the most important Latin theologian of the Church; his writings originate from pastoral practice, are easy to understand and perfectly executed. In his paper "De ecclesia unitate" C. stated that the Cathedra Petri was not only in Rome but in every church, headed by a legitimate bishop. According to C., the unity of the Church could be achieved if everyone followed their bishop. C. compared the Church with the undivided cloth of Jesus – The primacy understood C. in such a way that every bishop was a successor of Peter, but that Rome had no active jurisdiction because Peter also had no jurisdiction over the apostles.

Legends: C. demands the members of his congregation pay the hangman 15 gold pieces as salary. – Due to the confusion with the magician, C. of Antioch, numerous other legends exist: C., still a pagan, tries with the aid of demons to arouse the love of the Christian Justine for a noble pagan young man but the demons declare that they can do nothing to the Christian virgin. – C. recognizes Christ as the stronger God and is baptised. – C. burns his books of magic.

Patronage: invoked against the plague.

Veneration and cult sites: canon saint, relics in Compiègne, Kornelimünster (head), Lyons (since 860). Veneration particularly in Africa, Rome, Constantinople and Spain.

Superstition: C.'s blessing helps the bewitched and livestock. – C.'s magic books were written in blood and were therefore very powerful. – C. prayers, used in Spain, protect against the devil's temptations and sins.

Representation in Art: *Apparel:* as bishop in vestments (Chartres, southern portal, fig., circa 1225). *Attributes:* bishop's crosier, book (Siena, Pinacoteca Nazionale, painting by Sano di Pietro, 1449); Panisellus (Codiponte near Lucca, SS Cipriano e Cornelio, painting by the master of Ristonchi, 15th century); palm tree, sword (Vaduz, Collection of Liechtenstein Castle, painting, 16th century); astronomical equipment (Città del Vaticano, Bibliotheca Vaticana, Urb. lat. 63, book illustration, 15th century). *Special scenes:* C. in the study (Città del Vaticano, Bibliotheca Vaticana, Urb. lat. 63, book illustration, 15th century); C.'s arrest (Ninove,

Notre-Dame, painting attributed to J. B. Mille, 18th century). *Cycles:* (only in confusion with C. of Nicomedia): Sarnstein, Tyrol, frescoes, 15th century.

Cyriacus of Rome

(Kyriakus) Deacon, Martyr, Helper in need, saint

Feast-day: 8th August (translation feast on 16th March).

Life: C. suffered martyrdom under Diocletian (305).

Legends: Pope Marcellus ordains C. as deacon. C. lives for a short while as a hermit in Lindenberg, Pfalz. – The emperor sentences C. to forced labour to build the Roman bath. – C. and five companions are thrown into prison. – Through the experience of lights and a divine voice, the prison warden, Spronianus, becomes a Christian and is beheaded by the prefect. – Arthemia, the daughter of Emperor Diocletian, is possessed by an evil spirit which only succumbs to C.'s power. – C. cures Arthemia. – The Persian king requests from Diocletian that C. be allowed to cure his possessed daughter too. – C. sails to Babylon and cures her. – After Diocletian's death, Emperor Maximilian orders hot tar to be poured over C.'s head and his torture because C. refuses to sacrifice to idols. – C. is beheaded. – When the pagan, Carpsius, takes C.'s head and with nineteen friends feasts and bathes at the baptismal site, they all die suddenly.

Patronage: invoked against evil spirits; possession; in the Pfalz patron saint of wine; protects young grapes.

Veneration and cult sites: his mortal remains were buried at the seventh milestone of the Via Ostiense; relics are in Altdorf, Alsace (13th century); Neuhausen near Worms (since 874); Bamberg, Cathedral (arm relic, in 936–973 brought to Bamberg by Emperor Otto the Great). Pilgrimage to Lindenberg,

Pfalz, crowning the statue with wreaths of the first grapes; Neuhausen near Worms; C. veneration in Speyer Cathedral; patronage of Bad Boll; Sulzfeld, Franconia etc.

Superstition: infirm or weak children get stronger if they are weighed on the Neuhausen C. scale, drink C. water and if the parents give the weight of the child in grain.

Representation in Art: *Apparel:* as deacon in dalmatic (Strasbourg, Cathedral, stained glass, 2nd half of the 13th century). *Attributes:* book of exorcisms (Hanover, Regional Museum, fig. by T. Riemenschneider, circa 1510); palm tree (Quedlinburg, Castle Church, reliquary, fig., circa 1510); sword (Frankfurt, Städel, painting, circa 1530); devil at his feet (Cologne, Wallraf-Richartz Museum, painting by the master of the holy clan, 1493/94); dragon (Frankfurt, Städel, epitaph of Charles of Hymperg, painting, circa 1500); Arthemia at his feet (Stuttgart, Regional Museum, fig. by the master of the Thalheim altar/D. Mauch (?), 1515); Arthemia with a stole around her neck (Frankfurt, Städel, Heller altar by master MGN, 1509/11); Arthemia as child on his arm (Bühlau, Thuringia, painting, 16th century); axe (Lauterbach, Austria, Church, painting, 1739); two women (Stuttgart, Regional Library, Stuttgart Passional, circa 1130); chains, cross, doves (Lindenberg, Pfalz, 15th century). *Special scenes:* curing of the possessed Arthemia (Niederndorf, Bavaria, painting by J. G. Bergmüller, circa 1720). *Martyrdom:* Venice, S Marco, Breviary Grimani, circa 1475.

Cyril of Alexandria

Patriarch, Doctor of the Church, saint

Feast-day: 27th June (nomination to Doctor of the Roman Church); until 1892: 28th January; from 1892 until the calendar reform: 9th February; in the rites of the Eastern Church: 9th June.

Life: born circa 380 in Alexandria; through his uncle, Theophilos, patriarch of Alexandria, admitted to the clergy, C. was involved in Theophilos's intrigues against John Chrysostom during the so-called "auto-synod" (in the monastery, in the oak forest, near Chalcedon). In 412 he became patriarch as his uncle's successor. Characteristic of C. were his inconsiderate actions towards the Alexandrian Novatians and Jews. In the calmer period of his term of office he fought the doctrines of Arius and Nestor who denied the unification of the divine and human nature in Jesus Christ. Under his chairmanship of the 431 third Council of Ephesus, Nestor was removed from office and excommunicated. In his papers C., writing without excitement or elegance, described both natures of Christ as being very close together, true and real, but during his time terms were not defined clearly which ultimately led to confusion. C. wrote treatises about the Old Testament, the Holy Trinity, the incarnation of God and Mary giving birth to God. he died on 27th June 444. In 1882, Pope Leo XIII nominated him as a Doctor of the Church.

Veneration and cult sites: relics in Rome, S Maria in Campo Marzio.

Representation in Art: *Apparel:* as bishop of the orthodox rites in polystaurion with omophorion and a typical cap (Venice, Tesoro di S Marco, Pala d'Oro, enamel, circa 1100); as bishop in imaginary vestments in the manner of the Byzantine rites (Rome, S Maria Maggiore, Capella Paolina, painting by G. Reni, circa 1605/10. *Attributes:* Codex (Venice, Tesoro di S Marco, Pala d'Oro, enamel, circa 1100); dove on his shoulder (Rome, S Clemente, painting by P. Rasina, 18th century). *Special motif:* the mother of God appears to C. (Paris, Bibliothèque Nationale, illustration according to J. Callot's Les Images des Saintes..., copperplate engraving, 17th century).

Cyril of Jerusalem
Archbishop, Doctor of the Church, saint
Feast-day: 18th March
Life: born c. 313. In 348 ordained as bishop of Jerusalem by Acacius, Arian Metropolitan of Caeserea. C. soon became an adherent of the Nicene faith and was in conflict with Acacius and twice banished on the decision of the 357/360 synod. In 367, he was deposed and banished by Emperor Valens. He lived 11 years in exile, until 378. He participated in the 382 Council of Constantinople. He died in 387. In his doctrines, C. avoided the use of Homoousios, introduced by the Council of Nicaea, with which the council had defined the unity of God's son with the father, because this term was not mentioned in the bible. His catecheses, preached by C. in the Jerusalem Entombment Church in 348 (or 350), are famous. The subjects cover the fields of sin, penitence and faith and explain the symbol of baptism. C. later explained the sacraments of baptism, confirmation and Eucharist by using, within the context of the sacrificial and mystic character of the Eu-

charist, the term "transsubstantiation" and the service in the church for the first time. In liturgical history it is also important that he mentioned the epiclesis and memory of the dead Christ. In 1882 nominated as a Doctor of the Church by Leo XIII.

In the Western Church no known portraits.

Cyril (Constantine) and **Methodius**
Apostles of the Slavs, Bishops, saints
Feast-day: 14th February (in the rites of the Eastern Church: 11th May; in Slav countries; 5th July; in orthodox-Russian rites: C. 14th February, M. 11th May)
Life: C. was born in 826/27 in Thessalonica as Constantine, brother of M. He studied in Constantinople. After he was ordained as a priest he worked as a librarian and teacher of philosophy. By order of the emperor, C. and M. travelled in 860 as missionaries to Mora-

via on the Don and the lower reaches of the Volga. In Cherspon they found the mortal remains of Pope Clement I, moved in 863 to Moravia because Prince Ratislav requested missionaries speaking the Slav language to free his land from the Salzburg influence. Introduction of the Glagolitic liturgy. In 866, through missionary work and with the support of Prince Kozel they converted Pannonia (Western Hungary, Eastern Austria). They had differences with the Bavarian bishops because of the language of the liturgy. In 867, Pope Hadrian acknowledged the Glagolitic alphabet. In 868 the mortal remains of Pope Clement were translated to Rome. C. joined a monastery of Greek monks and became Cyril. He died on 14th February 869.

Legends: selection according to the Pannonic legends, written after C.'s death (869) but before 885 by M.'s pupils: at the age of seven, in a dream, C. selects wisdom as his bride. – C. refutes the doctrines of Islamic Saracen scholars and is rescued from poisoning. Among the Khasars, C. disputes with Jewish scholars, amongst them the Jew Kagan who, after a long discussion, is converted to Christianity and baptised. C. and M. fell an idol tree, an oak grafted onto a cherry tree.

Patronage: Europe (since 1980); all Slav people (since 1863), patron saint of Bohemia, Moldavia, Bulgaria, of numerous dioceses in the Balkans and the Prague Emmaus monastery.

Veneration and cult sites: the mortal remains are in Rome, S Clemente. The cult moved from Rome to Serbia and was revived, in 1688, in the Pec Union Contacs; in Bulgaria in context with the national awakening (since the 18th century); in Bohemia after the Benedictines moved, on the orders of Emperor Charles IV, from Dalmatia to the Prague Emmaus monastery and maintained the Glagolitic liturgy.

Representation in Art: *Apparel:* as Latin bishops in mass chasuble with mitre (Olmütz, Chapter Library, Cod. 45, book illustration, 1466); as bishops in Greek rites (Brno, Cathedral, pulpit, reliefs by A. Schweigl); as monk or archbishop (Prague, Thein Church, fig. by E. Max, before 1846); as Czech of Slovak (Prague, Karls' Bridge, fig, by K. Dvork, 1928/38). *Attributes:* book, cross on pole (Prague, St Vitus, Triforium, fig. by Master Hermann, circa 1375); book or chalice (Rome, S Clemente, lower Church, fresco, after 869); painting with Day of Judgement (Prague, Thein Church, fig., after 1846). In literature often used *Attributes:* converted pagans at the feet of angels with two plates, coming out of the clouds, cannot be proved. *Special scenes:* missionary work on the orders of Tsar Michael III (Rome, S Clemente, lower Church, fresco, after 869); C. and M. before Pope Hadrian (Rome, C. and M. Chapel at S Clemente, fresco by F. Nobili, late 19th century). *Cycles:* Vienna, Edition Tusch, coloured wood carvings by M. Hiszpanska-Neumann, 1973.

D

Damasus I

Pope, saint

Feast-day: 11th Dec

Life: * c. 305 in Rome, accompanied Pope Liberius into exile as deacon during the Aryan controversy. At times, D. sided with the anti-pope Felix but later made it up with Liberius. His rule as pope (366–384) was marked by violent internal clashes as a result of the lengthy schism with the anti-pope Ursinus. D. was falsely accused of murder, but acquitted in 378 at a synod in Rome. With the Decretum Gratiani in 378, D. raised the legal status of the bishop of Rome to a new level acknowledged by imperial law throughout the west. D. strove to reconcile a Christianity riven by the Aryan dispute, but nonetheless passed 24 anathemas against the false doctrines of the Donatists, Aryans, Apollinarians and Pneumatomachians. D. commissioned Jerome to revise the Latin Bible translation (the Itala), from which the Vulgate emerged. D. edited the Acts of the Martyrs from papal archives, and had numerous tombs of the martyrs restored. D. composed the epitaphs himself, and commissioned the calligrapher Furius Dionysius Philocalus to inscribe them on marble tablets, 59 of which have survived. During D.'s rule, the title church of S Lorenzo e Damaso was endowed with a building for ecclesiastical archives. † 11th Dec, 384.

Patronage: against fever.

Veneration and cult sites: body interred in Coemeterial church on the Via Adretina, erected by D. near the catacombs of SS Marcus and Marcellinus; translation to SS Lorenzo and Damaso; 1645 discovery of the bones.

Representations in Art: *Apparel:* in papal regalia with tiara and crosier (monastic library, Montecassino, illumination in MS 90, 1072); throned in exedra (Vatican City, 16C fresco by G. Romano). *Attributes:* diamond ring as name sign for Adamas (Sistine Chapel, Vatican City, 15C fresco); diamond, book (Avila Cathedral, painting by P. Berruguete, end 15C). *Special scenes:* handing over the Vulgate to Jerome (Bibliothèque, Dijon, 15C illumination in MS 15).

Demetrius of Sirmium

Martyr, saint

Feast-day: 26th Oct

Life: D. suffered martyrdom under Maximian (286–305) in Sirmium, capital of Illyria, c. 303/304.

Patronage: Soldiers.

Veneration and cult sites: 5C basilica of St D., Thessaloniki; cult spread to west by crusaders. Considered a Myrophore. Relics in Anagni Cathedral since 1199.

Representations in Art: *Apparel:* as young, beardless soldier in chiton and chlamys (An-no shrine, Siegburg, late 12C fig., extant in painted copy); as a soldier in coat of mail, leg mail and cloak (Strasbourg Cathedral, late 13C stained glass); armed with coat of mail, uniform, boots (Museo Civico, Sassoferato, mosaic icons from 1st half of 14C); at prayer in chiton, chlamys with tablion (Halberstadt Cathedral, 11C reliquary); as soldier on throne (S Marco, Venice, icons on reliefs c. 1200); on horseback (only in eastern representations). *Attributes:* cross (S Maria Antiqua, murals c. 649); shield, lance (Museo Civico, Sassoferato, mosaic ikons fr. 1st half of 14C); drawing his sword (S Marco, Venice, icons on reliefs c. 1200). *Special scenes:* D. kills the Bulgarian czar Colojan with his lance when he attacks Salonica (S Biagio, S Vito dei Normanni, 14C fresco). *Cycles:* on several Byzantine vitae icons.

Dionysius of Paris

(Denis, Denys) Bishop, martyr, Holy Helper, saint

Feast-day: 9th Oct

Legends: acc. to Gregory of Tours, D. was an apostle in Gaul and first bishop of Paris who was martyred by beheading in the 3rd cent. – The 5C Passion names Rusticus the priest and Eleutherius the deacon as companions, names wh. are mythological epithets for Dionysus, the ancient god of antiquity. They appear here as anti-Aryan propaganda, a symbol of the Trinity at the moment of death. Richly endowed by King Dagobert I, the monastery of St Denis lends D. political importance as a national saint, and Hilduin therefore composes a new Passion – binding for the Middle Ages – taking over the Golden Legend, backdating the martyrdom to the 1st cent. and including a personal union of D. Areopagitica and D. of Paris. In Hinkmar's "Gesta Dagoberti" further posthumous miracles are recorded. – A forged Caro-

lingian privilege reveals that Charlemagne appeared to D. in a dream and promised intercession to benefactors of St Denis. – The episodes in detail: D. is converted to Christianity by the apostle Paul. – D. is baptised with his wife Damaris. – For three years, D. is instructed in Christian doctrine. – D. is consecrated as bishop of Athens. – When he speaks of the hierarchies and orders of angels and heavenly powers, D. is so ecstatic that he is exalted to the third heaven. – D. prophesies to the banished St John in Patmos an early return. – D. is present at the death of Mary. – When he learns of the martyrdom of Peter and Paul, D. renounces the bishopric of Athens and travels to Rome. – D. is sent by Pope Clement I to Paris with Rusticus and Eleutherius. – D. converts many Parisians to the faith, builds numerous churches and consecrates priests. – When idolatrous priests stir up the populace, the priests are unable to keep up their wild doings at the sight of the saint and fall at D.'s feet. – When the Devil sees his effectiveness declining, he incites Domitian to start persecuting the Christians. – The Roman prefect Frescennius has D. beaten with fists, spat on and mocked. – D. is thrown in chains and scourged by 12 mercenaries. – D. is placed on a fiery grill. – D. is thrown to wild beasts, who become tame and docile at the sign of the Cross. – Finally, D. is nailed to a cross, but then taken down again. – In the night, Christ appears to D. in prison and strengthens him. – D. and his companions are beheaded as they profess the most sacred Trinity (variant: the executioner misses the head). – D. takes his head and, led by an angel, carries it two miles to Montmartre (= mons martyrum) (older variant: Catulla steals the body and buries it in St Denis). – Larcia hears choirs of angels, is converted and is immediately beheaded by the pagans and baptised in her blood. – A woman invites the pallbearers with the bodies of D.'s companions to

supper and steals the bodies during the meal. – Without knowing of their martyrdom, Bishop Regulus of Arles mentions D. and his companions during canonical prayers, at which three doves with the signatures of the saints written in blood on their breasts land on the altar cross.

Patronage: Neustrian and French royal houses, bowmen, keepers of the church flag of St-Denis, which, known as 'oriflamme', served as the war banner of the French kings (accompanied by the war cry "Montjoie St-Denis"); against headaches, dog bites and syphilis.

Veneration and cult sites: St-Denis, dateable from 475, from 639 burial site for Neustrian and French kings. Another church dedicated to D. in Rome refers actually to the eponymous pope. Relics in St Emmeram, Regensburg.

Superstitions: in France, onset of winter weather; in the canton of Vaud, St D.'s Day is when secret policemen elected annually relinquish their offices; in many places, it is the day for changing field-guards.

Representations in Art: *Apparel:* as bishop in a chasuble (tympanum sculpture, Enger, late 12C); as bishop in pluvial (altar of mercy, Vierzehnheiligen, fig. by J. M. Feichtmayr 1784); a novice apostle with long, belted tunic and pallium cloak (Acton Collection, Florence, painting by Cimabue school c. 1300); as a headless bishop (main doorway, west facade of St-Denis, 12C fig.); bishop with 2nd head in his hand (Notre-Dame, Paris, rose in S transept, stained glass c. 1265); as bishop at prayer (Rijksmuseum, Amsterdam, painting c. 1505); as a kneeling bishop (St-Jean-St François, fig. by G. and B. Marsy 1858); as a bishop pointing at his neck wound (Chapelle St-Grat, Luceram, 15C mural). *Attributes:* headless bishop with a mitre-covered head in his hand (Bamberg Cathedral, fig. c. 1235); second head in his hand, both heads with mitre (St Emmeram, Regensburg, reliquary shrine, fig. c. 1440); with calotte in hand as representation of relic which the chapter of Paris Cathedral claimed to possess (south doorway of Notre-Dame, Paris, fig. c. 1260); mitre with calotte (St Kunibert, Cologne, mural c. 1250); head of D. in the style of a Johannine chalice (late 19C fig. by A. Rodin). *Special scenes:* D. as witness to coronation of Mary (Westerland, Sylt, fig. c. 1460); D. preaching in Paris (MS 2, Bibliothèque, Chateauroux, illumination c. 1400); baptism of Lisbius (National Gallery, Washington, late 15C painting by St-Gilles Master); D. receiving eucharist (Bibl. Nationale, Paris, lat. 9436, 11C illumination); D. with escort of angels (W. doorway of Rheims Cathedral, 1st half of 13C); King Dagobert's dream (tomb of Dagobert, St-Denis, fig. c. 1260). *Martyrdom:* Louvre, Paris, early 15C painting by J. Malouel; Panthéon, Paris, late 19C fresco by Bonnat. *Cycles:* numerous, e.g. W. doorway of St Denis, c. 1135; Bourges Cathedral, stained glass, 1st half of 13C; St Gereon, Cologne, 13C mural.

Dominic of Caleruega

(Domingo de Guzmán) Founder of the Dominican Order, saint

Feast-day: 8th August (until 1558: 5th August, until 1972 : 4th August; Feast of his translation 24th May since 1233, in Soriano 15th September)

Life: * born around 1172 in Caleruega in Castille, a scion of the noble family of Guzmán. He studied at the cathedral school in Palencia; from 1199 he was a canon at the cathedral church in Burgo de Osma; in 1201 he was sub-prior, from 1206 he was in Rome together with his friend Bishop Didacus of Azevedo; there he learnt of the unsuccessful mission against the heretical Waldensians and Albigensians. Didacus (Diego) introduced the itinerant preaching ministry of priests, who lived in poverty, as a new missionary method. After the death of Bishop Didacus in December 1207 D. settled with his companions in the mission station founded by Didacus in Prouille. In 1215 he founded a community of preachers in Toulouse, which in 1216 received a Rule according to St Augustine, renounced all income and lived from alms, was placed under the authority of the Diocesan Bishop and dedicated itself to the teaching and conversion of heretics. In 1217 D. changed the society of pious women founded by Didacus for the same purposes into a Augustinian monastery. D. also urged the thorough study of theology and systematic preparation for preaching the Gospel. From 1218 the Order expanded into the whole of Europe. In 1217 Pope Honorius granted the Order privileges under the designation "Preaching Friars". † 6th August 1221. Canonised 3rd July 1234.

Legends: Before Dominic's birth his mother dreams she has in her body a puppy carrying a burning torch in its mouth and after it has emerged from her body, it sets the whole world aflame. – The godmother, who lifted D. up for baptism, sees on the forehead of the child a shining star lighting up the whole earth. – D. shuns wine for ten years. – As a student D. sells his books to help the hungry. – In Toulouse D. converts a landlord from heresy. – D. flagellates himself in the Grotto of Segovia. – When D. writes a tract against the Albigensians, they propose that when the books of the two opposing doctrines are thrown into the fire, those of the othodox teaching would remain undamaged. At this D.'s book leaps from the fire three times while the Albigensian book is burnt. The Mother of God gives D. the Rosary. – When D. asks Pope Innocent III for confirmation of

his Order, the Pope sees D. in a dream supporting on his shoulders the Lateran Basilica, which was threatening to collapse. – While D. is at prayer in St Peter's Cathedral, Peter and Paul appear to him and order him to preach in the world through the presentation of book and staff. – Through the prayers of Francis and D., Mary averts the wrath of Christ from mankind. – In a dream D. sees Christ fighting for the world with three lances against vanity, unchastity and greed. – D. miraculously saves drowning pilgrims of Santiago from the Garonne. – D. raises the nephew of Pope Nicholas Orsini, after he fell to his death in a grave during a boisterous game. – D. protects himself and his friars from the rain by making the sign of the cross. – D.'s books accidentally fall into the river. When a fisherman pulls them out three days later, they are completely dry. – When the food runs out, D. receives bread from angels to feed his 40 friars. – On D.'s death, the prior of the Dominicans of Brescia, Gwilis, sees the heavens open. He watches as angels on two ladders held by Jesus and Mary bring D. into heaven sitting on a chair. – In Hungary a noble visits D.'s relics kept in Similou. His son dies on the journey, but is raised again at the altar of the church.

Patronage: Patron saint of Bologna since 1306, Cordoba, Palermo; all tailors; against fever, in Bolsena against hail.

Veneration and cult sites: Buried in Bologna, St Niccolò, which was renamed after D.'s canonisation St Domenico. Toulouse, Bologna, otherwise only within OP Orders and their branches.

Representation in Art: *Apparel:* in the dress of the Order with long white robe, dark leather belt, white scapular, dark open coat with hood, sometimes biretta (Copenhagen, National Museum, painting, 1517); as bearded ascetic in the dress of the Order (Krems, Dominican Church, mural, circa 1300); as young monk in the dress of the Order (Pisa, Museo Civico, painting. by J. Carreno de Miranda 1661); as preacher (Budapest, National Museum, painting, by J. Carreno de Miranda, 1661); as Bishop in the Pontificalium (Madrid, Prado, painting, by B. Bermejo 1474/77). *Attributes:* Lily (Basel, Historical Museum, tapestry, 15th century); cross (Stuttgart, State Museum, figure, end 15th century); book, lily, star (Venice, I Gesuiti, painting by G. B. Piazzetta, 17th century); golden star, golden lily (Soriano, painting, by M. Calorese, 16th century); dog (Wimpfen, Dominican Monastery, figure, circa 1480); dog with torch in mouth (Dresden, copperplate engraving, wood cabinet, end 15th century); dog on book (Schloss Landsberg near Meiningen, stained glass, 1653). *Special scenes:* D. sells his books (Bologna, St Domenic's, relief, by A. Lambardi, 14th century); D. burns heretical writings (Madrid, Prado, painting, by P. Berruguete, 15th century); D. preaches before Albigensians (Florence, St Mary's Novella, fresco, by S Martini, 1355); D. sits before an auto-da-fé (Madrid, Prado, painting, by P. Berruguete, circa 1500); Mary takes D. and his Order under her mantle as patroness (Cologne, St Andrew's, painting, 1474);

Mary presents the Rosary (Bologna, Pinacoteca Nazionale, painting, by L. Carracci, circa 1600); Mary presents D. and Catherine of Sienna with the Rosary (Rome, St Sabina's, painting, by Sassoferrato, 1685); D. and Peter the Martyr receive the Rosary from Mary (Cologne, St Andrew's, painting, 1474); dream of Pope Innocent of D. supporting the collapsing church (Rimini, Pinacoteca Comunale, painting, by J. Tintoretto, 16th century); Peter and Paul commission D. to itinerant preaching (Pisa, Civic Museum, painting, by F. Traini, 14th century); Mary averts Christ's wrath upon the intercession of D. (Milan, Brera, painting, by P. Bordone, 1558); Mary averts Christ's wrath upon the intercession of D. and St Francis (Welden, Swabia, fresco, by B. Gozzoli, 1452); D. sees Christ with the three lances (Lyons, Museum, painting, by P. P. Rubens, circa 1600); the saving of the drowning from the Garonne (Vichy, Episcopal Museum, painting, by L. Borassa, 1415); raising of the nephew of the Pope (Rome, St Clement's, painting, by S Conca, 16th century); Mary heals Reginald of Orleans on the intercession of D. and presents him with the dress of the Order (Bruges, Great Seminar, Codex 55/171, illumination, 14th century); angels serve D. with food (Venice, Museum Correre, painting, by L. Bassano, after 1600); death of D. (Graz, Johanneum, painting, by G. Pietro de Fromis, 17th century); vision of the ladders of heaven (Darmstadt, State Museum, painting, by Master of the Dominican Legend, 1493/4); D. protects seafarers (Poznan, Museum Wielkopolskie, painting, by B. Daddi, 138); appearance at Soriano (Speyer, St Mary Magdalene, painting, beginning 18th century); D. appears to St Catherine (Perugia, S Dominico, painting, by Giancola di Paolo, 1494). *Cycles:* Florence S Marco, fresco, by Fra Angelico, 15th century; Pisa Civic Museum, painting, by F. Traini, 14th century; Bologna S Dominico, gravestone, by Fra Guglielmo da Pisa, 13th century.

Dorothy of Caesarea

Virgin, martyr, saint
Feast-day: 6th February
Legend: numerous, romantic versions of the legend.
Important Episodes: D.'s parents, Theodorus and Theodora, and her sisters, Crysta and Callista, flee from the persecution of Christians at Rome to Caesarea, where D. is born. – During the persecutions under the Emperor Diocletian, D. is thrown into prison in Caesarea for refusing to marry the Prefect Fabricius, because she wants to belong only to Christ. – D. is placed in a cauldron of boiling oil, but is unharmed; she feels only that she is being anointed with balsam. – D. is now locked in a dark cell without food for nine days, but she steps out of the dark dungeon in heavenly beauty. – D. asks God for a sign and an angel throws an idol down from its pedestal, at which the people hear the screaming of devils in the air. – D. is hanged by the feet and whipped, which she feels as stroking with peacock feathers. – Afterwards D.'s breast is singed with torches. – Overnight her wounds heal and D.'s body is unharmed. – D.'s apostate sisters are converted and burnt. – D. declares to the judge that she would accept any suffering for her Lord, in whose garden she will pick roses and apples eternally. – Thereupon the Clerk of the Court, Theophilus, mocks her and asks D. to send him a basket of roses and apples after her death. – After D.'s execution a boy with a basket appears to Theophilus in the winter and is translated before his eyes. – Theophilus is converted and beheaded after his baptism; his body is thrown to the animals.
Patronage: Florists, brides, women in childbed, newly married, brewers, miners.
Veneration and cult sites: Relics in Rome and Bologna; in Germany called upon in many situations as an auxiliary saint, particularly between the 14th and 16th centuries; Diocese of Görlitz.

Representation in Art: *Apparel:* as a virgin in contemporary long, girded robe (Cologne, Wallraf-Richartz Museum, painting, by Master of the Holy Family, 1493/94); with hair put up (Graz, Museum, Rottaler Epitaph, painting, 1505); with veil (Split, Museum, painting, from the circle of G. Bellini, circa 1500 [?]). *Attributes:* crown (Oberwesel, St Mary's Church, high altar, figure, circa 1331); palm branch (Wismar, St Jürgen, mural, 2nd half 15th century); peacock feather (Cologne, St Andrews, painting, by Master of St Severin, circa 1510); sword (Schlanitzen, Austria, painting, circa 1500); book (Rethwisch, figure, 15th century); cross (Malchin, painting, circa 1400); lily (Klosterneuburg, Albrecht's Altar, painting, circa 1440); basket with roses (Cologne, Wallraf-Richartz Museum, painting, by Master of St Severin, 1505/10); basket with roses and apples (Eton College, mural, circa 1480); basket with roses which the Christchild shows (Cologne, Wallraf-Richartz Museum, painting, by Master of the Holy Family, 1493/94); messenger with apples in apron, roses in basket (Cologne, Wallraf-Richartz Museum, painting by Master of the Holy Family, 1414/15); messenger giving the basket (Altena, Thomée Collection, figure, by J. Beldensnyder, early 16th century); messenger as Christchild with halo (Malta, Carinthia, parish church, mural, 13th century); naked messenger (Basel, Museum, D. – Monstrance, 15th century); messenger with toy (Washington, National Gallery, wood engraving, circa 1450); winged messenger as *putto* (Darmstadt, Hessen State Museum, painting by C. Dolci, 17th century); rose petals (Graz, Lech Church, stained glass, circa 1330); rose branch in hand (Gdansk, St Catherine's, painting, circa 1525); rosebush (Munich, Staatl. Graphische Sammlung, wood engraving, circa 1410); messenger sitting on bush (Darmstadt, Hessen State Museum, Ortenberger Altar, painting, circa 1400); rosary on head of child (Dresden, Gallery of Old Masters, painting, by L. Cranach the Elder, 1506); roses in D.'s aproned garment (Modena, Library Estense Horae BMV, illumination, circa 1387); three blossoms (Berlin, former German Museum, painting, circa 1350); three apples (Palermo, Museo Nazionale, painting by A. v. Dyck, 1624); plate with roses and fruits (Seville, Museum, painting. by F. Zurbaran, circa 1640); strawberry plant (Münster, State Museum, painting, by Conrad of Soest, circa 1400); cherries (Frankfurt, Städel, painting, by Master of the Garden of Paradise, circa 1410). *Special scenes:* D. takes the messenger by the hand (London, National Gallery, painting, by Francesco di Giorgio Martini, 15th century); conversion of Theophilus (Vienna, Kunsthistorisches Museum, drawing, by T. Pock, 1657). *Martyrdom:* beheading of D. in winter landscape (Prague, Narodni Museum, painting by H. Baldung-Grien, 1516); martyrdom and sending of messenger (Augsburg, State Art Collection, painting, by H. Holbein, 1499). *Cycles:* Levoca St Jacob, mural, 1400/20.

Dustan of Canterbury

Bishop, Benedictine monk, saint
Feast-day: 19th May.
Life: Born in 909 in Glastonbury near Bristol of a noble family; D. was educated by Irish monks and was a skilled craftsman able to cast bells, make musical instruments and carve crucifixes. D. joined the household of his uncle Athelm and then the court of King Athelstan, until his expulsion following an intrigue. At around 940 D. became a monk in Glastonbury and was ordained priest; in 945 he became abbot and adviser of King Edred. Due to reproaching King Edwy for leading an immoral life, D. was banned to Ghent for two years. King Edgar made him bishop of Worcester in 957, in 961 archbishop of Canterbury; Pope John XII appointed

him Legate of the Holy See. – D. insisted that his clerics had a good command of a trade or a skill, thus to instruct the people also in these matters. D. in 988.

Patronage: Patron saint of goldsmiths, armourers, blacksmiths.

Veneration and cult sites: his cult sprang up immediately after his death; feast-day ordered in 1039.

Representation in Art: *Apparel:* as archbishop in pontifical vestments with chasuble, pallium and mitre (London, British Museum Royal Ms.10, book illumination, circa 1200); as bishop in pontifical vestments with chasuble, pluvial and mitre (Stonyhurst, Lancashire, embroidery, circa 1400). *Attributes:* crosier, book (Canterbury, Royal Window, stained glass, circa 1470; golden vessels, metalworker's tools (Stonyhurst, Lancashire, embroidery, circa 1400); holding the devil by the nose with a pair of tongs (Oxford, Bodleian Library, stained glass, circa 1300).

E

Edmund of Abingdon

(Edme Rich) Bishop, saint

Feast-day: 16th November

Life: Born circa 1170/1180 in Abingdon; studied in Paris; in 1214 professor of theology in Oxford; from 1222–233 Canon and Treasurer of Salisbury Cathedral; as of 1227 papal chaplain for England in the crusades; in 1233 archbishop of Canterbury; in 1240, after being banned by King Henry III during disputes regarding the rights of the Church, E. was taken in by the Cistercian monks at the abbey of Pontigny. On his way to the Cistercian monastery at Soissy, E. died on 16th November 1240. E. was canonized in 1246.

Patronage: Diocese of Portsmouth.

Veneration and cult sites: buried in Pontigny; venerated mainly in the Cistercian Order, and in England.

Representation in Art: *Apparel:* as bishop in pontifical vestments with mitre (London, British Museum, Historia Anglorum, drawing, 1259); as archbishop with pallium (London, British Museum, Carmelite Missal, book illumination, 14th century); as bishop in pontifical vestments with pluvial (Wilhering, collegiate church, fresco by B.Altomonte, circa 1740). *Attributes:* crosier (London, British Museum, Historia Anglorum, drawing, 1259); Lily, book, crown (Neuburg/Styria, fresco, 18th century). *Special scenes:* E. worshipping at the Miraculous Image of the Virgin Mary (Zwettel, collegiate church, painting, 18th century).

Edmund Campion

Jesuit priest, martyr, saint

Life: Born on 25th January 1540 in London as son of a bookseller; in 1553, as young pupil, C. held a Latin oration on Queen Mary. C. studied in Oxford, became a Junior Fellow and orator. Despite his leanings towards Catholicism, C. was ordained deacon of the Church of England. Despite being persecuted for his Catholic beliefs, after five years of solitary life in Ireland C. returned to England under an assumed name, but soon left for Douai (Flanders) to study theology. In 1573, C. joined the Society of Jesus, taught in Brünn and Prague, was ordained priest in 1578. Together with Robert Persons and Theodore Cottam, disguised as Irish merchants, C. returned to England and wrote his famous "Decem Rationes" (10 reasons), a statement against the Anglican Church. The book created a great sensation. On 12th July 1581, C. was betrayed and arrested. On 1st December 1581, after all attempts to induce him to conform had failed, following terrible torture and a mock trial, C. was hanged, drawn, and quartered in Tyburn, together with Alexander Bryant SJ and the seminary priest, Ralph Sherwin. Their address to the people led to many of the listeners later returning to the Catholic Church. C. was canonized in 1970. No representation in Art.

Edmund of East Anglia

King, saint

Feast-day: 20th November.

Life: born circa 840, in 855 king of East Anglia; E. was regarded a virtuous ruler; captured in 870 in the battle near Thetford during the Danish invasion. E. refused to save his life by denying the Christian faith, was tied naked to a tree, shot with arrows and beheaded.

Legends: after his death, a bear (or wolf) guarded the head severed from the body, calling "hic, hic" (= here, here).

Patronage: Patron saint of England; invoked against the plague.

Veneration and cult sites: in 1020, King Cnut ordered the abbey of Bury St Edmunds to be built over E's shrine.

Representation in Art: *Apparel:* as youthful king (Amiens Cathedral, stained glass, 13th century); as bearded king in long garment and cloak fastened with frog at the chest (Vienna, St Stephan, reredos painting, early 15th century); as king with trunk-hose, girded doublet, fur-trimmed cape and crown (Nördlingen, church of Our Lord, figure, late 15th century); as king in armour (Juslenville, chapel, figure by E.Theux, 18th century); as king in ermine (London, National Gallery, Wilton Diptych, painting, 1380/1400). *Attributes:* arrow (London, National Gallery, Wilton Diptych, painting, 1380/1400); standard (Vienna, St Stephan, reredos painting, early 15th century); sceptre (Long Melford, Suffolk, stained glass, late 15th century); bear (wood cut from the Saints of the Family, Friends and Relatives of Emperor Maximilian I, 1516); bag on belt, book (Nördlingen, church of Our Lord, figure, late 15th

century); sword, crown at feet (Juslenville, chapel, figure by E.Theux, 18th century); *Special scenes:* E's birth (London, British Museum, book illumination by Harvey, 1433); E's coronation (Holford, Missal, book illumination, 12th century). *Martyrdom:* piercing with arrows and beheading (Kent Cathedral, mural painting, 13th century); piercing with arrows by three lords (London, British Museum, Carmelite Missal, book illumination, late 14th century). *Cycles:* New York, Pierpont Morgan Library MS 736, book illumination, circa 1130/35.

Edward the Confessor

King, saint

Feast-day: 5th January (until the Calendar reform 13th October as the Feast of his translation)

Life: * born around 1003 as son of King Ethelred II and his Consort Emma of Normandy, he was raised in his mother's native land. He was proclaimed king in 1042 and married Edith, the daughter of the influential Earl Godwin, in 1045. He encouraged monastic life and founded St Peter's Abbey, now Westminster Abbey. In his benevolence E. was not equal to the political battles between the Anglo-Saxons and the Normans. † 5th January 1066. Canonised 1161.

Legends: E. gives a beggar his gold ring. – E. sees the Christ-child in the Host on high.

Patronage: Patron saint of England, the English king, against king's evil (scrofula).

Veneration and cult sites: Translation of mortal remains in 1163 by Thomas Becket to Westminster Abbey.

Representation in Art: *Apparel:* as a king in a belted long undergarment, coat with an ermine-lined jacket, crown (London, National Gallery, painted circa 1380/1400). *Attributes:* Ring (Amiens, cathedral, stained glass, 13th Century); sceptre (London, Palace of Westminster, mural painting, 13th century);

leper (wood engraving as an illustration in the genealogical chart and relationships by marriage of Kaiser Maximilian 1, 16th century); sword (Wells, cathedral, stained glass, 1325/33). *Special scenes:* E.'s coronation (Palace of Westminster, mural painting, 13th century). *Cycles:* Cambridge, University Library, Ee. 3.59, book illumination, 13th century).

Edward the Martyr
King of England, saint

Life: born in 963 as eldest son of King Edgar the Peaceful; in 975, under the influence of bishop Dunstan, King of England. His violent death at Corfe on 18th March 978, was connected with the anti-monastic party led by his stepmother Elfthryth, who wanted her son Ethelred as king. His cult as saint and martyr began in 1001.

Veneration and cult sites: Diocese of Plymouth.

Representation in Art: *Apparel:* as king with long garment and overmantle (Westminster Abbey, figure, 12th century); as king with crown (Wells Cathedral, figure, 13th century). *Attributes:* dagger, cup with snake (wood cut from the Saints of the Family, Friends and Relatives of Emperor Maximilian I, 1516). *Martyrdom:* Treacherous Murder over Repast (private collection, copperplate engraving by J. J. Ebersbach, 1753). *Cycles:* Paris, Bibliothèque Nationale MS lat. 17249, book illumination, circa 1424/1435.

Eligius of Noyon
(Eloi) Bishop, saint

Feast-day: 1st December (25th June Feast of his translation)

Life: * born around 588 in Chaptelat near Limoges. E. was a goldsmith and mintmaster under the French kings Clothar II and Dago-

bert I and was also their counsellor. E. founded numerous churches and monasteries, including one in Solignac in 632. Together with his friend Audoin, he left the royal court in 639 and became a priest, becoming Bishop of Noyon in 641. He pursued missionary work in Flanders. † 1st December 600 in Noyon.

Legends: An eagle reveals the saintliness of the child to his mother in a dream. – E. had learned the blacksmith's craft and himself takes a horse behaving in an unruly manner to take his horseshoe off and afterwards reshoe him. (Variation: Unknown to E. Christ or Peter works as an apprentice and performs the miracle with the horse's foot, to cure E. of pride). – E. seizes a devil in his smithy by holding his nose with tongs. (Variation: E. is visited by a devil in female form sent to tempt him. – E. drives off the devil with a burning coal in his face.) – E. earns the trust of the king, because from one piece of gold entrusted to him he instead creates two throne chairs and proves their gold content using a pair of scales. – E. buys freedom for slaves. – E. begs the king's pardon because in his allotment at the monastery he has mistakenly measured one foot too many. – On the translation of the mortal remains of Saint Martialis, he himself opens the dungeon doors for a prisoner amnesty. – During a town fire E. saves the church of Saint Martialis from the fire. – E. heals the lame. – E. gives a drink to the poor, cares for prisoners and buries the executed. – E. raises an unjustly hanged man from the dead. – During a sermon E. exorcises a demon. – E. is interred in the robes of Queen Chlothilde. – After death several men are unable to bear E.'s body to Chelles, but he is carried quite easily to Noyon, to the Church of St Loup.

Patronage: Farmers, miners, armourers, goldsmiths, smiths, cutlers, locksmiths, metal workers, clockmakers, engravers, waggoners, coachmen, coach-makers, lamp

makers, saddlers, horses, horse dealers, grooms, basket makers, tenant farmers.

Veneration and cult sites: His body lies in Noyon cathedral, his head in Chelles, St André, cult expanded over the whole of Europe.

Superstition: Women offer crosses to E. to obtain a children's blessing. – In a Swabian horse blessing, E. is referred to as speaking "when a horse does not wish to allow himself be shod".

Representation in Art: *Apparel:* as bishop in pluvial with mitre and crosier (Cologne, Wallraf-Richartz Museum, painted by a south German master in the second half of the 15th century); as a bishop wearing a mass chasuble in the goldsmith's workshop (Amsterdam, Rijksprentenkabinett, copperplate engraving by master Bileam, circa 1450); as a nobleman in elegant national costume with a fur-lined robe, coat and biretta (Erfurt, Barfüsserkirche, painting, end 14th century); as a blacksmith in work clothing in an undershirt with rolled-up sleeves, close-fitting trousers and leather apron (Kressbronn, E. chapel, Figure circa 1750). *Attributes:* Confessor's cross (Palermo, Capella Palatina, Mosaic, 12th century); book (Köwerich, Figure by J. Manternach, 1624); hammer and nail (New York, Kress Foundation, painted by a Master Della Culla, 15th century); hammer with a crown (Bruges, St Saveur, painting attributed to J. van Oost, 17th century); tongs (Florence, Oratorio S Michele, figure by N. di Banco, 1410); goblet (Salzburg, St Peter, painting circa 1490); chalice (Augsburg, Staatliche Gemäldegalerie, painting, 15th century); horseshoe (Tarragona, Diocesan Museum, painting, 15th century); anvil (Schuld, parish church, vault copestone, relief, circa 1500); work iron (Borgo S Sepolcro, Pinacoteca, standard of the Signorelli workshop, circa 1505); horse's hoof (Erfurt, Barfüsserkloster, painting, circa 1410); horse (Lodi Vecchio, S Bassanio, mural, 14th century); horse with a cut leg (Beaune, Hôtel-Dieu, tapestry, circa 1500). *Special scenes:* E. working in the workshop (Bern, museum, painting by N. M. Deutsch, 1515); the devil, in the form of a woman, attempting to seduce E. (Paris, Bibliothèque Nationale, French manuscript, 183, book illumination, 14th century); attempted seduction by the devil (Le Mans, cathedral, stained glass, 13th century); miracle of the horseshoes in the smithy (Passau, diocesan museum, painting, 1490); E. in the goldsmith's workshop, making a chalice (New York, Oppenheim collection, painting by P. Christus, 1449). *Cycles:* Cagliari, museum, painting, end 15th century; Antwerp, cathedral, painting by H. Francken, 1588; Bologna, S Maria della pieta, painting by G. Cavedoni and A. Tierini, 17th century.

Elizabeth of Hungary

(Elizabeth of Thuringia) countess, saint
Feast-day: 19th November (date of burial)
Life: * born in 1207 in Burg Saros-Patak near Kaschau or in Pressburg (Bratislava) as daughter of King Andreas II of Hungary and his consort Gertrud of Andechs. Having lived in Wartburg since 1211, in 1221 she married Ludwig, son of the Count of Thuringia. Elizabeth's father confessor, Rüdiger OFM, and the extremely severe Konrad von Marburg, who was inclined towards fanaticism, had a strong influence on her. From 1266 E. practised heroic acts of charity from Wartburg, for instance she suffered no food unjustly extorted from farmers to be placed on her table. After the death of her husband in the Crusades in 1127, E. went to Marburg of her own free will as a tertial of the Third Order, and in 1128/29 there founded a hospital. She herself performed services for the poor, the sick and lepers. † 17th November 1231 in Marburg. Buried in Marburg, canonised in 1235 by Pope Gregory IX.

Legends: Childhood: During a singing contest a bell prophesies Elizabeth's birth in Wartburg in 1207. As a child E. reads in the missal (Reading as signs of intelligence and education, a comparison with the Mother of God). – E. gives away an apple she has won to her female companion. – E. hastens from playing to pray in the church. Through her prayers E. delivers her murdered mother from purgatory. Numerous legends are based on acts of compassion E. performed, such as: During the famine in 1226 in Eisenach E. gives a drink to the thirsty, whereby the beer in a pitcher does not run dry. – E. receives the tertial rule from St Francis in person. – E. gives away clothing she has made herself. – E. covers a dead body with her finely woven lace veil. – E. washes the poor, whom she has received, as Christ washed their feet, whereby Christ appears to her in the poor. – Her spouse Ludwig sees the crucifixion in place of a leper, whom E. is tending in their matrimonial bed. – An angel brings E. a robe, because she gave it away to him. – E. catches a fish from a stream for a sick person. During a reproach by her father-in-law, the bread in E.'s apron turns into roses out of season. With composure she shows this to her spouse Ludwig. – E. receives an offer of marriage from Kaiser Friedrich II, which she declines for Christ's sake. – Legends after death: E. raises a drowned maiden from the dead. – E. heals a brother of the OFM in Reinhardsbrunn. – A small sapling which E. cuts down, retains the spherical shape of the crown even after the death of the saint. – Through three great fires in Hörselberg near Eisenach in 1389 E. reveals the great murders there in Würzburg in 1390.

Patronage: Patron saint of the Third Order of OFM, Teutonic Order, Cistercians (1236) and Dominicans (1244) charity, associations with Elizabeth, bakers, beggars, widows, orphans, persecuted innocents, lacemakers and veil weavers.

S. ELISABETHA VIDVA REGINA.

Veneration and cult sites: Reliquary in Marburg circa 1235. Pre-Reformation pilgrimage there from Bremen, Magdeburg and across Hungary in cycles of the pilgrimage to Aachen. In 1236 her mortal remains were raised and the head of the deceased was crowned with a crown by Kaiser Friedrich II. The skull reliquary donated by Friedrich II located since the 13th century in Mainz, emerged in Würzburg in 1631, and is today in the Stockholm History Museum (Inv. No.1). After the introduction of the Reformation in Marburg, in 1539 translation of the head to Besançon and the body to the Elizabeth Convent, Vienna III Landstrasse. Chief sites of veneration: Marburg, Kaschau (Hungary), Thuringia, Silesia, Spain, Mexico, Winchester.

Superstition: A stream near Schröck (Amöneburger province), in which E. washed her linen, receives special powers of purification at Whitsuntide.

Representation in Art: *Apparel:* As a young princess (Assisi, S Francesco, painting by S. Martini, circa 1325); as a widow in simple garb (Marburg, Elisabethenkirche, E. – shrine, relief, circa 1235); as a duchess with a duchess' hat (Klosterlechfeld, painting, 18th century); with a crown (Prague, Charles Bridge, figure by F. M. Brokoff, 1707); with a bonnet and conventional apparel (Münnerstadt, Magdalenkirche, figure by T. Riemenschneider, 1492); as a Franciscan tertiary with a grey habit and cingulum (Cologne, cathedral, stained glass, circa 1500). *Attributes:* Book (Naumburg, cathedral, relief, circa 1240); model of a church (Magdeburg, cathedral, relief, circa 1340); sceptre (Ludlow, church, stained glass, 15th century); angel with a crown (Marburg, Elisabethenkirche, stained glass, 13th century); childlike representation of a crowned soul (animula) (Marburg, St Elizabeth, relief, circa 1300); with two crowns (Cologne, Wallraf-Richartz Museum, painting by a Master

of Holy Family, 1500/1504); with three crowns, one on her head and one set inside the other in her hand (Berlin, Kaiser Friedrich museum, painting by a Master of Holy Family, circa 1500); a crown on her head and two crowns, one inside the other, on a book (Eisenach, Wartburg, painting by B.Bruyn, circa 1540); three crowns, piled on top of each other like a tiara, in her hand (Kalkar, painting, second half of the 15th century); three crowns, piled on top of each other like a tiara, on a book as a symbol of the secular crowns which E. had renounced, namely those of countess, sovereign and princess (New York, Frick Collection, painting by J. van Eyck, circa 1435); discarded crown at her feet (Liechtenstein Castle, gallery, painting, 15th century); bread (Strasbourg, Cathedral, figure, circa 1350); breadbasket (privately owned, Bavarian figure, circa 1490); bread and fishes (Rottweil, St Lorenz, figure, 15th century); plate with two fishes (Hamburg, museum, figure, circa 1430); bread and grapes as a reference to the sacrament (Nuremberg, Spitalkirche, relief, 1524); bowl and spoon with which E. is feeding the sick (Ismetleren kelyröl, painting, circa 1430); pitcher with which E. is giving the sick a drink (Frötuna Kyrka, Sweden, figure, 15th century); with a golden chalice (Barnham Broom, Norfolk, painting, 15th century); with a robe which she is giving to the poor (Frankfurt, Städel, painting, early 14th century); with bread and a robe (Oberwesel, stained glass, circa 1420/30); with coins (Rott am Inn, statue, by I. Günther, circa 1760), comb with which she is attending to the hair of lepers (privately owned, Swabian painting, circa 1430); beggar (Klagenfurt, museum, figure, 1510); cripple (Ulm, museum, painting, by M. Schaffner, 1525); lepers (Munich, Alte Pinakothek, painting, by H. Holbein the Elder, 1516); with roses (Perugia, Pinacoteca, painting by B. di Lorenzo, circa 1450); roses and lilies in clusters on her garment (Arezzo S Francesco, fresco, 14th century). *Special scenes:* Bread in E.'s apron changing into roses during a reproach by her father-in-law (Frankfurt, Städel, painting, early 14th century); E. distributing bread during a famine in Spital (Bad Mergentheim, Schlosskirche, painting, by G. Pittoni, 1734); E. feeds a poor person (Löcse, painting, 1493); E. feeding a sick person (Karlstein, painting, by master Theoderich, 14th century); E. giving a drink to a poor person, where the beer in the pitcher does not run dry (Rottweil, St Lorenz, figure, 15th century); E. giving away clothing she has made herself (Mainz, Dom Memorienpforte, figure, by M. Gerthener, circa 1410); E. tending to a sick person in hospital (Perugia, Pinacoteca, painting, by B. di Lorenzo, 15th century); E. washing and combing the hair of a leper (Kaschau, figure, 14th century); E. washing the feet of the poor (Reval, Heilig-Geist-Spital, painting, attributed to B. Notke, 1483); Ludwig seeing the crucifixion in place of a leper in the matrimonial bed (Marburg, Elisabethenkirche, mural painting, circa 1300); Ludwig seeing three roses in place of lepers (Laufen, deanery, painting, circa 1490); Hungarian emissary receiving payment for the benefit of widows from E., who is sitting at a spinning wheel (Eisenach, Wartburg, tapestry, 1475); Christ appearing to E. (Eggenburg, parish church, painting, 1521); E. at a table refraining from unjustly acquired food (Paris, Bibliothèque Ste. Geneviève, book illumination, circa 1250); E. taking off her crown before a crucifix (Überlingen, Cathedral, mural painting, circa 1490); bringing a drowned maiden back from the dead (Perugia, Pinacoteca, painting by P. della Francesca, middle of the 15th century); curing a brother in Reinhardsbrunn (Bonn, St Elizabeth, stained glass, early 20th century); E. receiving the tertiary rule from Francis (Kassel, Museum Wilhelmshöhe, painting, by F. Lippi, 15th century); *Cycles:* numerous, including Mar-

burg, Elisabethenkirche, E. shrine, reliefs, circa 1235; Lübeck, Hl. Geist-Spital, mural, circa 1420; Kaschau, E. altar, circa 1475; Bartfa, E. altar, circa 1486; Frankfurt, Deutschordenkirche, painting, A, 16th century; Marburg, Elisabethenkirche, painting by L. Juppe and J. v. Leyten, 1513; Eisenach, Wartburg, fresco by Moritz v. Schwind, 1855.

Elizabeth of Portugal

Queen, tertiary of the 3rd order of St Francis, saint

Feast-day: 4th July (8th July before the calendar reform)

Life: * born in 1270 as daughter of King Pedro III of Aragon and named after her great-aunt Elizabeth of Thüringen, she married King Dionysus of Portugal in 1282. She was brought up as a Christian wife and worked as a mediator between her husband and her son, giving financial assistance to the church and monasteries and churches in Lisbon, Almoster, Alenquer and Coimbra and hospitals in Santarém and Leira. After the death of her spouse in 1325 she entered the convent of St Clare in Coimbra. † 4th July 1336 in Estremoz while attempting to mediate between her son and the king of Castille. Beatified in 1516, canonised in 1625.

Legends: Through her prayers E. changes water into wine. –

Patronage: Patron saint of Portugal, Coimbra, Estremoz, Saragossa, women's assemblies, helper in trouble in war.

Veneration and cult sites: Her body lies in Coimbra, Sta. Clara, now a centre of pilgrimage.

Representation in Art: *Apparel:* in royal garb with headscarf and crown (Hoogstraten, St Katharina, stained glass, 1531/33); as a nun of the order of St Clare wearing a nun's habit (Coimbra, tomb, figure, circa 1330); as a Franciscan tertial wearing a nun's habit

(Coimbra, museum, Machado de Castro, figure, middle 16th century). *Attributes:* second crown in her hand (Hoogstraten, St Katharina, stained glass, 1531/33); wine vessel, roses (St Nicolas Waes, church of Antonius, figure, 18th century); book, pilgrim's pocket (Coimbra, tomb, figure, circa 1330). *Special scenes:* E. distributing alms (Bologna, S Elisabetta, painting, 17th century); E. comforting the sick (Madrid, Palazzo Real, drawing by F. Goya, circa 1800); translation of mortal remains (Coimbra, Novo de S Clara, painting, 18th century).

Emmeram of Regensburg

bishop, martyr, saint
Feast-day: 22nd September
Life: Bishop of Regensburg mission, probably appointed to Regensburg by an Agilulfinger Duke and worked in Bavaria. According to the biographer Arbeo von Freising, E. was falsely accused by duke Theodore's son of seducing his sister Uta. He was attacked on a journey in Kleinhelfendorf near Aibling and was tortured to death by terrible mutilation to his body. † 652.
Patronage: Patron saint of Regensburg diocese as 2nd diocesan patron.
Veneration and cultic sites: His body lay in the Peterkirche of Aschheim, then in the Georgskirche, and was later transferred to the Benedictine abbey church named by E. in Regensburg. A solemn translation into the East crypt under Bishop Gaubald (739–760).
Representation in Art: *Apparel:* as a bishop in pontifical mass vestments with a chasuble (Regensburg, St Emmeran, figure, circa 1050); as a bishop in pluvial, mitre, crosier (Mühlberg, Oberpfalz, pilgrim's church of St Anna, figure, circa 1500). *Attributes:* Ladder (Spalt, parish church, figure, 18th century). *Martyrdom:* Two torturers beat him on a ladder, E. being bound hand and foot (Stuttgart, Landesbibliothek, Stuttgarter Passio-

S. EMMERAMMVS M. ET PONTIFEX RATISBON.

nale, book illumination, 12th century); E. is being beheaded when God lets down a ladder from heaven (Regensburg, St Emmeran, fresco by C. D. Asam, 17th century).

Ephrem of Syria

Doctor of the Church
Feast-day: 9th June (until 1920 1st February, until 1969 18th June, in Greek rites 28th January, in Syrian rites the first Saturday after the great fast, in the Pauline calendar 9th July)
Life: * in the 4th century in Nisibis, taught by Bishop Jacob of Nisibis, greatly influenced by Bishop Vologese with the characteristic linking of promotion with education. E. became deacon in his home town, which he left after the Persian invasion of 363 and emigrated to Edessa. There he worked as a teacher. † 373. – E. is respected as a classical writer of the Syrian church. His

writings are partly composed in poetical form of metric speeches, which consist of verses of any length with lines with equal numbers of syllables, mostly seven. Moreover E. created Madrasche, singable hymns, whose verse is a series of stanzas ending in a refrain. In his exegetical writings E. clarifies the text in a literal sense according to the Antioch school and here remains prosaically academic, as the annotations on Genesis and Exodus show. E. fought heretics, such as Bardesanes, Marcion and Mani, his hymns are important for liturgical feast days and as an exhortation to asceticism. In 87 hymns E. deplored the disputes about the Trinity. In his Christianity E. is dependent on a Jewish or rabbinical way of thinking and therefore according to Greek understanding uses an inadequate terminology. The characteristic of the Holy Ghost as Ignis and Spiritus is noteworthy. – On account of his poetic art E. receives the appellation "God's harp". Appointed Doctor of the Church in 1920.

Legends: E. accompanies his bishop to the Nicene Council and visits monks in Egypt. – E. meets Basil the Great.

Representation in Art: Rare in the West, B. as a monk (Siena, Pinacoteca, painting, by Sano di Pietro, 1444).

Erasmus

(Elmo, Telmo) Bishop, martyr, saint

Feast-day: 2nd June

Life: uncertain information, he was probably a bishop in Antioch, Syria.

Legends: E. was brought to trial and imprisoned. E. was freed by an angel and brought to Syria. – In Sirmium he was martyred for the sake of his belief, but was once more freed from the dungeons by archangel Michael and taken to Formiae in Campania, where he worked zealously for seven years. – E. died in 303 in Formiae. – Additions of the 15th century: E. was boiled in a cauldron of pitch. – E. has awls forced under his fingernails. – E.'s entrails are drawn from his body with a rope.

Patronage: Patron saint of Gaeta, helper in time of need, seafarers in France, Portugal and Spain, since the 15th century Baltic seafarers, thread-winders, ropemakers, wood turners, against stomach ailments, cattle plagues, childbirth.

Veneration and cult sites: Supposedly buried in Formiae, translation in the 9th century to Gaeta, relics in Rome, Gubbio and Naples.

Superstition: A stick bound with flaxen thread must be offered to St E. against stomach poisoning in children. – E. is venerated under the name of Elmo in Italy, Spain and Portugal and gave his name to so-called St Elmo's Fire, a light which hovers around tall objects when the air near dark clouds holds a strong electrical charge; in superstitions St Elmo's Fire burns on the yard-arms of a ship as a bad omen. – also predicts the weather. – Breton sailors regard St Elmo's Fire as the souls of the drowned. German sailors believe that St Elmo's Fire only appears where a man has fallen overboard from a ship. –

Representation in Art: *Apparel:* As a bishop in pontifical Mass vestments with a chasuble (Kaufbeuren, Blasius chapel, figure, early 16th century); as a bishop in pontifical robes with pluvial (Aschaffenburg, Johannesburg Castle, National Gallery, painting, L. Cranach the Elder school, 16th century); in bishop's vestments of the Orthodox church (Palermo, Capella Palatina, mosaic, 12th century). *Attributes:* Coiled entrails with entrails looped around his hand (Munich, Alte Pinakothek, painting by master Mathis (MGN), circa 1518); a cauldron in his hand (Neustadt, Mecklenburg, figure, 15th century); standing in a cauldron (Gaeta, Easter pharos, relief, end 13th century); with awls forced under his fingernails (Vienna, Kunsthistorisches Museum, painting by a Master

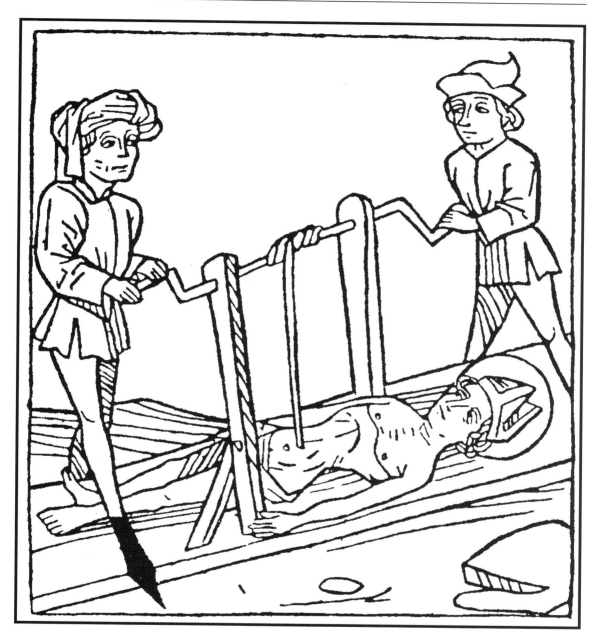

of the Holy Martyrs, circa 1490); candle (Messina, museum, painting, early 16th century); the attributes mentioned in literature of a ship's rope, anchor rope and a weaver's shuttle are fictions and have not been verified. *Martyrdom:* E. standing in a cauldron while while his entrails are coiled up (Taivassalo, Finland, mural, 15th century); E. lies naked on a board while an executioner draws out his entrails (Löwen, St Peter, painting by D. Bouts, 1458). *Cycles:* inter alia Gaeta, Easter pharos, reliefs, 13th century.

Ethelbert of Kent

(Aethelberct, Edilbertus) king, saint
Feast-day: 24th February
Life: King between 560 and 616; through his Christian wife Bertha, a grand-daughter of King Chlodwig, E. came in contact with the Christian faith, but delayed his baptism. In a letter, pope Gregory the Great reproached Bertha for not having converted him. In 596, E. received Augustine of Canterbury and the missionaries sent by pope Gregory in a friendly manner and encouraged the Christianisation of England. In an encouraging letter, Gregory congratulated E. on his contributions towards conversion and even compared him with Emperor Constantine.
Veneration and cult sites: Buried in Kent, church of SS Peter and Paul; cult in the dioceses of Westminster, Southwark and Northampton.
Representation in Art: as king with a vision of Ecce Homo (wood cut from the Saints of the Family, Friends and Relatives of Emperor Maximilian I, 1516).

Ethelburg of Barking

(Aedilburh) Virgin, abbess, saint
Feast-day: 11th October
Life: Supported by her brother Erkenwald, E. built the Benedictine monastery of Barking

in Essex and was appointed abbess. D. in 664.
Representation in Art: *Apparel:* as nun in black habit (Oxford, Bodleian Library MS Auct. D intra 2.11, book illumination, circa 1430/1440); as nun in grey habit with crown (Cambridge, Fitzwilliam Museum MS T 57, book illumination, circa 1490). *Attributes:* staff, book (Oxford, Bodleian Library MS Auct. D intra 2.11, book illumination, circa 1430/1440); coat of arms with three crowns, three lilies, three roses (London, British Museum, book of hours of Oldhall, book illumination, 15th century).

Etheldreda of Ely

(Aethelthryth, Ediltrudis, Aeldrith, Aetheldryte, Aetheldreda, Audrey) virgin, queen, abbess, saint
Feast-day: 23rd June
Life: Daughter of Anna, queen of Mercia; married to Tondberht, ealdorman of the South Gyrwas, but remained a virgin; retired to the Isle of Ely near Cambridge after his death; married again, for political reasons, to Egfrith, the young king of Northumbria, but again remained a virgin; 12 years later, E. left Egfrith and became a nun in the Benedictine monastery at Coldingham; founded a double monastery at Ely in 673 and was appointed as its abbess by Wilfrid, bishop of York. D. on 23rd June 679 of the plague.
Legends: The miraculous raising of the sea prevents E's abduction from the monastery by Egfrith. – On the way to Ely, a staff breaks out in leaf. – On E's intercession, Brithantus is freed from capture.
Veneration and cult sites: Body buried on the Isle of Ely; in 695, her body was found incorrupt; until the Reformation, her shrine remained a place of pilgrimage.
Representation in Art: *Apparel:* dressed as Benedictine nun (New York, Pierpont Mor-

gan Library, book of hours of Sarum, book illumination, mid 15th century); as crowned Sister of the Order (Eton, College Chapel, wall-painting, 1479–1488); in contemporary garments (Cambridge, Fitzwilliam Museum MS T 57, book illumination, circa 1490); as queen with crown and ermine (Rome, St Maria Maggiore, Capella Paolina, fresco by L. C. Cigoli, 1612). *Attributes*: book, branch in flower (London, British Museum MS Add.49598, book illumination, circa 975/980); staff (Stamford, St John, stained glass, 15th century); crown at feet, trunk (wood cut from the Saints of the Family, Friends and Relatives of Emperor Maximilian I, 1516). *Special scenes*: E. received by Edda of Coldingham (Boston, Museum of Fine Arts, figure, 15th century). *Cycles*: London, The Society of Antiquaries, painting, circa 1425; Ely Cathedral, reliefs, 1322–1336.

Ethelwold of Winchester

(Aethelwold) Bishop, Benedictine monk, saint

Feast-day: 1st August (2nd August in Abingdon); translation, 8th and 23rd October.

Life: Born 908 (912?) in Winchester; became a monk and, later, a prior under Dunstan in Glastonbury; in 941, E. restored the derelict abbey of Abingdon; became bishop of Winchester in 963 and founded a Benedictine convent at the cathedral, in addition to restoring monasteries such as Milton, Peterborough, Ely and Thorney. His support of craftwork and architecture led to the golden era of the so-called "Winchester School". D. on 1st August 984.

Veneration and cult sites: Buried in Winchester; in 996 remains taken from the tomb and relics translated to Ely, Thorney and Deeping.

Representation in Art: *Apparel*: as bishop in pontifical vestments with chasuble, pallium and mitre (London, British Museum MS Cotton Tiberius A. III, book illumination, 11th century). *Special scenes*: E. consecrates Winchester Cathedral (London, British Museum MS Add. 49598, book illumination, circa 980).

Eusebius of Vercelli

bishop, martyr, saint

Feast-day: 2nd August (16th December before the calendar reform, own feast day in Vercelli on 1st August)

Life: * around 283 in Sardinia, lector in Rome and first bishop of Vercelli. As first bishop E. inaugurated a Vita Communis for his clergy. In 355, as an emissary of Pope Liberius, E. procured the convocation of the synod of Milan, which the still condemned Athanasius attended; for that reason E. was banished to Skythopolis,Palestine and to Cappadocia and lastly Thebes. In 362 Julian the Apostate allowed all those who had been banished to return. E. was a participant in the synod of Alexandria, called about then for the Nicene Creed, but could not prevent a schism. After 363 E., together with Hilarius of Poitiers, worked in his diocese against Arianism. † 1st August 371.

Legends: During baptism E. is lifted from the font by an angel. – E. is so beautiful that a woman wants to force her way into his sleeping chamber, but an angel is watching over the doors. – E. serves an angel during Mass. – When on E.'s arrival at Vercelli Arians barricade the church doors, these spring open for the bishop by themselves. – On the way to the synod of Mailand E. sails a boat across the river without a helmsman. – A document with the banned signatures of Arian bishops burns by itself on being presented to E. – For this reason E. is whipped by the Arians, dragged across the street and ill-treated. – In exile E. is thrown into the dungeons, which are so narrow that he is forced to sit in a cramped position and cannot stretch out his legs. – After returning to Vercelli E. is stoned by the Arians.

Veneration and cult sites: Vercelli, cathedral.

Representation in Art: *Apparel:* As a bishop in Mass vestments (Vercelli, cathedral, treasury, book cover, 9th century). *Attributes:* A book (Vercelli, cathedral, treasury, book cover, 9th century). *Special scenes:* E. being taken prisoner in exile (Vercelli, cathedral, painting by G.B. Bernero, 18th century).

Eustace

(Eustachius, Eustathius) martyr, saint

Feast-day: 20th September

Legends: romantic, compiled from various sources: Placidus, a military commander under Emperor Trajan, was converted through a vision of a stag with an image of the crucifixion in his antlers, the more so since Placidus learns from the stag's mouth that in the works of charity which he has performed he has unknowingly venerated Christ. – Also Placidus' wife has a vision of Christ, which calls upon the family to receive baptism. – Placidus receives the baptismal name Eustathius from the Bishop of Rome, and is baptised with his wife Theoptista and his sons Theoptistus and Agapitus. – E. sees the stag for a second time, and it heralds future sufferings like those of Job. – E.'s servant and maid die, his horse falls down dead and a thief robs E. – E. and his family flee in the night to Egypt, where all his goodness is reduced to nought. – E. travels by boat, when the ferryman Theista demands and avails himself of fare. – E. has to leave his wife and wants to carry his children one by one across a raging river, but one child is taken by a wolf and a second by a lion. – Farmers hunt the wolf and shepherds hunt the lion with the living child and rescue him without E. knowing anything about it. – E. enters into service as a servant. – During recruitment of soldiers, a soldier's servant comes to E., and recognises him as his erstwhile commander. – E. is appointed to his station by the Emperor and besieges the enemy with an army. – E.'s sons are also serving in the army; E. finds them again and his wife, who unknown to E. and his sons has taken lodgings nearby. – After the death of Emperor Trajan E. has to present an offering of thanks for the victory. – E. refuses, and is thrown into the arena with a wild lion who, however, becomes tame and meek. – E. and his family are pushed into a brass bull in which a fire is lighted, they perish but their bodies do not burn.

Patronage: Patron saint of helpers in times of need, hunters of Paris and Madrid, tinsmiths, foresters, grocers, stocking knitters, cloth merchants.

Veneration and cult sites: The undamaged bodies lie in Rome, S Eustachi, relics are in Rome, Paris, St-Eustache (since the 12th century), veneration spread in the 15th century, later succeeded by Hubert of Liège.

Representation in Art: *Apparel:* As an armed warrior in roman soldier's attire with a chlamys and greaves (Rome, Palazzo Venezia, ivory relief, 10th century); as an armed warrior in a suit of armour (Città del Vaticano, Vatican Museum, ivory relief, 11/12th century); as a warrior in armour (Munich, Alte Pinakothek, painting, by A. Dürer, 1502); as a warrior on horseback (Belforte del Chiente, painting, by G. Boccati, 1468); as a nobleman in distinguished, elegant attire (Wenigumstadt, Lower Franconia, painting, circa 1520); as a nobleman with a diadem (London, Victoria and Albert Museum, reliquary, relief, 13th century); as a hunter (Ambierle, abbey, stained glass, circa 1470/85); in classical fantasy apparel with puffed sleeves (Vierzehnheiligen, figure, by J. M. Feichtmayr, 1764); *Attributes:* Cross,

sword (Rome, Palazzo Venezia, ivory, 10th century); lance (Paris, Louvre, Harbaville triptych, ivory relief, late 10th century); sword (Rome, S Lorenzo fuori le Mura, mural painting, 13th century); standard (Munich, Alte Pinakothek, painting, by A. Dürer, 1502); bugle (Ambierle, abbey, stained glass, circa 1470/85); palm branch (Sanseverino, S Lorenzo in Dolio, fresco, by L. Salimbeni, 1407); stag with a crucifix in his antlers (Florence, Accademia, painting, by B. di Lorenzo, 15th century); stag's head with a crucifix in its antlers (Munich, Alte Pinakothek, painting, by H. Burgkmair the Elder, 1528); stag's antlers with a crucifix (Vienna, St Stephan, choir stalls, figure, 1484). *Special scenes:* E. on the stag hunt (London, National Gallery, painting, by Pisanello, 15th century); E. kneeling before the stag (Berlin, Kupferstichkabinett, copperplate engraving, by A. Dürer, 1505); E. and his son (Brozzi, S Andrea, painting, by P. di Stefano, 15th century); E. and his family (Florence, Uffizi, painting, by F. Lippi, 1491); his sons being abducted by wild animals (Rouen, cathedral, relief, 14th century); lion in the arena licking E.'s feet (Venice, S Staè, relief, 18th century); E. and his family in a burning bull (Chartres, cathedral, south portal, relief, 13th century); E. on the road to the place of execution (Paris, St Eustache, painting, by S. Vouet, circa 1635). *Cycles:* inter alia Vienna, Österreichische Nationalbibliothek, cod. 370, book illumination, 14th century; Sens, cathedral, stained glass, 12th century; Pomposa, abbey, mural painting, 1351; Salzburg, Nonnberg, faldisterium, ivory reliefs, first half of the 13th century.

F

Fabian

Pope, Martyr, saint

Feast-day: 20th January (in Greek Rite 5th August)

Life: reigned 236–250 AD. In time of peace until the persecutions under Emperor Decius, F. consolidated the organisation of the church by separating Rome into seven administrative districts with seven deacons. † on 20th January 250 AD as one of the first victims of the new persecution of Christians.

Legend: By chance F. is at the meeting of Christians in Rome to elect a new Pope, when a white dove comes down onto his head. At this F. is chosen to be the new Pope. – The Roman Emperor Philip the Arab is excluded from the Easter celebrations until he has confessed his sins.

Patronage: Potters, tin founders,

Veneration and cult sites: Body in the Catacombs of Callixtus, relics in St Sebastian fuori le mura and St Andrea della Valle, Rome, formerly in the Fabian Chapel, Hornbach (until the Reformation).

Representation in Art: *Apparel:* as Pope in non-liturgical dress of office with cassock, rochet, cape with cowl and tiara (Hoyer, Denmark, painting, 15th century); in liturgical Pontiff's dress with amice, dalmatic and pluvial, tiara (Landstuhl, Pfalz, Orphanage, painting, beginning 16th century); as bishop in Pontiff's dress with mitre (Sinalunga, painting, by B. di Giovanni, 1509). *Attributes:* crosier (Sigmaringen, Hohenzollern Collection, painting by H. Strub, beginning 16th century); sword (Leipzig, Grassi-Museum, figure, by P. Breuer, circa 1500); palm (Tyassula, Vigilius' Church, mural, end 15th [?] century); angel with martyr instruments (Rome, St Sebastian's, figure, by F. Papaleo, 18th century). *Martyrdom:* Sinalunga, Predella, painting, by B. di Giovanni, 1509.

Felicitas and her seven sons

Martyr, saint

Feast-day: 23rd November (with her sons 10th July)

Life: F. and the seven martyrs Januarius, Felix, Philip, Silvanus, Alexander, Vitalis and Martialis, probably not real sons, suffered martyrdom together under Emperor Marcus Aurelius in 162.

Legend: The preserved Passion is not authentic. Rather it is a legend based on that of the seven Maccabean brothers (2 Macc. 7): The Roman Prefect Publius had the faithful sons killed before the eyes of their mother.

Patronage: Women, mothers.

Veneration and cult sites: originally a canonised saint, her name was replaced under

Pope Gelasius I. (492–496) by Perpetua and Felicitas.

Representation in Art: *Apparel:* as matron in cloak and with scarf (Vreden, Collegiate Church, relief, 16th century); as orantin in antique ladies' costume with her sons (Rome, Catacombs of Maximus, mural, 6th century); as enthroned mother (Florence, S Felicia, painting, by N. di Bicci, 1476). *Attributes:* palm, sword (Lüdinghausen, figure, 15th century); book, palm (Vreden, Collegiate Church, relief, 16th century); bowl with the heads of her sons (Admont, Chapel, Tutonis opusculum, illumination, mid 12th century); heads of her sons on a square tray (Berlin-Dahlem, relief, 1510/20); heads of the sons impaled on the edge of the sword (Nuremberg National Museum, stained glass, late 15th century); sons attributive at feet (Cologne, Wallraf-Richartz Museum, painting, by Master of the Bartholomy Reredos, circa 1500). *Special scenes:* condemning of the mother and sons (Ottobeuren, fresco, by J. Zeiller, 1763). *Martyrdom:* Florence S Felicia, painting, by N. di Bicci, 1476. *Cycles:* Rome, Oratorium by the Baths of Titus, frescoes, 5th century.

Fiacrius of Meaux

Hermit, saint

Feast-day: 30th August

Life: * circa 610 in Ireland. Bishop of Meaux brought into his diocese Irish monks, including F., who had lived as a hermit in Breuil. † 670.

Legend: As F. received a plot of ground from Bishop Faro and touched it with his staff, flowers bloomed.

Patronage: florists, gardeners, lattice-makers, box-makers, coppersmiths, knife-makers, sewers, packers, stocking makers, potters, tile makers, tin founders, carriage drivers (fiacres) who had their stands in front of

Evangelists, Fathers of the Church, early martyrs

27 *St John on Patmos, by Hans Burgkmair the Elder, Munich, Alte Pinakothek*

28 *Translation of the Bones of St Mark to Venice, by Paolo Veneziano, Venice, Museo di S Marco*

29 *St John Chrysostom, mosaic, Istanbul, Hagia Sophia*

30 *The four western Church Fathers: (L. to r.) Jerome, Augustine, Gregory the Great and Ambrose, by Michael Pacher, Munich, Alte Pinakothek*

31 *St Laurence distributing Alms, fresco by Fra Angelico, Vatican, Capella Niccolina*

32 *St Stephan, relief, Arles, cloister of St Trophime*

33 *Temptation of St Antony, by Joachim Patinier, Madrid, Prado*

28

ΙΩΑΝΗΣ Ο ΧΡΥCΟCΤΟΜΟC

29

31

33

the F. church in Paris and hence are named after F., notaries, against skin diseases.

Veneration and cult sites: body in the Cathedral of Meaux, church patron in Paris.

Representation in Art: *Apparel:* as hermit in farmers' garment with long open-fronted cassock and cloak (Karlsruhe, Kunsthalle, painting of the monogramist JS, 16th [?] century); with uncovered leg full of abscesses (Stuttgart, State Museum, figure, 1470); as notary (Bruges, Groeningenmuseum, painting, by Q. Massys, 15th century). *Attributes:* model of church (Lens, St Remi, figure, 17th century); rosary, spade (Karlsruhe, Kunsthalle, painting of the monogramist JS, 16th [?] century); cross, flower (Bruges, Groeningenmuseum, painting, by Q. Massys, 15th

century). *Cycles:* Notre Dame du Terte de Châtelaudren, chapel, painting, 16th [?] century.

Fidelis of Sigmaringen

(Marcus Roy) Capuchin, Martyr, saint
Feast-day: 24th April
Life: * 1578 as son of the mayor Roy of Sigmaringen. Studied at the University of Freiburg. 1603 awarded Doctor of Philosophy, 1611 Doctor of Laws. 1611–12 official of the Government of Lower Austria in Ensisheim, where F. was considered the advocate of the poor. 1612 ordination to the priesthood, entry to the Capuchin convent in Freiburg in Breisgau. 1617 preacher in Altdorf on the

century). *Attributes*: palm, sword, club (on meditational pictures of the 17th century). *Special scenes*: F. crushes heresy with Joseph of Leonesse (Parma, National Gallery, painting, by G. B. Tiepolo, 18th century). *Martyrdom*: Engen Town Hall, painting, by J. I. Wegscheider, 1729.

Firmin of Amiens

Bishop, Martyr, saint
Feast-day: 25th September
Legend: * in Pamplona and student of St Honestus. – F. is consecrated Bishop of Amiens by Honoratus. – F. a missionary in Angers and Beauvais, where the procurator has F. whipped and thrown into prison. – After being freed F. comes to Amiens, where two blind men and two lepers are healed. – F. is the first Bishop of Amiens. – Thrown into prison again, F. is martyred by decapitation. – F.'s body is discovered by Bishop Salvius.
Patronage: city patron of Amiens, Pamplona; bathers, coopers, wine-merchants, bakers, children; against scurvy and shingles.
Veneration and cult sites: body in the Cathedral of Amiens, relics in Pamplona since 1186.
Representation in Art: *Apparel*: as bishop in chasuble and mitre (Amiens, Cathedral, west portal, figure, 1225/30); as bishop in pluvial (Vienna, Austrian National Library, Cod. 2857, drawing, by J. Kolderer, 16th century); Cephalophore – carrying his head (Amiens, Cathedral, west portal, figure, circa 1375). *Attributes*: book (Innsbruck, Court Church, grave of Maximilian, figure, 16th century); man on feet (Amiens, Cathedral, west portal, figure, 1225/30); crown, sword, head, whip (Vienna, Albertina, Saints of the Family, Friends and Relatives of the Emperor Maximilian, wood engraving, 1516/17). *Cycles*: Amiens Cathedral, choir screen, relief, 14th century; Amiens Cathedral,

Vierwaldstättersee. 1618–1619 Guardian in Rheinfelden near Basel, 1619–1620 Guardian in Feldkirch in Vorarlberg, 1621–1622 in Altdorf and Freiburg in Switzerland. During the attempts to re-Catholicise in Grisons region, F. was treacherously cut down with a sword and killed with a club on the 24th April 1622 in Seewies in Prättigau after being invited to preach by Calvinist farmers. Beatification 1729, canonised 1746.
Patronage: Hohenzollern, second diocese patron of Feldkirch, jurists.
Reverence and Cultic Sites: Body in Chur crypt of the cathedral, relics in Feldkirch Capuchin church (head) and Stuttgart St Fidelis' Church.
Representation in Art: *Apparel*: in Capuchin habit (Burg Steisslingen, painting, 17th

stained glass, by Steinheil and Coffetier, 1854.

Florian and companions
Martyr in Lorch, saint
Feast-day: 4th May
Life: F. was a Roman administration official and was martyred in 304 with about forty other Christians.
Legend: F., of Celtic descent, is born in Zieselmauer near Vienna. – F. is an officer in the Roman army and President of the Chancellery of the Procurator Aquilinus. – As 40 Christians are tracked down and incarcerated in Lauriacum (Lorch) at the beginning of the Diocletian persecution 303/04, F. wants to stand with them (variant: free them) and is himself seized. – After refusing to sacrifice to idols, F. is to be thrown into the Enns. – Although no-one wants to make a mistake with the officer, F. is thrown into the river by a soldier. – At this the soldier loses his sight. – The body, weighted down by a stone, floats out of the water and is guarded by an eagle. – F. appears to a matron in the night and asks her to bury his body. – As the oxen pulling the cart with the body become exhausted with thirst, a spring rises up before them. (later addition: As a child F. extinguishes a burning house with a bucket of water. – A villain tried once in vain to set light to the chapel over his grave.)
Patronage: Upper Austria, Chapel and market of St Florian, Cracow, Bologna; against fire and flood, storm, on drought and barrenness of fields; brewers, coopers, stove-fitters, chimney sweeps, smiths, soap-boilers, firemen.
Veneration and cult sites: grave in the Chapel of St Florian; in the 11th century translation to Rome, from there to Cracow by St Kasimir.

Superstition: On F.'s Day one may not light a fire or smoke tobacco. – If it is bright on F.'s Day there will be many fires in the year. – The saying: "St Florian, protect our house, set another alight" is merely the result of a joke.
Representation in Art: *Apparel:* as a long-bearded old man in chlamys (Salzburg, Stift Nonnberg, mural, mid 12th century); as young knight in chain mail and cloak (St Florian, Museum, figure, circa 1300); in plate armour (Wroclàv, Corpus Christi Church, painting, 1497); as armed duke in duke's hat (Leutschau, St James', painting, 2nd half 15th century); as Roman soldier with breastplate and cocked helmet (Niederaschau, figure, by I. Günther, 1766). *Attributes:* banner (Salzburg, Stift Nonnberg, mural, mid 12th century); sword, shield with cross (St Florian, Museum, figure, end 13th century); lance bedecked with banner (Stuttgart, State Museum, painting, by B. Zeitblom, circa 1500); red and white cross (St Florian, Stift Library, Cod. III 205 A, illumination, circa 1310); palm branch (Neukirchen near Lambach, figure, circa 1700); millstone (Seifriedswörth, painting, circa 1700); water tub (Ljubljana, Museum, painting, by A. Cebej, mid 18th century); pouring water from a tub onto a burning house (Kefermarkt, figure, by Master of Kefermarkt, circa 1490); a burning house in his hand (Sterzing, Museum, figure, by H. Multscher, 15th century). *Martyrdom:* Munich, Bavarian State Art Collection, painting, beginning 18th century). *Cycles:* originally St Florian near Prien, now in Florence Uffizi; Nuremberg German National Museum; Prague Narodni Galleri; Berlin, private collection, painting, by A. Altdorfer circa 1520/25; St Florian Convent Church, frescoes, by A. Gumpp and M. Steidl, 1690.

Frances of Rome

widow, founder of the Order, saint

Feast-day: 9th March

Life: * 1384 in Rome; 1396 married to Lorenzo de Poziani, to whom she bore 4 children in 40 years of marriage. Benefactress for hospitals and the needy. 1425 founded the female branch of the Olivetan Order at the Church of St Mary Nuova, whose members joined together for a communal life in the Torre de Specchi, and since the are called "Nobili Oblati di Tor de Specchi". 1437 entry to the Order and its head. † 9th March 1440. Canonised 1608.

Legend: F. is tempted by the Devil in the form of St Onuphrius. – F.'s dead son, Raphael, appears to her and shows her the poor souls. – The Madonna lets F. carry the Christ Child. – The Oblates are taken under the protective gown of Mary opened out by Benedict and Mary Magdalena. – F. is in intimate contact with her protecting angel. – During contemplation, F. feels the five wounds of Christ. – The Apostle Peter gives F. the Eucharist in the presence of the Apostle Paul. – At F.'s communion the name of Jesus shines out.

Patronage: city patroness of Rome, women, women car drivers (since 1925); against the torment of Purgatory, plague.

Veneration and cult sites: body in Rome St Mary Nuova.

Representation in Art: *Apparel:* as nun in Benedictine habit with girdle and white veil (Paris, Louvre, painting, by P. Mignard, 17th century; the Marquess of Maintenon serves as a model for F.). *Attributes:* book, protecting angel (Monastery Gate de Specchi, fresco, 15th century); protecting angel as deacon (Rome, St Francesca Romana, marble relief, by E. Ferrata, mid 17th century); the bread basket and bundle of wood referred to in the literature are not attested in depictions. *Special scenes:* protecting angel helps F. (Rome, private possession, painting, by G. Galli gen.

La Spadarino, 17th century). *Cycles:* New York Lehmen Collection; Baltimore Walters Art Gallery, panel cycle, mid 15th century; Rome Monastery gate de Specchi, frescoes, by circle of Antoniazzo Romano, circa 1469; Rome Monastery gate de Specchi, monochrome painting, 1485.

Francis of Assisi

(Giovanni Bernadone) Franciscan, founder of the Order, saint

Feast-day: 4th October (within the Franciscan Order further feast days: remembrance of the stigmatisation 17th September; confirmation of the Rule of the Order 16th April; consecration of the church of St Francis in Assisi 25th May; canonisation 16th July; indulgence of Portiuncula 2nd August; rediscovery of the body 12th December)

Life: * 1181/82 in Assisi the son of the cloth merchant Pietro Bernadone and Johanna (?) Pica, probably from the area of Marseilles. After the father returned from France the name "Francesco" (= Francis) was added to the baptismal name "Giovanni". F. learnt to read and write in the parish school of S Giorgio. F.'s youth was noted for poetical sensitivity, lavish generosity and extravagance in clothing. F. became involved in a conflict between the towns of Assisi and Perugia and landed in prison in 1202, where he became seriously ill. After recovering freedom and health in 1204/05 pilgrimage to Rome, on which he travelled as poverello to experience beggary. F. wanted to attain knighthood in the Papal army of Count Walter of Brienne, but allegedly frightening dreams caused his return. F. detached himself gradually from the friends of his youth. F. retreated to prayer in the secluded grotto of Assisi. In St Damiano F. heard the directive to restore the fallen Church, for which he sold clothing material from his father's store. 1206/07 his enraged father elegant him, at which F. removed his distinguished clothes in public and threw them at his father's feet. F. lived among the poor and lepers in imitation of the abasement of God in the Incarnation. In the guise of a hermit F. renewed the chapel of St Damian and St Peter della Spina in 1206/08. On 24th February 1208 F. heard the Gospel of the commissioning of the disciples: "take neither purse nor scrip nor shoes", and recognised in that his future lifestyle. Twelve companions joined him, for whom F. drew up the first Rule, which Pope Innocent III confirmed orally on the intercession of Cardinal John of St Paul. In 1209 F. had to accept the tonsure and deaconate on the orders of Pope Innocent III. The first convent was set up in Portiuncula, once called the Chapel of St Mary degli Angeli of the Benedictines, then "Portiuncula". 1212 meeting with Clara of Assisi, with whose help F. founded the female branch of the Order (acceptance of Clara as novice on 18/19th March 1212). F. sent his brothers out as missionaries, he himself going to Dalmatia (1212) and Spain (1213–1215). Illness prevented him from missionary work among the Mohammedans in North Africa. F. was a private observer at the Fourth Lateran Council. In 1216 F. requested a special indulgence on the consecration of the church in Portiuncula from Pope Honorius III. During the Fifth Crusade F. moved the General Chapter of the Order with the crusaders to Egypt and tried with the Brothers of the Order of Illuminatus to convert Sultan Al-Malik al Kmil. Difficulties in the organisation of the Order caused F. to ask Pope Honorius III to give him Cardinal Ugolino as Protector. The source of the crisis lay in the charismatic personality of the founder, who opposed monastic structures. Nevertheless, monastic forms, such as the novitiate, had to be introduced. In 1219 an editorial reworking of the Rule was made in the famous so-called "Matten Chapter", whose imbalance brought about a revision in 1223 by F. and brothers Leo of Assisi and Bonitus of Bologna. On 29th November 1223 after difficult negotiations Pope Honorius III ceremonially confirmed this. In the meantime F. became ill; malaria, Egyptian eye disease, and degradation of the spleen and liver caused F. to give up the leadership of the Order. Thus F. appointed Peter Cattani Vicar General in 1220 and Elias of Cortona in 1221. 1221 granting of the third Order for laity who lived in the world. 1223 in a mystical display F. recreated the events of Bethlehem before the improvised crib in Greccio. In the summer of 1224 F. withdrew to Monte Alverna for a forty day fast in honour of the Virgin Mary. In an ecstatic display of a crucified seraph on Monte Alverna about 14th September 1224 F. received the stigmata of the Lord. 1225 an attack of trachoma in St Dalmiano with his sister Clara, F. was obliged by Cardinal Ugolino to let himself by treated by an ophthalmologist at the Papal Court in Rieti, which was unsuccessful. † in Assisi 3rd October 1226. Canonised 16th July 1228. The brotherhood around St Francis drew their spiritual strength from a closeness to the divine word in the Gospels; thereby came an easy simplicity, coupled with a rigorous radicalism, which showed itself in a dependence on divine providence, in an earthly homelessness, in penitence, in the testimony of their own modesty, and in the universal understanding of fraternity. The Franciscan Apostolate lives according to its own example and not from the pressure of others. The historical importance of F. in his own time lay in the message of poverty of the heart in the midst of conflict between Emperor and Pope, citizen and noble, "Ghibelline and Guelphs", in the arising early capitalism. The meaning for today lies in a radical following of Christ, an optimistic view of the world and the drawing of the whole of creation and creativity into the work of Christian love (e. g. in the sunrise).

Legend (Selection): F. is born in a stable. – A mysterious pilgrim predicts his moral greatness. – F. is threatened in winter by two robbers, who cast him into the snow. – F. gives his cloak to a poor knight. – In a dream Christ shows F. a great heavenly palace bedecked with flags, revealing to him a spiritual rather than a worldly calling. – A mysterious questioning voice in Spoleto causes F. to leave knightly service and return from Rome. – F. sees a mystic meeting with Christ in the kiss of a leper. – Pope Innocent III's confirmation of the Order comes after the Pope has a dream, in which he sees how the falling Lateran Basilica is supported by F. on his shoulders. – F. sees coming towards him in the street three women in the virtues of, the Order: poverty, chastity and obedience: they greet him with the words "Welcome is the Lady Poverty" and disappear. – An angel with a flask of water appears to F.; from the vision F. concludes that the soul of a priest must be as clear water and for this reason withdraws from consecration. – The Brothers in Rivotorto have a vision of a fiery wagon, which contains the ball of the sun, and they see in this the soul of F. – F., with the longing for martyrdom, wants to sail to Syria, but a storm casts him up in Dalmatia. – Around 1214 F. resists the nightly attacks of Satan in St Pedro di Bovara, by rolling naked in the snow, making seven snowballs and recommending them to the Devil as his family. – In an attack by the Devil, F. throws himself into thorns, which become roses. – F. does public penance for a fast broken through illness. – In order to punish himself for his sins, F. asks his Brother Bernardo to kick him three times. – in 1215 at Pian d'Arca F. preaches to the birds, who listen to him in silence and let themselves be stroked. – In favour of their Brothers, F. and Dominic refuse the office of bishop when offered by

the later Pope Honarius. – In Gubbio F. commands a wolf not to be seen in the town and not cause the inhabitants fear and trembling. – F. commands his Brother Silvester to drive the Devil out of the town of Arezzo, which is in a fraternal feud, so that the people may be able to live in peace again. – Before the Sultan in Egypt, F. undergoes a test by fire and passes unscathed through the flames, while the Imans refuse to follow. – During the sermon, F. appears in a dream to his Brother Pacificus with two crossed swords on his head and dew on his brow (dew is a heraldic symbol the Minorite life and has connections with the Aaronic blessing). – F. wrote down the Order as Christ dictated it. – In Arles in 1244, during the sermon of St Anthony of Padua, F. appears to his brothers. – After the death of F. the lark sings in the middle of the night. – 1449 Pope Nicholas discovers the burial place and at night finds F. with the stigmata preserved in the grave.

Patronage: Franciscans of all branches, Italy (since 1939), Bishopric of Basel, Assisi; the poor, the blind, prisoners, the lame, the shipwrecked, flax merchants, cloth merchants, traders, tailors, weavers, social workers, environmentalists.

Veneration and cult sites: on 4th October 1228 body taken in wooden coffin with painted lid to the nuns of St Clare in St Damiano; afterwards laid in the crypt of F.'s home parish church; translated 1230 into the newly built Lower Church of Assisi; burial cell open for special visitors until 1442 (1476?), under the orders of Pope Sixtus IV the entrance walled up in 1476; the exact burial place lost; on 12th December 1818 rediscovery, on contact with the air the body disintegrates into dust with the exception of the skull and some ribs and pelvic bones; relics of these in Rome SS Apostoli, Assisi, Kriens St Gallus, relics of clothes in Assisi St F. and St Chiara, Cortona, Arezzo, Florence (St Croce). Laying of the foundation stone of the double church in Assisi by Pope Gregory IX on 14th July 1228, 1832 partial collapse of the vaulting during an earthquake, 1836–40 restoration.

Representation in Art: *Apparel:* unshod in long cord-belted blue habit with white sleeve and hood (Marburg, St Elizabeth's stained glass, circa 1250); in dark dress of the Order without stigmata (Subiaco, Sacro Speco, Chapel of Gregory IX, fresco, before 1228); in dark dress of the Order, habit with hood and stigmata (Assisi, Museum of St F., painting, circa 1270); in dark dress of the Order, habit with hood (as a Mozetta) laid in folds, stigmata (Assisi, St F. Lower Church, painting, by S Martini, circa 1326); as true effigies according to the description of Thomas of Celano (Assisi, St F. Lower Church, painting, by G. Cimabue, 13th century); as hermit in the country (Rome, St Cecilia's, fresco, by P. Bril, 1599); as preacher before a bird-bath (Maxdorf, cemetery, figure, by T. Hauck, 2nd half 20th century). *Attributes:* crucifix (Florence, Uffizi, painting by A. del Sarto, 1517); book (Assisi, St Mary

degli Angeli, painting, circa 1230/40); death's head (Madrid, Prado, painting, by El Greco 1577/80); lamb (Dublin, National Gallery, painting, by P. P. Rubens, 17th century); globe (Lyons, Museum, painting, by P. P. Rubens, 17th century); chalice (Milan, Poldi Pezzoli Museum , painting, by C. Crivelli, 15th century). *Special scenes:* F. gives his cloak to a poor man (London, National Gallery, painting, by Sassetta, 15th century); F. renounces his father (Montefalco, St F., fresco, by B. Gozzoli, 1452); the dream of Pope Innocent (Berlin, State Museum of Prussian Culture, reliefs, by B. da Maiano 15th century); marriage of F. with Lady Poverty (Chantilly, Museum Condé, painting, by Sassetta, 15th century); the test of fire before the Sultan (Munich, Alte Pinakothek, painting, by T. Gaddi, 14th century); F.'s sermon to the birds (Königsfelden, stained glass, circa 1325/30); F.'s sermon before Pope Honarius in Rome (Assisi, St F. Upper Church, fresco, by Giotto 1296/99); F.'s sermon before the fishes (Nantes, Museum, painting, by L. O. Merson, 19th century); F. requests the Indulgence of Portiuncula (Portiuncula, chapel, fresco, by N. Alluno, 15th century, overpainted by F. Overbeck, 19th century); F. rolls in the thorns, which become roses (Rome, St Lawrence in Lucina, painting, by S Vouet, 17th century); F.'s vision of the Child Jesus, whom the Mother of God lays in his arms (St Petersburg, Hermitage, painting, by P. da Cortona, 17th century); F.'s vision of the angel with the flask (Madrid, Prado, painting, by K. J. Ribera, 17th century); F. kisses Jesus' feet on the Cross (Perugia, National Gallery, painted panelled cross, 1272); F. protects the world (Brussels, Royal Museum of Fine Arts, painting, by P. P. Rubens, 1633); F. under the cross (Bologna, St Mary della Carit, painting, by A. Carracci, 16th century); veneration of the cross by F. (London, British Museum, etching by Rembrandt, 1657); F. catches blood from the wound in the side of Christ (Milan, Poldi Pezzoli Museum, painting, by C. Crivelli, 15th century); F. kisses the wounds on Christ's feet (Bologna, Pinacoteca Nazionale, painting, by A. Carracci, 16th century); F. weeps for the dead Christ taken from the Cross (Parma, National Gallery, painting, by A. Carracci, 16th century); F. embraces the Crucified so-called Amplexus (Seville, Museum, painting, by B. E. Murillo, 1674/76); the crucified seraph appears to F. in rocky landscape (Assisi, St F. Lower Church, fresco, by P. Lorenzetti, 14th century); rays come down on to F. from the wounds of the Crucified (Washington, National Gallery, painting, by F. Pesellino, 15th century); the stigmatised F. in ecstasy (Vicenza, Civic Museum, painting, by G. B. Piazetta, circa 1732); the stigmatised F. hears the tune of an angel playing a violin (Madrid, Prado, painting, by F. Ribalta, early 17th century); F. receives a vision of the eternal continuance of the Order (Genoa, Palazzo Bianco, painting, by B. E. Murillo, 1645); the blessing of Assisi by F. (Paris, Louvre, painting, by L. Benouville, 19th century). *Cycles:* numerous, include Pescia St F., painting, by B. di Berlighiero 1235: Assisi St F. Upper Church, fresco, by Giotto, 1296–99; Florence St Croce, Bardi Chapel, fresco, by Giotto, 1317–20; Florence Academy, painting, by T. Gaddi, 14th century; Munich Bavarian National Museum, stained glass from Regensburg Minorite Church, late 14th century; Florence, Ognisanti, fresco, by J. Ligozzi, circa 1600.

Francis of Paola

(Francesco de Paola) founder of Order, saint
Feast-day: 2nd April
Life: * born 1436 in Paola, Calabria; at 13 educated by the Franciscans in Marco, Calabria; later other like-minded ones came to F. 1454 built a monastery in Cosenza under the name "Hermits of St Francis of Assisi", to-

day known as the "Lowest Brothers" or Minimites. Rule approved by Pope Sixtus in 1474. In 1482, at the request of the Pope prepared the ailing King Louis XI for his death. Lived in France. † 2nd April 1507 in Plessis-les-Tours. The Order spread rapidly in Italy, France, Spain and Germany. Canonised 1519.

Legend: F. considered a great miracle worker with numerous healings and raisings from the dead: F. raises his sister's son from the dead. – F. heals plague victims. – F. holds burning coals in his hand without injury. – F. crosses the Straits of Messina standing on his cloak, after the captain of a ship turns

him away. – When the French king offers him money to build a monastery, F. refuses it because the people's blood sticks to it and it has been extorted by the king; as proof a gold coin jumps up and drops of blood flow out.

Patronage: hermits, Italian seamen; against plague and barren marriages.

Representation in Art: *Apparel:* in black Capuchin habit with long wide sleeved robe, short scapular with hood and cord girdle (Altbunzlau, Martinitz Chapel, figure, 1662). *Attributes:* staff with inscription "Caritas", disc surrounded with rays (Meschitz, Castle Chapel, figure, 1770). *Special scenes:* F. heals plague victims (Munich, Alte Pinakothek, painting, P. P. Rubens, circa 1600); Christ appears to F. (Venice, St Mary del Giglio, painting, by J. Tintoretto, 16th century); F.'s vision of an angel carrying a disc (Bologna, Pinacoteca Nazionale, painting, by U. Gandolfini, 18th century); F. travels over the sea on his cloak (Paris, Church of the Minimites, painting, by N. Coypel, circa 1700); F. with King Louis (Château de Plessis-les-Tours, painting, by J. de le Romain, 1730); F. with King Charles VIII in Amboise (St Denis Hors-Amboise, painting, by C. Vignon, 17th century); F. prophesies a child to Louise of Savoy (Paris, Louvre, painting, by T. of Thulden, 17th century); F. in ecstasy (Venice, St Benedetto, painting, by G. B. Tiepolo, 18th century); raising of a child (popular devotional pictures of the 17th century); F.'s death (Toulon, Museum of Art and Archaeology, painting, by T. de Loo, 17th century). *Cycles:* Paris Church of the Minimites, painting, by S. Vouet, 17th century; Kloster Neudeck, 76 copper engravings.

Francis de Sales
Bishop, Doctor of the Church, saint
Feast-day: 24th January (before the calendar reform 29th January)

Life: * 21st August 1567 in Câteau de Sales near Thorens (Savoy), 1582–88 study in Paris: law and theology. During a crisis of faith under Calvinistic influence F. felt himself predestined to eternal damnation. However he found faith in the love of God through prayer before a statue of the Mother of God. 1589–91 continuation of studies, Doctor of Both Laws, 1594 consecration as priest. As a missionary in Chablis, dominated by Calvinism and dangerous for priests, F. achieved the re-Catholicisation of the region. 1599 Coadjutor of the Bishop of Geneva, who lived in Annecy. 1602 Bishop of Geneva, carried out faithfully the principles and decisions of the Tridentine Council. 1604 became spiritual director of St Joanna Francisca of Chantal. 1610 founding of the Order of the Visitation of Mary. F. preached Lenten sermons in Chambéry, Dijon, Grenoble and Paris in 1618; 1622 at the Court in Avignon and Lyons. Founded the Academia Florimontane at Annecy in his diocese. During a sermon in Lyons 24th December 1662 F. suffered a stroke, † 28th December 1622. Beatified 1661, canonised 1665, Doctor of the Church since 1877. His writings: Theotimus, On the Love of God and Philotea, Introduction to the Spiritual Life experienced a world-wide distribution and took a place similar to "Imitation of Christ" by Thomas Kempis. F. analysed Calvinism and refuted its conception of men being predestined to salvation of judgement in the sense of the Jesuit Luis de Molina, who emphasised the freedom of Christians to do or leave the good. F. successfully used this thought as a spiritual weapon against Calvinism.

Patronage: city patron of Annecy, Chambéry, Geneva, the Societies and Orders named after him, authors, Catholic Press.

Veneration and cult sites: body in Annecy, Visitation of Mary since 1623.

Representation in Art: *Apparel:* as bishop in cassock, rochet and Mozetta (Paris, St Louis-

François de Sales Euesque a Prince de Geneue

en-l'Île, painting, by N. Halle, 18th century); as bishop in pontifical costume with mitre (Berendrecht, Castle of Delft, figure, 18th century). *Attributes:* heart bound with thorns (St Lomer, figure, 17th century). *Special scenes:* presentation of the Rules of the Order to the Visitants (Paris, St Louis-en-l'Île, painting, by N. Halle, 18th century); F. receives the anointing of the sick (Paris, St Nicholas de Chardinnet, painting, by L. Durameau, 1767).

Francis Xavier

(Francisco de Jassu y Javier) Jesuit, saint
Feast-day: 3rd December
Life: * 7th April 1506 at Castle Javier near Sangüesa as the son of the Chairman of the Royal Council of Navarra; however F. grew up in a poor family. 1525 study of theology in Paris. 1533 F. joined Ignatius of Loyola, 1537 consecrated priest, 1539 helped to formulate the new statutes of the Order. On 7th April 1541 commissioned by the king as Legate of Lisbon to India, landed 6th May 1542 in Goa, worked two years among the Portuguese and converted about 30,000 heathens; worked then with the Parava pearl fishers in Travancore; 1545 travelled from Mailapur via Madras to Malacca; 1546 on the Moluccas Islands, as counsellor on the islands of Amboina, Halmahera, Morotai and Rau. Working from the island of Ternate, active missionary work. 1547 return to Malacca. F. receives news of the newly discovered islands of Japan. 1548 travels to Cochin (Vietnam); 1549 travelled further to Kagoshima (Japan); learnt Japanese and formed a small congregation of 100 Christians. F. wanted to meet the Japanese Emperor, but would not be allowed into Miako. In Yamaguchi near Hondo a Christian congregation flourished after discussions with Bonzes and scholars. A commission to be the first Provincial of the Indian province of the Order finally reached him and F. returned to India. F. carried out a mission to China in 1552, travelled to Sancian, an island off Canton, where the Portuguese could live in a free port, but foreigners were forbidden entry to China, so no-one dared take F. over. Consumed with grief and disappointment, † 3rd December 1552. Beatified 1619, canonised 1622.
Legend: F. raises a dead man to life and so is gazed at in reverence by the natives. – In a vision F. experiences Christ showing him his wounds. – On leaving the Molucca island of Amboina a small crucifix falls into the sea; the next day a crab comes to F. on the island Boranura with the cross in its mouth.
Patronage: India (appointed in 1748 by Pope Benedict XIV), Society for the Propagation of the Faith (appointed in 1904 by Pope Pius X), mission (appointed in 1927 by Pope Pius XI).

Veneration and cult sites: body brought to Goa in 1553, relics in Rome, Il Gesù (right arm brought by General of the Order, Claudius Acquaviva), Bavaria, Diocese of Eichstätt, Austria, Jesuit Order.

Representation in Art: *Apparel:* in belted gown, superpelliceum, stole (Traunstein, Aukirche, painting, by J. A. Schöpf, 1736); in belted gown and protecting cloak (Groß-Pöchlarn, figure, 1773). *Attributes:* cross, heart, coming out of flames (Starnberg, parish church, figure, by I. Günther, circa 1766); pilgrim's staff (painting, by G. Salvi gen. Sassoferrato: Künstle, Fig. 117); kneeling Indian (Poritsch, St Gall's Church, 18th century); Indian prince (Prague, Charles Bridge, figure, by F. M. Brokoff, 1711); native (Hamburg, Museum of Art and Crafts, figure, by I. Günther, 1766/70). *Special scenes:* F.'s sermon (Vienna, Kunsthistorisches Museum, painting, by P. P. Rubens, circa 1617); baptism of King Neachile (Düsseldorf, Art Museum, figure group, by A. Pozzo, 17th century); raising of the woman of Langerima (Paris, Louvre, painting, by N. Poussin, 17th century); baptism of Indians (Naples, Jesuit Church, painting, by L. Giordano, 17th century); healing of plague victims by F. (private possession, painting, by P. Troger, 17th century); F.'s death (Prague, St Nicholas', painting, by F. X. Palko, 18th century); F.'s death and apotheosis (Rome, Il Gesù, painting, by C. Maratti, 17th century). *Cycles:* Goa Jesuit Church, reliefs by G. B. Foggini, 1691–1697; Vienna Kunsthistorisches Museum, F.'s miracle, painting, by P. P. Rubens, circa 1617.

Fremund the Hermit

Martyr

Feast-day: 11th May

Life: A hermit killed in 866 during the Danish invasion.

Legends: Traditional account with many motifs: three days after her birth, F's oldest sister prophesies her brother's birth and name.- At the birth of F., son of Offa, king of Mercia, a rainbow appears over the royal palace. – F. abdicates as king and retires to the solitude of Ilafaye; the sea crossing is accompanied by many miracles. – F. is visited and asked to fight the Danes. – F. obeys after an angel appeared in his dream, ordering the return to the palace. – F. defeats the Danes near Radford. – During his prayers of thanksgiving, F. is decapitated by duke Oswy; E's blood sprays over the murderer, burning him to death. – Oswy asks for forgiveness and F's severed head grants absolution. – Supported by angels, F. carries his head. – Where his sword touches the soil, a fountain springs from the ground. – F. cleanses his wounds in the fountain and dies. – At his grave in Offchurch, three women are healed. – An angel orders the women to unearth and carry the body to the river Cherwell. – The women mark the grave with a branch which, on their return, has grown to a tree. – An angel tells the women that F. was buried by God Himself. – In Jerusalem, the pilgrim Edelbertus has a vision of F's grave. – After refusing to believe in this vision, an angel dislocates his arm and declares that, in order to be healed, the pilgrim has to find F's grave. – The pilgrim receives the pope's permission to search for the grave. – He finds the place seen in the vision and presents the papal permission to bishop Berinus of Dorchester, who orders the relics to be taken from the grave. – Bishop Berinus translates the relics to a new shrine.

Veneration and cult sites: relics in Dunstable, Bedfordshire; cult also in Cropredy.

Representation in Art: *Attributes:* Cephalophore with head resting on the hands (Dunstable Priory, seal relief, 13th century). *Special scenes:* Duke Oswy watches as the decapitated F. lifts his head from the ground (New York, Pierpont Morgan Library, Cruerdon Psalter, book illumination, after 1262). *Cycles:* London, British Museum Harleian MS 2278, book illumination, 1433).

Frideswide of Oxford

(Frévise) Virgin, abbess, saint
Feast-day: 19th October
Life: Born circa 680 as daughter of sub-king Dida and his wife, Safrida. F. was the first abbess of the double monastery she founded in Oxford. D. circa 735.
Patronage: Patron saint of the town and University of Oxford.
Veneration and cult sites: Remains and shrine in Oxford; relics at the abbeys of Reading, New Minster (Winchester), St George's Chapel, Windsor; cult also in Bomy, diocese of Thérouanne.

Presentation in Art: *Apparel:* as abbess in the habit of the Order (Oxford, nave of the cathedral, relief on the keystone, early 13th century); in black habit (New York, Pierpont Morgan Museum, book of hours of Kildare, book illumination, circa 1425). *Attributes:* flower, open book (Oxford, Christ Church, seal relief, 13th century); staff (Oxford, Bodleian Library Rawlinson MS D 939, book illumination, circa 1370); kneeling ox (Oxford, Magdalen Collage MS 223, book illumination, circa 1529). *Special scenes:* F. crosses a river on the back of an ox (New York, Pierpont Morgan Library, book of hours of Kildare, book illumination, circa 1425); F. cures the blinded messenger of Prince Algar (Kidlington, stained glass, mid 15th century).

Fridolin of Säckingen

Abbot, saint
Feast-day: 6th March
Life: F. counts as one of the first missionaries of Alemannia; probably of Frankish origin, Abbot in St Hilary's monastery in Poitiers; stood in union with King Chlodwig. F. was a peregrine monk and founder of monasteries on the Moselle, in Alsace, Chur and finally on the island of Säckingen in the Rhine, endowed by the king. † in Säckingen.
Legend: F. is born in Ireland – F. appears before court with the dead Urso as witness, after a large gift of land from Urso is legally challenged by his brother, Landolf.
Patronage: Canton Glarus, Säckingen, tailors, cattle, for fruitful weather, protector from water damage and fire, against cattle plague and childhood illnesses.
Representation in Art: *Apparel:* as Abbot in wide sleeved woollen garment (Kaysersberg, St Michael's, figure, circa 1520); as peregrine monk (Zürich, Swiss State Museum, mural,

beg. 15th century). *Attributes:* Urso small as a child (Dijon, Museum, painting, Master of Carnations, circa 1500); dead Urso with document (Galganen, Jodokus' Chapel, painting, 1550); dead Urso as skeleton (Stuttgart, State Museum, figure, mid 18th century); pilgrim's staff, hanging bag (Glarn, State Banner, embroidery, 1388). *Special scenes:* the testimony of Urso (Unterlunkofen, Aargau, mural, beg. 14th century); F. brings in the skeleton of Urso as testimony before the court (Zürich, private possession, painting, by a Master of Basel, circa 1500). *Cycles:* Säckingen Minster, reliefs on High Altar, circa 1500; Säckingen Cathedral, fresco, by F. J. Spiegler, 1752/53.

G

Gabriel

Archangel, saint

Feast-day: 29th September (from 1921 to 1969 24th March)

Biblical Testimony: G. appears as the herald of God's decrees. G. interprets to Daniel the vision of the ram and the goat (Dan 8:16–26) and the seven weeks of years (Dan 9:21–27). G. announces John's birth to Zachariah (Lk 1:11–20) and promises Mary the birth of Jesus as the coming Messiah (Lk 1:26–38).

Legend: G. prevents the demolition of a chapel near Meisenbühl by the devil.

Patronage: telecommunications, news service (since 1951), messengers, postal workers, stamp collectors.

Veneration and cult sites: rare patron of church, including: Rome St Gabriel Archangel, St Gabriel in Provence (since 858).

Representation in Art: *Apparel:* as thronal assistant in tunic and pallium (Berlin, Early Christian and Byzantine Collection, mosaic, from Ravenna, St Michael in Africisco, 6th century); as guard in tunic and chlamys (Ravenna, St Apollinare in Classe, mosaic, 6th century); as boy without wings and halo (Rome, catacombs of St Peter in Marcellino, mural, 1st half 4th century); as winged and haloed boy (Rome, St Mary Maggiore, mosaic, circa 432/40); as winged ruler in tunic and loros (Cefalú, Cathedral, mosaic, 12th centu-ry); in tunic, divitision, chlamys and loros (Monreale, Cathedral, mosaic, 12th century); in antique costume related to the peplos (Rome, St Mary degli Angeli, painting, 1534); in pluvial (Speyer, St Louis, painting, by Master of the Boaweiler Altar, circa 1480/90); in pluvial with stole (Florence, Uffizi, Portinai-Triptychon, by H. van der Goes, 1475); in dalmatic as deacon (Stuttgart, Art Gallery, Ehing Altar, painting, by A. Bouts, 1476/85); in dalmatic with deacon's stole crossed over the shoulder (Dijon, Museum of Fine Arts, painting, by Vrancke van der Stockt, 1470/80); in alb girdled with cingulum (Cracow, National Museum, painting, by Master of the Annunciation of Mary Gulbencian, circa 1480); as boy with feminine features (Cologne, Wallraf-Richartz Museum, painting, by Master of the Glorification of Mary, circa 1470); with diadem (Florence, Uffizi, painting, by H. van der Goes, 1475); with ribbon and jewel (Cefal, Cathedral, mosaic, 12th century); as girl-like boy with flowery crown as diadem (Florence, Uffizi, painting, by S. Martini, 1333); as girl-like boy with wings of peacock feathers (Dresden, Gallery of the Old Masters, painting, by F. Cossa, 15th century); as orant (Rome, St Arcangelo, mural, 12th century); as unicorn hunter (Weimar, Castle Museum, painting, 1st quarter 15th century). *Attributes: messenger's staff (Parenzo, Basilica, mosaic, circa 540); labarum with thrice 'Holy' (Ravenna, St Apollinare in Classe, mosaic, 6th century); crosier (Berlin, Museum of Late Antique and Early Christian Art, bronze cast, 6th century); sceptre (Cologne, Wallraf-Richartz Museum, painting, by the Master of George's Legend, circa 1485); scroll swung on sceptre (Cologne, Wallraf-Richartz Museum, painting, by B. Bruyn the Elder – disciple, circa 1555); scroll and sceptre in separate hands (formerly Berlin, painting, by the Master of Schöppingen, before 1457); sceptre and floating scroll (Iserlohn, Lutheran City Church, painting, by the Master of the Iserlohn Life of Mary, circa 1455); globe (Aachen, Cathedral, Shrine of Charlemagne, figure, 1200/15); lily (Ghent, St Bavo, Ghent Altar, by Jan v. Eyck, 1432); censer (Padua, Cathedral treasure, relief, 1228); sword (Pyrgi, fresco, circa 1310); dove as spirit (Berlin, copper plate cabinet, copper engraving, by G. de Jode, 16th century); standing over a dragon (Torcello, mosaic, cir-

ca 1200); blowing a hunting horn (Weimar, Castle Museum, painting, 1st third 15th century); Mary putto (Munich, Berg am Laim, figure, by J. B. Straub, 1767). *Special scenes*: expulsion from paradise (Cleveland, Ohio, Museum of Art, ivory box, relief, 13th century); interpretation of Daniel's vision (Dijon, library, Bible, illumination, 12th - century); Annunciation to Zachariah (London, British Museum, MS Harley 2788, illumination, circa 800); annunciation to Mary (Reims, Cathedral, west port, figure, circa 1245/55).

Gall

Monk, evangelist, saint
Feast-day: 16th October
Life: * circa 550 in Ireland, monk in the monastery at Bangor, Ulster. 590 missionary journey together with Columban to France, where Columban founded the monastery of Luxeuil. G. and Columban travelled on further to Metz and Zürich. 612 G. remained behind at Lake Constance with fever, while Columban went on to Italy. G. remained in the Alemanian region and founded a hermitage at Mühletobel. 614/5 G. was offered the Bishopric of Constance, which G. declined. G. gathered a large number of disciples around him, living according to the Rule of St Columban. † 16th October 645, aged 95. The monk's cell developed into the Abbey of St Gallen, into which Abbot Otmar brought the Benedictine Rule in 720.
Legend: On the river of Lindemacus and on Lake Turicinum G. and Columban meet people who practice an inhuman superstitious cult, destroy their cultic sites and throw their idols into the lake. – The incensed pagans take hold of G. and C., but their fearlessness converts the perplexed crowd. – G. and C. row across Lake Constance. – After his illness G. finds the way to the priest Willmar, where the deacon Hilti-

bald knows all places suited to hermits. –
Hiltibrand sends G. with Magnald to a
mountain with clear water. – On the way the
Devil tries to hinder them by fire and to dis-
courage them by showing them the endless-
ness of the way. – On the way Magnald asks
to rest; G. wants to press on, but stumbles
and takes this as a sign to stay. – In Steinach
they eat cooked fish and spend the night in
the open. – A bear wants to take the rest of
the meal, and G. commands the beast to
bring wood for a chapel (variant: G. endears
himself to the bear by removing a thorn from
its paw). – During the building one beam
proves to be too short, but it lengthens in a
miraculous way during the mid-day break. –
In a vision G. sees the death of Columban
and holds a requiem for him.

Patronage: Diocese and Canton of St Gallen;
fever patients, cocks, hens, geese.

Veneration and cult sites: body in St Gallen,
pilgrimages there until the Reformation,
blessing of wine common into the 19th century; patron of numerous churches in Germany and Switzerland.

Superstition: beginning of the Indian summer; strict prohibitions, probably based on
the synonym "Gall" (bitter), including:
meat may not be transported on this day,
otherwise it perishes. – A pig may not be killed. – Children born on the feast day walk in
their sleep, in many places they are were-
wolves.

Representation in Art: *Apparel:* as Benedictine in wide sleeved, closed woollen garment
with hood (Stuttgart, State Library, double

Passionate, illumination, circa 1147); as Abbot with staff in Pontifical Mass costume (Vinnenberg, relief, early 16th century). *Attributes*: mitre (Dresden, copper engraved cabinet, drawing, by Hans v. Kulmbach, 16th century); bear with wooden beam on its shoulder (Augsburg, St Stephen's, figure, end 15th century); bear passing bread to G. (St Gallen, parish library, ivory, circa 900). *Cycles*: St Gallen parish library, Cod. 602, illumination, 1452; Adelwil chapel, painting, by K. Meglinger, 1634; St Gallen St Gall's Chapel, painting, by J. Hersche (?), circa 1666; St Gallen Cathedral, reliefs, by J. Ch. Wenzinger, 1757/59.

Gangolf

(Galgolf, Gandoul, Gangloff, Gangwulfis, Gignoux, etc.) nobleman, martyr, saint
Feast-day: 11th May
Life: perhaps the same as Gangvulfus, who is attested as the owner of his own monastery in Varennes-sur-Ammance near Langres in 716–731.
Legend: According to the Vita of the 9/10th century: G. is a noble (Comes) at the Merovingian Court. – By a miracle G. translocates a well, bought in the Champagne, to his home in Varennes, the well following his staff through the air. – When G. returns home from a military expedition under King Pepin, he convicts his wife, by the ordeal of the well, of adultery with a priest. – G. is murdered in revenge by the priest.
Patronage: tanners, cobblers.
Veneration and cult sites: Eastern France, Lothringen, Alsace, Franconia, Bamberg, Burg (Diocese of Langres), Toul, pilgrimage in Neudenau, Baden with sacred spring, also Lautenbach, Alsace.
Superstition: G. wells have healing powers including: Cruchten in the Eifel helps against abscesses, in Merl against hysteria, in Bastendorf against leg wounds, in Milseburg for eyes.

Representation in Art: *Apparel*: as nobleman in narrow leggings, short pleated jacket, narrow doublet and short cloak fastened at the breast (Stuttgart, State Library, double Passional, illumination, circa 1147); as knight with cap, armour and shield (Landberg, Thuringia, figure, 15th century); as knight with helmet (Wolpertswende, reliquary bust, 18th century); as rider on horse (Nancy, Historical Museum Lorraine, figure, 15th century). *Attributes*: lance (Lautenbach, Alsace, figure of the protector of the well, 17th century); lance, sword (Hiedinghausen, painting, circa 1500); shield (Pailhe, St Fontaine, figure, 16th century); staff (Neudenau, G.'s Church, painting, 15th century). *Cycles*: Neudenau St G.'s Church, painting, 15th century; Schweighaus, Alsace, painting, 15th (?) century; Amorbach, frescoes, by J. Zick, 18th century.

Genevieve of Paris

(Genoveva) virgin, saint
Feast-day: 3rd January
Life: * 422 in Nanterre, at 6 years old consecrated to God by German of Auxerre. Helped the people during an attack of the Huns in 451. G. is considered the benefactor of the Church of St Denis. † 3rd January 502.
Legend: As a child G. protects poor farmers from Nanterre sheep. – When Bishop German of Auxerre blesses the children, he gives G. a copper medallion with the Cross of Christ as a prediction of her future holiness, and exhorts her to think only of the Cross. – G. often goes to church; when her mother tries to prevent this and strikes her on the cheek, she goes blind; at this G. brings water three times from the well, blesses the water with the sign of the Cross and so heals her blindness. – On the way nocturnal devotions, the devil extinguishes the candle in G.'s

hand; an angel immediately re-lights it. – G. spends her life in care for the poor and sick in Paris. – When the Franks besiege the city and a famine breaks out, G. brings food in ships. – G. saves a four year old boy from a deep well. – Through her prayers in a time of drought, G. brings rain to the land. – When the wine runs out for the farm workers at the Church of St Denis, G. prays over the empty vessel, which immediately fills itself again. – G. protects the city of Paris from destruction by the Huns in 451.

Patronage: city of Paris, the Orders named after her and all women's associations, shepherds, milliners, makers of wall coverings, wax-drawers, vintners; against danger from fire, plague, fever, misfortune, eye diseases, sieges, for good weather, for rain.

Veneration and cult sites: King Chlodwig I built a church over her grave, renovated in the 12th century by Stephen of Tournai. 1750 reconstruction of the Genovefaner (branch of the Augustinian Choristers) near the old church, which was turned into a Pantheon in 1791. Relics publicly melted during the French Revolution on 21st November 1793, 1803 old Church of Genevieve demolished. Today main veneration in Paris, St-Etienne-du-Mont.

Representation in Art: *Apparel:* as virgin of secular standing in a subdued contemporary costume without coif (Cologne, Wallraf-Richartz Museum, painting, by Master of the Holy Family, circa 1500/1504); with headscarf (Bankau, Silesia, painting, mid 15th century); with crown (Augsburg, State Art Collection, painting, 15th century); with chaplet (Vilnius, St Jakob's, painting, early 16th century); in long pleated cloak (Paris, National Library, Ms. lat. 1171, illumination, early 16th century); as hermit in hermit's garb (Ronda, Malaga, parish church, painting, 17th century). *Attributes:* devil blowing bellows and angel lighting candle (Paris, National Library, office book of Duc du Berry, illumination, 14th century); devil extinguishing candle with bellows (Vienna, Wolfram Collection, painting, by H. van der Goes, 15th century); with angel and book (Paris, Louvre, figure, circa 1220/30); stalk (Altsimonswald, figure, by S. Lainberger, 15th century); container (Darmstadt, Hesse State Museum, tapestry, 15th century); skull (Ronda, Malaga, parish church, painting, 17th century). *Special scenes:* G. as patron protects the city and people of Paris (Paris, National Library, Ms. lat. 1023, illumination, 13th century); G. looks after sheep (Paris, St Merri, painting of the school of Fontainebleau, 16th century); German of Auxerre presents G. with a medallion (Paris, St Thomas Aquinas, painting, by L. Lagrene, 18th century); St Medard gives G. a palm branch on Palm Sunday (Nantes, Museum, painting, by Corneille the Elder, 17th century); G. prays for rain while looking after sheep (Paris, Louvre, painting, by P. de Champagne, 11th century); procession with the reliquary shrine with prayers for the end of rain (Paris, St-Etienne-du-Mont, painting,

by J. F. de Troy, 1725); devotional picture of
G. against conflagration (Nîmes, Museum of
Fine Arts, painting, by J.B. Corneille, 17th
century); G. appears to the sick during an
epidemic in Paris (Paris, St-Roch, painting,
by G.F. Doyen, 1767). *Cycles:* Paris, Panthéon, painting, by P. de Chavannes, 19th century.

George of Cappadocia

Martyr, helper in need, saint
Feast-day: 23rd April
Life: probably martyred by beheading under
Diocletian, circa 305.
Legend: According to the Passio of the 5th
century: G. comes from Cappadocia. – G.
serves as a high ranking officer in the Roman
army. – G. exorcises the hell-hound Apol-
lyon. – In battle G. defeats a dragon, which
lives by the town of Dilena in Libya and daily eats a virgin, so freeing the king's daughter, chosen by lot. – The dragon, half dead
from the lance wound, is dragged into the
town by the king's daughter using her girdle,
at which the inhabitants are baptised. – G.
finally kills the dragon and has it dragged
into the sea by five oxen. – As a Christian, G.
is thrown into prison, where Christ appears
to him and predicts a seven year tribulation.
– G. is examined by Diocletian. – G. causes
the temple, where he should sacrifice, to collapse (variant: fire from heaven destroys the
temple). – G. is given a cup of poison, but the
drink does him no harm. – G.'s head is pul-
led off. – G. is bound to a wheel, but angels
break it. – 60 nails are knocked into G.'s
head. – G. is quartered by horses. – G.'s
hands and feet are cut off, but Christ heals
him (variant: angels). – In prison G. heals
one possessed by the devil. – G. receives
weapons as a gift from heaven. -G.'s body is
sawn up. – G. is tortured by glowing iron
claws. – G. is placed in a cauldron of molten
lead. – G. is beheaded.

Patronage: German Orders, Order of the
Swan of Frederick II of Brandenburg, military nobility, crusaders, chevaliers, crusading mission in north Russia, numerous G.
brotherhoods, brotherhoods of marksmen,
Catholic scouts, town patron of Ferrara,
Genoa, Novgorod, Georgia; banks of Genoa,
hospitals, English royal house, peasants,
horses, working animals; against plague,
leprosy, syphilis, snakebite, witches.
Veneration and cult sites: reverence began
in Lydda/Diospolis, today Lod, Israel.
Church destroyed in 1010, rebuilt by crusaders, burnt down in 1191 by Sultan Aladin,
since 1873 a Greek Orthodox church on the
site. 16th century relics revered in Gaul,
including Limoges, Le Mans, Rome, St
George's in Velabro (skull since 8th century), Reichenau (transferred from Rome in
896), Siegburg (head relics since 1750), Chie-
ri St George (head relics since circa 1300),
Prague St Vitus', Venice S Giorgio Maggiore,
Rougemont (1390 brought from the East).
Since 12th century numerous patronages including: Limburg, Prague, Bamberg east
choir of the Cathedral.
Superstition: G.'s day is the beginning of
spring, beginning of grazing, prediction day
for the harvest (e.g. if the wood is green before G.'s day, harvest will be early). G.'s day
is favourable for love potions, burying treasure.
Representation in Art: *Apparel:* in tunic
(Windisch-Matrei, Tyrol, mural, 13th century); in tunic and chlamys (Bamberg, State Library, Vita Henrici, illumination, 12th century); in ermine padded cloak (Serfaus, St
Georg, reliquary, figure, 13th century); as
knight in simple court robe with narrow leggings and hooded cloak (Siegburg, portable
altar, figure, 12th century); as knight in
chain shirt and tunic (Limburg [Lahn], Cathedral, mural, circa 1250); as knight in plate
armour and cloak (Bamberg, Cathedral, St
Mary's Gate, 2nd half 13th century); in an-

tique dress (Vierzehnheiligen, Grace Altar, figure, by J. M. Feichtmayr, 1764); in helmet (Wismar, St Georg, choir stalls, figure, mid 15th century); on horseback fighting dragon (Stockholm, Storkyrka, figure, by B. Notke, 1483/97). *Attributes:* martyr's palm (Siegburg, portable altar, figure, 12th century); lance, sword (Freiburg, Cathedral tower, figure, end 13th century); lance with flag (Munich, Alte Pinakothek, painting, by A. Dürer, 1498); broken lance (Paris, Louvre, painting, by A. Mantegna, 1495/96); dragon with lance through head at feet (Munich, Bavarian National Museum, figure, circa 1400); foot on the dragon (Oberstadion, Württemberg, painting, 1458); dead dragon, (Munich, Alte Pinakothek, painting, by A. Dürer, 1498); flag (Karlsruhe, Kunsthalle, painting, by H. Holbein the Younger, 16th century); princess (London, Victoria and Albert Museum, painting, by Marzal de Sax, 1420); lamb (Sudomer, epitaph, by J. Repicky, relief, 15th century); angel with victory garland and crown (Avignon, Cathedral, painting, by S. Martini, early 14th century). *Special scenes:* the fight of G. with the dragon (Paris, Louvre, painting, by Rafael, circa 1502); angel helps G. in fight with dragon (London, Buckingham Palace, painting, by P. P. Rubens, 1629/30); angel strengthens blow of lance (Washington, National Gallery, painting, by P. Uccello, 15th century); G. as Defensor Mariae (Weltenburg, monastery church, fresco, by C. D. Asam, 1721); G. as patron of Joris Riflemen on setting off (Antwerp, Museum, painting, circa 1500); G. helps the Christian army under Jaime I to victory over the Mohammedans at Puig in 1237 (London, Victoria and Albert Museum, painting, by Marzal de Sax, 1420). *Martyrdom:* Martyr cycle (Amay/Belgium, G.'s shrine, reliefs, circa 1230/40); single martyr: G. is broken on the wheel (Chartres, Cathedral, stained glass, 13th century); G.'s skin raked with iron combs (Stuttgart, State Li-

brary, double passional, illumination, circa 1147); G. is beheaded (Bayonne, Museum Bonnat, painting, by A. van Dyck, 17th century). *Cycles:* numerous, including Verona St Anastasia, painting, by Pisanello, 15th century); Venice St George degli Schiavoni, painting, by Carpaccio, 1507.

Gerhard of Csand

(Gherardo, Gellert) Benedictine, bishop, saint

Feast-day: 24th September

Life: * around 980 as offspring of the Venetian family of Sagaredo. Entered the Benedictine monastery of St George in Venice, where he later became Abbot. Circa 1015, while on a pilgrimage to the Holy Land, G. came to Hungary, where King Stephan I appointed him tutor to his son Emmerich. 1023 withdrew to Benedictine convent of Bakony-Beel. Eventually King Stephan appointed G. first bishop of the newly instituted diocese of Csand. During an uprising of pagans, G. was murdered on 24th September 1046 in Ofen by stones and lances. Canonised 1083.

Legend: G. was placed in a barrel by pagans and rolled into the river.

Patronage: Tutors.

Veneration and cult sites: Hungary, translation of the bones 1083. The place of martyrdom is today called Mount G.

Representation in Art: *Apparel:* as bishop in vestments with mitre and staff (Paris, St –Etienne-du-Mont, painting, by Girolamo di St Croce, 16th century); as Benedictine in dress of the Order (Haren, St Elisabeth's, mural, 15th century). *Attributes:* hand holding heart bored through with an arrow (meditational picture, copper engraving, Hollstein X 141 by L. van Leyden, 1517); spear (Haren, St Elisabeth's, mural, 15th century); cross (Budapest, G. Memorial over the Danube, figure, by F. Zanelli, 20th century).

Martyrdom: Padua St Giustina, painting, by J.C. Loth, 1677/78. *Cycles:* Vatican City, Vatican Library, cod. Vat. 8541, illumination, circa 1330.

Gertrude of Nivelles

Abbess, saint

Feast-day: 17th March

Life: * as daughter of King Pepin the Elder, ancestor of the Carolingians, entered the monastery of Nivelles, founded by her mother. G. called Irish peregrine monks and founded a hospital for the "perigrini monachi". G. brought liturgical books from Rome. † 659.

Legend: G.'s mother, Itta, cuts off her hair. – G. finds the body of St Foillian, murdered by robbers in 655. – G. saves a knight, who has made his soul over to the devil and hangs the devil on the gallows. – G. extinguishes the burning monastery at Nivelles. – G. raises a drowned child. – G. helps the sick and beggars. – G. helps her subordinates in a miraculous way during a stormy voyage and accommodates them in her hostel. – In the form of a mouse, the devil vainly tempts G. to impatience or anger. – At G.'s command the mouse has to bite off the thread during spinning. – G. accommodates the dead in paradise on the first night after their death.

Patronage: Hospitals, travellers, pilgrims, helper during plagues of mice and rats.

Veneration and cult sites: body in Nivelles, since 1272 in a precious reliquary, destroyed 1940. In the Benedictine monastery of Neustadt am Main, on the basis of a legendary sojourn of G., the idea developed that she is a sister of Charlemagne, and reverence for G. was carried over to the legendary G. of Karlburg.

Superstition: G. day is important for prediction of the weather. – G. as summer bride and sets the garden in order. – G. drives out mice. – During plagues of mice in Cologne, Mouse Processions are held from St Cunibert's to St G.'s, attested in 1759 and 1822, with a votive offering of a silver and a gold mouse respectively. – Water from the well of Nivelles drives out mice. – On leave taking and at sea, a drink is consecrated to G. for good lodgings and peace (attested 11th century at Ruodlieb in the monastery at Tegernsee).

Representation in Art: *Apparel:* in distinguished secular clothing with crown (Lübeck, St Mary's, figure, 1499); with prince's hat (Hamburg, Museum of Art and Crafts, stained glass, circa 1300); as Abbess in simple girdled dress, open cloak, wimple, veil with staff (Cologne, Wallraf-Richartz Museum, painting, by Master of St Severin, circa 1505/10). *Attributes:* book (New York, Pierpont Morgan Library, office book of

Catherine of Cleve, illumination, 1st half 15th century); crown (Nivelles, G.'s Shrine, figure, 1298); crown carried by angel (Saints of the Family, Friends and Relatives of Emperor Maximilian, wood carving, 1516/17); model of church (Magdeburg, Cathedral, relief, circa, 1350); mouse on book (Vienna, St Stephen's, choir stalls, figure, 15th century), one mouse at feet of the saint, one climbing up the staff (Kuringen, Register of the Brotherhood of G., illumination, beg. 16th century); mouse on cloak (St Goar, Lutheran church, mural, end 15th century); mice at feet (Trondheim, Norway, museum, painting, circa 1500); mice biting off spinning thread (private possession, single piece wood engraving, 1470); model of a hospital (Wismar, St Mary's, ceiling painting, 14th century); model of church (Elmenhorst, figure, mid 15th century); palm (Klosterneuburg, stained glass, beg. 14th century); cup (Vorst, Antwerp, pilgrimage flag, 17th century); healing well, devil (Brussels, Historia St Gertrudis, copper engraving, 1637); lily, ship, sea monster (Paris, National Library, copper engraving, by J. Callot, 1636). *Cycles:* Nivelles, G.'s Shrine, reliefs, 1298; Stade St Kosmas', painting, circa 1500.

Gervase and Protasius of Milan
Martyrs, saints

Feast-day: 19th June

Legend: GP. are twins, sons of St Vitalis and the blessed Valeria. – GP. share their possessions with poor after their parents have been martyred. – GP. live with St Nazarius, who has the boy Celsus as an assistant. – GP. are arrested as Christians and taken to Milan. – As Count Astasius comes to Milan to take the field against the Marcomans, the pagan priests explain their statues will give no answer until GP. bring their sacrifice. – GP. refuse to sacrifice. – G. is whipped to death

with lead blocks tied to rods, P. is beheaded. – The bodies of GP. are secretly buried.

Patronage: Milan; by flow of blood or urine, against theft.

Veneration and cult sites: Bishop Ambrosius of Milan found the bones on 17th June 386 in the basilica of SS Nabor and Felix. The vague memory of two old men and an ampoule (of blood?), together with the healing of blindness during the investigation, were taken as evidence of authenticity. This is the first example of an "inventio" of martyr's bodies. Ambrosius was buried in the grave of GP. in 397. The cult spread through Martin of Tours, Augustine of Hippo, and others. The relics in Breisach are dubious, probably procured at the time of the Stauffens, the transmission by Reinald of Dassel legendary.

Representation in Art: *Apparel:* as youthful and aged martyrs (Milan, St Ambrogio, mosaic, 4th century); as youths (Ravenna, St Apollinaire Nuovo, mosaic, 6th Century); as nobles (Milan, S Ambrogio, mosaic, 2nd half 12th century); as deacons (Le Mans, Cathedral, stained glass, mid 13th century); as secular youths (Palermo, Palatine Chapel, mosaic, 12th century); as warriors (Ravenna, S Vitale, mosaic, 6th century). *Attributes:* victor's garland (Ravenna, S Apollinare Nuovo, mosaic, 6th century); cross (Naples, Cemetery of S Severo, mural, 4th/5th century); sword and palm branch (Lucca, Pinacoteca Nazionale, painting, by A. Pucinelli, 1350); whip and sword (Breisach, Minster, figure, by Master HL 1526). *Cycles:* Le Mans, Interpolations in the Legend of Nazarius, stained glass, 1160/1260; Breisach, silver shrine, reliefs, 1496; Paris, Hotel de Ville, carpet weaving, by Le Sueur, Bourdon and P. de Champaigne, 1625.

GISALA MATER S. EMERICI.

Gisela of Hungary

Queen, Benedictine, blessed

Feast-day: 7th May

Life: * circa 985 Schloss Abbach as daughter of Duke Henry II and Gisela of Burgundy, sister of Emperor Henry II. Aged 10 married to King Stephan of Hungary, mother of Emmerich. Decisive influence in the Christianisation of Hungary, allegedly sponsor of the cathedral in Veszprém. 1038 after the death of her husband, severe hostility and persecution as a pagan reaction. 1045 liberated by King Henry III and brought to Passau, G. became a nun in the Benedictine Convent Niedernburg, later Abbess there. † 7th May 1060.

Veneration and cult sites: buried at Niedernburg, original gravestone from the 11th century remaining, above that the raised grave of 15th century. The Cross of Gisela now in Munich; the Hungarian coronation robe came from the magnificent Chasuble of Stuhlweissenburg.

Representation in Art: *Apparel:* as queen with crown (Budapest, Hungarian coronation robe, embroidery, 11th century). *Attributes:* model of church (Budapest, Hungarian coronation robe, embroidery, 11th century); model of church, rosary (Bern, Historical Museum, house altar, end 13th century).

Gregory VII

Pope, Benedictine, saint

Feast-day: 25th May

Life: * as Hildebrand 1020/25, probably in Tuscany; came early to the Lateran. Whether G. entered the monastery of St Mary on the Aventine as a Benedictine is uncertain, probably first in 1048 in Cluny, especially since in 1047 G. accompanied Pope Gregory VI into banishment at Cologne, to where the Emperor Henry III had exiled him. Leo IX, called to the throne of St Peter at the end of 1048 by Emperor Henry III at Worms, sent G. to Rome in 1049. G. sought to free the church of simony, concubinage among priests and reliance on secular power, according to the spirit of Pope Leo IX. G. was decisively involved in the Papal Election Decree, according to which the election of the Pope is entirely in the hands of the Cardinals. On 22nd 1073 elected Pope in spite of personal reluctance. G. set himself behind the reformation plans of Cluny and carried the model of monastic freedom over to the freedom of the church. This culminated in the formulation of the 27 principles in Dictatus Papae and thereby removed the centuries-old established right of German royalty to select bishops. King Henry IV reacted in 1076 with a sharp written reply and declared the Pope deposed. At this G. excommunicated Henry IV and released the subjects from their duty of loyalty to the king. In 1076 the German princes met together and renounced the king if he had not been restored before 2nd February 1077. Henry crossed the Alps in winter to Canossa, where G. was staying on the journey to Augsburg. Henry submitted to ecclesiastical penance by standing in the penitential garb at the door for three days, and was eventually released from excommunication. 1077 election of Rudolf of Swabia as rival king, which G. confirmed in Rome 1080. He also renewed the excommunication of Henry IV. Henry named William of Ravenna as anti-Pope Clement III, who conquered Rome in 1083/84. Henry was crowned Emperor by him. G. fled to Engelsburg and was freed by Duke Guiscard and the Normans. In the following plundering of the city G. had to flee to Salerno. † 25th May 1085. The conflict on investiture was only finally ended under Callixtus II in the Concordat of Worms in 1122. Canonised 1606.

Veneration and cult sites: grave in the Cathedral of Salerno; reverence strongly disputed particularly in the time of absolute monarchy, the French Revolution and the Napoleonic times.

Representation in Art: *Apparel:* as Pope with simple tiara (London, Victoria and Albert Museum, painting, circa 1400). *Attributes:* figure of virtue (Vatican City, Stanza, fresco, by Raffaelino del Colle, 16th century). *Special scenes:* G. releases Henry IV from excommunication (Vatican City, Sala regia, painting, by F. Zuccari, 17th century); G.'s expulsion, banishment and death (Jena, University Library, Chronicle of Otto of Freising, illumination, 1143/46).

Gregory the Great

Pope, Doctor of the Church, saint

Feast-day: 3rd September (before calendar reform 1969: 12th March).

Life: * 540 in Rome of senatorial rank; after the death of his father converted the house on Clivus Scauri into a Benedictine monastery dedicated to St Andrew and withdrew there with 12 companions in 575. From his inheritance in Sicily endowed a further six monasteries. Appointed superintendent of the seven counselling districts of Rome by either Pope Benedict I or Pelagius II, 579 apocrisiary at the imperial court in Constantinople, 585/86 return to Rome, advisor to the Pope. 590 Pope. During his reign, G. endeavoured to halt the decline, which the wars and invasions of the 6th century had brought, and to improve the commercial relations in the city by re-organising the church. With diplomatic skill G. reached a peaceful agreement with the Lombards when they threatened Rome in 592/93; he had friendly relations with France and to the Visigoths in Spain, who had turned from Arianism in 586. Further, G. succeeded in the Christianisation of the Anglo-Saxons with 40 companions. In the so-called Three Capital Conflict, G. attained recognition of the decisions of the Council of Chalcedon of 451, which ended the schism in Milan. G. sought to have all bishops and patriarchs submit to the primacy of the Pope, included in the Papal title "servus servorum dei" and personally declined the title "universalis papa". – In his writings G. shows himself as a counsellor. In the "Liber regulae pastoralis" G. describes the ideal picture on a shepherd of souls, in the "Moralia in Job" he expounded the Biblical text historically as well as allegorically and morally; for G. the Type of the Redeemer is embodied in Job, in his wife the life of the flesh, and the seven virtues lived in his seven sons. G. influenced theology from the Venerable Bede and Alcuin until Albert Magnus and Thomas Aquinas. Further, he described miracles, prophecies and visions in the ancient form of the dialogue, in order to show, that not only the Orient, but also Italy had brought forth asceticism. This collection had a great authority in the Middle Ages. Moreover G. renewed liturgy and church music. † 12th April 604.

Legend: Twice G. gives silver coins to a poor shipwrecked man; when there is nothing left in the house, he gives him a silver bowl from his mother's inheritance. – After his election to Pope, which G. does not want to accept, G. is brought out of Rome in a barrel, but a pillar of light, up and down which angels climb, betrays him. – During a petitionary procession during the bubonic plague, G. sees over the gravestone of Hadrian an angel sheath his bloody sword and interprets this as the end of the plague. – In St Peter's G. is weeping over the death of Emperor Trajan, who must suffer in Purgatory despite his mildness, when a voice declares to him the release of the Emperor. – G. has 30 Masses said in 30 consecutive days for the dead monk Justus, who suffers in Purgatory for breaking the oath of poverty. – G. allows 12 poor pilgrims to eat at the table, and sees suddenly that, as 13 are there, that Christ (variant: the Angel of the Lord) is among them. – When the Empress Constantia asks G. for relics, her legation receives only a dalmatic of St John the Evangelist, which she rejects as ineffective; at this G. cuts into the dalmatic with a knife and blood immediately flows out. – G. banishes the doubt of a bakerwoman about the Real Presence of Christ during Mass, in that the bread turns to flesh before her eyes. – During the celebration of the liturgy by G., Christ appears, climbs from the Cross and pours his blood into the Chalice. – A writer sees through a hole in the curtain, how the Holy Ghost in the form of a dove sits on G.'s shoulder and inspires him. – G. appears to the mortally ill little Fina, who carries her suffering with great patience, and prophecies that she will die on his feast day.

Patronage: learned men, teachers, pupils, students, schools, choristers, choir schools, singers, musicians, masons, button makers, lace makers.

Veneration and cult sites: Rome St Peter's, venerated in Rome St Gregory's. As a custom, the Gregorian Mass (30 Masses for a deceased person on 30 consecutive days) has been sanctioned by the Church since 1884, but the indulgence is limited to that altar on which, according to the legend, G. read the 30 Masses for the monk Justus.

Superstition: In the Middle Ages G.'s day was a school holiday, often with the election of Child Bishops.

Representation in Art: *Apparel:* in liturgical Mass robes with pallium (Rome, St Mary Antiqua, mural, 705/07); as Pope in liturgical Mass dress with simple tiara (Karlsruhe, State Museum, figure, from Kloster Petershausen, 1175); in pluvial (Subiaco, Sacro Speco, mural, by Master of the Gregorian Chapel, 1228); in threefold tiara (Capri, mural, ascribed to A. Alberti da Ferrara, 15th century); in the Pileolus (Bologna, St Paul the Great, painting, by Il Guercino, 1647); in non-Pontifical dress (Vicenza, Old Refectory

in the Santuario di Monte Berico, painting, by P. Veronese, 1572); as Doctor of the Church in Papal vestments (Chartres, Cathedral, Confessors' Gate, figure, 1215/20); as church author at pulpit (Rome, National gallery, painting, by C. Saraceni, beg. 17th century). *Attributes:* open book (Seville, Provincial Museum, painting, by F. Zurbarán, 17th century); crosier (Wells, Cathedral, stained glass, 1325/33); open scroll (Subiaco, Sacro Speco, mural, by Master of the Gregorian Chapel, 1228); spirit dove (Prague, National Gallery, painting, by Master of Wittingau, circa 1380); angel (Venice, S Marco, baptistery, mosaic, 14th century); model of church (Onate, painting, circa 1530); the released Roman Emperor Trajan, raised by the hand of G. (Munich, Alte Pinakothek, painting, by M. Pacher, 1482/83); a bloody host, in reference to a local legend that G. gave one of three bloody hosts (Andechs, Benedictine monastery, painting, 15th century). *Special scenes:* G. refuses the Papacy (Philadelphia, J.G. Johnson Gallery, painting, by a follower of Fra. Angelico, 15th century); a writer watches through a bored hole the inspiration of G. by the Holy Ghost (Trier, town library, single piece, by Master of the Gregorian Registry, late 10th century); G.'s meal with the beggars (Vicenza, Refectory of the Monastery of Monte Berico, painting, by Veronese, 1572); appearance of the Archangel Michael on the Castel Santangelo (Vatican City, Pinacoteca Vaticana, painting, by the circle of T. Gaddi, 14th century); blood from the tunic of St John the Evangelist (Vatican City, Pinacoteca Vaticana, painting, by A. Sacchi, 1625); G.'s intercession for the poor souls in Purgatory (Bologna, St Paul's, painting, by Il Guercino, 1647); the release of Emperor Hadrian from Purgatory by G. (Bologna, Pinacoteca Nazionale, painting, by J. Avanzo 1365); the introduction of church music by G. (Berlin, former Kaiser Friedrich Museum, ivory relief, last quarter 10th century), the G. Mass: the Man of Sorrows appears on the Altar during G.'s Mass (Cleveland, Ohio, Cleveland Museum of Art, painting, by H. Baldung-Grien, circa 1511). *Cycles:* Florence St Mary Novella, frescoes, by Master of the Gondi Chapel; Rome St G. the Great, reliefs, by L. Capponi, end 15th century; Rome St G. – Barbara Chapel, frescoes, by A. Viviani, 1602.

Gregory of Nazianzus

Bishop, Doctor of the Church, saint
Feast-day: 2nd January
Life: * circa 329/30 on the property of Ariance near Nazianzus as son of Bishop Gregory the Elder and his mother Nonna; became a Christian under the influence of his father. Studied at the rhetoric school of Caesarea, Cappadocia, the pagan academy of Athens 356/57, friendship with Basil. 361/62 ordained priest against his desires at the urging of the congregation, G. fled into solitude to escape the duties, soon returned. In the framework of a new division of counselling, consecrated Bishop of Sasima by Basil 372. G. never took on this office. 374 brief administration of the Diocese of Nazianzus after the death of his father, 375 into solitude in Seleucia, 379 leader of the Nazianzite church in Constantinople, 381 confirmed bishop at the 2nd General Council, but confusion and intrigues, which resulted in a dispute about the election of bishops, denied him the office so that G. became ill and returned to Nazianzus. After a short while holding office in Nazianzus, spent the rest of his life on his farm. † 390. – Humanly speaking, G. was enthusiastic and could carry men with him, but as his life showed he was easily discouraged and unstable. G.'s theological service lies in the elaborating of the differences in the three persons of the Godhead. Contrary to Basil, G. clearly defined the divinity of the Holy Ghost. In his Christology,

G. confirmed the unity of the Person of Christ with the formula "one from two", that is, two natures united themselves in his Person to One, the natures themselves are both fully present, even the human nature of Christ. G. spoke clearly of the serious consequences of Adam's sin and emphasised the real presence at the Eucharist. The teaching is laid down in five theological lectures (out of 45), which G. gave in 380 in Constantinople. A further 245 personal letters and poems of G. exist, describing the searching, errors, loves and hopes of his soul.

Patronage: poets, fruitfulness.

Veneration and cult sites: relics in Constantinople, since 8th century in Rome St Mary on the Field of Mars and in the Oratorio of St G. 1580 stimulus of reverence by Pope Gregory XIII, translation of the relics to St Peter's.

Representation in Art: *Apparel:* as bishop of the Greek Byzantine Rite with sticharion, epitrachelion, phelonon, omphorion (Palermo, Palatine Chapel, mosaic, 12th century); as bishop of the Latin Church in pontifical garb (Gotha, Museum, drawing, by P.P. Rubens, 1600). *Attributes:* book of Gospel (Cefal, Cathedral, mosaic, 12th century); angel, who points to God the Father (Rome, St Mary on the Field of Mars, fresco, 1638/1721); Lucifer as symbol of heresy at his feet (Gotha, Museum, drawing, by P.P. Rubens, circa 1600).

Gregory of Nyssa
Bishop, Doctor of the Church, saint
Feast-day: 9th March

Life: * as brother of Basil circa 335, rhetorical training, entered the monastery at Pontus on the Black Sea founded by Basil, against his will was appointed Bishop of unimportant Nyssa; 376 removed from office after the slanderous accusation of squandering church property, 378 returned as bishop, Visitor of the Diocese of Pontus and Metropolitan of Sebaste; 381 one of the best defenders of orthodoxy at the Council in Constantinople. † shortly after 394. – In his theological works G. repudiated, in the small treatise "On Enthusiasm About the Trinity" and "Oratio catechetica" amongst other works, the possibility that the human spirit can raise itself to the immediate presence of God in anticipation of the blessing of heaven, in the sense of Plotinus, who had not only propagated a knowledge of God rising from sensory to supersensory. Like Gregory of Nazianzus, G. emphasised the reciprocal exchange of the natures in Christ, which remained intact. In his eschatology, G. taught the view of the remaking of all things in the sense of the original and the Transubstantiation of the bread into the Body of the Logos. Further works remaining include those against specific heresies, exegetical works on the books of the Old Testament and short tracts on ascetism.

Veneration and cult sites: relic (head) in the monastery of Ivrion, Athos.

Representation in Art: as bishop of the Greek Orthodox Rite, as Gregory of Nazianzus with book (Palermo, Palatine Chapel, mosaic, 12th century).

Guthlac of Crowland
Hermit, saint
Feast-day: 11th April
Life: * in 673 of royal blood; G. became a soldier in 689 and, in 698, a monk at the monastery of Repton; in 700, he became a hermit at Crowland, Lincolnshire on 11th April 714.

Legends: A selection based on pseudo-Ingulph's Life of Guthlac: During his solitary life, G. suffers annoyances, including violent temptations and attacks by devils. – G. is visited by an angel and the Apostle Bartholomew and led to the gates of Hell. – In his cell, G. uses a scourge given to him by Bartholomew as defence against diabolical attacks. – By tying his belt around a man possessed, G. exorcises the devil. – G. is ordained priest by bishop Hedda. – At the saint's shrine, King Ethelbald has a vision of G. – In 851, during a pilgrimage to G's shrine, Ceolnoth, archbishop of Canterbury, is cured of ague by the saint.

Veneration and cult sites: After the body was found incorrupt in 715, the shrine at Crowland became a place of pilgrimage; cult also in Mercia, St Albans, Westminster and Durham.

Representation in Art: *Apparel:* as monk in the habit of the Order (Crowland, abbey church, figure, 13th/14th century). *Cycles:* London, British Museum Harleian Roll Y.6, drawings, late 12th century; Market Deeping, Lincolnshire, church of St Guthlac, stained glass, 20th century.

H

Hedvig of Andechs (Silesia)
(Avoice, Jadwiga) duchess, saint
Feast-day: 16th October
Life: * 1174 at Castle Andechs as the daughter of Count Berthold IV of Andechs-Merania; aunt of St Elizabeth of Thuringia. After being educated in the Benedictine convent at Kitzingen H. was married at 18 to Duke Henry I of Silesia, to whom she bore 7 children; widowed in 1238. 1241 the eldest son, Henry, fell in battle against the Mongols. H. called several Orders to Silesia and founded the Cistercian convent at Trebnitz. Commended for her piety, charity, social commitment and following the way of the Cross. Lived in the convent at Trebnitz until her death. † 1243. Canonised 26th March 1267.
Legend: Selection from the major legends: H. blesses the Crucifix at Trebnitz. – H. goes barefoot in winter, only wearing shoes at the behest of her confessor, in order not to cause offence in the court. – H. obtains exemption from tribute in favour of the people. – H. speaks on behalf of the poor at court. – H. gives poor girls a trousseau for the wedding. – When her husband, Henry, burns down a village during a military campaign, H. asks him husband to give compensation. – H. brings candles to prisoners in their cells. – H. honours the nuns at Trebnitz, kisses their prayer stools and handkerchiefs. – H. bathes her children in the water used for washing the feet of the nuns. – H. praises her husband's abstinence.
Patronage: Berlin, Silesia, Poland, Wrocláv, Cracov, Trebnitz, Andechs, Diocese of Görlitz, bridal pair, exiles, Europe.
Veneration and cult sites: Body in Trebnitz, relics in Kloster Andechs, pilgrimage to Andechs increased since 1945. Encouraged by here husband's family, the veneration spread to Poland, Hungary, Bohemia, Austria, as well as Berlin and France.
Superstition: H.'s loaf, baked on H.'s day, also called H.'s soles, is a shaped bread in the form of a shoe, as H. often went barefoot out of humility, and it is buried in the grave with women who died in childbirth.
Representation in Art: *Apparel:* as young married matron with long, girdled dress, cloak closed at the breast, wimple, "Weihel", scarf (Prague, St Thomas, Sacristy, fresco, mid 14th century); as Duchess with duke's hat (Wrocláv, Ursuline Monastery, figure, circa 1440); as Duchess with crown (Passau, Monastery of the English Lady, figure, circa 1420); as Cistercian in Sisters' costume (Trebnitz, H.'s Chapel, painting, by T. Hamacher, 19th century); as barefooted matron (Liegnitz, town archives, codex a 353, illumination, mid 15th century). *Attributes:* Crucifix (Monastery Arouca, figure, by J. Viera 1720/30); in form of Mary (Rauden, abbey church, figure, by J.M. Österreich, mid

18th century); book (Zielenzig, St Nicholas, figure, circa 1520); rosary (Wrocláv, cathedral, west porch, figure, mid 15th century); shoes (Muszyna, Parish church, figure, circa 1470); model of the Trebnitz church (Wrocláv, cathedral, lower church, keystone, relief, 2nd half 14th century); model of cross-shaped monastery church with ridge turret (Trebnitz, monastery church, figure, 2nd half 18th century); H.'s bread (Breckerfeld, Lutheran Parish church, figure, 16th century); giving food to a beggar (Trebnitz, figure, 2nd half 18th century); prisoner in a wheelchair (Ludwigshafen, St H., relief, by F. W. Müller-Steinfurth, 1993). *Special scenes:* battle with the Mongols at Wahlstatt with the decapitated body of Henry (Liegnitz, Piast Mausoleum, fresco, 1677/79). *Cycles:* Aachen Collection Ludwig, Schlackenwerth Codex, illumination, 1353; Wrocláv Museum of Pictorial Art, painting, circa 1430; Wrocláv St Matthew's, fresco, by J. M. Rottmayr, 1704/06; Wahlstatt fresco, by C. D. Asam, 1733.

Helen

(Helena) Empress, saint
Feast-day: 18th August
Life: * circa 225 in Depanon in Bythinia as daughter of lower class; became concubine of Constantine Chlorus († 306). Circa 285 her son Constantine was born; after Constantine was proclaimed Emperor by the army, he protected his mother. After the victory at the Milvian Bridge in 312 became an important patroness of the Christians. H. built numerous churches, such as the Church of the Nativity in Bethlehem. † 330 in Nicomedia.
Legend: The discovery of the Cross is ascribed to H. since the 4th century: H. travels to Jerusalem and searches for the Cross of Christ. – H. takes council from wise Jews, who deny all knowledge. – H. commands the

Jews to be burnt and they hand Judas over to her, who had appealed to his father and told the other Jews in secret, that no-one must discover the location of the Cross, or else the Faith of the Fathers would be destroyed. – H. takes Judas, threatens him with starvation and throws him into a well. – On the 7th day he asks H. to help. – When Judas prays at the right place, where a temple to Venus had been erected by the Emperor Hadrian, the earth moves and sweet smelling smoke rises up. – H. has the temple destroyed and makes Judas dig. – 20 paces under the earth (variant: in a cistern) three crosses are found. – In order to determine the true Cross, they place all three in the middle of the city and wait for a sign. At the ninth hour a deceased young man comes back to life when the third cross is placed on his shoulder. (Variant: Macarius, Bishop of Jerusalem, has a mortally ill woman lay the crosses one after the other on her shoulders and she is healed by the third). – H. searches for the nails from the Cross of Christ and Judas, now baptised, called Quiriacus and Bishop of Jerusalem, finds them during prayer when the nails suddenly shine as gold in the earth.
Patronage: Bishopric of Trier, Bamberg and Basel, Archdukedom of Austria, Frankfurt, Ascoli, Pesaro, Colchester; nail-makers, nail-smiths, dyers, miners, treasure hunters; revealing theft, discovery of lost items, against lightening, fire.
Veneration and cult sites: grave in Rome, later in Constantinople; relics in Hautvillers, Paris St Leu (since the end of the 18th century), Trier (head). Further veneration in connection with the Theban Legion and the Pilgrimage of the Holy Vestments in Trier.
Representation in Art: *Apparel:* as Augusta in antique lady's costume (Rome, St Croce in Gerusalemme, figure, 4th century); as Empress in a contemporary noble costume (Wrocláv, Diocesan Museum, painting, end

ni, Palazzo dell' Arrengo, mural, 14th century); cross with titule (Nuremberg, German National Museum, painting, 2nd half 15th century); cross on shoulder (Hampton Court, painting, by Chiadorolo, 16th century); three crosses (Paris, National Library, MS lat. 9474, illumination, by J. Bourdichon, 15th century); three nails of the Cross (Milan, Cathedral, figure, late 14th century); crown of thorns (Barcelona, Cathedral, painting, 14th century); medallion of Christ (Neuilly-sur-Seine, stained glass, by D. Ingres, 19th century); Church of the Holy Sepulchre as a model (Xanten, Cathedral, figure, circa 1350); model of church of Cologne (Cologne, St Gereon, stained glass, 14th century); book (Stuttgart, Landesmuseum, figure, from Ottenbach, circa 1510). *Special scenes:* Constantine and H. flanking the Cross (Venice, St Giovanni in Bragora, painting, by C. da Cornegliano, 1502); H. kneels before the Cross (Bonn, Cathedral, figure, circa 1660/70); discovery of the Cross with H. (Albi, Cathedral, fresco, 15th century); H. and Constantine with Pope Sylvester (Brussels, Royal Museum of Fine Arts, painting, by B. van Orley, 1515/20); trial of the Cross (Arezzo, St Francesco, fresco, by P. della Francesca, 1452/66); H. and Constantine at the trial of the Cross (Graz, Landesmuseum Johanneum, painting, by the Master of Laufen, 1440); H. single-handedly takes on the trial of the Cross (Stratford-on-Avon, Trinity Chapel, mural, 15th century); H. sees the Cross of Christ in a dream (Washington, National Gallery, painting, by P. Veronese, circa 1570); H. shows Constantine the Cross (Cuenca, Cathedral, relief, 16th century). *Cycles:* according to the Legenda aurea: Bártfa (Hungary), Altar of the Cross, painting, 1480/90.

15th century); in ermine cloak (Freising, Neustift, figure, by I. Günther, 1764); in fantastic oriental dress (Augsburg, State Art Collections, painting, by H. Burgkmair, early 16th century); as widow without crown (Milan, Cathedral, figure, late 14th century); as widow with cap (Munich, Alte Pinakothek, painting, by C. Engelbrechtsen, 16th century); as princess with prince's hat (Brandenburg, Cathedral, painting, 1502); as portrait of the Margravine Sibyl Augusta of Baden (Rastatt, Castle Church, figure, 1723); as portrait of Queen Marie-Thérèse (Créteil, painting, 18th century). *Attributes:* sceptre (Donaueschingen, Fürstenbergische Sammlungen, painting, circa 1500); small handheld cross (Valcabrère, St Just, figure, 12th century); large cross standing near her (Rimi-

Hemma of Gurk

Widow, saint

Feast-day: 27th June (before the calendar reform under Bishop Gurk 29th June)

Life: * circa 980 as Countess of Friesach-Zeltschach; married to Count Wilhelm von der Sann, who died on a pilgrimage in 1016. 1036 murder of her two sons by rebellious miners, after which H. gave all her possessions for spiritual causes, particularly the Benedictine house of Gurk. † 29th June 1045. Beatification 1287, cult ecclesiastically confirmed 1938.

Legend: The stone on which H. sat during the building of the Cathedral of Gurk suddenly takes on the form of a chair. – H. pays the builders from a purse from which she, in a miraculous way, cannot pay out more than they have earned.

Patronage: State of Carinthia, against eye disease, general illnesses.

Veneration and cult sites: body in the crypt of the Cathedral of Gurk since 1174, relics (ring, pendant) also in Gurk. Pilgrimage of the Slovenians to Gurk.

Representation in Art: *Apparel:* as founder in widow's dress and widow's veil (Gurk, Cathedral, mural, 1220); in Hungarian-Croatian costume with padded cap and chain of the Order of the Swan (Gurk, Cathedral chapter, painting, beginning 16th century); in court dress with hair free (Edelschrott, St Hemma, painting, 17th century); as nun (Gurk, Cathedral, painting, by H.G. Pfisterer, 1745). *Attributes:* Model of church (Zweinitz, mural, 15th century); crown (Hirschegg, figure, 1643); purse (Friesach, Church of the German Orders, figure, 16th century); pendant, ring (Vienna, Mariahilferkirche, painting, by W. Posch, 1937); roses (Edelschrott, painting, 17th century). *Cycles:* Gurk Cathedral, reliefs, by L. Pampstl, 1515; Edelschrott, Hemmakirche, painting, 17th century and frescoes 1731.

Henry II and Cunigunde

Imperial couple, saints

Feast-day: 13th July

Life: H. * 6th May 973 as the son of Henry the Quarrelsome of Bavaria, educated by Bishop Wolfgang and Abbot Ramwold of Regensburg. 995 Duke of Bavaria, 1002 elected German king. 1004 Italian crown, 1014 crowned Emperor by Pope Benedict VIII. Zealous proponent of church reform, extension of the system of Imperial churches, which joined with the monastical reforms pursued from Gorze and Trier by St Maximine. 1004 renewal of the Bishopric of Merseburg, 1007 foundation of the Bishopric of Bamberg; distinguished by enterprise and diplomatic ability; which showed itself in the alliances with the pagan Liutzes in Mecklenburg and Pomerania, among other things. † 13th July 1024 in Grona near Göttingen. – His wife C., daughter of Count Siegfried of Lützelburg, married H., but the marriage was without fruit; after H.'s death C. withdrew to the Abbey of Kaufungen, which she established, † there 1033. H. canonised 1246, C.1200.

Legend: Bishop Wolfgang appears to H. and prophecies to him, what was fulfilled six years later at the Imperial coronation. – H. and C. are crowned by Christ himself. – H. wins the battle against the Polish king Boleslav with the help of St Lawrence. – In the form of a young man, the devil tempts C. in her bed. – C. is questioned by her husband. – H. brings C. to trial, which is to be by fire. C. passes unharmed over the glowing ploughshares. – H. apologises to C. – C. attends a Mass and hangs her glove on a sunbeam. – C. pays builders from her miraculous bowl. – Benedict removes kidney stones from H.'s body. – H. and C. thank Christ for his help in H.'s recovery. – A broken glass goblet is repaired at H.'s prayer. – After the death of H., St Lawrence saves H.'s soul at the weighing by the Archangel Michael, by

S. KVNEGVNDIS IMPERATRIX, CONIVNX, VIRGO.

S. HENRICVS IMPERATOR.

placing in the pan of good works a chalice, which H. had donated on the deathbed of St Lawrence.

Patronage: Bishopric of Bamberg, city of Bamberg, Basel.

Veneration and cult sites: H. is buried in Bamberg, C. in Kaufungen, bones transferred to Bamberg in 1201. C. relics in Eichstätt (since 1501), Vienna St Steven's Cathedral, Kloster Andechs, Luxembourg (circa 1600), Lisbon, Jesuit Church (since 1587).

Representation in Art: *Apparel:* H. as Emperor with crown (Munich, Bavarian State Library, clm 4456, illumination, circa 1002/14); H. as founder (Paris, Musée Cluny, so-called Basel Antependium, relief, circa 1018); as bearded Emperor of middle age in robe and cloak (Bamberg, Cathedral, Adam's Door, figure, circa 1237); as young Emperor (Basel, Cathedral, figure, 1st half 13th century); in armour (Munich, Alte Pinakothek, painting, by B. Bruyn, early 16th century); in the robes of the Order of the Golden Fleece (private collection Spetz, figure, by H. Hangenower, 16th century); in armour and cloak (Rott am Inn, figure, by I. Günther, 1759); C. as Empress in long undergarment, girdled upper garment with cloak wrap (Bamberg, cathedral, Adam's Door, figure, circa 1237); C. in imperial robes with crown, head scarf together with H. (Nuremberg, St Lorenz, tapestry, late 15th century); C. with veil (Bamberg, Cathedral, sidepiece on choir stalls in the west Choir, 14th century); C. as Benedictine in dress of the Order (St Lamprecht, figure, 15th [?] century); C. as widow in simple dress, wimple, "Weihel", scarf (Oberstadion, Württemberg, painting, 1458). *Attributes:* H. with sceptre and Imperial orb (Munich, Bavarian State Library, clm 4452, illumination, 11th century); C. with crown and sceptre (Bamberg, Cathedral, Imperial grave, by T. Riemenschneider, 1499); C. with Imperial orb (St Leonhard in Lavanttal, stained glass, 14th century); H. with sword

and holy lance (Munich, Bavarian State Library, clm 456, illumination, circa 1002/14); laurel wreath near H. (Dieppe, St Jacques, painting, by C. Vignon II, circa 1650); model of church near H. (Moosburg, figure, by H. Leinberger, circa 1511); model of Bamberg Cathedral near H. (Rott am Inn, figure, by I. Günther, 1759); model of church near C. (St Lambrecht, figure, 1638); model of Bamberg Cathedral near C. (Bamberg, Cathedral, Adam's Door, figure, circa 1237); model of Bamberg Cathedral held in hands of H. and C. (Dresden, copper engraved cabinet, drawing, by H. v. Kulmbach, late 15th century); church model in hands of H. and C. (Nuremberg, St Lorenz, tapestry, late 15th century); document near H. (Passau, Cathedral, figure, circa 1500); lily near H. (Florence, Palazzo Pitti, painting, by F. Mancini, 17th century); Greek cross near C. (Basel, Cathedral, relief, 13th century); ploughshare in C.'s hand (Forchheim, hospital chapel, painting, circa 1480); ploughshare at C.'s feet (Mallersdorf, figure, by I. Günther, 1768/70); bowl and money near C. (Klosterneuburg, Albrecht's Altar, painting, circa 1440). *Special scenes:* Vision of H. from St Wolfgang (Angoulême, St André, painting, by C. Vignon, 1627); Benedict gives H. and C. the miraculous image of the old chapel at Regensburg (Regensburg, Old Chapel, fresco, by G. B. Götz, 1762); re-establishment of Polling by H. (Polling, relief, by F. X. Schmädel, 1765); weighing of H.'s soul and help of St Lawrence (Vamlingbo, Gotland, mural, circa 1240); C. passes over the glowing ploughshares (Munich, Bavarian National Museum, painting, by W. Katzheimer, circa 1495; C. hangs her glove on a sunbeam (Basel, Art Museum, enamel, 14th century); healing of H.'s stones by St Bendict (Bamberg, Cathedral, Imperial tomb, relief, by T. Riemenschneider, 1501/13). *Cycles:* Regensburg Old Chapel, frescoes, by C.T. Scheffler, 1752; Munich Bavarian National Museum,

Annunciation Altar, painting, 16th century;
Bamberg, Cathedral, Imperial tomb, reliefs,
by T. Riemenschneider 1501/13.

Heribert of Cologne

(Ariberto, Eriberto) Archbishop, saint

Feast-day: 16th March (in Cologne 30th August).

Life: * circa 970 as son of Count Hugo of
Worms and Tietwidis of the house of Count
of Alemania; educated in the cathedral
school of Worms and in the monastery of
Gorze. 995 consecrated priest. As an intimate of Emperor Otto III, appointed Chancellor of Italy already in 994, from 998 also of
Germany; 999 elected Archbishop of Cologne. In the year 1000 participation in the
festive opening of the grave of Charlemagne
in Aachen by Emperor Otto. After Otto's
death in 1002, H. led the transfer of the body
from Paterno to Germany, but was captured
by Duke Henry of Bavaria and held until H.
declared himself prepared to give up the Holy Lance, which belonged to the Imperial insignia and which H. had sent to the Palatine
Count Ezzo. After the burial H. laid down
the office of Chancellor. 1002 foundation of
the Benedictine monastery at Deutz, 1020
consecration of the church. His relationship
to Emperor Henry II was cool; H. accompanied him to Rome and in 1007 promoted the
foundation of the Bishopric of Bamberg. †
16th March 1021. Canonised apparently in
1046/48.

Legend: according to the H.'s Vita by Lantbertus and Rupert of Deutz: Count Hugo
and the wise Jew Aaron foresee in a dream
the birth of H. – Emperor Otto III presents H.
with the staff of St Peter. – In his humility
H. enters Cologne as its new Bishop barefoot. – At the informative process before the
consecration as bishop the book of the Gospels opens itself in front of H. of its own ac-

cord. – At the consecration itself the altar
opens itself in front of H. and Mary appears
with H.'s friend, Pilgrim, and both instruct
H. to found the monastery at Deutz. – When
the builders can bring no suitable wood, H.
sees a cross in a pear tree in his orchard at
mid-day and has the tree felled to build the
monastery. – During a procession for rain
held in Cologne from St Severin to St Panthaleon, a dove circles over H.'s head, visible
to all, and then it rains, – H. heals a possessed man during the sermon of Palm Sunday. – Emperor Henry II appears in Cologne .
He is angry, but a dream shows him that he
and H. will shortly see each other for the last
time and after the mid-day Mass he asks H.
for forgiveness.

Patronage: Town of Deutz, for rain.

Veneration and cult sites: body buried in Deutz. 1147 raising of the bones by Archbishop Arnold I to be taken to the Shrine of Heribert; local veneration in Cologne.

Representation in Art: *Apparel:* as historical bishop in Pontifical dress with mitre (Cologne, St Gereon, mural, 13th century); as historical bishop in Pontifical dress without mitre (Düsseldorf, city archives, seal, relief, 1003); as bishop with halo in Pontifical Mass dress with pallium (Cologne-Deutz, St Heribert's, Shrine of Heribert, relief, circa 1170); as bishop in pluvial (Cologne, St Apostles', painting [destroyed], mid 15th century); as Elector of Cologne (Cologne, Cathedral treasure, Shrine of Engelbert, figure, 1633). *Attributes:* two monks with scroll (Cologne, city archives, Theoderic Codex, illumination, circa 1150); personification of the virtues of humility and charity (Cologne-Deutz, St Heribert's, Shrine of Heribert, relief, circa 1170); model of church (Cologne, Wallraf-Richartz Museum, painting by the Older Master of the Holy Family, circa 1420); model of Cologne St Apostles' (Cologne, St Apostles', painting [destroyed], mid 15th century); sword, mitre at feet, roll (Cologne, Cathedral treasure, Shrine of Engelbert, figure, 1633). *Cycles:* Cologne St Heribert's, Shrine of Heribert, enamel medallion, circa 1170.

Herman Joseph of Steinfeld

Premonstratensian, saint

Feast-day: 21st May (before the calendar reform 7th April)

Life: * 1150 in Cologne; entered the Premonstratensian monastery in Steinfeld in the Eifel at the age of 12, studied in Mariengarten (Friesland). Important preacher, spiritual director in nunnery. † 7th April 1241 (or 1252) in Hoven, Eifel. Confirmation of cult on 11th August 1958, veneration as saint allowed from 15th January 1960. – HJ. counts

as one of the important mystics. Writings include: hymns to Mary in honour of her five joys, the well-known "Heart of Jesus" hymn "Summi Regis Cor" ("heart of the supreme king").

Legend: As a child HJ. gives an apple to the figure of Mary in St Mary in the Kapitol at Cologne as a present for the Boy Jesus. – Mary helps him climb over the closed choir trellis and gives him, in the presence of Joseph and John the Evangelist, the Christchild to play. – Christ appears to HJ. with an axe to destroy a corrupt monastery, while HJ. prays for its sparing and a story of execution. – In a mystical vision HJ. marries the Mother of God with the assistance of angels.

Patronage: Mothers, children, watchmakers.

Veneration and cult sites: body buried in Kloster Steinfeld, Eiffel; veneration encouraged since 1728 by Pope Benedict XIII. Patronages in Flossdorf and Ripsdorf.

Representation in Art: *Apparel:* as schoolboy (private possession, house altar, painting, by E. v. Steinle, 1860); as Premonstratensian in white tunic, white scapula with white cappa and cowl (Kloster Steinfeld, figure, 16th century); in choir dress with rochet, almutia and biretta (Wilten, Parish church, figure, by F.X. Nissl, 1776). *Attributes:* keys on girdle (Münster, State Museum, painting, 15th century); chalice out of which grow three roses (Berlin, Kaiser Friedrich Museum, painting, by the Master of the Life of Mary, 15th century); chalice without roses (Cologne, Cathedral, portal, relief, by E. Mataré, 1943); book (Kloster Steinfeld, cloister, stained glass, 16th century); knife (Kloster Steinfeld, figure, by Master Tilman, 15th century); Child Jesus on his arm (Kloster Steinfeld, figure, 1683). *Special scenes:* HJ. passes the Child Jesus an apple (Wahlen, chapel, painting, 1689); the mystical marriage of HJ. to the Mother of God (Vienna, Kunsthistorisches Museum, painting, by A. van Dyck, 1630).

Hilary of Poitiers
Doctor of the Church, saint

Feast-day: 13th January (before the calendar reform 14th January, feast of translation 29th June)

Life: * circa 315 as son of a noble pagan family with sound rhetorical and philosophical education. H. came to Christianity through questioning of the meaning of life and was baptised circa 345. 350 elected Bishop of his native city of Clerus. H. did not attend the Synods of Arles in 353 and Milan in 355, which renewed the deposition pronouncements against Athanasius, instead organis-

ed the resistance of the Gallic bishops to Arianism and the Arian- minded Metropolitan of Gaul, Saturnius of Arles. For this reason H. was exiled by the Emperor Constantius to Asia minor, where he remained from 356 to 359. Here he wrote the great theological treatise "De Trinitate". After the Synod of Seleucia in 359 H. went to the Emperor in Constantinople, to submit to a public disputation with Saturnius, which however did not take place. Being an irritation to the Arians in Asia Minor, H. was sent back to Gaul. In 361 H. carried through the excommunication of Saturnius at the Synod of Paris. After Emperor Valentine came to power in 364 attempt to remove the similarly Arian Bishop of Milan, which failed. † circa 367. – H. counts as one of the most prolific opponents of Arianism, and made the arguments of the Eastern Church known in the Latin West through memoranda, as he had come to know them during his exile. A significant exegete, as shown through his writings, such as the commentary on the Gospel of St Matthew and his tract about the Psalms. In the dogmatic books "De Trinitate" H. defended the consubstantiality of the Son of God. Belief in the divinity of Christ represented to H. a fundamental truth of the church; he derived this speculatively from the eternal generation; yet for H. the body of Jesus was no earthly body, but a heavenly one, because the Lord had made his body without human aid inside the body of the Virgin. The Transfiguration and walking on the water showed, for H., the true state of the body of Christ. H. also composed hymns.

Legend: On his exile H. comes to Galinaria, an island full of snakes, which must flee before him; H. sets a border post, which the snakes cannot pass, between them and the rest of the island. – In Poitiers an unbaptised child dies which H. raises. – H. awakes in his daughter the love of chastity, but fears she will not be able to keep to this resolution and so asks God to take her to him as a virgin. – H. also wins through prayer a blessed death for his wife. – Uninvited, H. attends the Council of Seleucia, where the ground upon which he sits rises up to form a seat. – H. disputes with the heretical Pope Leo, who immediately falls ill with dysentery and dies miserably during the Synod.

Patronage: La Rochelle, Lucon, Poitiers.

Veneration and cult sites: relics in Poitiers (missing since 409, discovered by Fridolin of Säckingen), Le Puy, Paris St Denis, Parma. Doctor of the Church since 1851.

Superstition: In Swabia H. bread is baked on H. Day.

Representation in Art: *Apparel:* as bishop (Parma, Museum, painting, by C. Caselli, 1499). *Attributes:* book (Parma, Museum, painting, by C. Caselli, 1499); staff (Poitiers, Notre-Dame la Grande, figure, 12th [?] century); dragon, snake (Karlstein, Chapel of the Cross, painting, by Master Theoderic, 1367); feather, thunderbolt (Niederalteich, sketch for fresco, by W. A. Heindl, 18th century).

Special scenes: uninvited, H. visits the Synod of Seleucia (Chantilly, library, Office Book, illumination, by J. Fouquet, circa 1450); death of the heretical Pope Leo (Semur-en-Brionnais, relief, 12th century); H. raises a child for it to be baptised (Stuttgart, State Library, fol. 57, illumination, 12th century); H. consecrates St Troecia to the service of God (Poitiers, museum, relief, 12th century); death of H. (Poitiers, St Hilary, capital relief, 12th [?] century); H.'s burial by his disciples Leonnius and Justus of Limoges (Melle, St Peter's, capital relief, 12th century). *Cycles:* Poitiers St Hillary-de-la-Celle, reliefs, 12th century; Vatican Library, Ms. 8541, illumination, late 14th century.

Hildegard of Bingen

Benedictine, abbess, saint

Feast-day: 17th September

Life: * 1098 in Bermersheim near Alzey as daughter of the nobleman Hildebert of Bermersheim; educated in the convent of Disibodenberg as pupil of the blessed Jutta. After her death in 1136 H. led the community of ladies; 1147/50 founding of a convent on Rupertsberg near Bingen and 1165 of a daughter convent in Eibingen near Rüdesheim. Her extensive correspondence made H. the counsellor of kings, princes, bishops, members of Orders; many travels to Cologne, Trier and southern Germany. Her speculative writings showed an unusually poetical gift. H. considered as founder of scientific natural history in Germany. † 17th September 1179.

Patronage: philologists, Esperantists (because of her speaking in tongues!).

Veneration and cultic sites: body on Rupertsberg, relics in the convent church at Eibingen.

Representation in Art: *Apparel:* as Benedictine in dress of the Order with long robe, scapular, open cloak, wimple, veil (Oberwesel, St Mary's Church, mural, 15th century); as prophetess writing (formerly Wiesbaden [destroyed], Sci-vias Codex, illumination, 13th century). *Attributes:* Abbess' staff, book (Bonn, St Elisabeth, fresco, by M. Schiestl, beg. 20th century); flames above her head (Lucca, State Library, Cod. 1942, illumination, circa 1230); model of church (Brussels, Musée Cinquentenaire, antependium, circa 1230); light, tiara, Emperor's and king's crown (Metten, fresco, by W.A. Heindl, 18th century). *Special scenes:* visions of St H. (Lucca, State Library, Cod. 1942, illumination, circa 1230); H. dictates to Volmar of Disibodenberg (Heidelberg, University Library, Sci-vias Codex, illumination, 2nd half 12th century); H. speaks with Emperor Frederick Barbarossa in Ingelheim (Bingen, Rochus Chapel, relief, circa

1900). *Cycles:* Bingen Rochus Church, painting, 18th century.

Hippolytus of Rome

Bishop, martyr, saint

Feast-day: 13th August

Life: * before 170 in Asia minor; possibly a student of Irenaeus and Roman Presbyter under Pope Victor. Tensions about the Logos theory led to open conflict when he accused Pope Callistus of too great leniency toward sinners. H. became Presbyter of a small schismatic church until exiled by a successor of Callistus, Pope Pontian. There they were reconciled. † in exile in Sardinia. – H. wrote an extensive treatment to refute all heresies and itemised 33 Gnostic systems. His chronicle began with the creation of the world and ended in the year 234. Among his exegetical writings, the commentary on Daniel was composed after the experiences of the persecution of Septimus Severus.

Legend: The themes come from various saints of the same name and add up to a person who has nothing in common with the historical H.: H. is a soldier and officer and functions as the prison warder of St Lawrence. – H. is converted by St Lawrence and baptised. – After his burial H. together with his nurse, Concordia, and his whole household suffer martyrdom by beating, lacerating with hackles, being bound to four horses, quartered, finally beheaded.

Patronage: Diocese and city of St Pölten, St Pilt/Alsace, prison warders, horses.

Veneration and cult sites: H. buried on 13th August 235/36 in the Cemetery on the Via Tiburtina, since 4th century honoured as martyr. Through Fulrad of St Denis relics brought to St Denis, St Pilt in Alsace, Paris St Hippolyte, also to Tegernsee and Salz-burg. Foundation of the monastery St Hippolyt in St Pölten.

Representation in Art: *Apparel:* as philosopher (Apt, Cathedral, sarcophagus, relief, 4th century); as martyr (Ravenna, St Apollinare Nuovo, mosaic, 6th century); as bishop in Pontifical dress with pluvial (Ulm, Cathedral, painting, by M. Schaffner, 1521); as youth in Byzantine court dress (Venice, St Mark's, mosaic, 13th century); as soldier in armour (Rome, St Lorenzo al Verano, mural, 13th century); as knight in armour with cap (Cologne, Wallraf-Richartz Museum, painting, by the Master of Bartholomy's Altar, 1498/99); as rider (Friedersbach, stained glass, 15th century). *Attributes:* crown (Ravenna, St Apollinare Nuovo, mosaic, 6th century); scroll (Vatican Museum, relief, 3rd century); book, bishop's staff (Ulm, Cathedral, painting, by M. Schaffner, 1521); lance (Rome, St Lorenzo al Verano, mural, 13th century); sword (Vichy, Cathedral, figure, 15th century); shield (Monreale, St Castrense, figure, 17th century); palm branch (Morlach, St H., figure, 15th century); cudgel, hackle, strap, rope (Cologne, Wallraf-Richartz Museum, painting, by Master of Bartholomy's Altar, 1498/99); rope on his hands, small horses at his feet (Ambierle/Loire, stained glass, 1470/75). *Special scenes:* H. guards Lawrence, buries him and receives the Communion from Justinus (Rome, St Lorenzo al Verano, fresco, 12th century); Lawrence baptises H. (art trade, painting, 15th century). *Martyrdom:* H. naked bound to wild horses (Brauweiler, Chapterhouse, mural, circa 1200); H., clothed, torn by wild horses (Ovre Dråby, Denmark, mural, circa 1450); H. quartered by four horses (Bruges, St Sauveur, painting, by D. Bouts, 1450); H. is beheaded (Mantua, painting, by L. Gambara, 16th century). *Cycles:* Tamara, reliefs, beg. 16th century.

Hubert of Liège

Bishop, saint

Feast-day: 3rd November

Life: * presumed circa 655, Bishop of Maastricht-Tongern; H. transferred the relics of his murdered predecessor, Lambert, and the seat of the Bishopric to Liège. H. carried out missionary work in the Ardennes region. † 727.

Legend: According to a Vita of the 12th century: H. is nephew of St Oda and has a high place in the court of Pepin of Herstal. – In his youth H. comes to the court of Theoderic in Paris, where he is made a Count Palatine. – H. must flee from the majordomo Ebroin of Neustria to Metz, where Pepin entrusts him with the office of Senior Master of the Royal Household. – H. is married to Floribana, a daughter of the Count of Louvain, his son,

Floribert, also becomes Bishop of Liège later. – On Good Friday, H. hunts a stag, which has a cross between its antlers, which led H. to change his life. – 695, after the death of his wife, H. withdraws for seven years into the remote forests of the Ardennes. – At the command of an angel, Pope Sergius stet H., while he is on a journey to Rome 702/03, to be the successor of the murdered Lambert. – Angels bring staff and mitre from heaven to the consecration as bishop. – H. receives from Peter the keys for healing of rabies. – With the sign of the cross, H. overcomes the murderers of St Lambert who follow him. – As bishop H. heals many possessed and sick. – H. is saved from a shipwreck. – An angel tells H. of his coming death. – H. dies of a wound accidentally received while fishing. – Even after his death, H.'s keys, kept by the

monks of St Hubert-en-Ardennes, retain the power of healing rabies.

Patronage: Ardennes, Bishopric of Liège, Augsburg, Dukedom of Jülich, H. Orders of Knighthood and Brotherhoods, hunters (since 10/11th century), turners, manufacturers, foundrymen, manufacturers of mathematical instruments, butchers, metalworkers, opticians, bell-makers, hunting dogs; against rabies, dog bites, possession by demons.

Veneration and cult sites: Body in Liège St Peter's, on the 3rd November 743 raising of the undecayed body; 825 translation to St Hubert-en-Ardennes, pilgrimage there.

Superstition: Using red-hot H. keys, people bitten by rabid dogs had a mark burnt on their foreheads; a thread from the stole of St H. was placed in the wound. The wound remained bound for nine days, and the Sacraments were to be taken on the following nine days; on the 10th day the bandage was removed and burnt. – It was a duty to join the H. Brotherhood after the healing procedure. In the 19th century this widespread custom led to many legally attested conflicts between the public health authorities and vicars, such as in the Diocese of Speyer.

Representation in Art: *Apparel:* as bishop in Pontifical dress (Antwerp, Museum of Fine Arts, painting, by D. Bouts disciple, 15th century); as hunter in tight leggings, half length robe , cloak, cap (Münster, Landesmuseum, figure, circa 1500); as nobleman in lily cloak (Brussels, Royal Museum of Fine Arts, painting, after J. Brueghel the Elder, circa 1600); as rider (Bascy-Thy, parish church, figure, 18th century). *Attributes:* book (Cologne, Wallraf-Richartz Museum, painting, 1512/15 or 1580[?]); stag on a book (Munich, Alte Pinakothek, painting, by S. Lochner, mid 15th Century); stag at feet (Cologne, St Mary in the Capitol, stained glass, 15th century); stag's head (Staffel, parish church, figure mid 17th century); hunting horn (Han-

over, State Museum, painting, by H. Raphon, 16th century); keys (Lendersdorf near Düren, relief, 16th century); hunter and dogs (Louvain, St Jacques, figure, 16th century); hunting rifle (Veltrum, parish church, painting, 16th century). *Special scenes:* H.'s vision of the hunt (Vienna, Copper Engraving Collection, wood engraving, circa 1460/70; H.'s vision of the Cross (Breda, Altar of the Cross, painting, 17th century); appearance of the stag in the forest (Berlin, State Museum, painting, by J. Brueghel the Elder, circa 1600); appearance of the angel with the heavenly stole (London, National Gallery, painting, by Master of the Life of Mary, circa 1470/80); Peter delivers the H. keys (Meditational picture, engraving, by A. Opdebeek, 18th century); H. heals one with rabies, H. distributes bread and wine as precaution against rabies (Donaueschingen, Fürstlich Fürstenbergische Sammlung, painting, by a Swiss the Master, 15th century). *Cycles:* include: Sint-Huibrechts-Hern parish church, mural, 13th century; Paris, Bibliothèque Nationale, MS fr. 424, illumination, 15th century; Elewijt parish church, painting, circa 1620.

Hugh of Lincoln

Carthusian monk, bishop, saint

Feast-day: 16th November (17th November before the Reformation)

Life: Born in 1140 in Avalon as son of the Seigneur de Avalon, Imperial Burgundy, H. was educated and made his profession in the priory of Austin Canons at Villarbenoît, becoming a deacon; after visiting La Grande Chartreuse H. became a Carthusian monk, was ordained priest in 1165 and later procurator. He was invited by King Henry II to become prior of his languishing Charterhouse at Witham in Somerset. In 1186 Henry chose him as bishop of Lincoln. H. projected himself as an ardent reformer and won the respect of three Plantagenet kings, despite relentlessly repudiating their encroachment on the freedom of the Church. H. extended Lincoln Cathedral, sometimes working on it with his own hands. D. on 16th November 1200. H. was canonized in 1220.

Legends: With his own hands, H. carries stones to the Cathedral. – H. rescues King Henry II from peril at sea. – H. brings a child back to life. – A very shy swan is so attached to H. that the bird announces his arrival days in advance. – During mass celebrated by H., a cleric sees the infant Jesus rising from the chalice.

Veneration and cult sites: In 1280, his relics were translated to a new shrine in the Angel Choir of Lincoln and became a place of pilgrimage; his cult was spread in Germany, England, Flanders, France and Spain by the Carthusian Order.

Representation in Art: *Apparel:* as monk in Carthusian habit with long tunic and sleeveless robe with side-slits and fastened at the knees with a frog (Cologne, Wallraf-Richartz Museum, painting by a Cologne Master, circa 1475/80); as bishop in pontifical vestments with pluvial and mitre (Abbeville, De Signiéres Collection, painting, 15th century); as bishop in pontifical vestments with pluvial, mitre and crosier (St Gotthard parish church, figure, 1727); with mozetta (Pavia, Certosa, fresco by D.Crespi, 1630). *Attributes:* mitra, crosier (Charterhouse, Prüll, figure, 1605); crosier (Erfurt, Carthusia church, figure, 1728); swan (Oxford, St Mary, figure, early 14th century); chalice with the infant Jesus (Cologne, Wallraf-Richartz Museum, painting by A.Woensam, 1535); book (Puschendorf, Upper Franconia, painting, 1489). *Special scenes:* H. carried to his grave by the kings of England and Scotland (Lincoln Cathedral, stained glass, 13th century); H. bringing a child back to life (Naples, St Martino, painting, 1652). *Cycles:* Bruchsal chapel, fresco by C. D. Asam, 1729.

The Fourteen Holy Helpers

34 *Pilgrimage church, Vierzehnheiligen, Germany*

35 *Martyrdom of St Florian, by Albrecht Altdorfer, Florence, Uffizi*

36 *Martyrdom of St Sebastian, by Andrea Mantegna, Vienna, Kunsthistorisches Museum*

37 *St Christopher, fresco, Augsburg cathedral, Germany*

38 *St George, figure by Egid Quirin Asam, Weltenburg, Germany*

39 *St Catherine, painting on glass by Peter Hemmel, Darmstadt, Germany, Hessisches Landesmuseum*

40 *St Margaret, by Titian, Madrid, Prado*

41 *Sermon of St Denis, miniature, Paris, Bibliothèque Nationale*

35

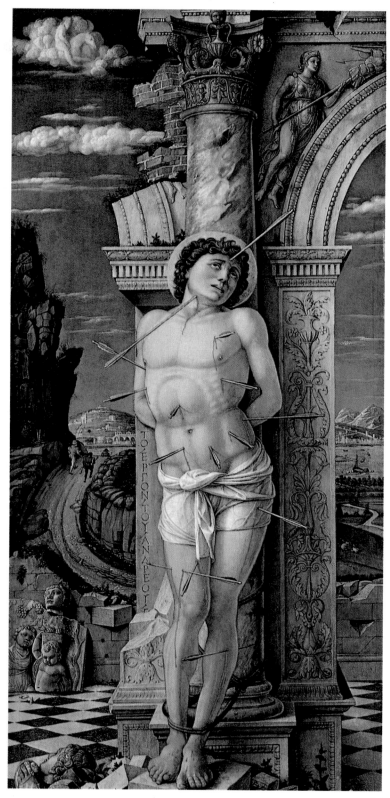

37

39

40

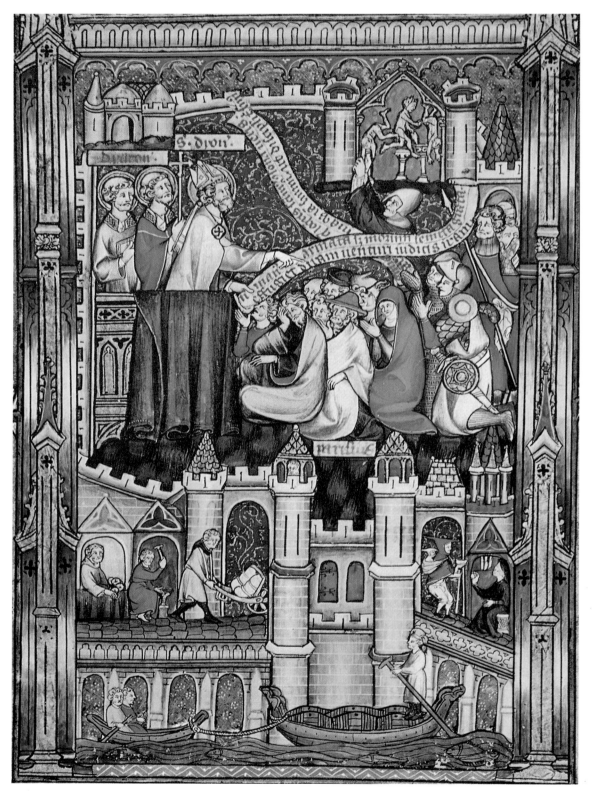

41

Hyacinth of Cracow

(Jacek) Odrowaz, Dominican, saint

Feast-day: 15th August (in Görlitz, Berlin, Gurk, Klagenfurt 17th August)

Life: * before 1200 as offspring of the noble family of Odrowaz at Schloss Gross-Stein; studies in Cracow, Prague, Bologna with Doctor of Theology. 1218 after acquaintance with Dominic, entry to the Dominican Order; from 1219 in Poland, founder of a series of Houses, such as Cracow 1222, Friesach 1221, Kiev 1223, Danzig 1227. Preaching ministry in southern Russia and Prussia. † 15th August 1257. Canonised 1594.

Legend: H. raises drowned boy. – With the monstrance in his hand, H. drives the Tartars back. – H. flees from burning Kiev before the Tartars by crossing the river dry-shod. – The Mother of God appears to H. in a dream and says that all H.'s prayers will be heard. – H. experiences the resurrection of Dominic and is introduced to him. – On his stretched out cappa, H. brings his Brothers over the river near Visograd. – H. heals blind twins. – H. saves many people when a bridge collapses. – H. drives a demon out of a tree.

Patronage: Poland, Lithuania, Pomerania, Prussia, Russia, Wrocláv, Cracow, Kiev; for an easy delivery, by danger of drowning.

Veneration and cult sites: tomb in the Dominican Church, Cracow, veneration widespread throughout the Dominican Orders.

Representation in Art: *Apparel:* as Dominican in long girded robe, scapular, cappa with hood (Tepozotlán, Mexico, Museum of Religious Art, figure, 18th century). *Attributes:* book (London, National Gallery, painting, by F. Cossa, 16th century); monstrance (Stein, parish church, painting, 18th century); ciboreum, statue of Mother of God (Friesach, Dominican Church, figure, 18th century); picture of Mother of God (Hattstadt, Alsace, figure, 17th century); lily (Cracow, gravestone, figure, 18th century); angel with lily (Wrocláv, Adalbert Church, figure, 1725); inscription of the promise of Mary (Ferrara, St Antonio in Polesine, relief, by C. Bonone, 17th century). *Special scenes:* Mary appears to H. (Paris, Louvre, painting, by L. Carracci, 1594); rescuing at collapse of bridge (Vienna, Kunsthistorisches Museum, painting, by F. Guardi, 18th century); H. drives a demon out of a tree (Cracow, Dominican Church, painting, by Dolabelli, 17th century). *Cycles:* Rome, St Sabina, frescoes, by F. Zuccari, circa 1600; Siena, St Spirito, frescoes, by V. Salimbena, circa 1600.

I

Ignatius of Loyola

(Inigo) Jesuit, founder of the order, saint
Feast-day: 31st July
Life: * born in 1491 in the castle in Loyola near Azpéitia, Northern Spain, to the Basque family Onaz y Loyola as the youngest of 13 children. His baptismal name was Inigo, he later called himself I. From 1506–1517 he was educated at court in the house of the chief treasurer of Queen Isabella of Castille, Don Juan Velasques de Cuellar, in Arevalo and Valladolid. From 1518–21 he was an officer of the Spanish viceroy of Navarra, leading a carefree secular life, but in 1515 with his brother Don Pedro he had to answer for some nocturnal mischief to the police in Guizpucoa. A great change in his life took place during the defence of the Pamplona fortress against French invaders, when I. was severely wounded by a cannon ball on 20th May 1521 and on his sickbed at the Vita Christi of Ludolf of Saxony he began to read, at first out of boredom. After recovery he made a pilgrimage to Aránzazu and Montserrat, and he read in solitude in Manresa for almost a year, when the book of spiritual practise, *Spiritual Exercises* emerged from this spiritual experience. In 1523/24 he travelled as a beggar through Rome and Venice to the Holy Land, after which as an adult he began a school career at the Latin school in Barcelona from 1524 to 1526. He attended the University of Alcal and Salamanca in 1526/27, where I. was cited as an Alumbrado zealot suspected of heresy before the Inquisition and twice placed under detention, as well as from 1528 to 1535 in Paris. In Paris I. lead the first six companions, among them Francis Xavier and Petrus Faber, to form a permanent community. On 15th August 1534 in the Mary Chapel of the Montmatre the solemn vows, including the new and characteristic fourth one, placing themselves at the disposal of the Pope for any use whatsoever, were laid down. In 1535 he completed his theological studies and in 1537 was ordained as a priest. In Rome he established a community near the half ruined church of La Storta, which community was adopted by the benevolence of Pope Paul III and redesignated as an Order, which the received Papal confirmation on 27th September 1540. On 8th April 1541 I. was chosen as superior general. The founding statutes of the Order were drawn up in 1539 and the constitutions 1544/48. † 31st July 1556 in Rome. Beatified in 1609, canonised in 1622. Jesuit orders spread rapidly across Europe, colleges and school were founded for the education of neglected young people. – What is new is the fundamental spiritual formation according to spiritual exercises with 30 daily spiritual exercises in all possible seclusion and under the composure of all forces.

Self-sanctification and apostleship form a unity, it is important that every member understands his life as a "contemplative in action", that is constantly spent in the holy work of Christ. Moreover I. renounced the typical organisation of an Order with communal prayer, habits and abstention from specific activities, Jesuits are active everywhere where it appears most important for the kingdom of God.

Legends: Peter the apostle appears to the wounded I. lying in his sickbed near Pamplona. – While convalescing I. experiences a vision of Mary. – On the road to Montserrat I. encounters a Moor, with whom he carries on a debate. – I. gives his costly garments to a beggar. – I. lays down his sword before the Mother of God in Montserrat. – I. is tormented by visions of devils while praying in the solitude of Manresa. In Manresa I. sees the figure of Christ in the Host during Mass. – I. is inspired into belief in a cave at Cardoner. – I. prays on the Mount of Olives before the footprints of Christ. – I. is brought back to the monastery by a watchman as he has stayed too long on the Mount of Olives. I. gives away the money for his journey to a beggar. – In Paris I. escapes an attempt on his life on the intervention of angel. – In Rome I. experiences a vision of God the father and Jesus Christ. – I. pleads for the innocent in court. – While at prayer I. is disturbed by his secretary. – During an encounter Philipp Neri sees a halo around I.'s face. – I. quenches a fire. – I.'s shirt heals the paralysed arm of the washerwoman as she presses it.

Patronage: Patron saint of Jesuits, spiritual exercise, soldiers, expectant mothers, children, against demons, witchcraft, scruples.

Veneration and cult sites: Grave since 1587 in Rome, Il Gesù, veneration in Jesuit Orders very widespread.

Representation in Art: *Apparel:* As a student (Madrid, Weisburger Collection, painting, 16th century); as an ordinary cleric in black robe and coat with a Roman biretta (Chateau de St Landry, painting, by F. Zurbarán, 17th century); in liturgical Mass apparel with a chasuble (Straubing, Ursulinenkirche, figure, by E. Q. Asam, 1738); as a knight (Rome, Il Gesù, painting, 17th century); as a pilgrim with staff (Paris, Bibliothèque Nationale, Cod.Par.lat. 9477, book illumination, 1693); as superior general of an Order (Puerto de S Maria, figure, by J. de Mesa, 17th century); in ecstasy (Rome, Il Gesù, fresco, by Il Baciccia, 17th century). *Attributes:* Armour at his feet (Vatican Museum, painting, attributed to Rubens, early 17th century); standard (Puerto de S Maria, figure, by J. de Mesa, 17th century); IHS symbol (Seville, university, painting, 17th century); IHS symbol in flames (Harlingen, S Michael, silver vessel, circa 1679); heart in flames (Santiago de Compostela, figure, by V. G. Fernández, 17th century); globe, personification of the continents (Munich, National Collection of Graphics, engraving, by C. Blomaert, middle of the 17th century); dragon (Vatican Museum, painting, end 16th century); book of the constitution (Loyola, Basilica, figure, by F. de Vergara the Younger, 1741); demon (Haastrecht, St Barnabas, Missal cover, relief, 17th century); crucifix (Madrid, Prado, painting, by B. Peréz, 17th century); crowned skull (Alcomàn, church, painting, 17th century); tears (Seville, University chapel, figure, 17th century). *Special scenes:* Vision of Mary of La Storta (Lucerne, Kunstmuseum, painting, by J. Ch. Storer, circa 1657); I. as a worker of miracles (Vienna, Kunsthistorisches Museum, painting, by P. P. Rubens, circa 1617/18); Christ giving I. his banner (Rome, Il Gesù, painting, on tomb altar, by A. Pozzo, 1699); I. receiving Franz of Borgia into the Jesuit Order (Frascati, Il Gesù, painting, by A. Pozzo, 1681/84); Pope Paul III confirming the Order rule (Rome, Il Gesù, painting, 17th century); I. being canonised (Rome, S Ignazio, relief, by B. Cametti, end 17th century); I. writing the book on spiritual exercises under the inspiration of the Virgin Mary (Ghent, Jesuitenkirche, painting, by G. Seghers, 17th century); *Cycles*: inter alia Rome, Casa Professa, frescoes, by A. Pozzo, 17th century; Rome, S Ignazio, frescoes, by P. de Lattre, 17th century; Rome, Il Gesù, tapestry, 1744; Rome, Il Gesù, tomb altar, reliefs, by A. Pozzo, circa 1695; Rome, S Ignazio, frescoes, by A. Pozzo, circa 1680.

Ignatius Theophorus of Antioch

Bishop, martyr, saint

Feast-day: 17th October (before the calendar reform 1st February, in Greek rites 20th December, feast of his translation on 22nd, 28th, 29th January)

Life: After Eusebius of Caesarea, circa 110/117, during the persecution of Christians under Emperor Trajan I. was taken from Syria to Rome and was there devoured in the arena by wild beasts. – On the journey to Rome I. wrote seven missives, four in Smyrna on the communities of Ephesus, Magnesia and Tralles, in which he gave thanks that they had allowed him to be received by an emissary on his Way of the Cross, as well as one on the Romans, in which he did not take any measures for his release by the Emperor. In Troas I. learnt that the persecutions in Antioch had ceased. He wrote to Polycarp in Smyrna, and to the congregations of Philadelphia and Smyrna, asking them to pass on his good wishes to his brethren in Antioch on heaving achieved peace. – The letters are importance evidence of the shared faith of the early Church. I. stood for the monarchic constitution of the Church, founded by Christ, with a bishop vested by God, through Christ, with full powers as authentic proclaimer of the teachings of Christ. Subordinate to the bishop, and in an advisory role, was the Council of Elders. To the Christian congregation in Rome he conceded precedence in matters of faith and charity, but expressly denied its primacy. With I. the term "Catholic Church" appears for the first time, to indicate the Christian community as a whole. In Christianity I. represents, inter alia, the incarnation of the divine Logos, his virgin birth by Mary, and redemption through his death on the cross. I. established the real presence of Jesus and His sacrifice on the cross in the Eucharist, that in Jesus Christ the divine and human nature are different and unmixed but united in one person, so that the eternal Logos possesses human characteristics and Jesus the man possesses divine characteristics. **Veneration and cult sites:** Mortal remains carried from Rome to Antioch, where they were interred at Hieronymus in Coemeterium on the Porta Daphnitica. Under Emperor Theodosius II (408–450) translation to the temple to Fortune which had been converted into a church. According to Latin tradition the mortal remains were brought back to Rome during a Saracen invasion in the 6th/

7th century and rest in Rome, S Clemente; relics in Naples; the head, which had been conveyed to Paris, was returned to Rome, Il Gesù, in 1559. Canon saint.

Representation in Art: *Apparel:* As a bishop of orthodox rite with sticharion, phelonion, omophorion (Palermo, Capella Palatina, mosaic, 12th century); as a young bishop with a wound on his breast (Montefalco, S Francesco, painting, circa 1400). *Attributes:* Lion at his feet (Mainz, St Ignaz, figure, by J. J. Jurcker, 1772); IHS symbol on his breast (Seville, University church, painting, 17th century). *Special scenes:* Christ recovering the heart of the dead I. (Florence, Uffizi, painting, by S. Botticelli, circa 1500); I. being condemned before Trajan (Rome, S Clemente, painting, by G. D. Piastrini, 18th century). *Martyrdom:* Vienna, Kunsthistorisches Museum, painting, by J. Kreuzfelder, 17th century.

Ildefonsus of Toledo

(Alfonso) Archbishop, Benedictine, saint
Feast-day: 23rd January.
Life: * born around 606, monk, later abbot of the monastery of S Cosma y Damiàn in Agli near Toledo, probably a pupil of Isidor of Seville, 657 archbishop of Toledo. † 667 – I. is included amongst the most important writers of late Roman literature in Visigothic Spain, inter alia I. provided a kind of early Christian literary history, which tells of eight writers. Unusual in his time I. was a worshipper of the Virgin Mary and defended the virginity of the Virgin Mary against three heretics in the writing "Libellus de viriniate Sanctae Mariae".
Legends: I. holds a debate with Jovian. – I. argues with Jews. – I. talks with an angel. – The Mother of God appears to I. and presents him with a divine Mass chasuble. – During the prayers of the bishops, I. raises the body of the town patron Leocadia, buried in an un-

known place, from the depths, the lid of the coffin flies open and Leocadia appears. – By the request of the people, using the sword of the King of the Visigoths, Reccesvinth (649–672), I. cuts off a piece of the green coat of Leocadia.

Patronage: Patron saint of Toledo, Zamora.
Veneration and cult sites: Relics taken in the 8th century to Zamora, highly venerated in Spain and the Netherlands.
Representation in Art: *Apparel:* As a monk in Benedictine apparel with a long, fully pleated long-sleeved woollen robe and cowl (Salzburg, St Peter, figure, 1782); as a bishop in pontifical Mass vestments with chasuble and mitre (Paris, Bibliothèque Nationale, Ms. lat. 2833, book illumination, early 12th century); as a bishop in pluvial with mitre and crosier (Saragossa, S Catarina, painting, of the Aragon school, 1554); in rochet and mozetta (Ilescas, hospital church, painting, by el Greco, 1603/05). *Attributes:* Plate with a picture of the Immaculate Conception (Salzburg, St Peter, figure, 1782); hovering angel with a book in his hands (St Trudpert, abbey, figure, 18th century). *Special scenes:* I. at his writing table with a picture of the Virgin Mary beside him (Ilescas, hospital church, painting, by El Greco, 1603/05); the Mother of God giving I., who is already dressed in a chasuble, a divine chasuble (Zamora, cathedral, painting, by F. Gallego, circa 1467); the Mother of God giving I., who is kneeling before her in rochet and mozetta, a divine chasuble (Vienna, Kunsthistorisches Museum, painting, by P. P. Rubens, 1631/32); the Mother of God giving I. a divine chasuble in the open air (Paris, Louvre, painting, by a Master of S Ildefons, circa 1490); the miracle of the veil on the coffin of St Leocadia (Zamora, cathedral, painting, by F. Gallego, before 1468). *Cycles:* Madrid, National Library, Ms. 10087, book illumination, circa 1200; Parma, Biblioteca Palatina, Ms. lat. 1650, book illumination, circa 1100.

Irenaeus of Lyon

bishop, martyr, Doctor of the Church, saint

Feast-day: 28th June (until 1960 28th June, then up until the calendar reform 3rd July, in Greek rites 23rd August)

Life: * born around 130 in Asia Minor, he was a pupil of Polycarp of Smyrna and around 170 he was a priest in Lyon. He preached against Montanism, the movement, which predicted the approaching end of the world argued for great rigour in ethical questions. I. was sent to Rome with a missive to Pope Eleutherus, in 177/78 he was a bishop in Lyon, probably returning to missionary activity in East Gaul. Around 190 I. induced Pope Victor I to yield to the bishops of Asia Minor, who on account of their non-acceptance of the western Easter term, were to remain excommunicated. The date of his death is not known, he was possibly martyred. – I. is respected as the most important theologian of the 2nd century. His principal work, written in his Greek mother tongue, is the "Exposure and Refutation of the False Gnosis," which dates from 180–185. In this I. gives a presentation of the gnostic manner of thinking, and a survey, beginning with Simon Magus, followed by a refutation in which he deploys arguments of common sense, the tradition and teachings of the apostles, and above all, the Word of God. In these writings, I. offers a principle of tradition based on the apostolic succession, then, using the example of the Roman church, expounds the faith which is common to all individual churches, and to which Gnosis is completely opposed. It is true that I. was not thus conceding the primacy of Rome, but he probably provided a first, theologically incomplete, justification for the leading position of Rome among the Christian communities, when he spoke of Rome's effective leadership, as a community founded by one of the apostles and based on the double apostolate of Peter and Paul.

Legends: In 202, because he will not make sacrifices to false gods, I. is thrown into prison and suffers the death of a martyr.

Patronage: Patron saint of the Diocese of Lyon.

Veneration and cult sites: His body lay in Lyon above the meeting place in the church founded in the town by the first Christians, destroyed in 1562 by the Huguenots.

Representation in Art: *Apparel:* as a bishop of the Latin Rite with a mitre and crosier (Ambierle, stained glass, 15th century); as a bishop in pseudo-Greek vestments (Rome, S Maria Maggiore, fresco, by G. Reni, 1611/ 12). *Cycles:* Lyon, cathedral, stained glass, 15th (?) century.

Isidore of Seville

archbishop, Doctor of the Church, saint

Feast-day: 4th April

Life: * born around 560 in Cartagena of a distinguished family, which was expelled from the town by the Byzantine authorities and settled in Seville, I. was educated by his brother Leander, who he succeeded as bishop around 600. He presided over the Council of Seville in 619, and that of Toledo in 633. As a bishop I. promoted science and founded schools and monasteries with good libraries, and promoted the scientific and ascetic training of the clergy. † 4th April 636 in Seville. Canonised in 1598, appointed a Doctor of the Church in 1722. In his works I. appeared close to Boëthius and Cassiodor as a teacher of the Middle Ages, but his works consist mainly of mosaic-like compilations from other writings. As a result of his clear, easily understood expressions and the breadth of the themes chosen, such as the "Etymologiae" in 20 volumes, he provides a current encyclopedia of world and spiritual knowledge of his time.

Patronage: National saint of Spain, patron saint of the Spanish army in battle.

Veneration and cult sites: Buried in Seville, shortly before 1063 his body was conveyed by King Ferdinand to León, the I. church was consecrated in 1063.

Representation in Art: *Apparel:* As a bishop in vestments (León, S Isidoro, figure, 13th century); as an archbishop with pallium (Burgos, S Lesmes, painting, by P. Ricci, 17th century); as a horseman (León, museum, standard, 12th/13th century). *Attributes:* Cross, sword (León, museum, standard, 12th/13th century). *Special scenes:* I. praying to Christ (Chartres, Bibliothèque, Ms 69, book illumination, 11th century); I. giving a messenger a missive (Santiponce, S Isidoro, fresco, attributed to D. Lopez, 15th century); the death of St Isidor (Seville, S Isidoro, painting, by J. de las Ruelas, circa 1613,16).

Ivo of Brittany
(Ivo [Yves] Helory) lawyer, saint

Feast-day: 19th May (before the calendar reform 17th October, or 19th March)

Life: * born 17th October 1253 in Minihy-Tréguier, Brittany, he studied theology in Paris and canon law in Orléans, worked as a lawyer in Rennes and Tréguier and as a church official. In 1284 he was ordained as a priest and parish priest of Trédrez, 1292 of Louannec. He resigned in 1297/98 and retired to his paternal residence in Kermartin. As a lawyer I. represented the helpless and the oppressed in court and was a benefactor of the poor. † 19th May 1303. Canonised in 1347.

Patronage: Second national patron saint of Brittany, the University of Nantes, legal faculties of the late Middle Ages, the poor, turners, court ushers, lawyers, ministry officials, notaries, parish priests, priests, barristers, judges, orphans during trials, as a sign of the virtue of equality.

Veneration and cult sites: His body was buried in the cemetery in Tréguier, and he was venerated by all in France.

Representation in Art: *Apparel:* As a judge in then contemporary apparel, in robes and beret (Paris, St Yves, figure, 14th century (destroyed)); in scholars robes and biretta (Freiburg, Cathedral, stained glass, 1524); as a cleric in soutane, cingulum, coat (Maria Bühel, Wallfahrtskirche, figure, 1764); as a deacon in Dalmatia (Florence, Accademia, painting, by G. di Marco gen. da Ponte, 15th century). *Attributes:* Book (Empoli, Museum, painting, by Maestro del Bambino Vispo, early 15th century); banderole (Salamanca, Chapel of S Caterina, painting, early 15th century); feather, scroll (Barcelona, cathedral, painting, 15th century); scroll and book (Quimper, Musée Breton, figure, 16th century); allegory of Justice at his feet (Prague, Charles Bridge, figure, by M. B. Braun, 1714); palm (Villy-le-Maréchal, figure, 16th century); chalice (Lübeck, Katharinenkirche, upper choir stalls, second half of the 15th century). *Special scenes:* I. healing the poor (Löwen, Museum, painting, by P. P. Rubens, 1633); the poor pressing towards I. as a deacon (Rome, S Ivo alla Sapienza, painting, 1685); I. surrounded by a divine light during Mass (Castelnovo (Carellón), parish church, painting, end 15th century); the poor standing before I. in a judges seat with a petition and a rich person with a moneybag (Brussels, Musées Royaux des Beaux-Arts, painting, by H. de Clerck, circa 1600). *Cycles:* Moncontour-de-Bretagne, stained glass, 1537.

J

James the Great

(the Elder, son of Zebedee, brother of St John)
Apostle, martyr, saint

Feast-day: 25th July (originally 27th Dec)

Life: in the New Testament, James is mentioned as the son of Zebedee and Mary Salome (Mt. 27, 56) and was called as a disciple by Christ together with his brother John (Mt. 4, 12); his presence was mentioned during the raising of Jairus's daughter from the dead by Jesus Christ (Mk. 5, 37), in the Transfiguration on Mount Tabor (Mt. 17, 1ff.) and in the Garden of Gethsemane during the seizure of Jesus (Mt. 26, 36). Beheaded in 44 under Herod Agrippa (Acts 12, 2).

Legends: first records of the journeys of the apostles appeared in the 5C and were translated into Latin by Julius Africanus. A more comprehensive version was written by Honorius of Autun: J. preaches in Judea and later unsuccessfully in Spain. – The high priest Abiathar turns to the sorcerer Hermogenes, who sends his pupil Philetus to turn J. from his faith. – Philetus is converted by the miracles, so Hermogenes renders him immobile. J. sends him a sudarium, which releases him from the magic spell. – Hermogenes sends demons to capture J., but they obey J. and bring Hermogenes in chains to J. – On J.'s orders, Philetus releases Hermogenes. Hermogenes is converted and receives J.'s pilgrim's staff as protection against demons.

– Hermogenes's books of magic are thrown into the sea. – Abiathar hands J. over to Herod Agrippa. – On his way to execution, J. cures a paralytic, at which the thug Josias is converted and is beaten by Abiathar with his fists. – Before his death, J. baptises Josias, who suffers martyrdom by beheading together with J. – Two of his pupils purloin the body and put it in a boat without oars which is guided by angels to the northern coast of Spain. – A rock hollows itself out as J.'s grave. – Wild bulls transport J.'s body to the castle of the pagan queen Lupa, who is then converted. – J.'s grave is re-discovered in 825. – According to a version from 1165 wrongly attributed to Archbishop Turpin of Rheims, J. appears in a dream to Charlemagne, showing him how to find the hidden grave by following the stars. Posthumous pilgrimage legends according to the 12C pilgrim's book: c. 1090, an innkeeper hides a silver chalice in the clothing of pilgrims on their way to Compostela; when they leave, he reports a robbery and the youngest son is hanged. – When the pilgrims return 36 days later, they find the son alive because J. supported his feet. (1st var: the innkeeper's daughter falls in love with the young pilgrim and takes revenge by hiding the silver chalice because her love is not returned). – (2nd var: when the news is brought to the judge that the executed young man is still alive, he says he is no more alive than the roast chicken on my table, at which the chicken flies off.) – During the battle of Clavijo (c. 844), J. appears on a white horse and puts the Moorish army to flight. – Mary appears to J. on a pillar in Zaragoza, demanding missionary work.

Patronage: Order of St J. Knights of the Sword in the fight against the Moors in Léon; of hospices, hospitals, brotherhoods of St James, orphans, pilgrims and the grain crop.

Veneration and cult sites: Santiago de Compostela, after Jerusalem and Rome the most important pilgrimage centre in the west; pilgrimage routes, including hospices and hospitals in Germany, France and Northern Spain; patron saint of numerous churches in Europe, esp. in Galicia and S America.

Superstitions: St J.'s Day is a momentous day when conclusions are drawn as to how the crop is doing. – In Silesia and Bohemia a ram is thrown from the church tower on St J.'s Day. The blood is distributed as a remedy against disease. – In the Tyrolean Alps, on St J.'s Day blacksmiths hammer on cold anvils after work to reinforce the Devil's chains (which have worn thin on this day) to ensure that he cannot free himself. – St J.'s candles help people digging for treasure and drive away evil spirits during it.

Representations in art: *Apparel:* as an apostle in a belted tunic and coat (Moissac [Tarn-Garonne], cloister relief c. 1100); as an apostle with pilgrim's hat (Bavarian National Museum, Munich, fig. by Hans Leinberger, 1525); as a pilgrim in a belted robe and tight cloak (Erfurt Cathedral, fig c. 1350); as a knight in full armour (Toledo Cathedral, 16C fig. by D. Gutiérrez de Cárdena); as a mounted figure and slayer of Moors (Santiago de Compostela, cloister tympanon, 11/12C relief; Tepotzotlán, Mexico, Museum of Christian Art, 17C fig.); as a nobleman (St John's, Marchena, early 17C painting by Zurbarán). *Attributes:* book or scroll (Bourg-Argental [Loire], 12C doorway sculpture); two tree stumps (St Sernin, Toulouse, S door, 12C fig.); pilgrim's staff (Santiago de Compostela Cathedral, fig. prob. 1188); shell on bag, staff, book (Mimizan, 12C fig.); staff with shell tied to it (Castle Library, Aschaffenburg, book illumination, c. 1400); shell on coat (antechurch of Paderborn Cathedral, fig. c. 1250); calabash on his back (Musée des Beaux-Arts, Dijon, 15C standard of Charles the Bold); calabash on a staff (St Jakobus, Schifferstadt, fig. c. 1450); rosary (St Jakob, Straubing, late 15C high altar fig.); pilgrim (S Cernin, Pamplona, 13C fig.); sword (Cologne Cathedral, early 13C relief on Ephiphany shrine by Nicholas of Verdun); crowns placed by J. on the heads of pilgrims (Palatinate Historical Museum, Speyer, 14C fig.). *Personifications with J.:* Emperor Charles V as Matamoros (Museum, Worcester, Mass., painting by Cornelius Cornelisz,

c. 1530); Stanislas Leczynski as J. the Pilgrim (National Museum, Warsaw, painting by J. B. Oudri, 1st half of 18C); Compostela pilgrim as J. (Maximilianstrasse, Speyer, fig. by Martin Mayer, 1990). *Special scenes:* chicken miracle (Winnenden Castle Church, relief by Riemenschneider school, c. 1520); Mary on the pillar (Benediktbeuern monastery, St James Chapel, early 18C painting); J. shows Charlemagne the way (Aachen Cathedral, Treasury, late 12C shrine of Charlemagne); J. as a helper of suffering mankind (Graphische Sammlung, Munich, early 18C cartoon for fresco by C. D. Asam. *Cycles:* Chartres Cathedral, choir window, early 13C stained glass; S Antonio, Padua, fresco by Altichiero de Zevio and Jacopo d'Avanzo, 1376–1379; Louvre, Paris, painting by Lorenzo Monaco, 1387/88; Pistoia Cathedral, mid–14C reliefs by Giulio da Pisa; St Jakob, Rothenburg o.T., high altar by Friedrich Herlin, 1443; Kereszteny Muzeum, Esztergom, 15C painting.

James the Less
(the Younger, son of Alphaeus) Apostle, saint

Feast-day: 11th May (originally 1st May. Changed to 3rd May after Pius XII introduced the feast of James the Labourer, then changed again by calendar reform)

Life: mentioned in the New Testament as son of Alphaeus (Mt. 10, 3) or as James the Less (Mk. 15, 40), in Galatians 1, 19 as the brother of Paul's master. The Eastern Church distinguishes between the J. of the Gospels and J. the master's brother. After Peter's escape from Jerusalem, J. became the leader of the Jerusalem Church and host to the Council of Apostles in Jerusalem discussing the issue of integrating pagan Christians into the young Church; J. carried through the Clauses named after him, that a Christian should not eat meat from pagan sacrifices, in order to avoid trouble. Author of the Epistle of St James, he was killed in 62 by order of the high priest Annas because of J.'s very successful Jewish missionary work.

Legends: on the Day of Preparation, J. vows to eat nothing until Christ has risen from the dead. – J. first receives communion from the resurrected Christ. – J. preaches for seven days before the high priest Caiaphas when a man incites the crowd to stone J. J. is then thrown from the pulpit, after which he walks with a limp. J. frees an innocent merchant from prison. – J. assists a pilgrim in distress. – J. is taken up to the pinnacles of the Temple in Jerusalem, thrown down and stoned. – As he is still not dead, they club him to death with a fuller's stick.

Patronage: patron saint of Friesia and local saint of Dieppe; of hatters, grocers, pie makers and fullers.

Veneration and cult sites: a church of St J. was built at the site of his martyrdom in Jerusalem; under Justinian (?), his relics were translated to the St J. church in Constantinople; historical evidence of body in SS Apostoli, Rome in 6C, together with body of St Philip.

Superstitions: on St J.'s Day (1st May), fertility magic with 'majes' stuck on the houses of marriageable girls. – On St J.'s Day (1st May) no darning should be done in Bavaria.

Representations in art: *Apparel:* as an apostle in tunic and pallium (St Trophime, Arles, west door, late 12C fig.); as a bishop of the Orthodox rite (S Giorgio di Greci, Venice, icon by E. Tzanes, 1683). *Attributes:* crown in hand (S Giovanni in Fonte, Ravenna, mid–5C); book (Ravello Cathedral, bronze door, 1179); scroll (Vatican Museums, Rome, predella by Niccolo da Foligno, 1466); fuller's stick (Aachen Cathedral, shrine of St Mary, fig. 1237); wool plate = pierced piece of wood on a long stick (Blutenburg, Munich, castle chapel, late 15C fig.); club (St Ursula, Cologne, slate c. 1275); opening a church

with a key (Old Church, Sodra Rada, Denmark). *Martyrdom:* Sedlec nr Kuttenburg, Czech Republic, painting by Leopold Willmann, 1701; S Marco, Venice, early 13C mosaic. *Cycles:* S Antonio, Padua, Capella del beato Luca, late 14C frescoes by Giusto di Menabuoi.

Jane Frances Fremyot de Chantal
Salesian nun, saint

Feast-day: 21st Aug, 12th Dec

Life: * in 1572 in Dijon, daughter of the president of the Burgundian Parliament, Baron de Fremyot. At her confirmation, a second Christian name, Frances, was added. In 1592 she married Baron Christophe de Rabutin de Chantal, with whom she lived happily for eight years. In 1600, after the death of her husband, she was in an uncomfortable situation with four children and a difficult father-in-law; in 1604, she met Francis de Sales during his Lenten sermons in Dijon. He told J. not to search for holiness in ascetic activities but in the fulfilment of her daily duties. In 1610, she founded the Salesian Order of the Visitation in Annecy. According to the original plan, nuns were not to live in seclusion but to devote themselves to the education of girls. † 13th Dec 1641 in Moulins. Beatified in 1751, canonized 1767.

Patronage: educators, young girls.

Veneration and cult sites: body in Annecy, Order of the Visitation.

Representations in art: *Apparel:* in the habit of the Order (Convent of the Visitation, Turin, painting 1636). *Special scenes:* robing of J. by Francis de Sales (Accademia Carrara, Bergamo, 18C painting by Boverini); presentation of the Rule to J. by Francis de Sales (Saint-Louis-en-Ile, Paris, early 18C painting by Noel Halle; J. worshipping Jesus's heart (art trade, 18C painting by Corrado Giaquinto).

Januarius of Benevento
(Janiver, Gennaro, Jenaro) Bishop, martyr, saint

Feast-day: 19th Sept (day of martyrdom), 1st May, 2nd May, 19th Oct, 16th Dec (translation feast)

Life: arrested on 19th Sept 305 and beheaded near Pozzuoli during the persecutions under Diocletian – together with his companions Acutius, Desiderius, Eutyches, Proculus and the deacons Festus and Sosius – because of their refusal to make a pagan sacrifice.

Legends: J. is thrown into a fiery furnace but emerges unhurt. – Wild animals unleashed at J. settle tame at his feet.

by angels, lions at his feet (St Stephan, Vienna, St J. altar by M. Altomonte, 1715); phials of blood in the hands of angels (Prado, Madrid, painting by Andrea Vaccaro, c. 1650); Vesuvius (S Gennaro, Naples, fresco by Domenichino, 1632). *Martyrdom:* Kunsthistoriches Museum, Vienna, 17C painting by S. Compagno); Pozzuoli Cathedral, painting by A. Gentileschi; Naples Cathedral, painting by J. Ribera. *Special scenes:* Apotheosis of St J. (Certosa di S Martino, Naples, painting by Battistello Caracciolo).

Jean de Brebeuf
Jesuit, martyr, saint

Feast-day: 16th March, in the Roman calendar together with Isaac Jogues and his companions on 19th Oct, orig. 18th Oct

Life: sent in 1625 with companions of his Order as missionary to the Iroquois and Huron Indians in the border region between Canada and the American colonies; between 1642 and 1649, seven missionaries suffered martyrdom, J. during a Huron rebellion in 1649. Beatified in 1925, canonized 1931.

Representations in art: *Martyrdom:* J. at the stake (engraving in Tanner, Societas Jesu, Prague 1675).

Jean-Baptiste Vianney
Priest of Ars, saint

Feast-day: 9th Aug (4th Aug, local feast in the see of Bellay)

Life: * 8th May 1786, the son of a peasant farmer in Dardilly nr Lyons, took his first communion secretly during the French Revolution; failed theological studies but was admitted, because of his great piety, to ordination, 1815 ordained, priest in Ecully, after 1818 priest of Ars; lived in great poverty but was widely famous as a father confessor, 1855 Legion d'Honneur. † 4th Aug 1856. Beatified 1905, canonized 1925.

Patronage: patron saint of Naples; invoked against volcanic eruptions and earthquakes.

Veneration and cult sites: 413 or 431 body transferred from Pozzuoli to the catacombs in Naples. – 831 body in S Maria in Gerusalemme, Benevento, 1154 in the abbey of Monte Vergine, 1497 in Naples Cathedral; 25th Feb 1964 ceremonial recognition by Archbishop Alfonso Cataldo, in a bronze urn dated 1511 at the main altar of the Cathedral. 871 relics on Reichenau island; since 985 chapel of St J. – Blood miracle documented since 1389 but scientifically not yet explained. Two phials of St J.'s blood liquefies at certain times if it is brought near the head (on the Saturday before the 1st Sunday in May and on 19th Sept).

Representations in art: *Apparel:* in tunic with cloak (Naples, upper catacomb, 5C fresco); as a bishop with pallium (Naples, lower catacomb, 10/11C fresco). *Attributes:* crown, palm tree, sword, bishop's crosier presented

Legends: J. prays in the parental stalls. – As a shepherd he prays in the fields in the Chante-Merle valley. – J. is haunted by the Devil.

Patronage: French pastoral workers. Invocation in the All Saints' liturgy before the ordination of priests.

Veneration and cult sites: the body is intact in a shrine in Ars; church dedications in France in churches built after 1945 such as Rueil (Nanterre), Lille, Arras, Villefranche-sur-Saône.

Representations in art: *Apparel:* as a father confessor with rochet, violet stole around his neck, Geneva bands (Ars, 20C fig. by E. Cabuchet). *Cycles:* Ars, 20C painting by Paul Borel).

Jerome

(Hieronymus) Doctor of the Church, saint

Feast-day: 30th September (Bamberg 3rd October; Basel 1st October)

Life: * 340/350 in Stridon in Dalmatia as son of a wealthy family. Studied grammar, rhetoric and philosophy in Rome around 354, Donatus Grammaticus became J.'s teacher, Rufin of Aquileia was his student colleague. Baptised towards the end of the study time in Rome; probably under the influence of ascetics from Trier decided on an ascetic life in Aquileia. 373/74 pilgrimage to Jerusalem; but an illness detained him in Antioch. J. heard exegetical lectures from B. Apollinarius of Laodicea and learnt Greek thoroughly. 375–78 hermit in the Chalcis, learnt Hebrew from a monk of Jewish ancestry. Paulin of Antioch ordained J. as Presbyter. Residence in Constantinople, where J. heard Gregory of Nazianzus translated into Latin. 381 friendship with Gregory of Nyssa. 382 participation at the Roman synod at the invitation of Pope Damasus, to end the Melitian schism. 382–85 residence in Rome as secretary of the Pope; beginning of the revision of the Latin

text of the Bible; centre of an ascetic circle of noble Roman ladies, such as Marcella, Paula and Eustochium. After the death of his patron Pope Damasus 384, openly attacked and his ascetic friends suspected. After disturbances following the death of the daughter of Paula due to too strict fasting, for which J. was blamed, J. left Rome and went to Alexandria. After visiting the monks in the Nitric desert 386, permanent residence in Bethlehem, characterised by polemic conflicts over Pelagianism. Strong in spirit and belligerent until his end † 30th September 419/20. – J. was no speculative theologian, his foundations rested on the Scriptures, tradition, liturgy, life and practise. As regards the doctrine of inspiration, J. expounded the view of a historical grammatical meaning of the text without moving completely away from the Alexandrine allegorical exposition. For this reason contradictions remained, e.g. when J. held to the absolute infallibility of the Holy Scriptures, but still that only the original text was inspired. As regards freedom and grace, as opposed to the heresy of Pelagius, he sought to prove that only God can be without sin and a man can only attain this state for a certain time with the help of the grace of God. With great energy J. emphasised his love for the church, the teaching of which could only be given by the Roman See. Among his works, as well as the outstanding achievement of the Vulgate translation, are commentaries on books of the Bible and precisely formulated, polemic broadsheets, aggressive to the point of offence, against John, Rufin us the friend of his youth, and against Pelagianism.

Legend: during his time of study a great fever comes over J. and he sees himself already standing before the throne of God, where he is asked about his faith. When J. insists he is a Christian, it is claimed he is in truth a follower of Cicero and for this reason he is struck by an angel with a rod. – In the night his opponents lay by his bed a lady's dress, which he inadvertently puts on in the dark and so is mocked by the people of the church. – J. can only survive the hermit's life with difficulty, because sexual desires plague him and he believes himself to be surrounded by beautiful girls. – For this reason J. strikes himself on his sinful breast. – Near to the monastery in Bethlehem, J. finds a limping lion and takes out a thorn. – The now tame lion must protect a donkey, but when the lion comes back without the donkey, it is thought that the lion has eaten it and he is used as a beast of burden. – The tame lion comes suddenly upon a caravan, scares the people and drives the camels and donkeys to the monastery. – Later the merchants admit to J. that they had stolen the donkey from the sleeping lion. – The lion licks the feet of the dying J. – Sulpicus Severus, the author of the Vita Martini, sees in a vision, how Christ bears J.'s soul into heaven accompanied by angels. At the same hour J. appears to St Augustine, just as he is about to write a eulogy to J. – After his dean, J. appears in a dream to Eusebius, his pupil, as sectarians spread views different from the teaching of the church. J. tells Eusebius to inform Bishop Cyril of Jerusalem, that he should spread over three men, who had died in the night, the cloak that J. had last worn. With this the dead come back to life and can report the truth on hell, purgatory and paradise. – J. calls Cardinal Andrew, who is to be punished by God for his effeminate lifestyle, back to life, so that he may warn his brothers. – Sabianus passes off his own work as that of J. and is chastised by Bishop Sylvanus with the words, that he is prepared to die if the deceased J. does not give his own opinion within day; when nothing happens Sylvanus is to be killed by the sword, but J. appears and holds the sword fast, while Sabianus' head is removed without human intervention. – J. saves two Roman pilgrims con-

demned to death in Constantinople, in that the axe can do nothing to them and when they are hanged supports them until someone frees them.

Patronage: Dalmatia, Lyons, Orders of St Jerome, ascetics, teachers, scholars, translators, correctors, theologians, universities, scientific societies, Bible Societies.

Veneration and cult sites: late 13th century, body brought to Rome St Mary Maggiore, since 1343 Doctor of the Church.

Representation in Art: *Apparel:* in priestly robes with chasuble (Chartres, Cathedral, confessors' portal, figure, 1215/20); in bishop's robes (Bilbao, Sacrestia di Santiago, figure, by G. de Beaugrant, 1545); as Cardinal in red cappa with cardinal's hat (Cologne, Wallraf-Richartz Museum, painting, by Master of Batholomy's Altar, 1500/01); as Cardinal in rochet, with hat (Münster, Landesmuseum, figure, 18th century); as Cardinal in the likeness of Albrecht of Brandenburg (Darmstadt, Hessen State Museum, painting, by L. Cranach, 1525); as learned man in the study (Cologne, library of the Archbishop's priests' seminary, Hs 1a, illumination, 10th century); as secretary of Pope Gregory the Great, holding his tiara during Mass (Cologne, Wallraf-Richartz Museum, painting, by Master of St Severin, 1500/05); as penitent in torn garment (Cologne, Wallraf-Richartz Museum, painting, by Master of St Severin, circa 1488); as penitent in penitential shirt (Florence, Collection of the Conte Contini Bonacossi, painting, by G. Bellini, circa 1477/78); as naked penitent in loincloth (Murcia, monastery St Jeronimiano de la Nova, figure, 18th century);. *Attributes:* crosier with double crossbar garment (Cologne, Wallraf-Richartz Museum, painting, by Master of the Holy Family, after 1484); crosier with simple crossbar garment (Cologne, Wallraf-Richartz Museum, painting, by Master of Bartholomy's Altar, 1498/99); crucifix (Diessen, figure, by J. Dietrich, 1738); book

garment (Cologne, Wallraf-Richartz Museum, painting, 1440/50); books (Cologne, Wallraf-Richartz Museum, painting, by Master of Bartholomy's Altar, 1500/01); holding tiara (Cologne, Wallraf-Richartz Museum, painting, by Master of St Severin, 1500–05); putto, carrying cardinal's hat (Diessen, figure, by J. Dietrich, 1738); stone (Cologne, Wallraf-Richartz Museum, painting, by Master of St Severin, circa 1488); death's head (Salzburg, Stift Nonnberg, figure, 18th century); lion (Munich, Alte Pinakothek, painting, by M. Pacher, 1483); scorpion (Florence, St Annunziata, fresco, by A. del Castagno, 15th century); dove (Munich, Alte Pinakothek, painting, by M. Pacher, 1483). *Special scenes:* J. in house (Detroit, Institute of Arts, painting, by J. van Eyck, circa 1442); healing of the lion (Bologna, St Mary dei Servi, fresco, by V. da Bologna, circa 1350); J. in the dry desert (Sienna, Pinacoteca Nazionale, painting, by Maestro dell'Osservanza, 1436); J. in the stony desert (Florence, collection of the Conte Contini Bonacossi, painting, by G. Bellini, circa 1477/78); J. in a forest desert (Vienna, Kunsthistorisches Museum, painting, by L. Cranach the Elder, 1502); J. in panorama landscape (Madrid, Prado, painting, by J. Patinir, 16th century); J. is tempted by unchastity (Reggio di Emilia, Museum, painting, by Il Guerino, circa 1620); J. hears the trumpet of judgement day in the desert (San Diego, California, Gallery of Arts, painting, by F. de Zurbarán, 17th century); J. with ladies of Rome living ascetically (Munich, Alte Pinakothek, painting, 1440/50); J. and the lion (Birmingham, Barber Institute, painting, by Giambelino, circa 1500[?]); J.'s last communion and death (New York, Metropolitan Museum, painting, by S. D. Botticelli, circa 1500); J. helps the hanged on the gallows (Paris, Louvre, painting, by P. Preugino, circa 1500); J. appears to Cardinal Andrew (Paris, Louvre, painting, by P. Perugino, circa 1500); an angel appears to J. (London, National gallery, painting, by Domenichino, 17th century); John the Baptist shows the sleeping J. the Mother of God with Child (London, National Gallery, painting, by Parmigiano, circa 1527); J. receives the vision of the Holy Trinity (Venice, St Nicolo da Tolentino, painting, by J. Liss, early 17th century); J. appears to St Augustine (Paris, Louvre, painting, by Sano di Pietro, 15th century). *Cycles:* include Paris National Library, Vivian's Bible, Codex. lat. 1, illumination, circa 846; Assisi St Francesco, Upper Church, fresco, circa 1280; Paris Louvre, painting, by Sano di Pietro, circa 1440; Montfalco, frescoes, by B. Gozzoli, circa 1450; Venice St Giorgio degli Schiavoni, frescoes, by V. Carpaccio, 1502; Rome, S Maria del Popolo, frescoes, by Pinturicchio (?), 16th century.

Jerome Aemiliani

(Hieronymus Aemiliani, Girolamo Miani) layman, founder of Order, saint

Feast-day: 8th February (before the calendar reform 20th July)

Life: * 1486 in Venice, Venetian nobleman, 1508 was taken prisoner, converted in prison in 1508 and freed in miraculous way. Since 1528 life of heroic penitence under the spiritual direction of Giampietro Caraffa, later Pope Paul IV; cared for the sick and neglected, founded orphanages in Venice, Brescia, Begamo, Verona, Como and Milan. In Somasca founded the Order of Somasca for care of orphans, an institute for regular clerics. † 1537 of plague in Somasca. Beatification 1747, canonisation 1767.

Legend: J. extracted water for his charges from a rock.

Patronage: Treviso, Venice, lost and orphaned youth (since 1928), founders of schools, orphanages, reformatories for fallen girls.

Representation in Art: *Apparel:* stylish Venetian costume (Venice, Museo Correr, painting, by L. Bassano, late 16th century). *Attributes:* crucifix, book, chain, orb (Pavia, S Felice, painting, by P. A. Magatti, circa 1743); orphans (Venice, Medallion of the Doge Alvise Mocenigo IV, relief, 1768). *Special scenes:* Mary frees J. from prison (Rome, S Alessio and St Boniface, painting, by J. F. de Troy, 1749); J. extracts water from the rock (Villa di Zanigo, mural, by G. D. Tiepolo, 16th century.

Joachim

Father of the Blessed Virgin Mary, saint

Feast-day: since 1622 jointly with St Anne on 26th July; 1522–1568 20th March (translation feasts on 16th Sept and 9th Dec), 16th Aug (individual feast-day since 1913, earlier 15th Aug)

Legends: not a historical figure; mentioned in 2C proto-gospel of St James; his legend was popularised via *Speculum humanae salvationis* and Jacobus de Voragine's Golden Legend in connection with the Mary Legend: because of his childlessness, priests turn J. away at the sacrificial altar. – J. lives in solitude with the shepherds. – An angel orders J. to go to the golden gate. – J. meets Anne at the golden gate. – Out of gratitude, J. sacrifices a lamb three months after Mary's birth. For further information, see under Anne and Mary.

Veneration and cult sites: Choziba monastery in the 4C; popular services in Southern Germany since the 18C in connection with the veneration of Joseph.

Representations in art: *Apparel:* long robe, cloak or wrap (St Georg, Tosens, early 16C); as a shepherd in narrow trousers, short robe, shawl, turban-like headdress (former monastery church at Amorbach, fig. c. 1750). *Attributes:* book (Thalkirchen, Munich, fig. by I. Günther, 1748/49); reading a book (Kunst-

historisches Museum, Vienna, painting by M. Woutiers, 1646); scroll (St Peter convent, Schwyz, 1774); walking stick (St Maria, Gelnhausen, St Anne retable, 1500); Tau staff (Kreuzherren Church, Prague, fig. by J. Süssner, 1690); shepherd's crook (pilgrimage church, Birnau, fig. by J. A. Feuchtmayer, 1749; two doves in hand (Collegiate Church, Tiefenbronn, 16C Holy Family retable); two doves on closed book (St Laurentius Chapel, Miltenberg, fig. c. 1500), two doves in small basket (Collegiate Church, Engelszell, fig. 1760); lamb on arm (Schwerin Museum, late 15C painting; gambolling lamb (Arnsdorff, Austria, Parish Church, fig. 1755); lamb at his feet (Pelplin Cathedral, early 17C fig.); infant Mary on arm (Gräfrath Parish Church, 1690); prayer cord (Stuttgart Staatsgalerie, painting 1516). *Special scenes:* J. worshipping the Immaculata (Hildesheim Cathedral, fig. at the Immaculata altar by Paul Egell, 1713; a branch with a madonna grows from J.'s breast in the manner of a Jesse tree (Musées Royaux des Beaux-Arts, Brussels, 17C painting by Cornelis van Coninxloo). *Cycles:* see Anne and Mary.

Joan of Arc

Virgin, saint

Feast-day: 30th May (France: 1st Sunday after Ascension Day)

Life: * 6th Jan 1412 in Domremy, the daughter of simple peasants, received a Christian upbringing but no education. At the age of 13 she heard her first voices accompanied by visions; after 1428, J. heard voices electing her as liberator of France but especially of Orleans. J. was to make possible Charles VII's coronation. – On 23rd Feb 1429, J. dressed in men's clothes and met the Dauphin, whom she succeeded in convincing of the sincerity of her mission. In May 1429, J. occupied Orleans with a small army, liberated the regions of Loire, Troyes and Châlons and led

Charles VII to his coronation as King of France in Rheims. Charles was not interested in continuing the war, however, J. was unable to take Paris and was injured in the battle. On 28th March 1430, J. left court and, following the guidance of her voices, was captured by Burgundians during a raid from Compiègne and sold at a high price to the English. A witchcraft trial in Rouen, to establish – at the behest of the English – that Charles's coronation had been an act of witchcraft. On 25th May 1431 condemned to the stake, recanted but subsequently revoked her retraction; burned on 30th May 1431 as a lapsed heretic. On 7th July 1456, the sentence was lifted after a re-examination by Pope Calixtus II. Beatified in 1909, canonized 1920.

Patronage: France, Orleans, Rouen, patron saint of telegraphy and broadcasting (because of the disembodied voices that reach her!).

Veneration and cult sites: after the German victory over France in 1870, her role as liberator of France was recalled.

Representations in art: *Apparel:* in women's clothes (Musée de l'Histoire de France, Paris, drawing 1429); in women's clothes on horseback (Grenoble Museum, 15C book illumination); in full armour (Musée de l'Histoire de France, Paris, 15C book illumination); in gilded armour on a horse (Musée Dobrée, Nantes, 15C book illumination by A. du Four); in classical armour (former 15C votive picture of Charles VII for J.); in contemporary women's dress (Musée Jeanne d'Arc, Orleans, painting, 1581); on numerous engravings, in mixed knightly and fashionable outfits variously combined. *Attributes:* drawn sword (Musée Jeanne d'Arc, Orleans, painting, 1581); standard and sword (Musée de l'Histoire de France, Paris, drawing by C. de Fauquembergue, 1429); lance (engraving in the Cosmography by A. Thevet, 1575); French coat of arms (engraving by L. Gaultier, 1606);

laurel wreath (equestrian statue, Paris, by A. Mercie, 1885). *Special scenes:* J. as shepherdess, hearing voices (Louvre, Paris, 19C fig. by F. Rudé); J. praying (North Carolina Museum, Raleigh, painting by P. P. Rubens); battle scenes (Musée Johannique, Orleans, 19C painting by B. de Monvel); Galerie des Batailles, Versailles, 19C painting by H. Scheffer); coronation scenes (Louvre, Paris, 19C painting by J. A. D. Ingres). *Martyrdom:* Wadsworth Museum, drawing by J. Ensor; plinth of the equestrian statue in Place du Martroy, Orleans, 19C relief by V. Dubray). *Cycles:* Château d'Epinal, 17C tapestry; Commercy Museum, 19C ivory carving.

John I
Pope, confessor, saint
Feast-day: 18th May
Life: 523–526 bishop of Rome during the rule of the Ostrogoth King Theodoric; in the disputes with the Arians, Theodoric tried to support and protect the latter from persecution by the Byzantine Emperor, Justinian I. Against his will, Pope J. was included in the delegation sent to Justinian by Theodoric. After the failure of the mission, J. was held in Ravenna by the distrustful Theodoric and † there a few days later. 530 body transferred to Rome.

Representations in art: *Apparel:* as pope (S Paolo fuori le mura, Rome, 19C fresco). *Special scenes:* J. in prison (S Maria in Porto Fuori, 15C fresco).

John the Almsgiver of Alexandria
Bishop, saint
Feast-day: 23rd Jan (Byzantine rites 12th Nov)
Life: * in 2nd half of 6C in Amanthus, Cyprus. After the death of his wife and children

he became an ascetic. 610/11 elected patriarch of Alexandria, becoming a fervent fighter against the heresies of Monophysitism; venerated for his charity. 619/20 died fleeing from Persian troops. Buried in Cyprus beside Bishop Ticon.

Legends: J. sees compassion in the form of a virgin with a green wreath made of olive leaves, and selects her as his bride sent by Christ. – J. has the arms of his servants drawn in a book. – The patrician Nicetas filches church money but J. recognizes the fraud during Sacrament. – J. waives the interest and taxes of a grocer, although he has insulted his nephew. – J. sells his sheets for the poor. – J. receives alms from Africa. – J. adopts a boy whose father has become impoverished from giving alms. – J. supports an impoverished merchant and protects his ship. – J. leaves his grave unfinished so as to be always reminded that he does not know the day and hour of his death. – A courtesan who for shame could not voice her sins and wrote them down a few days before J.'s death on a piece of paper, receives absolution for them at J.'s grave.

Patronage: charity, merchants, boatmen, beggars.

Veneration and cult sites: mainly in the eastern Church; in the west, relics in S Giovanni in Bragora, Venice (since 1247); in Buda (through Matthias Corvinus, 1489); Bratislava Cathedral (since 1632), Poland, Hungary.

Representations in art: *Apparel:* as a patriarch (S Giovanni in Bragora, Venice, high altar, 18C fig. by G. Marchiori); as a cardinal (S Giacomo, Levoca, relief c. 1520); as a hermit (copper engraving in Villeforte, Patri, Amsterdam, 1714). *Attributes:* crosier, giving beggar alms (S Giovanni Elemosinaria, Venice, painting by Titian); Tau staff, purse (Cracow Museum, painting c. 1504). *Cycles:* Cracow Museum, polyptych of the Cracow school, c. 1504.

John the Apostle

Apostle, evangelist, favourite disciple of Jesus, saint

Feast-day: 27th Dec, 6th May (martyrdom at the Porta Latina)

Life: acc. to the New Testament, he was the son of Zebedee and Mary Salome, younger brother of James the Great (Mt 4, 21). Worked as a fisherman with his father, belonged to the disciples of John the Baptist and, together with Andrew, attached himself to Jesus (Jo. 1, 38–40). He belonged to the inner circle of disciples, was present at Jesus' transfiguration on Mount Tabor (Mk. 9.2), the revival of Jairus's daughter (Mk. 5, 37), and during Jesus's arrest on the Mount of Olives (Mk. 14, 33). On the cross, Jesus gave his mother into J.'s care. After the Resurrection, J. went with Peter to the tomb. He and Peter healed a man born lame at the Golden

Gate of the Temple in Jerusalem (Acts 4, 13); was in Samaria and during his last years in Ephesus; under Domitian (81–96) exiled to the island of Patmos, where he wrote the Book of Revelation (Rev. 1, 9). Under Nerva he returned to Ephesus and died during the reign of Trajan.

Legends: sources are the apocryphal 3C writings of St John and the Golden Legend: at the Porta Latina in Rome, J. is led before Domitian, who has him scourged and put in a barrel of boiling oil but J. remains unhurt. – On Patmos, his dead female companion Drusiana, is brought to him and he revives her. – J. instructs the philosopher Craton who, as a sign of his contempt for the world, orders two of his disciples to break jewels, which are joined together again when J. prays. – J. destroys the Temple of Artemis in Ephesus by prayer. – After making the sign of the Cross over it, J. drinks a cup of poison handed to him by the pagan priest Aristodemos, without being hurt. – J. brings a priest of Artemis back to life, who is then converted to Christianity. – J. meets a young man who has murdered his father after he told him to live a pure and decent life. J. revives the father. The son castrates himself to remove the part of his body which made him a murderer, and becomes J.'s disciple. – J. brings back the couple Cleopatra and Lycomedes from the dead. – J. destroys a portrait of himself commissioned by one of his disciples. – J. is called to Smyrna. – J. instructs a young man who laughs at J. because he saw him playing with a tame partridge, and says neither a bow nor the human soul should be held in tension for too long. – In an inn on the way from Laodicaea to Ephesus, J. dismisses from the room the bugs that are irritating him in his bed, and they stay outside until morning. – On Patmos, the Devil steals J.'s inkwell. – Posthumous. Legends: J. gives the empress Galla Placidia his slipper as a relic for the Church of St John in Ravenna. – J. gives Edward the Confessor his ring back, which he had given to a poor pilgrim.

Patronage: miners (in Carinthia), sculptors, bookbinders, printers, booksellers, glaziers, engravers, candlemakers, portrait painters, basket makers, notaries, paper manufacturers, saddlers, authors, writers, mirror makers, speculative theologians, vineyard workers, for maintaining friendship, blessing the harvest; invoked against epilepsy, bad feet, poisoning, burns and hailstorms.

Veneration and cult sites: relics in Constantinople, Saint-Jean-d'Angely (head), Magdeburg (piece of clothing), Premonstratensians, Order of St John, Knights of St John, Ephesus, Patmos, monasteries of St John, Bologna, S Giovanni in Monte, Parma, Pesaro, Pistoia, S Giovanni Evangelista (Ravenna), San Giovanni in Oleo and San Giovanni a porta latina (Rome), San Juan de los Reyes (Toledo), Besançon, Bar-le-Regulier, s'Hertogenbosch, Johannesberg near Hersfeld, Meissen Cathedral, St Matthias (Trier), Cappenberg, Kleve, Prummern.

Superstitions: St J's wine or St J's beer serves as a remedy, wards off demons, protects against lightning, sorcery, poisoning, drowning, enhances beauty, health and a happy marriage. – The beginning of St J.'s Gospel is a blessing of the weather. – The first words of St J.'s Gospel are inscribed into the weather bell. – On Judgement Day, J. leads children who died unbaptised, into heaven. – In Jugenheim on the Bergstrasse, J. sits in a well and plays a song to innocent children on a fiddle.

Representations in art: *Apparel:* as a bearded old apostle (Vienna, Viennese Coronation Gospel, 9C book illumination); as a young apostle in tunic and cloak (S Prassede, Rome, Zeno Chapel, mosaic 822); in a cassock (Enger, Enger Antependium, weaving-mill, early 14C); as a deacon in dalmatic (Landesmuseum, Hanover, 16C fig. by T. Riemenschneider); as a fisherman (Carthage, gilt glass

base, Early Christian period). *Attributes:* scroll (Freiburg, Golden Gate, fig. 1225/30); palm tree (Museum Ferdinandeum, Innsbruck, mid–15C fresco from Wilten); Aristodemos with the poisoned cup (Chartres, central south door, fig. 1210–1215); oil barrel (shrine of St Elizabeth, Marburg, fig. c. 1240/50); poisoned cup with dragon (Toledo Cathedral, painting by El Greco); poisoned cup with snake (Kalkar Parish Church, shrine of St John, fig. 1543); chalice with host (Termini, Collegio Casa Gallegro, polyptych by Gaspare da Pesaro); ceremonial goblet with pagan deity (Steinfeld, Drautal, painting by P. Troger; quill (Omisali Parish Church, painting by Jacobelle del Fiore, 1st half of 15C); with the writer Prochoros (only in Byzantine art, e.g. Bibliotheca Vaticana Cod. vat. gr. 1156 fol. 1); golden diadem in allusion to Polycarp (Musée de la Société Archéologique, Avesnes, book illumination, 2nd quarter of 12C); dove of Holy Spirit (St Maria, Lübeck, early 16C fig.); townscape as symbol of continent of Asia (S Francesco, Assisi, upper church, late 13C vault fresco); seven personifications of the apocalyptic communities (Landesbibliothek, Dresden, MS A 94 fol. 122 v, book illumination, last quarter of 12C); angel of the communities (Bibliothèque Nationale, Paris, bible by S. Pedro de Roda, 11C book illumination); hovering eagle (St Ursula, Cologne, painting 1275); eagle in roundel (Strasbourg Cathedral, St Catherine Chapel, late 14C stained glass); eagle on book held in left hand (Wurzen Cathedral, fig. c. 1513; eagle at his feet (Orsoy Parish Church, 15C retable painting); eagle as Atzmann (Cologne Cathedral, St Peter's door, late 14C); eagle with inkwell in its beak (Schweisweiler (Donnersberg), mid–18C ceiling painting); eagle with book in its claws (Gernsdorf near Siegen, 18C fig.); cauldron (Städt. Graphische Sammlung, Augsburg, thesis page by J. Klauber, copper engraving, c. 1760); lion throne (Erla, 15C Spanish painting); glass pane with Christ-child (Limburg (Lahn), Cathedral Museum, late 13C stained glass). *Special scenes:* J. as a evangelist in a rowing boat (Museo Profano e Cristiano Lateranense, Rome, fragment of 4C sarcophagus relief). – St John Agape: J. at Christ's breast (Dahlem, Berlin, sculpture collection, fig. c. 1320); J. alone under the cross (Städel, Frankfurt, altar from Rimini, c. 1400); J. brought as the first apostle to the dying Mary and welcoming her at the gate (Museo de l'Opera del Duomo, Siena, painting by Duccio, 2nd half of 13C); J. gives the dying Mary provisions for the journey (Georgianum, Munich, painting 1481); J. presents Mary with a palm shoot from paradise (Dadesjö, Sweden, fresco c. 1260); J. on Patmos (Schätzler Palace, Augsburg, painting by H. Burgkmair, 1502); visions of the apocalypse (St J. Hospice, Bruges, painting by Hans Memling, 1479); after mass, J. steps into his tomb (Tivoli Cathedral, 12C fresco); J. gives Galla Placidia his slipper as a relic (Brera, Milan, painting by Rondinelli). *Cycles:* numerous, e.g.: Ste Chapelle, Paris, 13C stained glass; S Maria Donnaregina, Naples, mid–14C frescoes; Dominican monastery, Friesach, St J. altar, c. 1500.

John the Baptist

Forerunner of Jesus, saint

Feast-day: 24th June (birthday), 29th Aug (beheading), 23rd Sept (annunciation to Zacharias), 24th Feb and 25th May (discovery of head)

Life: according to the accounts in the four Gospels, Archangel Gabriel foretold the birth of the future prophet to elderly parents, Elizabeth and Zacharias, * six months before Jesus in a Judean mountain town. J. withdrew into the desert as an ascetic. At about 30, he began his eschatological preaching in the Jordan valley and administered baptism of repentance, preparing the way for the

| John the Baptist | John the Apostle | Sebastian | Antony of Egypt |

coming of the Messiah. When J. baptised Jesus, he proclaimed Him as Messiah. Arrested and beheaded by Herod for political reasons, perhaps at the instigation of his wife Herodias, whose daughter Salome allegedly demanded his head.

Legends: Elizabeth and the young J. visit Mary and the infant Jesus in Bethlehem. – Elizabeth flees with the young J. into the mountains to escape the Massacre of the Innocents; there, a rock cave opens up and closes behind them to hide them from their pursuers. – Zacharias is murdered because he refuses to hand over his son to the pursuers. – The angel Uriel carries the young J. into the desert. – The angel gives J. clothes which grow as he does. – In the desert, J. meets Jesus and his parents returning from Egypt. – An angel summons J. to the Jordan. – In limbo after his execution, J. prophesies of the Redeemer to the forefathers. – J. appears to St Augustine and Jerome. – J. appears to St Frances of Rome on her deathbed. – Julian the Apostate has J.'s body cremated.

Patronage: Burgundy, Malta, Provence; patron saint of Florence and Amiens; church dedications, e.g. in S Giovanni in Laterano, Rome, 4C basilica major, baptistries; held up as a good example of the ascetic life for the Carmelites and the Knights of St John; brotherhoods for the support of the condemned; of weavers, tailors, tanners, furriers, shepherds; invoked against headache and epilepsy.

Veneration and cult sites: head relic in S Silvestro, Rome (c. 1400), Maastricht, Quarante, Montpellier (c. 1440), Brussels (reliquiary, 1624/25), St Bavo, Ghent, St Johann, Burtscheid, Aachen; robe and chalice in S Giovanni in Laterano, Rome. Imperial relics in Imperial Palace, Constantinople (the finger of his right hand was used during the coronations of Byzantine emperors), Schatzkammer, Vienna (the imperial treasures include a tooth relic).

Superstition: Midsummer's Eve – a day of blessing and a lucky day; J. as a person scarcely features in the traditions of the day such as St J.'s fire and similar events, nor in numerous purification and fertility cults such as couples rolling on the ground, nakedness magic etc. Exceptions: in Leobschutz, J. himself blesses the flowers picked in his honour on St J.'s Eve. In Bohemia, J.'s flowers are mixed in animal fodder after a prayer is said to J. as they are picked – A child baptised on St J.'s Day is more blessed than if it gets 1000 thalers. – Children weaned on St J.'s Day are lucky and walk in the sunshine of life. On St J.'s Day there is a good opportunity for those who have fallen out to be reconciled.

Representations in art: *Apparel:* in a coat as a Cynic philosopher (Crypt of Lucina in the Callixtus catacomb, Rome, late 2C/early 3C mural); in tunica exomis (Arian Baptistry, Ravenna, mosaic c. 500); in a loincloth (S Silvestro, Venice, painting by J. Tintoretto, c. 1580/84); as a prophet and preacher of repentance, in a camel-hair robe with a leather belt (Siena, fig. by Donatello, 1st half of 15C); in a leopard skin (basilica of Euphrasius, Parenzo, 6C mosaic); in a wether's skin, partly with head and claws (Schalding, Lower Bavaria, fig. c. 1520); in a camel-hair robe under a fabric cloak (Cathedral opera, Florence, 15C fig. by Michelozzo); in clothes made from fabric (Florence Baptistry, mosaic c. 1235/40); as an ascetic (Landesmuseum, Karlsruhe, fig. c. 1300); as an ascetic with St John the Evangelist in a landscape (Regensburg Municipal Museum, painting by A. Altdorfer, 1510); as an ascetic with angels' wings (Parma Cathedral crypt, 15C painting); as a young ascetic (National Gallery, London, 16C Manchester Madonna by Michelangelo); as a hermit (Gemäldegalerie, Berlin, late 15C painting by Geertgen tot Sint Jans); as a child in fur (Bargello, Florence, 15C fig. by A Rosselino); as a young man, drinking from a spring (Lyon Museum, early 17C painting). *Attributes:* Lamb of God in halo (Magdeburg Cathedral, fig. c. 1230); Lamb of God in rectangular frame (Rouvres-en-Planche, 13C fig.); a lamb on a book (Kaufbeuren, fig. by J. Lederer, 1518); a lamb in his arms (Albi Cathedral, 13C fig.); a lamb at his feet (Accademia, Venice, 16C painting by Titian); a lamb with a chalice of blood at his feet (Unterlinden Museum, Colmar, Isenheim altar by the monogrammist MGN, 1513/15); lamb with breast wound and blood chalice (Germ. Museum, Nuremberg, early 14C fig.); boy playing with a lamb (public art collections, Basle, painting by Caravaggio); shepherd's crook (Arian Baptistry, Ravenna, c. 500); crosier with crux gemmata (Orthodox Baptistry, Ravenna, 430/458); crosier with banderole (Louvre, Paris, painting by the Botticelli workshop); crosier with Agnus-Dei plate (Brera, Milan, painting by Francesco del Cossa, 1472/73); hand crucifix (Lateran Baptistry/Rome, 640–642); hat on a book (art trade, Burgundian fig. 2nd half of 14C); book (Boston Museum of Fine Arts, early 16C fig.); bowl, chalice, shell, ointment bottle (Atri Cathedral, 15C fresco, Pinacoteca Nazionale, Siena, painting by Pinturicchio, 2nd half of 15C); axe on tree (Capella Palatina, Palermo, 13C); baptismal child (Senlis Cathedral, west door, 12C fig.); bowl with severed head (Mantlach, Central Franconia, fig. 1485); Christ-child on paten (only in Byzantine art);

honeycomb (Berlin, fig. by Michelangelo workshop); rising against Herod (Contini Collection, Florence, 14C painting by Giovanni del Biondo); lantern (Enschede Church, 16C painting by J. Prevost); candle (Kampen Church, 16C painting by E. Maeler); lily (Alte Pinakothek, Munich, 15C painting by D. Bouts); apple with palm growing from it (Siena, dorsal by Guido da Siena, c. 1270). *Special scenes*: annunciation of J. to Zacharias (British Museum, London, gospel by the court school of Charlemagne, book illumination, c. 800); birth of J. (Bay. Staatsbibliothek, Munich, lectionary by St Erentrud, 11C book illumination); naming of J. (Berne Museum of Arts, painting by Nelkenmeister, c. 1495); Mary leaves Zacharias's house (Urbino, fresco by Salimbena, 1415); circumcision of J. (Auxerre Cathedral, SW door, 13C); Elizabeth and J. visit Mary in Jerusalem (Germ. Nationalmuseum, Nuremberg, altar painting c. 1400); hiding place of Elizabeth and J. in the rock (Boymans-van Beuningen Museum, Rotterdam, painting by the Master of the St Johns' altar, 1480/90); J. in the desert (National Gallery, Chicago, painting attrib. to Giovanni di Paolo); angel bringing fur to J. (Berne Museum of Arts, 14C); John undresses to put on hermit's clothes (Kress Collection, Washington, painting by Domenico Veneziano, 1438); J. says goodbye to his parents (National Gallery, Chicago, painting attrib. to Giovanni di Paolo); God's word comes to J. (Duomo, Milan, predella painting by Gentile da Fabriano); J. and his parents meet Jesus in the desert (painting collection, Staatl. Museen, Berlin, painting by the Lippi school); J. with the holy family in Nazareth (Pinacoteca Nazionale, Siena, early 16C painting by Pinturicchio); J. preaches repentance to the people (Alte Pinakothek, Munich, painting by J. Breughel the Elder, 1503); mass baptism in the Jordan (St-Barthelemy, Liège, font by Reiner of Huy 1107–1118); J. by the Jordan pointing to Jesus (Berne Art Museum, predella by the master of the Louvre Nativity, 2nd half of 14C); baptism of Jesus (Pisa Baptistry, lintel relief c. 1200); Herod's banquet, Salome dancing (S Zeno, Verona, 12C doorway relief); seizure of J. (Pisa Baptistry, lintel relief c. 1500); composite scene of Herod's banquet, J.'s beheading and presentation of J.'s head to Salome (Aachen Cathedral, Liuthar Gospel, Reichenau book illumination c. 990); Julian the Apostate has J.'s body cremated (Kunsthistorisches Museum, Vienna, painting by Geertgen tot Sint Jans, 1484); arrival of J.'s head relic in Amiens (Amiens Cathedral, 12C choir cabinet relief); St John's chalice (Naumburg Cathedral, early 13C fig.). *Martyrdom*: Speyer Cathedral Treasury, in Palatinate History Museum, 15C painting by the Cologne master of the St Mary legend; Städel, Frankfurt, painting by Rogier van der Weyden; St John's Hospital, Bruges, painting by H. Memling. *Cycles*: very numerous, e.g. Fossacesia in the Abruzzi, 13C doorway relief; Peruzzi Chapel, Florence, frescoes by Giotto; Urbino, frescoes by L. and J. Salimbena, 1415; Stams in Tyrol, ceiling painting by J. J. Zeiller, 1757; Blaubeuren, altar, 1493.

John-Baptist de La Salle

Priest, founder of order, saint

Feast-day: 7th Apr, orig. 15th May, in the Congregation 26th Jan

Life: * 30th Apr 1651, tonsure at age of 11, 1678 ordained, foundation of the Congregation of Brothers of Christian Schools; successfully established schools for the poor in which corporal punishment was forbidden, lessons were held in the mother tongue rather than Latin, and moreover a kind of early vocational education for workers was instituted; introduced seminars for teachers. His reforms encountered resistance, particularly in ecclesiastical circles. † 7th Apr 1719. Beatified in 1888, canonized 1900.

Patronage: schools for the poor.

Veneration and cult sites: 1734 body brought to crypt of St Yon Chapel, Rouen; 1937 transferred in an urn to Rome, to the Congregation building. Relics in Milan Cathedral, France, Brothers of the Christian Schools.

Representations in art: *Apparel:* in mid life (Congregation building, Rome, painting by P. Leger 1733); translation of the body to Rome (Collegio S Giuseppe, Rome, apse painting in chapel); transfer of relic to Milan Cathedral (chapel of Istituto Gonzaga, Milan, 19C stained glass). *Cycle:* Vatican, Rome, painting by C. Mariani and G. Gagliardi.

John of Beverley

Bishop of York, Benedictine monk, saint

Feast-day: 7th May (translation 25th October)

Life: Born in Harpham (Humberside) as son of a noble family, L. was educated by archbishop Theodore of Canterbury and became a monk at the Benedictine monastery of Whitby, Yorkshire. In 687, J. was consecrated bishop of Hexham, in 705 bishop of York. After founding the monastery of Beverley, J. retired there in 718. D. on 7th May 721. J. was canonized in 1037.

Legends: J. cures a mute boy. – The victory of Agincourt of the English in 1415 is ascribed to the intercession of J. and John of Bridlington.

Veneration and cult sites: his body is buried in Beverley; on J's canonization in 1037, Aelfric, bishop of York, ordered the translation of the relics to a new shrine; in 1292, a further shrine was ordered and consecrated in 1308; relics in Arundel in Sussex. In 1416, after the victory of Agincourt, the feast-day was given greater significance by bishop Chichele; fictitious connection with the University of Oxford.

Representation in Art: *Apparel:* as bishop in pontifical vestments with chasuble and mitre (Beverley, St John, seal relief, 13th century); as archbishop with pallium (York Minster, stained glass, 1338). *Attributes:* crosier, book (Oxford, chapel of All Souls College, stained glass, circa 1441). *Special scenes:* curing a mute boy (Dublin, Hunt Collection, crosier, ivory relief, mid 11th century); at St John's altar, King Athelstan invokes his intercession for victory in the 934-937 battle against the Scots (York Minster, stained glass, 1410/1427); King Athelstan presents J. with a letter of endowment for the church at Beverley (Beverley, St Mary, keystone relief, circa 1445).

John Bosco

Priest, founder of order, saint

Feast-day: 31st Jan

Life: * 16th Aug 1815 in Becchi nr Turin, the son of poor peasants; 1846 after his ordination in Valdocco, Turin, he built a settlement for 700 neglected children and young people, which took on a model character; 1857 founded the Salesian Order, a congregation of priests and laymen named after St Francis of Sales and intended for the upbringing and education of young people; together with Maria Domenica Mazzarello, founded the Daughters of Our Lady, Help of Christians; reformed education system in Italy and after 1875 in S America. † 31st Jan 1888.

Patronage: schoolchildren, young people, publishing houses.

Veneration and cult sites: pilgrimages to Becchi, where he was born; dedications of numerous parish churches in Germany after 1945.

Representations in art: *Apparel:* as a priest in a cassock (St Johannes Bosco, Unterpfaffenhofen, fig. by M. Moroder 1981); as a priest (Milan Cathedral, 20C painting). *Attribute:* children (St Johannes Bosco, Unterpfaffenhofen, colour lithograph by W. Persey 1956). *Cycle:* S M Ausiliatrice, Turin, 20C altar painting)

John of Bridlington

(John de Thwing) Austin Canon, confessor, saint

Feast-day: 10th October

Life: Born circa 1320 at Thwing near Bridlington; in 1340 J. became a canon at St Augustine's monastery, Bridlington, later precentor and lastly prior from 1361 until his death on 10th October 1379. Some of his words have been preserved, among them comments on the Psalms and several homilies. J. was canonized in 1401.

Patronage: patron saint of the House of Lancaster.

Veneration and cult sites: In 1404, his relics were translated to a shrine at Bridlington priorate church; relics at Durham Cathedral and Eton College; patronal objects in Dover and Sandwich, Kent.

Representation in Art: *Apparel:* in long superpallium, fur almutia with biretta and shoulder cape (Beauchamp Chapel, Warwick, stained glass, circa 1470); with black doctor's cap (New York, Pierpont Morgan Library MS M 105, book illumination, circa 1425). *Attributes:* staff, book (Hamstead, Norfolk, stained glass, mid 15th century).

John of Capestrano

Apostle of Europe, Franciscan preacher, saint

Feast-day: 23rd Oct

Life: * 24th June 1386 in Capestrano in the Abruzzi, 1405/06 began law studies in Perugia and became a judge, 1413 adviser to Perugia Podesta; 1415 imprisoned and, after a failed escape attempt in 1416, entered the Franciscan order of Observants; from 1417 a

restless inquisitor, disseminator of the Observance, itinerant preacher in Italy, France, the Netherlands, Austria, Germany, Bohemia, Poland and Hungary. Along with Bernardino of Siena, he promoted devotion to the Holy Name of Jesus. Had a decisive role in the victory of the Christian army led by Janos Hunyadi against the Turks nr Belgrade in 1456. † on 23rd Oct 1456 in Ilok, Croatia. Initially buried in the cemetery and transferred eight days later into a side chapel of the Franciscan church; body lost after the Turkish occupation in 1526. Beatified 1622, canonized 1690.

Legends: St Francis of Assisi appears to J. and persuades him to join the Order. – During celebration of mass in Hungary, an arrow with the message "Giovannis noli timere" falls on the altar. – During a sermon in Aquila, J. exorcises a possessed soul with the monogram of the Name of Jesus. – J. walks over water. – St Leonard as patron saint of the monastery of Granz (founded at the instigation of J.) presents the crusader standard to J. **Veneration and cult sites:** St John of Capestrano, Munich, petrified Statio Orbis erected in 1960 during the Eucharist World Congress.

Representations in art: *Apparel:* in Franciscan habit (Wartenberg, East Prussia, Franciscan church, early 18C). *Attributes:* book, flag with cross (Louvre, Paris, painting by Bartolomeo Vivarini, 1459); monstrance with monogram of Christ in his hand (Bamberg Museum, painting by S. Bopp); flag with cross, crucifix, star above his head, monstrance carried by angels (Schutzengel church, Straubing, early 18C painting by Johann Caspar Sing); war trophies and standing on a defeated Turk (St Stephan, Vienna, fig. 1737). *Special scenes:* J. walks over water (Museum of Fine Art, Antwerp, 17C painting by Peter van Lint); St Leonard's presentation of the flag with the cross to J. (St Stephan, Vienna, tomb of Friedrich, relief 1478–1485); burning of heretical papers by J. (16C copper engraving by Hans Schäuffelin); J. burning vanities during a sermon (Bamberg Museum, painting by S. Bopp); J. as patron saint of Europe and the triumph of St J. (St John of Capestrano, Munich, J. memorial by J. Henselmann, 1960). *Cycles:* Museo Civico, Aquila, 16C polyptych by Sebastian di Cola da Casentino).

John Chrysostom of Constantinople

Doctor of the Church, patriarch, saint
Feast-day: 13th Sept in the Roman feast calendar, 27th Jan (return of body to Constantinople), 30th Jan (three hierarchies), 15th Dec (consecration as bishop); 14th Sept (birthday).

Life: * of a noble family in Antioch between 344 and 354, after the death of his father, brought up by his devout mother, Anthusa. His teachers were the philosopher Andragathius and the rhetorician Libanius. Baptised as an adult, lived for six years as an ascetic in the mountains nr Antioch. Theological instruction from Diodorus together with Theodore of Mopsuestia, returned due to health reasons to Antioch where 381 became deacon, 386 presbyter and preacher at the main church. In this church he held his famous sermons on the 'Statues' during the 387 rebellion against tax increases, when the crowd overturned statues of the emperors. Thanks to intervention by him and bishop Flavian's, an amnesty was granted. 397 with some trickery on the part of the emperor Arcadius, he was abducted and brought to Constantinople where, against his will, he was made patriarch and deposed the Simonist bishops. In the turmoil following the ousting of Eutropius the minister in 399 by the empress Eudoxia, urged on by opposing bishops, esp. Theophilus of Alexandria, who was afraid of losing his pre-eminence, in 403 J. was deposed and exiled. In the shock following an accident in the palace, J. was recalled the next day. At Easter, the empress deployed soldiers to prevent an evening baptismal service, but the assassination attempt was foiled. Exiled again by imperial decree of 9th June 404, J. went to Cucusus in Armenia. As he was later being brought to Pityus on the Black Sea, he died on 14th Sept 407 in Comana in Pontus. On 27th Jan 438, Empress Theodosius II had the body solemnly buried in the Church of the Apostles, Constantinople. In his writings, J. advocates faith in two distinct natures (human and divine) found in Christ. Also important is his doctrine on Communion in asserting the real presence in the sacrament. He saw the Eucharist as a sacrifice identical to the sacrifice on the Cross. J. related the papal primacy only to the position of St Peter. In the orthodox "Divine Liturgy", attributed to J. since the 8C, only the Anaphora originates from him. Doctor of the Church (since 1568).

Patronage: preachers (since 1908).

Veneration and cult sites: in the Orthodox world, a feast-day since 428 celebrating the translation of his body to Constantinople; relics on Mount Athos, in Moscow, Kiev, Messina, Venice, Dubrovnik, Clairvaux, Paris, Bruges, Mainz.

Representations in art: *Apparel:* as a patriarch of the Orthodox rite (Vatican, Rome, Nicholas II Chapel, fresco by Benozzo Gozzoli); in a polystaurion (Stilo Cattolica, 11C fresco); as a bishop of the Latin Church (Hospital Library, Kues, fresco c. 1500); as an author at work (S Giovanni Crisostomo, Venice, painting by S. da Piombo). *Special scenes:* penance of J. (part of a Florentine poem of the 14C in which a robber Shirano, who had raped a woman and thrown her into a well, does penance as a naked ascetic; the name of the robber as later handed down was Giovanni Boccadoro, which led to confusion with J.) (Albertina, Vienna, engraving by Hans Sebald Beham; Cucusus, Bethlehem forest, fig. by M. Braun, 1726).

John of the Cross

Carmelite, Doctor of the Church, saint

Feast-day: 24th Nov (until 1732, 24th Dec)

Life: * 1542 in Avila; after an impoverished childhood, he entered the Carmelite Order in 1563 and, after studying in Salamanca, reformed the Order with the help of Theresa of Avila. 1572 – 1577 confessor in the monastery of the Incarnation in Avila, mystic studies, 1578 arrested by opponents of Theresa's reforms, 1588 prior in Segovia following disputes about monastic reform in Ubeda, where he died in 1591 after suffering degrading treatment. Beatified 1675, canonized 1726, 1926 proclaimed a Doctor of the Church.

Veneration and cult sites: body in Segovia since 1593, relics in various Carmelite monasteries.

Representations in art: *Apparel:* as a Carmelite friar in a belted robe, scapular and coat with hood (Scharding, abbot's mill, fig. by J. P. Spaz, 1677). *Attributes:* open book (Avila, 17C fig. by G. Hernandez); crucifix, dove on his shoulder (art trade, 17C Spanish fig); cross, eagle at his feet, angel with banderole (prayer, Carmelite Church, 17C fig.); lily, books (Cabinet des estampes, Paris, 18C engraving by A. Wierix). *Special scenes:* vision of Christ carrying the cross (Carmelite Church, Paris, fresco by W. Damery, c. 1640); the imprisoned J. sees a vision of the Mother of God (Provincial Museum, Mechelen, 19C painting by V.-H. Janssens). *Cycles:* Brussels, 60 copper engravings accompanying to Jerome de Saint-Joseph, Tableau racourcy de la vie de Jean, 1678.

John Damascene

(John of Damascus) Doctor of the Church, monk, saint

Feast-day: 4th Dec (form. 29th Nov, 6th May, since 1890 27th March, abolished in the recent calendar reform), in the Byzantine rite 29th Nov

Life: * c. 675 in Damascus of a noble family (his father was the caliph's chief treasurer). 690 after a careful education, became the caliph's general logothete, before 700 or by 715 entered the monastery of St Sabas nr Jerusalem. Shortly after the Byzantine iconoclastic controversy over the theology of Christian art broke out, he wrote benchmark tracts limiting the Old Testament ban on images to depictions of the invisible God but repudiated the worship of paintings. He composed several hymns to St Mary, participated in the 7th Council of Nicaea of 787. Considered a saint in the early 9C, 1890 proclaimed a Doctor of the Church.

Legends: J. is educated by the monk Cosmas. – A denunciation prompts the iconoclastic Byzantine Emperor Leo to have J.'s arm broken by force, but Mary heals it (origin of the Mary Tricheirousa type of icon); J. sells baskets in Jerusalem on behalf of the impoverished abbey.

Patronage: pharmacists in Milan, painters of icons and pictures of saints, carvers of crucifixes.

Representations in art: *Special scenes:* healing of J.'s broken arm by an angel (S Maria Maggiore, Rome, Capella Paolina, fresco by G. Reni). *Cycle:* Milan Cathedral, 16C stained glass, donated by the grand master of the pharmacists, N de Varella.

John Eudes

Founder of order, saint

Feast-day: 19th Aug

Life: * 14th Nov 1601 in Ri (Normandy), 1623 entered the Oratory in Caen, 1625 ordained, from 1632 a popular missionary (he is supposed to have organised 110 popular missions); 1643 foundation of the "Religieuses de Notre Dame de Charte du Refuge", a world priest association for the education of priests; he also founded the "Sisters of Christian Love, now known as the "Sisters of the Good Shepherd". Promoted the cult of the Hearts of Jesus and Mary. † 19th Aug 1680. Beatified in 1909, canonized on 31 May 1925.

No definite iconography.

John Fisher

Bishop, martyr, saint

Feast-day; 2nd June

Life: * 1469 in Beverley (Yorkshire), the son of a merchant; 1482 went to Michaelhouse, Cambridge (now Trinity College), 1491 ordained, 1494 Master of Michaelhouse, Doctor of Theology and Vice-Chancellor, 1501 Chancellor of Cambridge University, 1504 bishop of Rochester, father confessor and teacher of Margaret Beaufort, wife of Henry VII, who helped him found Christ's College and St John's College. In his writings, J. defended the primacy of the pope and the theology of tradition against Luther. 1527 confirmed the validity of Catherine of Aragon's marriage with Henry VIII, and in the House of Lords attacked the anti-ecclesiastical laws of 1530 and the king's claim to be the head of the English Church. In 1534 he refused to take the Oath of Succession, was imprisoned in the Tower and, whilst there, nominated a cardinal by Pope Paul III. Beheaded 2nd June 1535. Beatified 1886, canonized 1935.

Veneration and cult sites: Body buried in the cemetery, All Hallows, Barking, later transferred because of the great veneration he attracted, to St Peter in Vincula in the Tower of London. Dedication of numerous English churches.

Representations in art: Windsor Castle, portrait by H. Holbein the Younger, between 1528 and 1532.

John of God of Granada

Founder of hospital, saint

Feast-day: 8th March

Life: * 8th March 1495 in Montmemor o Novo, Portugal. He ran away from home and lived the life of an adventurer, working as a shepherd and mercenary in King Charles V's war against France and the Turks, and served an exiled Spanish nobleman in Africa. In 1538 in Granada, where in 1540, after a sermon by John of Avila, he founded a hospital and lived the life of a strict ascetic. † 8th March 1550. 1584 his colleagues at the hospital drew up a rule of conduct which was published in 1585 and approved in 1586 as the rule of the Order of the Brothers of Mercy (Fatebenefratelli) as their maxim. Beatified 1630, canonized 1691.

Legends: (selection from Franciscus de Castro): J. sells prayer-books and catechisms in the street and at church doors. – J. begs for his hospital by hanging two baskets to a yoke and asking for alms. – The bishop of Tuy and chancellor of Granada, Don Sebastian Ramirez, gives him the cognomen 'of God'. – J. washes the feet of a sick man and recognizes Jesus. – On a stormy night, assisted by the Archangel Raphael, J. carries a sick beggar to his hospice. – Mary appears to J. in Guadelupe and shows him the infant Jesus. – During a fire at his hospice, J. personally carries patients from the flames. – Christ crowns J. with the crown of thorns. – J. appears to a sick woman and cures her.

Patronage: patron saint of Granada, of hospitals, the sick and book-sellers.

Veneration and cult sites: body in S Juan de Dios, Granada, 18C urn by Miguel de Guzmán; pilgrimage to Montmemor o Novo,

Portugal; a church was built where he was born; Brothers of Mercy of St J. of God.

Representations in art: *Apparel:* in simple habit (Granada, woodcut accompanying vita, 1585); in the habit of the Order of the Brothers of Mercy with a long skirt, leather belt and scapular-like upper robe (Granada Hospital, fig. pre–1609). *Attributes:* crown of thorns (Imbach Parish Church, fig. 1700); crucifix (Museo de Arte Moderno, Madrid, 20C fig. by J. Higueras); pomegranate (Granada Cathedral, 18C fig. by Agustin Ruiz); infant Christ with the Devil at his feet (Cadiz Hospital, 17C fig.); beggar on his back (Malaga Cathedral, 17C choir-stall relief by P. de Mena); beggar at his feet (Seville Cathedral, 17C painting by C. Giaquinto); collection box (copper engraving in Weigel's Columnae, Nuremberg, 1725); patients at his feet (Oberberg-Eisenstadt, fig. 1726). *Special scenes:* all the motifs in the legends can be found individually (not in cycles) on copper engravings and paintings in Spanish and Italian art.

John Leonardi

Founder of order, saint

Feast-day: 9th Oct (originally 6th Oct)

Life: * 1543 near Lucca, became an apothecary's assistant, studied theology, 1571 ordained, worked in hospitals and prisons in Lucca, trying, at the behest of the Council of Trent, to teach young people religion, 1574 published a handbook for religious instruction. He founded a lay confraternity to help him in his work, 1574 founded his Clerks Regular of the Mother of God, later merged with Joseph Calasanz's Piarists. The reforms provoked hostility and he had to leave Lucca. In Rome, developed the hospital and school systems. Appointed Visitator and Reformer of Orders by Pope Clement VIII, 1603 founded the Roman College for the Education of Missionaries, which later became the

Sacred Congregation of Propaganda. † 9th Oct 1609 in Rome. Beatified 1861, canonized 1938.
Veneration and cult sites: buried in S Maria in Portico, Rome, 1662 body moved to Campelli to the church of his congregation. No reliable iconography.

John of Matha

Founder of order, saint
Feast-day: 8th Feb (orig. 17th Dec)
Life: * in 1160 in Faucon, Provence, studied in Paris, gaining a doctorate in theology. In 1194, J. and Felix of Valois founded the Order of the Most Holy Trinity to Redeem Christian Slaves (OST) in Cerfroid (Aisne). 1198 rule confirmed by Pope Innocent III. 1199 great successes in Morocco, followed by a surge in the Order's popularity, with 30 convents in Spain, France and Rome. † 17th Dec 1213 in Rome. His cult was approved as harmless in 1694.
Legends: Mary foretells J.'s birth to his parents. – During the celebration of his first communion, the Archangel Michael appears to J. with two prisoners, which leads to the foundation of the Order. – Pope Innocent III has the same vision: while raising the host, he sees an angel dressed in white clothes and with a red and blue cross on his chest. – J. withdraws to the solitude of Gandelu nr Meaux, where he meets Felix of Valois. After three years of fasting and prayer, a deer appears to them at a forest well with a red and blue cross in its antlers. – In Tunisia, J. suffers humiliation and is tortured. – J. escapes from Tunisia by boat, the mast and rudder broken by barbarians, and arrives at the port of Ostia by using his coat and the coats of his companions as sails.
Patronage: Order of the Most Holy Trinity for Redeeming Prisoners, religious prisoners, galley slaves.

Veneration and cult sites: body in S Tomaso, Formis. In 1665, Spanish brothers of the Order brought it secretly to the OST monastery in Madrid.
Representations in art: *Apparel:* in the habit of the Order, with a long, belted skirt, scapular with blue-red cross on the front and coat (Salvator Church, Binabiburg, fresco c. 1750). *Attributes:* chain in his hands (St Salvator, district of Griesbach, fig. 1782); deer with crucifix in its antlers (Salvator Church, Binabiburg, fresco c. 1750); prisoners (Charles Bridge, Prague, fig. by F. M. Brokhoff, 1714). *Cycles:* in various museums, formerly in the OST Church, Madrid, painting by Vincente Carducho, 1632; St Gilles, Bruges, 18C painting by J. Garemijn.

John of Nepomuk

Patron saint of Bohemia, martyr, saint
Feast-day: 16th May
Life: * c. 1350 in Nepomuk (southern Bohemia), studied law in Prague and Padua; 1370, cleric and notary of the Prague court chancery; 1377 head of chancery, 1370 ordained, 1389 vicar-general of the archdiocese of Prague under bishop John of Jenzenstein; canon at St Vitus's; on the orders of King Wenceslas (Vaclav) he was tortured on the night of 20/21st March 1393 for reasons unknown and drowned in the river Vltava. Beatified 1721, canonized 1729.
Legends: a light announces J.'s birth. – The sick J. is cured by the Mother of God. – J. makes a pilgrimage to Altenbunzlau [Czech name?] and prays at the shrine. – In a sermon, J. condemns the cruelty of King Wenceslas/Vaclav. – J. hears the confession of the queen. – King Wenceslas/Vaclav gives J. the choice between the episcopal insignia and torture. – J. refuses to break the seal of confession for King Wenceslas/Vaclav. – J. is tortured with torches. – Thrown from the Vltava bridge, J.'s body is carried by the water

amid a brilliant light. – The Mother of God throws J. stars from her crown.

Patronage: patron saint of Bohemia; 2nd patron saint of the Jesuits; dedicatee of episcopal chapels in Brühl and Mirabell nr Salzburg; patron saint of bridges, the seal of confession, boatmen, raftsmen; invoked against the dangers of water transport and defamation.

Veneration and cult sites: tomb in St Vitus, Prague; 1719 tongue found intact, relics in numerous locations. Cult spread through Europe by the Bohemian aristocracy. Processions and floating lights in Bamberg, Passau, Heidelberg and Walten, South Tyrol.

Superstitions: stone Nepomuk tongues cure ailments of the tongue and protect from defamation. – Gt. variety of supernatural tales associated with bridge figures of St J.

Representations in art: *Apparel:* as a canon in rochet, soutane, amice or mozzetta, biretta (Alzenau Parish Church, altar fig. by J. P. Wagner 1769). *Attributes:* book (Prague Cathedral door, relief by G. Bendl 1620/30); crucifix, palm branch, crown of five stars (Prague, stone bridge, fig, model by M. Rauchmiller, 1683); clouds (Mautern, fig. by J. Th. Stammel 1740); contemplation of the Cross (Andechs, fig. by F. X. Schmadl 1755); crown of stars with "TACUI" (I was silent) in the centre (Bavarian National Museum, Munich, sketch by F. A. Zeiler c. 1750); tongue (Narodni Galeri, Prague, painting by A. Kern 1735/37); angel motioning for silence, and fish (Rotthalmunster, fig. by W. Jorhan 1730/40); seal, lock, key (Municipal Graphic Collection, Augsburg, copper engraving by Klauber, c. 1755); water (Vilshofen, fig. by E. Q. Asam c. 1746); personification of the Vltava (Freising Diocesan Museum, fountain fig. by J. B. Straub, 1751); bridge (Erding Museum of Local History, bridge fig. by Ch. Jorhan the Elder 1765); personification as an allegory of defamation (State Graphic Collection, Munich, drawing by G. B. Götz, c.

1750); in a ship (Neubeuern, processional mace of the boatmen's guild). *Special scenes:* J. at the Madonna of Altenbunzlau (St Stephan/Vienna, painting by M. J. Schmidt, 1722); J. hears the confession of the queen (Pinacoteca, Turin, 18C painting by Giuseppe M. Crespi); J. thrown from the bridge (St Peter, Vienna, group of sculptures by L. Matelli, 1729); Madonna throws stars from her crown to J. (Messkirch, Baden, painting by C. D. Asam 1738); J.'s body in brilliant light (Narodni Galeri, Prague, 18C painting by F. X. K. Palko); recovery of the body (St Thekla, Welden nr Augsburg, painting by F. Sigrist 1758/59); J. interceding and helping (new monastery church, Wiener Neustadt, 18C painting by P. Troger). *Cycles:* e.g. Lateran, Rome, painting by A. Massucci 1729; St Vitus Cathedral, Prague, tomb relief 1736; St John Nepomuk, Munich, frescoes by C. D. Asam, c. 1740.

John Nepomuk Neumann
Bishop, Redemptorist, saint
Feast-day: 5th January
Life: Born on 28th March 1811 at Prachatitz (Bohemia), JN. studied in Budweis and Prague. Due to an abundance of priests, he emigrated to the United States, where he was ordained priest in 1836, working at the North American mission for German emigrants near Buffalo. In 1840, JN. joined the Redemptorist Congregation and became a travelling mission-preacher in 1848. For his outstanding pastoral work he was consecrated bishop of Philadelphia in 1852 and had 100 churches and 80 Catholic schools built, as well as founding a seminar for priests. Worn out with his labours, JN. died on 5th January 1860. Beatification in 1963, and canonization in 1977.

Veneration and cult sites: Shrine in St Peter, Philadelphia; cult in the USA, Czech Republic and Germany, for instance, at the Catholic College community of Mainz. No representation in Art.

John and Paul of Rome

Martyrs, saints

Feast-day: 26th June

Legends: compilation from the legends of St Gallican of Ostia and the martyrdom of the officers Juventinus and Maximin in 363: the brothers J. and P. came from a noble family and served as palace officials to Constantia, the daughter of Constantine the Great. – J. and P. refuse to accept service under Julian the Apostate. – In 362, on Julian's orders J. and P. were secretly beheaded in their house on the Coelian Hill and their bodies buried. – Discovery of the bodies following the martyrdom of SS Crispin and Crispinian.

Patronage: patron saints of the weather, the main feature of this being the reading of the Gospel during the Stations of the Cross on the Friday after Ash Wednesday in their church in Rome (Mt. 5, 43–48): "The Lord makes his sun to rise on the evil and the good, and sends rain on the just and unjust." In addition, the feast coincides with the summer solstice, when prayers are said for protection against lightning, hail and the plague and for or against rain and sunshine.

Veneration and cult sites: a church was built over J. and P.'s house in Rome in the 4C; false relics in Rome, Venice, Veroli, Avignon, Tours, Vienna, Mittelzell (Reichenau) and Fulda; admitted to the Roman Canon of the Mass among the Communicant saints, in the All Saints' litany and weather blessings; stations church in Rome on Friday after Ash Wednesday; on SS J. and P.'s Day, black weather candles; Rogation procession since the 16C in which weather poles are carried bearing J. and P.'s portraits.

Superstitions: weather bells bearing pictures of J. and P. ward off lightning. – The other customs are more connected with the summer solstice than with the saints personally.

Representations in art: *Apparel:* as martyrs in long tunics, pallia (S Apollinare Nuovo, Ravenna, 6C mosaic); as ostiaries in court dress (Maria in Via Lata, Rome, late 9C fresco); as East Roman soldier saints (Monreale, 12C mosaic); in contemporary princely dress (Walchstadt, 15C fig.); as knights (Kirchdorf nr Bad Aibling, fig. 1619); as Roman soldiers (St Peter and Paul, Lienz, fig. c. 1510). *Attributes:* hand cross (Capella Palatina, Palermo, 12C mosaic); spear, shield, sword (Monreale, 12C mosaic); club, spear (Reichenau-Mittelzell, reliquary shrine, early 14C relief); palm branch (S Croce, Florence, Bardi Chapel, 16C painting by Giovanni del Biondo); halberd (Kirchdorf, fig. pre–1619); sword, cloud with lightning and rain cloud with hailstones (Margarethenberg, Alz, altar fig. c. 1750); sun and dark rain cloud (St Martin, Eugendorf nr Salzburg, high altar fig. 1683); key, laurel wreath, sword, palm tree (St Johann nr Kitzbühel, St Antony Chapel, fig. by Benedikt Faistenberger 1674); grain sheaf (art trade, 18C fig.). *Martyrdom:* Musée des Augustins, Toulouse, painting by Guercino 1632. *Cycle:* SS Giovanni e Paolo, Rome, frescoes c. 390.

Josaphat Kuncewycz of Polotsk

Archbishop, martyr, saint

Feast-day: 12th Nov

Life: * 1580 in Wlodzimierz (now Vladimir, Ukraine), the son of a town councillor, apprenticed to a merchant in Vilnius, 1604 admitted to Basilian Order, went over to the Ruthenian Church and its Roman rite, 1614 abbot in Vilnius, 1617 co-adjutor of the archbishop of Polotsk with right of succession, which succession took place a year later. Promoted union with the Roman Church, and was therefore hated by Orthodox Poles and nicknamed "robber of souls". 1623 killed horribly by a fanatical mob. Beatified 1643, canonized 1867.

Veneration and cult sites: Ruthenia, Vilnius, Lithuania.

Representations in art: Jesuit College, Vilnius, 17C portrait.

Joseph Calasanz

Founder of order, saint

Feast-day: 25th Aug (formerly 27th Aug).

Life: * 11th March 1556 at Peralta de la Sal (Aragon), theological studies and promotion, 1583 ordained, vicar-general of the see of Urgel, 1592 in Rome working for Cardinal Marcantonio Colonna; cared for the urban poor, esp. for their education, 1597 founded a free elementary school in the vicarage of S Dorothea in Trastevere; founded the Order of Piarists (Clerks Regular of the Christian Schools), 1617 recognised by the pope, 1621 after promulgation of the Order, he became its general. † 25th Aug 1648. Beatified 1748, canonized 1767.

Veneration and cult sites: body in S Pantaleone, Rome, highly venerated in the Piarist Order.

Representations in art: *Apparel:* in the habit of the Order with black talar (S Pantaleone, Rome, 16C painting by Giovanni Maria Morandi). *Attributes:* lily, mitre and cardinals' hat as a sign of honours refused (Archivio Hist. de la Ciudad, Barcelona, 19C copper engraving). *Special scenes:* the last communion of St J. (Piarist Church, Madrid, painting by Francisco Goya, 1819); vision of the Mother of God (Collegio Nazareno, Rome, 19C painting by P. Gagliardi).

Joseph of Nazareth

Foster-father of Christ, saint

Feast-day: 19th March (since 1621), 1st May Joseph the Labourer (since 1955)

Life: according to the New Testament, * of lineage of David, lived as a carpenter in Nazareth where he became engaged to Mary. When he wanted to break the engagement to Mary, an angel enlightened him in a dream. J. went to Bethlehem for a census and Christ was born there. J. fled to Egypt from Herod's Massacre of the Innocents, and after his return lived in Nazareth. Visited the Temple in Jerusalem with Jesus (then 12 years of age), returned to Nazareth, where Jesus was subject to his parents. No further mention during the public work of Jesus.

Legends: when Mary is 12, widowers of the town put sticks on the altar, and the owner of the stick which blooms takes Mary as his bride (variant in the proto-gospel of St James: a dove flies from J.'s stick). – J. becomes engaged to Mary (the 'sposalitio'). – Anne's scribe discovers Mary's pregnancy, gives J. and Mary water to prove them and sends them into the desert, whence they return unharmed. – J. searches for a midwife for the forthcoming birth. – When the child is born, Mary has to make a nappy from J.'s trousers. – Jesus helps J. in his workshop. – For further legends, see under Mary, Mother of God.

Patronage: patron saint of the Church (elevated in 1870 by Pope Pius IX) and labourers (since 1955 by Pope Pius XII); Mexico (1550), Philippines (1565), Canada (1624), Bohemia (1654), Bavaria (1663), Austria (1675), German Palatinate, Peru (1828); for a good death, chastity, people in Orders, marriage and family, orphans, inns, those seeking shelter, refugees, carpenters, woodcutters; patron saint of numerous brotherhoods and congregations.

Veneration and cult sites: cult promoted particularly by the Jesuits as the husband of Mary and foster-father of Christ (cf. the Jes-

uit invocation: Jesus – Mary – Joseph). Admitted to the Roman Canon Missae by Pope John XXIII. 1254 false relics (J.'s garments) brought back by crusaders to Joinville, since 1649 parts of them in Feuillant church, Paris and Chalons Cathedral, a ring of Joseph's in Perugia (brought from Jerusalem in the 11C), Semur-en-Auxois, Anchin, St Salvator Abbey and Notre Dame in Paris; staff in S Maria degli Angeli, Florence, further relics in S Alessio, Rome, Orvieto, Frascati. Earliest dedication 1074, oratory at Parma Cathedral. Expansion of the cult of St J. in the 18/19C.

Superstitions: On St J.'s Day, spring is in the air, so Bohemian children play ball for the first time in the year. In Upper Bavaria, dough is woven into St J. rings, to protect young girls' virginity. – St J. rings are carried by young married couples against unchaste temptations. – J. lilies and J. oil are used against swine erysipelas and skin burns.

Representations in art: *Apparel:* as a beardless young man (Dottighofen, early 15C fig.; in a long or medium-length robe with cloak and hat (Cologne Cathedral, mid–14C high altar table); in classical dress, often with belted tunic and pallium (Freiburg Cathedral, St Anne's altar, fig. c. 1520); as a craftsman with close-fitting leg garment, boots, short skirt and coat (St Laurentius Chapel, Freudenberg, epitaph 1650); as a Jew with Jewish hat (in Tree of Jesse portraits and depictions as a patriarch); with turban-like, Oriental headdress (Gemäldegalerie, Dahlem, Berlin, Flemish painting 1410–15); as a wine-grower (Limburg Cathedral, 13C fresco). *Attributes:* staff (Alte Pinakothek, Munich, 16C painting by Hans von Kulmbach); auger (Louvre, Paris, painting by Georges de La Tour); auger and axe (Dottighofen, late 15C fig.); saw (St Mary's Chapel, Cologne, fig. c. 1500); set square (Ferschnitz, fig. pre–1770); work bench (Gemäldegalerie, Dahlem, Berlin,

painting 1410/15); vine (Limburg (Lahn) Cathedral, 13C fresco); lily (Diocesan Museum, Cologne, late 15C braid trimming with embroidery); flowering stick (S Croce, Florence, 14C fresco by T. Gaddi); Christ-child on his arm (Landesmuseum, Mainz, fig. by Sebastian Pfaff, 2nd half of 18C); pilgrims' bottle at the belt (Kunsthalle, Hamburg, St Petri high altar, nativity by Master Bertram 1383); pilgrims' bottle in hand and biting a bread roll (loc. cit., Hamburg, the Flight into Egypt); bath jug (Udine Cathedral, 14C fresco by Vitale da Bologna); small basket with two doves (scene of Jesus in the Temple, counting redemption money (Hessisches Landesmuseum, Darmstadt, altar painting by Stephan Lochner 1447); stirring a bowl of porridge (Netze Parish Church, triptych, 1370/80); fanning embers (Landesmuseum, Hanover, Golden Panel 1410/18); with lamp (St Ludwig, Speyer, Bosweil altar, late 15C); with candle (S Maria Maggiore, Rome, relief by Mino da Fiesole, 2nd half of 15C). *Special scenes:* J.'s workshop (Tate Gallery, London, 19C painting by J. Millet); Jesus holds a candle for his father to work (Besançon Museum, painting by Georges de La Tour); J. washes and hangs clothes on a line (Old Masters Gallery, Dresden, 17C painting by F. Albani); J. removes his nether garment to cover the Christ-child (Ferdinandeum Museum, Innsbruck, painting c. 1370/72); Jesus on J.'s lap, playing with Mary (Convento del Angel Custodio, Granada, 18C painting by Alonso Cano); death of J. (Steierisches Landesmuseum, Graz, painting by P. Troger 1740); coronation of J. by Christ, a Jesuit analogy to the coronation of the Virgin (S Domenico Maggiore, Naples, painting by L. Giordano); Pius IX presents to J., as patron saint of the Church, a model of St Peter's (St Joseph, Speyer, stained glass 1914). *Cycles:* St Joseph, Grussau, late 17C frescoes by M. Willmann; Waldniel Church, early 20C stained glass by W. Brenner.

Jude (Thaddaeus)

Apostle, saint

Feast-day: 28th Oct (with St Simon), 19th June (Orthodox rite)

Life: mentioned in passing in the New Testament in Mk. 3, 18, Mt. 10, 3, Jo. 14, 22 and Acts 1, 13. The image of the apostle as a polemicist and powerful figure is derived from the last epistle in the New Testament, the General Epistle of St Jude, written by J.

Legends: J. is sent by Thomas to King Abgar of Edessa. In Abgar's presence, J.'s face gleams in divine light. – J. cures Abgar of leprosy by pressing to his face the letter sent by Jesus to Abgar. – J. preaches in Mesopotamia, Pontus and Persia. – Contrary to the prophesies of two sorcerers, J. makes the hostile army of Indians submit to the Persians without battle. – Using magic, sorcerers strike all the lawyers in the town dumb, but when J. holds a cross up to them, they are able to speak again. – J. sends serpents, which bite the magicians but suck out the poison again on J.'s orders so that the men are cured after three days. – J. tames two wild tigers that escape. – J. reveals the innocence of a deacon accused of fathering a maidservant's child, because at J.'s behest the baby confirms the innocence of the deacon but does not make reveal the maidservant's guilt. – J. suffers martyrdom by stoning and is clubbed to death.

Patronage: hopeless and difficult causes.

Veneration and cult sites: fake relics in St Peter's, Rome; cults in the church in the Hof zu den neuen Choren der Engel, Vienna, Dobling i. d. Krim, St Joseph in der Leimgrube (18C). Widespread dedications in parish and monastic churches since 19C.

Representations in art: *Apparel:* barefoot in long, belted tunic with pallium or cloak fastened at the breast (Orthodox Baptistry, Ravenna, mid–5C mosaic). *Attributes:* lance (Aachen Cathedral Treasury, apostle antependium c. 1481); club (Paderborn Cathedral, Westphalia Chapel, 1517); halberd (St Jakob, Straubing, late 15C stained glass); medallion of Christ (St Veit am Vorgau, Styria, fig. c. 1750); stones (St Ursula, Cologne, late 13C painting); sword (Rab, Dalmatia, enamel relief 1170); axe (Amiens, west door of Cathedral, fig. 1220/25); set-square (Kunsthistorisches Museum, Vienna, painting by A. van Dyck, 1st half of 17C); model of the city of Edessa (Rab, Dalmatia, enamel relief 1170); three sticks (Bamberg Museum, portable altar, c. 1170). *Special scenes:* casting down pagan idols (S Marco, Venice, 13th–14C mosaics); a serpent bites the sorcerers (S Staè, Venice, 18C painting by G. B. Mariotti); Abgar legend (Vich Museum, 15C painting by Luis Borrassas. *Martyrdom:* Austrian Gallery at the Belvedere/Vienna, painting by F. A. Maulpertsch, c. 1760).

Judoc

(Josse, Just, Joos, Jost, Jobst, Jox)
Pilgrim, saint

Feast-day: 13th Dec (11th June, 25th July translation feast)

Life: came from a noble, probably princely, Breton family, Founder of the Runiac hermitage, pilgrim to Rome. † c. 669. Nr the hermitage, the Benedictine monastery of St-Josse-sur-Mer was built.

Legends: A Breton prince like his elder brother who has joined a monastery, J. rejects power. – J. flees, and joins a group of pilgrims. – J. settles as a hermit in Runiac, where the fish and fowl he feeds become tame. – When Christ appears to him three times in the shape of a beggar, he divides his

bread until nothing is left. – J. recognizes Jesus, and sees through the window ships arriving with food. – During his pilgrimage to Rome, J. meets St Martin. – J. is often tempted by the Devil. – A snakebite drives J. from his hermitage. – During a mass, J. has a vision showing him the heavenly crown he will gain.

Patronage: pilgrims, sailors, infirmaries, the blind, bakers, parental duties and the blessing of children, pets, harvests, invoked against grain mites and other cereal pests, fire, plague and fever.

Veneration and cult sites: Benedictine abbey of St Josse-sur Mer, Premonstratensian monastery of St-Josse-sur-Bois, Prüm (Eifel) (9C); Walberberg (11C); cult spread from Brittany throughout Europe by Anglo-Saxon monks, particularly in the Moselle valley, Scandinavia and Switzerland.

Superstitions: A day of great import. On St J.'s Day, the harvest must be blessed against blight, lightning and hail. – In Switzerland, J. finds husbands for women.

Representations in art: *Apparel:* as a young pilgrim with hat (Hofkirche/Innsbruck, tomb of Maximilian, early 16C fig. by P. Godl); in allusion to James the Great (Palatine Historical Museum, Speyer, fig. 1462); as a cleric with biretta and abbot's crosier (Stockholm History Museum, 15C triptych); with crossed priest's stole under a pilgrim's coat (Salzburg Museum, late 15C fig.). *Attributes:* pilgrim's bag, pilgrim's staff, St James's shell, rosary (St Goar Protestant Church, mural 1469–1479); crown taken off and carried (late 15C engraving by Israhel van Meckenem the Younger); crown taken off, sceptre at his feet (Schweidnitz, retable 1492); crown on book (French Collection, New York, 16C tapestry); crown on arm (Our Lady, Bruges, late 15C painting by the Master of the Godelieve Legend); a crown at his feet and a crown in his hand as a symbol of the heavenly crown (Berne, privately owned early 16C painting); small ox, pig and sheep (Biever nr Trier, fig. 1750). *Cycles:* St Jost Chapel, Obergass, 15C mural; Stockholm History Museum, triptych, 15C predella reliefs.

Julian the Hospitaller

Penitent, saint

Feast-day: 29th Jan

Legends: following the classical Oedipus myth, interwoven with motifs from the Christopher and Eustace Legends: * in the 7C in Ath, Belgium (var: of Spanish descent). – A deer foretells to J. that he will kill his parents. – J. flees his home to make this crime impossible and marries the daughter of a baron abroad. – When J. is out hunting, his parents come to his house, and J.'s wife offers them the marital bed for the night. – J. thinks he has discovered his wife in flagrante and kills the guests. – When J. recognizes his mistake, he does penance and builds a hospice in the Gard in Provence. – One night, J. carries a leper over the river, who reveals himself as Christ.

Patronage: ferrymen, boatmen, fishmongers, carpenters, tilers, inns, travellers, pilgrims.

Veneration and cult sites: S Giuliano, Flemish church in Rome; false relics in S Giuliano, Florence, arm relic in Macerata.

Representations in art: *Apparel:* as a young aristocrat with biretta and ermine (S Spirito/Florence, painting by Maso di Banco, 1st half of 14C); with cape (S Elisabetta/Barga, late 14C painting); as a nobleman (English art trade, painting by Perugino); as a soldier (Jarves College, New Haven, 15C painting by A. Gaddi); as a pilgrim (Flemish Hospice of St Julian, Rome, 18C fig. by C. F. Pevcke; as a penitent (SS Annunziata, Florence, fresco by Andrea del Castagno, c. 1555); as a falconer on horseback (Museo del Seminario, Lerida, painting by J. Ferrer II, 2nd half of 15C). *Attributes:* sword (Museo, Empoli, terracotta

by the della Robbia workshop); falcon (Salemi, Sicily, fig. by Francesco Laurana c. 1470); angel (Museo Civico, S Gimignano, 15C painting by the St Julian master); sailing boat and oar (St-Remacle-au-Pont, Liège, 16C fig.). *Special scenes:* J's murder of his parents (Alte Pinakothek, Munich, painting of the A Gaddi school); *Cycles:* mainly stained glass in French cathedrals, e.g., Chartres, stained glass, c. 1220; Rouen, stained glass, late 13C (this window inspired Flaubert's novel on Julian); Trento Cathedral, 14C frescoes; Collegium Castiglione, Florence, predella by B. della Gatta, 1468, and portrait of J. carrying Christ; S Maria Maggiore, Rome, Uffizi, Florence and Musée Ingres, Montauban: altar painting and predella by Masolino de Panicale.

Juliana of Nicodemia

Virgin, martyr, saint

Feast-day: 21st Feb (eastern Church rite: 21st Dec)

Life: martyred in 305 under Diocletian.

Legends: J. rejects the pagan judge Eulogius as a husband. – She suffers martyrdom by being stripped naked and beaten with sticks. – Molten lead is poured over her head before she is thrown into prison. – Disguised as an angel, the Devil tries to persuade J. to make a pagan sacrifice. – J. throws the Devil to the floor and thrashes him the chain she is bound with. – J. takes the Devil with her to execution and throws him into a latrine on the way. – J. is stretched on the wheel, which an angel destroys. – J. is put into a cauldron full of hot lead but remains unharmed. – In the end she is beheaded. – The judge who sentences J. drowns on a ship with 30 people.

Patronage: patron saint of Italian Cistercian convents, invoked against temptations and the wiles of the Devil.

Veneration and cult sites: relics in Pozzuoli, 568 taken to Cumae to escape the Lombard

invasion, on 25th Feb 1207 transferred to Naples. Other relics, e.g. in Santillana del Mar, pre–1376 head relic now in Metropolitan Museum, New York.

Representations in art: *Apparel:* as a martyr in robe with deep folds and fastened tight at top (Bankau Protestant Church, retable painting, 2nd half of 14C); as a patron saint with protective cloak sheltering Cistercians (Pinacoteca, Perugia, fresco 1376). *Attributes:* martyr's crown on a cloth (Januarius catacomb, Naples, 9/10C fresco); hand cross (S Giuliana, Perugia, 13C fresco); Devil held by angels with chain (Worms Cathedral, late 12C choir pier); Devil in chains (Kunsthistorisches Museum, Vienna, early 17C painting by Domenico Fetti); whip to beat the Devil (Havelberg Cathedral, choir screen relief, 2nd half of 14C); open book (S Juliana, Vigo di Fassa, early 16C fig.); palm tree and book (Santillana del Mar, 18C fig.); dove (Siones nr Burgos, 12C relief); sword, whip, palm tree (Graphische Sammlung, Munich, 16C copper engraving by J. Sadeler after Marten de Vos); lily (Pinacoteca, Siena, painting in the Lorenzetti manner). *Martyrdom:* Landesmuseum/Stuttgart, Stuttgart Passional, book illumination c. 1130; Heiligenkreuz Abbey Library, Cod. 11, book illumination c. 1190; Pinacoteca, Perugia, 14C fresco; Musée du Château, Sceaux, 16C fig. *Cycles:* S Giuliana, Livorno, painting influenced by Cimabue, 1295/1305; Santillana del Mar, Collegium, 15C painting.

Julitta and Cyricus

(Quiricus, Cyr, Cyriacus, Cerdre, Cergue, Querido) of Tarsus or Antioch
Martyrs, saints
Feast-day: 16th June, 30th June (eastern Church rite 13th or 15th July).
Legends: J. and C. come from Iconium, where the mother and her three-year-old son flee from the persecution of Christians. – J.

and C. are arrested in Tarsus. – J. and C. refuse to renounce Christianity. – J. and C. are roasted over a fire but the fire goes out. – In prison, J. and C. are visited and comforted by Christ. J. has a nail hammered into her head but an angel helps her. – J. is beaten with straps in front of C., wherepon C. scratches the judge's face with his nails and bites him on the shoulder. – From his throne, the judge throws C. to the floor, where he dies. – J. is flayed alive and hot tar poured over her body. – J. is beheaded (var: C. exclaims that he is a Christian too, and is tortured and killed like J., by dismemberment).

Patronage: doctors (only in eastern rite, esp. Epirus, Castoria).

Veneration and cult sites: false relics in the cathedrals of Nevers and Burgos; local veneration in Florence and Toulouse.

Representations in art: *Apparel:* J. and C. as orants (S Maria Antiqua, Rome, fresco, 1st half of 8C); J. with C. in her arms (Barcelona, 12C antependium). *Attributes:* hand cross, crown (Monreale Cathedral, 12C mosaic); dagger, nails, saw (Barcelona, 15C painting by P. Garcia). *Cycles:* Museo de Arte de Cataluna, Barcelona, 12C antependium; Issoudun Abbey, 15C stained glass. For individual portraits of C., see Cyricus.

Justin the Philosopher

Martyr, saint
Feast-day: 1st June
Life: came from a Greek family in Flavia Neapolis (Nablus) in Palestine, † c. 165, considered the most important writer of Apologies of the 2C. Repelled by Stoic philosophy, he turned to the ideas of Plato, but was in the end convinced of the inadequacy of all philosophies and became a Christian, powerfully defending Christian beliefs. In his Apologies he refutes the accusations laid against Christianity and justifies the content of

Christian teaching. In the dialogue with Trypho, a Jewish scholar (probably Rabbi Tarphon), J. shows that Jewish ceremonial law has only transitional validity, that worshipping Jesus is not a contradiction of monotheism and that pagans too are called to Christ. The disputation underlying the writings must have been conducted during the Bar-Kochba uprising (132–135).

Veneration and cult sites: S Pudenziana/ Rome (grave presumed there).

Representation in Art: J. hands over his Apology to the Emperor Hadrian (copper engraving by J. Callot 1636).

L

Ladislas of Hungary

("László", Ladislaus, Ladislav) king, saint
Feast-day: 29th July (before the calendar reform 27th June)
Life: * circa 1040 as the son of King Béla I of Hungary and the Polish Duchess Ryksa. 1077 proclaimed king after the death of his brother, but did not allow himself to be crowned. L. had to deal with rebellious dukes and uprisings, such as 1063 with the deposed King Salomon, with whom L. could be reconciled for a short time, but who sought the aid of Emperor Henry IV to recover power. L. fought against the heathen Cumans, who ravaged the land in 1071/72. Eventually L. was able to restore order through harsh laws. L. supported the Pope against Henry IV in the conflict over investiture. 1090 foundation of the Bishopric Agram (Zagreb) in Croatia, 1091 victory over the Petchenegens and removal of the ravaged bishop's seat of Bihar, which Stephan I had founded, to Groawardein. † 29th July 1095 near Neutra. Canonised 1192.
Veneration and cult sites: body in Nagyvrad in the Cathedral Szüs Mária, which he founded, reliquary (bust reliquary) in the Cathedral of Györ 1192, reliquaries in Zagreb and Dubrovnik.
Representation in Art: *Apparel:* as knight in king's cloak (Zdigra, parish church, mural, circa 1270/80); as rider (Eger, Cathedral, painting, by J. L. Kracker, 1773). *Special scenes:* L. commits his wife and children to the Mother of God (Budapest, Szépmüveszeti Museum, painting, by B. Strigel, circa 1511/12). *Attributes:* crown, sceptre, Imperial orb (Siegendorf, parish church, figure, 17th century); halberd (Budapest, Szépmüveszeti Museum, painting, by B. Strigel, circa 1511/12). *Cycles:* include Zigra parish church, mural, 14th century; Bögöz parish church, mural, circa 1300; Gelence, mural, circa 1320/30; Bántorny frescoes, by J. of Aquila, 1383; Pozsony chapel of the Archbishop's Palace, frescoes, by F. A. Maulpertsch, 1781.

Lambert of Maastricht

Bishop, martyr, saint
Feast-day: 18th September (before the calendar reform 17th September, translation feast 31st May)
Life: * 2nd quarter 7th century; as bishop involved in the party political fight of his time. After the death of King Childeric L. was driven out by the majordomo, Ebroin and spent seven years in the monastery at Stablo as exile. After his recall by King Pepin, L.'s followers killed two men, who had profaned church property. For this Dodo took blood revenge and had L. killed in Liège.

Legend: L. is brought up by Landoald. – The young L. brings water out of the ground with a switching rod. – L. is commanded by the superior of the Order to bring burning coals. – the young L. carries the coals to the altar in the lap of his choir shirt. – When L. accidentally makes a noise at night, the culprit is called upon by the Abbot to go to the Cross, which L. obediently does. – L. feeds the poor. – L. drives a demon out. – St Landrada appears to L. and shows her burial place. – L. makes representations to Pepin about adulterous relations with Alpais. – L. refuses to say a blessing over Pepin's wine. – L. is woken from sleep by Baldevous as his bloodhound approaches and approaches him with incantations. – Demons fall upon L.'s murderers and they kill each other.

Patronage: Carolingian House, Salier; town patron of Arnoldstein, Seeburg (Mansfeld), Seeon, Liège, Freiburg, Lambrecht (Palatinate), Oldenburg; the lame, those with eye diseases, farmers, surgeons, wound-dressers, dentists, woodcutters of Antwerp, linen weavers of Wachtendonk, masons of Maastricht; against epilepsy, cramp, at need in birth, cattle fever.

Veneration and cult sites: In Liège a church at the place of his martyrdom, body taken first to Maastricht, brought back to Liège by Bishop Hubert when his seat was moved, destroyed there 1794 during the French Revolution. Head relic in Freiburg Cathedral (since late 12th century).

Superstition: In Münster the eggs of hens are presented for L.'s favour. – Also a popular day of games with L. games, L. dance and L. nuts as a feast day gift.

Representation in Art: *Apparel:* as bishop in Pontifical robes with chasuble (Stablo, Remaclus' Shrine, figure, 1266); as bishop in chasuble with rational (Brussels, Museum of Art and History, figure, late 15th century); as bishop in pluvial (Waldfeucht, parish church, figure, end 15th century); as knight

Early Christian saints and popes

42   *SS Vincent, James the Great and Eustace, by Antonio Pollaiolo, Florence, Uffizi*

43/44   *St Agnes and St Cecila, detail from a painting by the Master of the St Bartholomew Altar, Munich, Alte Pinakothek*

45   *St Martin, illumination from the Ambrosian Missal, Milan, Bibliotheca Braidense*

46   *SS Elmo (Erasmus) and Maurice, by Matthias Grünewald, Munich, Alte Pinakothek*

47   *Adoration of the Trinity by Pope Clement I, by G. Tiepolo, Munich, Alte Pinakothek*

48   *Pope Leo repelling the Huns, relief by Alessandro Algardi, Rome, St Peter's*

49   *Shrine of St Quirinus, Neuss cathedral, Germany*

42

43

45

47

48

49

in armour and boots with pluvial on top (Malines, St Rombaut, painting, by J. B. le Saive, 1624); as Benedictine in pluvial (Lille, Museum of Fine Arts, painting, by B. Flémalle, 17th century); in gown and monk's scapular and cap (Parike, St Lambert, pulpit, figure, circa 1700); in fantastic garments (Heist-op-den-Berg, pulpit, reliefs, by G. I. Kerricx, 1737). *Attributes:* mitre, staff on floor (Lille, Museum of Fine Arts, painting, by B. Flémalle, 17th century); hand-sized cross (Stablo, Remaclus' Shrine, figure, 1266); sword with blade upwards (Kassel, State Art Collection, pilgrim's drawing, relief, 15th century); dagger with point on hand (Tondorf, Eifel, figure, 18th century); arrow (Ellingen, Luxembourg, St Lambert, relief, 18th century); model of church (Coesfeld, St Lambert, figure, 15th century); knotted cloth, coming out of flames (Louvain, Bollandisten, incunabulum, wood engraving, 1499); cowering man held down by the tip of the bishop's staff (Affeln, figure, 16th century); two men with helmet and sword stretched out (Bure, St Lambert, figure, 17th century); one man at feet (Liège, Hospital of Bavire, painting, 1641); half raised man (Hasselt, Our Beloved Lady, figure, 17th century). *Special scenes:* Mass of St L. (Kempen, Collegiate Church, Anthony's Altar, figure, circa 1520); L. is crowned by Mar (Ste-Foye, parish church, painting, 17th century); L. carries burning coals (Ostercappeln, baptismal font, relief, 12th century); L. carries coals in garment bolster (Gent, St Bavo, painting, by P. van Huffel, 1808); L. prays barefoot before the Cross at night in Stablo (Parike, St Lambert, pulpit, figure, circa 1700). *Martyrdom:* L. is killed with an arrow by a murderer (Stuttgart, State Library, passional, illumination, 12th century); L. is killed before the altar (Bockenheim (Palatinate), branchwork font, relief, circa 1500); angel brings L. the palm of victory (Woluwe-St-Lambert, painting, by T. van Loon, circa 1616). *Cycles:* Trier Cathe-

S. LAMBERTE / ORA PRO NOBI

dral, choir stalls, mural, 13th century; Treuchtlingen parish church, painting, by Master Hans, early 16th century; Liège St Paul's, bust reliquary, reliefs, by Hans of Reutlingen; 1512; Lige St Martin's, stained glass, 16th century; Affeln St Lambert's, painting, 16th century.

Lawrence of Brindisi

(Laurentius, Giulio Cesare Russo) Capuchin, Doctor of the Church, saint

Feast-day: 21st July

Life: * 22nd July 1559 Brindisi; studied as one-parent child and oblate with the Convent Franciscans, 1575 entered the Capuchin convent in Venice. Exegetical studies with knowledge of Hebrew, 1582 consecrated priest, gifted preacher, 1590–1592 Provincial in Tuscany, 1594–1596 in Venice, 1598 in Switzerland, 1613–1616 in Genoa, Definitor General of the Order 1596, 1599, 1613, 1618. L. instigated the Capuchin Order in Germany and Austria, founder of the Capuchin monastery in Vienna 1600. L. played a great part in the victory at Stuhlweissenburg against the Turks on 11th October 1601, as L. had the task of calling the army together. L. took part in the campaign as chaplain. L. helped Maximilian I of Bavaria to impose church law in Donauwörth 1607 and at the formation of the League of Catholic Princes of Germany for the preservation of the peace in the Imperial lands and the protection of the Catholic religion. † on a diplomatic mission in Lisbon 22nd July 1619. Beatified 1783, canonised 1881, Doctor of the Church since 1959. – His works consist mainly of sermons, in Mariology building up the principle of the Motherhood of God consistently carried out.

Patronage: the Capuchin Orders.

Veneration and cult sites: buried in Villafranca de Bierzo, north-west Spain.

Representation in Art: *Apparel:* as Capuchin in typical dress of the Order (Koblenz-Ehrenbreitstein, Capuchin church, painting, 18th century); drying the tears with his own handkerchief (Antwerp, archives of the Capuchins, drawing, by M. Snejders, 17th century). *Attributes:* picture of Mary, book, death's head (Antwerp, archives of the Capuchins, drawing, by M. Snejders, 17th century); quill pen, book, death's head, angels' heads (Rome, Museum Francescano, OFM Cap., copper engraving, by Garofalo, 1783); crucifix, lily, angel with crown (Koblenz-Ehrenbreitstein, Capuchin church, painting, 18th century). *Special scenes:* L. in the battle of Stuhlweissenburg (Vatican Museum, painting, by F. Grandi, 1882); L. is sent to Germany by Pope Paul V (Forli, Capuchin church, painting, by P. Randi, 19th century); L. as Nuncio with Maximilian I (Rome, Museum Francescano, OFM Cap., engraving, by A. Gregori, 19th century); L. heals sick (Forli, St Mary del Fiore, painting, by P. Randi, 19th century).

Lawrence of Rome

(Laurentius) deacon, martyr, saint
Feast-day: 10th August

Ecclesiastical background: Cyprian of Carthage remarked in his 80th letter, that on the 6th June 258 Pope Sixtus II and four deacons were martyred. In the mid 4th century there was already a tradition, which had L. as the Archdeacon of Pope Sixtus, who was executed a few days after the Pope.

Legend: L. is born in Spain and discovered by Pope Sixtus on his journey to the council at Toledo (which took place in 589!) and brought to Rome. – As Archdeacon L. carries out innumerable good works. – L. washes the feet of the poor. – L. heals the virgin Cyriaca of her headaches. – L. and Sixtus together destroy the temple of the god Mars. – When Pope Sixtus is to be executed for his faith, he gives the responsibility for the church's money and valuables to L. – The Emperor has L. arrested and commands him to hand over the enormous church treasure. – L. asks for three days, in which he gives the wealth of the church to the needy. – Then L. comes with a great crowd of poor, blind and sick before the Emperor and presents these as the imperishable treasure of the church. – The Emperor, who feels he has been deceived, has L. whipped with lead lumps and beaten with cudgels, finally laid on a grill and held there with iron forks. – After a while L. tells the Emperor that one side is done, now he must be turned. – The horrified Emperor turns away and L. dies. – After his translation to heaven L. descends every Friday into Purgatory to free a soul. – During the weighing of souls by Michael, L. saves the soul of Henry II by placing on the scale of good works a chalice, which the Emperor had donated on the death bed of St Lawrence.

Patronage: National saint of Spain (since Philip II, who had the Escorial laid out in a grid form in honour of L.); the poor souls in Purgatory, schoolchildren, students, poor, administrators, librarians (as administrator of the church's books!), all professions which are involved with fire, such as brewers, firemen, glaziers, cooks, bakers, launderers, innkeepers, vintners; against burning, lumbago, fever.

Veneration and cult sites: L. Feast was celebrated as early as 354, grave in Rome in the Coemeterium on the Via Tiburtina, with the Basilica of S Lorenzo fuori le Mura built over it; bones raised in 1447; in Rome a further 5 churches with patronage of L. Relics in Florence St Lawrence's (head), Rome S Lorenzo in Luzina (cuttings from the grid). In Germany the victory over the Hungarians on the Lechfeld on 10th August 955 is ascribed to L. Numerous pilgrimages, including one up the Laurenziberg near Gau-Algesheim.

Superstition: Decisive day for the weather in the coming autumn. On L. day great efforts to protect the harvest and plantings from fire. – Shooting stars in August are called L.'s tears, because even heaven itself weeps over the martyrdom of L. In folk medicine there is the L. blessing against burning and burns.

Representation in Art: *Apparel:* like the Apostles in white pallium cloak (Ravenna, Mausoleum of Galla Placida, mosaic, 5th century); as deacon with dalmatic (Rome, S Lorenzo fuori le Mura, mosaic, 6th century); as sub-deacon with maniple (Fasano, SS Lorenzo, crypt, fresco, 11th century); as deacon with stole (Cefal, Cathedral, mosaic, 12th century); with sudarium (Atri, Cathedral, fresco, by A. Delitio, dating?). *Attributes:* crosier, book, open cupboard with Gospels, grid (Ravenna, Mausoleum of Galla Placidia, mosaic, 5th century); book (Perugia, Fontana Maggiore, figure, 13th century); rotulus (Vatican Museum, gold glass, 5th century);

chalice filled with gold pieces (Paris, Louvre, painting, by the Lorenzo Monaco school, 15th century); purse (Schwimmbach, Franconia, painting, circa 1510); palm, scroll (Montecassino, Chiesa della Assunta, painting, by G. da Recanati, 15th century); grid (St Petersburg, hermitage, painting, by F. Zurbarán, 1636); persecutor under the grid (Syracuse, Museo Bellomo, painting, by Master of St Martino, 14th century); liturgical items of the Eastern Church (Monreale, Cathedral, mosaic, 12th century). *Special scenes*: L. distributes the church treasure (Venice, St Nicolò da Tolentino, painting, by B. Strozzi, 17th century); L. in Purgatory to free poor souls (Porciano, S Lorenzo, painting by D. di Michelino, 15th century); the weighing of Emperor Henry's soul (Florence, S Maria Novella, painting, by A. di Orcagna, 14th century). *Martyrdom*: L. is bound to the gallows and burnt with torches (Berching, church, painting, circa 1515); L. is whipped with hooks (Lau, S Lorenzo, painting, by P. Aertsen, 17th century); L. is burnt on the grid (Venice, Jesuit church, painting, Titian, 1548/57). *Cycles*: numerous, including Bourges cathedral, stained glass, 13th century; Fabriano church, fresco, by A. Nuzi, 14th century; Castiglion d'Olona, frescoes, by M. da Panicale, 15th century; Vatican City, Cappela Niccolina, frescoes, by Br. Angelico, 15th century; Munich Alte Pinakothek, L. Altar, painting, by M. Pacher, 1462/63.

Leo the Great
Pope, Doctor of the Church, saint

Feast-day: 10th November (before the calendar reform 11th April, in the Greek Rite 17th or 18th February).

Life: L. came from Tuscany and was Archdeacon under Pope Coelestin, 440 successor to Sixtus III; L. was not only the protector of orthodoxy, but also of true occidental culture in the western half of the empire. L. journeyed to Attila, the King of the Huns, and persuaded him to turn back. 455 L. obtained from Geiseric protection from burning and murder for the city of Rome, but could not prevent the plundering. – L. fought chiefly against the Pelagians, Manicheans and Priscillians, whose heresies he refuted in a didactic writing. 449 refutation of the monophysite teaching of Eutyches; his writing formed the basis of the Doctrine of the Twin Nature, as set down at the Council of Chalcedon 451. † 10th November 461. Designation Doctor of the Church 1754.

Legend: L. places a letter, which he has written against Flavian and other heretics, on the grave of Peter, with the prayer for corresponding correction. In vision Peter tells him what he has changed and improved.

Patronage: Musicians, singers.

Representation in Art: *Apparel:* in tunic with pallium (Rome, St Mary Antiqua, mural, 7th/8th century); as bishop of the Orthodox Rite with phelonion, stricharion, epitrachelion and omophorion (Palermo, Palatine Chapel, mosaic, 12th century); as Pope in Papal vestments with tiara (Chartres, Cathedral, Confessor's Portal, figure, 1215/20); as Pope in pluvial with threefold tiara (Kloster Andechs, Holy Altar, painting, 1495); as Pope riding (Vatican City, Stanza d'Elidoro, fresco, by Rafael, 1512). *Attributes:* book (Stuttgart, State Library, Cod. hist 2x415, illumination, 12th century); lunula with host (Kloster Andechs, Holy Altar, painting, 1495). *Special scenes:* L. goes against Attila and shows him the Apostle princes protecting Rome (Rome, St Peter's, relief, 1648); Eudoxia brings L. the chains of Peter (Vienna, Austrian National Library, Cod. 444, illumination, 12th century); Mary heals L.'s hand after he had struck it to resist the temptation to unchastity (Dublin, Museum, painting, by Antonezzo Romano [?]).

S. LEO IX P. O. M.

32

S. Leonardus Abbas Ord. S. Ben.

Misit me prædicare captivis remissionem Luc. 4. 18.

C.P.S.C.M.   Ios. et Ioa. Klauber Cath. Sc. et exc. A.V.

Leonard of Noblac

Abbot, confessor, saint

Feast-day: 6th November

Life: * probably in 6th century. Supposed to have founded a cell in St-Léonard-de Noblac near Limoges.

Legend: according to the Vita of 1030 from a distinguished Frankish family under the Merovingian Chlodwig. – L. is educated and baptised by Bishop Remegius of Reims. – L. declines an office at the court and begins a life as a hermit and missionary. – L. helps Queen Chlotilde give birth when the birth pains come unexpectedly while her husband is away hunting. – As a reward L. does not ask for money but a piece of woodland, where he can serve God far away from the treasures of the world. – L. has a well dug, which fills with water at his prayer. – Whatever prisoner calls upon L. is freed from his chains; many bring them to him as a votive gift. – L. drives out a devil. – L. frees a prisoner, who has been chained in a grave by a tyrant and is watched by armed guards; the house collapses and buries the guards.

Patronage: farmers, miners, coopers, butter traders, drivers, hammer-smiths, copper-smiths, coal carriers, load carriers, fruit dealers, locksmiths, smiths, stable boys, women in labour, prisoners, horses, cattle.

Veneration and cult sites: numerous places of pilgrimage such as Inchenhofen (14th/15th century), Aigen am Inn, Dietramszell, Ganacker, Tamsweg; horse rites and cattle blessings (Tölz, Siegertsbrunn, Fischhausen).

Superstition: rich in customs, including: as votive offerings iron cattle are given to L. In Ramsach (Zillertal) virgins net their hair with water from the font of the L. Church to protect their cattle from plague. – In Gaishof horses are led round the church three times on L. day and their heads pushed through a hole in the church wall. – In Aigen L. logs serve as a test of strength and conscience.

Representation in Art: *Apparel:* as abbot in well pleated wide-sleeved woollen garment, large cowl and biretta (Möllbrücken, St L., painting, 16th century); as Abbot in pontifical dress (Wismar, St George's, painting, 15th century); as Abbot in pontifical dress with pluvial without mitre (Würzburg, Cathedral, figure, 14th century); in pontifical dress with mitre (Rothenburg, St Jacob's, figure, by F. Herlin, 1466); as deacon in dalmatic (New Haven, dossal, circa 1265); as knight (Palermo, Palatine Chapel, mosaic, 12th century); robe half black, rest serrated pattern (Loreto, St Casa, fresco, late 15th century); in secular clothing (Forst, fresco, by M. Günther, 18th century). *Attributes:* book (Paris, Louvre, figure, beg. 16th century); prison chains (Inchenhofen, Pilgrimage Church, figure, circa 1755); cow (Paitzkofen, figure, 17th century); horse (Untereching near Salzburg, figure, 17th century); prisoner in stocks (Junkersdorf, fresco, circa 1450); prisoner at feet (Zug, painting, by P. Lorenzetti, 14th century); shepherd's crook (Obergrafendorf, figure, end 15th century). *Special scenes:* L. drives out a devil (Bad Aussee, L.'s Chapel, painting, mid 15th century). *Cycles:* numerous, including: Amiens Cathedral, stained glass, 13th century; Regensburg Cathedral, stained glass, 1365; Zickenberg, Carinthia St L. mural, circa 1400; Linz museum, L. Altar, reliefs, 16th century; Inchenhofen Pilgrimage Church, fresco, by I. Baldauf, 18th century.

Louis IX the Saint

King of France, saint

Feast-day: 25th August

Life: * 25th April 1214 in Poissy as son of King Louis VIII and Blancas of Castille, crowned aged 11 in 1226. As Regent for many years his mother brought him up to a rigorous life of prayer under the influence of Spanish mystic asceticism. 1230 married

Marguerite of Provence. The dominant factors in his Life: love of peace, love of neighbour, industry, simplicity and crusading spirit, led to a reorganisation of the administration, which was strictly controlled. Through the reform of the money system and the foundations of trade, L. made France's kingdom the most powerful in Europe. 1257 through the donation of the Aluminates, played important paint in the foundation of the Sorbonne. L. encouraged the mendicant Orders, founded hospitals and sought to defend the King's right over the bishops. 1243/48 building of the Sainte Chapelle in Paris for the relics obtained from Constantinople. 1248–54 7th crusade, on which L. was taken prisoner and had to pay a high ransom to regain freedom. 1250–1254 in Palestine, 1267 new crusade, on which he died on 25th August 1270 of a fever which had broken out in the army before Tunis. Canonisation 1297.

Patronage: Orders bearing his name, the 3rd Order of St Francis, scientists, barbers, the blind, bakers, builders, bookbinders, printers, brush binders, fishermen, hairdressers, plasterers, farriers, tradesmen, button makers, linen sellers, embroiderers, pilgrims, tailors, quarrymen, wallpaperers, weavers, carpenters; against blindness, loss of hearing.

Veneration and cult sites: muscle parts in Monreale, in 19th century in Tunis, skeleton in St Denis, 1308 numerous relics; first church patronage in 1298 in Garches; all French ambassadorial chapels throughout the world have L. as Name Saint; venerated in Germany since 17th century, in 19th century building of St Louis' Church in Munich by King Ludwig I of Bavaria.

Representation in Art: *Apparel:* as king with crown and collared wide sleeved over-garment (Kamenz, Saxony, Lutheran monastery church, figure, 1513); in straight cowled cloak with slits for the arms (Paris, National Library, MS fr. 5716, illumination, beg. 14th century); in coronation robe with fleurs de lys (Dijon, town library, MS. 568, illumination, circa 1260); in king's robe as chasuble-like wrap, fastened at the side with a fibula (Paris, Provincial Archives of the Capuchins, wood cut, by L. Gaultier, 16th century); rearwards falling parade cloak over a tunic (example in the catalogue 'The France of Saint Louis', Paris, 1970, fig. 212); short cloak with fur collar and shoulder pelerines (Paris, Provincial Archives of the Capuchins, copper engraving, by J. C. Guttwein, 18th century); in armour covered by magnificent robe (Paris, Provincial Archives of the Capuchins, copper engraving, by J. C. Guttwein, 18th century); in Franciscan habit with king's robe over (Paris, National Library, Arms Book of Guillaume d'Auvergne, illumination, 15th century); in Franciscan habit (Montefalco, fresco, by B. Gozzoli, 15th century); in dress of the Dominican Order (Poissy, Dominican Convent, wood cut, 1755).

Attributes: sword, lance crown, sceptre carried by angels (Paris, Provincial Archives of the Capuchins, copper engraving, by J. C. Guttwein, 18th century); hunting bird (ivory figure from the back of a mirror, 14th century, shown by the Circle of St Louis, Paris, 1970, fig. 8); Imperial orb (Assisi, St Francis, Martin's Chapel, fresco, by S. Martini, before 1344); ring (illumination, 2nd half 13th century, example in the catalogue 'The France of Saint Louis', Paris, 1970, fig. 148); lily (royal seal of 1330, shown by the Circle of St Louis, Paris, 1970, fig. 1); three lilies in shield (Grisaille, illumination, by J. Pucelle, 1325/28); five lilies (Vienna, St Stephen's, choir stalls, figure, 15th century); a nail (Würzburg, Cathedral, figure, 1662); relic of the Cross (Paris, National Library, Ms fr. 5716, illumination, circa 1330/40); crown of thorns (Senlis, Cathedral, figure, 14th century); crown of thorns with nails round (Munich, Theatine Church, figure, circa 1680);

opens prison doors (Paris, Palace of Justice, painting, by O. Merson, 19th century); L. gives alms (Paris, Louvre, painting, by L. Tristan, 17th century); L. touches the scrofulous (Paris, Les Invalides, relief, by p. Magnier, 18th century); L. barefoot in procession with the crown of thorns (Paris, Les Invalides, relief, by J. van Cleve, 18th century); lily miracle when the Cistercian Abbot of Les Vaux-de-Cernay greets L. and his wife (Versailles, Chapel of the Petit Trianon, painting, 18th century); St Francis presents L. and Elizabeth of Thuringia the statutes of the Third Order (Volterra, St Girolamo, relief, by A. della Robbia, end 15th century); vision of L. with the Child Jesus (Madrid, Prado, painting, by C. Coello, 17th century). *Cycles:* very numerous, including: Paris Ste-Chapelle, Under Church, painting, 14th century; Paris National Library, MS fr. 5716, illumination with 24 scenes, circa 1330/40; Paris, Panthéon, mural, by Cabanel, 19th century.

Lucia of Syracuse

virgin, martyr, saint

Feast-day: 13th December

Life: martyr, no certain testimony.

Legend: according to the Passio of the 5th/6th century, L. lived in Syracuse during the persecutions of Diocletian. L. is engaged when she accompanies her sick mother to the grave of St Agatha and implores healing for the sick. – Agatha appears, heals the mother and informs L. of her martyrdom. – At this L. gives her goods to the poor and renounces the marriage (variant: L. tears out her beautiful eyes so that they can never again seduce a man and sends them to her fiancé). – The disappointed groom denounces her as Christian. – L. remains true to the faith before the court. – L. is to be brought to a brothel, but her body becomes so heavy that even the strength of several oxen is not enough to move her from the spot. – The at-

nails interwoven in the crown of thorns with covering cloth (Plougastel-Daoulas, St Gunol, figure, 17th century); hand cross (Bergamo, Pinacoteca dell'Accademia Carrara, painting, by Borgognone, 15th century); laurel wreath (Innsbruck, lithograph, by J. Grader, circa 1820); model of church of Sainte Chapelle (Paris, Louvre, figure, circa 1370); hand of judgement (Lyons, town library, Missal, illumination, 1340/50); belt of the Third Order (Florence, Bardi Chapel, fresco, by Giotto, before 1337); book (Paris, Museum of Cluny, figure, end 13th century); flagellant (copper engraving in: Sedulius 'Imagines Sanctorum OSF' circa 1600); chain of honorary Order (La Feuille, parish church, figure, beg. 18th century). *Special scenes:* (selection, as most belong to the genre): L. is taught by a monk (New York, Pierpont Morgan Library, illumination, 13th century); L. is crowned and anointed (Poissy, Dominican Church, stained glass, 14th century); L.

tempt to burn her fails. – L. predicts the coming death of the Emperor and the future peace of the Church. – Eventually her neck is pierced with a sword.

Patronage: farmers, the blind, repentant prostitutes, glaziers, coachmen, knifesmiths, sewers, notaries, beadles, saddlers, tailors, writers, doorkeepers, weavers; against eye disease, blindness, sore throats, infection.

Veneration and cult sites: inscription on a grave of 5th century in Syracuse, canon saint; in Rome St L. in Selce built under Pope Honorius (625–638); popular saint in Germany.

Superstition: until the Gregorian calendar reform L. day was mid-winter's day, important prediction day, quarter day for contracts, end of school year; nightly processions (bride L. with crown and candles in the north with play on the name, first attested in 1780, renewed in connection with the anniversary of the death of Alfred Nobel in Sweden on 10th December 1896). In the popular imagination L. shows partly some witch-like traits, partly she is a bringer of gifts, like the Christchild. In Hungary a cake is baked for each member of the family and a feather placed inside; if it burns, the person concerned will die in the coming year. – No stranger may be sheltered on L. day in Hungary, otherwise he will take the look of the household with him.

Representation in Art: *Apparel:* as martyr (Ravenna, St Apollinare Nuovo, mosaic, 6th century); as virgin in virgin's garb of contemporary style, mostly with long girdled robe, wide sleeved over-garment (Munich, Bavarian National Museum, tapestry, circa 1500); chaplet (Prague, Rudolfinum, painting, by H. Holbein the Elder, circa 1500); fashionable hat (Siersdorf, figure, early 16th century); crown (Munich, Georgianum, painting, end 15th century); cloak (Mühlbeck, Saxony, painting, circa 1500). *Attributes*: double cross (Rome, St Sebastiano al Palatino, mural, 8th/11th century); palm (Gaeta, St L., painting, by G. Sagittano, 1456); crown in the hand (Ravenna, St Apollinare Nuovo, mosaic, 6th century); chalice with Host (Perugia, National Gallery, painting, by Perugino, 16th century); book (Fossa, St Mary ad Cryptas, mural, 15th century); burning lamp (Apiro, painting, by A. Nuzi, 1366); candle (Atri, crypt, mural, 15th century); vase with flowers (Syracuse, Cathedral, figure, by P. Rizzo, 15th century); hand pierced with sword (Inzighofen, monastery church, painting, by Master of Sigmaringen, 1505); neck pierced with sword (Cologne, Wallraf-Richartz Museum, painting, by B. de Bruyn the Elder, 1530/35); sword in the hand (Settignano, Berendson Collection, painting, by S. Martini, 14th century); flames at feet (Cologne, former Nelles Collection, 2nd half 15th century); eyes in a box (Art dealer, formerly Amsterdam, painting, by J. del Casentino, 14th century); lamp with eyes (Florence, St L. dalle Rovinate, painting, by P. Lorenzetti, 14th century); tray with eyes (Florence, Academy, painting, by G. del Biondo, circa 1378); bowl with eyes (Vichy, Cathedral, figure, by P. Iller, 15th century); eyes bound to branch (Art dealer, painting, by F. Cossa, 2nd half 15th century); eyes on point of dagger (Bergamo, Pinacoteca dell'Accademia Carrara, painting, by Bergognone, circa 1700); mask with two eyes (Fossa, St Mary ad Cryptas, mural, 15th century). *Special scenes*: oxen attempt in vain to pull L. into a brothel (Venice, Apostles' Church, painting, by G. B. Tiepolo, 18th century). *Martyrdom*: Berlin State Museums, Art Gallery, painting, by P. Veneziano. *Cycles*: include Melfi Grotto of St L., mural, 12th century; New York Metropolitan Museum of Art, painting, by L. di Niccolo, 15th century; Amsterdam Rijksmuseum, painting, by Master of the L. Legend, before 1480.

Luke

Evangelist, saint

Feast-day: 13th October

Biblical testimony and tradition of the Church Fathers: L. is traditionally the author of 3rd Gospel and the Book of Acts, from the first-person narratives (Acts 16:10–17; 20:5–21,18; 27:1–28:16); from these his accompanying of the Apostle Paul on the 2nd missionary journey, circa 51, can be deduced: L. remained in Philippi and went on to Rome with Paul six years later (2 Tim 4:11); according to Clement of Alexandria, Paul's secretary in Rome. According to Col 4:14 L. was a doctor, with Antioch in Syria as his home town according to Eusebius and Tertullian. According to Gregory of Nazianzus, after the death of Paul work, in Achaia, Egypt and Thebias, Patras and Thebes. † traditionally 63.

Legend: L. painted the picture of the Mother of God.

Patronage: doctors, painters, notaries, sculptors, sewers, lace-makers, bookbinders, butchers, gold-workers; bulls, cattle.

Veneration and cult sites: relics in Constantinople Apostle's Church (since 357); discovery of relics 552; relics in Orthosias near Arca (since 5th century); Padua, St Giustina (since 1177, from early 14th century in alabaster sarcophagus); Rome Vatican (head relic); Rome St Peter's and St Martin's; Venice, St Giobbe (since 1464); Rome St Andrew's; Ostia, Naples, Fondi, Brescia, Nola, Barcelona, Valencia, Espina near Valladolid, Sens (until 1793), Valence, Douai, Paris St-Germain, Tournai, Malines.

Superstition: The beet harvest begins on L. day. – L. notes containing magic formulae can be laid on the sick and they will be healed, even when the doctors have given them up.

Representation in Art: *Apparel:* as young evangelist in Apostle's dress with long girded tunic, cloak pallium (Ravenna, Archbishop's Museum, Maximian's Cathedral, ivory relief, 6th century); as bearded evangelist in Apostle's dress (Ravenna, St Vitale, mosaic, 6th century); as learned man in humanist dress (Berlin-Dahlem, State Museum of Prussian Culture, painting, by M. Schaffner, 16th century); as learned man with Doctor's sash over the shoulder (Cologne, Wallraf-Richartz Museum, figure, mid 15th century); as learned man with biretta (Cologne, Wallraf-Richartz Museum, painting, by S. Lochner, circa 1445); l. half bull, half man (Lucca, Capitolare Library, Cod. 2, illumination, 12th century). *Attributes:* book (Florence, Cathedral, figure, by G. di Antonio di Banco, circa 1410); globe (Venice, S Giorgio Maggiore, figure, 1593); doctors' instruments (Rome, Comodilla Catacombs, mural, 7th century); scalpel (Brussels, Royal Library, Ms. 1, illumination, 11th century); standing on a bull (Strasbourg, Cathedral, figure, circa 1230); sitting on a bull (Paris, Louvre, relief, by J. Goujon, 16th century); bull with inkpot hanging from horns (Haarlem, Pannwitz Collection, painting, by L. von Leyden, 16th century);bull holding inkhorn (Paris, Arsenal Library, Cod. 591, illumination, 12th century); bull supporting the picture of Mary (Rome, S Maria del Popolo, painting, by Pinturicchio, beg. 16th century); realistic bull (Berlin-Dahlem, figure, by T. Riemenschneider, 1492); bull in the hand (Liège, Diocesan

Museum, figure, end 14th century); winged bull (Florence, S Croce, relief, by L. della Robbia, circa 1445); easel, mortar, healing herbs (Hofkirchen an der Tür, parish church, fresco, by W. A. Heindl, 1754); Mary panel with Boy Jesus (Cologne, Wallraf-Richartz Museum, painting, by S. Lochner, circa 1445); Mary panel with Boy Jesus (Paris, National Library, Ms lat. 9474, illumination, end 15th century); statue of Mary (Prague-Old City, St Clement's, figure, by M. B. Braun, circa 1715); angel carrying brush (Appenweier, St Michael's, fresco, by B. Gambs, 18th century); mallow on girdle (Cologne, Wallraf-Richartz Museum, painting, by S. Lochner, 1445). *Special scenes:* L. cuts the quill to size (New York, Pierpont Morgan Library, MS 333, illumination, 10th century); L. tests a quill (Venice, St Zachariah's fresco, by A. del Castagno, 1442); the Mother of God dictates the Gospel to L. (Lübeck, St Annen Museum, painting, by H. Rode, 1484); L. presents the Childhood Gospel to the Boy Jesus on the lap of the Mother of God (Nördlingen, Town Museum, painting, by F. Herlin, 1488); L. paints the Mother of God in the type of Eleous (Nuremberg, German National Museum, painting, by Master of the Augustine Altar, 1487); L. paints the Mother of God as lactans (Cambridge/Mass., Fogg Art Museum, painting, by Master of the Holy Blood, circa 1515/20); L. paints the Mother of God near the lectern (Valencia, Provincial Museum, painting, by F. Ribalta, circa 1600); L. paints the Mother of God standing (Bern, Art Museum, painting, by M. Deutsch, 1515); an angel grinds the colours for L. (Münster, State Museum, painting, by D. Baegert, circa 1490); L. treats the sick (Madrid, Prado, painting, by J. de Levi, 15th century); L. heals a child (Segorbe, Diocesan Museum, painting, of the school of Valencia, 15th century); L. in the doctor's practice (Freiburg, Augustine Museum, silver altar, 1st half 18th century). *Cycles:* Lübeck St Annen Museum, painting, by H. Rode, circa 1485.

M

Marcellinus and Peter

Martyrs, saints

Feast-day: 2nd June

Life: during the Diocletianic persecution of the Christians M. and P. suffered their martyrdom in Rome. The year of their martyrdom fluctuates (299, 303, 305).

Legends: according to the Golden Legend: P., according to Roman tradition an exorcist, is released in prison from his double chains, appears to the prison warden, Anthemius, and cures his daughter from evil spirits. – Anthemius and his family are baptised by a priest. – The prefect orders M. to lie naked on pieces of glass and P. to be chained to a pole. – During the night, M. and P. are led into Anthemius's house by angels. – M. celebrates in the catacombs; M., P. and Anthemius are found by pagans. – Anthemius is stoned, and M. and P. beheaded in a dark forest. – The hangman, Dorotheus, sees that the saints' souls are carried into heaven by angels. Further miracles and legends are in Einhard's report on the relic translation to Seligenstadt.

Veneration and cult sites: the mortal remains are buried in Rome, "Coemeterium ad duas Lauros" and Via Labicana. Constantine the Great built a basilica on the site with the mausoleum of St Helen. In 827, Einhard, the head of Charlemagne's school of scholars, translated relics to Seligenstadt and buried them in a crypt. M. and P. are mentioned in the Roman mass canon (canon I), in the prayer "Nobis quoque peccatoribus" (= to us sinners also), after the consecration in the request of communion with the saints, together with seven male and seven female martyrs in the prayer.

Representation in Art: *Apparel:* as early Christian martyrs (Rome, catacomb, SS Pietro e Marcellino, mural painting, 4/5th century); as priests in mass chasuble and exorcist in tunicella (Seligenstadt, Einhard Basilica, fig. by B. Zamels, circa 1720). *Attributes:* scroll, book (Rome, Pontian catacomb, mural painting, 6th century); palm tree, cross (Cremona, Cathedral, fig. by Benedetto Briosco, 16th century); sword, book (Chokier, SS Pietro e Marcellino, fig. 15th century); chalice and book (Seligenstadt, Einhard Basilica, fig. by B. Zamels, circa 1720). *Martyrdom:* Brauweiler, Chapter Hall, mural painting, 12th century.

Margaret of Antioch

(Marina) Virgin, Martyr, saint

Feast-day: 20th July

Legends: M., daughter of a pagan priest, is baptised by her wet-nurse. – Her father therefore disowns her. – The town's prefect, Olibrius, meets M. looking for a lost sheep and wants to marry her for her prettiness if she deserts her faith. – M. remains a Christian and is interrogated twice. – During the

305 Diocletianic persecution of the Christians, M. is, on the orders of Olibrius, tortured and hanged, her body cut open with iron combs and she was beaten with canes; finally she is thrown into prison. – In prison she is comforted by a dove. – The tempter appears to M., impersonating a dragon, overcomes her and tries to devour her. – M. makes the sign of the cross above the dragon and it disintegrates (var: in the Golden Legend: the dragon devours M. but it disintegrates after M. draws the sign of the cross on its body). – The devil appears to M., this time impersonating a man, but she conquers him by putting her foot on his head. – Because she refuses to sacrifice to the pagan gods, she is burned with torches and put in hot water. – After a violent earthquake, M. comes out of the water tub unharmed. -The miracle converts 5000 people to Christianity. – The judge then orders M. to be beheaded. – Following the execution, the hangmen fall down dead. – Angels bring the palm of victory to M. – At her grave, cripples are cured miraculously.

Patronage: wet-nurses, farmers (because the Sachsenspiegel included the regulation that the yield of a field belongs to those who have cultivated it before St M.'s day), virgins, married women, pregnant women, invoked against infertility of women.

Veneration and cult sites: M. is one the 14 Holy Helpers. Relics are in Montefiascone near Bolsena.

Superstition: women, having difficulties giving birth, measure their girth and light a candle for the saint. – In Starzedel near Guben, women who have just given birth sacrifice the dry umbilical cord of their six week-old infants to St M. – In Salzburg, girls born illegitimately had to carry M.'s name as an additional Christian name to ensure that they grew up well. -In Estonia, a child born on M.'s day must never keep watch over livestock, otherwise the wolves will maul the herd. – During M. week no snakes must be killed because M. looks after them. – On her feast-day, M. releases the flies, the doors should therefore be closed. – On M.'s day one should sow autumn turnips. – Rain on M.'s day brings a poor nut harvest. – In connection with Margaret numerous oracles exist, for instance, by plucking off leaves one can recognize the profession of a future husband or determine the number of future children.

Representation in Art: *Apparel:* as young martyr in noble dress: long girdled dress with coat or wrap (Regensburg, Cathedral, stained glass, late 14th century); as lady of the court (Fraunenburg, Castle, painting, circa 1400); in contemporary, civilian clothes

(London, National Gallery, painting by F. Zurbarán, 17th century); with 'schapel' (Mesum, Westphalia, fig., circa 1450); with turban (Themar, Town Church, painting, late 15th century); bonnet, embroidered with pearls (Nuremberg, Germanic National Museum, relief, circa 1520); as shepherdess (New York, privately owned, Franconian tapestry, circa 1560). *Attributes*: palm tree (Paris, Bibliothèque Nationale, Par. let. 12055, Miserale of Cologne, book illustration, 12th century); cross (Palermo, Capella Palatina, mosaic, 12th century); crown (Florence, Accademia, painting by the Magdalen master, circa 1260); crown, dove (Methler near Hamm (Westphalia), mural painting, 2nd half of the 13th century); book, cross (Vich, Episcopal Museum, painting, 15th century); palm tree, comb (Heiligenkreuztal, stained glass,, circa 1320); torch (Chomle, Bohemia, fig., circa 1500); dragon, small cross, crown, palm tree (Strasbourg, Cathedral, fig., circa 1250); dragon on a book (Lübeck, St Peter's Church, relief, 1425); dragon at her feet (Metz, Cathedral, stained glass, circa 1525); dragon at a lead (Krecov, Bohemia, painting, circa 1500); dragon with cross crosier in its mouth (Mainz, Cathedral, fig. at the memory gate, circa 1400); dragon with end of cloth in its mouth (Munich, Alte Pinakothek, painting by the master of the Bartholomew altar, circa 1500). *Martyrdom*: M., tortured with burning torches (Osnabrück, Cathedral, fig., circa 1510), M. alights from a disintegrated dragon (Madrid, Prado, painting by Titian, 1550–1552); M. stabs the dragon with a cross on a pole (Berlin, Copperplate Engraving Cabinet, drawing by M. Schongauer, 15th century); M. points to dead dragon (Pisa, Cathedral, painting by Andrea del Sarto, after 1500). *Special scenes*: St John and M., because during difficult births where the mother's life was endangered, St John's prologue and M.'s martyrdom from the legends of the saints were read to the women (Munich, Alte Pinakothek, painting by the master of the Bartholomew altar, circa 1500); M.'s mystic engagement with the Christ-child (Lugano, Thyssen Collection, painting by the circle of Pacher, circa 1490); Mary gives the Christ-child to M. (Bologna, Pinacoteca Nazionale, painting by Parmigianino, 16th century); M. with spindle, looking after sheep (Paris, Louvre, book illustration in the Heures d'Etienne Chevalier by Jean Fouquet, 1452/60. *Cycles*: numerous, amongst others, Vich, Museum, painting, 12th century; Tournai, Cathedral, fresco, circa 1200; Fornovo near Parma, relief by the Antelami workshop, early 13th century; Chartres, Cathedral, stained glass, 1220–1227; Torpe, Norway, Church, painting, 14th century; Montici near Florence, S Margareta, painting by Giotto' circle, 14th century; St Florian near Linz, painting by L. Beck, 1510.

Margaret of Hungary
Queen, saint

Feast-day: 18th January

Life: born in 1242 (?) in Clissa, the daughter of King Bélas IV and the Greek princess Mary Lascaris, niece of St Elizabeth of Thuringia. In 1246 she joined the Dominican convent in Veszprém, where she was educated. In 1246 she joined the convent on Margaret Island (Rabbit Island), and made her profession in 1254 after refusing marriage to King Boleslav VI Pobozny, of Poland, Ottokar II of Bohemia and Charles of Anjou. From the hand of the archbishop of Gran, she publicly took the veil and lived a strictly ascetic life in poverty combined with intensive worship of Christ's suffering and heroic dedication to the infirm. She died on 18th January 1270. Beatified 1776, canonized 1943.

Legends: during the 1241 Tartar invasion, her parents dedicate their still unborn child, M., to God. – The Tartar Great Khan dies and the Tartar leader, Batu, returns with his hordes to Central Asia to secure his share of the inheritance. – Because of his attempted marriage arrangements for her, M. lectures her father.

Veneration and cult sites: since 1789 in the Hungarian dioceses; since 1804 in the Dominican Order.

Representation in Art: *Apparel:* as Dominican nun (Esztergom, Christian Museum, woodcut, circa 1500); in a coat covered with stars (Bibliotheca Sanctorum). *Attributes:* book, lily (Basle, History Museum, tapestry, late 15th century); crown of the kings refused in marriage (Bibliotheca Sanctorum), stigmata (London, National Gallery, predella by Fra Angelico's circle, 15th century); stigmatized Christ seraph (Perugia, S Domenico, fresco, 1368). *Special scenes:* M. under the cross (Pest, University, relief by Pándikiss, 19th century), St M.'s stigmatisation (Città di Castello, S Domenico, fresco, 15th century). *Cycles:* Piliscsaba, Parish Church, painting by A. E. Falkoner, 1772; Augsburg, copperplate engraving by Klauber, 18th century.

Margaret Mary Alacoque

Salesian (Visitation) saint

Feast-day: 16th October (before 1970: 17th October)

Life: born on 2nd July 1647, the daughter of a judge and notary public in Lauthecour near Vérosèvres, Burgundy. After the death of her father, M., at eight years of age, was sent to the Claris convent near Charolles. At the age of 10 she contracted polio which was cured when she was 14. In 1665, she showed mystic tendencies. In 1667, following a private revelation, she decided, against the wishes of her family, to join an Order. In 1671, she joined the Paris Visitandine convent, founded by Francis de Sales and Jane Francis de Chantal. In the Order her 'ecstatic revelations' continued. On 16th June 1675 she had a powerful vision of Sacred Heart in which she was instructed to introduce a feast-day in its honour. She was influenced by her spiritual guide, the Jesuit Claude de Colombire, who recorded M.'s revelations in his book "Retraite spirituelle" which was published in 1682, two years after his death. In the convent, M. suffered many humiliations by other nuns and Mother Superiors. In 1684, the new Mother Superior, Melin, nominated M. as her assistant and mistress of the novices. In 1689, the Jesuit P. Jean Croiset took up M.'s request and assisted her in spreading the new devotion to the Sacred Heart. In 1685, M. wrote an autobiography. She died in 1690. Beatified on 24th April 1864, canonized on 13th May 1920.

Veneration and cult sites: relics are in Paray-le-Monial, Chapelle de la Visitation where her visions were read at the table for the first time in 1684.

Representation in Art: *Apparel:* in black habit of the Visitandines, hands crossed at the breast (Paris, Bibliothèque Nationale, painting by G. Delangle, 19th century). *Special scenes:* looking in ecstasy at the Sacred Heart (Munich, former branch of the Niederbronn Sisters, painting by A. Hess, late 19th century).

Margaret of Scotland

Queen, saint

Feast-day: 16th November (day of her death, formerly 10th June, translation feast 19th June)

Life: born circa 1046 as daughter of King Edward the Atheling and Princess Agatha of Hungary in Reska near Nsad during the period when her father was banished from England. At the age of 11 she moved to the court of her great uncle, Edward the Confessor. In 1066, after the battle of Hastings, she fled to Scotland where, in 1070, she married King

Malcolm III of Scotland. Together with the king and Archbishop Lanfranc of Canterbury she reformed ecclesiastical life, removed Celtic customs, founded Dunfermline Abbey and was a great benefactress of the poor. She died in 1093 in Edinburgh. Canonized in 1249.

Patronage: patron saint of Scotland.

Representation in Art: *Apparel:* as queen (Edinburgh, Scottish National Gallery, painting, 19th century); as nun (London, Jesuit Church in Farm Street, fig., 20th century). *Attributes:* crown at her feet (Città di Castello, Pinacoteca Communale, painting by L. Signorelli, late 15th century); the infirm (copperplate engraving by Callot, 1636).

Mark

Evangelist, Martyr, saint

Feast-day: translation feast on 31st January; M.'s appearance in Venice on 25th June; further feast-days on 9th April; 23rd September; 3rd October; 8th October; in the Greek Church on 11th January.

Life: M., according to the Apocr. 12.12 John with the epithet Mark wrote, at the request of the Romans, the oldest Gospel. At the beginning of the 2nd century, Papias called him the "Hermeneut of St Peter". According to Apocr. 12.25, M. was, together with his nephew Barnabas, Paul's companion on his first missionary journey to Antioch and his esteem of M. was reported in Col. 4.10, Phm 24.2 and Tim 4.11. Contrary to Barnabas's request, Paul refused to take M. on his second missionary journey and both of his companions left him (Apocr. 13.13). Later they were seemingly reconciled because the letter to the Philemons included M.'s greeting to Paul. M. was probably the bearer of the second letter to the Colossians (Col. 4.10). In Peter 1, 5.3, Peter referred to M., in the transferred sense, as his son. In 63/64, M. lived with Peter in Rome. Paul mentioned M.'s missionary work in the Orient in 2 Tim 4.11.

Legends: according to Dionysius bar Salibi, M. and his sister Rhode are the children of Mary, the wife of Peter. After Peter's miraculous escape from prison, he finds shelter in her house (var: M. is the son of the Mary in whose house the early Jerusalem congregation met). According to the Arab tradition, during M.'s baptism, the mother of God herself lays her hands on him. – M. belongs to Jesus's 12 disciples. – M. is the water-carrier, mentioned in Mk 14.13, who leads the disciples into the Communion hall. – M. is the young man who flees naked when Jesus is arrested (Mk 14.51). – M. is a Levite, like Barnabas, and originates therefore from a priest's family. – M. mutilates his finger to be unsuitable for Levite service in the temple. – M. is a missionary in Lorch (Enns) and Aquileia. – M. is the nephew of the protomartyr, Stephen, and therefore visited Alexandria. – When a belt of his shoe loosens itself in Alexandria, the shoemaker, whilst repairing it, injures his hand badly with the awl; M. cures and converts him. – As the first bishop after foundation of the Egypt and Abyssinian patriarchate, M. suffers martyrdom in Alexandria. – During his Alexandria Easter service, M. is arrested and dragged on a rope through the town and thrown into prison. – The following day, M. is dragged on a rope to death (var: M. is burned). – Bad weather prevents the mob from burning the mortal remains and he is buried honourably in Bucoles. – In 829, the Venetians bring the mortal remains by ship to Venice, using a cunning trick: they hide the remains under pork, regarded as impure in Muslim countries.

Patronage: writers; notaries; glass painters; glaziers; basket and rug-makers; builders; bricklayers (because of his rescue miracle during the construction of the Venetian church of S Marco); lantern makers; invoked against impenitents on the deathbed;

scabies; for good weather and good harvest; (the Rogation procession on M.'s day originates from the older Roman tradition of Robigalia, a procession against the demon Robigo who causes grain rust).

Veneration and cult sites: patron saint of Venice (blessing of M.'s bread = marzipan); patron saint of Albania and Corfu; relics are in Venice, S Marco; Aquileia; Reichenau-Mittelzell (presented in 830 by bishop Ratold of Verona to abbot Erlebald); Badajoz; Valencia; Zente; Lorch (Enns); Huy; Limours (Seine-et-Oise); Trèves; Prague; Florence; Wittenberg (part of his kneecap). Early patronage of churches in Bedburg near Kleve; Beringhausen; Padberg near Paderborn; Bredeney near Essen; Godesberg near Bonn.

Superstition: M.'s day is an important annual day, particularly so for the growth of fruit. On M.'s day the salt is blessed and given to the livestock as they are driven out to the grazing land.

Representation in Art: *Apparel:* in traditional dress with chiton and himation (Florence, S Lorenzo, stucco tondo by Donatello, 1434/37); in contemporary dress (Udine, Cathedral, painting by G. Martini, early 16th century); as archbishop with robe and pallium (Stuttgart, Governmental gallery, painting by the master of the Maulbronn altar, 15th century); as bishop of orthodox rites (Venice, S Marco, mosaic in the Narthex, 13th century); as Oriental with turban (Deventer, Town Hall, painting by H. ter Brugghen, 1621); with turban (Paris, Bibliothèque de l'Arsénal, book illustration, 15th century); as scholar (Paris, Bibliothèque Nationale, hour-book of Anne of Brittany); as scholar with spectacles (Antwerp, Museum, painting by L. van Leyden, early 16th century). *Attributes:* closed book (Nuremberg, Germanic National Museum, golden Echternach Gospel book, book illustration, 11th century); open book, M. writing (Copenhagen, Museum, altar reredos from Preez, circa

1450); scroll (Munich, Alte Pinakothek, painting by A. Dürer, 1526); writing quill, writing equipment (Berlin, Governmental Museums, Sculpture Collection, fig. by Chr. Jordan, 1760); lion without wings (Ravenna, S Vitale, mosaic, 6th century); winged lion at his feet (Cologne, Wallraf-Richartz Museum, painting by S. Lochner, 1445); springing lion (Unterrissdorf, Saxony, fig., 15th century); lion, resting on the book (Neusitz, Saxony, fig., 1515); lion held in hand (Liége, Diocesan Museum, fig., 15th century); winged lion on a round pane, held in hand (Wismar, St Jürgen, fig., 15th century); M. riding on a lion (Admont, Collegiate Library Cod. 115, book illustration, circa 1457); lion with Gospel book (Venice, Palazzo Ducale, painting by V. Carpaccio, 15th century); lion pulling a wagon, with portrayal of the resurrection (Rome, Biblioteca Casanatense MS 1404, book illustration, early 15th century); inspecting lion (Prato, S Maria delle Carceri, tondo by Andrea della Robbia, circa 1500);

hand of God as source of inspiration (New York, Minster Library, gospel by York, book illustration, late 10th century); fig tree without fruit (Venice, Accademia, painting by M. Basaiti, early 16th century); lion with open book beside Christ, rising from the grave (Munich, Governmental Library, Clm 4454, book illustration from the Reichenau, early 11th century); city architecture (London, Victoria and Albert Museum, ivory relief, 11th century). *Special scenes:* a) painting of the evangelist M.: M. writing (St Gallen, Collegiate Library, cod. 51, Irish book illustration, 8th century); Sophie dictates the Gospel to M. (Rossano, Archiepiscopal Museum, book illustration, late 6th century); M. writes as Peter dictates (Münster Westphalian Governmental Archive, MS VII, book illustration, early 12th century); Peter's presentation of the Gospel to M. (Prague, Chapter Library, Cim. 2, book illustration, late 9th century); M.'s presentation of the Gospel to Christ (Perugia, Chapter Library, Ms. 2, book illustration, 8/9th century); M., resting from writing, thinking about the text (Frankfurt, Städel, painting attributed to A. Mantegna, circa 1449); M. in the scholar's office (Tegernsee, evangelist altar by G. Mäleskircher, 1478). b) motifs from the vita: M., preaching in Alexandria (Milan, Brera, painting by Gentile Bellini, 1507); M., baptising the shoemaker Anianus (Venice, Scuola di S Marco, relief by Tullio Lombardo, 16th century); M. cures the hand of the shoemaker Anianus (Berlin, Emperor-Frederick Museum, painting by Cima da Conegliano, 15th century); M. preaches before the Sultan (Venice, Accademia, painting by G. Mansueti, circa 1500); arrival of M.'s mortal remains in Venice (Venice, S Zaccaria, fresco by A. Celesti, 1684); rediscovery of St M.'s mortal remains in the Cathedral (Milan, Brera, painting by J. Tintoretto, 1566); M. rescues a slave from martyrdom by descending from heaven and destroying the executioner's equipment (Venice, Accademia, painting by Tintoretto, 1548); M. cures a young man of cancer (Venice, Accademia, painting by Tintoretto, 1566); M. rescues Venice, together with George and Nicholas (Venice, Accademia, painting by Giorgione, finished by Bordone and Palma Vecchio, 1510); discovery of M.'s ring by a fisherman and presentation to the doge Gradenigo (Venice, Accademia, painting by Paris Bordone, 1534); St M.'s glory (Rome, S Marco, painting by G. F. Romanelli, 17th century). *Martyrdom:* Florence, S Marco, painting by Guillaume Courtois, 17th century. *Cycles:* mostly in Venice and environs. Venice, Tesoro di S Marco, Pala d'Oro, 1102/05; Venice, S Marco, mosaics, 1260/70; Viterbo, S Marco, predella by G. Francesco d'Avanzarano, 1512; Venice, Accademia, 11 paintings by Tintoretto.

Mark Carlo Domenico (Cristofori) of Aviano

Capuchin friar, servant of God

Life: born on 17th November 1631 in Aviano, Friule. He studied at the Gorizia Jesuit college and became a Capuchin novice in 1648 and was ordained as a priest in 1655. He was a famous preacher and supported the Hungarian Maria Poc's veneration and ordered the translation of the Madonna to Vienna, St Stephan. He was regarded as a faith-healer in his blessing of the infirm. He contributed considerably to the 1683 liberation of Vienna from the Turks. He died on 13th August 1699 in Vienna.

The process of beatification was begun in 1912.

Representation in Art: mainly on engravings and popular devotional pictures with his portrait (numerous examples in Rome, Museo Francescano OFM Cap.), also in portraits of the Turkish occupation of Vienna.

Martha of Bethany

Sister of Lazarus, saint

Feast-day: 29th July, also on 19th January, 17th October and 17th December (in the rites of the Eastern Church on 4th June or 6th June).

Life: when Jesus visited the sisters Mary and M. in Bethany, Mary listened to Jesus as Martha served the guests (according to Lk 10, 38–42). Mary and Martha were present during Lazarus's revival by Jesus. M. declared her faith before Jesus as Messiah and Son of God (Jo 11, 1–45). According to Jo 12, 1–11, Jesus visited Lazarus's house six days before the paschal feast where Martha served the guest but Mary anointed Jesus's feet.

Legends: M. is the sister of Mary Magdalene. – M. converts Mary Magdalene. -According to Ambrose of Milan, M. is the bloodstained woman who touches Jesus's clothes. – M. is one of the three women who go to the grave on Easter morning. – M. and their brothers and sisters travel by ship to Marseilles (see under "Mary Magdalene"). – M. conquers Tarascus, the man-eating dragon in the Rhône valley with the cross and holy water. – M. revives a young man who falls into the Rhône trying to hear her sermon. – M. exorcizes demons. – On M.'s deathbed, Mary Magdalene, who died eight days earlier, lights the candle blown out by demons. – M. is buried in Tarascon by bishop Fronto of Périgueux. – Christ leads bishop Fronto of Périgueux to M.'s Tarascon funeral.

Patronage: housewives, cooks, maids, housekeepers in vicarages, alpine herdsmen and herdswomen, laundrywomen, female labourers, hospital managers, landlords, painters, sculptors, those dying of haemophilia.

Veneration and cult sites: relics in and pilgrimages to Tarascon, Wittenberg. Church patronages are found often in Tuscany, Nuremberg and the Speyer old peoples' home of St M. for housekeepers in vicarages.

Superstition: in the Czech Republic, those who make butter on M.'s day and give some of it to the church for the lamps will have plenty of milk during the year.

Representation in Art: *Apparel:* in simple, girdled dress, coat and headscarf (Gelnhausen, tympanon relief, 1225/30); in contemporary dress (Ath, Hennegau, fig. 15th century); as housewife with apron (Léau, St Leonard, altar painting, 15th century); in dress with ermine (Iravalls, S Martha, painting by R. Destorrents); in noble dress with crown (Strasbourg, Cathedral, Catherine Chapel, stained glass, circa 1350); *Attributes:* wooden spoon (Mühlhausen, Thuringia, Blasius Church, painting, 15th century); cutlery, bowl at her belt (Munich, Alte Pinakothek, painting by B. Zeitblom, circa 1500); bowl with cooked chicken and jug (Weimar, Library, painting, 16th century); ointment container (Autun, Lazarus' grave, fig., circa 1170); dragon, tied up with a belt (Barga, Conservatorio di S Elisabetta, painting of the Daddi workshop, 1st half of the 14th century); holy water frond and font in hand (Berlin, Kaiser Friedrich Museum, painting by the Master of the Holy Family, 2nd half of the 15th century; book, rosary (Iravalls, S Martha, painting by R. Destorrents). *Special scenes:* M. and her sister, Mary, welcome Jesus (Brussels, Bibliothèque Royale, MS 466, book illustration, 1st quarter of the 13th century); M. watches Mary Magdalene, anointing Jesus's feet (Padua, Museo Civico, painting by J. Tintoretto, 1526); Jesus with Mary and M. with kitchen still-life in the foreground (Vienna, Art History Museum, painting by Pieter Aertsen, 1552); M. declares her faith before Christ (Florence, Uffizi, painting by N. Fromment, 1461); revival of Lazarus (Hildesheim, Bernward Evangeliar, book illustration, early 11th century); M.,as bloodstained woman, touches Jesus's clothes (Paris, Bibliothèque Nationale, Fr. 24955, book illustration by Godfredus Batavus, circa

1520); M.'s fight with the dragon (Arles, St Trophîme, Chapter relief, 12th century); Mary Magdalene lights the candle at M.'s deathbed (Nuremberg, Germanic National Museum, painting, 2nd half of the 15th century). *Cycles:* amongst others in Nuremberg, St Martha, stained glass, 1407; Wroclàv, Diocesan Museum, altar from Langendorf, circa 1420; Nuremberg, St Lorenz, altar, 1517; Tarascon, Franciscan Church, painting by J. M. Vien, 1750.

Martialis of Limoges

Bishop, saint

Feast-day: 30th June

Life: Besides Gregory of Tours one of the seven bishops sent to Gaul during the reign of Emperor Decius (249–251).

Legends: According to a Life written in the 10th/11th century, M. is one of the 72 disciples sent out by Jesus Christ (variation: sent out by St Peter). – As a child, M. listens to Jesus Christ's sermon. – M. is baptized by St Peter. – St Peter sends M. to Gaul, together with Austriclinianus and Alpinianus. – M. is given a staff by St Peter, with which he can raise the dead, and raises Austriclinianus from the dead. – M. has a vision of Christ, ordering him to go to Limoges.- On her refusal to marry Duke Stephan, the virgin Valeria is sentenced to death, prophesying the death the next day of her executioner and, after the execution, carries her head to M. – After the death of the executioner, Duke Stephan implores M. to raise him from the dead and, on M's miracle, agrees to be baptized. – M. raises the son of the Count of Poitiers from the dead, who had been strangled by the devil. – M. orders the destruction of heathen images and temples and builds churches. – Touching him with his staff, M. cures Duke Siegbert of Bordeaux. – Christ predicts the death of SS Peter and Paul to M. – M. ordains Aurelianus as his successor as bishop of Li-

moges. – M's soul is received in heaven by Christ, the Virgin Mary, John the Baptist and SS Peter, Paul and Stephen. – Angels sing at M's grave. – Cripples are cured at M's coffin. – With M's staff, Siebgert's wife extinguishes a conflagration in Bordeaux. – Alpinianus covers the sick with M's shroud, thus curing them.

Veneration and cult sites: In 848, the Benedictine abbey of St Martial was erected on the site of M's grave. Special cult at the diocese of Limoges.

Representation in Art: *Apparel:* as bishop in pontifical vestments with chasuble, crosier and mitre (Paris, Louvre, reliquary, emaille, late 12th century); as bishop with pluvial, crosier and mitre (Limoges, St Joseph, figure, 18th century). *Attributes:* book (Limoges Cathedral, figure, late 14th century). *Special scenes:* The raising of Austriclinianus from the dead (St Julien (Haute-Vienne), wall-painting, late 13th century); at the Last Supper, M. presents a cup of wine to Christ (Léon, Real Colegiata de S Isidoro, wall-painting, 11th century); using both hands simultaneously, M. writes two letters (Paris, Bibliothèque Nationale MS lat.5296 A, book illumination, circa 1100); Valeria carries her severed head to M. (Limoges Cathedral, stained glass, 15th century); Valeria and her mother before M. Paris, Ste Clothilde, fresco by J. E. Lenepveu, 1868); M's elevation (Venice, S Marziale, painting by J. Tintoretto, 1548). *Cycles:* Avignon, Papal Palace, fresco by M. Giovanni da Viterbo, circa 1345; Tours Cathedral, stained glass, circa 1260; Bordeaux, St Seurin, reliefs, 15th century.

Martin I

Pope, Confessor, saint

Feast-day: 13th April (formerly 12th November)

Life: born at Todi, Umbria. He was Apocrisiarius (= diplomat, representative of the pope) in Constantinople. Was elected and ordained as pope in 649 but his election was not acknowledged by Emperor Constantine II. During the 649 Lateran synod, M. condemned the error of Monothelitism, was arrested on 17th June 653 in the Lateran basilica by Exarch Theodoros Kalliopas and taken to Constantinople. Because of his alleged participation in the rebellion of Exarch Olympios who, in Rome, renounced the Byzantine emperor and survived for three years, M. was sentenced to death but, at the request of Patriarch Paulos II of Constantinople, was pardoned and banished to Cherson (= Sebastopol), Crimea. During the lifetime of the exiled pope, Pope Eugen I became his successor. He died on 26th September 655 as a result of his banishment and imprisonment.

Patronage: in the united Greek rites as patron saint of the faithful.

Representation in Art: *Apparel:* as pope (Assisi, S Francesco, Martin's Chapel, stained glass, early 14th century).

Martin of Porres

Dominican laybrother, saint

Feast-day: 3rd November (before the calendar reform, 5th November).

Life: born on 9th December 1569 in Lima, illegitimate son of the Spanish knight Juan de Porres and the Mulatto Anna Velásquez. Because of his dark skin, M. was socially spurned, became at the age of 12 a barber-surgeon, was a surgeon and pharmacist and in 1603 joined the Dominican Order as a doctor. For the first time in Latin America, he did not distinguish between the social standing of the infirm nor colour of the skin and founded numerous charitable organisations in Lima. He died on 3rd November 1639 of typhus. Beatified in 1837, canonized in 1962.

Patronage: patron saint of sick livestock, of the Peruvian 'social weeks', nurses and care assistants, invoked against rats and mice.

Representation in Art: *Apparel:* as dark-skinned Dominican (Pavia, S Rosa da Lima, painting, 17th century). *Attributes:* cross, rosary, bread basket with mice, angel with a whip and chain (Pavia, S Rosa da Lima, painting, 17th century). *Cycle:* copperplate engraving by Goetz-Klauber, Annus Dierum, circa 1750).

Martin of Tours

Bishop, Confessor, saint

Feast-day: 11th November, Ordination: 4th July, translation of the relics: 12th May, in the Byzantine-Greek rites: 12th October.

Life: born in 316/17 in Sabria/Pannonia (now Szombathely), the son of a Roman tribune. He was educated in Pavia and, at the age of 15, joined the Roman army and served in the Gallic guard under Emperor Constantine II and Julian. M.'s donation of his coat by cutting it in half took place at this time, at the gates of Amiens. M. was baptised at 18, left the army a year later, became a disciple of Hilary of Poitiers and received the Acolyth ordination. After working as a missionary in Illyria, M., because of the resistance against the Arians, withdrew as a hermit to the island of Gallinaria near Genoa. In 360, after his return to Poitiers, M. met Hilary again. In 361, M. founded the first monastery in Gaul in Ligugé, which was simultaneously the first western Coenobite monastery. M. extended his missionary work to the Danube region. There is evidence that he worked in Chartres, Amboise, Levrous, in the region of Sens and in Paris. In Vienne he met Victricius and Paulinus of Nola. In 371, the people elected him as bishop of Tours. In 375 he founded the Marmoutiers monastery. In two journeys to Trier, M. supported Priscillianus's rapturous-ascetic movement, originating from Spain, but could not prevent Priscillianus's execution (385). He died on 8th November 397 during a missionary journey to Candes near Tours. M. was the first saint not to suffer martyrdom.

Legends: M. gives half of his officer's coat to a beggar at the gates of Amiens. During the night, Christ appears to him, wrapped in this part of the coat. – M. offers to Emperor Julian to face the enemy without arms, only with the crucifix in his hand, but the enemy submits before he can do so. – On a journey to his parents, M. is robbed and tied up by alpine robbers. – M. converts the robbers to Christianity. – In Milan, M. conquers the devil. -M. overcomes hellebore poisoning with the power of his prayer. – M. revives a dead catechist shortly before his baptism. – M. discovers that a location, venerated as the grave of a saint, is the grave of a robber. – M. revives a young man before pagans. – M. goes as petitioner to Emperor Valentin's throne and shows him God's power through fire. – M. drives flames from the roof of a house, the flames are then carried away by the wind. – M. orders the tree of an idol to be cut down. – M. banishes two dogs, hunting a hare, and the dogs become paralysed temporarily. – M. cures a leper by embracing and kissing him. – The mother of God and St Thecla appear in M.'s cell. – The apostles Peter and Paul appear to M. – At the table of Emperor Maximus, M. only sips only from the wine presented to him. – M. reads a mass in an old, short robe but angels lengthen it with decorated ribbons. In Agaunum, M. collects the blood of St Mauritius. – Tours and Poitiers dispute over M.'s mortal remains. – M.'s relics are brought to Tours by ship. – During a mass in Milan, Ambrose of Milan is carried away to be present at M.'s funeral.

Patronage: patron saint of the Merovingians, the Frankish empire (France), the diocese of Eisenstandt, Mainz, Rottenburg, Hildesheim, of the Eichsfeld region, and the canton of Schwyz. Amongst others, patron saint of Aschaffenburg, of numerous churches, soldiers, cavalry, riders, blacksmiths, armourers, horses, weavers, tailors (because of the division of his coat), teetotallers (because of the legend of Emperor Maximus's banquet), town criers, beggars, coopers, broom and brushmakers, prisoners, tanners, beltmakers, glove-makers, herdsmen, hoteliers, hatters, millers, travellers, dealers in sheepskin, drapers, winegrowers.

Veneration and cult sites: relics in and pilgrimages to Tours; coat relic in Paris, Ste-Chapelle (the word chaplain originates from the chaplains working there); Limousin (head relic); Marcolés (Cantal) relic statue.

Superstition: final day of the business year, final day of the contract of employment, market day. – The Martin's goose was the last banquet before the Christmas quarter and Advent. – From the goose's breastbone, the weather can be foreseen for the following winter. – With the goose, Martin cakes, mostly croissants are eaten. – The first new wine is tasted. – It is a begging day for the young people who ask, during processions, for eggs, bacon and cakes. – In the Ardennes, women of marriageable age go with their boyfriends to springs to catch their future husbands by throwing a needle into the water. – In Hungary, people who dream during M.'s night will be happy. – In Hungary, people who get drunk on M.'s day by drinking too much wine will not have headaches or stomach pains the following year. – People who eat only turnips on M.'s day will become incontinent. – On M.'s day people can steal what they can get.

Representation in Art: *Apparel:* as bishop (Weltenburg, Monastery Church, fig., circa 1720); in tunica (Ravenna, S Apollinare Nuovo, mosaic, 6th century); as bishop in full armour (Rozebeke, Belgium, fig., 15th century); as soldier in trousers, tunic, coat and beret (Munich, Bavarian National Muse-

um, fig. from Zeitlar, circa 1480); as soldier in full armour and coat (Wismar, St Jürgen, fig., early 15th century); in full armour, coat and helmet, decorated with feathers (Aschaffenburg, Castle Chapel, fig., early 17th century); as rider in national Magyar dress (Bratislava, Cathedral, fig. by G. R. Donner). *Attributes:* book, model of a church (Mainz, Cathedral's Commemoration, tympanon relief, early 13th century); beggar at his feet (Mainz, Cathedral, commemorative portal, fig., circa 1410); coin as alm (Grossengstingen, fig., circa 1500); two dogs at his feet (Chartres, confessor's portal, fig., circa 1220); goose on a book (Tyrol Castle, reredos, circa 1500); goose at his feet (Weltenburg, Monastery Church, fig., circa 1720); goblet – so-called double goblet (Amberg, St Martin, fig., circa 1500); jug (Purg near Pöggstall, fig., early 16th century). *Special scenes:* as bishop, M.'s donation of his coat (Risstissen/Württemberg, Cemetery Chapel, fig., 1483); as soldier on foot, dividing his coat (Gotha, Castle, Erfurt Brakteat, circa 1170); as soldier on horseback, dividing his coat with the sword (Bassenheim, Parish Church, fig. by the Naumburg master, circa 1250); donation of the whole coat to a beggar (Rostock, St Nikolai, fig., 2nd half of the 15th century); alms donation to a beggar (Obernzell, Lower Bavaria, fig., 18th century); Jesus appears to M. in a dream (Correggio, S Quirino, painting by D. Feti, early 17th century); M.'s vision of the mother of God, Thecla, Agnes, Peter and Paul (Paris, Louvre, painting by Eustache le Sueur, circa 1655); M.'s cutting down of the tree of idols (Vézelay, Chapter relief, 12th century); M. kisses a leper (Tours, Maladerie de St-Lazare, Chapter relief, 12th century); M. collects the blood of St Mauritius (Angers, Musée des Tapisseries, tapestry, early 16th century); M. cures a possessed soul (Brussels, Musée des Beaux-Arts, painting by J. Jordaens, 1630); celebration in old clothes (Paris, Louvre,

painting by Le Sueur, 17th century); M. revives a dead child (Vienna, Kunsthistorisches Museum, painting by C. Ferri, 17th century); veneration of M. by the faithful (Szombathely, Episcopal Palace, painting by F. A. Maulpertsch, 18th century); St M.'s death (St-Benoît-sur-Loire, Chapter relief, 12th century); St M.'s funeral by Ambrose of Milan (Milan, S Ambrogio, mosaic, 12th century).

Cycles: numerous, amongst others, Chartres, Cathedral, stained glass, circa 1220; Paris, Musée Cluny, embroidery from Iceland, 13th century; Tours, Cathedral, stained glass, 2nd half of the 13th century; Assisi, S Francesco, lower Church, fresco by S. Martini, early 14th century; Liége, St Martin, antependium, 15th century.

Martyrs of Kaschau

(Mark Stephen Körosy, Stephen Pongraz SJ, Melchior Grodziecki SJ) beatified

Feast-day: 7th September

Life: born in 1580 in Krizêvci Körös, Croatia, M.'S.K. studied theology at the Jesuit Ferdinandeum college in Graz. Between 1611 and 1615 he studied at the Roman Germanicum in Rome. After he was ordained as a priest, he worked in Croatia. In 1616 he became, as the successor of Peter Pázmány SJ, archbishop of Gran and was appointed professor and rector of the Tyrnau seminary. After 1619 he was a popular missionary in the entirely protestant region of Kaschau and administrator of the Széplak Benedictine abbey near Kaschau. M.'S.K. became friends with the other two Jesuits after they had jointly celebrated religious Ignatian exercises. – S. P. was born in 1582 in Alvinc Castle in Transsylvania. He studied in Prague and Graz and worked in Ljubljana and Klagenfurt as a teacher. After 1615, he was a teacher and pastoral worker at the Homonna College and became, in 1618, a popular missionary in the Kaschau. –

M. G. was born in 1584 in Teschen/Austria/Silesia and originated from a Polish family. In 1603 he joined the Brünn Society of Jesus and became S. P.'s co-novice. He studied in Neuhaus (Bohemia), Prague and Brünn. In 1614 he became the director of Prague's Wencelas College. After 1619 he worked as a military pastoral worker and popular missionary in Kaschau. When prince Gabriel Bethlen tried to become king of Hungary, following the death of Emperor Mathew, they suffered martyrdom, because Bethlen ordered the Calvinist, Georg Rákóczi, to subjugate the northern regions. On 5th September 1619, Rákóczi forced Kaschau to surrender, following a surprise attack. Rákóczi's agreement to spare the Catholic people, demanded by the Calvinist councillors and the Calvinist priest, was explicitly not extended to the three priests. On 7th September 1619, they were arrested and tortured horribly to death by soldiers and the mob. S. P. did not die from his injuries until 8th September. The mortal remains were thrown into the sewers. Countess Catherine Pfaff, wife of the paladin Sigmund Forgasch, recovered the mortal remains and gave them a dignified burial. Beatified in 1905 by Pope Pius X.

Veneration and cult sites: in 1636, the mortal remains were translated to the Jesuit Church at Tyrnau.

Representation in Art: *Martyrdom:* engraving by Matthias Tanner SJ, Societas Jesu usque ad Sanguinis et vitae profusionem militans in Europe, Africa, Asia et America, Prague 1674.

The first **martyrs of Rome**
saints

Feast-day: since 1969: 30th June, local Roman feast since 1923

Ecclesiastical history: commemoration day for the Christians who suffered martyrdom under Emperor Nero after the rumour was spread in the Roman population, following the terrible fire on 18th/19th July 64, that the mad emperor had burned down the city himself so as to rebuild it more to his liking. The Roman Christians were therefore blamed for this rumour. The Christians had a bad reputation because they worshipped a nameless God and were regarded as atheists because they refused to put their God into the Pantheon, to be worshipped with the other Gods, as ordered by the government. Many Christians were, as Tacitus reported, selected from the martyrs and executed to entertain the public.

Representation in Art: *Apparel:* Nero's living torch (Cracow, National Museum, painting by H. Siemiradzki, 1876).

Mary the Blessed Virgin
Mother of God, saint

Feast-day: 8th. December, high feast of the Virgin and Mother of God, Immaculate Conception (in the 9th century from Constantinople to Southern Italy as a liturgical feast, introduced by Anselm of Canterbury who introduced the feast in his diocese; in 1476 adopted by Pope Sixtus IV for the Roman Church; on 8th December 1854 declared as obligatory and defined doctrine and dogma by Pope Pius IX. 1st January high feast of Mary, mother of God (Mother of the Church, oldest Roman Marian feast); 2nd February, feast of the portrayal of the Lord (on the 40th day after Christmas, since the early 5th century in Jerusalem; since 650 in Rome, but there more celebrated as "The Purification" in accordance with Jewish law; since 1960 the character of the Lord's feast is emphasized); 11th February, commemoration day of Our Lady of Lourdes (permitted in 1891 by Pope Leo XIII and in 1907 extended to the entire Church by Pope Pius X; commemorates the visions in 1858 of the shepherdess, Bernardette Soubirous, in a cave near Lourdes in which Mary invited the people to make pilgrimage but particularly encouraged them to prayer and penitence); 25th March high feast of the Annunciation (since 550, in the Eastern Church observed nine months before Christmas; in Rome, introduced in the 7th century); the Saturday following the 2nd Sunday after Whitsun, feast of the Immaculate Heart of Mary (stipulated in 1944 by Pope Pius XII after he had dedicated, on 31st October 1942, on the occasion of the feast of Fatima, all mankind to the Immaculate Heart of Mary, until 1970: 22nd August); 31st May, feast of Mary's Visitation (introduced in 1263 by Bonaventura for the Franciscan Order and fixed on the day of the octave of John the Baptist, 2nd July; in 1389 extended to the entire Western Church; since 1970 only observed in Germany on the original day); 16th July, commemorative day of Our Lady of Mount Carmel (originally the feast of the Carmelite Order with Mary's legendary scapula presentation to the general of the Order, Simon Stock, and therefore connected with the Scapula feast; since 1726 in the Roman feast calendar); 5th August, commemorative day of the consecration of the Roman basilica Santa Maria Maggiore (formerly celebrated as Our Lady of the Snows as commemoration of the legend of the miraculous snowfall in August with which Mary indicated the site on the Esquiline where she wanted her church to be built; celebrated within the Church since 435 in commemoration of the Council of Ephesus which confirmed and explicitly declared the title Mother of God for Mary); 15th August, high feast of the Assumption (a feast on Mary's death, observed in the Eastern Church in accordance with the Council of Ephesus, the feast-day was acknowledged by Emperor Mauritius (582–602) and observed in the Roman Church since the 7th century; on 1st November 1950, Pope Pius XII defined it as binding dogma that Mary's body and soul were admitted to heaven); 22nd August commemoration day of Mary the Queen (introduced by Pope Pius XII at the end of the Marian year (1954) and celebrated on 31st May; since 1970 moved to the octave of Assumption); 8th September, The Nativity of the Blessed Virgin (originally the consecration day of St Anne Church, Jerusalem, but introduced as a Roman feast by Pope Sergius (687–701); 12th September commemoration day of the Name of Mary (introduced in the 16th century in Spain, in 1683 adopted for the Roman Church by Pope Innocent XI as commemoration of the Viennese victory over the Turks, deleted from the Roman feast calendar in 1970; in Germany still observed because of the name celebrations on this day); 15th September, feast of the seven sorrows (a veneration originating from the Middle Ages, in the 15th century a feast in Erfurt and Cologne, since 1667 a feast-day of the Order of Servites, in 1814 introduced as a general feast-day by Pope Pius XII); 7th October, feast-day of Our Lady of the Rosary (rosary prayer began in the 15th century and was spread by the Dominicans and later by the Jesuits, in 1572 introduced as a feast by the Dominican Pope, Pius V in commemoration of the victory over the Turks in the sea battle near Lepanto (7th October 1571) and, at the request of Charles V, extended on 5th August 1716 to the entire Church following the victory near Peterwardein, Hungary); 8th October, Mary mother of Hungary, 21st November day of Our Lady of Jerusalem (since the 6th century consecration feast of St Mary's Church, Jerusalem; in the Roman Church only introduced in the 14th century and connected with the legendary Marian sacrifice, originating from the Protogospel according to St James.

Life: in Paul's letter to the Galatians (Gal. 4.4) he mentioned Christ's mother without name but emphasized the importance of

M.'s motherhood as the place where the transition of the eternal son of God into human nature and history occurred. That is regarded as M.'s special role. In the Gospel according to St Mark it was handed down that the family could not understand Jesus and intended to withdraw him from public life (Mk 3, 20 fol). Gospels written later slightly adapted Mk 3.13 to increase M.'s dignity. Matthew and Luke gave M. much attention in their history of Christ's childhood. M. was engaged to Joseph, originating from the House of David, but M. received Jesus from the Holy Spirit and Jesus was born of M., though still a virgin. The family's home was Nazareth. In the Gospel according to John, M. is mentioned in the report of the wedding of Cana. Under the cross, John took care of M. (Jo 19, 26–27). According to the Apocryphal New Testament Story, M. was present during the effusion of the Holy Spirit. From the beginning, the secret of the faith of the mother of God was connected to her virginity and later to M.'s privilege in having no personal sins. M.'s special standing in ecclesiastical life was traditionally seen as the Church's self-recognition in M.

Legends: Proto-Gospel according to James regarding Christ's childhood: an angel predicts M.'s birth to Anne. – Anne makes M.'s nursery into a sanctum and does not permit M. to eat anything profane or unclean. – M.'s playmates are the pure daughters of Hebrews. – At the age of three, M. is brought to the temple where she is placed on the third step of the altar by the high priest. God gives M. grace and she dances before the priest. M. lives in Jerusalem as a temple virgin and receives her food there from angels. – M. becomes engaged to Joseph after his staff began to sprout before the high priest after Israel's widowers had placed them on the altar. – M. sews a new curtain for the Jerusalem temple using purple and scarlet fabric. – The Archangel Gabriel appears to M., sitting at the distaff, and announces the conception of the Holy Spirit. – M.'s pregnancy is revealed to Joseph and the divine secret is revealed to him in a dream by an angel. – Because of M.'s defilement, Annas, the scribe, gives Joseph and M. a drink with cursed water and orders them to go into the desert. Both of them return unharmed, Annas cannot sentence them because God has revealed no sin. – At Christ's birth, M. is assisted by a wet-nurse who tells the servant, Salome, about the miracle of the conception by a virgin; Salome only believed this after she has examined M.'s condition but her hands burn as on fire; an angel appears and cures her. -Legends on M.'s death and ascent to heaven according to the Legenda aurea and Transitus Mariae: to M., at 72 years of age, an angel appears who predicts her death and presents her with a

palm branch from paradise. – M. requests that the apostles should be present when she dies. – Clouds pick them up and bring them to her door in Ephesus. – Christ comes with an army of angels and the patriarch to pick up his mother's soul. – On Christ's orders, the apostles carry M.'s mortal remains from Mount Sion to the Josaphat valley. – The Jewish high priest wants to prevent M.'s funeral by armed force but his hands remain attached to the bier and can only be removed after St Peter intercedes (var: a Jew wants to desecrate the mortal remains on the bier but God's angel cuts off both his hands). – The people accompanying the high priest are blinded by angels but cured after St Peter orders the high priest to hold the palm branch, brought from paradise, over the people. – Christ unifies M.'s soul again with her body and M. is admitted into heaven with body and soul, carried there by angels. – Thomas is not present when M. dies and does not believe the miracle but M.'s belt suddenly falls from heaven. – M., as imperial bride, sits at her son's right side as he blesses and crowns her. – Further legends under Caesarius of Heisterbach.

Patronage: patron saint of Hungary, Poland, Bavaria (feast of Patrona Bavariae on 14th May), Rhineland, Westphalia, Lower Italy, Sicily, Spain, Southern France, Altötting, Einsiedeln and many others; German Order, Servites, Marian Congregation, numerous Marian brotherhoods all over the globe, fishermen, sailors, grinders in Hallgarten, Rheingau with a painting belonging to their trade association ("the beautiful Hallgarten maid", late 14th century), of virginity, chastity, members of Orders, of pregnant women, M. is a helper in all kinds of distress and danger, M. is always helpful, is a powerful and kind patron, is the salvation of the infirm, of travellers, invoked in battle and at war, and for problems of infertility.

Veneration and cult sites: relics are, amongst other locations, in Aachen, Cathedral Treasury (dress, napkins of the Christchild); Saturday as St Mary's day; Rome, Santa Maria Maggiore; patron saint of numerous Episcopal Churches worldwide. Numerous St Mary pilgrimages and Madonnas. In Germany St M. pilgrimages to (amongst others) Aachen, Cathedral; Altötting, Andechs, Mount Aren (mother in pain); Aufhofen (mother in pain); Maria Beinberg; Berching; Berchtesgaden; Beuron; Bidlesheim; Maria-Birnbaum; Birkenstein; Birnau; Blieskastel (vespers painting); Bochum-Stiepel; Dettelbach; Dieburg (vespers painting); Dorfen; Ettal; Führbrück; Freystadt; Fulda; Gaweinstein; Gräfinthal; Mariahilf ob Passau; Hohenpeissenberg; Kevelear, Klosterlechfeld; Kolmerberg; Ramsau; Sammarei; St Mürgen; Sossau; Telgte; Tuntenhausen; Vilsbiburg; Waghusel, Würzburg; Käppele. Pilgrimages in France to (amongst others) Agen; Aigouillon; Aix (Haute Vienne); Aix (Bouches-du-Rhône); Albi; Amiens; Angoulême; Antibes; Chartres; Clermont-Ferrand; Notre-Dame-du-Port; Notre-Dame-du-Folgoet; Honfleur; Notre-Dame-de-la-Delivrande near Bayeux; Notre-Dame de Boulogne; Lourdes; Marseille, Notre-Dame-de-la-Garde; Paris, Notre-Dame-des-Victoires; Puy, Notre Dame; Rocamadour; Saintes Maries de la Mer. Pilgrimages in Hungary (amongst others) to Abos (to the rosary queen); Maria-Pócs; Maria-Radna; Szepesvádralja on Mount Leutschauer; Mariazell in Styria (preferred by Hungarian pilgrims); Gjyüd; Maria Kemend near Fünfkirchen; Maria Könnye; Csiksomlyö; Sasvar; Maria Schlossberg; Turbek near Szigetvár; Ohegy; Zolyom; Radvány; Königsberg; Neutra; Dubnicz; Visnyó; Rust; Kópháza; Téth-Szent-Kut; Radafalva; Vasvár; Röth; Kertes; Maria-Bodaik; Maria-Einsiedeln near Ofen; Hétkápolna near Waitzen; Maria Besnyö near Gödöllö; Andocs; Remette; Hajos. In Great Britain M. pilgrimages (amongst others) to Walsingham.

Superstition: M.'s feasts are important annual days. Numerous, barely comprehensible customs connected with nature. – Maria Läng (Long), expressed as a measure, serves as a remedy against harm and danger (see the Regensburg Maria-Läng Chapel) and for labour. – Small Mariazell pictures to swallow cure many diseases and can be, if needed, cut from a roll and swallowed individually. – In Hungary a lamp burns on Christmas night to ensure that M. comes to bring luck. – Those who catch a swallow on Nativity must take a stone from its stomach and eat it as a remedy against epilepsy.

Representation in Art: *Apparel:* as child (Frankfurt, Städel, painting by J. de las Roclas, 17th century); as Roman matron in tunica and palla (Rome, Santa Sabina, relief on the wing of the door, circa 430); as Hodegitria or Glykophilousa in Paenula (bell-like wrap with a hood on the upper part) and shirt-like dress (Cologne, St Maria in Kapitol, fig., circa 1180); in chiton, above maphorion (veil, covering breast and shoulders), hood over hair (Hildesheim, Cathedral Treasury, book illustration, Bernward Evangeliar, 11th century); as queen in purple dress (Rome, Santa M. in Trastevere, icon Madonna della Clemenze, 7th century); as crowned queen (Siena, S Maria dei Servi, painting by Coppo di Marcovaldo) as empress (Liège, St Jean, fig, circa 1200); as Christ's bride without child (Cologne, Cathedral's Choir, fig., 13th century); as bride of the Holy Spirit (Tegernbach, fig, circa 1750); as pregnant woman with belt (Augsburg, Cathedral, painting, circa 1470); as pregnant woman with the child, made visible on her body through a mandorla (Utrecht, Diocesan

Museum, painting by the master of the Friedberg altar, circa 1410); as woman who has just given birth, lying in child's bed (Georgsmarienhütte-Oesede, fig,. circa 1440); as mother praying to her child (Florence, Uffizi, painting by Correggio, 1524/26); as mother castigating her child (privately owned, painting by Max Ernst, 1926); as nursing mother (Siena, Pinakotheca Maria Lactans by Ambrogio Lorenzetti, circa 1330); praying (M. Orans) (Rome, Oratory of S Venetius, mural painting, before 642); as priestess with Jesus as server (Paris, Louvre, painting from Amiens, 1437); lying, having fainted (Ebernburg, Catholic Parish Church, fig, circa 1400); as mourning widow (Cologne, Schnütgen Museum, fig., circa 1420); as mother breaking down with grief (Osnabrück, Diocesan Museum, fig., early 16th century); as mother, suffering (Düsseldorf, St Lambertus, fig. circa 1700); accusing Mary as vesper painting with her dead son on her lap (Soest, Nikolai Chapel, fig., circa 1400); in full armour as warrior (Klosterneuburg, painting, circa 1440); as helms man on a ship (page for New Year, woodcut, before 1450/60); in a dress of sheaves (Soest, Maria zur Höhe, painting, circa 1470); as good shepherdess (Thaining, St Wolfgang, painting, 18th century); in protective coat (Berlin, Governmental Museums, fig. by Friedrich Schramm, 1480); in wreath of flowers (Munich, Alte Pinakothek, painting by J. Breughel the Elder; as companion of souls on the divine ladder (Siena, S M. della Scala Hospital, fresco, 16th century); as Annunziata (Munich, Alte Pinakothek, painting by Antonello da Messina, circa 1470); as Assunta (Munich, Alte Pinakothek, painting by Lippo Memmi, 1310); as Mater Dolorosa (Madrid, Prado, painting by Tiepolo, late 18th century); as apocalyptic woman (Munich, Alte Pinakothek, painting by P. P. Rubens, 1626); in a wreath of light (Kloster Oelinghausen, fig., circa 1500); as Mary the victorious (Weyarn, fig. by I. Günther, circa 1764); as Mater et Magistra (Munich, Frauenkirche, fig. by E. Diez, 1959); as saint at pillar (Munich, Marienplatz, fig., 1638), giving milk to saints (Grosskarlbach, relief at the pulpit, 16th century); as black mother of God (Czestochowa), pilgrim painting). *Attributes:* sceptre (Paris, Notre-Dame, Anne's portal, relief, after 1160); rose sceptre (Osnabrück, Cathedral Treasury, fig., circa 1450); crown (Aachen, Cathedral Treasury, fig., circa 1280); crown of oak leaves (privately owned, painting by the master of the coloured Nimus, 15th century); headband (Kalkar, St Nikolai, fig., 1475/80); globe (Cologne, Cathedral, book illustration in the Pontifical by St Vaast in Arras, circa 1050); necklace (Westphalian Art Society, fig., circa 1520); necklace with charm (Munich, St Moritz, fig. circa 1400); small cross (Lemberg, Dominican Church, fig., late 14th century); small cross with tools of torture in the hands of angels (Venice, S Giorgio dei Greci, icon by E. Tzanfournaris, late 16th century); cross crosier, pointed at the Christ-child by the child, John (Cologne-Marienburg, Cremer Collection, painting, circa 1550); crucifix (New York, Metropolitan Museum, Madonna shrine, circa 1300); crucifix, carried by angels (Florence, Uffizi, painting by Andrea Rizzi, 16th century); open book (Nuremberg, Germanic National Museum, painting by Hans Burgkmair, Madonna with the dove, 1510); eagle lectern with book (Cologne, Cathedral, fig., after 1473); dove as symbol of the Holy Spirit (St Florian, Collegiate Church, painting by C. Dolci); seven doves as symbol for the gifts of the Holy Spirit, lions as symbol of the apostles and both St Johns' (Gurk, Western Gallery, mural painting, 1260/70); bird, presented to his mother by Jesus (Paris, Louvre, fig. from Coulombs, late 13th century); goldfinch as play on words, originating from Italian, cartelline = scroll, cardellino = goldfinch (Böllenborn,

Pilgrimage Church, fig., 1517); jay as messenger bird (Zurich, Swiss National Museum, master of the Bremgarten altar, circa 1510); great tit (Nuremberg, Germanic National Museum, painting by Hans Burgkmair, 1509); nightingale (Nuremberg, Germanic National Museum, so-called Gossenbrotmadonna, 1499); parrot, as this bird can say 'ave' (Nuremberg, Germanic National Museum, painting by Hans Baldung-Grien, 1527/28); swallow (Madrid, Prado, plate of the word of God, by Fra Angelico, circa 1430/50); siskin (Berlin, Governmental Museums, painting by Albrecht Dürer, Madonna with the siskin, 1506); unicorn (Weimar, Castle Museum, painting, 1st half of the 15th century); lamb (Paris, Louvre, painting by Leonardo da Vinci); flowers (Florence, Museo Nationale di Bargello, relief by Lucca della Robbia, circa 1440); aquilegia (Erfurt, Cathedral, painting of the mystic unicorn hunt, circa 1420); eland (Cologne, Wallraf-Richartz Museum, painting by Joos van Kleve, 1515); apple as sign of redemption (Cologne, Wallraf-Richartz Museum, painting by Stephan Lochner, circa 1448); anemone, arnica, arum, lily of the valley, iris etc. (Frankfurt, Städel, painting by the Master of the small paradise garden, circa 1410); pear (Aachen, Suermondt Museum, fig. circa 1410); wooden clove or Carthusian clove reminiscent of nails and therefore passion (privately owned, master from the Upper Rhine, preaching to Mary); thorns (Essen, Folkwang Museum, painting by Petrus Christus, 1444); dill (Chantilly, Musée Condé, Ingeborg Psalter, portrait of Christ's birth, circa 1200); strawberry (Solothurn, Municipal Museum, painting by the Upper Rhine master of the Madonna with the strawberries, circa 1425); fig tree, lady's slipper, carnation, camomile (Stuppach, painting by the master of the MGN, called Grünewald, 1517/19); pomegranate or paradise apple (Düsseldorf, Museum of Art, fig. circa

1400); cherry as symbol of pardonned sins (Münster, Regional Museum, painting by Hermann tom Ring, circa 1550); lily in hand as sign of the Immaculata (Alzenau, Parish Church, fig. by P. Wagner, circa 1760); lily in vase by a portrait of preaching (Mainz, Regional Museum, painting by the so-called house-book master, after 1500); peony (Colmar, Dominican Church, painting by M. Schongauer); larkspur (Ghent, St Bavo, Ghent altar by Hubert and Jan van Eyck, 1432); rose (Trier, Episcopal Museum, fig. by Peter Wederath, after 1500); rose hedge (Colmar, Dominican Church, painting by M. Schongauer); celandine (Munich, Alte Pinakothek, praying of the kings by Rogier van der Weyden, 15th century); violet (Cologne, Archiepiscopal Diocesan Museum, painting by Stephan Lochner, circa 1439); picture-puzzle carnation (Nuremberg, Lorenz Church, altar painting, 1310); vine (Marburg, Elizabeth Church, tympanum relief, 1283); grape as symbol of Jesus, born of M.'s womb as noble fruit (Kälberau, Pilgrimage Church, fig., circa 1450), sweet pea (Cologne, Wallraf-Richartz Museum, painting by the master of St Veronica, circa 1410/20); Madonna with a flower of a sweet pea, wide spoon and bowl (Hemstede, v. Pannwitz Collection, painting by G. David, circa 1500); egg (Milan, Brera, painting by Piero della Francesca); cut lemon as sign of the passion (Essen, Krupp Collection, painting by Joos van Cleve, early 16th century); burning Grail chalice (S Clemente de Tahull, painting, circa 1123); dummy or sucking bag (Nuremberg, Germanic National Museum, painting by Hans Holbein the Elder, circa 1505); pearl, glass container with light shining through, candlestick, water-bowl with clear water as sign of virginity, fruit (Frankfurt, Städel, painting by Jan van Eyck, 1st half of the 15th century); divine city (London, British Museum, book illustration in Cod. Add. Ms. 28681, early 13th century); concave mir-

ror (Speyer, St Ludwig, Bossweil altar, circa 1490); Church building, rainbow, bee hives (Stuppach, painting by the master of the MGN, called Grünewald, 1517–18, chalice with host (Paris, Louvre, painting by Ingres, 1840); coral necklace (in the art trade, painting by Marinus van Reymerswaele, circa 1500); prayer cord (Cologne, Wallraf-Richartz Museum, painting by the master of St Veronica, circa 1410/20); rosary (painting by Murillo, 17th century); girdled sword (Niederstetten, Cemetery Chapel, fig., 13th century); sword at the breast, tear cloth (Munich, Herzogspital Church, fig. by T. Pader, 1651); seven swords (Munich, Bavarian National Museum, from the Kria Collection, 18/19th century); sun (London, National Gallery, painting by Pisanello, 1440); crescent moon (Lübeck, St Mary's Church, fig. from the Antwerp altar, 1518); globe as plinth, paradise serpent (Brussels, St Gudula, sound screen of the pulpit, 1695/99); dragon at her feet (Cologne, Schnütgen Museum, fig., circa 1240). *Special scenes:* Mary with all symbols of the Laurentian litany (Bonn, Regional Rhine Museum, water barrel altar; 1420; Mainz, Regional Museum, painting by C. Crayer, 17th century; Munich; Residenz, Hofkapelle, stucco, 1614/30; Altenburg, Pilgrimage Church, frescoes, 1711); a selection of (amongst others) sun, moon, starfish, mirror without marks, Gideon's fur moistened by dew, ivory tower, divine Jerusalem, the entrance to heaven, closed gate, sealed spring, spring of salvation, well of life (Essen, Krupp Collection, painting by S. Botticelli, late 15th century); closed garden, rose bush, lily under thorns, magnificent olive, rice 'jesse', Aaron's flowering staff, almond branch, unicorn hunt (St-Jean – Saverne, tapestry, 15th century); Madonna rosary (Nuremberg, Lorenz Church, fig. by Veit Stoss); Luke paints M. (Munich, Alte Pinakothek, painting by Rogier van der Weyden, 1435/40); gift of a rosary to St Dominic

(Speyer, St Magdalena, painting, 17th century); Marian appearances can be found under the individual saints; numerous local miracles and events during and for pilgrimage. *Cycles:* amongst others in Chartres, King's portal, Chapter sculpture, 1150; Chartres, western portal, 1150; St Gilles, left gate, 2nd half of the 12th century; Paris, Notre Dame, Anne portal, 12th century; Tournai, St Mary's Shrine by Nicholas of Verdun, 1205; Pisa, Museo Nazionale S Matteo, M. plate, late 13th century; Padua, Arena Chapel, frescoes by Giotto; Orvieto, Cathedral, frescoes by Ugolino d'Ilario, 1357–1364.

Mary of Egypt
Anachoretine, saint

Feast-day: 2nd April (in the Greek-Orthodox Church rites 1st April)

Life: lived as a hermit in the 4th century.

Legends: reports partially mirror the penitent life of St Mary Magdalene: M. lives for 17 years in Alexandria and works as a prostitute. – During a voyage with pilgrims to the Jerusalem Holy Cross she offers her body to the sailors instead of paying her fare. – Because of her impurity, an invisible power denies her access to the pilgrimage Church. – Before a Madonna, M. is converted and able to enter the Church. – A man gives her three pennies which she uses to buy three loaves of bread. – A voice orders M. to cross the Jordan which she does. – M. lives for 47 years in the desert and during this time eats the three loaves of bread, bought in Jerusalem. – When searching for a holy old man, abbot Zosimas discovers M., her clothes by then gone. – M. begs for Zosimas's coat to cover herself. – Before Zosimas's eyes, M. is lifted from the earth in prayer. – M. requests Zosimas to bring the body of the Lord to her in the desert every year. – M. walks over the Jordan to receive the body of the Lord from Zosimas. – M. takes only one hour for the thirty day return journey into the desert. – One year later Zosimas finds her mortal remains. – M. writes in the sand to ask Zosimas to bury her. – A lion digs the grave for Zosimas because he has brought no tools.

Patronage: penitents.

Veneration and cult sites: relics in Rome, Naples, Tournai, Antwerp. Since the 6th century, her grave has been a location for pilgrimages. Since 614, her cult was brought to Rome, Calabria and Southern Italy by Palestinian refugees.

Representation in Art: *Apparel:* as a naked, young woman, her entire body covered by hair (Aachen, St Paul, fig. at the confessional, 1665); in long dress, coat with headscarf, turban-like bonnet (Vienna, St Stephan, plinth of the pulpit, fig., early 16th century); naked, covered by Zosimas's coat (Bruges, St-Jans Hospital, painting by Hans Memling, 1480); As old, penitent hermit (Montpellier, Musée.)

Mary Goretti

Martyr, saint

Feast-day: 6th July

Life: born on 16th October 1890 in Corinaldo. She was the first of five children of a poor farmer. In 1899 they moved to the leased farm of the widower Serenelli. The son of the leaseholder, Alessandro, sixteen years of age, made advances to M. and tried to submit her to his will. On 5th July 1902 he stabbed her in blind fury with a knife. – M died of her injuries but forgave her murderer on her deathbed. – Beatified on 27th April 1947, canonized on 24th June 1950 in the presence of her mother.

Legends: in a dream, M. appears to Alessandro, sentenced to 30 years' forced labour, picks flowers and offers them to him.

Patronage: mostly of extreme conservative ecclesiastical unions, amongst others in Bavaria.

Veneration and cult sites: relics are in Nettuno, S Maria delle Grazie e S Maria Goretti.

No representation in visual art.

Mary Magdalene

One of the female followers of Jesus, saint

Feast-day: 22nd July

Life: according to biblical reports (Mk 16.9 and Lk 8.2), Jesus drove out seven demons from Magdala (now el-Mej-del on Lake Genezareth near Tiberius). Since that time, MM. followed Jesus, was present at Jesus's crucifixion and death (Mk 15.40, Mt 27.56 and Jo 19.25), when Jesus was taken from the cross and during his funeral (Mk 15.47, Mt 27.61). MM. belonged to the three Marys who went to the grave, after buying ointment, to anoint Christ (Mk 15.1) or to look after the grave (Mt 28.1) but found it empty (Jo 20.1). The risen Christ appeared to MM. but she thought it was the gardener (Jo 20.15). When MM. realized that it was the Lord, she told the disciples (Mk 16.10 and Jo 20.18).

Legends: Because of the exegetic interpretation of the Fathers of the Church, Ambrose of Milan, Cassian and Pope Gregory I, the biblical MM. merged in the west with M. of Bethany from the House of Lazarus as well as with a nameless sinner (Lk 7.37–50) who, during the banquet of the Pharisees anoints Jesus's feet and dries them with her hair. – Missionary legends after the Ascension of Christ: MM. preaches Christianity. – Together with Maximinus, her brother Lazarus, her sister Martha, her servant Martilla and Cedonius, born blind but cured by Christ, MM. is put into a rudderless ship by pagans and driven into the sea (older var: together with Maximinus, MM. escapes from the pagans on a seaworthy ship). – The ship lands in Marseilles but MM. is not admitted to the city. – MM. converts the pagan prince and princess by appearing to them three times during the night in a dream threatening them with divine punishment if they refuse to give her shelter. -In Marseilles, MM. preaches against pagan idols. – With her prayers, MM. ensures that the prince has an heir. – With his pregnant wife, the prince sails on a pilgrimage to Rome. – During childbirth, a violent storm breaks and the princess dies on the ship. – The dead princess and the living child are abandoned on an island. – On the island, MM. cares for the boy and makes, along with the revived princess, the same pilgrimage to Jerusalem as the prince has done with St Peter. – In Rome, the prince meets St Peter who assures him that his wife is only sleeping. – The prince and St Peter make a pilgrimage to the Jerusalem location of the Lord. – After their return Maximinus baptises the prince and the princess. – Both destroy the pagan temple in Marseilles. – MM. nominates Lazarus as bishop of Marseilles. – MM. later preaches in Aix (Provence) and nominated Maximinus as bishop there. – Legends regarding penitence: unrecognized, MM. lives for 30 years in the desert. – At the seven hours of prayer, angels lift MM. into the air to ensure that she can hear the singing of the heavenly hosts and so needs no earthly food. – A hermit priest who wants to fathom MM.'s secret has a sudden blackout and is therefore unable to observe MM.'s elevation. – MM. reveals herself to the priest, explains who she is and requests from him, because her end is near, that he go to Maximinus to tell him to be alone in the church during early mass because she would be brought there by angels (var: the priest gives his coat to the penitent MM. to ensure that she can go to him dressed). – In his church, Maximinus gives MM. the Lord's body and blood. – MM. dies next to the altar, her arms spread wide. – Angels carry MM.'s soul into heaven. – With the assistance of angels, Maximinus buries MM. – Selection of posthumous Legends: in the search for MM.'s mortal remains, the monk, Badilon, discovers the saint's sarcophagus near Aix, lavishly decorated with motifs of her life. – MM. appears in a dream to Badilon and orders him to bring her mortal remains to Vézelay. – There are numerous reports about miracles during MM. pilgrimages to Vézelay.

Patronage: Provence; by order of Charles of Anjou, since 1266 also patron of Sicily and Naples; penitent women; women in white habits; nuns of the Dominican Order; nuns of the Franciscan Order and other Orders named after her; prisoners; the seduced; women; hairdressers; comb-makers; gardeners; children who have difficulties in walking; perfume and powder manufacturers; ointment mixers; lead casters; coopers; glove makers; pupils; students, wool weavers; 'white' tanners; winegrowers; patron saint of mineshafts; the miners of Mareit; the water-carriers of Chartres; the Lübeck tailors; of the Bologna Drapieri, the Troyes shoemakers, invoked against eye disease, the plague, vermin and lightning.

Veneration and cult sites: since the 6th century the mortal remains are venerated in Ephesus; in 899 translated to Constantinople; Mary's grave, Lazarus's sister, is venerated particularly in Bethany; since the 9th century an important pilgrimage to the Vézelay Benedictine monastery, introduced by Girard de Roussillon as well as to Aix-en-Provence and St-Maximin near Aix. Relics are, amongst others, in Exeter and Halberstadt (10th century); Paris (1810). Veneration in Burgundy and Provence. Patron saint, among others of Verdun (11th century); Paris, Ste-Madeleine and of hospitals and churches on the pilgrimage routes to Compostela; pilgrimages to Autun; Vézelay; St-Baume-en-Aix; Lübeck (after the victory over the Danes in the battle of Bornhöved, 1227).

Superstition: if the plaits of young girls are cut on MM.'s day, they will have beautiful long hair. -MM.'s day is regarded as an unlucky day, one should therefore avoid weddings, journeys, important new business or embarking on a voyage because "9 will be hanged, 9 will fall down and 9 will drown". Moreover, one should not climb mountains or go swimming because "MM. wants a swimmer and a climber".

Representation in Art: *Apparel:* in traditional, long, girdled dress and coat with covered head (Autun, Lazarus grave, fig., circa 1170); in dress, decorated with braiding (Weitensfeld/Carinthia, stained glass, 1175); in rich Byzantine clothes (Cividale, S Maria della Valle, mural painting, late 12th century); with bare head (Venice, Accademia, painting by Lorenzo Veneziano, 1337); in secular, fashionable clothes with flowing hood (Hamburg, Kunsthalle, Grabow altar by master Bertram, 1379); as princess in court clothes (Cologne, Wallraf-Richartz Museum, painting by Lucas Cranach the Elder, 16th century); in dress with ermine collar (Bamberg, Staatsbibliothek, HS. his 149, book illustration, circa 1330); as penitent in hair shirt (Karlsruhe, Staatl. Kunsthalle, painting by the Coburg circle pages, late 15th century); as penitent, covered in hair (Florence, Galleria dell' Accademia, painting by the MM. master, circa 1280); as penitent her body covered with hair, except breasts and knees (Munich, Bavaria National Museum, fig. from Münnerstadt by Tilman Riemenschneider, circa 1490); as naked, captivating penitent in the countryside (Parma, National Gallery, painting by Correggio, before 1517); in ecstasy (Rome, Galleria Doria Pamphili, painting by Wybrand de Geest, circa 1620). *Attributes:* closed ointment container (Komburg, Monastery Church, relief fig. of the light crown, circa 1130/40); open ointment container (Antwerp, Museum, painting by G. Massys, circa 1500); incense barrel (Gernrode, holy grave, relief, circa 1100); heads of devils as indication of possession (Freiburg, Minster, northern transept, stained glass, middle of the 13th century; palm branch as indication of Palestinian origin (Basle, Copperplate Engraving Cabinet, pen-and-ink drawing by H. Holbein the Elder, after 1500); removed crown (Nuremberg, Germanic National Museum, altar of the Bethany brothers and sisters, 2nd half of the 14th century); MM. with ointment container and divine crown on her head (Vich, Museum, painting by Master of Fonollosa, late 14th century); penitent MM. with divine crown on her head (Oberwesel, Liebfrauen Church, mural painting, circa 1500); MM.'s crowned soul (Chartres, Cathedral, stained glass, circa 1200); prayer cord (Palma de Mallorca, Beata Cataline convent, painting, circa 1365); scroll as indication of missionary work (Amsterdam, O. Lanz Collection, painting of the Florentine school, circa 1350); book (London, National Gallery, painting by Rogier van der Weyden, circa 1423/34); crown of thorns (Játiva, S Felix, paining attributed to Juan Rexach, 2nd half of the 15th century); whip (Berlin, Staatsmuseen, painting by P. P. Rubens); crucifix (New York, Metropolitan Museum, paint-ing by Titian, 1530/35); skull (Pomssen/Saxony, painting, circa 1510); skull, crucifix, books, snake, light at night (Paris, Louvre, painting by Georges de La Tour, circa 1640); flowering branch (Gubbio, Cathedral, painting by T. Viti, 1521); mirror (Nuremberg, Germanic National Museum, choir vestment embroidery from Gdansk, circa 1430); musical instruments (Poznan, National Museum, painting by the master of the female half figures, 1st third of the 16th century). *Special scenes:* MM.'s wedding with John in Cana, nominated by Jesus as his disciple (Frankfurt, Museum of Arts and Crafts, foundry relic, 1st half of the 12th century); MM. riding to a hunt (Berlin,

Staatsmuseen, painting by the MM. Master of the Hat Legend, 1510/20); MM. with lovers (Paris, Bibliothèque Nationale, HS. Fr. 24955, circa 1520); MM., anointing Jesus's feet (S Angelo in Formis, mural painting, 11th century); MM, drying Jesus's feet with her hair (Dresden, Gallery of Old Masters, painting by D. Gabbiani, 19th century); MM. anoints and dries simultaneously Jesus's feet (Bourges, Cathedral, stained glass, 1st quarter of the 13th century); MM. mourns under the cross (Padua, Arena Chapel, fresco by Giotto, circa 1350); MM. anoints the wounds of Jesus's mortal remains (Feldkirch altar by Wolf Huber, 1521); MM. with other women at Jesus's funeral (Cologne, Wallraf-Richartz Museum, painting, early 15th century); MM. goes, together with other women, to the grave (Studernheim (Pfalz), Noli-me-tangere plate, side motif, circa 1480); MM. receives at Christ's tomb, together with other women, the angel's message (Esztergom, Keresztény Múseum, painting by the Ausgburg Master, before 1477); MM. meets the resurrected Christ in the garden – the so-called Noli-me-tangere presentation (Cologne, Wallraf-Richartz Museum, painting by the master of the golden plate, 1st third of the 15th century); MM. at Christ's Ascension and the sending of the Holy Spirit (Neckartailfingen, St Martin, mural painting, 1st quarter of the 14th century); MM.'s departure by ship on a missionary voyage with Maximinus, Lazarus and others (Troyes, stained glass, 1st half of the 16th century); MM. at sea (Karlsruhe, Regional Library, book illustration in Cod. St Georgen 66, 15th century; MM. and her companions at sea in an unseaworthy ship (Châlons sur Marne, St-Alpin, stained glass, 1st half of the 16th century);MM. and her companions in a long, unseaworthy ship at Marseilles (Tiefenbronn, MM. altar by Lucas Moser, 1430); Christ appears to the penitent MM. (Ferrara, S Domenico, painting by I.

Scarsellino, circa 1595); God the father and angels crown the penitent MM. (Gdansk, St Mary's Church, St James's Chapel, painting, circa 1425); MM. and the penitent sinners with Christ (Munich, Alte Pinakothek, painting by P. P. Rubens, 1615/18); MM. lifted from the ground by angels (Strasbourg, Museum of the Women's Refuges, fig. from Niederehnheim, circa 1400); MM. as Christophory corresponding to Mary Platytera, perhaps an indication of the burning love of the Lord (Worcester, Mass., Museum of Art, painting by Paolo Veneziano, middle of the 14th century); MM. fed by angels (Berlin, Kaiser Friedrich Museum, painting by L. di Credi, circa 1500); MM., fed by angels during elevation (Esztergom, Archiepiscopal Gallery, painting by L. die Credi, c, 1500); in front of the cave, a bishop offers communion to MM. (Münnerstadt, St Magdalena, relief by Tilman Riemenschneider, 1490/92); MM. receives communion from a priest in the church (Philadelphia, Museum of Art, predella painting by S. Botticelli, circa 1500); MM. receives communion whilst angels play music (Valencia, Museum, painting by J. Espinoza, 17th century); at communion, death waits for MM. (Genoa, S Maria di Carignano, painting by F. Vanni, circa 1600); MM. on her deathbed, angels receive her soul (Vich, Museum, painting by the master of St Georg, circa 1450); MM. dies on the steps of the altar (St Korbinian, Tyrol, painting, 1498); MM.'s funeral, assisted by angels (Münnerstadt, St Magdalena, relief by Tilman Riemenschneider, 1490/92); MM.'s funeral in the desert (Vercelli, mural painting by G. Ferrari, 1532); opening of MM.'s sarcophagus to test the authenticity of the relic (Semur-en-Auxois, stained glass, 1225/79. *Cycles:* numerous, amongst others, Chartres, southern aisle, stained glass, circa 1200; Semur-en-Auxois, stained glass, 1225/79; Florence, Galleria dell'Accademia, painting by the MM. master, circa 1280); Assisi, lower church, mural painting by the Waltensburg master, 2nd quarter of the 14th century; Gdansk, St Mary's Church, choir vestments embroidery, circa 1430); Erfurt, Ursuline convent, tapestry, late 15th century; Tiefenbronn, MM. Church, altar by L. Moser, 1432; Mareit (Ausserridnaun) near Sterzing, altar by M. Stöberl, 1509; Lübeck, Annenmuseum, altar, circa 1519.

Mary Magdalene dei Pazzi

Carmelite nun, saint

Feast-day: 25th May (Carmelite Order 29th May)

Life: born on 2nd April 1566 in Florence as Catherine of the noble family, Pazzi. In 1582 she joined the Florence Carmelite convent S Maria degli Angeli. One year later, whilst ill, she made her vow. She had deep depressions, inner temptations and the feeling that God had not supported her for five years. With her special veneration for the suffering of Christ, MM.'s soul reached a mystic unity with Christ. Her visions, recognized by the other nuns, encompassed wide fields of Christian spirituality, the secret of the Holy Trinity and the incarnation of Jesus. She finally became mistress of the novices and vice-prioress. She died on 25th May 1607. Beatified in 1626, canonized in 1669.

Patronage: Florence, Naples, Order of the Barefooted.

Veneration and cult sites: the mortal remains, still not decomposed, are in Carecci, in a magnificent sarcophagus, made by G. B. Foggini.

Representation in Art: *Apparel:* as noblewoman (Florence, privately owned, painting by Santi di Tito, 16th century); as Carmelite nun (Lille, Carmelite church, painting by J. van Oost the Younger, 17th century). *Attributes:* Christ-child (Toledo, Capuchinas, painting by G. Brandi, 17th century); tools of torture (Naples, S Maria Maddalena, paint-

ing by L. Giordano, late 17th century); stigmata, crown of thorns, cross, lily (Rogny, Parish Church, relief medallion, 7th century); burning heart, chain, spiritual dove (Paris, St Joseph, fresco by G. Damery, 17th century); heart in the right hand (Cologne, S Maria in der Schnurgasse, fig., 1683); whip (Maxglan, fig., 1772). *Special scenes:* MM. led into paradise by St Peter and Mary Magdalene (Lille, Carmelite church, painting by J. van Oost the Younger, 17th century); Christ and Catherine crown MM. with the crown of thorns (Granada, Museum, painting by P. de Moya, 17th century); MM.'s stigmatisation (Courtrai, St Martin, painting by L. de Deyster, 17th century); MM., exchanging her heart with Christ (Ghent, Museum, painting by Boeyersman, 17th century). *Cycles:* amongst others, Rome, S Maria in Montesanto, painting by L. Gemignani, 17th century; Florence, S Maria Maddalena, painting by. L. Giordano, 1685.

Matthew

Apostle, Evangelist

Feast-day: 21st September (translation feast in Salerno: 6th May), in Greek rites: 6th November and 16th December.

Life: M. was mentioned in all Apocryphal New Testament stories. In Mk 2.14, he was called Levi, son of Alphaeus of Capernaum. Jesus nominated M. as his disciple at a customs house. Following his nomination, M. gave a banquet and invited many customs officers and sinners. In about 120, Papias and Origen reported that M. was the author of the Gospel of the Jewish Christians. This Gospel, now the first in the New testament, was not written in this form by M. One can assume that M., as listener and observer of Jesus, had begun a Hebrew and Aramaic collection of quotations, used later by the author to write, in accordance with the Gospel according to St Mark and other legends,

the Gospels in the Greek language as they exist today.

Legends: irregular, often contradicting traditions: M. lives, according to Clement of Alexandria, as a vegetarian. – About 42, M. leaves Palestine to do missionary work in Ethiopia and Parthia (old var: M. goes to Persia to do missionary work). M. suffers martyrdom by burning (var: by stoning, beheading, by stabbing with a sword or spear) in Edessa (Syria), Beshbar (Arabia) or in Nadda ber i Senaar.

Patronage: patron saint of the city and diocese of Salerno; of tax-collectors, customs officers, accountants, money-changers, alcoholics, hospitals, invoked against fatal diseases, patron saint of the Lübeck fishermen sailing to Bergen, patron saint of ships.

Veneration and cult sites: his mortal remains are in Paestum; since 1084 in Salerno (M. pilgrimage); relics are in Benevento (arm); Veroli (hand); Rome, S Maria Maggiore, S Marcello, S Cosma e Damiano (11th century).

Superstition: an important annual day because on M.'s day the autumn storms and the winter begin. – People born on M.'s day must, on certain nights, carry the ghosts around at the cemetery. – In Hanover, young women make prophecies about their future marriage by floating paper or grain in water to interpret the water's movements.

Representation in Art: *Apparel:* in traditional dress of the apostles with girdled tunica and coat (Tübingen, Collegiate Church, fig., circa 1480); as scholar with biretta and doctor's sash (Munich, Alte Pinakothek, painting, before 1500); in coat with hood and biretta (Witzin, Mecklenburg, relief, late 15th century); in vestments (Lübeck, St Mary's Church, painting at the Bergfahrer altar, 1524); in cape, decorated with ermine (Vienna, Austrian Gallery in the Belvedere, painting by the master of the Frederic altar, 1435/40); as evangelist (Vienna, Art History Museum, painting by C. Carlone, 18th century); as evangelist with spectacles (Le Seca, painting by the Portillo master, 1st half of the 16th century). *Attributes:* sword in his back (Lüne Monastery, procession flag, middle of the 14th century); sword in hand (Cologne, Three King's Shrine, goldsmith's work by Nicholas of Verdun, early 13th century; halberd (Vienna, Art History Museum, painting by Hans, called Mair of Landshut, 15th century); wallet (Ulm, Minster, fig., 15th century); abacus (Lübeck, St Mary's Church, painting at the Bergfahrer altar, 1524); angle iron (Gärtingen, Swabia, fresco, 1665); axe (Munich, Bavarian National Museum, fig. by T. Riemenschneider, circa 1500); vanquished king at his feet (Chartres, central southern portal, fig., 1210–1215); angel in a glass pane (Oberwesel, Collegiate Church, Lettner fig., 1331); book (Vienna, Cathedral and Diocesan Museum, painting at the St Andrew altar, circa 1430); *Special* *scenes:* an angel dictates the Gospel to M. (Rome, Museo Capitolino, painting by Guercino, 1st half of the 17th century); angels assisting M. by writing the Gospel (Orvieto, Cathedral, fig. by Franqueville after a drawing by Giovanni da Bologna, 1595); angel holding light and an inkwell (Brescia, S Giovanni Evangelista, painting by G. Romanino, 16th century); nomination of the customs officer Levi at the customs house (Reims, Cathedral, internal western wall, relief 1250/60); nomination of the customs officer Levi at the money-table (Munich, Alte Pinakothek, painting by G. Vischer, 17th century); banquet given for Christ by the customs officer Levi (Venice, Accademia, former refectory of SS Giovanni e Paolo, painting by P. Veronese, 1572); M. conquers the dragon at Vadaber (Paris, Notre-Dame, southern rosary, stained glass, 12th century); M. revives the son of King Egippus (Prato, S Francesco, fresco by Nicolò di Pietro Gerini, late 14th century). *Martyrdom:* by stabbing in front of the altar (Rome, S Luigi dei Francesci, painting by Caravaggio, 1590/99). *Cycles:* Assisi, S Francesco, stained glass, 13th century; Florence, Uffizi, painting by Jacopo di Ciones, 1367–1369; Prato, S Francesco, frescoes by Gerini, 14th century; Prato, Galleria Communale, predella painting by Pietro di Miniato, 1413.

Matthias

Apostle, Martyr, saint

Feast-days: 14th May (since 1969, before, 24th February, in a leap year, 25th February) 7th February in Milan; 12th May (commemoration day of the election to apostle); 18th July (translation feast in Trier); in Greek rites: 9th August).

Life: in his election as apostle, M. was selected by drawing lots, to replace the traitor, Judas Iscariot, from the circle of the 70 disciples of Jesus. His opposing candidate was Joseph Barsabbas also known as Justus.

Legends: irregular legend tradition, mostly taken from legends of other apostles: M. is the abandoned child of Ruben and Cyborea. – M. grows up at court. – On the orders of Pilate, M. murders the successor to the throne. – After the murder of his father, M. marries his mother. – As penitence, M. follows Christ. – M. preaches in Jerusalem, Judea, Egypt and Antioch. – M. suffers martyrdom by stoning and beheading (var: M. is crucified). – Apostle Andrew rescues M. from the cannibals.

Patronage: patron saint of the diocese of Trier and of the towns of Goslar, Hildesheim, Hanover; patron saint of builders, blacksmiths, tailors, butchers, confectioners,; invoked against whooping cough, smallpox, infertility in marriage, patron of boys as they begin school.

Veneration and cult sites: grave in and pilgrimage to Trier, Eucharius Church, since 1127 to St Matthias; relics were brought to Trier as the gift of Empress Helena to Bishop Agricius. Relics are in Padua, S Giustina; Rome, S Maria Maggiore; Halle. Pilgrimages to Trier and Aachen; brotherhoods, amongst others, in Aachen. M. veneration was promoted by Emperor Charles V.

Superstition: the former feast-day in February was an important annual day for the spring weather (M. breaks the ice, if there is no ice he will make it). – In the Czech Republic, the trees must be shaken out of hibernation to ensure that enough fruit is grown. On M.'s day, the housewife carries a boy on her back through the garden, shouting M. – Water, scooped up during M.'s night between 11 and 12, changes to wine. – Those who see on M.'s night, a headless ghost at the cemetery, must die during the year. – There are numerous oracles connected with M.'s day, influenced by his election to apostle, amongst others, in Cologne where ivy-climbers are put into a bowl of water and sprinkled with salt; those whose climbers darken will die soon. – There are also traditional predictions of romance for girls.

Representation in Art: *Apparel:* as apostle in long, girdled tunica and coat (Munich, Alte Pinakothek, painting at the Heisterbach altar, 2nd quarter of the 15th century). *Attributes:* book (Munich, Bavarian Governmental Library, clm 23094, book illustration, 13th century); sword (Aachen, St Mary's Shrine, pieces of goldwork, 1237); stones (Ettal, Minster, fig. by J. B. Straub, circa 1760); cross (Grosslupenitz, Thuringia, painting, early 16th century); lance (Paris, Bibliothèque Nationale fr. 13091, book illustration in the Psalter des Duc du Berry, 14th century); halberd (Villach, St Martin, painting by master Frederic of Villach, 1435); axe (Munich, Blutenburg Chapel, fig., late 15th century). *Special scenes:* election to apostle (Florence, Rabbula Codex, book illustration, 6th century); M.'s sermon (Rome, S Maria Maggiore, mosaic, 1288–1296); Jesus visits the imprisoned M. (Stein a. d. Donau, Göttweigerhof Chapel, mural painting, 1st quarter of the 14th century); translation of the relics (Salerno, Sacramentar, book illustration, 14/15th century). *Martyrdom:* Kájow, Bohemia, painting, before 1500; Vienna, Art History Museum, painting by Jan de Beer, circa 1500; Tours, Museum, painting by F. Providoni, circa 1700. *Cycles:* Brussels, Musée des Beaux-Arts and Vienna Art history Museum, painting by Barend of Orley, 1515.

Maurice of Agaunum
Primicerius of the Theban Legion, Martyr, saint
Feast-day: 22nd September
Life: according to the report of Bishop Eucherius of Lyons, M. was Primicerius of a le-

gion of Christians, led by M. during Diocletian's persecution of the Christians (302–305) through Italy, over the alps to Octodurum (now Martigny), in the Rhône valley. In Acaunum (now St-Maurice d'Agaune), Emperor Maximian demanded a pagan sacrifice from them but the soldiers refused to carry out this order. Maximian therefore ordered that every tenth soldier be killed, and after repeating his order, the entire legion (despite the fact that Constantinus Chlorus, tolerant of Christianity, was in charge of Acaunum, Maximian apparently used his absence to order the blood-bath). It is not historically proven that the Legion was called the Theban Legion.

Patronage: patron saint of the holy Roman empire under Otto and the Salier; protector of the Langobards; protector of Otto's colonisation of the East; patron saint of the Kingdom of Burgundy; Valais; Magdeburg; Einsiedeln; Sitten; Chur; of crusaders; dyers (because of his red coat); clothiers; glass painters; hatters; merchants; cutlers; armourers; soldiers; infantrymen; cloth-weavers; laundrymen; vineyards; horses.

Veneration and cult sites: the relics are in St-Maurice d'Agaune, Magdeburg (in 937, on the orders of Emperor Otto the Great, translated by Bishop Udalrich of Augsburg); Vienne (head relic, crowned between 879 and 887 by King Boso); Vienna (sacred Treasury, M.'s spurs and M.'s sword as imperial insignia); further numerous relics are in Switzerland, Germany, Italy, France, Spain and South America; veneration along the old Roman military road to the Lower Rhine.

Representation in Art: *Apparel:* as soldier (Fröndenberg, Westphalia, fig., circa 1500); as soldier in tunic (Oberstadion, Württemberg, altar painting, 1458); as fair-skinned knight (Metz, Bibliothèque Municipale, Ms 1200, book illustration, 1276); as fair-skinned duke on horseback (St Maurice, Sigismund Shrine, relief, 12th century); as fair-skinned knight on horseback (Stuttgart, Landesbibliothek, Hirsau Passion, book illustration, 12th century); as Moor in coat of chain mail (Magdeburg, Cathedral, fig., circa 1240); as dark-skinned duke with hood (Hollern near Stade, fig., 13th century); as dark-skinned duke with hat, coat and armour (Vienna, St Stephan, Neustadt altar, fig., 1447); as dark-skinned nobleman with fur-lined coat (Schwerin, Staatsmuseum, stained glass, 1300/1310); as dark-skinned knight in full armour and coat (Halle, Staatsgalerie Moritzburg, fig. from the Town Hall, 1526); as dark-skinned knight in full armour (Bräunsdorf, altar relief, 1517); as dark-skinned knight in full armour with turban (Ingoldstadt, Liebfrau Minster, painting by Hans Mielich, 1572); as Moor on the Hippokampen (Lüneburg, Rathaus, centre-piece by the Augsburg goldsmith HM. circa 1660). *Attributes:* palm tree, London, British Museum, Harley 2889, book illustration, 12th century); sword (Munich, Alte Pinakothek, painting by master MGN, 1521/22); sceptre (Lausanne, choir-stalls of the Minster, fig., 15th century); dagger (Quittelsdorf, altar painting, circa 1420/30); flag on lance (Limbach, Church, painting by Hans Süss of Kulmbach, circa 1510/20); shield, lance (Halberstadt, Moritz Church, fig., circa 1480/90); shield with eagle (Magdeburg, Cathedral, alabaster fig., 1467); shield with head of Moors (Ebstorf, Lüneburg Heath, Monastery Church, late 13th century); dragon (Wiesentheid, Lower Franconia, fig. by J. v. d. Auwera, circa 1760). *Martyrdom:* Gerona, Museo Diocesano, Martyrologium, book illustration, ca. 1410; Munich, Alte Pinakothek, painting by P. de Mares, 1517; Karlsruhe, Badisches Landesmuseum, painting, circa 1515/25; Heilsbronn near Ansbach, Abbey Church, painting by Wolf Traut, 1502. *Cycles:* Essen-Werden, St Peter, mural painting, 12th century; Saanen, Mauritius Church, frescoes, circa 1480.

Maurus

Bishop, Benedictine, saint
Feast-day: 4th December
Life: born about 1000. At a young age he joined the Györszentmárton monastery, southeast of Raab. At 1030, he was elected abbot and in 1036 appointed bishop of Pécs where he built the first Cathedral. In literature, he described the lives of Ceodardus and Benedict. M. was a friend of King Stephan of Hungary and Emmerich. He died about 1070.
Veneration and cult sites: since 1848 liturgical feast in the diocese of Pécs and since 1892 in Györszentmárton.s
No representation in Christian art.

Maximilian Kolbe

Priest, Martyr, saint
Feast-day: 14th August (day of martyrdom).
Life: born on 8th January 1894 in Zdunska Wola near Lodz. On 5th September 1911 he made his profession in the Franciscan Minorite Order. In 1912 he studied in Rome and received his doctorate in philology in 1915. On 16th October 1917, he founded the Militia of Immaculata. The worldwide spread of this Order was his aim in life. In 1918 he was ordained as a priest; in 1919 he received his doctorate in theology and was briefly professor of ecclesiastical history in Cracow. Together with a Franciscan monastery, he founded the Niepokalanów 'press city' (over 700 members). In 1930 he went to Asia and founded, in Japan, the second 'press centre', Mugenazai no Sono (Garden of Immaculate Conception). In 1939 he was arrested by the Gestapo for the first time. In 1941 he was arrested a second time by the Gestapo and, in the Auschwitz concentration-camp, changed places with a family man who had been sentenced to death on the grounds of being a Catholic priest. On 14th August 1941 he died in the 'starvation bunker' after administration of a phenol injection. Beatified in

1982 by Pope Paul VI, canonized in 1982 by Pope John Paul II.

Legends: in M. K.'s childhood, the mother of God shows him white and red flowers in a dream (var: crowns) as an indication of innocence and martyrdom, demanded by the child. – The mother of God scatters flowers over M. K.

Patronage: families, journalists, the media, political refugees, prisoners.

Reverence: Franciscan Minorite Order; Poland; Germany; Japan.

Representation in Art: *Apparel:* in Franciscan habit with metal-rimmed glasses and short beard, physiognomy according to photographs with high, sloping forehead or as concentration-camp inmate in the striped clothes of a prisoner. *Attributes:* book, martyr palm (Rome, painting by Amore Del Vecchie, 1971); globe as indication of worldwide missionary work (fig. in Niepokalanów); red triangle and concentration camp number 16 670. *Cycles:* Niepokalanów, high altar, predella relief; Vienna, Commemoration Chapel at the Minorite convent in the Alser suburb by E. Degasperi, 1973.

Mechthild of Helfta

(von Hackelborn) Cistercian nun, saint
Feast-day: 19th November
Life: born in 1241, daughter of the noble von Hackelborn family. At the age of seven she joined the Rodersdorf convent-school, near Halberstadt where her sister, Gertrud, was already a nun. In 1258 she moved with the entire convent to Helfta near Eisleben. M. became the head of the convent-school. On the orders of the abbess, Sophie of Querfurt, her sister, Gertrud, and another nun wrote down M.'s mystic visions. The book "Liber specialis gratiae (book of special grace), was widely circulated and promoted the veneration, due to numerous Sacred Heart prayers. She died on 19th November 1299.

Early bishops and missionaries north of the Alps

50 *St Zeno driving out a demon, doorway relief, Verona, Italy, church of St Zeno*

51 *The cathedral of Fulda, Germany, burial-place of St Boniface*

52 *St Gerard, by Bertalan Székely, Pécs cathedral, Hungary*

53 *St Willibrord, Echternach*

54 *St Wolfgang praying for a miracle, by M. Pacher, Munich, Alte Pinakothek*

55 *St Corbinian makes the bear his beast of burden, by Jan Pollack, Freising, Germany, Diocesan Museum*

56 *St Ulric and St Afra, Augsburg, burial-place of St Ulric*

57 *The expulsion of St Adalbert from Prague, Budapest, National Gallery*

50

51

52

53

55

57

Veneration and cult sites: Engelszell convent.

Representation in Art: *Apparel:* as Cistercian nun (Engelszell, fig., 1759). *Attributes:* scale, sword (Venice, book illustration for Liber specialis gratiae, 1522); book (Mauterndorf, St Gertrud, painting, circa 1750).

Michael

Archangel, saint

Feast-day: 29th November, anniversary of the consecration of S Michele at the Roman Via Salaria by Pope Leo the Great; 8th May, appearance of M. at the Monte Gargano; 8th November, consecration of the Constantinople M. Church; 16th October, M.'s appearance on Mont-Saint-Michele. In the Greek rites, commemoration of the Chonai miracle: 6th or 29th September.

Attestation: the name of the archangel Michael (= "who is like God") was mentioned in the Book of Daniel in the Old Testament as one of the first Kings of heaven, as protector of Israel. In the Apocalypse 12.7 the fight between Michael and Satan was described. In the epistle according to St Jude, the dispute with the devil was mentioned regarding the mortal remains of Moses. The Fathers of the Church, like Irenaeus of Lyons, regarded M. as the leader of the heavenly hosts. Origen explained M.'s task as having to present the prayers of the people to God, and Gregory the Great emphasized M.'s special tasks, given by God. According to Gregory of Tours, he is the companion of the souls of the dead; even after Mary's death, Christ gave him the soul of his mother. According to Pseudo-Meliton, M. is the King of paradise and assessor of souls at the Last Judgement.

Legends: M. appears at Chronis in Phrygia. – M. directs a poisoned arrow, shot at an escaped bull, back to the bowman and appears to Manfredonia, the city's bishop, on Mont Gargano. – M. orders the bishop of Tumba to build a church and moves two rocks to make sufficient space. – During a pilgrimage, M. rescues a pregnant woman from the floods to ensure that she can give birth at sea. – To avert the 950 plague, Pope Gregory the Great orders a large procession. When he looks at Hadrian's Castle he sees that an angel has inserted the sword into the sheath. When the number of nuns declines in the Mülberg convent near Meissen and the singing is too weak, the wooden M. painting joins in the singing.

Patronage: protector of the Holy Roman Empire (the M. flag was carried in front at the 955 battle against pagan Hungarians at the Lechfeld); protector of the Church; the German nation; of poor souls; people dying and for a good death. Patron saint of the order named after him; of pharmacists; people adjusting weighing-scales; weight-makers; merchants (because of the scale); bakers; bankers (since 1958); turners; glaziers, painters, radio specialists (since 1958); knights; tailors; soldiers; gilders; lead and tin founders; invoked against lightning; storms (because of the flaming sword), patron saint of church yards.

Veneration and cult sites: since the early Middle Ages mainly in numerous pilgrimage churches in mountain areas, particularly important for Monte Gargano in Apulia (children's pilgrimage since 1456–1458); Ravenna, Rome; Engelsburg; Mont-Saint-Michel in Normandy (founded in 709 by Bishop Autbert of Avranches because of his vision).

Superstition: end of the grazing period for livestock; day when interest must be paid; important annual day for the weather. – If the M. painting falls from the roof of the Michelstein monastery, one will find strangled livestock or restless bullocks in the stable. On M.'s day one should not thresh because the souls, flying through the air, could be injured. – A dead soul lives the first night with

St Gertrud and the second with St M. – In Hungary, the bier is called the horse of St M. **Representation in Art:** *Apparel:* as King of heaven in tunica and pallium (Berlin, early Christian-Byzantine collection, mosaic from Ravenna, S Michele in Affriciso, 545); in tunica and chlamys (Ravenna, S Apollinare in Classe, mosaic, 6th century); as ruler in tunica, divitison (magnificent dress, with trimming at neck and seam), loros (Monreale, Minster, mosaic, 1180/94; in tunica and loros (Cefalù, Cathedral, mosaic, 12th century); as general in short tunica, boots and full armour (Palermo, Capella Palatina, mosaic, 12th century); as warrior in full armour and beret (London, National Gallery, painting by Perugio, 1496); as warrior in full armour and helmet (Kaiserslautern, Pfalz Gallery, etching by L. Corinth, 1923); in liturgical robe with pluviale (Düsseldorf, Art Museum, copperplate engraving by M. Schongauer, circa 1480); in pluviale and full armour (Hamburg, Kunsthalle, copperplate engraving by Israhel of Meckenem, 15th century); in dalmatica and pluviale (Hamburg, Weber Collection, painting by the master of Liesborn, 2nd half of the 15th century); feathered creature in golden chain-mail (Chantily, Musée Conde, Les Très riches Heures du Duc de Berry, book illustration, circa 1415. *Attributes:* headband with cross (Hamburg, Kunsthalle, etching by Johann Weiner, 16th century); globe with the sign of the cross, messenger's stick with ball (London, British Museum, ivory relief, 6th century); labarum (Ravenna, S Apollinare in Classe, circa 549); spear (Paris, Louvre, painting by Raphael); lance (New York, Metropolitan Museum, Cloisters Apocalypse, book illustration, early 14th century); sword, shield (Augsburg, Municipal Art Collection, oil sketch, circa 1790); flaming sword (Naples, Chiesa dell'Ascensione a Chiaia, painting by Luca Giordano, 17th century); cross crosier (Munich, St Michael, painting by Christoph

Schwarz, 1587/88); shackle and chain (Heidelberg, University Library, Hortus Deliciarum, facsimile of the original burned in Strasbourg, last quarter of the 12th century); scale (Avignon, Museum, painting by Nicolas Fromment, late 15th century); disc (Monreale, Cathedral, mosaic, 12th century); dragon (former Baron Hüpsch Collection, painting by the master of the Kalkar St Mary's death). *Special scenes:* M. as assistant to the throne (Ravenna, S Apollinare in Classe, mosaic, circa 549); M. as assistant to Mary's throne (Berlin, Governmental Museums, stone relief, 12/13th century); M. as companion of the three holy kings (Hohenzollern Castle, relief, 1920); M. as divine representative (Milan, S Ambrogio, mosaic, 1st half of the 9th century); M. killing a dragon (Lucca, S Michele, tympanon relief, circa 1143); M. consecrates his arms to Mary (Nevers, St Pierre, painting by M. and L. Le Nain, 1633/40); fall of Lucifer and other angels by M. (Breslau, Cathedral, Elector's Chapel, fresco by C. Carlone, after 1726; as assessor of souls (Autun, portal relief, 1130/40); as rescuer of souls from purgatory (Lübeck, St Anne's Museum, Corpus Christi altar, painting, 1496); M.'s appearance and the end of the Roman plague (Rome, S Pietro in Vincoli, fresco, 15th century); in a vision, M. orders Gottfried of Bouillon to liberate Jerusalem (Rome, Casino Massimo, Tasso Hall, painting by F. Overbeck, 19th century). *Cycles:* cycle with biblical motifs (Monte S Angelo, bronze door relief, 1076); cycle with motifs of miracles at the Monte Gargano (Florence, S Croce, Vellituri Chapel); miracle of Chonai (only on Byzantine icons).

Monica of Tagaste
Mother of St Augustine, saint
Feast-day: 27th August (before 1976: 4th May).

Life: born in 332 in Tagaste, the daughter of Christian parents. As a young woman she married the pagan official Patritius (died in 371, a Christian) and had three children. She was very concerned about her son, Augustine, converted him to Christianity and, in 387, saw his baptism in Milan. She died in October 387 in Ostia.

Legends: at her last communion before her death, the Christ-child appears to M. – Martha presents her belt to M.

Patronage: ecclesiastical societies of mothers, women, mothers, gave her name to the so-called 'Brotherhoods of Belts'.

Veneration and cult sites: the relics are in the Arrouaise Augustine monastery and in Rome, S Agostino (since 1430).

Representation in Art: *Apparel:* as widow in black, girdled dress with widow's veil (Rome, S Maria del Populo, relief, 14th century); in protective coat, held by angels (Bagnoreggio, SS Annunziata, fresco). *Attributes:* book (San Gimignano, S Agostino, fresco by B. Gozzoli, 15th century); banner (Munich, Alte Pinakothek, painting by M. Pacher, 15th century); rosary (Stuttgart, Museum, fig., early 16th century); crucifix (Milan, painting by A. da Fabriano, 15th century). *Special scenes:* M. in ecstasy in Ostia (Paris, Louvre, painting by Ary Scheffer, 19th century); mother of God gives her belt to M. (painting of the brotherhood) (Naples, S Maria Egiziaca a Forcella, painting by F. Solimena, 18th century). For further motifs see the chapter on Augustine of Hippo. *Cycles:* Rabastens, Church, middle of the 14th century; Padua, Chiesa dei Eremitai, frescoes, 1338 and in connection with further Augustine cycles.

Nereua and Achilleus of Rome

martyr, saint

Feast-day: 12th May

Life: N. A. were praetorians and court soldiers, who suffered martyrdom during the persecution of Christians under Emperor Diocletian.

Legends: N. A. were eunuchs and servants of the bedchamber of the niece, Domitilla, of Emperor Domitianus. – N. A. converted Domitilla, who renounced her bridegroom to live a virginal life. – The incensed bridegroom allowed N. A. to be deported into banishment on to Pontus island. – There N. A. had to make sacrifices to false gods but they refused because they had been baptised by Peter and Paul. Thereupon N. A. were beheaded. – The bridegroom, who attempted to rape Domitilla, suddenly could not stop dancing and fell down dead. – Thereupon Domitilla and her maid were burned in a fire in her chamber.

Veneration and cult sites: Buried in the Domitilla catacombs, translation to a church bearing her name at the end of the 16th century, relics in S Maria in Vallicella.

Representation in Art: *Apparel:* As virginal martyrs (Florence, S Salvatore al Monte, painting, by G. da Ponte, 15th century); as martyrs in classical apparel with older physiognomies (Rome, S Maria in Vallicella, painting, by P. P. Rubens, circa 1608); as soldiers (Unterfischen, Upper Bavaria, figure, 16th century). *Attributes:* Lances (Cleveland, Ohio, Cleveland Museum of Art, book illumination, 15th century); swords (Unterfischen, Upper Bavaria, figure, 16th century).

Nicholas of Flue

hermit, saint

Feast-day: 25th September

Life: * born around 1417 in Flüeli, near Sachseln, as a child he showed a tendency to solitude. N. was a soldier in the wars against Zurich (1140744) and the Thuringian campaign. The salvation of the Diessenhofer monastery from destruction by Swiss soldiers fighting against the Austrians is attributed to N. After 1460 N. married Dorothea Wyss, who bore him 10 children. He worked as a farmer, administrator and judge. On 16th October 1667 he left his wife and children and wandered as a hermit, following an inner compulsion, returning after early trials as a wandering pilgrim in Listal near Basle, on the Klisterli Alp in Melchtal, where curious neighbours troubled him, then in Ramft, close to his estate. N. probably came under the influence of a mystic circle in Engelberg monastery, and also under the influence of the religious Haimo am Grund in Kriens and Oswald Isner in Kerns. He had a good word for those seeking counsel, but could also be very unfriendly towards visitors. – In his seclusion N. had a great influence on politics, for example it was by his efforts that the court hearing came to Stans, on the Vierwaldstätter See, before a permanent schism existed. – † 21st March 1487. Equipollent beatification in 1669, canonised in 1947.

Legends: At 16 years of age N. has a vision of a tower, whose top disappears into the clouds. – N. lives for 19 years in Ramft without any food or drink. – N. has to survive a struggle with the devil, who throws him into the briers. – The Mother of God appears to N.

Patronage: Switzerland· (First national patron saint).

Veneration and cult sites: Body rests in the parish church in Sachseln, highly venerated as a worker of miracles. Immediately after N.'s death a pilgrimage was established.

Representation in Art: *Apparel:* As a bearded hermit, with bare feet and long, unbelted robe (Sachseln, charnel house, figure on tomb, 1518). *Attributes:* Stick, garland of roses (Untere Ramftkapelle, figure, 1504); cross (Herrenberg, choir stalls, relief, 1517). *Cycles:* Untere Ramftkapelle, mural painting, circa 1520.

Nicholas of Myra

Bishop, saint

Feast-day: 6th December (9th May in Byzantine rites)

Life: * born in Patras in Lycia. N. was Bishop of Myra in Lycia. † probably on 6th December 343/50 or 345/52.

Legends: Only three days after birth N. stands upright in his bathing tub. – N. refuses to accept his mother's breast on Fridays. – N. loses his father Euphemius and his mother Anna in a plague epidemic and distributes his entire fortune amongst the poor. – N. throws three golden balls into a room occupied by three maidens, whose impoverished father wishes to force them into prostitution, but with this gold as a dowry they can now marry well. – His uncle Nicholas the Elder was Bishop of Myra, educates N.,

founds a monastery and establishes N. as abbot. – After the death of his uncle, N. makes a pilgrimage to the Holy Land and after his return is proclaimed as the new bishop by the people of Myra because they had resolved that whoever first entered the following morning would become Bishop of Myra. N. is ordained as a Bishop. – N. has to suffer greatly during the persecution of Christians under Galerius around 310, for which reason he receives the appellation of the Confessor. – N. appoints 325 members to the Council of Nicaea, where he with other bishops defends the identical nature of the three divine beings. – Christ and the Mother of God return the bishop's insignia to N., which N. had taken off on account of the insult of Arius by the Emperor at the Council of Nicaea. – While taking part in the Council seamen appear to N. and he rescues them from distress. – The seamen reach Myra and there recognise him again. – N. saves a small child from boiling bathwater. – N. brings back to life three scholars, who were killed by an innkeeper and pickled in barrels. – N. fells a tree which is consecrated to the cult of the goddess Diana, whereupon Diana takes revenge on N. when she, disguised as a pious woman pilgrim, gives a bottle of oil, which she should pour out in his church as a consecration gift. N. appears, seeing through the deception and pours the bottle into the sea, which immediately bursts into flames. – N. prevents the execution of three noblemen, Ursus, Nepotian and Apilion, who are innocent but accused by the emperor Constantine of high treason, by appearing to Constantine in a dream and threatening him with the wrath of God if he allows the innocent to be executed. – N. appears in a dream to the Eparch Eulalius. – N. saves the boy Dimitri from the Dniepr; on the following day his parents find him on the steps of the cathedral. – N. saves three innocent children when the forester of Myra wishes to allow them to be put to

death, because N. tears the sword from the hand of the executioner and frees the children from their bonds. – During a famine in his diocese N. sends a ship laden with corn to the town and allows the corn to be distributed. As the ship continues on its voyage it does not sink under its load. – A Jew has entrusted his money to the protection of the saint. When it is stolen the Jew beats the form of the saint, whereupon N. appears to the thief and he has to return the money. The Jew then undergoes a conversion. – N. brings a deceitful Christian, run over by a carriage, back from the dead on being entreated by a deceived Jew, whereupon the Jew allows himself to be baptised. – A man who wishes to have a son promises a golden beaker but breaks his promise after the fulfil-ment of his wish, but contributes something of lesser value, whereupon the child drowns in a well on the road to Myra and N. raises the child from the dead for the remorseful father. – The young Adeodatus is taken prisoner by a heathen ruler and appointed to be his cupbearer, but in his homesickness the boy prays to N. who seizes him by his hair and returns him to his father. – A boy is strangled by the devil in the guise of a beggar, but N. gives him back his life. – The lame are healed on N.'s grave.

Patronage: Patron saint of Russia, Lorraine, Hanse, Bari, Myra, Novgorod, lawyers, apothecaries, ribbon makers, farmers, beer brewers, choirboys, ministrants, travellers, coopers, firemen, fishermen, fishmongers, raftsmen, prisoners, maidens, children, button-makers, linen weavers, butchers, notaries, scent merchants, pilgrims, voyagers, judges, distillers, scholars, teachers of arithmetic, teachers of writing, bargees, seamen, buyers of spices, lace merchants, cloth merchants, weavers, innkeepers, wine merchants, candlemakers, quarrymen, stonemasons, helpers in times of need.

Veneration and cult sites: Buried in Myra, on 4th September 1087, conveyed from Myra to Bari by merchants, up until the present oil pours forth from his grave. Cult recorded since the 6th century in Myra and Constantinople, a N. basilica was erected in Rome in the 9th century, cult promoted in Germany in the 10th century by Theophanu, proceeding from the Rhineland in the 11th century. In France and England veneration of N. recorded, around 2,000 church patronages, place-names, etc.

Superstitions: There are special N. customs proceeding from the legends, the basis being in connection with medieval school practices, in monastery schools to accept dominion and to choose a children's bishop on the feast day of innocent children, though in the 9th century these practised customs were ineffectively prohibited until the 16th century, in the 13th century N. day was moved to the same day as Christmas day. Many dramatisations of the school theatre exist. Moreover there are seasonal myths of nature, especially in Alpine areas.

Representation in Art: *Apparel:* as a bishop of the Latin Rite in pontifical Mass robes with chasuble and pallium (Limburg, cathedral, fresco, 13th century); as a bishop of the Latin Rite in pluvial and mitre (Lübeck, Jakobikirche, painting, 1488); as a bishop of the Greek Rite with sticharion, epitrachelion, enchiron, phelonion and omophorion (Karlsruhe, Landesbibliotek, Evangeliar des Speyerer Domes, book illumination, 12th century); in a rochet (Venice, S Sebastiano, painting, by Titian, 16th century). *Attrib-*

utes: Christ and Mary as small figures at the side (Bisceglie, Apulia, painting, 13th century); angel with mitre (Venice, S Sebastiano, painting, by Titian, 16th century); three golden balls on a book (Florence, Uffizi, painting, by B. Daddi, 14th century); three golden balls in his hand (Lieberhausen, Evangelist parish church, mural painting, early 15th century); three balls at his feet (Venice, S Sebastiano, painting, by Titian, 16th century); three gold ingots (Schwerin, museum, figure, end 15th century); three gold bars (Rostock, Nikolaikirche, predella, circa 1450); three apples (Kortrijk, O.-L-Vrouwenkerk, painting, by J. van der Asselt, 15th century); with money purse (Brussels, figure, reproduced by R. van Linden, icon of Saint Nicholas in Flanders, Ghent, 1972, Abb.347); three small moneybags (Putte, Nikolauskirche, figure, 19th century); three loaves of bread on a book (Strasbourg, cathedral, figure, 1522); three kneeling scholars (Antwerp, St Jakob, painting, by A.Francken I, 1592); three scholars standing in a tub (Lübeck, Jakobikirche, painting, 1488); three scholars standing out of a tub (London, National Gallery, painting, by G. David, circa 1500); child in swaddling clothes (Elzach, Baden, stained glass, by H. Gitschmann von Ropstein, 1524); child holding his hair (Atri, cathedral, mural painting, 15th century); three maidens at his feet (Soest, Nikolaikirche, painting, 14th century); three maidens in a wayside shrine (Lieberhausen, Evangelist parish church, mural painting, 15th century); three maidens and three scholars (Brussels, Bibliothèque Royale, Hs. 15.082–83, book illumination, 15th century); maiden and a boy prepared for execution with a rope around his neck (Naples, Museo Capodimonte, painting, by A. de Salerno, 13th century); anchor (Lübeck, Marienkirche, painting, end 15th century); boat (Westkapelle, St Niklaas Kirche, figure, 19th century). *Special scenes:* N. in a Sacra Conversatione, in which a child is reaching for balls (Florence, Uffizi, painting, by S. Botticelli, 15th century); the young N. throwing three golden balls through a window (Vatican Museum, painting, by G. da Fabriano, 14th century); N. in conventional apparel throwing three balls through a window (Antwerp, Musée Royale de Beaux-Arts, painting, by O. van Veen, circa 1600); N. being ordained as a bishop (Chantilly, book illumination, by J. le Fouquet, 15th century); the deliverance of seamen from the sea (Löwen, St Peter, painting, by J.B. van der Kerckhoven, 18th century); N. fells a tree consecrated to Diana (St Louis, painting, by P. di Cosimo, circa 1500); the prevention of the execution of three innocents (Moscow, Tretyakov Gallery, painting, by I. J. Repin, 19th century); the redeemed bringing N. gifts (Geraardsbergen, St Bartholomäus, painting, by C. de Crayer, circa 1640); the salvation of Myra from famine (Bruges, Museum Groeninge, painting, by J. Prevost, circa 1500); the legend with the golden chalice (Frankfurt, Städel, painting, circa 1460); N. recommending children to the care of the Mother of God (Brescia, Galleria Martinengo, painting, by A. Moretta, 1539); N. as refuge for those seeking help (Poigern bei Dachau, N. chapel, fresco, 18th century). *Cycles:* very numerous, including Zedelgem, Laurentiuskirche, reliefs, circa 1125: Chartres, cathedral, south portal – tympanum, 13th century); Tours, cathedral, stained glass, 13th century; Asissi, S Francesco, crypt, frescoes, after Giotto, 1310; Gdansk, Marienkirche, painting, 15th century; Grimma, Saxony, Nikolaikirche, painting, by L. Cranach the Elder, 16th century.

Nicholas of Tolentino
Augustin hermit, saint

Feast-day: 10th September

Life: * born in 1245 in Sant Angelo in Pontano, he entered the Augustine Order of Hermits in 1255/56 in a monastery in the town of his birth. N. worked successfully as a preacher, father confessor and carer of sick souls in the Ancona borderlands and as a novice master in S Elpidio. After that he spent 30 years in Tolentino. † 10th September 1305. Canonised in 1466.

Legends: N. is revered as a great worker of miracles. Parents pray for a son on the grave of St N. in Bari. – After a sermon N. resolves to enter an Augustine hermitage. – N. rescues a someone unjustly hanged from the gallows. – N. bring a woman back from the dead. – N. rescues a boat in distress. – N. heals those possessed. – N. sends away a bird offered to him during an illness, whereupon the roasted creature flies up from the plate. N. is cured of a fever in a miraculous manner by bread. – N. experiences a vision on his sickbed. – N. catches in his hand the plague arrow which God has hurled at the town from Heaven. – During a Mass held by N. angels bring the souls of the poor out of purgatory. – Near N.'s death a light comes to him on the path ahead to the Oratory.

Patronage: Patron saint of Rome, Cordoba, Venice, Genoa, Antwerp, Lima, Bavaria, Brotherhood of Poor Souls, scholars, freedom from thunderstorms.

Veneration and cult sites: Body buried in Tolentino, above which a basilica has been erected; on his grave 301 miracles took place up until 1325, which became recognised on canonisation. Arm relics probably 1325, on which the miracle of blood took place, which were brought in connection with the church historic events, the last being in 1939. The remaining mortal remains were not heard of for a long time and were rediscovered in 1926 during excavations. In the

century); burning plate/stars with an angel's head on his breast (S Gimignano, S Agostino, fresco, by B. Gozzoli, 15th century); star above his head (Munich, Graphics Collection, woodcut, end 15th century); star in his hand (Perugia, Pinacoteca Nazionale, fresco, 14th century); flying bird and a roasted bird on a plate (Munich, Graphics Collection, woodcut, end 15th century); partridge taking wing from a plate (Cologne, Wallraf-Richartz Museum, painting, by a Master of the Holy Family, 1493/94); a pigeon on a plate (Salamanca, painting, by G. Lanfranco, 17th century); fever bread (Rattersdorf, painting, by Frater Jonas, end 18th century); devil at his feet (Perugia, Pinacoteca, painting, by Rafael, circa 1501); model of a town (Montefalco, S Agostino, fresco, attributed to O. Nelli, 15th century). *Special scenes:* N. catching the plague arrow shot by Christ (Empoli, Museo della Collegiata, painting, by B. di Lorenzo, 15th century); N. holding the plague arrow shot by an angel (Pisa, S Nicola, painting, 14th century); N. looking at purgatory with the souls of the poor, who are being delivered by an angel (Barcelona, cathedral, painting, by A. Llonye, 15th century); N. delivering a hanged man from the gallows (Amsterdam, Rijksmuseum, painting, by Z. Machiavelli, 15th century); N. saving the shipwrecked in a boat (Philadelphia, Museum of Art, painting, by G. di Paolo, 15th century); a vision of the Virgin Mary on his sickbed (Cadiz, museum, painting, by J. de Sevilla, 17th century); distribution of the fever bread Ghent, Augustinerkirche, painting, by C. de Crayer, 17th century). *Cycles:* inter alia Tolentino, N. basilica, mural painting, circa 1340; Naples, S Giovanni in Carbonara, frescoes, 15th century; Vicenza, Oratorio di S Nicola, painting, by Fr. Maffei, 1655/56.

16th century up until the 18th century he was the most venerated saint in Europe and America.

Superstitions: The "Panis S Nicolas de Tolentino", bread blessed according to a special rite on N. day by Augustine hermit Orders helps all kinds of privations and suffering. N. bread thrown into the flames controls conflagrations.

Representation in Art: *Apparel:* As an Augustine hermit in a long, belted robe with a leather strap and a cowl (Cologne, Wallraf-Richartz Museum, painting, by the Master of the Holy Family, 1493/94). *Attributes:* lily stem, book, stars on his coat and a halo around him (Tolentino, S Nicola, painting, by a master of Tolentino, circa 1340); crucifix (Gent, Palazzo Bianco, painting, 15th

Norbert of Magdeburg
Premonstratensian, bishop, saint
Feast-day: 6th June

Life: * born around 1082 in Xanten to the family of noble von Gennep. N. was subdeacon and canon in St Victor in Xanten, but led a secular life at the house of the Archbishops of Cologne, Frederic I and Emperor Henry V. A. stroke of lightning while riding, probably in 1115, led to a changing of his ways. – As a penance N. entered the Benedictine monastery in Siegburg under the spiritual guidance of Abbot Kuno and Liutolf, the recluse. N. was ordained as a priest and travelled around the country as an itinerant preacher. In 1118 he entered the monastery of St Gilles, and was granted full authority as a preacher by the then exiled Pope Gelasius II. On petitions by Bishop Bartoloméus de Joux of Laon, N. settled in the valley of Premontré in 1120, where he developed the Order of Premonstratensian according to the Rule of St Augustine, which in 1126 received Papal confirmation. In 1121 was the second foundation in Floreffe near Namur, in 1124 in Antwerp an appearance against the religious zealot Tanchelm, who denied the church hierarchy and the Sacraments. In 1126 the Archbishop of Magdeburg, the head of the Order received N.'s pupil Hugo of Fosses in 1128. † 6th June 1134. Canonised in 1582.

Legends: There are no independent legends, because canonisation was not anticipated and therefore no reports were compiled on miracles, late themes: N. drinks a poisonous spider, which has fallen into a chalice and which escapes after through his nose Mass. – The Mother of God dictates the Rule of the Order to N. – N. brings a dead child back to life.

Patronage: Patron saint of Prague, Strahov Monastery, Bohemia, Premonstratensians and the Sisters of the 3rd Order of St Norbert, all communities associated with his name.

Veneration and cult sites: Buried in the Liebfrauenkirche in Magdeburg. Translation of his mortal remains to Strahov Monastery in 1628.

Representation in Art: *Apparel:* As a Premonstratensian in the garb of the Order with a long robe, scapula, cap and cowl (Orvieto, S Severo, fresco, 14th century); as a bishop in pluvial with a mitre and crosier (Berlin, Staatliches Museum, painting, by B. Strigel, early 16th century); as a bishop in choir robe and mozetta with pallium (Doksany, painting, by K. Liska, 18th century). *Attributes:* Angel with mitre (Duisburg-Hamborn, abbey, painting, circa 1700); chalice (Altengönna, Thuringia, painting, circa 1500); monstrance (Rostock, S Marien, painting, early 16th century); staff with a double cross (Münster, cathedral treasure, Missal, copperplate engraving, 1632); the heretic Tanchelm at his feet (Antwerp, Jakobskirche, painting, C. de Crayer, 17th century); the devil at his feet (Pouch, painting, circa 1500); palm branch (Duisburg-Hamborn, abbey, painting, circa 1700); model of a church (Sankt Salvator, Lower Bavaria, parish church, figure, 1782). *Special scenes:* The Mother of God dictating the Rule to N. (Parma, Pinacoteca, painting, by G. Mazzola, 16th century); In a dream Gereon instructs N. to raise up his mortal remains (Witów, St Marcina, painting, 17th century); N. preaching against Tanchelm (Munich, Alte Pinakothek, painting, by B. van Orley, before 1515); The Mother of God presenting N. with the apparel of the Order (Lüttich, Notre-Dame, painting, by W. Damery, 17th century); N. receiving the monstrance and the church implements (Antwerp, Musées Royaux des Beaux-Arts, painting, by C. de Vos, 17th century); N.'s conversion through a stroke of lightning (Löwen, St Peter, painting, by J. Bergè, 1742). *Cycles:* inter alia Milevsko, Southern Bohemia, painting, by J. J. Haering, circa 1628; Prague, Strahov Monastery, frescoes, by J. V. Neunherz, 18th century; Schus-

ssenried, abbey, frescoes, by J. Zick, 1745; Osterhofen, monastery church, fresco, by C. D. Asam, 18th century.

Notburga of Rattenberg

Serving maid, confessor, saint

Feast-day: 13th September (before the calendar reform 14th September).

Life: * born around 1265 in Rattenberg am Inn, she was a serving maid in the castle of Count von Rattenberg.

Legends: A driverless pair of oxen brings her body to Eben through the Inn, which parts before them.

Patronage: Patron saint of serving maids, farmers, respite from labour, the end of the working day, for a successful birth, against illnesses in cattle and all destitution of agriculture.

Veneration and cult sites: Grave in the cemetery also a destination already in the Middle Ages for those seeking assistance and pilgrims, venerated in Southern Germany, the Tyrol and Austria.

Representation in Art: *Apparel:* In the rustic costume of her class with shoes, stockings, half-length dress, apron, bodice and jacket (Nuremberg, Germanic National Museum, figure, 18th century). *Attributes:* sheaf of grain, hay rake, tin vessel (Horin, Bohemia, cemetery, figure, 18th century); sickle, bunch of keys on her belt (Birkenberg nr Telfs, Ex Voto, painting, 19th century); loaves of bread (Rott am Inn, figure, by I. Günther, 1762); a poverty-stricken person at her feet (Sexten, South Tyrol, figure, 18th century).

S. NOPPVRGA

O

Odilia of Hohenburg

(Ottilia) Abbess, saint

Feast-day: 13th December

Life: * circa 660 as the daughter of the Alsatian Duke Attich. Together with her father, O. founded on the Hohenburg the Augustinian Ladies' Choir Convent, later named Odilienberg after her. O. was the first Abbess. After 700 foundation of the Ladies' Abbey Niedermünster. † circa 720.

Legend: Her father wants to kill O., who was born blind, but the mother Bethsvinda succeeds in having the nurse bring her into the monastery at Palma (variant: O. is placed on the water by her father, saved by a miller, whom she later helps in a miraculous way by extending an axle beam that is too short). – O. receives her sight when Bishop Erhardt of Regensburg is sent to her by an angel and baptises her. – O.'s younger brother brings her into the family, but Attich casts him down. – O. hides from her pursuing father in Arlesheim by closing a rock round her and the falling rocks injure Attich severely. – O. flees on, but reconciles herself with her recovered father, who allows her to build a monastery on the Hohenburg. – When Attich dies, he must do penance in purgatory, but the continuous prayers of O. bring his release. – When O. dies, it is during a prayer of the choir of other nuns and without the Last Rites; at the sincere prayers of the Sisters,

the soul returns to the body again; O. takes the chalice herself and dies.

Patronage: Alsace (since 1632); eye sicknesses, poor souls in Purgatory, dying.

Veneration and cult sites: grave in St John's Chapel on the Odilienberg with pilgrimages, pilgrimage customs (including drink from the supposed chalice of O.).

Superstition: When Alsatian ladies walk seven times round the Chapel of Tears on the Odilienberg, they will be still married in seven years. – The evil-smelling shirt of O's father is kept in the church and worn every year by a priest on the two days before the O. Festival when he goes among the people.

Representation in Art: *Apparel:* in dress of a secular maiden (Strasbourg, Minster, stained glass, end 13th century); in fashionable dress of the time (Rottalmünster, cemetery church, figure, 16th century); as Duchess with crown (Algen am Inn, St Leonard's, figure, circa 1520); as nun in dress of Augustinians, in long girdled robe, scapular, cloak, wimple, veil (Salzburg, Nonnberg Convent, painting, circa 1475); as Benedictine (Miltenberg, St Lawrence's Chapel, figure, 16th century). *Attributes:* palm (Münster, State Museum, painting, by K. of Soest, circa 1410); eyes on book (Regensburg, St Emmeram, Shrine of Dionysius, silver work, circa 1440); eyes floating above chalice (Metz, Cathedral, stained glass, 15th century); eyes in

the hand (Stuttgart, State Museum, figure, from Altshausen, circa 1390); eyes on pate (contrary to details in the literature, attribute not attested); cockerel (St Wolfgang, painting, by M. Pacher, 1481); cockerel in the hand (Darmstadt, Hessen State Museum, painting, 15th century); cockerel on book (Munich, Bavarian National Museum, painting, by B. Zeitblom, circa 1500); cockerel on chalice (Zeilen near Emmingen, mural, 15th century); chalice (Weilen unter den Rinnen, parish church, figure, 1520); Attich at feet (Oberwesel, St Mary's Church, mural, 15th century). *Special scenes:* baptism of O. by bishop Hildulf and Erhard (Monastery Moyenmoutier, Niello, 12th century [lost] copy); baptism of O. by Erhard in presence of the Ducal family (Salzburg, St Erhard's Church, painting, by J.M. Rottmayr, 1692); the miracle of the axle (Prague, National Gallery, painting, by H. Holbein the Elder, 1509); release of Attich from Purgatory by an angel (Ladenburg (Neckar), St Gall's Church, mural, 12th century). *Cycles:* include Strasbourg, tapestry, embroidery, 15th century; Plochingen parish church, mural, 1432 (whitewashed 1928); Möschenfeld near Munich O. Church, painting, mid 15th century; Mörsach parish church, reliefs, circa 1530; Prague National Gallery, painting, by H. Holbein the Elder, 1509.

Oliver Plunket

Archbishop of Armagh, martyr, saint

Feast-day: 11th July

Life: Born in 1629 in Loughcrew (co. Meath) of a noble family, he studied at the Irish College of the Sapienza University, Rome, from 1645, was ordained priest in 1654 and, in 1657, became professor of theology at the Propaganda College and procurator of the Irish bishops. In 1669, O. was consecrated archbishop of Armagh and Primate of All Ireland. Due to the Anglican schism created by King Henry VIII, and despite the leaning towards Catholizism of King Charles II (1660–1685), the pressure exerted by the parliamentary opposition had severely increased the penal laws against Catholics (so-called Test Act of 1673). As of 1674, O. was only able to carry out his work in secrecy. The panic caused by the false allegations of the Anglican cleric Titus Oates, claiming a conspiracy of the Jesuits to kill the king and to reinstate the Catholic Church by force led to the arrest of 35 Catholics, among them O. who was imprisoned in Dublin in 1679 and moved to Newgate, London. The false evidence of two apostate Irish friars, together with the bias of the court, led to accusations of collaboration with the French and the preparation of an uprising, resulting in a conviction for high treason. On 11th July 1681, O. was hanged, drawn and quartered at Tyburn. He was beatified in 1920 and canonized in 1975.

Veneration and cult sites: His body was taken to Lambspring Abbey near Hildesheim, Westphalia in 1683; translated in 1883 to the Benedictine abbey of Downside in Somerset; his head was first kept in Rome and, in 1722, translated to Drougheda (C. o. Louth), where it now rests at the church of St Oliver. No representation in Art.

Onuphrius the Great

ascetic, saint

Feast-day: 12th June

Life: O. lived in 4th/early 5th century; after education in the monastery of Hermopolis, 60 years as a hermit in Thebais. Paphnutius was at O.'s death.

Patronage: Munich, weavers, cattle.

Veneration and cult sites: O. is one of the few desert fathers with his own veneration in the Latin Church. Skull relics sent by the Pope to Henry the Lion, transferred in a cel-

Georgianum, painting, late 15th century); skull, crown (St Petersburg, hermitage, painting, by J. Ribera, 17th century); host in hand (Schweidnitz, Catholic Church, painting, 1492); angel with host (Freiburg, Cathedral, stained glass, 14th century); staff, prayer cord (Zürich, State Museum, painting, circa 1514/15); crown (Galatina, St Catherine's, fresco, 15th century); sceptre (Schwäbisch Hall, St Michael's Church, painting, 1521). *Special scenes*: burial of O. bound in a sack by Paphnutius with the help of two lions (Pisa, Camposanto, fresco, by Maestro del Trionfo della Morte, 14th century); Paphnutius flees, because he takes O. for an animal (Florence, Accademia, painting, by L. Monaco, circa 1400); childhood of O. (Nuremberg, German National Museum, painting, by H. Schäufelein, circa 1515/20). *Cycles*: Rome St Onofrio al Giancolo, frescoes, 16th/17th century; Barcelona Cathedral, Predella, 15th century.

Oswald

King, saint

Feast-day: 5th August

Life: * circa 604, king of Northumbria. His father died in battle at an uprising of the Britons; O. had to flee to the monastery founded by Columba on Iona Island and was there baptised. 634 victory over Caedwall, King of the Britons, reconquest of the land, 635 founding of the Monastery of Lindisfarne, which became the centre point of missionary work. O. fell in the battle of Maserfelth (today Oswestry) against Penda, King of Mercia.

Patronage: English royal house, city and Canton of Zug; crusaders, reapers, cattle; weather; also as helper in need.

Legend: At the coronation of O. as king, there is no chrisam oil, which a raven brings in a valuable vessel with a sealed letter; afterwards it is consecrated by St Peter himself;

ebratory procession to the Castle Chapel, Munich, on 14th June 1158, since 1180 in Brunswick.

Representation in Art: *Apparel:* naked, body covered by beard (Monreale, mosaic, 12th century); as naked old man, whole body covered with hair, loincloth of leaves (Schweidnitz, Catholic Church, painting, 1492); in robe of leaves (Zürich, State Museum, painting, circa 1514/15); in plaited shirt (Madrid, University, painting, by F. Collantes, 17th century); as kneeling penitent in solitude (Escorial, painting, by J. Ribera, 17th century). *Attributes:* chain wrapped round body (Schloss Unterelkofen, painting, 1517); hand cross (Bominaco, St Pellegrino, mural, 1263); cross (Escorial, painting, by J. Ribera, 17th century); large standing cross (Munich, another raven gives him a letter and ring for the engagement with the king's daughter, which O. is able to do only after difficult conflicts with the pagan father. – At a feast the king is told that many poor are asking for a gift, so O. did not only give them the food, but also cut the valuable tableware into pieces and distributed it.

Veneration and cult sites: Cult propagated by Scottish monks. Relics in: monastery Bardney, Abbey of Weingarten (of skull relics since 1098), Hildesheim Cathedral Treasury (Oswald reliquary); pilgrimage chapels in Black Forest, also in poems, such as the Minstrel's Epic "Sant Oswalt uz Engellant" or become popular through his bridal and heroic journeys.

Representation in Art: *Apparel:* as king in well pleated undergarment and open cloak (Hildesheim, Cathedral Treasury, O. reliquary, niello, 12th century); in princely dress, smooth leggings, robe (woodcut from the Sainte of the Family, Friends and Relatives of Emperor Maximilian I, 16th century); as knight in armour (Graz, Gallery of the Staatsmuseum, painting, circa 1450); as reaper (Fertörákos, Hungary, wayside shrine, relief, 1643). *Attributes:* palm branch (Bergues, town library, MS 19, illumination, circa 1100); covered vessel (Freiburg, figure, circa 1300); double tankard (Hinterzarten, O. Chapel, figure, circa 1550); raven on hand (Untermais, parish church, mural, 1444); raven on orb (Nonnberg Convent near Salzburg, painting, 15th century); raven covered vessel (Zug, St Michael, figure, 1689); raven on book (Seefeld, Tyrol, figure, circa 1500); raven at feet with ring and letter in beak (Hinterzarten, O. Chapel, figure, circa 1550); ring in hand (Zug, Historic Antique Collection, painting, 16th century); ears of grain (Fertörákos, Hungary, wayside shrine, relief, 1643). *Special scenes:* O. gives alms (New York, Pierpont Morgan Library, MS 710, illumination, 13th century); scenes from the epic: the raven brings the Chrisam oil (Munich, Bavarian National Museum, painting, circa 1470); O. presents his wife to Christ dressed as a beggar (Bolzano, St Vigil's, mural, circa 1420). *Cycles:* Otterswang near Schussenried, mural, by A.M. of Ow (Au) 1778; Katal St Catherine's, painting, 1493.

P

Pancras of Rome

Martyr, saint

Feast-day: 12th May

Life: P. suffered martyrdom probably during Diocletian's persecution of the Christians. His name was mentioned in the 354 calendar.

Legends: according to the Passio of the 6th century, P. is born the son of a wealthy Phrygian. – After the early death of his parents, P. goes with his uncle, Dionysios, to Rome where he is baptised. – Despite the personal intervention of Diocletian, the 14 year old young man remains steadfast in his faith. – P. is beheaded. -His mortal remains are buried by the senator's wife, Octavilla.

Patronage: children receiving their first communion, German knights, French children, protector of young seeds and flowers (ice saints).

Veneration and cult sites: first Roman church above P.'s grave on the Via Aurelia, built by Pope Symmachus (498–504), decorated under Pope Honorius I (625–638), since 1517 S Pancrazio fuori le mura. Veneration all over Central Europe, sometimes belongs to the 14 Holy Helpers.

Superstition: according to the Golden Legend, if somebody commits perjury then the devil will enter his bones, rendering him mad and he will be unable to reach the doorstep.

Representation in Art: *Apparel:* as young knight in full armour, coat and beret (Rappoltstein Castle, altar fig., 2nd half of the 15th century); in traditional soldier's dress with helmet (Paderborn, Market Church,

fig., 18th century); in noble dress with tunica and chlamys (Halberstadt, College Library, so-called Hamersleben bible, book illustration, 12th century). *Attributes:* palm tree (Velbern near Beckum, Westphalia, baptismal font relief, 12th century); sword (Nuremberg, Germanic National Museum, stained glass, circa 1320); lance and pennant (Paris, privately owned, tapestry from Nuremberg, circa 1450); heart plate (Rome, Basilica S Pancrazio, fig. 20th century). *Special scenes:* P.'s baptism (Città del Vaticano, Museums, painting by Mariotto di Nardo, 15th century?); P.'s education by Pope Cornelius (Ranst, fig., 18th century). *Martyrdom:* Ebreuil (Allier), St-Léger, mural painting, 12th century. *Cycles:* Ranshofen, frescoes by Ch. Lehrl, circa 1700.

Pantaleon of Nicomedia

(Panteleimon) Doctor, Martyr, saint

Feast-day: 27th July

Life: P. suffered martyrdom in the 305 Diocletianic persecution.

Legends: according to the Passio of the 5th century, following the characteristics of the invincible saint: P. is born in Nicomedia (now Izmir, Turkey), son of a pagan father and a Christian mother. – P. is personal physician of Emperor Maximianus Herculeus. – P. is baptised by the priest Hermolaos. – P. cures a child bitten by a snake. – Out of spite, a colleague brings a charge against P. who is tortured. – P. is tied to a wheel which breaks. – P. is thrown to wild beasts, Christ appears and comforts him. -P. is thrown into water with a millstone around his neck but the waves carry him to the shore. – B. is tied to a dead olive tree and hit with thorns until he bleeds. When his blood drips on the trunk, the tree turns green and begins to bloom. – At the soil around P.'s feet lilies, roses and violets grow. – Faced with the miracle, the observers are converted to Christianity. – The angry executioners nails P.'s hands to his head. – P. prays for pardon for the executioners and a divine voice calls him "Panteleémon" (=compassion for all people). – During P.'s beheading milk flows from his wounds instead of blood.

Patronage: doctors, midwives, invoked against headaches and consumption, locusts, witchcraft, loneliness, accidents, for real penitence; patron saint of livestock, of the Dillingen medical faculty, in Merscheid (Rhineland), helper for crying children, in Hamburg the patron saint of the school feast of Lutheran (!) children.

Veneration and cult sites: Vercelli, Cathedral (skull); Venice (arm); relics amongst other locations in Arles, Lyons, Benevento, Borobia, Brindisi, Genoa, Lucca, Oviedo, Porto, Ravenna, Vercelli, St-Denis, Verdun, Andechs, Buchhorn, Petershausen, Salem, Unkel on Rhine, Weissenau, Zwiefalten. Blood and milk relics (so-called changing relics) in Constantinople, Bari, Lucca, Madrid, Naples, Ravello near Naples, Rome, Venice. P. pilgrimages to Wilfingen near Säckingen, Oberrottweil at the Kaiserstuhl. Patronage amongst others of Constantinople (of the P. Church, built by Emperor Justinian, 1st half of the 6th century); Jerusalem (P. monastery in the Jordan desert); Cologne (St Pantaleon, 9/10th century).

Superstition: in Italy, P. gives favourable lottery numbers in dreams. – In the Campagna, bandages exist with spells to guard against witchcraft.

Representation in Art: *Apparel:* as martyr in long dress (Cologne, Municipal Archive, evangeliar, book illustration, 12th century); as doctor (Ceské Budejovice, Ales Gallery, painting, circa 1530); in narrow trousers and skirt, reaching to the knees (Regensburg, St Emmeran, Emmeran Shrine, relief, middle of the 15th century). *Attributes:* ointment spatula, surgical instruments (Vienna, Art History Museum, relief, 12th century); surgical instruments, the infirm at his feet (Dolianova, Parish Church, painting, before 1503); surgical instruments, palm tree (Cologne, St Pantaleon, seal relief, 1267, 1480); sword (Cologne, St Pantaleon, stained glass, 1622); nail in hand (Hanover, Kestner Museum, woodcut, circa 1500); hands nailed on the head (Sülzenbrücken/Thuringia, embroidery, before 1400); whip and canes (Cologne, Municipal Archive, evangeliar, 12th century). *Special scenes:* curing of a child (Venice, S Pantaleo, painting by P. Veronese, 1587). *Martyrdom:* hands nailed on the head (Regensburg, St Emmeran, Emmeran Shrine, relief, middle of the 15th century); tied naked to a horizontal beam (Grünow, Mecklenburg, fig. 16th century); P.'s beheading and glory (Venice, S Pantaleo, fresco by G. A. Fumiani, 17/18th century). *Cycles:* Sant'Angelo in Formis, mural painting, 11th century; Wolfenbüttel, Library, Cod. ang. 4,11,2, book illustration, 1st half of the 12th century; Chartres, Cathedral, stained glass, circa 1250; Unkel on Rhine, relic shrine, reliefs, circa 1460; Dolianova, Parish Church, painting, before 1503; Granada, Provincial Museum, painting by Juan de Seville, 1675/80.

Paschalis Babylón

Franciscan laybrother, Confessor, saint
Feast-day: 17th May
Life: born on 16th May 1540 in Torrehermosa. Initially he worked as a herdsman and in 1564 joined the Montforte Franciscan monastery (near Alicante) as laybrother. He worked in humple service in the refectory and as door-keeper. He was well-known for his love of the poor and his devotion to the Eucharist. P. had mystic visions. He died on 17th May 1592 in Villarreal (Castellón de la Plaña). Beatified in 1618, canonized in 1690.

Patronage: diocese of Segorbe-Castellón de la Plaña (since 1961); of Eucharist congresses and unions (since 1897); sacramental brotherhoods; herdsmen; chefs; in Italy the patron saint of women.
Veneration and cult sites: grave in the Villarreal monastery near Valencia. During the Spanish Civil War, the grave was devastated and the relics burned. Votive temple of the Eucharist world congresses in Villarreal.
Representation in Art: *Apparel:* in Franciscan habit, rope belt, hood (Ehingen, Liebfrauenkirche, fig., 18th century); as shepherd (Villeforte Padri). *Attributes:* shepherd's crook, garden shovel (Aranjuez, P. monastery, painting by G. B. Tiepolo, circa 1769); Pyxis (Ehingen, Liebfrauenkirche, fig., 18th century); worshipping the monstrance (Straubing, Church of the Guardian Angel, painting by C. D. Asam, early 18th century); with penitent's chain (Villeforte Padri). *Special scenes:* P.'s acceptance to the Order (Körtinghausen/Westphalia, Fürstenberg Collection, painting by G. Odazi, 18th century).

Patrick

(Patricius) Bishop, saint
Feast-day: 17th March
Life: born about 385 in Bannavem Taberniae, probably now Ravenglass, Cumberland as son of the decurio and deacon Calpurnis. In 401, at the age of 16, he was carried off to Ireland as a slave and worked as a herdsman. He was spiritually cleansed and escaped in 407. Back at home, he studied on the mainland, lived as a monk, probably in the Lérins monastery near Nice, later as cleric in Auxerre and visited Italy and the monastic colonies on the Tyrrhenian Sea. In 432 he went as missionary to Ireland and became bishop and successor of Palladius. P., protected by the High King Laoghaire and many tribal kings, created a church organisation with

the episcopal see in Armagh and other dioceses. He died circa 416.

Legends: with the help of a trefoil P. explains the secret of the Holy Trinity to pagans.

Patronage: apostle of Ireland; of the Tullow S P.brotherhood (since 1808) and the Kiltegan missionary society for foreign missions (since 1932); of lost souls; miners; coopers,; hairdressers; blacksmiths; livestock.

Veneration and cult sites: Ireland, Rouen, Lérins, North America, Australia, Eastern Styria, pilgrimage to Lough Derg (Ireland), Croagh Patrick (Ireland), Hohenstadt (Swabia).

Superstition: in Ireland on St P.'s day it is always good weather ensuring particularly good celebrations. – On St P.'s day, a black cockerel should be sacrificed.

Representation in Art: *Apparel:* as bishop (Hohenstadt, Swabia, fig., late 14th century). *Attributes:* snake (Dublin, National Museum, relief, 15/16th century); trefoil (New York, St Patrick, stained glass by H. Clarke, 20th century); livestock (Rouen, St Patrice, stained glass, 16th century). *Special scenes:* curing of the infirm (Padua, Museo Civico, painting by Tiepolo, 18th century).

Paul

Apostle of the Gentiles, Martyr, saint

Feast-day: 29th June (together with Peter); 25th January P.'s conversion; 18th November (consecration of the Basilica S Paolo fuori le mura); 16th April (translation of his head); 6th July (P.'s first arrival in Rome); 1st September (P. got his sight back); 21st February (Maronite rites); formerly 30th June (own feast, after the liturgical and calendar reform feast of the Roman martyrs).

Life: P. letters and the Apocryphal New Testament story are the main sources: born about 5–10 A. D.as Saul, of a Jewish Diaspora family in Tarsus and belonged to the Benja-

min tribe (Romans 11.1). Educated in Jerusalem by Gamaliel the Elder (Apocr. 22.3), as an Aramaic and Greek speaking Pharisee, he studied intensively the bible and Jewish tradition. According to Jewish customs, P. worked as a tent maker (Apocr. 18.3) to earn his living. Later, this craft made him self-sufficient in society. Initially, he was a fervent supporter of the law and a deadly enemy of the young Church (Apocr. 5, 34 – 39) and, according to Apocr. 7.58 present when deacon Stephan was stoned. By order of the Synedrium he travelled with a letter of introduction from Jerusalem to Damascus (1 Cor. 15.8, Gal. 1,15–16). In 33/34 or 35/36 his life changed when he was converted near Damascus and nominated as apostle. P. said he should not have been born (Romans 15.15 – 16). Shortly before the first missionary journey, Saul changed his name to Paul. As a popular missionary, he later made three missionary journeys; 44 – 49 with Barnabas and

Mark (Apocr. 14.1 ff); 50 – 52 with Timothy and Silas (Apocr. 15, 26 ff); and his third journey between 53 – 58 (Apocr.18.23 ff). Between 58 and 60 he was arrested under Felix and Festus in Caesarea. In 61 he travelled to Rome where he was arrested and imprisoned until 63 (Apocr. 28.17 ff). He then travelled to Asia Minor. In the first letter of Clement another journey to Spain was reported, together with Sergius, the first bishop of Narbonne. His second arrest under Nero in Rome (64) and his beheading cannot be proved historically. According to Eusebius he died in 67. P. saved the Christian communities from abolishing the syncretic and gnostic doctrines and found opposition with the Jewish Christians because according to him there was no difference between Jewish and gentile Christians. He was a famous organiser, restricting his missions to centres from where the glad tidings of the Gospel could radiate into other regions. P.'s letters gave him great theological influence as he tried to comprehend God's word in thought and system. He is even regarded as the founder of speculative theology, for instance, in the letter to the Romans he dealt with the issues of the guilt of the people, their need for salvation, justification and grace as well as with Christ's death and resurrection.

Legends: according to the reports on Paul of the late 2nd century: during a sermon in Iconium, P. converts Thecla. – Her fiancé feels deceived by Thecla's abstinence and inflames the authorities against P. – P. is arrested and secretly visited by Thecla. It is discovered and P. is sentenced to death by fire but rain and hail prevent the execution. Thecla too is rescued. – In men's clothes, Thecla follows P. to Antioch and lives in Tripania's house where she meets a young man, Alexander, who falls in love with her. – Thecla is thrown to wild beasts but a lion defends her against the other animals. – Thecla is thrown into the sea but lightning kills

seals and other animals. Triphania women calm the water with spices. – Thecla is burned at the stake but remains unharmed. – In the context of the confession made to Christ by the imperial cupbearer, Patroclus, P. is arrested as ringleader by Nero and sentenced to death by the sword. – During execution, milk instead of blood falls on the soldier's clothes. – After execution on the road to Ostia, three springs erupt at the sites where his head fell to the ground.

Patronage: the Order and religious societies named after P., of labourers, tent makers, weavers, saddlers, rope-makers, basket and rug makers, swordsmen, theologians, doves, the catholic press, invoked against storms at sea, snakebites, for rain and productivity of the fields.

Veneration and cult sites: Rome, the Basilica S Paolo fuori le mura at the Via Ostiense, built by Emperor Constantine; the main relic is in Rome, Lateran basilica (since 16th April 1370), other relics are in S Paolo alle Tre Fontane at the Via Laurentina; SS Pietro e Paolo in Carcere; S Paolo alla Regola (arm relic); S Agnese at the Piazza Navona (cloth relic from Plautillas's eye bandage); S Ignazio (tooth relic); S Lorenzo in Damaso (penitent cingulum); S Matteo in Merulana; SS Eustacio e Prassede (fragments of clothes). Particular veneration in Tarsos, Rome, Malta, Corvey, Frankfurt/Main, London, Münster, Saragossa, Valladolid, Utrecht.

Superstition: P.'s feast-day plays no role in customs. But P.'s conversion (25th January) is the so-called mid-winter day, connected with the idea that all animals in hibernation turn over. – Important annual day: if it rains an expensive time approaches; if it is clear and bright a good year approaches. – With snow or rain, great bloodshed will soon come to man and livestock. – If it is foggy, plague will come. – Prophetic customs: young women should turn the mattress to the wrong side and request from P. that they

cannot see their belly. – If one lies the wrong way around in bed, one can see one's future marriage partner. – During the 1382 livestock plague at Galmaarde (near Ghent), P. appeared to the herdsmen and distributed small white balls for the livestock and the disease disappeared. Since that time there are P. buns and P. balls. P. buns protect against seed-borne disease.

Representation in Art: *Apparel:* as apostle in long, girdled tunica and coat pallium (Reims, portal of the Court of Justice at the north wing, fig., circa 1230). *Attributes:* sword (Hanover, Regional Museum, painting by A. van Dyck, 1618); two swords as analogy to St Peter's keys (Nuremberg, St Sebald, Sebaldus tomb, bronze fig. by P. Vischer, circa 1510); drawn sword (Florence, Uffizi, painting by G. Bellini, 15th century); scroll (Palermo, Capella Palatina, mosaic, 12th century); scroll in cingulum, Pan lying at his feet (London, Church of the Ascension, painting by F. Shields, 1888); book (Munich, Alte Pinakothek, painting by A. Dürer, 1526); scroll above the sword pommel (Eisenberg, Protestant Church, stained glass, circa 1900); upturned altar of the unknown God (Castelgandolfo, Villa Torolonia, fresco, by M. Seitz, 1835/44); three springs (Berlin, Governmental Museums, painting by the Master of Schöppingen, 1450/75); transparent blood container with lion as root of a flower (Rome, St Peter's Church, portal relief by A. Filarete, before 1445); with severed head in hand (Stuttgart, Landesbibliothek, Zwiefalten martyrdom, book illustration, 12th century). *Special scenes:* Traditio Legis (Tivoli, S Silvestro, fresco, 13th century), P. seated, writing a letter (Schwarzrheindorf, double Chapel, mural painting, 12th century); P. preaching before the receiver of the letters (Paris, Louvre, ivory relief, 6/7th century); P. folding a letter (Toledo, Greco Museum, painting from the Greco school, 16th century); presentation of the letter to the Galatians to

a messenger (Vienna, Albertina, woodcut by A. Altdorfer, 1533); P. with books in the countryside, in the background, ships capsizing on the sea (Leiden, Museum, painting by Lucas van Leyden, 1526); P. in the countryside (Paris, Louvre, painting by G. Ferrari, 1543); P. in prison (Stuttgart, Staatsgalerie, painting by Rembrandt, 1627); P. s sermon (Neustift near Freising, fig. by I. Günther, 18th century); P.'s sermon to the inhabitants of Lystra (Marostica, S Antonio, painting by J. and F. Bassano, 16th century); P.'s sermon at the Athens altar of the unknown God (Vienna, Art History Museum, painting by J. Zick, 18th century); P.'s conversion with angel descending from heaven (Madrid, Museo Cerralbo, painting by Juan de la Corte, 1642); P.'s conversion with frightened horse (Rome, S Maria del Populo, painting by M. Caravaggio, 1601); P.'s escape over the town wall (Naturns, Prokulus Church, mural painting, circa 770/80); P. and Barnabas, worshipped by the inhabitants of Lystra as Gods (Paris, Louvre, painting by M. Corneille le Père, 1644); shipwrecked at Malta (London, National Gallery, painting by A. Elsheimer, circa 1598); P. unharmed after the snakebite (Canterbury, Cathedral, fresco, 12th century); the curing of Publius's father (Lilienfeld Concordancia, Cod. 151, book illustration, middle of the 14th century); departure of the apostle prince (Graz, Johanneum Regional Museum, painting by M. J. Schmidt, circa 1778); P. stoned but unharmed (Marseilles, Musée des Beaux-Arts, painting by J. B. de Champaigne, 1667); P.'s sentencing and beheading (Paderborn, Diocesan Museum, Abdinghof movable altar by Roger of Helmarshausen, relief, circa 1100); beheading and miracle of the springs (Rome, S Paolo alle Tre Fontane, fig. by A. Algardi, 17th century); P.'s severed head (Münster, west transept section of the Cathedral, fig., circa 1225/35. *Cycles:* very numerous, among others in the Vatican, Biblioteca Vaticana,

MS Barb., lat. 4406, drawings of the cycle of S Paolo fuori le Mura; Monreale, Cathedral, mosaics, 12th century); Palermo, Capella Palatina, mosaics, 12th century; Chartres, Cathedral, stained glass, 13th century; Augsburg, Staatsgalerie, painting by H. Holbein the Elder, 1504; London, Victoria and Albert Museum, cartons for the tapestry of the Sistine by Raphael, circa 1525; London St Paul, painting on the dome by J. Thornhill, 19th century; Geneva, St Paul, painting by Maurice Denis, 1904.

Paul of the Cross

Founder of the Passionist Congregation, saint

Feast-day: 19th October (before the calendar reform: 28th April)

Life: born 1694 in Ovada, Piedmont, son of the impoverished noble Danai family. At the beginning he worked in the family business. At the age of 19 he joined the Venetian army to fight against the Turks. In 1716 he decided to live a pure life and in 1720 received the black clothes of the penitent from Bishop Francesco Arborio di Gattinari of Alessandria (Piedmont). He lived for 40 days in the solitude of Castellazzo where he wrote the rules of an Order whilst praying and doing penance. In 1725, Pope Benedict XIII gave him permission to found an Order. Between 1726 and 1728 he cared for the infirm in San Gallicano. Together with his brother he was ordained priest. In 1728 he founded the first Passionist monastery on Monte Argentario near Orbetello. In 1741, more moderate rules than in the first version were introduced and approved by Pope Benedict XIV. In 1769, P. became general of the Order and moved the headquarters to the Roman Giovanni e Paolo monastery. He died on 18th October 1775 in Rome and was buried in SS Giovanni e Paolo. P.'s mysticism and focus on the passion were inspired by Theresa of Avila, John of the Cross and Francis de Sales. He became a important preacher. Beatified in 1853, canonized in 1867.

Representation in Art: *Apparel:* in black soutane with the emblem of the Order. *Attributes:* skull, crucifix (Itri, Passionist Church, painting by S. Conca, 19th century.)

Paul Miki

(Michi) Jesuit, Martyr, saint

Feast-day: 6. February (day of martyrdom), before the calendar reform: 15th February.

Ecclesiastical history: during the 1549 persecution of the Japanese Christians by Shogun Toyotomi Hideyoshi, affecting locals and missionaries who had worked in Japan since 1549, twenty-six Christians (six Franciscans, three Jesuits and seventeen members of the Third Franciscan Order) were tied to crosses and killed on 6th February 1597 with lances. Further persecution began in 1614 and led to the Christian rebellion of 1637 resulting in the 1640 eradication of Japanese Christianity. Only in 1873 did Japan permit freedom of religion which was entered into the constitution in 1899. Of numerous martyrs, 205 are venerated as saints, amongst them the three Jesuits, Paul Miki, John Soan and James Kisai.

Life: Paul Miki, one of the Jesuit pupils, regarded as an excellent preacher and catechist, preached in Nagasaki before his death to the people as he hung on at the cross. – James Kisai (Ghisai) and John Goto were killed in the same way.

Representation in Art: *Apparel:* as Jesuit in black soutane (Tournai, S Nikola, painting, 18th century). *Martyrdom:* only of the three Jesuits on the cross (Munich, Staatl. Graphische Sammlung, copperplate engraving by A. Bolswert, 17th century); pierced by lances (Rimini, Museum, painting by Canlassi, called Cagnacci, 17th century); all Japanese martyrs (Milan, Brera, painting by A. Tanzio da Varallo, circa 1627).

Paul of Thebes

The first hermit, saint

Feast-day: 15th January (translation feast: 27th January).

Life: born in 228, the son of wealthy parents at the edge of the Thebaid. During the Decian persecution of the Christians he fled into the mountains and lived there for 60 years in a cave. At the age of 113 he was found by Antony of Egypt. When Antony returned for the second time, P. was already dead.

Legends: see "Antony Abbas"

Patronage: Order of St Paul, of basket and rug makers.

Representation in Art: *Apparel:* in shirt woven from palm leaves (Höchst, St Justinus, fig., circa 1460); in long skirt with hood and scapula (Nuremberg, Frauenkirche, painting at the Tucher reredos, middle of the 15th century); as penitent (Madrid, Prado, painting by J. Ribera, 17th century). *Attributes:* raven (Basle, Arts Museum, painting, 15th century); breaking bread (London, British Museum, painting by L. Limosin, 16th century). *Cycles:* see also under "Antony Abbas"; independent P. *Cycle:* Paris, Bibliothèque Nationale, Les belles Heures de Jean de France, book illustration, 14th century.

Paulinus of Nola

Bishop, saint

Feast-day: 22nd June

Life: born in 353/54, the son of a Christian senator near Bordeaux. P. received his Christian education from Ambrose of Milan and, apparently before 379, became governor of Campania. In 385, he married a Spanish woman Theresa, who gave him a son. In 390, P. was baptised in Bordeaux. After the early death of his son, P. decided to withdraw from the world and lived with his wife – but not in a marriage – in Nola near the grave of St Felix. According to the example of Martin of Tours, he founded a semi-monastic Order and constructed many buildings. In 409 he was elected as bishop. His contemporaries regarded him as an example of Christian renunciation. Of his 35 poems, P. dedicated 14 to St Felix and two to Ausonius, indicating particularly the difference between pagan and Christian culture. His correspondence with Augustine, Martin of Tours and Sulpicius Severus dealt, amongst other things, with the issue of liturgical and non-liturgical devotion. He died on 22nd June 431 in Nola.

Legends: in place of the son of a widow, P. goes voluntarily as prisoner of the Visigoths.

Patronage: patron saint of Nola, Regensburg and millers.

Veneration and cult sites: in the 7th or 8th century the mortal remains were in Benevento; translated in 1000 to Rome; in 1908 re-translated to Nola by Pius X.

Representation in Art: *Apparel:* as bishop (Stuttgart, Regional Library, Zwiefalten martyrdom, book illustration, 12th century). *Attributes:* shovel, basket, watering-can (copperplate engraving in Giulini, daily edification of a real Christian, Vienna, Augsburg, 1753/55).

Perpetua and Felicitas

Martyrs, saints

Feast-day: 7th March, before the calendar reform 6th. March, in the rites of the Eastern Church, 2nd February or 4th March.

Life: reports handed down by Perpetua and witnesses, reporting great religious zeal: P. was born the child of noble parents. P. had a son, was converted to Christianity and baptised as adult woman which was forbidden under Septimius Severus under sentence of death. P.'s father tried unsuccessfully to dissuade her from Christianity. – On 7th March 202/203, at the age of 22, on the occasion of an animal circus for the birthday of Publius Septimius, son of Emperor Septimius Severus, P. suffered martyrdom in the Carthage arena, together with other Christians. Confronted with their steadfastness, the prison warden, Pudens, was converted to Christianity. -F. was a slave, probably married to the prisoner Revocatus, and gave birth to a daughter, two days before her martyrdom. The child was brought up by one of her sisters as her own. In the arena, P. and F. were thrown before wild cows.

Veneration and cult sites: P. and F. belong to the canon saints, mentioned, together with six other martyrs, in the Roman canon (canon I) "Nobis quoque peccatoribus" (= to us who are also sinners), prayed after the transsubstantiation. Relics are in Beaulieu (Corrèze), Berry, Vierzon.

Representation in Art: *Apparel:* as women, P. in noble dress with necklace and headdress, F. in simple dress without jewelry and simple headscarf (Ravenna, Archiepiscopal Chapel, mosaic medallions, 6th century). *Attributes:* wild cow, child on lap (Vich, Episcopal Museum, painting, 15th century). *Cycles:* Barcelona, Diocesan Museum, antependium of the P. altar, 14th century.

Peter

Apostle, Bishop of Rome, 1st Pope, Martyr, saint

Feast-day: 29th June (together with Paul, the original feast of all twelve apostles); 22nd February (Cathedra Peter, since the 1960 rubric reform, introduced in the 4th century as Peter's 'chair feast' to drive out pagan commemoration of the dead; in Gaul since the 6/7th century on 18th January, commemoration of the transfer of the 'pastorate', therefore two feasts. In Rome, the feast of the transfer of the 'pastorate' was confused with P.'s assumption of office as bishop of Antioch). 1st August, anniversary of the consecration of S Pietro in Vincoli, Rome 432, called the feast of St Peter's chains.

Life: in the Gospels and the Apocryphal New Testament story, P. was mentioned 150 times: P. was born in Bethsaida/Galilee as Simon, son of Jonas or John. The name P. was given to him by Jesus during a promise at Caesarea Phillippi (Mt 16, 18 f).When Jesus called him, P. was married in Capernaum and worked, like his brother, Andrew, as a fisherman (Mk 1. 21–29). Jesus cured P.'s mother-in-law (Mk 1.30). P. belonged, besides John and James, to Jesus's most familiar companions. In the Gospels, P.'s special position as spokesman was clarified. P. was characterised as a man with a spontaneous and impulsive nature emphasized in Christ's Passion: on Christ's way to the Mount of Olives, P. wanted to give his life for Christ (Mk 14.31) and, during Christ's arrest, he hit out in wild rage at the high priest's servant (Jo 18.10) and then, after he denied Jesus, had to suffer a painful humiliation (Mt 26.29ff). After P. had declared his love three times, Jesus transferred the highest shepherd's power to P. (Jo 21.15–17). After his resurrection, J. appeared first to P. and then to all remaining disciples (1 Cor 15.5). After Whitsun, P. worked in the Jerusalem congregation, preached in Samaria, Lydda and Joppe; revived Tabitha from death (Apocr. 8–9) and had the vision of the pure and impure animals which led him to the belief that pagans are also destined for the glad tidings. In Caesarea he baptised the pagan Cornelius (Apocr. 10). In about 44 he was arrested by Herod Aggrippa and rescued in a miraculous way by an angel the night before his execution. He then went to Antioch. With Paul he had disputes over his ideas on the issue of pagan Christians.(Gal 2.11 ff). In 50/51 he participated in the Jerusalem apostolic council and later visited Asia Minor and probably also Corinth, which led to a split in the Christian congregation as indicated in Paul's letter to the Corinthians, written circa 57 (1 Cor 1.12). His visit to Rome is proven historically but an exact date and the duration cannot be proved conclusively. P. did not speak Greek and Latin fluently and Mark (Papias) was therefore his translator. In 64/67 he suffered martyrdom in Rome, crucified during Nero's persecution of the Christians.

Legends: according to P.'s Apocr. of approx. 200/210:with the help of his paralysed daughter P. explains that an alleged illness could be a gift from God to remain a virgin. – With a ship, P. sails to Rome, finally conquering Simon Magus. – P. cures a blind woman. – When P.'s life is endangered he leaves Rome at the request of his brothers, and meets Christ who tells him that he will go to Rome to be crucified again. P. returns to Rome immediately. – P. demands to be crucified head down to ensure that he will not die in the same way as Christ.

Patronage: patron saint of the Carolingians, patron saint of Geneva and the dioceses of Rome, Berlin, Lausanne-Geneva-Fribourg; of fishermen, sailors, mechanics, bridge builders, blacksmiths, butchers, quarry workers, watchmakers, invoked against fever, epilepsy, thieves and snakes.

Veneration and cult sites: Aedicula, circa 160/180 regarded as St P.'s place of burial; Sgraffiti in S Sebastiano on the Via Appia could also be the burial site of P.'s mortal remains. Two contradictory traditions which led to the hypothesis of translating mortal remains. – In the early 3rd century, the Christian congregation built the Tropaion as location of the martyrdom. Memorials are in Upenna, Henchir, Megrun, Orléansville, in Northern Africa. P. relics are in Rome, St Peter (Cathedra, since the 11th century, in fact the ivory throne, owned by Charles the Bold,

circa 870); Rome, S Prassede (P.'s altar table); Rome, S Maria in Trastevere; Rome, S Cecilia in Trastevere; Rome, S Maria in Campitelli; Rome, S Gregorio al Celio; Rome, SS Giovanni e Paolo; Jerusalem, St Peter in Gallicantu; Venice, S Pietro in Castello (P.'s Cathedra from Antioch); London, Cathedral (P.'s Antioch chalice); Rome, S Pietro in Vincoli (chains); Metz, Cathedral (chain links); Minden, Cathedral (chain links); Chambéry (nail from P.'s cross); Venice, S Marco (P's knife with which he had cut off Malchus's ear); Aachen, Cathedral Treasury (chain links); Limburg, Cathedral (part of the crosier with which P. revived Bishop Maternus); Cologne, Cathedral (another part of the crosier); Maastricht, Cathedral (P.'s key), 12th century); Lodi Vecchio (P.'s key); numerous P. churches, many famous, amongst others in Ravenna (4th century); Rome (S Peter), Rome (S Pietro in Montorio, is regarded since the 14th century as location of his martyrdom).

Superstition: P. is regarded as ruler of the weather. P. keys help against rabies and snakebites. – In Erfurt, nobody must be elected as town mayor with the Christian name of P. – On Peter's chair feast (22nd February), the spring begins with numerous spring customs which are not directly connected with P. (driving out of the winter etc.). – The 22nd February is in the Netherlands the day when children can demand things.

Representation in Art: *Apparel:* as apostle in long, girdled tunica and coat pallium (Munich, Alte Pinakothek, painting by A. Dürer, 1526); as preacher on the throne (Rome, S Peter, fig. by A. die Cambio, circa 1300); as pope in pluviale and tiara (Cologne, Wallraf-Richartz Museum, painting by the master of Mary's glorification, 2nd half of the 15th century). *Attributes:* key with large bit (Darmstadt, Hessian Regional Museum, painting by a Worms master, circa 1250); two keys as sign of binding and loosening

(Ballamont, Parish Church, fig. by Syrlin the Younger, 1496/99); tiara in hand (Regensburg, Cathedral,Trumeau pillar of the western portal, fig., circa 1425); crosier (Döbeln, Saxony, Nikolai Church, painting, circa 1515); small cross (Bamberg, Cathedral, Adam's gate, fig., circa 1240); cockerel (Doxan, Bohemia, Praemonstratensian Church, fig., 1708); fish (Regensburg, Nicholas Chapel in the Cathedral, relief on the final stone, late 15th century); flame of the Holy Spirit, key on the book (Vienna, Art History Museum, painting by R. Mengs, 18th century). *Special scenes:* P.'s vocation according to Mt 4.18–20 (Ravenna, S Apollinare Nuovo, mosaic, 493/526); curing of P.'s mother-in-law (Escorial, Codes Aureus Spirensis, book illustration, 11th); good fishing according to Lk 5.1–11 (Rome Sistine Chapel, painting by Ghirlandaio, 1481/83); P. as fisher of men (Florence, Uffizi, painting by Bellini, circa 1488); P.'s rescue from the sea according to Mt 14, 24–32 (Vatican City, Stanza della Cleopatra, painting by D. da Volterra, 16th century); the ship of the Church and P. are rescued by Christ, so-called Navicella (Rome, Museo Petrino, copy of a mosaic in the style of Giotto, 17th century); P. steers the ship of the Church (New York, Morgan Library, MS 799, book illustration, circa 1480); presentation of the key to the kingdom of heaven to P. (Munich, Bavarian Governmental Library, golden Gospel book of Henry II, book illustration between 1002 and 1014); P. receives the key from the Christ-child (Vatican City, painting by Crivelli, 1488); allegory "graze my sheep" (London, Victoria and Albert Museum, carton for the tapestries of the Sistine by Raphael, 1515/16); the miracle of the 'interest penny' in the fish according to Mt 17.24–27 (Liverpool, Museum, ivory relief of the Magdeburg antependium, circa 970); P. at Christ's transfiguration (Speyer, History Museum of the Pfalz, painting by the master of Mary's life,

circa 1470); P. refuses that Jesus washes his feet (Mainz, Landesmuseum, prayer-book of Cardinal Albrecht of Brandenburg, book illustration by Simon Bening, circa 1530); P. sleeps at the Mount of Olives (Mainz, Regional Museum, prayer-book of Cardinal Albrecht of Brandenburg, book illustration by Simon Bening, circa 1530); P. cuts off Malchus's ear (St Florian, painting by A. Altdorfer, 1518); during Christ's arrest, P. flees with the disciples (Mainz, Regional Museum, prayer-book of Cardinal Albrecht of Brandenburg, book illustration by Simon Bening, circa 1530); P. announces the denial of Christ (Paris, Louvre, painting by D. Tenniers, 17th century); P.'s denial in front of the maid (Naumburg, Westlettner, fig. by the Naumburg master, circa 1250/60); P.'s denial in front of the soldiers, sitting at the fire (Nantes, Musée des Beaux-Arts, painting by G. de La Tours, 1650); P.'s repentance

(Kattenhorn, St Peter's Church, stained glass by O. Dix, 1959); curing of the paralysed man (Munich, St Peter, fresco by J.B. Zimmermann, 1753); Ananias's and Saphira's death as penalty according to Apocr. 5.1–20 (Avignon, Musée Calvet, relief, late 4th century); P.'s release from Herod's prison according to Apocr. 4.3 (Vatican City, Stanza d'Eliodoro, fresco by Raphael, 1512); vision at Joppa (Rome, Comodilla catacomb, mural painting, 4/5th century); miracle of the shadow according to Apocr. 5.14–16 (Florence, S Maria del Carmine, Brancicci Chapel, fresco by Masaccio, circa 1425); P. fells Simon Magus according to Apocr. 8.9–24 (Munich, St Peter, painting by J. Pollak, circa 1490); revival of Tabitha according to Apocr. 9 (Florence, Palazzo Pitti, painting by Guercino, 17th century); Centurio Cornelius's baptism according to Apocr. 10 (Liége, St-Barthélemy, baptismal font, relief by Reiner of Huy, 1107/18); Traditio legis (Rome, S Costanza, mosaic, 4th century); curing of P.'s daughter (Bonn, Regional Museum, painting by Master Berthold of Nördlingen, 15th century); revival of the son of the Antioch governor, Theophilus (Florence, St Maria del Carmine, Brancacci Chapel, painting by F. Lippi, 15th century); baptism of Processur and Martinianus by P. (Rome, St Peter, painting by G. Passeri, 17th century);P.'s mass with Asprenus and Candida (Naples, S Pietro ad Aram, fresco, 15th century); P. meets Christ on his way to Rome (London, National Gallery, painting by A. Carracci, 16th century); erection of P.'s cross (Rome, S Maria del Popolo, painting by M. Caravaggio, 1601); P.'s crucifixion (Aulnay-de-Saintonge, tympanon relief, 12th century); P. as official at Mary's death (Pfullendorf, Hospital Chapel, painting by J. Stocker, circa 1500); P. as gate-keeper of heaven (Cologne, Wallraf-Richartz Museum, painting by S. Lochner, circa 1440. *Cycles:* Rome, old St Peter, mural painting, circa 681 (ruined);

Müstair, mural painting, circa 800; Munich, Bavarian National Museum, Kunigund coat, embroidery, early 11th century; Palermo, Capella Palatina, mosaics, 12th century; Monreale, Cathedral, mosaics, 12th century; S Pietro a Grado, frescoes, circa 1300; Beauvais, tapestries, circa 1460; Munich, St Peter, painting by J. Pollak, circa 1490 and frescoes by J. B. Zimmermann, 1653/56; Uffizi, painting by H. of Kulmbach, 16th century.

Peter Canisius
Jesuit, Doctor of the Church, saint
Feast-day: 27th April
Life: born on 8th May 1521 in Nijmegen, as son of the town mayor Jakob Kanijs. Between 1536 and 1546 he studied in Cologne. In 1538 he became Bachelor of Liberal Arts and in 1540 Master of Arts. In Cologne, P. met representatives of the Devotio moderna and German mysticism. Against the wishes of his parents he studied theology. In 1543 he received the Ignatian exercises by Peter Faber and joined the Jesuit Order. After 1544, P. gave lessons and translated Cyril of Alexandria's and Leo I's papers into German. In 1546 he was ordained as a priest and was the spokesman of the Catholics against Archbishop Hermann of Wied, who had converted to Protestantism. In 1547, Cardinal Otto Truchsess of Waldburg nominated him as private theologian of the Council of Trent. In 1548 he founded the Messina Jesuit college. In 1549, on the day of the Sacred Heart revelation, he was at the tomb of Peter of Rome. In the same year he was promoted in Bologna to Doctor of the Church. P. was the real instigator of the Counter-Reformation. Between 1549 and 1552 he was professor in Ingolstadt, between 1552 and 1554 professor and preacher at Vienna Cathedral, between 1571 and 1577 he lived in Innsbruck, and between 1556 and 1569 became the first provincial of the Upper German province

IHS

THEOLOGVS ✠ PETRVS CANISIVS SOCIE TATIS IESV

Qui docti fuerint, fulgebunt quasi splendor.
firmamenti; et qui ad iustitiam erudiunt
multos, quasi stellæ in perpetuas æ's
 iernitates. Dan. 12.

Hunc habuit Petrum felix Germania Patrem,
Quem stupuére olim Curia, Templa, Scholæ.
Nunc sculpta ære quidem fas est hæc ora tueri,
Illius at vita est suspicienda magis.

which included Southern Germany, Austria, Hungary and Switzerland. He founded numerous new Jesuit colleges in, amongst others, Munich, Innsbruck, Würzburg, Fribourg, Hall in Tyrol and Augsburg where education was free of charge. Amongst his papers was the 1555 catechism for students, followed by the 1556 catechism for children and the 1558 catechism for secondary schools which were very important and, during P.'s life, reached a circulation of 200 issues. Disputes with his successor, Paul Hoffaeus led in 1580 to P.'s transfer to Fribourg where P., by order of Pope Gregory XIII, founded the Gerome College. When the Jesuit general, Rudolf Aquaviva, wanted to recall him, the Fribourg people and clergy refused to let him go. He died on 21st December 1597 in Fribourg and was buried in the St Michael's Church. Beatified in 1864, canonized in 1925.

Patronage: apostle of Germany, since 1921 patron saint of catholic German school organisations, the diocese of Brixen (since 1925), the diocese of Innsbruck (since 1974).

Veneration and cult sites: in German provinces of the Jesuit Order; Fribourg, St Michael; in the dioceses of Berlin; Cologne; Lausanne-Geneva-Fribourg; Mainz; Meißen; Aachen; Augsburg; Eichstätt; Fulda; Regensburg; Feldkirch; Vienna; Sitten.

Representation in Art: *Apparel:* as Jesuit in black soutane (Fribourg, Cantonal Museum, stained glass, 1591); in coat (Munich, St Michael, painting, 17th century). *Attributes:* writing quill, catechism, crucifix (Manresa, painting by M. Coronas, 1903); hammer (malleus hereticorum) ('s-Heerenberg, painting, 18th century). *Special scenes:* P. preaches to cardinals and rulers (Fribourg, painting by P. Wuilleret, 1635); P. as teacher of the catechism ('s-Heerenberg, Boniface House, painting by F. Langenberg, 1912); P. as opponent of the Magdeburg Centuriators ('s-Heerenberg, painting by P. Gigliardi, 1865); P.'s Sacred Heart vision (Vienna, Jesuit College

at Mount Frein, painting by J. Kessler, 1875); Ignatius sends P. to Germany (Valkenburg, Ignatius College, painting by F. W. Hengelberg, 19th century); P. on his deathbed, comforted by the mother of God (Fribourg, St Michael, painting by F. Bonnet, 1864); P.'s triumph (Vienna, Jesuit College at Mount Frein, painting by P. of Deschwanden, 1864).

Peter Chrysologus

Bishop, Doctor of the Church, saint

Feast-day: 30th July (prior to calendar reform, 4th Dec.)

Life: * around 380 in Forum Cornelii near Imola, educated by Bishop Cornelius of Imola, 431 Bishop of Ravenna, closely associated with Pope Leo the Gr. in the struggle against the Monophysites, esp. Eutyches of Constantinople. Considered an outstanding preacher, wh. earned him the epithet Chrysologus (= gold-tongued). 183 of his sermons have been preserved. † 3rd Dec, 450 in Forum Cornelii. Declared Doctor of the Church in 1729.

Patronage: against fever and rabies.

Representation in art: *Special scenes:* P. with wafer in the epiclesis (Imola Cathedral, painting); P. dying at the altar (early 19C painting by P. Benvenuti, Ravenna Cath.).

Peter Damiani

Benedictine monk, cardinal, bishop of Ostia, Doctor of the Church, saint

Feast-day: 21st Feb. (prior to calendar reform, 23rd Feb.)

Life: * 1007 in Ravenna; after a deprived youth, his brother Damian enabled P. to study in Ravenna, Faenza and Parma. Adopted the cognomen Damian out of gratitude for this help. 1035 Benedictine monk in community of hermits at Fonte Avellana near Gubbio, 1043 prior. Determined reformer of spiritual life and the Church generally

1072 in the monastery of S Maria foris portam in Faenza. No formal canonisation, 1828 Doctor of the Church.

Patronage: against headache.

Veneration and cult sites: body transferred from S Michele, Faenza to the cathedral, feast-day celebrated since 1569 by the Camaldolese Benedictines, universally since 1828.

Representation in Art: *Apparel:* as bishop with mitre (13C fresco, S Guiliana, Perugia); as a cardinal with cappa magna (Rott am Inn, fig. by I. Günther 1763); as a hermit in the hermit's garb (Bishop's Palace, Faenza, painting by B. Gennari the Younger). *Attributes:* suspended cardinal's hat (Accademia, Ravenna, painting by A. Fabriano); crosier (Rott am Inn, fig. by I. Günther 1763); putto with cardinal's hat, skull, angel thrusting a torch between the jaws of a dragon, cross and scourge, baby Jesus and Mother of God with little hours of Our Lady in open breviary (Bishop's Palace, Faenza, painted by B. Gennari the Younger). *Cycles:* St P.'s Chapel, Faenza Cathedral, 19C reliefs.

beyond the community of his order. In his writings Liber gratissimus and Liber Gomorrhianus, P. attacked the dependence of the Church on the state, the bondage of the monasteries vis-à-vis ecclesiastical and temporal powers, simony in spiritual offices and worldly feudal behaviour within the Church. P. came into contact with the Curia and was appointed cardinal and bishop of Ostia in 1057 by Pope Stephen IX. As a skilful diplomat, P. mediated between Bishop Vido and the reform movement led by Deacon Arialdus in Milan in 1059–60; 1061–4 P. fought the anti-pope Honorius II; 1063 P. stood up for the monastery of Cluny against Bishop Macon; 1066 P. investigated charges laid by the monks of Vallombrosa against their simoniacal bishop; 1069 went to Mainz to dissuade the Emperor Henry IV from divorcing his wife; 1072 reconciliation of Ravenna with Pope Alexander II. † 22/23rd Feb,

Peter Louis Maria Chanel
Martyr and saint
Feast-day: 28th April
Life: * 12th July, 1803 in Potière (Ain), joined the Marists in 1831, three years after being ordained; after little success in Tahiti and the island of Tonga, finished up as a missionary on the Islands of Futuna in Oceania, one of the Fiji group. There taken up by Chief Niuliki. P. soon developed enemies in the chief's council of elders. When the chief's son became a Christian, Niuliki got his principal minister Musumusu to murder P. and two other men on 28th April, 1841. A few years later, the whole population was baptised. Beatification 1889, canonisation 1954.

No representations in Christian art.

Peter Nolasco

Mercerdarian monk, saint

Feast-day: 25th Dec. (prior to calendar reform, 31st Jan.)

Life: * c. 1182 in Recaudum south of Toulouse, P. was of knightly lineage. Aged 15, took part in the crusade against the Albigensians and grew up at the court of Jaime I of Aragon. Jointly with Raymond of Pennafort, founded the Order of the Blessed Virgin Mary for Ransoming Prisoners. P. redeemed altogether c. 900 prisoners. † 25th Dec. 1249 (or 1256) in Barcelona. Canonisation 1628.

Legends: Visions encourage P. to found Order. – P. receives apparel of Order personally from Mother of God. – Jesus Christ indicates El Puig's picture of Virgin to P. – Jesus prophesies to P. the seizure of Valencia. – P. is cast adrift by pirates in a rudderless vessel and sails to port with his cloak. – His patron saint appears to P. in a vision on the cross. – He opens the gate of heaven personally for P. on Christmas Eve.

Patronage: prisoners.

Representation in Art: *Apparel:* in the white habit of the Mercedarian Order with the arms of Aragon (Mercedarian Convent, Lima, painting by F. Martínez, 1st half of 18C); *Attributes:* flag (S Andres, Segovia, 17C fig.); liberated prisoners at his feet (Castellon de la Plana, 17C painting by F. Zurbarán); chain (copper engraving illustrating Weigel, Columnae militantis ecclesiae, Nuremberg 1725); staff with double cross (Barcelona, Archivio Historico de la Cuidad, 18C painting); olive branch, halo of stars (Madrid, Facultad de Veterinaria, 17C painting by G. de Crayer). *Special scenes:* birth of P. (Cordoba Museum, 17C painting by C. Guzmán); P. taking the habit of his Order (Chapelle de la Sorbonne, 17C painting by S. Bourdon); the Virgin hands the raiment of the Order to P. (St Amas, Soult (Tarn), 17C painting by F. Zurbarán); P. and the discovery of the picture of the Virgin by El Puig (Valencia Museum, painting by J. J. Espinosa, 1660); P. adrift in rudderless boat (Prado, Madrid, 17C painting by F. Zurbarán). *Cycles:* Seville Museum, painted by F. Pacheco, 1611.

Peter of Verona

Also Peter the Martyr, Dominican friar, saint

Feast-day: 6th April (prior to calendar reform, 29th April). Translation feast-day on 4th June

Life: * c. 1205 in Verona, the son of parents belonging to the Albigensian sect, pupil of St Dominic 1221–2 in Bologna, 1232 papal legate in Milano, 1240 Prior of Asti, 1241 Prior of Piacenza, 1251 papal legate in Cremona and prior and inquisitor in Como and Milano; popular as a preacher, but hated by the Cathars. Stabbed to death by two hired murderers in Farga on 6th April, 1252. Buried in S Eustorgio in Milan. Canonisation in 1253.

Legends: Selection from Golden Legend: the child P. refutes the heresies of his Cathar uncle. – P. makes the sign of the Cross to move a cloud between the sun and his audience and impress heretics. – P. heals a lame man with the sign of the Cross. – P. heals a growth on the son of a nobleman by covering the spot with his skull cap. – Stomach pains that seize the nobleman some time later disappear when the latter puts P.'s skull cap on his chest and crushes a dragon with two heads. – P. heals a dumb child. – P. heals the broken leg (variant: fractured foot) of a young man. – The Mother of God appears to P. at a fair. – P. awakes a drunken youth. – P. catches a runaway horse. – Miracle after the death of P.: the lamps on P.'s tomb light up of their own accord. – P. saves a heckler from suffocation. – P. saves a ship in distress. – P. brings a stillborn child back to life to restore marital peace. – Women in Utrecht market mock P., at which the yarn they spin becomes bloody. – A heckler of the Domini-

cans in Utrecht is overcome by violent fever and cured by P.

Patronage: patron saint of Lombardy and the duchy of Modena, of Como and Cremona, the Inquisition, new mothers; against headaches, lightning (for Rome and Piacenza), storm and tempest, for good harvests; in Selztal, Mitterndorf and Werfenau, against vermin in the fields.

Veneration and cult sites: relics in S Eustorgio, Milan (Order of St Dominic) and the Dominican monastery at Friesach (pilgrimage with healing spring), Graz, Vienna, Lienz (Tyrol).

Superstitions: willow boughs and small wooden crosses are dedicated to P. against storms, magic in the field and vermin. – In Luxembourg, children suffering from consumption are called "Peter of Milan's children". To cure them, the childen are weighed up in corn obtained by begging. – In Eutsch near Wittenberg, as a result of a confusion, 29th April is children's begging day.

Representation in Art: *Apparel:* as a Dominican monk in a long, cinctured robe, scapular, cap and cowl and gaping wound on the skull (St Andreas, Cologne, early 16C fig.). *Attributes:* sword piercing the right shoulder, palm, index finger to mouth (S Marco, Florence, 15C fresco by Fra Angelico); banner of the Cross (Perugia, Capella del Gonfalone, painting by Bonfigli 1464); scroll (S Domenico del Maglio monastery, Florence, 14C fresco by follower of Nardo di Cione); hand crucifix (S Domenico, Cingoli, painting by L. Lotto 1539); holding scimitar (St Andreas, Cologne, early 16C fig.); stabbed in the heart by dagger (Bergen Museum, 16C fig. from Opdal); three scimitars in the head, laurel wreath with three crowns (monastic church, Maria Medingen, fig. c. 1750). *Martyrdom:* Kunsthistorisches Museum, Vienna, 16C painting by G. Vasari). *Cycles:* Capella Portinari, S Eustorgio, Milan, murals by G. di Balduccio 1339; S Eustorgio, Milan, frescoes by V. Foppa 1468; S Maria Novella, Florence, 15C frescoes by A. Bonaiuti da Firenze.

Philip

Apostle, martyr, saint

Feast-day: 3rd May, together with James the Less (moved from 1st May to 3rd May in 1956 after the introduction of the feast of Joseph the Worker), in Greek rite 14th Nov, Armenian rite 17th Nov. Translation day 28th Feb, in Einsiedeln 4th May.

Life: P. came from Bethsaida and belonged to the disciples of John the Baptist; P. also brought Nathaniel to Jesus (John 1, 43–46) and was a friend of Andrew. Mentioned in the New Testament at the feeding of the 5,000 (John 6, 5–7), where he remarks that '200 pennyworth would not be enough [bread] for them'; enables several Greeks to meet Jesus (John 12, 21–22), and when he asks Jesus to show him the Father, is put right by Jesus: 'he that has seen Me has seen the Father' (John 14, 8).

Legend: often confused with Philip the Deacon mentioned in Acts; according to the Golden Legend, P. preached in Scythia for twenty years. – When P. is shown an idol and told to make a sacrifice, a dragon appears from under the image that kills the son of the priest and two tribunes and makes the crowd ill with its poisonous breath. – P. banishes the dragon and heals the sick. – P. has two daughters by whom many are converted. – At the age of 87, P. suffers martyrdom on the Cross. (Variant: P. is stoned to death.)

Patronage: Brabant, Sorrento, Philippeville, Dieppe, Luxembourg (the often mentioned patron saint Philip of Speyer is in fact the Blessed P. of Zell), hatters, grocers, pastrycooks, tanners, fullers; guardian angel in battle.

Veneration and cult sites: body supposedly buried in Ephesus; relics in SS Duodici Apostoli, Rome, S Giovanni, Florence, Paris, An-

dechs Monastery, Cologne (ebony relics from 1620), Prague, Toulouse, Troyes; pilgrimages to Pichl (Styria), St Philippen (Carinthia), Pisweg (Carinthia).

Superstitions: The eve of the original festival of St Philip, known as Walburga's Night or Witches' Night, is called the St Philip's Eve in Upper Austria, and revellers can get up to unbridled mischief with impunity (see entry for Walburga). – In Hungary, the custom of the maypole is traced back to P. and Walburga, apparently because both travelled through the land of the Hungarians, were reviled as they did so and as a sign against the slanderers stuck a branch in the ground, which immediately began to turn green.

Representation in Art: *Apparel:* as an apostle in a long, cinctured robe, pallium or cappa (abbey of St Denis, relief, pre 1151). *Attributes:* book (Ravello, 12C relief); sword (relief on shrine to the Virgin, cathedral treasury, Aachen, 1220/38); vanquished queen of Hieropolis at his feet (south door of Chartres, fig. c. 1210); lance (Wallraf-Richartz Museum, painting by Veronica Master, c. 1415); rock (Einsiedeln-Dorf, fig. c. 1500); serpent (National Museum, Copenhagen, mid–15C fig.); crown of pearls (Albertina, Vienna, copper engraving by Israhel of Meckenem, 2nd half of 15C); crux gemina with double crossbars (Narodni Galeria, Prague, painting from Wittingau altar 1385/90); crux commissa – T-shaped cross (collegiate church, Tübingen, fig. c. 1480); crux immissa – with one crossbar (Bavarian National Museum, Munich, fig. by T. Riemenschneider c. 1500); crosier (Kunsthistorisches Museum, Vienna, painting by J. U. Mayr 1653). *Special scenes:* P. asking Jesus to show him the Father (Accademia, Venice, painting by P. Veronese, 1st half of 16C); P. banishing dragon (S Maria Novella, Florence, fresco by P. Lippi 1502). *Martyrdom:* P. is scourged and stoned on the Cross (Brussels Museum, portable altar from Stavelot, relief 1150/60); erection of P.'s cross (St Veit, Krems, choir stall carving by J. M. Götz 1735); crucifixion upside down (S Maria in Trastevere, Rome, tomb of Cardinal Philip of Alençon c. 1400); crucifixion (chapel, Versailles, bronze relief by F. Ladatte 1732); stoning of P. (Sedlec, Bohemia, painting by M. L. Willmann c. 1701). *Cycles:* Chartres Cathedral, 13C stained glass; S Domenico, Arezzo, 14C frescoes by Spinello Arentino; Alte Pinakothek, Munich and Kunsthistorisches Museum, Vienna, paintings by Master of the St Philip Legend 1518.

Philip Neri
Oratorian, saint
Feast-day: 26th May
Life: * 21st July, 1515 in Florence, the son of a notary and alchemist, strongly influenced by the Dominicans of the convent of S Marco; initially apprenticed in business, 1533. 1551 in Rome as tutor to children of Galeotto del Caccia of Florence; while living in his house, cared for the physical and spiritual wellbeing of the sick. Studied theology. 1548 with his father confessor Perisano Rosa founded the Confraternity of the Holy Trinity for the Care of Pilgrims to Rome. 1551 ordained priest; P. joined a community of priests at S Girolamo della Carità, from which P.'s Oratory developed. 1583 removal of community to S Maria in Vallicella. The aim was the moral renewal of Rome. Promoted church music (e.g. the musical form of the oratorio as a spiritual-cum-musical portrayal derives its name from P.'s Oratory). P. encouraged Cardinal Baronius to undertake his Annals and Antonio Boasio to carry out archaeological research on the catacombs. Characteristic was his sunny nature. † 26th May, 1595 in Rome. Beatification 1615, canonisation 1622. Legend: P. cures Pope Clement VIII of gout. – P. protects a man from a dagger thrust.
Patronage: Oratorians.

the sick (S Procolo, Bologna, 18C painting by G. Graziani). *Cycles:* S Maria in Vallicella, Rome, painted by C. Roncalli ('Pomaranzio') before 1621; Gerolamini church, frescoes by F. Solimena c. 1700; S Prospero e Filippo Neri, Pistoia, 18C painting by G. Gambarini.

Pirmin

Benedictine monk, abbot and bishop, saint
Feast-day: 3rd Nov
Life: * either in Gaul or Spain, worked as founder of monasteries in upper Rhine area, Reichenau 724, Murbach 727, Hornbach nr. Zweibrücken 742; reformed numerous monasteries, including Schuttern, Gengenbach, Schwarzach. Author of a handbook for missionaries ("Scarapsus"). † 3rd Nov, 753 in Hornbach.
Legends: with his staff, P. drives out all vermin from the island of Reichenau. – With his staff, P. causes numerous springs to break forth.
Patron: German Palatinate, Alsace, monastery of Reichenau, Innsbruck; against rheumatism, eye complaints, plague, snakes and vermin, food poisoning.
Veneration and cult sites: body buried in Hornbach (grave now buried under Prot. church, memorial), 1558 to Speyer, 1576 to Innsbruck. Pilgrimage since 1953 to the Cath. church at Horbach; numerous dedications in diocese of Speyer, e.g. at St Ingbert, Pirmasens.
Superstitions: a spring near Esch in Luxembourg was blessed by P.'s staff at which scrofulous children are healed. – Pregnant women in the Palatinate used to put on a P.-girdle for a successful delivery.
Representations in Art: *Apparel:* as a priest wearing a chasuble (St Ursus, Solothurn, Hornbach sacramentary, 10C illumination); as an abbot with staff and mitre (Victoria and Albert Museum, London, enamel panel on abbot's staff, 1351). *Attributes:* model of

Veneration and cult sites: Body in Oratorio S Maria in Vallicella, Rome; death mask there and in Convento dei Gerolamini, Naples.
Representation in Art: *Apparel:* in black cassock and biretta (Oratorio, Bologna, portrait by F. Zuccaro 1593); in nursing garb with white apron over black cassock (S Spirito in Saxia, Rome, late 18C painting). *Attributes:* lily, angel with book (S Maria in Vallicella, Rome, fig. by A. Algardi 1640); acolyte (Akademie, Vienna, 18C painting by G. Giaquinto). *Special scenes:* P.'s meeting with Carlo Borromeo (Gerolamini church, Naples, painting by L. Giordano 1704); P. at prayer having vision of Our Lady (Padua Cathedral, 18C painting by G. B. Tiepolo); P.'s vision of the Cross (S Maria in Vallicella, Rome, 17C painting by G. Reni); P. nursing

S. PIRMINIVS EPISCOPVS.

church (cathedral archives, St Gallen, Kopi-albuch des Pfafers, illumination 1590); frog, snake (Reichenau, Mittelzell, stained glass 1556). *Special scenes:* P. drives out vermin (Nuremberg woodcut illustration by A. Koberger 1488).

Pius V
Pope, saint

Feast-day: 30th April (prior to calendar reform, 5th May)

Life: * 17th Jan, 1504 at Bosco near Alessandria as Michele Ghislieri; 1518 entered Dominican order, 1528 ordained, Dominican rector in Pavia, later preacher, prior, provincial for Lombardy and inquisitor for Como and Bergamo. 1551 appointed commissary general of the Roman Inquisition by Pope Julius III on the recommendation of Cardinal Giampetro Caraffa; 1556 bishop of Sutri and Nepi near Rome, 1557 cardinal, 1558 inquisitor general, 1560 bishop of Mondovi. After the death of Pope Pius IV, Carlo Borromeo came out for P., so that on 7th Jan, 1566 P. was elected pope. P. saw as his main task putting the Tridentine Council into effect; rooted out nepotism and summoned reforming clerics to the college of cardinals. Among other reforms, P. imposed a residency requirement on bishops and strict celibacy, 1566 published the Roman Catechism, 1570 a new missal. During his rule, the sea battle against the Turks at Lepanto was won on 7th Oct, 1571. In consequence, P. introduced rosary festival. † 1st May, 1572. Buried in S Maria Maggiore, Rome. Beatification 1672, canonisation 1712.

Representation in Art: *Apparel:* as a Dominican monk in white habit with red papal mozetta (Stonyhurst College, Blackburn, painting by F. Zuccari, end 17C). *Attributes:* cross and loosely dangling legs, in allusion to a poisoning legend (Dominican convent, Vienna, early 18C painting); cross (monastic church, Maria Medingen, fig. by F. K. Schwertle 1765); cross, rosary, key, tiara (St Paul, Antwerp, 16C reliquary bust by Colyn de Nole). *Special scenes:* sea battle at Lepanto with bestowal of rosary on Dominic (Prien, Chiemsee, fresco by J. B. Zimmermann 1738); P.'s flour-multiplying miracle in nunnery (S Niccolo, Prato, 18C painting); P. hands over to Polish legate relics in the form of earth from the catacombs (S Domenico, Perugia, 17C painting by G. Laudati). *Cycles:* S Maria Maggiore, Rome, reliefs on P.'s tomb by Silla Longhi da Viggiu and Gillis van den Vliete 1586.

Pius X
Pope, saint

Feast-day: 21st August

Life: * 2nd June, 1835 in Riese near Castelfranco (Venetia). Grew up in poverty as the son of simple parents, 1858 ordained, chaplain in Tombolo, 1867 priest in Salzano nr Mestre, 1875 chancellor in Trevisio and spiritual director of seminary, 1884 Bishop of Mantua, 1883 Patriarch of Venice; elected pope on 4th Aug, 1903 in conclave following the Austrian Emperor's veto of Cardinal Mariano Rampolla del Tindaro. P. sought cooperation between Church and state, 1905 reduced tension in the Italian situation after the loss of the ecclesiastical state, mediated in territorial conflict between Bolivia, Peru and Brazil, concluded missionary concordat with the Congo in 1906. Violent resistance in Germany against the Anti-Modernist oath and the encyclical on the 300th anniversary of Carlo Borromeo's death because of the application of certain biblical quotations against the Protestants. Failures in policies towards France (revocation of 1802 concordat), Portugal and Spain (termination of diplomatic relations 1910). In terms of religion, rigorous and aggressive action against humanistic and natural ideological currents

for fear of betraying the supernatural. P. lo-
wered the age for first communion, which
made the Pope popular. † 20th August, 1914.
Beatification on 3rd June, 1951, canonisation
on 29th May, 1954.

Patronage: Esperantists, Pontifical Society
of the Holy Childhood (since 1955).

Representation in Art: as pope (Frauenkirche, Munich, mosaic by Sepp Frank 1960).

Polycarp of Smyrna

Bishop, martyr, saint

Feast-day: 23rd Feb (prior to calendar reform,
26th Jan, among Melchites 25th Jan).

Life: appointed by John the Apostle as Bishop of Smyrna: c. 155, P. negotiated with
Pope Anicetus in Rome about the date and
content of the Easter festival, but without
reaching agreement. A letter from P. to the
Philippians has survived (probably a compilation of two epistles) as well as a letter from
Ignatius of Antioch to Polycarp. The record
of P.'s martyrdom constitutes one of the oldest reliable accounts of a martyrdom to survive; written by Marcion shortly after P.'s
death in the form of an epistle from the community at Smyrna to the church of Philome-
lium in Phrygia: Whereupon the rabble demanded the sacrifice of P. on the occasion of
the festival. Before the crowded theatre in
Smyrna, the 86-year-old P. declared his belief in Christ, was condemned to the stake,
but was executed with a dagger on 23rd Feb,
155/156.

Legends: P. condemned to death on the
stake but remains untouched by the flames
of the pyre, as the fire curves round him like
a sail.

Veneration and cult sites: According to the
martyrdom account, the body of P. was buried on Mount Mustasia near Smyrna. – Pilgrimages there every year with remembrance of the death as a birthday celebration (oldest evidence of veneration of saints in the
history of the Church). Relics at S Ambrogio
della Massima in Rome.

Representation in Art: *Apparel:* as martyr (S
Apollinare Nuovo, Ravenna, 6C mosaic); as
bishop (Lyons Cathedral, 13C stained glass).
Special scenes: P. meets St Ignatius of An-
tioch of the road to Rome (S Clemente,
Rome, 18C painting by G. Triga). *Martyr-
dom:* Upper Austrian Provincial Museum,
Linz, painting from 1515.

Pontianus

Pope, saint

Feast-day: 13th Aug

Life: * the son of Calpurnius the Roman;
230–235 Roman pope. A schism developed
in 217 under Pope Callixtus I, because Hippolytus the Priest accused him of a dishonest
way of life; the schism continued into P.s'
time. 235 the Emperor Maximus Thrax
ended it in a rather drastic fashion by banishing both P. and his rival Hippolytus to the
mines of Sardinia. There, Hippolytus renounced his claims and returned to the unity of
the Church; P. died in exile.

Patronage: Patron saint of the town of Velletri.

Veneration and cult sites: Body transferred
by Pope Fabian to Rome, found in 1909 in
the Callixtus catacombs.

Representation in Art: *Apparel:* as pope (S
Paolo fuori le Mure, Rome, fresco from the
papal picture cycle). *Special scene:* translation of relics (Velletri Cathedral, 14C/15C
fresco).

Q

Quiricus of Tarsus

Martyr, saint

Feast-day: 16th June (Orthodox rites, 13th or 15th July).

Legends: the three-year-old son of St Julitta, and as little inclined as his mother to abjure the Christian faith, Q. is smashed by the Roman governor Alexander on the steps of his throne, while Julitta is crucified and beheaded. (Variants: nails are driven into Q's head./Q. is sawn up.). – The bodies of Q. and his mother are burnt.

Patronage: in Orthodox rites, jointly w. Julitta the patron saint of doctors.

Veneration and cult sites: relics in cathedrals of Nevers and Burgos. Cult in Florence, Toulouse and Spain.

Representations in Art: *Apparel:* in loincloth (St Nicolas du Chardonnet, Paris, painting by Louis Durameau 1767); in ancient child's toga on the arm of his mother Julitta (Museo de Arte de Cataluna, 12C antependium); as orant (S Maria Antiqua, Rome, mural, 1st half of 8C). *Attributes:* nails, saw (Diocesan Museum, Barcelona, 15C painting by P. Garcia); martyr's palm (Bavarian National Museum, Munich, panel of Tramine altar c. 1500); child's rattle (Jarze, Anjou, 15C fig.). *Martyrdom:* nails are driven into Q.'s head (Lisbon Museum, 16C painting by J. Affonso); Q. is sawn up (Musée Municipal, Nevers, tapestry from 1521). *Cycles:* only in connection with Julitta.

Quirinus of Neuss

Martyr, saint

Feast-day: 30th March (translation day 30th April)

Legends: according to the legendary, historically untenable 5C/6C Vita, as tribune under the Emperor Hadrian (117–138) Q. is supposed to guard captive Christians, including Pope Alexander I. – Q. is converted when he finds Hermes and Alexander, who had been kept separate, together in a cell. – An angel guides. A. to Hermes in prison. – Pope Alexander cures Balbina, Q.'s daughter. (Variant: A. has Balbina look for the chains of Peter, after whose kiss Balbina recovers completely.) – Q. and Balbina are baptised by Alexander. – Both suffer martyrdom by dismemberment. – A hawk which is thrown Q.'s cut-off tongue leaves it untouched.

Patronage: Patron saint of town of Neuss, knighthood, against pestilence, gout, rheumatism, headache, skin diseases, patron saint of horses and cattle.

Veneration and cult sites: relics in Rom, 1050 transferred to the Benedictine convent in Neuss as present from Pope Leo IX to Abbess Gepa; now in cathedral of Q. Pilgrimage to Neuss after the siege of the town by Charles the Bold 1475; Scandinavia before the Reformation.

Superstitions: The notion that St Grein (popular name for Q.) is particularly good at healing fistulas and pox; becomes a curse es-

pecially in Luxemburg if Grein's pox is invoked on someone. – A marksman in Cologne gets the pox when he curses the saint. – Anyone who drinks water from the St Q. fountain on the west side of the old abbey from the beaker-shaped skull of St Q. has his ailments alleviated. – In Nuremberg, the Q. potion helps cure headaches. – In Luxembourg, St Grein's water is blessed on the 4th Sunday after Easter and taken away in bottles against scrofula and other illnesses. – In Neuss on 30th April, consecrated water helps to close open wounds and protect horses from disaster. – Mounted and ambulant processions on the 30th April in the Aachen area and the Eifel region are linked with consecration of water, esp. in Zülpich. – Girls in Neuss who are still unmarried at 30 have to go and scrub St Q., i.e. scratch the back of the copper statue on the dome of the Cathedral.

Representations in Art: *Apparel:* as a Roman warrior (Hessisches Landesmuseum, Darmstadt, illumination in 15C Lochner prayer book); as a knight in armour, cloak and cap (Alte Pinakothek, Munich, 15C altar painting by Stephen Lochner); as a Roman officer (Stadtmuseum, Regensburg, votive image from Kraslice/Bohemia 1798). *Attributes:* escutcheon with nine balls as arms of Neuss, standards (parish church of St Goar, fresco c. 1475); spear and shield (art trade, 16C painting from Aachen); saw (Camblain [Nord], pilgrim's badge); invalid, angel bearing arms of Neuss, votive offerings (Staatliche Graphische Sammlung, Munich, 15C copper engraving by the monogrammist M); prospect of Neuss (Clemens-Sels Museum, Neuss, 17C painting). *Special scenes:* votive pictures with horses and cattles. *Martyrdom:* S Maria della Quercia nr Florence, 15C fresco. *Cycles:* former Dominican nunnery at Lambrecht, 15C fresco; St Kunibert, Cologne, 15C altar painting; Evang. parish church, Wimpfen a.B., early 16C St Q. altar.

Canonised rulers and rebels

58 *Reliquary of the sainted King Stephen, cathedral, treasure-room, Kalocsa, Hungary*

59 *Reliquary of St Ladislas, cathedral of Györ, Hungary*

60 *St Louis (king Louis IX of France), miniature, Paris, Musée du Petit Palais*

61 *Shrine of Charlemagne, Aachen cathedral, Germany*

62 *St Elizabeth of Thuringia, painting on glass, Marburg, Germany, church of St Elizabeth*

63 *Scenes from the life of St Hedwig, by the Langdorf Master of the Death of Mary, Warsaw, National Museum*

64 *St John Nepomuk hearing the confession of the Queen, by Filippo Evangelisti, Prague, National Museum*

65 *The murder of Thomas Becket, fresco in the church of S Giovanni e Paolo, Spoleto, Italy*

66 *St Joan of Arc, memorial, Paris*

59

ELIZABETH

Quirinus of Siscia

(Sisak, Croatia) Bishop, martyr, saint
Feast-day: 4th June
Life: martyred during the persecution of Christians by Diocletian.
Legends: the bishop of Siscia (Sisak) on the river Sava south-east of Zagreb, Q. is seized in flight during the persecution of Christians under the eastern emperor Galerius and brought to the governor of the province of Pannonia Inferior, Maximus (actually Maximinus). – Q. refuses to offer incense and is beaten up. – Three days later, he is handed over to Amantius, governor of Pannonia Superior. In Sabaria (Szombathely, west Hungary) following cross-examination and torture, a millstone is hung around his neck and he is drowned in the river Sibaris (Gyongyos) on 4th June, 308/9. – The body is recovered and buried in the basilica at Szombathely. Transferred to the Platonia at S Sebastiano on the Via Appia nr Rome end 4C/early 5C.

Patronage: Isola Abbey.
Veneration and cult sites: relics in S Maria in Trastevere, Rome since 1140, Milan Cathedral, Aquileia, Hungary.
Representations in Art: *Apparel:* as Roman martyr (St Cecilia's Crypt, Callixtus catacombs, Rome, 5C mural); as deacon (Germanisches Nationalmuseum, painting by H. L. Schäufelein 1506/7); as bishop with mitre and staff (Isola Abbey, painting by Sano di Pietro 1471). *Attributes:* book (St Q., Quer, fig. c. 1500); millstone on book (St Wolfgang, Lower Bavaria, fig. 1738); millstone at feet (Accademia Carrara, Bergamo, painting by Borgognone c. 1500). *Special scenes:* Q. swims on the millstone and blesses the faithful (Isola Abbey, painting by Sano di Petro 1471). *Martyrdom:* Österreichische Galerie, Vienna, 18C painting by F. A. Maulbertsch.

R

Raphael

Archangel, saint

Feast-day: 29th September

Biblical testimony: R. is mentioned in the book of Tobit, where he functions as a companion of the young Tobit and tells him to catch the dangerous fish and take the liver. With this R. exorcises the demon, Asmodaeus, which is plaguing the wife of Tobit and heals the older Tobit of blindness.

Patronage: apothecaries, emigrants, miners, roofers, the sick, pilgrims, travellers, sea-

men, Society of R. for the protection of Catholic emigrants (since 1871).

Representation in Art: *Apparel:* in tunic, divitision, chlamys, and loros (St Angelo in Formis, mural, 12th century); in the costume of a nobleman (Florence, St Spirito, painting, by F. Botticini, 15th century). *Attributes:* leading the little Tobit by the hand (Paris, National Library, copper engraving, by G. de Jode, 16th century); ointment jar in the hand (Turin, Gallery, painting, by A. del Pollaiuolo, 1465); Arma Christi (Cologne, Shrine of the Three Kings, figure, by N. of Verdun, circa 1200). *Special scenes:* the departure of Tobit and R. (Budapest, Szépmüvészeti Múzeum, painting, by D. Bleker, 17th century); Tobit and the fish (London, National Gallery, painting, by Domenichino, 17th century); wedding of Tobit and Sarah (Cologne, Wallraf-Richartz Museum, painting, by H. Terbrugghen, 17th century); the return of Tobit (Paris, Louvre, painting, by Hemessen, 18th century); R. leaves Tobit (Paris, Louvre, painting, by Rembrandt, 1637); R. knocks the crown from the head of the Synagogue (Parma, Cathedral, relief, by B. Antelami, 1178/79).

Raymond of Peñafort
Dominican, saint

Feast-day: 7th January (before calendar reform 23rd January)

Life: * circa 1176/80 in Villafranca del Panads near Barcelona; studied in Barcelona and Bologna, where he became Doctor Decretorum and Professor of Church Law and composed a collection of laws, rediscovered in 1877. 1220 returned to Spain and took over a canonicate; 1222 composition of the statutes for the Mercedarians founded by Peter Nolascos; entry to the Dominican Order, 1223–1229 teacher at the Order's college. 1230 called by Pope Gregory IX to be Chaplain and Penitencer of the Curia, where he had the task from the Pope of collecting and collating all Papal decrees; 1234 published. 1238 R. completed a Casuistic, in which he presented all the details necessary for the Confessors in an easily usable form. Great influence on the work of confession and penitence of the church. 1238–1240 first General of the Order, new codifyng of the statutes of the Order, worked as legal advisor and confessor to King Jaime I of Aragon, Together with Raymond Lull organisation of the mission to the Moors and Jews; founding of a school for the study of Oriental languages. R. encouraged Thomas Aquinas to compose the "Summa contra gentiles". † 8th January 1275 in Barcelona. Beatified 1553, canonised 1601.

Legend: R. sailed from Majorca over the Mediterranean on his spread out cappa using his staff as a sail. – R. raised a dead boy.

Patronage: Scholars of Church law (since 1847).

Veneration and cult sites: buried in Barcelona; after a miracle of dust at the gravestone 1297 translation.

Representation in Art: *Apparel:* as Dominican in dress of the Order (Barcelona, marble grave, figure, 14th century). *Attributes:* lily stem (Bern, Dominican Church, mural, 1495); keys (Palermo, Museo Pepoli, painting, by V. Carrera, 1602); hand crucifix (Friesach, Domincan Church, 18th century). *Special scenes:* R. before picture of the Mother of God (Maria Medingen, nun's choir, painting, circa 1720); miraculous voyage (Bologna, St Dominic's, painting, by L. Carracci, circa 1610); raising of the dead boy (Florence, St Maria Novella, painting, by J. Ligozzi, 16th century).

Remigius of Reims

Bishop, saint

Feast-day: 13th January

Life: * circa 436 near Laon from a leading Gallo-Roman family; at 22 Bishop of Reims, stood by Chlodwig I, King of the Franks, from his coronation and in a letter of good will on that occasion encouraged him to work together. Christmas 498/99 baptism of Chlodwig and beginning of the mission to the Franks. R. founded the Dioceses of Arras, Laon, Throuanne and Tournai-Cambrai; 514 synod. † 13th January 533 in Reims.

Legend: The birth of R. is prophesied by a blind hermit, who prays for the peace of the church in France; but R.'s mother, Clima, does not believe this, as she is too old. – On the day of R.'s birth, the hermit receives his sight again. – R. is so gentle, that as a young bishop the birds trust themselves to fly onto his table and take crumbs from his hand. – When R. is visiting a lady, the wine runs out; R. goes to the cellar and makes the sign of the cross over a barrel, so that it is filled again and flows over. – At Chlodwig's baptism, there is no Chrisam, which is brought by a dove from heaven in an ampoule. – R. heals the possessed in Toulouse. – R. heals a blind man. – R. punishes drunken farmers, who have burned the corn stores before a famine predicted by R., that in future all their male descendants will be cripples and the female get goitre.

Patronage: city and Diocese of Reims; against plague, epidemics, fevers, sore throats, snakes, religious complacency, despair, temptations.

Veneration and cult sites: buried in the Abbey church St Remi in Reims; translation of the reliquary in 565, 852, 1650, 1st October 1949. Under the reliquary the Holy Ampoule was found (destroyed 1793) with the anointing oil for the baptism of Chlodwig, according to the legend, which led to a joining of the veneration of R. to the primacy claim of the Bishops of Reims to anoint the king. Further relics include Remigiusberg in the north Palatinate.

Superstition: In the Allgäu pilgrims go to R. in Rohdorf near Isny for seriously ill children, and during the Mass lay two clothes of the sick child and a coin under the altar; the clothes and prayer note must stay nine days under the pillow of the child, until healing or death.

Representation in Art: *Apparel:* as bishop with bell, chasuble and pallium (Reims, St Remi, figure, 1180); as bishop in chasuble, dalmatic, alb, mitre (Sentenhart, parish church, figure, 16th century); bishop in pluvial, mitre (Weiler, parish church, figure 16th century). *Attributes:* ointment jar (Aachen, Suermont Museum, figure, 2nd half 12th century); dove with ointment jar, sitting on open book (Private collection, copper engraving, 1st half 16th century); staff, lamp (Sentenhart, parish church, figure, 16th century); kneeling girl (Weiler, parish church, figure, 16th century). *Special scenes:* miracle of anointing oil (Amiens, Museum of Picardy, ivory, 10th century); baptism of Chlodwig (Chartres, Cathedral, relief, 13th century); baptism of Chlodwig and his followers (Rome, St Luigi dei Francesi, fresco, by G. Siccolante, 16th century); healing of the blind (Rome, St Luigi dei Francesi, painting, 16th century); healing of the possessed (Reims, St Remi, lapidarium, relief, 14th century); R. blesses a wine barrel (New York, Metropolitan Museum, painting, 15th century); R. punishes the farmers (New York, Metropolitan Museum, painting, 15th century); birds eat from R.'s table (Munich, Bavarian State Library, clm 6, illumination, 1362). *Cycles:* Reims Cathedral, Callixtus Portal, relief, 1225/30; Chartres Cathedral, stained glass, 13th century.

Richard

(wrongly called "King of the English")
Pilgrim, confessor, saint

Feast-day: 7th February (translation celebrated in Eichstätt)

Life: The father of SS Willibald, Winnibald and Walburga of Heidenheim, Richard left his native Wessex with his sons on a "Pilgrimage for the Sake of Christ" to the Holy Land, but died in Lucca in the autumn of 720.

Legends: Richard was the king of the English. – R. is present at the consecration of St Willibald as bishop. – A sick man is cured at R's tomb.

Veneration and cult sites: His body is buried in the church of S Frediano near Pisa; translation circa 1150; relics in Eichstätt since 1154; local cult there.

Representation in Art: *Apparel:* as king in royal garments with crown (Eichstätt, St Walburga, figure, 1501); as pilgrim with sandals, trunk-hose, calf-length coat, overmantle, hat (Innsbruck, royal chapel, figure by L. Magt, 1517/18). *Attributes:* sceptre (Eichstätt Minster, figure, 1470/1480); sons and sick man (wood cut from the Saints of the Family, Friends and Relatives of Emperor Maximilian I, 1516); rosary, staff, crown at feet (Vienna, National Library of Austria ser.nov.4711, book illumination by J.Kölderer, 16th century).

Rita of Cascia

Augustine hermit, saint

Feast-day: 22nd May

Life: * circa 1380 in Roccaporna near Cascia, east of Spoleto. Was married against her wishes to a brutal man. After his murder and the death of the two sons, entry to the Augustinian Hermit Monastery in Cascia after several rejections. R. distinguished herself by her deep mystical veneration of the Crucified. 15 years before her death received the stigmata of the crown of thorns. † 22nd May 1457 in Cascia. Beatification 1627, canonisation 1900.

Legend: After the death of her husband, R. asks God to take her sons to himself to prevent blood revenge, – On her death bed in January R. prays to see once more before her death a rose from her parent's garden, which was found blooming in the middle of winter.

Patronage: Sisters of R.; charitable works named after her; helper in dire need.

Veneration and cult sites: buried in Cascia, 1703 body discovered undecayed; on F. day consecration of R. roses.

Superstition: R. oil is used as a popular medicament, especially by Augustinians, e.g. in Würzburg.

Representation in Art: *Apparel:* as nun in dark cloak with white veil (La Granja, parish church, figure, by L. S. Carmona, 17th century). *Attributes:* forehead wounds, crucifix (La Granja, parish church, figure, by L. S. Carmona, 17th century); palm branch with three crowns in the hand (Lisbon, Museum, painting, 18th century); thorn (examples at Kaftal, Iconography of the Saints in Central and South Italian Schools of Painting, Florence, 1985, fig. 1138 and 1139); rose, bees (Cascia, Painting, by F. Ferrazzi, 20th century); two children (Barcelona, Historical Archives of the Ciudad, woodcut, 17th century). *Special scenes:* wounding of R. by the thorn of Christ (Bologna, copper engraving from C. Rabbi da Bologna, Vita della R., 1774). *Cycles:* Cascia, Augustinian Hermit Monastery, painting, by F. Ferrazzi, 20th century.

Robert Bellarmin

Jesuit, Cardinal, Archbishop of Capua, Doctor of the Church, saint

Feast-day: 17th September (before the calendar reform 13th May)

Life: * 4th October 1542 in Montepulciano, nephew of Pope Marcellus II; educated at the Jesuit College in his home town; 1560 entered the Society of Jesus, studied in Rome, Padua, Louvain; 1570 consecrated priest; until 1576 Preacher and Professor of Theology at Louvain. Author of the "Index Haereticorum" and a theology of the Sacraments, amongst other works. 1576 called by Pope Gregory XIII to Rome, where he worked as Controversy Theologian; at this time he wrote his main work, the "Disputationes de controversiis christianae fidei adversus huius temporis haereticos" (= Discussion on Controversial Issues of the Christian Faith against the Heretics of This Time); supervised Aloysius of Gonzaga, whose Beatification he advocated. 1592 Rector of the Roman College, 1594/97 Provincial of Naples. Called by pope Clement VII 1597 as Consultor of the Holy Office to be Rector of Penitencers at St Peters; 1597 publication of the Smaller Catechism for the people. 1599 Cardinal; called to be Archbishop of Capua because of differences in the conflict about the Doctrine of Grace. There engaged in social action; R. committed himself on the question of parcelling land and brought in measures to make work for the poor. From 1605 in Rome again as a member of the Holy Office, Protector of the Celestins and the Collegium Germanicum. 1607 Administrator for the Diocese of Montepulciano. Involved in the conflict between Pope Paul V and the Republic of Venice and in the controversy around King James I of England about the introduction of his anti-Roman oath of allegiance. 1610 R. wrote a work about the plenary power of the Pope in temporal matters, was commissioned to inform Galileo of the judgement of the Copernican World System by the Index Commission. 1615–1620 Chairman of Text Revision of the Greek New Testament. – Personally, R. led an ascetic life; friendly relations with Francis de Sales and Philip Neri. † 17th September 1621. Beatified 1923, canonised 1930, Doctor of the Church 1931.

Veneration and cult sites: Rome, Il Gesù; 1923 carried to St Ignatius'.

Representation in Art: *Apparel:* as Cardinal with mozetta and birett (Madrid, Jesuit College, painting, by B. Passarotti).

Rochus of Montpellier
Confessor, saint

Feast-day: 16th August

Legend: * 1295 in Montpellier, at an early age R. loses his parents. – R. gives his possessions to the poor. – 1317 R. goes an a pilgrimage to Rome. – On the way R. cares for plague victims and heals them through the sign of the cross. – On the return journey R. himself catches the plague, is strengthened by an angel in a hut in the forest of Piacenza and is brought bread by the dog of Gothard, an easy-going citizen. – The angel heals R. – R. is incarcerated as a spy in Montpellier, because he is silent about his distinguished origins out of humility. – After 5 years in prison R. dies on 16th August 1327. – Christ reveals in a mysterious writing on the wall, that R. is a helper in afflictions of plague.

Patronage: Montpellier, Parma, Venice; apothecaries, doctors, farmers, brush-binders, surgeons, gardeners, prisoners, art-dealers, plasterers, joiners, gravediggers; hospitals for incurables, hospitals; against plague, cattle plagues.

Veneration and cult sites: 1485 translation of the supposed bones from Montpellier to Venice; relics in Antwerp, Arles, Lisbon, Venice. Occasionally numbered among the helpers in need; very popular saint; numerous pilgrimage chapels, including on the Rochusberg near Bingen.

Superstition: Pilgrims to St R. must offer coins, straws or straw brooms according to the number of sores on the body, a gift

based on sympathetic or homeopathic foundation.

Representation in Art: *Apparel:* as young pilgrim in pilgrims' garb, shoes, boots, cloak with collar on shoulder (Zülpich, figure, circa 1500). *Attributes:* wound on leg with pointing gesture (Deruta, St Francis', mural, by F. di Lorenzo, 1478); sword, ointment jar (Gubbio, Pinacoteca Comunale, painting, by O. Merlini, 16th century); pilgrim's bag (Obersimonswald, figure, end 15th century); pilgrim's bottle (Kiedrich, St Valentine's, end 15th century); pilgrim's staff (Cologne, Wallraf-Richartz Museum, painting, by Master of the Holy Family, 1493/94); angel (Cologne, Wallraf-Richartz Museum, painting, by Master of the Holy Family, 1500/1510); angel with ointment jar and spatula (Mainz, Gutenberg Museum, incunabulum, woodcut, 1459); angel and dog with bread in mouth (Munich, Alte Pinakothek, painting, by Q. Massys, end 15th century); dog (Utrecht, Archbishop's Museum, figure, beg. 16th century). *Special scenes:* Christ appears to R. (Arezzo, Civic Museum, gonfalon [oblong flag], painting, by B. della Gatta, 15th century); dog brings bread to R. (Florence, St Felicity's, painting, 16th century); incarceration and death of R. (Modena, Estense Gallery, painting, by G. Reni, 17th century); R. as patron of those with plague (Alost, St Martin's, painting, by P.P. Rubens, circa 1600). *Cycles:* Antwerp St Jacob's Church, altar, 1517; Bruges City Museum painting, 16th century; Venice, St Rocco, painting, by J. Tintoretto, 16th century.

Romuald of Camaldoni
Founder of Order, Camaldolite, saint
Feast-day: 19th June
Life: * circa 952 in Ravenna; offspring of a noble family, probably Onestri. After a worldly youth, entered the Benedictine Order in St Apollinare in Classe. 975 R. left the monastery, lived as a hermit and joined the hermit Marinus. 978 R. fled with the fallen Doge Pietro Orseolo into the Pyrenees and in the monastery of Cux, near Prades gathered a group of hermits around him; 987/88 return to Italy. Emperor Otto III gave him the title of Abbot of St Apollinare in Classe, which he laid down again a year later. Circa 1012 reform of Camaldoli near Arezzo, which became the original home of the Camaldolites, a branch of the Benedictine Order. † 19th June 1027 at the monastery Val di Castro. 1032 canonised.

Patronage: Camaldolites.

Veneration and cult sites: 1466 bones raised in Val di Castro, 1481 taken to Fabriano.

Representation in Art: *Apparel:* as long bearded old man in white habit of the Camaldolites (Treviso, St Nicholas', fresco, by T. da Modena, 14th century); in dress of the Benedictines with black habit (Venice, Correr Museum, painting, by A. Zanchi, 18th century); as Abbot in pontifical dress (Borselli, St Margaret di Tosina, painting, M. di Nardo, 15th century). *Attributes:* walking stick (Camaldolites Treviso, St Nicholas', fresco, by T. da Modena, 14th century); T. staff (Florence, Academy, painting, circa 1365); open book, model of hermitage (Fabriano, St Mary del Popolo, fresco 1473); death's head (Venice, Academy, painting, by J. C. Loth, 17th century). *Special scenes:* Benedict presents the Rule of the Order to R. (Florence, Galleria degli Uffizi, painting, 14th century); R.'s vision of the ladder to heaven (Jérez de la Frontera, church, painting, by B. E. Murillo, 17th century); R. interprets for his brothers the vision of the ladder to heaven (Vatican City, Vatican Museum, painting, by A. Sacchi, 17th century); angel points R. to the ladder to heaven (Venice, Correr Museum, A. Zanchi, 18th century); Mary holds the ladder to heaven (Rio de Janeiro, St Bento's, painting, by R. de Pilar, 1684); Guarinus of Cux and Peter Ursoleus

before Abbot R. (Venice, Correr Museum, painting, by G. da Asola, 16th century); angel wards off demons (Ravenna, Gallery of the Academy, painting, by Guercino, 17th century); R. denies entry to the church to Otto III because on his unexpiated murder of Senator Crescentius (Antwerp, Royal Museum of Fine Arts, painting, school of Fra Angelico, 15th century). *Cycles:* include Florence St Mary degli Angeli, frescoes, by D. Mascagni, circa 1600; Fabriano SS Biagio and R., frescoes, by P. Rossi, 1674 and L. Malatesta circa 1500; Bielany, frescoes, by Dolabella, 1643.

Rosa of Lima

Dominican (Third Order), saint

Feast-day: 23rd August (before the calendar reform 30th August)

Life: * 20th April 1586 in Lima as daughter of Gasparo de Florez and Maria de Oliva. R. is supposed a great to have shown a extraordinary zeal for prayer, even as a child. Was plagued by numerous illnesses and experienced a miserable feeling of neglect. R.'s sufferings were accompanied by mystic visions. R. lived in her parents' house; the last three years of her life she spent in the house of the royal official Gundisalvi. † 24th April 1617. Beatified 1688, canonised 1671.

Legend: At the Beatification of R. a shower of roses fell.

Patronage: America, Peru, Philippines, West Indies, Lima, florists, gardeners.

Representation in Art: *Apparel:* as young Dominican of the Third Order, with black veil of the 2nd Order (Madrid, Prado, painting, by C. Coello, 17th century). *Attributes:* garland of roses, rosary chain (Lima, St Rosa, painting, by A. Medoro, 1617); garland (Florence, Palazzo Pitti, painting, by C. Dolci, 1668); rose, crown of thorns (Lima, St Domingo. figure, by M. Cafa, 17th century);

Christchild sitting on bouquet of roses (Lima, St Catherine's, painting, 17th century); child on arm (Antwerp, St Paul's, figure, by A. Quellin the Younger, 17th century); anchor (Sittard, R. Chapel, painting, 17th century). *Special scenes:* R. is garlanded with roses by the Boy Jesus (Madrid, Prado, painting, by C. Coello, 17th century); R. with white and native Peruvians (Rome, St Maria sopra Minerva, painting, by L. Baldi, 18th century); R. is confirmed by Turibius of Mongrovejo (Mayorga, parish church, figure, 17th century).

Rupert of Salzburg

Bishop, saint

Feast-day: 24th September (before the calendar reform 24th March); together with Modestus 24th November (before the calendar reform 27th September).

Life: R. came from the family of the Robertin of Worms, there consecrated bishop. In connection with the missionary attempts of the Carolingian major domo, 696 to Bavaria, founded the Benedictine monastery of St Peter in Salzburg and the ladies' nunnery on the Nonnberg; there the first Abbess was R.'s niece Erentrud. Preaching tour in Austria; founded churches in Seekirchen on the Wallersee, Pongau, Bischofshofen, Maxglan. As bishop R. was the monastery bishop in the Irish way with no strictly defined diocese. † 27th March 718.

Legend: R. converts Duke Theodore. – R. does missionary work in Enns, Regensburg and Lorch. – R. endows the miraculous image of Altötting. – R. translocates the relics of St Amandus. – R. consecrates St Vitalis as bishop. – R. dies during the Mass at the altar.

Patronage: City of Salzburg, State of Salzburg, Carinthia salt-mines; against rabid dogs, red rain.

Veneration and cult sites: body 774 in the Cathedral of Salzburg built by Bishop Virgil.

S . RVPERTVS .

15

Representation in Art: *Apparel:* as bishop in pontifical Mass dress with chasuble and pallium (Salzburg, St Peter's Convent Library, antiphonary of St Peter, illumination, 12th century); as bishop in pluvial with mitre (Vienna, Kunsthistorisches Museum, figure, 1518); in protective cloak of miners (Dürnberg, figure, circa 1740). *Attributes:* crosier (Munich, Bavarian State Library, clm 15812, illumination, 12th century); salt bucket in hand (Vienna, Kunsthistorisches Museum, figure, 1518); salt bucket on book (Kirchloibersdorf, figure, circa 1500); salt bucket at feet (Salzburg, Nonnberg Convent, figure, end 15th century); miner at feet (Dürnberg, figure, circa 1740); miraculous picture of Altötting in hand (Ettal, figure, by J. B. Straub, 1757/82). *Cycles:* Salzburg St Peter's, mural, by T. Sing, 1660 and F. König, 1757.

S

Scholastica

Benedictine nun, abbess, saint
Feast-day: 10th Feb
Life: * c. 480 in Nursia, sister of St Benedict; even as a child, she was a devout virgin and lived in the nunnery of Roccabotte near Subiaco, then in Piumarola, and finally near Montecassino. S. used to meet her brother Benedict once a year for a spiritual conversation. † c. 547 in Nursia.
Legends: according to the Life and Miracles of St Benedict by Pope Gregory the Gr., on the occasion of S.'s last meeting with her brother, the prayers and tears of S. bring on such a rainstorm that Benedict is forced to stay with her much longer. – At the death of S., Benedict sees her soul entering heaven in the shape of a dove.
Patronage: Benedictine nuns, patron saint of Le Mans, Vich (Catalonia), Subiaco; against lightning and for rain.
Veneration and cult sites: the bones of S. and Benedict supposedly transferred to Fleury in 2nd half of 7C, subsequently to St-Benôit-sur-Loire and Le Mans; 874 parts of the body given as relics to Juvigny-sur-Loison. After discovery of the grave of St Benedict under the high altar of Montecassino in 1960, this translation of relics can be considered of little historical worth. Monastery of S Scolastica in Subiaco.

Representations in Art: *Apparel:* in black habit of Benedictine nuns (Sacro Speco, Subiaco, late 13C fresco by Conxolus); in long robe, cloak open in front, wimple and veil (Stift Nonnberg, Salzburg, 16C fig.); in broad-sleeved fleece gown (Mallersdorf Abbey, fig. by I. Günther 1768/80). *Attributes:* hand crucifix (Capella Palatina, Palermo, 12C mosaic); palm (Brera, Milan, 15C painting by A. Mantegna); book, abbess's staff (Morgan Library, New York, Catherine of Cleves's Book of Hours, illumination 1st half of 15C); dove (high altar, Blaubeuren, fig. by G. Erhard 1493/4); dove at breast (monastic church of Amorbach, fig. c. 1749). *Special scenes:* death of S. (S Giustina, Padua, 17C painting by L. Giordano). *Cycles:* Sacro Speco, Subiaco, 14C/15C frescoes; Stift Raigern, painting by J. Führich, post mid–19C; for further scenes, see under Benedict.

Sebald

Pilgrim, hermit, saint
Feast-day: 19th Aug
Life: no historically delineable personality. Canonisation on 26th March, 1425.
Legends: acc. to late 14C/early 15C tradition (typical motifs from the life of a pilgrim saint): S. is born the son of the king of Denmark (variants: S. comes from Franconia,

S. SEBALDVS PEREGRINVS.

France or upper Tisza region of Hungary). – S. is sent to Paris to be educated and later marries a French princess. – S. abandons his bride on their wedding night to live as a hermit. – After 15 years as a hermit, S. sets off on a pilgimage to Rome, where he meets the Irish missionaries Willibald and Wunibald and joins their mission. – When the three are starving, S. turns stones into bread (variant: angels bring the three missionaries bread from heaven). – In Vicenza, a man vituperates against S. during the sermon, whereupon the earth swallows him up. – At the solicitation of S., the earth releases the man, who is converted. – S. crosses the Danube on his outspread cloak. – In an inn where the host is mean with the wood, the sick S. freezes and turns icicles to firewood. – Against the order of the pagans, S. gets a fish to eat from a man, who goes blind in consequence but is immediately cured by S. – S. lives in a hermitage near Nuremberg and tells a man looking for his lost cattle to go on looking despite the darkness, when suddenly the raised hands of the man emit light and the cattle are found in the undergrowth. – S. provides help against bandits. – S. helps a ship in distress. – S. asks a woman to put his body on an ox cart after he dies and to bury him where the beasts stop. The oxen stop in Nuremberg on the spot where St Sebald's church is later built. – Numerous miracles take place at the tomb of S.

Patronage: patron saint of Nuremberg, Holy Helper in many matters.

Veneration and cult sites: tomb and relics in St Sebald, Nuremberg, pilgrimages thither with tradition of cures (creeping under the coffin; the principal relics are brought before women in travail), St S.'s Chapel, Schwäbisch-Gmünd 1505, pilgrimage centre in Egling/Upper Bavaria since 1512, St S.'s Grotto at Heiligenstein near Steyr 1413.

Representations in Art: *Apparel:* as a pilgrim in pilgrim's cloak and hat with turned-up brim and shell (Schwäbisch-Gmünd, stained glass 1506). *Attributes:* pilgrim's staff, model church (tomb of St Sebald, St Sebald's church, Nuremberg, fig. by P. Vischer 1519); ash cakes (saints of the extended family, relatives and cousins of Emperor Maximilian I, woodcut by L. Beck 1518). *Cycles:* Germanisches Nationalmuseum, Nuremberg, tapestry, 1st qtr of 15C; St S. altar in Germanisches Nationalmuseum, Nuremberg and Heiligkreuz, Schwäbisch-Gmünd, painting from 1508; tomb of St Sebald, St Sebald's church, Nuremberg, fig. by P. Vischer 1519.

Sebastian

Martyr, saint

Feast-day: 20th Jan

Life: acc. to Ambrose of Milan, born in Rome and martyred there, presumably in 2nd half of 3rd cent.

Legends: acc. to the 5C Passio, S. was born in Narbonne and grew up in Milan. – His noble bearing induces the Emperor Diocletian and his co-emperor Maximian to appoint him officer of the bodyguard. – S. is a Christian and uses his office to help persecuted Christians. – At the request of the mother, S. visits the twin brothers (variant: at the request of their mothers, the two young Christians) Marcellianus and Marcus who are prisoners in the house of Nicostratus and are due to be beheaded. – An angel holds the book for a reading of the scriptures. – S. converts Zoe, wife of the householder, and cures her of a serious illness. – Sebastian heals the senior knight in Rome, Cromatius, after the latter has allowed all his idols to be smashed. – Accused before Diocletian, S. is ordered to be tied to a tree and run through by Numidian bowmen. – After being left for dead, the widow of the martyr Castulus nurses him back to health. – Cured, S. goes to the Emperor and lectures him on the senselessness of his persecutions. – S. is clubbed to death and his body thrown in the Cloaca Maxima. – S. appears to the Christian Lucina in a dream and shows her the spot. – The body is interred in S Sebastiano ad catacumbas.

Patronage: one of the 14 Holy Helpers, plague saints after a plague epidemic in Rome in 680, patron saint of cattle, archers, marksmen societies, soldiers, hunters, gunsmiths, firemen, tinsmiths, stonemasons, gardeners, upholsterers, ironmongers, tanners, crusaders, invalids of war, potters, clothworkers, frail and sickly children, the dying, against the enemies of religion.

Veneration and cult sites: original tomb in Rome a small loculus at the entrance to the catacombs in the Via Appia; 4C basilica of the Apostles erected thereon, now S Sebastiano; early 5C during Innocent's time, enlarged to a confession; during reign of Pope Sixtus II (432–440), veneration extended to whole Church. Pope Gregory IV (827–844) transferred the head to the church of S Quattro Coronati, the bones to St Peter's; 1250 arm relic to the Franciscan friary in Hagenau (Alsace); further (non-genuine) relics in St Medard, Soissons since 826, part of cranium in monastery of Ebersberg nr Munich, in Florence, Moret, Basle, Muri, Berne, Schwyz, Zwiefalten, Speyer, Koblenz. Numerous pilgrimage centres and plague columns, societies of Sebastian.

Superstitions: metal S.-arrows provide protection from plague (sold 1630 by Jesuits in Munich). – Wine in which S.-arrows are dipped has the same protective effect. – Cattle must fast on St S.'s Day to remain immune to illness. – On St S.'s Day, trees are sacred and may not be cut. – On St S.'s Day the sap in tree trunks begins to rise.

Representations in Art: *Apparel:* as a youth in a white tunic (Callixtus catacombs, wall-painting c. 495); as a bearded man (Capella Palatina, Palermo, 12C mosaic); as an old warrior in Byzantine dress (S Giorgio in Velabro, Rome, 13C wall-painting); as warrior

in armour (St Maria im Kapitol, Cologne, mural, 2nd half of 15C); in elegant bourgeois costume (Barfüsserkirche, Erfurt, painting 1445); with arrows in clothed body (Pinacoteca, Camerino, painting by G. di Giovannni 1463); as a nude tied to a tree and arrows in body (Hopital, Beaune, painting by R. v.d. Weyden c. 1430); as a freestanding nude without arrows (Chiesa dell'Ospidale, painting by P. della Francesca c. 1450); as freestanding nude with cloak (cathedral treasury, Regensburg, silver fig. 1505); as nude tied to tree but without arrows (Empoli, fig. by A. Rosellino, 2nd half of 15C); as kneeling nude bound to tree with arrows in his body (Palencia Cathedral, painting by El Greco c. 1580); as nude sinking to ground under impact of arrows (Neue Pinakothek, Munich, painting by A. Weisgerber 1912/13); in protective cloak as plague saint (S Agostino, San Gimignano, mural by B. Gozzoli c. 1465). *Attributes:* hand crucifix (S Sepolcro, Barletta, 13C mural); sword, shield, spear (Freiburg Minster, late 13C fig.); crown (S Pietro in Vincoli, Rome, mosaic c. 680); two arrows in hands (Pinacoteca, Sanginesio, painting by S. Folchetti 1492); tree trunk in his hand (Rethwisch/Mecklenburg, mid–16C fig.); bow and arrow (Barcelona Cathedral, late 15C painting by P. Alemany); palm (Museum Mayer-van-den-Bergh, Antwerp, painting by A. di Puccinelli, 1st half of 14C); sword (Louvre, Paris, early 15C painting); shield with plague arrows (Schliersee, flag embroidery 1731). *Special scenes:* S. helps Marcellianus and Marcus (S Sebastiano, Venice, painting by P. Veronese 1558). *Martyrdom:* S. is pierced by arrows from bowmen (Wallraf-Richartz Museum, Cologne, painting by Master of Holy Family c. 1500); angels untie S. from tree (Louvre, Paris, painting by A. van Dyck, 1st half of 17C); Irene nurses S. (Tours Museum, 17C painting by Le Sueur). *Cycles:* numerous, e.g. Florence Cathedral, painting by G. del Biondo, 2nd half of 14C;

Museo Civico, Padua, 15C murals; St S.'s Chapel, Venanson, wallpainting c. 1481; St Florian, paintings by A. Altdorfer 1518; parish church of Amorbach, painting by J. Zick 1753.

Servatius of Tongeren

Bishop, saint

Feast-day: 13th May

Life: identical with Sarbatios, one of the chief opponents of the Arians at the Synod of Sardica (Serdica) in 342; already bishop at Tongeren (Belgium) by 345, embassy of the anti-emperor Magnentius to Constantius II in Edessa. 359–360 participant at the Synod of Rimini, where S., like the other bishops, agreed under pressure from imperial officials to vaguely formulated phrases such as "the similarity of the Son to the Father". 366 and 384, journeys to Rome. † 384 in Maastricht.

Legends: S. is a grandchild of Esmeria, the sister of St Anne, and thus a member of the Holy Family. – S. receives a key from St Peter on which filings of St Peter's chains are found (variant: the key falls from heaven out of the clouds). – With the key, S. can gain access to eternal life for anyone who asks. – An angel brings S. the pontificalia from heaven. – In Speyer, S. strikes a spring from the ground. – S. kills a dragon. – S. falls into the captivity of Attila the Hun, where an eagle protects S. in his sleep. – Seeing this miracle, Attila is converted. – S. predicts the Vandal incursion of 406. – S. suffers martyrdom by having clogs thrown at him. – Angels cover S.'s body. - Thieves that break into vineyards belonging to the sepulchral church are turned to stone and can only move again after appealing to S.

Patronage: Maastricht, Quedlinburg, Goslar, Limburg/Lahn, Tongeren, diocesan patron of Worms, patron saint of joiners, metalworkers, against foot complaints, frost damage (as frost saint), fever, swine erysipelas, lameness, plagues by mice and rats.

Veneration and cult sites: S.'s tomb in Maastricht; object of pilgrimages by Charles Martel, Charlemagne, Emperors Henry II and III, Maximilian of Austria, the Emperor Charles V, St Norbert of Xanten and Bernard of Clairvaux. Great expansion of cult in western Europe after Vandal attack of 406, particularly the Moselle and Rhine areas.

Superstitions: S. is one of the frost saints. If it rains on St S.'s Day, the corn will grow up to the stalk. – S's grave is green even in winter and is never covered by snow. – St S.'s water is a cure for fever, especially if it is drunk in the week after the festival. – S. brought a spring bubbling from the ground in Speyer after making the sign of the Cross on the ground. – Cattle born on St S.'s Day in Westphalia suffer accidents.

Representations in Art: *Apparel:* as bishop in pontifical robes (Gurk Cathedral, mural c. 1220); in pluvial and mitre (St Veit, Eifel, fig. c. 1500); in a habit (castle church, Quedlinburg, reliquary c. 1200). *Attributes:* key (St Servais, Liege, 14C fig.); banner on crosier (Morgan Library, New York, Catherine of Cleves's Book of Hours, illumination from 1st half of 15C); dragon (Carmelite church, Boppard, 15C stained glass); male figure at his feet (Schwimbach, Mid-Franconia, painting from 1511); clogs (Germanisches Nationalmuseum, Nuremberg, painting by S. Striegel 1528). *Special scenes:* S. in the scriptorium (Germanisches Nationalmuseum, Nuremberg, painting by B. Striegel 1528); St Peter handing over the silver key to S. (Salvatorkirche, Duisburg, early 15C mural). *Cycle:* Portico of St S's church, Maastricht, 12C relief.

Seven Servite Founders

(Sette SS Fondatori) saints

Feast-day: 17th Feb

Life: Buonfiglio dei Monaldi, Giovanni di Buonagiunta, Benedetto dell'Antella, Bartolomeo degli Amidei, Ricoverino dei Lippi-Ugoccioni, Gheradino di Sostegno and Alessio de' Falconieri joined a confraternity of the Blessed Virgin, and in 1233 founded a hermitage at Monte Senario near Siena. They called themselves the Order of the Servants of Mary (Servites); 1240 accepted Augustinian rule and the black habit. Using the Dominican rule as a basis, the first Prior General Buonfiglio drew up the Constitutions, confirmed in 1249 by Pope Innocent IV. In 1276, Pope Innocent V dissolved the order, but Nicholas IV had it re-established in 1290; 1304 the foundation solemnly confirmed by Pope Benedict XI. Since 1424, the Servites considered a mendicant order. Canonisation in 1888.

Veneration and cult sites: relics at Monte Senario since 14C.

Representations in Art: *Apparel:* black habit of order (S. M. Annuziata, Florence, painting by T. Gaddi 1332). *Attributes:* scourge, skull, monogram of Mary, rule book (S. M. dei Servi, Bologna, painting by G. M. Crespi c. 1700); lilies, rosary (S. M. Annunziata, Florence, 18C painting by A. Allori). *Special scenes:* the founders under the protective cloak of Our Lady (S. M. Annunziata, Florence, fresco fr. 2nd half of 15C); Mary handing over scapular (S. M. Annunziata, Florence, painting by N. Nannetti, 1st half of 18C). *Cycles:* cloister at Pistoia, painting from 1602; cloister of S. M. Annunziata, Florence, painting by Occetti 1604; Monte Senario, 18C painting by A. Pillari.

Seven Sleepers of Ephesus

Martyrs, saints

Feast-day: 27th July, 27th June (Germany and France), 2nd Aug, 22nd/23rd Oct. (Byzantine rites), 22nd Oct. (eastern Christians).

Legends: acc. to 5C Syrian legend, the SS were young Christians (variants: shepherds, eight youths) who hid in a cave on Mount Ochlon near Ephesus to avoid making sacrifices to pagan idols. – When Decius ferreted out their hiding place, he had the entrance to the cave sealed off, leaving the SS to starve. – The SS simply fell asleep and awoke in 437 (variant: 443) and so were able to bear witness to the resurrection of the dead. – Only then did they finally fall asleep for ever.

Patronage: Sailors, against fever, sleeplessness.

Veneration and cult sites: Ephesus, as attested by church constructed there betw. 408 and 450 by the emperor Theodosius II; pilgrimage to Panajir Dagh and Arbisos (Cappadocia) and Brittany with Christian-Islamic pilgrimages. Relics in St Victor, Marseilles, Guadix (Spain), Stegaurach. Veneration in Arras, Esslingen, Faras (Egypt), Höllerich, Kiev, Marmoutier, Marseilles, Mohn, Mont nr Malmedy, Noirmoutier, Obersimonswald (Baden), Pontpierre, Prüm (Eifel), Paphos (Cyprus), Rome, Rotthof (Lower Bavaria), Stephansfeld, Stiffel (Côtes-du-Nord), Salerno.

Superstitions: The SS's Day is a day for a change in the weather. – In Austria, vervain is picked on SS's Day against headache and hypersomnia.

Representations in Art: *Apparel:* as youths asleep (chapter house, Brauweiler, wallpainting from 3rd quarter of 12C); as soldiers in stalactite cave (Rotthof, stucco fig. by J. B. Modler 1757); as children (Landesbibliothek, Stuttgart), Stuttgart Passional, illumination c. 1130); as standing youths (crypt of St Victor, Marseilles, 3rd cent. relief); as orants (oratory on Via Appia, Rome, 1st half of 12C [destroyed]). *Attributes:* shepherd's purse or provender pouch (baroque fig. at Stegaurach). *Special scenes:* The SS leave the cave (Bibliothèque Nationale, Paris, lat. 245, 15C illumination by J. Foucquet circle). One of the SS using Decius's coinage to buy bread in Theodosius era (Bibiliothèque Nationale, Paris, lat. 242, illumination c. 1375). – The SS forewarn King Edward the Confessor of approaching disaster by turning in their sleep (Westminster Abbey, London, chapel of Edward the Confessor, early 15C relief).

Severin of Noricum

Abbot, saint

Feast-day: 8th Jan

Life: S. lived as a monk in the east, after the death of Attila came to Noricum and worked as missionary in Favianis (= Mautern, Danube?) as political and spiritual leader of an orthodox minority opposing the Arian Rugiers. S. succeeded in establishing religious harmony among the quarrelling parties. His welfare work assuaged poverty among the populace, and he founded a monastery in Favianis, Lauriacum (Lorch, Enns) and Bojotro (Passau). † in Favianis on 8th Jan, 482.

Legends: S. brings priest Silvinus back to life. – Maximus of Noricum wanders through the Alps led by a bear, in order to see St S. – The dead S. appears during the exorcism of a woman and drives out the devil. – S. warns Bishop Constantius of Lorch of an attack by the barbarians. – S. distributes olive oil in the basilica among the starving populace. – S.'s words avert corn diseases called down by God on citizens for their stubbornness in refusing to pay tithes.

Patronage: Bavaria, archduchy of Austria, diocesan patron of Linz; for the fertility of vine stocks.

Veneration and cult sites: Body at the siege of the Romans of Noricum by Prince Odoacer, transferred to Naples, to S Leo, Montefeltre nr San Marino, afterwards to Castellum Lucullanum nr Naples; on 10th Oct. 910 to SS Severino e Sossio, Naples; since 1807 at Frattamaggiore nr Aversa. Esp. vene-

S. SEVERINVS.

rated in the dioceses of Passau, St Pölten and Vienna.

Representations in Art: *Apparel:* as a pilgrim (St Severin, Passau, fig. c. 1470); as a monk (Monreale Cathedral, 12C mosaic); as a bishop (Altstädten, mid–18C fig. by A. Sturm); as abbot with pannisellus (Passau Cathedral, Trenbach Chapel, fig. from 1519). *Attributes:* oil pitcher (Lorch, 20C medallion by F. Mayr); symbols of Eucharist (Salzburg Cathedral, sculptures in doorway by G. Manzu 1958). *Cycles:* SS Severino e Sossio, Naples, mid–15C predellae; Lorch (Enns), doorway sculpture by P. Dimmel 1971.

Sigismund of Burgundy

King, saint

Feast-day: 1st May (2nd May in diocese of Freising (Munich) and Sitten)

Life: under the influence of Bishop Avitus of Vienne, in 496/99 S. transferred his allegiance from Aryan to orthodox confession; 516 after the death of his father Gundobald he took over the kingdom. 516/522 had his son Sigrich by his first marriage with his wife Ostrogotha strangled at the instigation of the second wife, because the latter claimed (falsely) that the son wanted to seize power. S. did penance for the crime in the monastery of St-Maurice (Valais); endowed a perpetual choral chant. 523 defeated in the war against the Franks after support from the Ostrogothic king Theodoric the Gr. failed to materialise, and taken captive by Frankish king Chlodomir, brought to Orleans and drowned in a well in Coulmiers (Loiret) together with members of his family. 535 buried in the abbey of St Moritz, the bodies of his sons in the parish church of St Moritz.

Patronage: diocesan patron of Freising and Cremona; against marsh fever and fractures.

Veneration and cult sites: body in abbey of St Johannes, St Moritz, relics in (e.g.) Matzenheim, Alsace (cranium, originally in St Sigismund since 676), in Benediktbeuern (11C), Stablo, Gorze (Lorraine), Trier (12C), Himmerod, Zwiefalten, Plock, Oberlana; St Emmeram, Regensburg (13th. cent.), Prüfening, Ranshofen, St Vitus (Prague), Freising (transferred from Alsace to both churches 1354 by the emperor Charles IV), Vienna (16C), Heiligenstein (Pfalz) (20C). Venerated since early Middle Ages in Burgundy, France, Switzerland, Germany, Italy and Spain; centre of veneration until 18C was Freising.

Representations in Art: *Apparel:* as youthful king (cathedral treasury, Hildesheim, Oswald reliquary, late 12C relief); as an old, bearded king with crown (Alte Pinakothek, Munich, 16C painting by H. Burgkmair); as king with hat and barret (Kunsthalle, Karlsruhe, 16C painting by H. Burgkmair); as a monk in a habit with insignia (Kadan, Bohemia, painting c. 1470); in Roman apparel (Tempio Malatestiano, Rimini, fig. by A. di Duccio c. 1450); in Roman apparel with crown (S Frediano, Lucca, relief by J. della Quercia c. 1420); in armour and cloak (Freising Cathedral, fig. by P. Dirr 1624). *Attributes:* sword (w. tower of Freiburg Minster, fig. c. 1300); imperial orb (Staatsgalerie, Stuttgart, painting from Mühlhausen 1385); palm (parish church of Heiligenstein (Pfalz), 18C fig.). *Martyrdom:* Casole College, Colle di Val d'Elsa, painting by A. di Nicolo 1498). *Cycles:* reliquary shrine, abbey church of St Moritz, reliefs fr. 3rd qtr of 14C; Freising Cathedral, painting by H. Wertinger 1498; parish church of St-Sigismond nr Orleans, 19C stained glass.

Silvester I

Pope, saint

Feast-day: 31st Dec. (in eastern church rite 2nd Jan.)

Life: pontificate 314–335.

Legends: S. is instructed in the faith by Cyrinus the priest. – S. takes in the missionary

Timothy. – After the latter's martyrdom, S. is ordered by the judge Tarquin to worship idols; when he refuses, the judge has S. thrown into jail. – A bone sticks in the judge's gullet while he eats, at which he dies. – S. is freed from prison and after the death of Pope Malachi is elected his successor by the populace. – S. introduces Ember Days and regular fasting on Wed, Fri and Sat. S. flees from Constantine, who is persecuting Christians, and hides in a mountain. – When Constantine is struck down with leprosy, pagan priests advise sacrificing 3,000 children, but he refuses to do so when faced with the sorrowing mothers. – Peter and Paul appear to the Emperor in his sleep and order him to fetch S. from Mount Sirapte (i.e. Soracte), who will show him a spring in which he must immerse himself three times. – The Emperor identifies the apostles who have appeared to him by means of two pictures that S. shows him. – Constantine gets S. to teach him the faith, and is baptised. – At the command of the Empress Helen, S. emerges victorious in a debate with 12 Jewish scribes before a court of arbitration consisting of the pagans Kraton and Zenophilos. – The Jewish scribe Zambri kills a bull by pronouncing the name of God according to Deuteronomy 32, 39, but S. demands that he bring it back to life on the basis of the same biblical text, which he fails to do. S. of course manages to do so, bringing the wild beast back to life and moreover making it tame. – Helen is converted on the strength of the bull miracle. – Using a thread, S. ties up the devil in the form of a dragon and stops its jaws with the seal of God. – S. is present when St Helen finds the True Cross. - The Emperor Constantine hands over to S. the insignia of the crosier and tiara as symbols of papal office. – The Emperor leads by the rein the horse on which S. rides (ceremony of stratorial service). – Constantine gives the Church a gift, out of gratitude for being cured of leprosy. This makes all churches in the world – including the four patriarchates – answerable to the Pope, declares the Lateran Church the head of all churches, presents the Pope with the Lateran Palace and bestows imperial insignia and dignities on the Pope, raises cardinal-level clerics to senatorial rank and qualifies them for the patriciate and consulate, and moreover makes over the whole western world to the Church as state territory.

Patronage: former Papal States, pets, good harvest.

Veneration and cult sites: body interred in Catacombs of Priscilla on the Via Salaria, 762 transferred to S Silvestro e Capite; another version speaks of the translation of the bones to the abbey of Nonantola nr Modena. Earliest verifiable veneration in Germany in 11C in Bamberg. For political reasons, the cult of S. was practised in the Papal States until under Pope Paul V the Gift of Constantine was shown to be a forgery.

Superstitions: generally connected with the New Year. On St S.'s Day, a glimpse into the future is possible if numerous actions are undertaken that vary by region, such as looking through the keyhole of the church door or foretelling from figures made of cast lead, etc. – Anyone who on St S.'s Eve secretly buys a nutmeg and keeps it in his pocket for a year will not break his bones even in the most serious falls. – Anyone who on St S.'s Eve scratches moss from a wooden cross naked in the churchyard can cure gout. – Anyone who casts no shadow on St S.'s Eve will die.

Representations in Art: *Apparel:* as bishop in pontifical robes (St S.'s Chapel, Goldbach nr Uberlingen, 14C fig.); as a pope with the insignia tiara and red cloak (SS Quattro Coronati, Rome, fresco 1246); as pope in a golden pluvial (high altar, Blaubeuren, painting 1493/4). *Attributes:* book, crosier with three bars (Airischwand nr Freising, 16C fig.); bull (allusion to raising the bull from the dead) on the book (Siegertsbrunn, Upper Bavaria, 17C fig.); bull at his feet (Neufahrn nr Wolfratshausen, fig. c. 1500); bull looking upwards (Berghofen nr Sonthofen, early 15C fig.); serpent with the book (St Peter, Salzburg, painting c. 1490); mussels, as allusion to baptism of Constantine (Ellwangen, late 15C fig.); dragon (parish museum, Daroca nr Zaragoza, late 15C painting attrib. to Bermejo). *Special scenes:* S. holds up the Holy Cross (Lateran Baptistry, fresco by Maratta 1648/50); S. and Constantine venerate the True Cross found by St Helen (Emperor's stained glass window in St Lorenz's church, Nuremberg, 1477); S. baptises the Emperor Constantine (Samuel H. Kress Collection, Philadelphia Museum of Art, tapestry woven after Rubens 1622–30); S. awaits the Emperor Constantine on the steps (sacristy of SS Apostoli, Rome, fresco by D. Bruschi 1882); S. meets Constantine on horseback (Sala di Costantino, Vatican City, pre–1522 relief); Constantine and S. in triumphal chariot (Chartres Cathedral, 13th century stained glass window); S. removes a fishbone stuck in the prefect's gullet (Galleria Doria Pamphili, Rome, 15C predella by F. Pesselino); S. consecrates churches (La Mentorella hermitage at Capranica Sabina, 13C door relief); S. slays the dragon (Grotta dei Santi, Calvi nr Capua, fresco c. 1100). *Cycles:* SS Quattro Coronati, Rome, murals 1246; S Silvestro, Pisa, 13C reliefs; Bardi chapel, S Croce, Florence, 14C painting by Maso di Banco.

Simon Stock

Carmelite friar, saint

Feast-day: 16th May

Life: Simon, who came from Aylesford, Kent, is reputed to have lived as a hermit in a tree, thus his second name of Stock. In 1241/42, S. joined the Carmelite Order founded in Palestine and, since 1237, established in England. In 1245, S. was elected in London superior-general of his Order. S. was crucial to the development of the Carmelite Order and its popularity in the whole of Europe. D. on 16th May 1265 during a visit to Bordeaux.

Legends: in accordance with the Sanctorial of the Carmelite Order: in 1251, S. had a vision of the Blessed Virgin and received the brown scapular with the promise that whoever died wearing it would be saved.

Patronage: Bordeaux; Carmelite Order.

Superstition: Whoever dies wearing the Carmelite scapular, his soul will be released from purgatory the following Saturday (so-called "Sabbath Indulgence").

Veneration and cult sites: The Holy See approved his cult in Bordeaux in 1435, in Ireland and England in 1458, and for the Carmelite Order in 1564.

Representation in Art: *Apparel:* as Carmelite monk in the brown habit and brown scapular of the Order and white overmantle (Prague, St Gallus, painting by J. Kr. Liska, 1696). *Attribute:* dog having retrieved bread (Maikammer, SS Cosmas and Damian, relief by Möhring, attributed in 1765). *Special scenes:* the Blessed Virgin presents S. with the scapular (Rome, S Maria della Scala, painting by C. Roncalli, 1604/05); in the presence of several saints, S. receives the scapular from the Blessed Virgin (Merkelbeck, monastery of the Discalced Carmelites, painting by V. H. Janssens, late 17th century); Reading at a table, S. receives the scapular (Bologna, Pinacoteca Nazionale, painting by A. Tiarini, 17th century); Redemption from purgatory by the Blessed Virgin and S. (Ghent, church of the Discalced Carmelites, painting by C. de Crayer, early 17th century).

Simon the Zealot

Apostle, saint

Feast-day: 28th Oct

Life: mentioned in the Synoptic Gospels and Acts of the Apostles. S. is given the epithet Zealot to indicate his membership of the Zealot faction. Another epithet is 'Canaanite', which has caused him to be mistakenly identified as the bridegroom in the miracle at Canaa. S. was presumably active in the diaspora in Egypt and Armenia. Acc. to 1 Cor. 9, 5, Simon and Jude were still active in 57 AD.

Legends: S. and Jude-Thaddeus are active in Babylon and Persia for 13 yrs. S. and Jude prophesy to the ruler that the King of the Indians will send embassies to proffer his submission and avoid much blood-letting. – S. and Jude demonstrate to the magicians the ineffectiveness of their gods by picking up serpents in their hands and throwing them at the magicians. – S. and Jude command the serpent to suck the poison out of the bodies of the magicians again. – S. and Jude prove the innocence of a deacon by getting a newborn infant to prove the innocence. – In Suanir, S. and Jude drive evil spirits out of the idols in the shape of two moors, who go on to smash the images. – Thereupon S. and Jude are killed by the idolatrous priests in the town, S. with a saw, Jude with a club.

Patronage: S. societies in Austria, patron saint of Goslar town hall, dyers, tanners, lumberjacks, leatherworkers, masons, weavers and henpecked husbands (the 'Siemandl' Confraternity in Krems can be traced back to 1747).

Veneration and cult sites: relics in St Peter's, Rome, Hersfeld, Cologne, Reeken nr Münster, pilgrimages in Potsmos and St Simon nr Seeg.

Superstitions: St S.'s Day marks the end of the grazing season and the onset of winter weather. In Hungary, there is a saying, "St S.'s Day is coming, watch out if you're only wearing underpants". – An unlucky day because St S.'s Day is when the Flood began (cf. Schiller's William Tell: "The lake is raging and seeks its victim"). – On St S.'s Day, husbands should not contradict their wives. – If the wife gets up earlier than the husband on St S.'s Day, then she gives the orders for a year.

Representations in Art: *Apparel:* as an apostle in a belted tunic and pallium (parish church of Krems, fig. by A. Krimmer 1706); in cap and cowl (Blutenburg, Munich, late 15C fig.). *Attributes:* scroll (Ravello, 12C door relief by Bonanus of Pisa); book which S. is looking through (Prado, Madrid, painting by P. P. Rubens 1613); saw (high altar at Doberan, painting fr. 2nd half of 14C); open book, saw (Stiftskirche, Tübingen, fig. c. 1480); spear (Arbe Cathedral, late 12C enamel work); sword (south door of Chartres, fig. from 1210/15); axe (St Ursula, Cologne, mural c. 1280); anchor (Graphisches Kabinett, Benedictine abbey at Göttweig, copper engraving by Götz and Klauber c. 1750); glasses (cathedral treasury, Aachen, apostle antependium c. 1481). *Special scenes:* S. in the lion's pit and rescued by an angel (Vatican City museums, 17C painting by M. B. Mandl). *Martyrdom:* S. being sawn up (choir stalls at Krems town parish church, relief by J. M. Götz 1736); being beaten with cudgels, sword and halberd (Vatican City museums, 15C painting). *Cycles:* Chartres Cathedral, 13C stained glass; Archepiscopal Museum, Vich, painting by L. Borrassa 1414.

Sixtus II

(Xystus), Pope, martyr, saint
Feast-day: 7th August (before the calendar reform 6th August)

Life: S. reigned 257–258. Mellowed the discussions between his predecessor Stephen I and the North African bishops about the validity of baptisms performed by heretics. Arrested during the persecutions on 6th August 258 during the service in the Coemetrium of Callixtus and beheaded after a short trial.

Veneration and cult sites: buried in the Papal tomb in the Callixtus Coemetrium; in 6th century the church of St Crescentiana was renamed to St Sixtus; relics translated under Pope Leo IV 847/55. Relics in Verden. Canonical saint.

Representation in Art: *Apparel:* as martyr (Ravenna, St Apollinare Nuovo, mosaic, 6th century); as head carrier in Mass vestments with pallium and simple tiara (Stuttgart, State Library, Stuttgart Passional, illumination, 12th century); as Pope in pluvial with threefold tiara (Kanopiste near Prague, painting, in the following of B. Daddi, 14th century). *Attributes:* double crosier (Dörndorf, figure, circa 1520); threefold crosier (Wollmesheim, Catholic Church, figure, circa 1490); palm (Pisa, St Francis', painting, by S. Aretino, 15th century); purse (Dörndorf, figure, circa 1520); purse on book (Sindolsheim, figure, circa 1500); coin in hand (Polenfeld, figure, circa 1520); sword (Zumsweier, figure, 18th century).

Sophia

With her three daughters Fides, Spes, Caritas (Pistis, Elpis, Agape) of Rome, martyrs, saints
Feast-day: 30th Sept (mother), 1st Aug (daughters), in Greek rites 1st Aug or 17th Sept
Ecclesiastical historical background: ever since the exile of the Jews in Babylon, wisdom is seen as an inherent attribute of God or as a real form of manifestation in the midst of the world. The personification of

the attribute, that speaks to God as a person and stands at his side in the creation of the world or has pleasure in human kind, is suggested in the literature of wisdom, e.g. Proverbs 8, 22–36. Wisdom features correspondingly as an attribute of Christ (preamble to Gospel of St John), and churches dedicated to Christ bore this epithet, like Haghia Sophia in Constantinople, Kiev, Jerusalem, Novgorod, Thessaloniki, Ohrid (Macedonia) and Sofia.

Legends: acc. to the 7C Milan Passion, a person was created from the attributes of Christ: S. comes from Milan and after the death of her husband distributes her goods among the poor. – S. goes to Rome and is taken up by the high-ranking lady Thessaminia. – During Hadrian's reign, S. and her daughters are accused of being Christian. – After numerous miracles, the daughters suffer martyrdom by being flayed, having their breasts cut off, being thrown in the furnace, pierced and beheaded with a sword, and are buried by the mother. – S. dies three days later from natural causes.

Patronage: widows.

Veneration and cult sites: memorial to St S. and daughters in Rome beneath the church of S Pancrazio on the Via Aurelia; the three daughters are not mentioned by name. The Latin cult is concentrated on a tomb at Milestone 18 on the Via Appia and a 6C cult in the Catacombs of Callixtus with Sophia and her daughters, whose names are associated with expressions of virtue. Despite the poaching of the Via Appia names and legendary characteristics of the saints for the Via Aurelia site, the feast-days remain separate. Relics translocated during Pope Paul I's reign (8C) to S Silvestro in Campo Marzio; on 10th May, 778 further relics were obtained by Bishop Remigius of Strasbourg for the nunnery of Eschau in Alsace.

Superstitions: anyone in distress should have a St S. service read with their own service order and offer four candles in honour of the saint, a custom which is supposed to go back to a service by Pope Leo III in Paderborn in the Palatinate of Charlemagne.

Representations in Art: *Apparel:* as a matron in cinctured robe, cloak, wimple, headscarf or bonnet, daughters in girls' clothing at her feet (Eschau, late 15C fig.); as a matron carrying her daughters (Opperkofen, 15C fig.); daughters in long dress (Chapel of St Agnes, Cologne Cathedral, 14C mural). *Attributes:* crown concealed in S.'s veiled hands (Grotta di Salvatore, Vallerano, 9C/10C mural); palm bough in S.'s hand (St Stephan, Vienna, late 15C fig.); swords in the hands of the daughters (Chapel of St Agnes, Cologne Cathedral, 14C mural); S. with lily sceptre and crown, daughters with swords in hand, breasts on their arms, skin draped on arms (National Museum, Warsaw, painting c. 1460). *Cycle:* Szaszfalu/Sasova (Slovakia), painting c. 1440.

Stanislas of Cracow

Bishop, martyr, saint

Feast-day: 11th April (prior to calendar reform, 7th or 8th May)

Life: * c. 1030, studies in Gniezno, perhaps also in Paris; parish priest in Czembocz, canon and (post 1072) bishop of Cracow; after differences with the irascible king Boleslaw II of Poland, condemned as traitor on 11th Apr, 1079 and slain by Boleslaw's own hand at the altar during mass in St Michael's church outside the gates of Cracow. As a martyr for ecclesiastical interests, S. is of particular political importance. Canonisation in 1254 in Assisi.

Legends: S. reproaches King Boleslaw for his immoral way of life. – S. criticises Boleslaw for having recent mothers suckle young dogs instead of their children. – S. raises Piotrowin from the dead, who appears as a witness

(S Stanislas, Rome, painting by A. Gramatica c. 1594); resurrected man at his feet (Museum of Fine Arts, Wroclaw, 16C painting); resurrected man at hand (Wawel Cathedral, Cracow, relief 1510). *Special scenes:* judgment scene (Franciscan friary, Warta, painting by T. Dolabella, 1st half of 17C). *Martyrdom:* lower church, S Francesco, Assisi, 14C frescoes by school of Giotto; Stiftsgalerie, St Florian, painting by N. Breu c. 1508; Wawel Cathedral, Cracow, reliquary reliefs c. 1500; Plawno, early 16C altar reliefs; Szépmüvészeti Muzeum, Budapest, late 15C painting.

Stanislas Kostka

Jesuit, saint

Feast-day: 13th Nov. (As the saint's death coincided with the Assumption of the Virgin, for the sake of the patronage a feast-day was chosen which can be celebrated during the school year.)

Life: * 28th Oct, 1550 in the castle of Rostkovo (Masowie) of a Polish aristocratic family. 1564 after being educated at home, took up his studies at the Jesuit college in Vienna, journeying there with his brother Paul and tutor Bilinksi. In Vienna, S. lived for a year in the seminary for noble families, subsequently with the Lutheran Kimberker family. S. became a member of the Jesuit-run Confraternity of St Barbara for the Furtherance of the Worship of the Sacrament; six months later, sought admittance to the Jesuit Order as a novice, but the Austrian Vice-Provincial P. Maggi was afraid of difficulties with S.'s noble father and so turned his request down. S. fled to Peter Canisius in Dillingen, who because of the political problems dispatched S. to the General Superior Francisco Borgia in Rome. Borgia accepted S. into the novitiate on 28th Oct, 1567. Weakened by the strain of flight and travel, S. died on 15th Aug, 1568

before the king over the rightful acquisition of a piece of church land. – S.'s body is cut up over a pond and a fish swallows the finger. – In a posthumous miracle at canonisation, S. raises someone from the dead. S. provides aid at the battle of Grunwald. A further series of legends pursue the fate of Boleslaw: his excommunication and expulsion by Pope Gregory VIII, the pilgrimage to Ossiach and his service in the monastery kitchen, his confession and death.

Patronage: national saint of Poland, patron saint of archbishopric of Cracow.

Veneration and cult sites: Body initially in Skalka church in Cracow, 1088 transferred to Wawel cathedral.

Representations in Art: *Apparel:* as bishop in pontifical clothing (relief at Stary Zamsk, 2nd half of 13C); as bishop in pluvial and dalmatic (Narodnowa Catalogus Archiepiscoporum Gnesnensium et Cracoviensium, Warsaw, book illumination by S Samostrzelnik 1535). *Attributes:* sword, martyr's palm

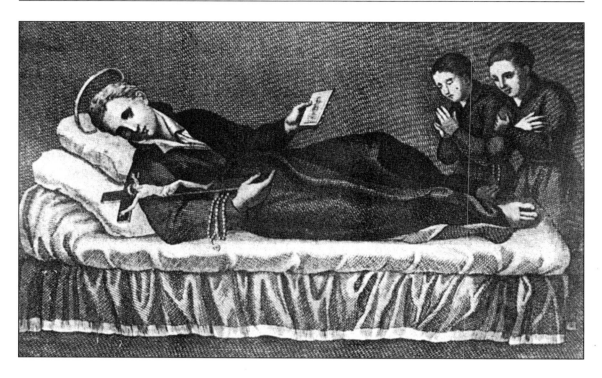

of malaria. S.'s purity and courage were praised. Beatification 1670, canonisation 1726.

Legends: in Vienna, S. endures abuse and hard words from his brother with the utmost patience. – S. receives holy communion from angels. – The mother of God appears to S. and places her child in his arms. – During the escape from Vienna, an angel holds back the horse of S.'s pursuing brother. – With his prayers, S. frees a colleague from temptations. – S. has to plunge into a spring to cool the mystic flush generated by prayer. – S. heals a dying lame man. – S. saves a boy who has fallen into a well. – After a sermon by Peter Canisius, S. takes the preacher's remark, that one should begin every month as if it were one's last, even when healthy, as a personal reference. – After his death, S. frees the town of Lublin from the plague.

Patronage: Poland (since 1671), patron saint of Warsaw, Poznan, Lublin, Lvov, Gniezno; of students and novice Jesuits; against fever, eye complaints, broken limbs.

Veneration and cult sites: Body in S Andrea al Quirinale, Rome, relics in Neuhausen-Fildern and Starowies.

Representations in Art: *Apparel:* as young ordinand in talar of Italian Jesuits with broad woollen cincture, cloak with stiff, upright collar (Opole Lubelskie, 18C painting). *Attributes:* lily, Madonna (Hofkirche, Dresden, fig. by L. Mattielli c. 1740); holding infant Jesus (Historisches Museum der Pfalz – cathedral treasury, Speyer, fig. by P. Egell c. 1730); crucifix, rosary (S Andrea al Quirinale, Rome, fig. by P. Legros 1703); walking stick. *Special scenes:* Mary shows S. the infant Jesus (S Andrea al Quirinale, Rome, painting by C Maratti 1687); S. liberating Lublin from the plague (St Peter's, Cracow, 18C painting). *Cycles:* S Andrea al Quirinale, Rome, painting by A. del Pozzo, 2nd half of 17C.

Stephen

Protomartyr, saint

Feast-day: 26th Dec. (observed since end of 4C, from 9C to 1955 festal week), 3rd Aug festival of discovery of his relics (observed from 9C to 1960).

Life: acc. to Acts 6, 1 to 8, 2, because of arguments between Jewish and Gentile Christians in Jerusalem, seven men were chosen to help the apostles with distributing alms, among them being S, who belonged among the Greek-speaking Jews. Missionary sermons by him in the libertine synagogue (the libertines were freed slaves and their offspring) and other synagogal communities (of which the Cyrenean, Alexandrian, Jewish Cilician and Asian are mentioned) caused uproar, which led to a charge of blasphemous speech against both temple and law at the sanhedrin. In accordance with Mosaic law (Levit. 24,11), S. was thereupon stoned to death.

Legends: selection from legends taken from Vita fabulosa of 10C/11C: shortly after his birth, S. is abducted by the Devil. – A changeling is found in the cradle instead. – S. is suckled by a hind, found by Bishop Julian and at the request of the hind adopted by Julian. – As a young man, he returns to his parents and exorcises the changeling, whereupon a demon with horns, bat's wings and a long tail escapes. – During a Passover meal at the house of his parents, the wine suddenly turns to blood as a sign of the martyrdom of the son. – After the stoning, wild beasts keep watch over the body. – Gamaliel and Nicodemus bury S. in one of Gamaliel's fields. – Selection of episodes from the 12C

English/Scandinavian Christmas Legends:
S. was a servant (variant: stable boy) at the
court of King Herod. – S. sees the star of
Bethlehem and interprets the event to
Herod. – At a banquet, a roast cock gets up
from the plate and crows "Christus natus
est". – Enraged, Herod has S. stoned. – Selection of posthumous legends from the Golden
Legend: in the year 415, Gamaliel appears to
Lucian the priest and reveals the lost grave of
S. – A sick pagan in the town of Martialis,
who has spent the night on flowers from the
St S. altar, asks to be baptised next morning.
Patronage: the diocese of Vienna, patron
saint of horses, stable boys, coopers, coachmen, masons, slingsmen, tailors, stonecar-
vers, weavers, carpenters; against headaches, stitch, and stones.
Veneration and cult sites: Body allegedly
found on 3rd Aug, 415 in Kafar Gamala, 15
km from Jerusalem (in 1916, the ruins of a
small church with a rock tomb were discovered by the Salesians, which might well be
the grave mentioned by Lucian). Translation
of relics to the church on Mt Zion, Jerusalem, to Constantinople; 560 relics to San Lorenzo fuori le mura, Rome, Zwiefalten since
1141 (left hand). Since the 5C, a place 350m
north of the Damascus Gate in Jerusalem is
mentioned as the martyrdom spot; a church
was erected there in 455/60 by the Empress
Eudocia, later burnt down by the Persians in
the 7C (excavated 1882 when the Ecole Bib-
lique was constructed). Canon saints; veneration spread along two routes from the east:
a) Ancona, Naples, north Africa, Rhône
estuary, Arles, Konstanz; b) north Italy,
Chur, Passau, Vienna. In the late Middle
Ages the cult of S. was promoted chiefly by
royal houses, esp. by King Stephen of Hungary.
Superstitions: invocations in numerous incantations and traditions. – In Silesia and Poland, after the service on St S.'s Day the
priest is showered with oats as he leaves the

Saints of monastic orders I

67 *St Benedict, miniature, Vatican Library*

68 *Monastery of Monte Cassino, burial-place of St Benedict and St Scholastica*

69 *St Hildegard, miniature, Lucca, Italy, state library*

70 *Bernard of Clairvaux preaching to the Devil, miniature, Paris, Bibliothèque Nationale*

71 *St Francis of Assisi preaching to the birds, detail of fresco by Giotto, Assisi, Italy, church of S. Francesco*

72 *Tomb of St Francis, crypt of S. Francesco, Assisi*

73 *St Clare having her hair cut by St Francis, painting on glass, former monastery church, Königsfelden, Germany*

74 *Church of S. Antonio, Padua, Italy; burial-place of St Antony*

69

74

church; in Beuthen, the congregation indulge in mutual throwing, probably in imitation of the stoning of S. – Early in the morning, girls' backs are beaten by the boys with switches or sometimes (e.g. in Bohemia) with plants. – Sometimes this happens the other way round or mutually, in the sense of a fertility rite. – The last person to get up in Viol/ Schleswig on St S.'s Day has to ride round to the neighbours on a pitchfork in a nightshirt amid general mockery, and is rewarded with a tasty morsel or two. – On the first day of school, the prayer of St S. is read to boys to make them eloquent. – St Stephen's potion has been around since Carolingian times, and is thus the earliest demonstrable love potion. St S.'s wine which is blessed in church must be red wine, and there must be a stone at the bottom of the glass. – In Württemberg, the poor used to get St S.'s bread for alms. – Flowers which are put on the St S.'s altar brought health to the sick. – Cloths from the St S's altar have curative effects. – Water dedicated on St S.'s Day is sprinkled by peasants on food, barns and fields against witches and evil spirits. – Salt consecrated on St S.'s Day is shaped into a block and hung in the stall. – Before the cattle are driven up to the high pastures in the New Year, they are given the salt to lick. – Peasants are supposed to lick St S.'s salt if they go on a long journey. – Game that licks St S.'s salt is easily caught by hunters. – Oats are consecrated on St S.'s day, and are given to horses as a protection against disease. – Blood-letting of horses on St S.'s day protects them from disease. – There is in addition a rich tradition of customs at Christmas and New Year not directly connected with S., such as the moving of objects or traditions of horseshoes as harbingers of good luck in the New Year, etc.

Representations in Art: *Apparel:* as a young deacon on a white tunic (S Lorenzo fuori le mura, Rome, 6C mosaic); as a deacon in an amice, alb, stole, maniple and dalmatic (chapel of Merton College, Oxford, stained glass c. 1300); in a richly patterned dalmatic (Rasini Collection, Milan, early 16C painting by V. Foppa); dalmatic with a stole worn over the robe (Städtischer Kunstbesitz, Goslar, late 13C). *Attributes:* gospel book, palm (Hessisches Landesmuseum, Darmstadt, mid– 13C painting); stones in a halo (S Cecilia in Trastevere, Rome, fresco by Cavallini c. 1293); stones on his head (book of hours by Rohan in Bibl. Nationale, Paris, lat. 9471, illumination, 1st half of 15C); stones in his hands (Bamberg Cathedral, Adam door, 13C fig.); stones on the book (Breisach, Münster, fig. by H. L. Master 1526); in the folds of a puffed dalmatic (Ghent altar, St Bavo, Ghent, painting by H. and J. van Eyck 1432); censer (Kansas Gallery of Art, early 16C painting by Carpaccio); incense boat (Museo Piersanti, Matelica, 15C painting by J. Bellini); elevated gospel (cloister of St-Trophime, Arles, relief fr. 2nd half of 12C). *Special scenes:* miracle of the wine in the house of S.'s parents (St-Etienne, Beauvais, stained glass 1526); tomb (Musée municipal, Arras, painting by E. Delacroix 1862). *Martyrdom:* S. lying beneath a pile of stones (fragment of book cover fr. Metz School, c. 850); kneeling S. being stoned (Louvre, Paris, painting by Carracci c. 1604); S. receives the martyr's crown and palm from angels (National Gallery of Scotland, Edinburgh, painting by A. Elsheimer c. 1602/5). *Cycles:* very numerous: a) story as per Acts of Apostles: Chartres Cathedral, south transept, early 13C fig.; shrine at Gimel, late 12C reliefs; Nicholas V Chapel, Vatican City, frescoes by Fra Angelico c. 1449; Szt Istvan church, Papa, painting by F. A. Maulpertsch 1782; b) legends and biblical scenes: Sens Cathedral, reliefs post 1268; Musée de Cluny, Paris, tapestries 1502; c) finding of relics and translation *Cycles:* Vatican City museums, 14C painting by B. Daddi; S Lorenzo fuori le mura, Rome, mural, 2nd half of 13C; d) Vita fabulosa version: Lentate Oratory, frescoes fr. 2nd half of 14C with 43 scenes; e) English-Scandinavian version of Christmas Legends: ceiling painting, Dadesjo (Sweden), end 13C; St George's Chapel Windsor, painting end 15C.

Stephen I

King of Hungary (Szent Istvan), saint

Feast-day: until 1969, 2nd Sept, today 16th Aug; in Hungary, 20th Aug (burial date and national holiday)

Life: * c. 970 as son of the Arpad prince Geza, probably in Esztergom. 996 (?) married Gisela, sister of the Emperor Henry II. 997 regent, Christmas 1000 crowned king of the Hungarians. S. embodied the concept of a rex et sacerdos, and gave his realm a Christian constitution. S. successfully fought off all pagan reactions and created an ecclesiastical structure of two archbishoprics and eight bishoprics. The royal throne was supplied to S. by Pope Silvester II. S. was considered a good, just and purposeful king. † 15th Aug, 1038, buried in the cathedral of Szekesfehervar. Canonised 1083 together with his son Imre by Pope Gregory VII.

Legends: S. baptised by missionary priest sent by Bishop Pilgrim of Passau. – S.'s nuptial journey to Scheyern. – S. is confirmed by St Adalbert of Prague. - S. cures the sick. – S. offers patronate of Hungary to the Virgin (Patrona Hungariae). – S. receives a bull from Pope Silvester conferring apostolic privileges, including the right to have the cross with double crossbar of archepiscopal rank borne before him (known since 1576). – The victory over the Turkish army nr Budapest in 1687 is attributed to S.'s intercession (foundation legend for the introduction of general liturgical veneration).

Patronage: national saint of Hungary, Order of St Stephen, horses.

Veneration and cult sites: Tomb in Szekesfehervar, relics in Budapest and Zagreb; shrine with relics of S., Laszlo and Imre in Aachen and Cologne, on analogy of the Three Kings.

Superstitions: Anyone using a shotgun on 20th Aug will, with S.'s help, always hit the mark. – On the name-day of the Virgin (26th Dec), the well at Postyen/Piestany (now Slovakia) reveals the name of a girl's future husband if she calls on her king as patron saint of the country (i.e. Hungary) and fills pitchers with water.

Representations in Art: *Apparel:* as an old king with crown and insignia (Bibliotetheca Vaticana, Vatican City, Hungarian coronation robe 1031); as a knight (Budapest, statue by A. Strobl 1906); Szekesfehervar, by F. Sidlo 1938; Györ by F. Medgyessy, 1940/50). *Attributes:* crown, globe and cross as symbols of missionary activity (Zsigra/Zehra, mid–14C mural); choir stalls in St Stephan, Vienna 1476). *Special scenes:* baptism of S. (Nemzeti Galeria, Budapest, painting by G. Benczur 1875); founding of Pannonhalma Abbey (Nemzeti Galeria, Budapest, painting by I. Dorffmaister 1792); S. with the Virgin Mary (Szt Ignac, Györ, painting 1643); S. offers the Mother of God the patronate of Hungary (Györ Cathedral, painting by J. L. Kracker 1773). *Cycles:* Szechenyi Library, Budapest, illustrations to Kepes Kronika c. 1360; Mateoc/Matejovce, painting c. 1450; royal chapel, Scheyern 1625 (on model of 1382); Vatican City, frescoes by A. Durante 1613.

T

Teresa of Ávila

(Theresia, Teresa of Jesus, the Great) Carmelite, saint

Feast-day: 15th October; as the day of T.'s death coincided with the feast of St Francis of Assisi, the feast was displaced to the next day, which became 15th October in 1580 after the calendar reform.

Life: * 28th March 1515 in Ávila as daughter of the nobleman Alonso de Cepeda and Beatrix de Ahumeda. As a child T. was very independent and self-confident; aged seven wanted to be martyred by the Moors. At 12 after the death of her mother, consecrated to the mother of God, following this, under the influence of a friend, worldly and non-religious phase, 1530 educated by the Augustinians, 1532 released for health reasons, 1535 entry into the Carmelite Monastery of the Incarnation in Ávila, became seriously ill; 15th August 1539 lay in a coma, then severely lame and could not walk even after three years. Mystic experiences: 1543 turned to mysticism under the influence of her confessor Vincente Baron. There were intrigues against T. 1556 in a vision a mystical engagement with Christ, since 1560 after a vision of hell, made an oath always to do the more perfect thing. With the help of Peter of Alcantara and against resistance from within the Order, beginning of the reform of the Carmelite Order with stronger emphasis on hermit aspect. At Ávila in 1562 T. founded a branch of the Order, the Discalced (barefoot) Carmelites. † 4th October 1582. Beatified 1614, canonised 1622, feast designated by Pope Clement IX with duplex character as the first feast day of a confessor who was not a martyr. – Rich in written works, T. sought in the work "The Interior Castle" to systematically compose her mystic experiences.

Patronage: Spain, city patron of Ávila, Alba de Tormes, Naples, Archbishopric of Mexico, Discalced Carmelites; in spiritual need, for the inner life, the poor souls in Purgatory, lace makers, against sorrow of the heart.

Veneration and cult sites: body first in Ávila, since 1586 in Alba de Tormes church of the Order.

Representation in Art: *Apparel:* as nun in Carmelite dress (Seville, Carmelite Convent, painting, by J. de la Miseria, 1576). *Attributes:* dove, spindle (Rome, Vatican Library, copper engraving, by F. Villamana, 1614); writing desk, quill, book (Madrid, National Library, copper engraving, by C. Galle, beg. 17th century); biretta and chain (Jan, Cathedral, relief, circa 1730); putto, arrow and flaming heart (Rome, St Peter's, figure, by F. della Valle, 1754); heart pierced with arrow (Dresden, Court Church, figure, by F. Matielli, 18th century); arrow (Vienna, Church

on Steinhof, stained glass, by K. Moser, 1907); book of the Rule (Ávila, Monastery Church, figure, 17th century); model of monastery (Aachen, Suermondt Museum, figure, 17th century); two branches growing out of T.'s breast (Paris, copper engraved cabinet, copper engraving, by J. Matheus, circa 1620). *Special scenes:* (selection): T.'s vision of the Holy Trinity (Aix-en-Provence, museum, painting, by Guercino, 17th century); vision of the dove (Rotterdam, Boymans van Beuningen Museum, painting, by P.P. Rubens, circa 1600); Christ appears to T. and appoints her to be his bride (Rouen, Museum, painting, by J. Jouvenet, circa 1700); Christ shows T. his wounds (Aix-en-Provence, Museum, painting, by P. de Champaigne, mid 17th century); T. receives a chain from Mary and a cloak from Joseph (Vienna, Kunsthistorisches Museum, painting, by C. de Crayer, 17th century); transverberation of St T. (Rome, St Mary della Vittoria, figure, by L. Bernini, 1646); T. receives communion from Peter of Alcantara (Madrid, Adanero Collection, painting, by C. Coello, 1670). *Cycles:* Madrid National Library, 60 engravings by A. v. Westerhout, 18th century.

Thecla

companion of the Apostle Paul, martyr, saint

Feast-day: 23rd September

Legend: according to the "Acta Pauli et Theclae" of the 2nd century, which are rejected by Tertullian and Jerome as Apocryphal: T. is converted in her home town of Iconium by

the Apostle Paul. – At this T. renounces her bridegroom. – Both mother and groom accuse her before the court. – P. is arrested, T. visits him in prison. – T. condemned to death on the pyre, but rain and hail save her. – T. is released and meets the Apostle Paul on the road to Daphne, joins him and comes to Antioch. – T. rejects another suitor, the Syrian Alexander. – T. is again accused and condemned to fight animals in the arena. – During the fight T. jumps into a moat to baptise herself (variant: T. is thrown into a moat with wild animals). – The animals do not touch T. – T. is released, returns to Iconium, converts her mother and fiancé. – In Iconium T. founds a society of virgins. – T. dies a blessed death (variant: one day T. disappears between rocks and is translated).

Patronage: the T. Brotherhoods, the dying, (which in 14th century was accepted into the dying prayer "Libera me" because she suffered torment three times) against plague, fire.

Veneration and cult sites: since 4th century in Seleucia (T. Church in Silifke), relics in Tarragona (since 1319), Bethphage near Jerusalem (church patron since 530); extension of veneration through upper Italy to Cologne and Bavaria, also to Spain around Tarragona, town patron of Este.

Representation in Art: *Apparel:* half naked bound to post (Kansas City, W. Rockhill Nelson Collection, marble relief, 5th century); as orantin in tunic (London, British Museum, Cologne glass bowl, 4th century); as virgin in long, girdled robe and cloak (Munich, Georgianum, painting, late 15th century); with maphorion (Copenhagen, Museum, altar, relief, circa 1140). *Attributes:* book (maphorion (Copenhagen, Museum, altar, relief, circa 1140); tame lion on line (cloak (Munich, Georgianum, painting, late 15th century); lion (Milan, Cathedral, figure, by Niccolò da Venezia, 14th century); lion, bear (Erfurt, Cathedral Museum, figure, 15th

century); dove, women in reverence (Milan, Cathedral, alabaster relief, 10th century); pillar with flames (Munich, private possession, figure, circa 1500); T. cross (Egea de los Caballeros, St Mary's, painting, beg. 16th century); relic of arm (Barcelona, Cathedral, painting, by P. Alemany, end 15th century); crucifix, snake (Maria Bühel, pilgrimage church, figure, 1769); palm branch (Washington, National gallery, painting, by El Greco, 1597). *Special scenes:* T. as orantin on the pyre (Stuttgart, State Library, Cod. 2x57, illumination, 12th century); T. on deathbed, surrounded by Christ and Mary (Welden, T. Church, painting, by P. Riepp, 1758); T. receives from heaven a bowl with bread (bread of the Eulogy) (Welden, T. Church, fresco, by J. B. Enderle, 1759); T. as patron against plague (Este, church, painting, by G. B. Tiepolo, 18th century); T. hears the sermon of St Paul (Augsburg, City Art Collection, painting, by H. Holbein the Elder, 1503). *Cycles:* Tarragona Cathedral, marble reliefs, 12/13th century; Tarragona, reliefs, by P. Johan, circa 1426.

Theodul of Sitten
bishop, saint
Feast-day: 16th March
Life: first Bishop of Wallis, 381 participant at the Synod of Aquileia, 393 Synod of Milan. According to Eucherius of Lyons, T. found the bones of St Maurice and buried them in St Maurice.
Legend: T. commands the devil to carry a bell which the Pope had given him in Wallis. – Charlemagne presented T. with sovereignty rights in Wallis.
Patronage: Wallis, Walser Region in northern Italy, Vorarlberg, Switzerland; bells, vintners, cattle and weather.
Veneration and cult sites: bones brought to Sitten presumably by Martinach; in 12/13th century in Valeria near Sitten, since 1798

disappeared. Pilgrimage in Valeria attested in the Middle Ages.

Representation in Art: *Apparel:* as bishop in pontifical dress with mitre and staff (Oberwesel, St Mary's Church, mural, 15th century). *Attributes:* sword (Sitten, Cathedral, figure, 16th century); sword pointing down and held by blade (Fribourg, Switzerland, Notre-Dame, figure, 17th century); small devil at feet (Zürich, Swiss State Museum, stained glass, circa 1510); grape in hand (Christberg, Vorarlberg, figure, 16th century); grape on book (Sitten, Cathedral, figure, 16th century); bell at feet (Bihlafingen, Württemberg, figure, end 15th century); mitre in hand (Oberfrütti in Val Formazza, chapel, figure, end 15th/beg, 16th century); devil and bell (Rottenburg, Diocesan Museum, figure, end 15th century); stone hammer and ore step (St Bartholomäberg, Vorarlberg, painting, circa 1525). *Special scenes:* devil carries T, who is sitting inside the bell (Altsellen, Jodernkapelle, painting, probably 13th century). *Cycles:* Sitten Valerie Church, painting, 1596.

Theresa of Lisieux

(Theresa of the Child Jesus) Carmelite, saint

Feast-day: 1st October (before the calendar reform 3rd October)

Life: * 2nd January 1873 at Alençon in Normandy as 9th child of Louis-Joseph-Stanislas Martin and Marie-Azélle Guin; at 4 years of age lost her mother and as a child showed an unusual religious earnestness, also survived a scrupulous phase. At 15 T. tried to enter the Carmelite Convent at Lisieux, but Bishop Hugonin of Bayeux refused her; her wish was first fulfilled on 9th April 1899. Her motive was the salvation of souls; 1893 2nd Novice Mistress; on the advice of her Superior wrote her autobiography; 1896 her mortal illness began, of which T. died on 30th September 1896. – During her illness T. suffered much under a feeling of being abandoned by God, but she sacrificed her inner suffering for the salvation of souls. T. sought as a remaining reward a "Little Way" to perfection through a completely normal ascesis and documented in the picture of a wheelchair the Omnipotence of God, which can be shared by even the weakest. Beatified 29th March 1923, canonised 17th May 1925.

Patronage: World missions, Peter's Work of the Propagation of the Faith (since 1927), France (since 1944).

Representation in Art: numerous authentic photographs, otherwise artistically inferior representations: *Apparel:* as young nun in dress of the Order (Rome, Propaganda Fide, figure, 20th century). *Attributes:* book, Boy Jesus, sweat-cloth, roses (Lisieux, Carmel, figure, 20th century). *Special scenes:* in shower of roses (Munich, once in German Society for Christian Art, painting, by F. Feuerstein, 1926).

Thibault of Provence

(Thibault, Theobald) hermit, priest, Camaldolite, saint

Feast-day: 30th June

Life: * 1017 at Provence; came from the family of the Counts of Brie and Champagne. T. refused to serve in the army, secretly left his parents to go with his friend Walter to St Remy. T. and Walter settled in Pettingen (Luxembourg), earned their keep as masons and builders. Pilgrimage together to Compostela and Rome; then settled as hermits at the Camaldolite monastery at Vangadizza near to Salanigo. Abbot Peter consecrated T. as priest, 1065 take the oath of the Order , † 30th June 1066/67, two years after Walter. Canonised 1073.

Legend: Bishop Thibault of Vienne prophesied the great grace of the new-born child. – hermit Burchard revealed to T. his future life as a hermit. – T. and Walter exchange their clothes for pilgrims' tunics. – By holding on to his leg, the devil tries to prevent T. from kneeling before St James in Compostela. – Soldiers try in vain to steal T.'s body.

Patronage: beltmakers of Paris, brewers, charcoal burners, the seven crafts in Luxembourg; against fever, gout, eye diseases, fits, spells of fear, dry coughs, barrenness.

Veneration and cult sites: body buried in Vicenza, translation to Vangadice, relics also in Provence by T.'s brother Arnulf, Benedictine Abbey of St Columba near Sens and Lagny, St T. des Vignes. Special reverence also in Vicenza, Luxembourg, in the Bishoprics of Dijon, Sens, Paris, Soissons, Meaux, Trier Cathedral.

Representation in Art: *Apparel:* as bearded long haired nobleman in parade dress, riding boots, spurs (Paris, Lithography of Perrot, circa 1830); as young hunter in tunic (Commarin, figure, H. P. Wier, 1653); as knight (Provence, St-T., figure, 12th century); as priest in Mass chasuble (St-T.-en-Auxois, Priory Church, figure, circa 1310); as hermit (St-Riquier, Abbey Church, figure, circa 1520). *Attributes:* falcon, hunting pouch (Commarin, figure, H.P. Wier, 1653); book, pilgrim's staff, canteen, crooked figure of devil (Huy, Church of the Brothers of the Holy Cross, relief, 17/18th century). *Cycles:* St-T.-en-Auxois Priory Church, reliefs, circa 1320/30; St-T.-en-Auxois Priory Church, altar reliefs, circa 14th century.

Thomas

Apostle, saint

Feast-day: 3rd July (before calendar reform 1969 21st December, in Greek Rite 6th October).

Biblical testimony: T. is the nickname of the Apostle, which is correctly translated "Didymus" (= Twin) in Jo. 11:16; the real name is not given; mentioned in the list of Apostles (Mt. 10:3, Lk. 6:15, Acts 1:13). In John's Gospel speaker three times: on the news of the death of Lazarus T. also expresses his readiness for death (Jo. 16); in the departure speech of the Lord he asked: "Lord, we do not know where you are going, how shall we know the way?" (Jo. 14:5). The best known scene is T.'s doubt about the resurrection of Christ and as proof being able to place his hands in the wounds in his side (Jo. 20:24–29).

Legend: contradicting details of his later life in the tradition of the Church Fathers: Missionary journey to Persia, to the Parthians, India. Whether T. was martyred by the sword in Calamina is doubtful, for Clement of Alexandria speaks of a natural death at Heraklion. According to the apocryphal Acts of St Thomas 3rd century: T. is the twin brother of Jesus, was also a carpenter and looked very similar to Jesus. – According to the Golden Legend: At the command of Jesus T. sets off for India, where King Gundaphar is seeking the best builder in the world. – T. takes part in a wedding which a king on the way has organised and invited everyone; at the wedding is a Jewish flute player, who recognises T. as compatriot and she sings a few verses in Hebrew. – As T. listens dreamily, he is struck on the cheek by a cupbearer, who is shortly after torn by a lion, a dog brings the right hand of the deceased to the guests at table. – At this miracle the Jewess and the bridal couple are converted. – T. is to build the palace in India, but instead distributes the money to the poor, preaches and converts many to Christianity, as he wants to build a heavenly palace. – When T. is thrown into prison on the return of the king, the king's brother, who has died and been briefly brought back to life, tells of the heavenly palace built by T. – T. calls the poor together, and a luminous appearance causes all the infirm fall to the ground, but T. heals them all. – After regaining freedom, T. preachers in the interior, converts Migdonia,

the sister of King Gundophor, and Sentice, the wife of the King's friend Carsius. – After T.'s sermon, Migdonia decides to live a chaste marriage. – In order to bring her from this decision the king sends his wife to her, and she also decides on a abstinent marriage. – Carsius has T. thrown into prison; T. is tortured, but glowing plates on which he must stand do not harm him, because a spring of water comes from him. – A fiery oven, into which T. is thrown, immediately cools down. – T. is led before the King to sacrifice to idols, but the idols melt as wax. – At this the pagan priests stab him from behind with a lance.

Patronage: East Indies, Portugal, city patron of Urbino, Parma, Riga, Pontifical State; Magistrato dei sei de la Mercanzia in Florence, Thomas Islands; those ready for marriage, architects, builders, surveyors, masons, quarrymen, carpenters, theologians.

Veneration and cult sites: grave in Mailapur-Madras on the Gulf of Bengal, translation of the bones on 3rd July to Edessa, relics in Rome St Croce (finger), Ortona near Chieti, Prato Cathedral (T. Belt).

Superstition: originally the feast day was the longest night of the year; many sinister happenings are associated with T. day, unlucky day when Lucifer was cast from heaven. – 1st harsh night of the Christmas custom. – T. day serves for the investigation of the future with many customs, such as: one puts papers with numbers on them in dumplings, and bets on the number which is in the first dumpling to float out of the boiling water. – On this night one should lie the other way round in bed, then he will dream the important events of the coming year.

Representation in Art: *Apparel:* in usual Apostle's dress with long girdled tunic and pallium cloak (Arbe, Cathedral, enamel plate, 12th century); as young Apostle (Ravenna, St Vitale's, mosaic, 6th century); as bearded Apostle (Siegburg, St Servatius', Shrine of Honoratus, figure, 1183); as priest in chasuble (Wienhausen, monastery, figure, circa 1520). *Attributes:* scroll (Monreale, Cathedral, door relief, by Barisanus of Trani, 2nd half 12th century); sword (Mettlach, parish church, relic of the Cross, niello, circa 1220/30); protractor (Cologne, Wallraf-Richartz Museum, painting, by Master of Bartholomy's Altar, 1499); stone cube (Schweinfurth, St John's Church, font, relief, 1367); stone in fold of garment (Kempen, Chapel of the Holy Ghost, fresco, 13th century); lance (Wimpfen im Tal, Convent Church, figure, end 13th century); King of India forced at his feet (Chartres, Cathedral, door panel, figure, 1210/15); chalice, book (Wienhausen, monastery, figure, circa 1520); heart (Buchau am Federsee, Convent Church, relief, 2nd half 18th century). *Special scenes:* Doubt of T. in the old type: Christ lifts his hand for T., without pointing directly at the wounds (Venice, St Mark's, mosaic, 12th century), doubt of T. in the middle type: Christ lets T. touch the wounds (Munich, Bavarian State Picture Collection, painting, by S. Cantarini, 17th century); Doubt of T. in the new type: Christ puts T.'s hand in the side wound (Cologne, Wallraf-Richartz Museum, painting, by Master of Bartholomy's Altar, 1498/99); doubt of T. in isolated type: Christ and T. alone, without the rest of the disciples (Berlin, copper engraved cabinet, Great Passion by A. Dürer, 1511); doubt of T. as meeting without touching the Resurrected (Seebüll, Ada and Emil Nolde Endowment, painting, by E. Nolde, 1912); doubt of T.: T. looks at the wounds in the hands (Antwerp, Royal Museum of Fine Arts, painting, by P.P. Rubens, 1613/15); belt given by Mary to T. (Berlin-Dahlem, State Museum of Prussian Culture, painting, by M. di Banco, 14th century); belt given by Mary to T. at the coronation of Mary (Vatican City, Vatican Museum, painting, by Raffael, circa 1503); belt given by Mary to T. at the Ascension of Mary (Siena, Oratorio di Bernardino, fresco, by Sodoma, 16th century). *Martyrdom:* T. is beheaded with a sword (Stuttgart, State Library, Cod. hist 2x415, illumination, 12th century); T. is stabbed with a lance by two dark skinned servants (Esslingen, St Dionysius', stained glass, end 13th century); T. is stabbed with a lance at the altar (Vienna, Kunsthistorisches Museum, painting, by B. van Orley, circa 1515); T. is stabbed in the back with a lance (from the Martyr Apostles, wood cut sequence, by L. Cranach the Elder, 1512). *Cycles:* numerous, include Wienhausen Monastery, carpet picture, circa 1380; Vercelli Cathedral, Archivio Capitolare, illumination, end 12th century; Semur-en-Auxois Priory Church, reliefs, circa 1240/50; Bourges Cathedral, stained glass, 13th century.

Thomas Aquinas

Dominican, Doctor of the Church, saint
Feast-day: 28th January (before the calendar reform 7th March)
Life: * circa 1225 at his father's castle Roccasecca near Montecassino (County of Aquino), as 4th son of the Lombard noble Landulph and Theodora, a noblewomen from Naples. At 5 years of age Oblate in the Benedictine abbey of Montecassino, at 14 study of Aristotelian philosophy, 1243/44 requested admission to the still young Dominican Order. T. spent time in Rome, then studied further in Bologna, Naples, Paris and Cologne, pupil of Albertus Magnus. 1252–59 teacher of theology in Paris, from 1257 in College of Professors; 1260 Chief Preacher of his Order and service at the court of Pope Urban IV in Orvieto and Pope Clement IV in Viterbo; 1265 leader of the Order's Study in St Sabina in Rome and Lector Curiae with Pope Clement IV; 1269–72 again in Paris as Professor. Pope Gregory X called T. to the Council of Lyons, but 1274 T. suddenly became ill. † in the Cistercian Abbey Fossanova on 7th March 1274. – In connection with scholastics his most important works are "Summa contra gentiles", a treatment of Arabian philosophy, and the "Summa theologica", which offers a brilliant synopsis and ordering of theological details. T.'s service lies in the introduction of Aristotelism to speculative theological thought and in the synthesis of Platonic thinking and the teaching of Augustine and Aristotle, also in striving for knowledge of natural and supernatural truth in a system of theoretical knowledge. Care in setting the question, clarity of thought, logic of proof and objectivity in presentation are characteristics of T.'s works. – To his contemporaries T. was seen as an outstanding thinker, but also of loveable and mellow nature. Pope Leo XIII obliged the seminarists by making the scholarly method of T. the content of their studies. T.

also composed hymns, including the Eucharist hymn "Pange lingua" and "Lauda Sion Salvatorem", which influenced church hymns of the late Middle Ages. Canonised 1323, since 1567 Doctor of the Church.

Legend: T.'s parents want him to become Prior of the Benedictine Monastery of Montecassino; when, against the will of the family, he joins the Dominican Order instead, he is kidnapped by his brothers and held in the family castle, where he is incarcerated with a young woman in his room; T. drives the woman away with a burning log. – T. is visited by two angels who put on him a chastity belt, so that he no longer has any bodily longing for a woman. – During his studies with Albert Magnus, called "The Dumb Ox" by his study colleagues, on account of his taciturnity and corpulent figure; at this Albert Magnus says once, "This dumb ox will one day bellow, so that the whole world comes together." – When T. is sitting at the table of Louis IX of France he, who is otherwise not averse to table talk, jumps up suddenly, bangs on the table so hard that the nuts from the table fall all around the room and cries to the shocked group, "That will finish them!": T. had refuted the Manichean heresy. – During a journey by boat T. calms a storm.

Patronage: Dominicans, Catholic schools (since 1880), theologians, youth studying, pencil makers, book dealers, brewers; of chastity, against storms.

Veneration and cult sites: body in Toulouse St Stephen's, relics in Toulouse St Sernin (skull), Rome St Mary sopra Minerva (arm).

Representation in Art: *Apparel:* as Dominican in dress of the Order with habit, girdle, scapular and cap with cowl and biretta (Wismar, St George's, figure, end 15th century); with black habit and white scapular (Ingolstadt, civic hall of Maria de Victoria, figure, by J. M. Fischer, 1763); black Magister's gown over dress of the Order (Nuremberg, German National Museum, painting, by H. Pleydenwurff, 15th century); with Magister's hat, which reaches over the ears (Dortmund, Provost Church, painting, by D. Bagaert, circa 1490); as large enthroned Dominican (Leipzig, Dominican Church, figure, circa 1400); with kappa covered with stars and crosses (Ravenna, Academy of Fine Art, painting, by N. Rondinello, circa 1500). *Attributes:* inkpot, book, quill (Bern, Abegg Convent, painting, by S. Botticelli, circa 1500); shining star on breast (Aachen, St Paul's Church, figure, 1652); precious stone (Siena, St Spirito, painting, by Sodoma, circa 1500); dove of the Holy Ghost (Coblenz, Dominican Monastery, figure, 17854); angel of inspiration (Niederaltaich, Benedictine Church, drawing for a fresco, by W. A. Haindl, circa 1720); Magister's chain with sun disc (Dillingen, Study Church, fresco, by T. Scheffler, 1750/51); golden chain with sun disc (Aachen, St Paul's, figure, 1652); rosary (St Katherinental, figure, by G.A. Machein, 1738); chalice (Wismar, St George's, figure, end 15th century); chalice with Host (Palencia, Cathedral, figure, 18th century); monstrance (Baroque mediational picture); IHS monogram (Baltimore, Walters Art Gallery, ceramic plate, circa 1520); mitre trod by feet (Wismar, St George's, figure, end 15th century); staff, double cross (Maria Medingen, figure, circa 1750); model of church (Vichy, Cathedral, figure, by P. Oller, end 15th century). *Special scenes:* the temptation scene in confinement (Bruges, Church of the Redeemer, painting, by C. de Crayer, 1644); T. is girded by two angels (Budapest, Szépmüvészeti Museum, painting, by Sasetta, 15th century); night time prayer of T. with elevation (Vatican Museum, painting, by Sasetta, 15th century); T.'s service on Passion Sunday (Florence, St Maria Novella, painting, by Orcagna, 14th century); T. at the table of King Louis (Basel, Public Art Collection/Art Museum, painting, by M. Deutsch, beg. 16th century); presentation of the celebratory office on Corpus Christi to Pope Urban IV (Orvieto, Cathedral, fresco, by U. di Prete Ilario, 14th century); visit to Bonaventura (Berlin, Kaiser Frederick Museum [lost in war], painting, by F. Zurbarán, 1629); Sacra Conversatione (Venice, St Maria del Rosario, painting, by S. Ricci, 1732/34). *Cycles:* include Ávila St Thomas Aquinas, painting, by A. Berruguete, 15th century.

Thomas Becket of Canterbury

Archbishop, martyr, saint

Feast-day: 29th December (Translation feast 7th July, feast of Regressio de exilio 1st December)

Life: * in 1118 as the son of a merchant in London; educated by the Regular Canons of Merton, then study in Paris. Archbishop Theobald of Canterbury took T. into his clergy in 1141; study of church law in Bologna and Auxerre; Archdeacon of Canterbury. 1155 Lord Chancellor and intimate of King Henry II; 1162 through his patronage raised to the Archbishop's throne of Canterbury. T. began an ascetic life, wore the Benedictine habit and gave the Chancellorship back to the king. Whereas before T. set himself for the king, now he stood for the rights and privileges of the church. Conflict between king and Archbishop 1164 on the subject of limits of jurisdiction of sacred and secular judgements, 1164 flight of T. to France be-

fore court proceedings. After an apparent reconciliation 1170 return to England, there on 29th December 1170 murdered in the Cathedral at Canterbury by four noblemen from the circle of the king. Canonised 1173. King Henry reconciled himself to the church on 27th September 1172, publicly repented at the grave of the Archbishop on 12th July 1174.

Legend: T. is the son of a Saracen princess, who has come to London and marries Gilbert Becket. – In order to mock T. his horse's tail is cut off. – T. gives ring and garland to Pope Alexander III (original nucleus of the legend lay in the rejection of T.'s offer of resignation). – T. experiences an appearance of Christ.

Veneration and cult sites: relics since 1220 in valuable shrine in Canterbury with pilgrimage; 1538 shrine destroyed by King Henry VIII of England and images forbidden. Venerated in all Europe.

Representation in Art: *Apparel:* chasuble with pallium (Monreale, Cathedral, mosaic, 12th century); with mitre (Anagni, Cathedral, fresco, 12th century [destroyed]); with rational and staff (Hadleigh, Essex, figure, 13th century); as head carrier, carrying skull in calotte (Wells, Cathedral, figure, 13th century); in gown and rochett (Gurk, Cathedral, figure, circa 1630). *Attributes:* model of church (Wismar, St George's, figure, end 15th century); palm (house belonging to Wittelbach, figure, by J. Seld, 1492); sword, crosier (Gurk, Cathedral, figure, circa 1630). *Special scenes:* Expulsion and mocking of T. (Hamburg, Kunsthalle, painting, by Master Franke, 1424). *Martyrdom:* Chartres Cathedral, relief, circa 1225; Munich Bavarian National Museum, mitre, embroidery, beg. 13th century; Spoleto Sts. Giovanni e Paolo, fresco, end 12th century. *Cycles:* numerous include Sens Cathedral, stained glass, circa 1206; London British Museum, Queen Mary Psalter, illumination, 13th century.

Thomas of Lancaster Earl

saint

Feast-day: 22nd March

Life: Born circa 1278, the nephew of King Edward I was leader of the ecclesiastical party in opposition to his cousin Edward II; after a short reconciliation, open rebellion broke out between 1318 and 1321, resulting in T's defeat in Burton-on-Trent and his imprisonment in Boroughbridge; in 1322, T. was executed in Pontefract Castle in the presence of the king.

Veneration and cult sites: Immediately after his death, T. was revered as saint; when Edward II was disposed in 1327, T's cult was recognized, but he was never officially canonized; relics in Durham and All Saints, York.

Representation in Art: *Apparel:* in armour (London, British Museum Egerton MS 3510, book illumination, 15th century). *Attributes:* shield, banner with coat of arms (Oxford, Bodleian Library MS Douce 231, book illumination, 14th century). *Martyrdom:* South Newington, wall-painting, 14th century. *Cycles:* London, British Museum, pilgrim's button made of lead, relief, 14th century.

Thomas More Lord Chancellor

martyr, saint

Feast-day: 6th July

Life: Born on 7th July 1478, Thomas More at the age of thirteen joined the household of John Morton, archbishop of Canterbury, who sent him to Canterbury College, Oxford, in 1492, where T. studied classics. In 1496 he entered Lincoln's Inn and was called to the Bar in 1501. In 1504, T. entered Parliament. He was married with four children and lived in Chelsea. More had already made friends with some of the leading men of the New Learning, especially Erasmus of Rotterdam, and artists such as Hans Holbein the Younger, who regularly met at his house. After incurring the displeasure of King Henry VII, More retired from public life and returned to his studies of the classics, which he pursued in Leuwen and Paris. On the death of Henry VII in 1509, T. returned to public life and, in 1510, was promoted by King Henry VIII to Under-Sheriff of London. In 1514, T. was raised to the peerage and received further promotion: envoy to Flanders in 1516, Privy Councillor and Master of Requests in 1518 and Lord Chancellor in 1529. Throughout his life, T. had remained true to his Roman-Catholic faith, publicly speaking out against the King's hostility to the Church and intentions towards divorce. Realising the fruitlessness of his endeavours, More resigned the chancellorship in 1532 and returned to private life. In 1534, after refusing to take the oath of Supremacy to the king as "Protector and Supreme Head of the Church of England", More was committed to the Tower. After a show trial and despite his excellent defence, T. was convicted of high treason and beheaded on 6th July 1535, two weeks after Cardinal John Fisher. More was beatified in 1886 and canonized in 1935. – In the most notable of his publications, Utopia, written in Latin in 1516, More castigated the political and social conditions in Europe, imploring, as the title indicates, the creation of an ideal commonwealth.

Representation in Art: *Apparel:* in full regalia (Windsor Castle, drawing by H. Holbein the Younger, 1528). *Attributes:* scroll, chain with Tudor Rose (New York, Frick Museum, painting by H. Holbein the Younger, 1527); Tudor Rose without chain (Madrid, Prado, painting by P. P. Rubens, 17th century); cross (Knole, Kent, Lord Sackville Collection, copy of a painting by H. Holbein the Younger, 16th century). *Special scenes:* Thomas More in conversation with Huthlodaye, Aegidius and John Clement (wood cut, Utopian edition Basle, 1516). *Martyrdom:* T's farewell to his daughter Margaret Roper, and execution (Blois, museum, painting attributed to A.Caron, 1590).

Three Kings
Wise Men from the East, saints
Feast-day: 8th January, called Epiphany
Biblical testimony: according to Mt 2;1–12, Magi from the east learn from a star of the birth of a king in Judea. They are sent on to Bethlehem by Herod. With the aid of the star they find the child there and bring him gifts. Being warned of Herod in a dream, they return home a different way.
Legend: Since Origen the number of Magi is accepted as 3, corresponding to the number of gifts. The gifts are related to Christ: gold = king, frankincense = god, myrrh = doctor (doctor of souls, resurrection). Their names are given as Caspar, Melchior and Balthasar. – The Magi are baptised by the Apostle Thomas on his missionary journey. – The Magi are consecrated bishops. – Immediately after celebrating Christmas together in the year 54 they die.
Patronage: Kingdom and later Free State of Saxony, city of Cologne, travellers, pilgrims, inns, manufacturers of playing cards, furriers, riders; against witchcraft, for a good death.
Veneration and cult sites: The bones were found by the Empress Helena, brought to Constantinople and given to Bishop Eustorgius of Milan (343–355). – His successor, Protasius, brought the bodies to Milan and buried them in a sarcophagus in St Eustorgio. – In 1158, after the capture of Milan by Frederick Barbarossa, the bones were taken by Reinald of Dussel, Imperial Chancellor and Archbishop of Cologne, by way of Chur and Speyer, to Cologne, arriving on 23rd July 1164; they are kept there now in the Shrine of the Three Kings. – a part of the relics were returned to Milan in 1904 by Anton Cardinal Fischer.

Superstition: numerous customs at the time of the Winter Solstice. – On Epiphany, houses are consecrated with an inscription, on the lintel, of the year and the letters CMB joined with three crosses, probably from a previous forbidden custom of the raw winter nights. – Singing, given new life from 1950 with the new aim of collecting money for charity in the mission field and developing countries. – Whoever steals on Epiphany and is not caught may continue to steal for the whole of the following year. – All Christmas cake must be eaten before Epiphany, or bad luck will follow. – On Epiphany a prediction of love through the throwing of a shoe is popular. – On Epiphany consecrated chalk for writing the holy names can also be used to heal cattle. – The farmer's wife adds consecrated TK.'s salt, originally used in baptismal water, to the milk in the stirrer. – TK.'s salt protects from child bed fever.

Representation in Art: *Apparel:* as Orientals in Persian costume, usually trousers with belted chitons, chlamys with Phrygian caps (Ravenna, St Apollinare Nuovo, mosaic, 6th century); as Orientals with tiara (Rome, St Mary Magdalene, mosaic, before 550); as kings in royal robes with royal crowns (Amiens, St Mary's Gate, figure, 1225/36); as Burgundian kings in three stages of life (Geneva, Museum, painting, by K. Witz, 1444); two white kings, one black (Cologne, Wallraf-Richartz Museum, painting, by Master of St Severin, circa 1512/15); as representatives of the three parts of the earth: Asia, Europe, Africa (Siena, Cathedral, pulpit, figures, by N. Pisano, 1266); TK. as bishops with mitres (Cologne, Klaren Altar, painting, end 15th century); two kings as bishops with mitres, one as cardinal (Vienna, Kunsthistorisches Museum, painting, by R. Fruehauf the Elder, end 15th century). *Attributes:* staffs (Ancona, early Christian sarcophagus, relief, 4th century); palm branches (Münster, Cathedral, lintel, relief, 13th century); three iden-

tical gifts (Freiberg, Cathedral, Golden Gate, relief, circa 1230); gifts in valuable reliquaries (Cologne, Wallraf-Richartz Museum, painting, 2nd quarter 15th century); gifts in golden cups (Cologne, Wallraf-Richartz Museum, painting, by a Cologne master, circa 1460). *Special scenes:* worship of the child (Cologne, St Mary in the Capitol, door relief, 11th century); appearance of the star (Rome, St Mary Antigua, mural, 8th century); appearance of the child in the star (Ulm, Cathedral, south-west portal, relief, circa 1330); prophecy of the miraculous bird (Bern, Cathedral, stained glass, 13th century); caravan of the TK. (Milan, St Eustorgio, painting, by Balduccio da Pisa, 1346); arrival in Bethlehem (Florence, Annunziata, cloister, mural, by A. del Sarto, circa 1500); TK. before Herod (Paris, Louvre, ivory casket, 10th century); dream of the TK. (Autun, Cathedral, relief on capital, 1120/30); meeting with the Apostle Thomas in India and baptism (Pigler I, 474); TK. as city patrons of Cologne (Cologne, Cathedral, painting, by S. Lochner, circa 1440). *Cycles:* Amiens Cathedral, medallions, relief, 13th century; Ulm Cathedral, south-west portal, reliefs, circa 1330; Florence, Uffizi, painting, by G. da Fabriano, 1423.

Timothy and Titus
Companions of the Apostle Paul

Feast-day: 26th January (before the calendar reform Timothy 21st, 22nd, 24th January/Titus 26th January)

Biblical testimony: In Phil. 2:19–22 Tim. mentioned as co-worker of the Apostle Paul, probably later Bishop of Ephesus, Tit. as disciple and companion of the Apostle, probably working in Corinth, Dalmatia and Crete.

Patronage: Tit. Crete, against free thinking.

Veneration and cult sites: 356 bones of Tim. transferred to Constantinople, relics of Tit. (head) in Venice St Mark's.

Representation in Art: *Apparel:* of Tim.: in tunic (Vatican Library, gold glass, 5th century); as bishop in Mass vestments (Paris, Cluny Museum, stained glass, circa 1150). Of Tit.: (Sao Paolo, Cathedral, figure, by T. Fiedler, circa 1955).

Turibio of Mongrovejo
Bishop, saint
Feast-day: 23rd March
Life: * 16th November 1583 in Mayorga de Campos, 1575 appointed Inquisitor of Granada, 1580 Archbishop of Lima. The Provincial Council called by him became the Charter of the South American Church. † 23rd June 1606 in Lima. Beatified 1679, canonised 1726.

Patronage: Lima, Peru.

Veneration and cult sites: body in the Cathedral of Lima.

Representation in Art: *Apparel:* as Archbishop (Mayorga, figure, 18th century). *Special scenes:* T. visits natives (Piacenza, gallery of the Collection of Alberoni, painting, by S. Conca, 18th century).

U

Ulrich of Augsburg

Bishop, saint

Feast-day: 4th July

Life: * circa 890 in Augsburg as son of the Alemannian noble Hupald, later Count of Dillingen. Aged 10 went to the monastery school at St Gallen; 908/909 consecrated priest by Bishop Adalbero of Augsburg; 28th December 923 consecrated bishop by Bishop Heringer of Mainz. Showered with gifts by King Henry I. 953/54 with armed force U. supported Henry at the rebellion of his son Liutolf, but could successfully mediate in the conflict between father and son. After repeated raids by the Hungarians U. had a strong wall built around Augsburg; during the attack by the Hungarians in 955 U. led the defence of the city and sent a team under the leadership of his brother, Dietpald, to Lechfeld, through which he helped Otto I to his victory over the Hungarians on 10th August 955. 962 retreat from all worldly business. U. dedicated himself from now on to the building up of his bishopric: visitation journeys; supported monasteries such as Benediktbeuern and founded 968 the Canonical Convent of St Stephan. Circa 940 U. brought the relics of the Thebaïd Legion to Augsburg. 972 U. attempted to renounce his office and enter a monastery, but the imperial Synod would not accept his request † 4th July 973. Canonised 31st January 993 in the first formal ceremonial canonisation of a saint by Pope John XV.

Legend: On Thursday U. gives the messengers of the Bishop of Constance a piece of meat to take with them; to bring ill repute upon U. they want to show it on the Friday, but the meat has changed in a miraculous way into fish. – During high water U. and his chaplain Herewig ride through the Wertach. – At the Easter festival U. has a love potion passed round. – Two angels bring chalice and paten from the altar to the aged and infirm U. – At the blessing of the Chrisam on Maundy Thursday U. appears at the right of the Lord surrounded by rays of light.

Patronage: City and Diocese of Augsburg; weavers, dying, wine growers, vintners, fishermen, wanderers; in danger from water, against floods, against plagues of rats.

Veneration and cult sites: since 1071 burial proved in the church of St U. and Afra in Augsburg; numerous church patronages in Bavaria, Württemberg, Allgäu, Alsace, Grödner Valley, Switzerland and Belgium.

Superstition: prophetic day for weather (if it rains on U. day the grain will give poor flour). – In Swabia U.'s poem helps against adversity. – U.'s wells are a medicament against eye diseases. – U.'s keys as with Hubert's keys: burning iron against rabies.

XXI

DEXTERA DÑI PERCVSSIT INIMICVM.

Wolf Kilian fecit.

Representation in Art: *Apparel:* as bearded bishop in pontifical dress with Mass chasuble (Augsburg, St U. and Afra, copper engraving, 1187); as bishop in pontifical dress with pluvial (Blaubeuren, rear side of High Altar, painting, 1494); as rider (Augsburg, Episcopal Seminary for Priests, painting, end 17th century). *Attributes:* fish on book (Munich, St Peter's, relief, end 14th century); rats (Cologne, St Andrew's, painting, circa 1540). *Special scenes:* the transformation of meat into a fish (Augsburg, State Painting Collection, painting, by H. Holbein the Elder, 1512); U. rides through the flooding Wertach (Stuttgart, State Library, Cod 2x58, illumination, 12th century); an angel presents U. with the victory garland in the battle on the Lechfeld (Augsburg, Cathedral, U.'s Cross, relief, by J. Seld, 1494); the battle on the Lechfeld (Zell near Eggenfelden, painting, 18th century). *Cycles:* Augsburg St U., Lenten Cloth, embroidery, 12th century; Kaufbeuren Blasius' Chapel, painting, circa 1485; Augsburg St U., painting, by Master of St U.'s Legend, 1453/55.

Urban I

Pope, saint

Feast-day: 25th May

Life: Urban reigned 222–230.

Legend: U. baptises Valerian, the bridegroom of St Cecilia. – U. buries St Cecilia. – U. overthrows idols, which kill 22 sacrificing priests. – U. and his companions are beheaded. – U. instructs the clergy that the chalice and paten are to be made from silver or gold.

Patronage: In Germany due to the correlation of the feast day with the end of the ordering of the vineyards, since 13th century patron of vintners (presumably carried over from Bishop Urban of Langers [5th century] to Pope Urban), against danger of frost.

Veneration and cult sites: place of burial, whether at St Callixtus or St Praetextat in Rome is unclear, under Pope Paschalis I translation to St Cecilia 849.

Superstition: in the Middle Ages in German Law key date for the possession of the produce of vineyards. Rich customs of processions of field and petition, U.'s rides, dipping of U. figures in streams, U.'s gift (from the custom of U.'s bread) in wine and produce of Rheingau vintners to the old and sick (arisen after 1945). U.'s poem after taking of a statue of U. around in Swabia. Also prophetic day for weather: sunshine on U. day gives a good vintage.

Representation in Art: *Apparel:* as Pope in pontifical vestments with tiara (Würzburg, Main Franconian Museum, figure of the beltmakers workshop, circa 1500); as vintner with crown (Waiblingen, town museum, relief print, 1822). *Attributes:* crosier, book (Strasbourg, Cathedral, stained glass, 13th century); as bishop with mitre and crosier (Püssberg, figure, circa 1530); sword (Huckarde, figure, beg. 15th century); grape (Fuchsstadt, figure, circa 1500); grape on book (Salz near Bad Neustadt an der Saale, figure, circa 1500); bunch of grapes (Vienna, St Stephen's, painting, 15th century); grape in cup (Gumperda, figure, 15th century); grape container (Waiblingen, town museum, relief print, 1822). *Cycles:* include St U. alla Caffarella Upper Church, frescoes, 11th century (destroyed); Rome St Cecilia, frescoes, 11th century.

Ursula and Companions

Virgin, martyr, saint

Feast-day: 21st October.

Church historical background: In the choir of the U. Church in Cologne there is an inscription of the 5th century, which states that a Clement was led out of the Orient by heavenly visions, and on the basis of a vow renovated the basilica, which had been raised on the place where holy Virgins gave their blood in the name of Christ. Presumably the time of this martyrdom was the persecution under Diocletian. Although the number and names of the martyrs are missing, later liturgical calendars know of 5, 8, and 11 saints, amongst whom is a Virgin Pinnosa or Ursula. In a sermon from 8th century there are 1000, since the 10th century the reference is to 11000 Virgins. The number is presumably due to an error in transmission: the abbreviation is probably "Ursula et XI.M.V" (= Ursula and 11 virgin martyrs) and was erroneously read as "Ursula et undecim mille virgines" (= Ursula and 11 thousand virgins).

Legend: Firstly a version of the 10th century; secondly a fantastically elaborated version of 11th century: accordingly, U. was the daughter of a British king, desired as wife by the pagan king's son Aetherius, in spite of a vow of chastity. – The king threatened war in the case of her refusal, so U. asks for a respite of three years and sets as a condition the

conversion of the groom to Christianity. – U. asks her father for 10 distinguished virgins to accompany her, along with 1000 further girls and ships. – U. sails from Britain with her companions, gets into a storm and is driven into the estuary of the Waal. – From there they travel up the Rhine to Cologne. – U. and her companions receive instruction from an angel to make a pilgrimage to Rome, so they travel to Basel by ship and go the rest of the way on foot; they are greeted by Pope Cyriacus and go the same way back to Cologne. – Just then the city is being besieged by the Huns, the virgins shot down with arrows, but U. desired by the king because of her beauty. – As U. refuses she is also killed by an arrow.

Patronage: Sorbonne University in Paris, Coimbra University, Ursulines, youth, bridal couples, women teachers, cloth traders, sick children.

Veneration and cult sites: veneration of U. encouraged by the Cistercians; 1106 bones found in a Roman cemetery are seen as the bodies of St U. and her companions; characteristics of the cult include: U. ships in the representation of a spiritual cargo of pious works, as signs of brotherhood and as a picture of life as an earthly pilgrimage.

Representation in Art: *Apparel:* as young king's daughter in fine clothes, girdled, with crown over free hair (St Wallpurgen, filial Church, stained glass, 13th century); in girdled robe with narrow sleeves hanging down the front and cloak with crown (Admont Convent, Liber matutinalis, illumination, circa 1180); long undergarment, richly decorated over garment with a cloak fastened in the middle with a gusset (Cologne, St Cunibert'a, stained glass, 13th century); in long robe and well pleated cloak (Linz, parish church, mural, 13th century); in fashionable dress of the time (Cologne, Wallraf-Richartz Museum, painting, Master of St Severin, 1505/10); with veil (Frankfurt, Städel, paint-

ing, ascribed to A. Vanni, 15th century); with head dressing (Amsterdam, Empire Museum, figure, by Master of the Female Stonehead, circa 1520/30); with loose hair, without head covering (Barcelona, Museum of Catalonian Art, painting, end 13th century); in protective cloak (Cologne, St Andrew's, fresco, circa 1340); as bust reliquary (Cologne, U. Church, Golden Chamber, reliquary, end 13th century). *Attributes:* arrow (Cologne, St Cunibert's, stained glass, 13th century); several arrows (Karlsruhe, Art Hall, painting, by H. Holbein the Elder, 1522); bow and arrow (Cardona, Collegiate Church, painting, 15th century); flag of the cross as standard (Taufers, St John's, mural, 14th century); ship (Sitges, Hospital of St John the Baptist, figure, circa 1544). *Special scenes:* U. in the group of 11000 virgins (Venice, St Lazzaro, painting, by J. Tintoretto, circa 1547). *Cycles:* numerous, include Cologne, Wallraf-Richartz Museum, U. Legend, painting, by the Cologne Master of 1456, 1455/60; Cologne, Wallraf-Richartz Museum, painting, by Master of the U. Legend, 1492/96; Bruges, St John's Hospital, U.'s Shrine, painting, by H. Memling, before 1489.

Valentine of Rätien

Bishop, saint

Feast-day: 7th January

Life: was bishop in the 5th century, the diocese is not known. † probably in Mais-Meran on the Zenoberg.

Legend: corresponds to that of V. of Terni or Rome. According to the anonymous Passaviensis (12th century), V. tried three times to work in Passau, but was driven out each time and so went to South Tyrol.

Patronage: Cripples, epileptics, also taken over from Bishop V. of Terni.

Veneration and cult sites: body in Mais-Meran on the Zenoberg, there Corbianian of Freising was also buried. Bones taken to Passau by Duke Thassilo III of Bavaria St Stephen's 764. Bones raised in 1120. Pilgrimages during the Middle Ages to Kiedrich and Mertesheim, etc.

Representation in Art: normally representations of V. in bishop's garments north of the Alps refer to V. of Rätien: *Apparel:* as bishop in vestments with staff (Schwerin, Museum, figure, circa 1435). *Attributes:* epileptic at feet (Nuremberg, German National Museum, painting, by a Master of the Danube School, circa 1520). *Special scenes:* sermon of V. against the Arians (Munich, St Boniface's, painting, 19th century). *Cycles:* Augsburg State Gallery, painting, by B. Zeitblom, circa 1500.

Valentine of Rome

Priest, martyr, saint

Feast-day: 14th February

Life: Not a historical person.

Legend: The Rhetor Craton seeks doctors with his sick son. – Craton offers V. money for the healing of his son. – V. prays for the healing of the son. – Craton is baptised. – V. is beheaded in the persecution of Emperor Claudius in 269.

Veneration and cult sites: body buried on the Via Flaminia, where in the 4th century two graves of two martyrs (the priest at the 2nd milestone in the city of Rome and the Bishop of Terni at the 63rd milestone) existed. Although the Roman Martyrologium proceeds on the assumption that there were two martyrs, it could be that there was only one person, as it is said that only the basilica at the 2nd milestone was called the Basilica of V., and it is possible an endower is behind that, so that all reverence on the 14th February must be assigned to V. of Terni.

Representation in Art: representations of V. in bishop's vestments south of the Alps refer to V. of Terni, north of the Alps to V. of Rätien: *Apparel:* as priest with chasuble (Rome, St Mary Antiqua, mural, 757/67); as head carrier in dalmatic (Stuttgart, State Library, Cod. hist 2°414, illumination, 12th century). *Attributes:* palm branch (Stuttgart, State Library, Cod. hist 2°414, illumination,

12th century); sword (New York, Pierpont Morgan Library, office book of Catherine of Cleves, illumination, 15th century). *Special scenes:* V. as priest baptises St Lucilla (Bassano, museum, painting, by J. Bassano, 16th century). *Martyrdom:* V. as priest is killed by two hangmen (copper engraving by Callot, 1636).

Valentine of Terni
Bishop, martyr, saint
Feast-day: 14th February
Life: Bishop of Terni, suffered martyrdom.
Veneration and cult sites: attested in 8th century on the Via Flaminia near Terni, basilica of St V. 1605 Relics transferred to the Basilica of Terni; also in Roufach/Alsace.
Representation in Art: usually representations of V. in bishop's vestments south of the

Alps refer to V. of Terni, north of the Alps only in Roufach in Alsace. *Apparel:* as bishop in pontifical vestments (Roufach/Alsace, reliquary, figure, 15th century). *Special scenes:* V. heals the son of Craton (Venice, St Luca, painting, by J.C. Loth, 17th century). *Martyrdom:* V. is beheaded (Venice, National Marciana Library, Grimani Breviary, illumination, 12th century). *Cycles:* Bussolengo near Verona, mural, circa 1400.

Veronica
Martyr, saint
Feast-day: 27th February
Legend: propagated since 4th century in the west: one of the weeping women on Jesus Way of the Cross, by the name of V. gives Jesus a cloth to dry his face. J. presses his face on it so that an imprint remained on it. – Lat-

er V. is identified with the woman with the flow of blood (Mt. 9:20) or with Martha of Bethany. According to the Acts of Pilate: when the seriously ill Emperor Tiberius sends messengers to Jesus to ask for healing, he discovers that Pilate has executed Jesus, and in his anger has Pilate arrested. – He calls to him the woman with the flow of blood, who had Jesus' face impressed in a cloth, is healed at sight of the image and is baptised. – The cloth comes into the possession of Pope Clement (variant: in 705 it comes under the relics of St Peter). – Finally V. works as a missionary in Médoc.

Patronage: linen weavers, linen traders, washerwomen, sewers in white, advocate for a good death, helper with serious wounds, bleeding.

Veneration and cult sites: body supposedly buried in Soulac, relics in Bordeaux St Sernin. V. legend component of all Ways of the Cross.

Representation in Art: *Apparel:* as dying matron with girded robe and cloak, with wimple and headscarf (Vienna, St Stephen's, choir stalls, 15th century); as standing matron with cap and thin veil (Cologne, Wallraf-Richartz museum, painting, by Westphallian Master in Cologne, circa 1415/20). *Attributes:* cloth with the face of Christ in hands (Munich, Alte Pinakothek, painting, beg. 15th century). *Special scenes:* the healing of Tiberius by V. with the cloth (New York, Lehmann Collection, Gobelin, circa 1510); grave and shrine of St V. (Soulac, Chapter, relief, 12th century); V. meets the Cross-carrying Christ (copper engraving, by M. Schongauer, circa 1479).

Vincent Ferrér
Dominican, saint
Feast-day: 5th April
Life: * circa 1350 in Valencia; at 17 entered the Dominican monastery there; study in Lrida and Barcelona, after consecration as priest circa 1375 worked as lecturer in philosophy, from 1377 as preacher, from 1385 also teacher in the Cathedral school in Valencia. Through VF.'s friendship with Cardinal Pedro di Luna, later Pope Benedict XIII, worked at Benedict's side at the time of the Papal Schism between 1378 and 1417, until the Council of Constance, where VF. saw the election of Urban VI as forced and therefore invalid. As a result of the Papal Schism VF. believed in an imminent end of the world and thus had difficulties with his Brothers and the Inquisitor Nicolaus Eymericus 1399/1409. Preacher of repentance in Catalonia, Marseilles, on the Riviera; serious conflict with Flagellants. 1412 brought a change for VF. as the Council of Pisa elected a third Pope, and VF. was convinced that his friend Benedict XIII must resign, but his influence over him was of no effect. Only when VF. was able to bring King Ferdinand I of Aragon, in the name of the Spanish kings, to renounce obedience, was the way free for the election of a new Pope, Martin V, who sent VF. to France as a preacher of repentance. † 5th April 1419 in Vannes. Canonised 1458.

Legend: The Bishop of Valencia predicts the birth of a son to his parents. – VF. drives a devil out of a woman and speaks the exorcism over John from Nantes. – After an attempted murder two men are lamed, are converted and healed. – A lunatic dismembers her only child, which VF. raises again. – VF. raises a dead young woman in Salamanca. – VF. bans storms. – At a celebration VF. works a miracle and feeds 200 men. – VF. is able to convert lawless men in the Valley of Destruction and sun worshippers. – VF. converts men under King Mohammed Aben Baha in Granada. – VF. dresses converted Moorish princesses as nuns.

Patronage: Valencia, Vannes, lead casters, roofers, woodworkers, tile makers; against headaches, epilepsy and undetermined symptoms of illness.

Veneration and cult sites: body buried in Vannes (Britanny); veneration encouraged by Emperor Charles VI in Austria and by name in Styria; widespread in the Dominican Order.

Superstition: VF. water, blessed by Dominicans, helps to ease sickness.

Representation in Art: *Apparel:* as Dominican in dress of the Order with long girded robe, scapular, kappa with cowl (Venice, SS Giovanni e Paolo, painting, by G. Bellini, circa 1464); as Dominican in preaching gesture with angels wings (Wimpfen am Berg, Dominican Church, figure, 18th century). *Attributes:* IHS monogram on breast, lily (Trier, Welschonnen Church, figure, 18th century); flame over head (Siena, St Spirito, figure, by G. Cozzarelli, circa 1500); flame in hand (cowl (Venice, Sts. Giovanni e Paolo, painting, by G. Bellini, circa 1464); sun (Prague, Charles bridge, figure, by F.M. Brokoff, 1712); open book with text from Revelation 14:7 (Recanati, St Dominic's, painting, by L. Lotto, 16th century); open book with text from Psalms 61:8 (Sanginesio, church, painting, by P. Alemanno, 1485); Cardinal's hat at feet, indication of renounced honours (Castelvetrano, St Dominic's, painting, 15th century); trumpet (Krems, Dominican Monastery, relief, by J. Gallo, circa 1730); Satan and flaming sword (Ehrenhausen, Styria, painting, 18th century); naked child in basin (Waidhofen an der Thaya, wayside shrine, figure, 18th century); spit (Friesach, Dominican Monastery, painting, 18th century); bell (Barcelona, Cathedral, painting, 16th century). *Special scenes:* VF. raises a child (Bologna, St Dominic's, painting, by D. Creti 18th century); VF. points to Christ as judge of the world (Budapest, Szépmüvészeti Museum, painting, by A. del Verrocchio Workshop, 15th century). *Cycles:* include Vienna Kunsthistorisches Museum, painting, by B. degli

Erri, 15th century; Florence, Stibbert Museum, painting, by D. Ghirlandaio school, 16th century; Castelvetrano, St Dominic's, painting, 15th century.

Vincent de Paul

Priest, founder of Order, saint
Feast-day: 27th September
Life: * 24th April 1581 at Pouy near Dax; study in Toulouse, consecrated priest, 1604 Baccalaureate of Theology, then to Rome. The imprisonment by the Moors in 1605/07 is questionable, 1608 Paris, 1612 priest in Clichy; made a vow to dedicate his life to the poor. 1617 undertook missionary work in the country, with world priests founded a missionary congregation which called itself "Lazarists" and a society of townswomen for the care of the poor and sick, from whom the Vincentians came. V. became the organiser of Caritas in France. During the bloody uprising of the Fronde, set up people's kitchens. V. saved whole provinces from poverty. V. was with King Louis XIII at his death. V. was a friend of Francis de Sales. † 27th September 1660 in Paris. Beatification 1729, canonised 1737.

Patronage: Lazarists, Vincentians, charitable organisations and societies, hospitals, orphanages, prisoners, clergy; for recovery of lost objects.

Representation in Art: *Apparel:* in Cassock (Paris, Mother House of the Lazarists, painting, by S. François, circa 1660); in Cassock with superpelliceum (Paris, St Etienne, painting, by S. Bourdon, 1649). *Attributes:* crucifix (Rome, St Peter's, figure, by P. Bracci, 17th century); child on arm (Paris, St Julien the Poor, figure, 18th century); flaming heart, child at feet (meditational picture, engraving, by L. Zucchi, 17th century). *Special scenes:* many numerous motifs including: vision of the globe during Mass (meditational picture, engraving, 18th century); V. is

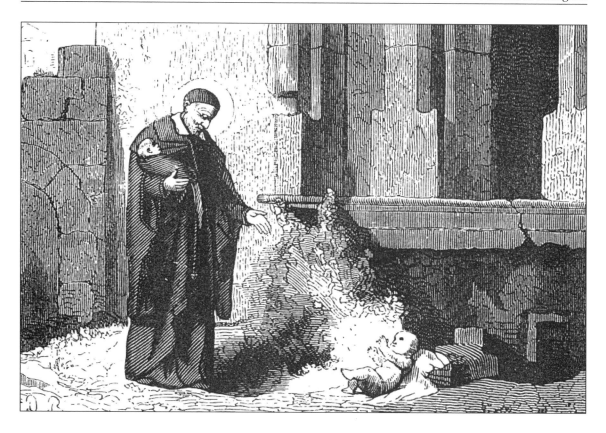

surrounded by angels during the sermon (Bergamo, St Catherine's, painting, by G. A. Petrini, 18th century); V. is appointed by King Louis XIII as Monseignior General of the galley slaves (Paris, St Margaret's, painting, by J. Restout, 18th century); V. as Monseignior General (Paris, Church of the Trinity, painting, by Lecomte de Nouy, 19th century); V. takes the place of a galley slave (Gaillac, St Michael's, painting, by F. Dufau, 19th century); F. de Sales presents V. with the Superiority over the Visitresses (Paris, St Margaret's, painting, by J. Restout, 18th century); V. gives the Visitresses a foundling child (Werl, Hospital Chapel, stained glass, by E. Lammers, 1951). All motifs collected by L. de Lanzac de Laborie, Saint V. , Paris, 1927.

Vincent of Zaragoza

Deacon, martyr, saint

Feast-day: 22nd January

Life: thrown into prison in Valencia during the persecution under Diocletian. V. was martyred in 304.

Legend: According to the Passio of Prudentius and the Legenda Aurea: V. is deacon with Bishop Valerius. – As V. can preach better than the bishop, he gives this function to V. – During the persecution V. and Valerius are incarcerated, to starve them, but they stand unmoved before the judge and refuse to sacrifice to idols (variant: V. overthrows the idols). – Valerius is exiled, V. however is tortured by being lacerated with hooks and pincers (variant: V. is stretched on a St Andrew's cross and covered in running blood). –

V. is roasted on a grid. – Brought back into prison, V. should rest on shards, but they change into soft flowers, causing the conversion of the prison warders. – V. should suffer more torments, but dies on his bed. – The body is laid in the open field and guarded by angels. – A raven drives a ravening wolf from the corpse. – The body, weighed down with a millstone, is thrown into the sea, but immediately returns to land. – Angels bury the body.

Patronage: Portugal, the vineyards of Vigneron, patron of vintners in Germany and France (because one saw erroneously in his name the word "vin" [= wine]), wine merchants in Paris, vineyard guards and protectors, wood cutters in Salzburg and Zaragoza, roofers, potters, French weavers, tile makers, seamen.

Veneration and cult sites: bones in Valencia, tunic relic since 531 placed by King Childebert I in Paris St Chapelle as matching piece to the cloak of St Martin.

Superstition: prediction day for weather, because with sunshine on V. day the wine flourished especially well; market day and dance festivals; also counted as the day of the birds' marriage.

Representation in Art: *Apparel:* in phaenula with orant gesture (Rome, Pontian Catacombs, fresco, 6/7th century); as deacon of the Byzantine Rite (Cefalù, Cathedral, mosaic, 12th century); as deacon of the Latin Rite in dalmatic (Rouen, St V. stained glass, 1525). *Attributes:* censor (Cefalù, Cathedral, mosaic, 12th century); book (Wroclav, Cathedral, painting, 1468); millstone (Wismar, St George's, figure, 15th century); prison tower, angel (Abeida, Huesca, painting, end 15th century); hoop (Lübeck, Hospital of the Holy Ghost, painting, end 15th century); raven at feet (Chartres, Cathedral, south portal, figure, 1215); ship (Belém, St Jerome's Church, figure, by N. Chanterene, 1517); two ravens on the ship (Montefalco, St Fran-

cis', painting, by A. Romano 15th [?] century); fiery hooks (Heiligenblut, figure, 1520); chain (Greenville, South Carolina, Collection of Bob Jones University, painting, by F. Goya, 18th century); St Andrew's cross (Barcelona, Museum of Catalonian Art, painting, by B. Martorell, 15th century); Moor at feet (Washington, Hispanic Society of America, figure, 14th century); grid (Wroclav, Cathedral, relief, 1591); staff with three barbs (New York, Pierpont Morgan Library, office book of Catherine of Cleves, illumination, 15th century); twig with flowers (Slavetin, Bohemia, mural, 16th century); mattock (Hallstatt, St Mary's Altar, figure, by Master Astl, circa 1515). *Martyrdom:* V. is hung from a beam and lacerated (Stuttgart, State Library, Cod. hist 2x54, illumination, 12th century); V. is roasted on the grid (Berz-la-Ville, mural, 12th century). *Cycles:* include Galliano near Como St V. mural, circa 1007; Bern Historical Museum, carpet, 1515; Barcelona Museum of Catalonian Art, painting, by J. Huguet, 1456/60.

Vitus

(Veit) Martyr, Helper in Need, saint
Feast-day: 15th June
Life: as person mentioned in the Martyrologium Hieronymianum circa 430.
Legend: * in Sicily as son of pagan parents; his father, Hylas, will use all means to bring V. away from the Christian faith. – V. is taken away by the Prefect Valerius. – When the executioners want to strike him their arms go lame. – V. heals the withered hand of the judge. – the father at home sees seven angels standing around his son. – The father is blinded by the supernatural light from the angels. – The blindness is not healed by the sacrifice of a bull to Jupiter. – At the command of the angel V. flees with his tutor, Modestus, and his nurse, Crescentia, to a distant

land. – An eagle brings food to the fugitives. – V. drives out a devil from one possessed before the Emperor Diocletian, because the devil had declared, he would only give way to V. – V. then refuses to sacrifice to idols. – An angel releases the chains of Modestus, Crescentia and V. – V. is thrown into a glowing furnace 'variant: cauldron of boiling oil', from which he climbs out unharmed. – V. tames a wild lion. – During a further torture the earth quakes ; the temple collapses. – In anger the Emperor feels himself to be overcome by a child. – An angel takes away V., Modestus and Crescentia to their home, where they die in peace.

Patronage: Imperial house of Saxony, Sicily, Bohemia, Pomerania, Saxony, Island of Rügen, Corvey, Ellwangen, Höxter, Krems, Mönchengladbach, Prague; youth, copper and cauldron smiths, brewers, actors, vintners, apothecaries, miners; for protection of chastity, against sleeping long, possession, frenzy, cripples, lame, deaf, dumb, blind, eye diseases, epilepsy ("St Vitus' dance"), dancing mania, hysteria, children's cramps, bedwetting, barrenness, dog bite, snake bite, lightening, storm, danger of fire, earthquake, sowing and harvest, hens, pets, dogs.

Veneration and cult sites: bones in Lucania, Sicily since 583, 756 brought by Abbot Fulrad to St Denis', 836 transferred to Corvey by Abbot Hilduin, Corvey gave Wenceslas of Bohemia an arm for Prague as a relic, for which St Vitus' was built. Charles IV also obtained for Prague relics once found in Pavia. Specially revered on the Island of Reichenau, in St Gallen, Bavaria, Carinthia, Friaul, 150 further places with relics; 1300 church patronages show the popularity of St V.

Superstition: before the Gregorian calendar reform V. day was mid-summer's day, popular market day, V. fire in the place of St John's fire. Numerous folk medicinal cures to heal St Vitus' dance.

Saints of monastic orders II

75 *St Dominic as founder of the Holy Inquisition, by Pedro Berreguette, Escorial, Spain*

76 *St Thomas Aquinas and St Dominic beside the Mother of God, Escorial, Spain*

77 *St Margaret of Hungary, woodcut, Esztergom, Hungary, Christian Museum*

78 *Tomb of St Ignatius of Loyola, Rome, Il Gesù*

79 *Miracle of St Francis Xavier, by Peter Paul Rubens, Vienna, Kunsthistorisches Museum*

80 *Ecstasy of St Theresa of Avila, by G. Bernini, Rome, S. Maria della Vittoria*

81 *Shrine of St Theresa of Lisieux, Lisieux, France*

82 *St Conrad of Parzham, silver figure, Altötting, Germany, Gnadenkapelle*

75

76

SEL. BRUDER KONRAD
BITTE FÜR UNS!

Representation in Art: *Apparel*: as boy in long, distinguished clothes, curled, long hair, cap (Nuremberg, German National Museum, painting, by H. Burgkmair, 1505); in half length, girded under-garment and cloak (Rottweil, St Lawrence's Chapel, figure, by J. Syrlin the Younger, circa 1500); in short, girded robe with cloak, (Vierzehnheiligen, figure, by J. M. Feichmayr, 1764); as knight in armour (St Goar, Lutheran Church, mural, 1475); as naked boy in cauldron (Schwaz, Tyrol, Miner's Chapel, figure, 16th century); as naked boy in cauldron with cap (Krems, Museum, figure, 1525); in ermine cloak with crown (Zelina, Bohemia, painting, 1526). *Attributes*: palm, sword (St Goar, Lutheran Church, mural, 1475); book (Eichstätt, Episcopal Chapel, figure, circa 1500); cockerel (Hirschaid, parish church St V., figure, circa 1750); hanging lamp (Schwaz/Tyrol, Miner's Chapel, figure, 16th century); cauldron by V.

(Morzg-Salzburg, figure, end 17th century); cockerel on pillar (Prague, St V., figure, circa 1700); cauldron in hand (Junkenhofen, figure, 15/16th century); Raven (Sünninghausen near Beckum, figure, 15th century); bird (Saretano, painting, by A. Niccolò, 15th century); lion, furnace, stick (Wismar, St George's, choir stalls, relief, 15th century); model of church (Mönchengladbach-Hardt, St Nicholas', figure, 1720/30); lion's head, hanging bag (Corvey, Monastery Church, figure, 18th century); oil lamp (Landsberg, parish church, figure, 15th century). *Martyrdom*: V., Modestus and Crescentia are martyred in a cauldron of boiling oil (Nuremberg, German National Museum, painting, 1487). *Cycles*: numerous including Wasenweiler Cemetery Chapel, mural, circa 1470; Morzg-Salzburg, painting, circa 1480; Vienna Austrian Gallery in Belvedere, painting, by Master of the Vitus Legend, circa 1480.

W

Walburga

Abbess, saint

Feast-day: 25th February

Life: * circa 710 as the daughter of Richard of England, sister of the saints Willibald and Wunibald of Eichstätt; educated in the convent of Wimborne near Bournemouth, together with St Lioba. On the wish of her uncle Boniface, she was sent out as a missionary into the mission field, worked first under Lioba in Tauberbischofsheim, from 751/52 in the double cloister of Heidenheim, where W. took over as leader after Wunibald's death in 761. † 25th February 779.

Legends: The devil arouses a storm at sea, which dies down at W.'s prayer. – When W. comes to Heidenheim, a divine light shines over the cloister. – W. heals the daughter of the lord of the castle and walks across the drawbridge without the dogs attacking her. – When W.'s bones are transported into the Cathedral in Eichstätt, the horses stop, by the Chapel of the Cross, so the body is laid to rest there.

Patronage: Diocese of Eichstätt, Oudenaarde, Belgium; farmers, peasants; for the prospering of fruits of the field, pets, against dog bites, rabies.

Veneration and cult sites: bones placed on 1st May 870 in the Convent Church of St W. at Eichstätt, so-called Myrophore, because oil comes out of the grave, which is drawn off into flasks. Since 893 relics in the nunnery at Monheim, Furnes, west Belgium, Walberberg, near Bonn (skull and staff), Walburg (Alsace), Lamberg near Cham, Ehrenbürg near Forchheim, Alfen, Wormbach, Scheer, Danube, Walburgisberg near Weschnitz, Chapel of the place of Recovery at Heilsbach near Schönau (Palatinate) (since 1983). Numerous church patronages in Franconia, Bavaria and Flanders. Pilgrimage in Eichstätt.

Superstition: Walpurgis Night or Witches' Night, on which the witches do their mischief on the Blocksberg in the Harz Mountains, originate in German ideas and has no connection with St W. other than her name.

Representation in Art: *Apparel:* as a Benedictine nun in wide sleeved woollen garment, with wimple and veil (Münster, State Museum, painting, circa 1170); in princely dress, long undergarment, shorter overgarment and closed cloak with slits for sleeves (Darmstadt, Hessen State Museum, painting, 15th century); in state robes with princely hat (formerly Boppard, Kloster Marienberg; now Cologne, private possession, painting, circa 1410); in chasuble-like cloak, long undergarment, long veil (Stuttgart, Sta-

DEUS AUTEM INCRE- MENTUM DEDIT

Io! eXVLtet! IVbIILet fLOREAT sVb Ioanne antonIo II. s.r.I. prInCIpe et epIsCopo MILLenarIa eVstettensIs eCCLesIa!

te Library, double martryology, illumination, 12th century); as Abbess with crown and staff (Eichstätt, St W.'s, tomb, figure, 15th century); as a wise maiden (Münster, State Museum, painting, by Master of the Fröndenberg Altar, circa 1420). *Attributes:* sceptre (Eichstätt, St W.'s, votive picture, 18th century); book (Münster, State Museum, painting, circa 1170); palm branch (Darmstadt, State Library, Hitde Cod. illumination, 11th century); burning lamp (Münster, State Museum, painting, by Master of the Frönberg Altar, circa 1420); apple (Eichstätt, St W.'s, figure, 11th century); large crown (Walburgskirchen, Lower Bavaria, figure, circa 1460); oil flask (Eichstätt, Cathedral, figure, end of 15th century); flowering branch in three parts (Regensburg, Cathedral, stained glass, 14th century); flower sceptre (Eichstätt, St W.'s, Luitger Chalice, enamel, 14th century); lily sceptre, ears of corn (Nuremberg, German National Museum, painting, by S. Lochner, 15th century); three ears of corn (Kisslegg, St Anna's, figure, 18th century); lily stem (Ulm, City Museum, painting, by F.A. Maulpertsch, circa 1749). *Special scenes:* St W.'s ship miracle (Leipzig, Museum of the Pictorial Arts, painting, by P.P. Rubens, circa 1610); translation of St W.'s relics (Eichstätt, St W.'s tomb, painting, 18th century); Charlemagne receives the relics for Furnes (Turin, Pinacoteca, painting, by B. of Orley, 16th century). *Cycles:* Maihingen, tapestry, circa 1455; Munich Bavarian State Library, Clm. 19 162, pen and ink drawings, 15th (?) century; Heilsbach near Schönau/Palatinate, painted Solnhof slate, by C. Winkler, 1983 (extensive and iconographically interesting, artistically unpretentious cycle).

Waldetrudis

(Waltraud, Waudru, Audru) Abbess in Mons, saint

Feast-day: 9th April

Life: * as daughter of the nobleman Walbert, sister of Saint Adelgundis, married to Vinzenz Madelgar and mother of four children, On her advice each of the children founded a cloister, she herself building a cloister in Castrilocus, the later "St Waudru" in Mons, Belgium. After the children moved away, she separated from her husband, who was likewise a founder of cloisters. In Mons W. took the veil of a nun from Bishop Autbert of Cambrai, eventually Abbess. † circa 688.

Veneration and cult sites: body laid to rest in Mons, elevation of the bones circa 1250; head contained in a special reliquary, that since 1349 is carried alongside other relics on Trinity Sunday in a splendid procession

through the town in a state coach. – After the Norman Invasion a Benedictine Abbey developed out of the cloister, later transformed into a convent of regular Augustinian Choir Women, eventually secular Augustinian Choir Ladies.

Representation in Art: *Apparel:* as a girl without veil with short cloak (Temse, Notre-Dame, relief, by P. Nijs, 1750); as noblewoman in state dress and rich jewellery around neck (Soignies, St Vincent Madelgaire, figure, 1715); as young Abbess in secular (!) dress (Gent, Augustinian Church of St Stephen, relief, 17th century); as Abbess with staff and book (Herentals, St Waudru, painting, circa, 1585); model of church (Antwerp, Museum Vleeshuis, figure, 16 century); model of church of Mons (Bruges, Museum Gruuthuse, stained glass, 17th century); as heavily veiled nun with girdle of the Order (Innsbruck, Silver Chapel, figure, by S. Godl, 16th century); with fashionable veil and small crown (Herentals, St Waudru, figure, end 17th century); in protective cloak spread over her daughters (Mons, Collection of Madame Marcel le Tellier, illumination, 2nd half 15th century). *Attributes:* daughters at her feet (Mons, Collection of Madame Marcel le Tellier, illumination, 2nd half 15th century); daughters in dress of the Order with book and palm branch, W. with staff and book (Herentals, St Waudru, painting, circa 1585); rosary (Ohain, St Stephen's, figure, 1759); chalice (Anderlecht, St Pierre et St Guidon, Grave of Ditmar, relief 1439). *Special scenes:* W. comes to England by ship (Brussels, Royal Library, Chroniques de Hainaut des Jacques Guise, illumination, 1455/68); W. with her daughters supervises the building of a cloister (Mons, St Waudru, relief, by J. Dubroeucq, circa 1540); W. receives a visit from Adelgundis (Moorsel, St Gudule, painting, by A. Blanckaert, 1661); the nuns invoke W.'s protection (Mons, St Waudru, painting, 1658).

Wenceslas

(Vaclav) duke, martyr, saint

Feast-day: 28th September

Life: * circa 903/905 in Altbunzlau of the family of Premysliden as the eldest son of Duke Wratislas and his wife Drahomira. Brought up under the influence of Ludmilla. After the death of his father in 921, his mother exercised the regency for her young son. Drahomira was filled with a deep hatred of Ludmilla and had her strangled. After taking over the regency in 922 W. had a complete change of life to have a great sense of righteousness. W. strived for the Christianisation of the land and leaned politically toward the German Empire and the Roman Church. In a pagan-nationalist revolt in 929 or 935, W. was murdered by his brother Boreslaw.

Legend: W. cuts down a gallows. – W. works as a labourer in a vineyard, sows, mows and threshes grain himself and bakes the Host, which he brings to the church. – W. singlehandedly brings wood for the poor and is mishandled unknowingly in the woods. – Through the sign of the Cross W. defeats the pagan Prince Radislas in a duel (variant: an angel intervenes and defeats Radislas with the Cross). – W. is led by angels at the Reichstag at Worms, when he is invited to be received by the German Emperor Otto, who gives him relics of St Vitus and St Sigismund for the new St Vitus' Cathedral. – After W.'s murder the blood cannot be washed away.

Patronage: National saint of the Czechs, Bohemia, helper in battle for the Bohemian army.

Veneration and cult sites: shortly after the murder rehabilitation and burial in St Vitus' in Prague resulted; tumulus cult rapidly spread to be the Bohemian national cult, venerated in Germany since 10th century; cult propagated by Emperor Charles IV as Imperial Saint. Relics in Prague St Vitus' Cathedral (helmet, armour, lance).

Representation in Art: *Apparel:* as beardless youth in narrow leggings, half length robe, widening from the thighs down, with white sleeves (Stuttgart, double Passional, illumination, 12th century); as bearded king in armour with duke's hat (Prague, St Vitus' Cathedral, figure, by P. Parler, 1373); as knight in plate armour (Vienna, St Stephen's, figure, end 15th century); as armoured rider (Prague, W. Square, figure, by J. Myslbek, 1904); as armoured knight with cloak and duke's hat (Wroclav, Corpus Christi Church, painting, 1497); with Elector's hat (Aachen, Minster, W. Altar, painting, 1387/1400); with helmet and armour (Erfurt, St Lawrence's, figure, 1445); with crown and armour (Vienna, St Stephen's, figure, late 15th century). *Attributes:* sword, lance, shield (Nuremberg, Frauenkirche, figure, late 14th centusry); eagle shield, lance with wimple (Wroclav, Corpus Christi Church, painting, 1497); sceptre, orb (Vienna, Austrian National Library, Cod. 370, pen drawing, 14th century); grape, press (Bardowieck, choir stalls, relief, 15th century); instruments of war (Tepl, Convent Museum, figure, 18th century); Mercy Image of the Madonna of Star Boleslaw (Prague, University, Thesis page of the Faculty of Philosophy, copper engraving, by J. J. Heintsch and B. Kilian, 1695). *Special scenes:* Christ crowns W. with the duke's helmet (Wolfenbüttel, Library, illumination, end 10th century). *Martyrdom:* Prague St Vitus' Cathedral, painting, by L. Cranach circle, 1543. *Cycles:* include Burg Karlstein, stairwell, mural, end 14th century; Prague St Vitus' Cathedral, mural, circa 1548.

Wendelin

(Wendalin, Wendel) hermit, saint
Feast-day: 20th October
Life: lived as hermit at the time of the Trier Bishop Magnerich, circa 570, in the woody mountains of the Vosges.
Legend: W. is born as a Scots-Irish prince. W. has settled down, following a pilgrimage to Rome, as a hermit and herdsman in Saarland. – W. in the service of a rapacious master, drives the cattle to a mountain seven miles distant, where he likes to pray, about which his master is angry, because the animals are destined for the table and cannot arrive at his court at the right time; but when the master has returned, W. has already arrived with his herd. – Frightened by that, the master builds him a cell near to a neighbouring cloister – The monks of the cloister of Tholey make W. their Abbot. – When W. has died, the body lies beside the grave the next day; they take this as a sign, put oxen, which had never before been harnessed, to a cart and let them pull it with the body; these bring W. to the mountain at which he prayed; the town of St Wendel towers there today.
Patronage: farmers, herdsmen, peasants, shepherds, for pasture and cattle, against cattle plagues.

Veneration and cult sites: body in the church of St W., 1360 transferred to the choir of the new church; the high grave came into being in the first half of the 15th century; characteristic folk healer with widespread reverence in the Alemannian and Franconian regions, through emigrants also in America, Hungary, and in Banat.

Representation in Art: *Apparel:* as monk in habit (St Wendel, parish church, figure, 14th century); as hermit (Kirchheim, figure, 16th century); as pilgrim with hat (Zellhausen, figure, circa 1500); as shepherd boy in breeches, boots, short jerkin (Saarbrücken, private possession, painting, by M. Schiestl, beg. 20th century); as young shepherd (Oberwesel, St Martin's, painting, circa 1450); as shepherd in hooded cloak (Reutlingen, parish church, figure, circa 1500); a bearded shepherd (Hurlach, figure, 17th century); as shepherd boy in peasant dress (Mönchsberg, parish church, figure, 18th century); as shepherd (Vierzehnheiligen, pilgrimage church, figure, by J.M. Feichtmair, 1764); as Abbot (Hatzenbühl, Palatinate, figure, 18th century); as bishop (Colpach, Luxembourg, figure, 18th century). *Attributes:* open book (Kleinheubach, Lutheran Church, mural, 15th century); closed book (St Wendel, parish church, grave tomb, relief, 14th century); staff, shell, horn (Rothenburg o.T., St Wolfgang the Shepherd's Church, figure, circa 1500); rosary (Nuremberg, German National Museum, figure, circa 1520); crown (Münstermaifeld, Convent Church, painting, 15th century); winnow (Pilgrimage Church Birnau, figure, by J. A. Feuchtmayr, 18th century); club, shepherd's purse (Frankfurt, Städel, painting, by H. Baldung-Grien, 1525); sheep and cow at feet (Miltenberg, parish church, relief, circa 1500); bugle, purse, pigs (Lautenbach, Alsace, relief, circa 1500); sheep (Hilzhofen, relief, 16th century); a sheep at feet (Riezlern, relief, 16th century); sheep leaping (Siessen, Saulgau, W.'s Chapel, figure, 1780); cow at feet (Niederburg, Upper Palatinate, figure, 18th century). *Cycles:* Nussbach (Baden) W.'s Chapel, mural, 15th century; Stalden near Zug W.'s Chapel, painting, circa 1700.

Wilgefortis

(Kummerus, Ontkommer, Kümmernis, St Gwer, Hülpe [Help], Liberatrix, Eutropia, Caritas) deleted as saint

Feast-day: formerly 20th July

Ecclesiastical history: when nobody understood the portrait of the crucified Christ in long precious clothes as a heavenly king, like Volto Santo in Lucca, a bizarre but regionally different legend developed. In the Martyrologium Romana listed as Wilgefortis (1506).

Legends: originate from minstrel poems for the bride of King Oswald of Northumbria. W., a pagan Portuguese princess, refuses all pagan princes because she has engaged herself to Christ – Mary and holy virgins appear

to W. – Her father orders W'.s imprisonment. At her request, Christ transformed her face with a beard. – W. is tortured with a fork and torches. – Her father orders her crucifixion (var: W. is banished into the wilderness). – From her cross, W. throws her golden shoe to a poor minstrel.

Veneration and cult sites: the Netherlands, Northern France, areas on the North and Baltic Sea, Rhineland, Franconia, Bohemia, Bavaria, Tyrol, Switzerland, South-East Spain.

Representation in Art: *Apparel:* as bearded virgin in long dress at the cross (Ghent, University Library, ms 2750, book illustration, early 16th century); in fashionable, baroque women's clothes (Axams, S Liberata, painting, 19th century); with crown (Seligenstadt, Einhard Basilica, fig., 15th century); with crown of thorns (Horst, fig., 1st half of the 16th century); as virgin without beard (Vienna, Art History Museum, dalmatic of the vestments of the Golden Fleece, weaving, circa 1440). *Attributes:* cross on arm (Bruges, St John's Hospital, painting by H. Memling, 1480); shoe (St Florian, Collegiate Gallery, painting, late 17th century); palm branch (Au, Hallertau, painting by G. B. Götz, 18th century). *Special scenes:* W. at the cross, with her father (Aschaffenburg, Castle Library, Perg. Man. 3.4, book illustration, circa 1400); C. with a suitor (Rostock, S Nikolai, mural painting, 15th century); W. and the minstrel (Bad Tölz, Museum, painting, 1690); Christ appears to W.on the cross (Brno, St Thomas, painting by J. G. Hensch, 1687. *Cycles:* Eltersdorf, Church, painting, 1513; Bevegen, East Flanders, painting, 1912.

William of Malavalle

Hermit, saint

Feast-day: 10th February

Life: 1153 W. withdrew himself as a hermit to the island of Lupavicio near Pisa, 1155

B. GVILELMVS PEREGRINVS.

went to a barren valley Malavalle near Castiglione. † 10th February 1157. 1202 confirmation of the cult. His disciples formed the Hermit Congregation, the Williamites, whose Rule was approved by Gregory IX.

Legend: W. has a boisterous youth and in a sudden change draws penitent's dress over the armour, helmet and chain which he has had made, goes on a pilgrimage of nine years to Rome and the Holy Land, and to Santiago di Compostela. – Only motive: W. is sent by the Pope to dissolve his excommunication for the sins of his youth to the Patriarch of Jerusalem. – W. distributes his possessions among the poor. – W. has a chain shirt for penitence made. – W. receives communion from St Bernhard of Clairvaux. – W. receives from the Monks in the wilderness the Augustinian habit. – A sick girl is healed through bread blessed by W. – W. is beaten by demons. – The Mother of God appears to W. with two virgins and heals his wounds.

Patronage: the Williamites

Veneration and cult sites: body in Castiglione di Pescara; head in the Dominican Convent Frankfurt/Main, then in the Jesuit Church in Antwerp; veneration in Malavalle and the Benedictine monastery Monte Fabali.

Representation in Art: *Apparel:* as hermit in cowl (Pisa, Civic Museum, painting, by G. di Jacopone, 1391); as hermit in chain shirt under cowl (Florence, St Apollonia, painting, by N. di Bicci, 15th century); as monk in habit of the Order (Orvieto, St Lawrence's, fresco, 14th century); in chain shirt forged onto the upper arm, helmet and barefoot (Freiburg, Augustinian Museum, relief, 15/16th century); in monk's dress over armour (Frankfurt, Städel, painting, by H. Baldung-Grien, circa 1520); in full armour with cowl and helmet (Nuremberg, German National Museum, painting, circa 1520); as pilgrim (Strasbourg, St W.'s, stained glass, 15th century); in armour with pilgrim's dress (Hoogstraten, St Catherine's Church, stained glass, circa 1530). *Attributes:* T. staff, iron bands over head covering, book (Pisa, Civic Museum, painting, by G. di Jacopone, 1391); standing on a dragon (Empoli, Museum, painting, by P. Francesco Fiorentino, 1474); T. staff with half-moon as grip (Frankfurt, Städel, painting, by H. Baldung-Grien, circa 1520); rosary, shield with lilies (Freiburg, Augustinian Museum, relief, 15/16th century). *Special scenes:* W. as penitent bound to a tree (Vienna, Kunsthistorisches Museum, painting, by S. Rosa, 17th century); the forging of the chain shirt (Strasbourg, St W. relief, 15th century); the healing of W. by the Mother of God (Rome, St Agostino's, painting, by G. Lanfranco, 17th century). *Cycles:* include Strasbourg, St W.'s, stained glass, 15th century; private possession, copper engraving, by A. Collaert, circa 1600 with false designation of the saint (W. of Aquitaine!).

Willibrord

(Clement) Benedictine, bishop, saint

Feast-day: 7th November

Life: * 658 in Northumbria; as a child given by his parents to the Scottish monks at the monastery of Ripon near York to be educated, which shortly afterwards took the Benedictine Rule under Abbot Wilfrith. In connection with the conflict between Wilfrith and Theodore of Canterbury, Wilfrith went in 678 to Frisia and W. to Ireland into the monastery of Ratmelsigi, there consecrated priest. 690 entry to the Frisian mission, whereby W. put himself under the protection of the Frank authorities and had his area of work designated by Pepin; 692 further commissioned by Pope Sergius, 695 consecrated bishop in Rome and addition of the Roman name Clement. W. erected the Cathedral in Utrecht, 698 founding of the monastery in Echternach. With the death of Pepin 714 the support for W. collapsed; new field in Thuringia, but first in 719 under Charles Martell and Boniface renewed missionary activity. † 7th November 739 in Echternach.

Legend: W. is supposed to have taken 30 boys from Schleswig-Holstein into Franconia in order to bring them up as Christians. – On the feast of St Wilgils, W. multiplies the wine in a miraculous way.

Patronage: church province of the Netherlands, Dioceses of Utrecht, Harlem, patron of the land of Luxembourg, the towns of Echternach, Deurne, Oss, Vlaardingen; bakers in Nijmegen, innkeepers in Amsterdam; against childhood diseases, epilepsy, skin diseases.

Veneration and cult sites: buried in Echternach, venerated in Belgium, Germany, the Netherlands where W. Sunday is celebrated throughout the land; spring procession in Echternach on Whit Tuesday; among the Old Catholics.

Superstition: W. water consecrated accord-

ing to a special formula in the Rituale Romanum, helps against the so-called "wild fire", also water that has been drawn from particular W. wells.

Representation in Art: *Apparel:* as bishop in pontifical vestments with Mass Chasuble and pallium (Nuremberg, German National Museum, book covering Cod. Aureus, relief, 983/991); as bishop in pluvial (Bruges, Museum Groeninge, painting, by L. Blondeel, 1574). *Attributes:* mitre, staff (Xanten, St Victor's, stained glass, 1535); child on book (Echternach, Basilica, bell, relief, 1512); child kneeling on book on floor (Lauterborn, Castle Chapel, painting, circa 1629); crosier, model of church (Amersfoort, Old Catholic Seminary, embroidery, circa 1520); model of Utrecht Cathedral (Huissen, Church of the Ascension of Mary, painting, by J. Bijlert, [destroyed], circa 1650); barrel with crosier inside (Bruges, Museum Groeningen, Altar Table of St George, painting, beg. 16th century); barrel with child (Longuich, St Maxim, figure, 18th century); two wine pitchers (Huissen, Church of the Ascension of Mary, painting, by J. Bijlert [destroyed], circa 1650); canteen (Wulpen, pilgrimage flag, applied copper engraving, 1657); spring (Gouda, St John the Baptist, painting, by J.F. Verzijl, 1639); well (Amsterdam, Imperial Museum, embroidery, circa 1510). *Special scenes:* W. meets Pepin (Geijsteren, Castle, fresco, 1660); W. destroys an idol (Amsterdam, St Francis Xavier, painting, by J. Collaert, 1621); W. receives Charles Martell in Echternach (Echternach, Basilica, painting, circa 1640); W. brings forth a fresh water spring in Heiloo (Heiloo, parish church, painting,

1631); W. blesses the Echternach Spring Procession (Echternach, Basilica, painting, by A. Stevens, 1604). *Cycles:* include; Kortrijk St Mary's, Counts' Chapel, relief, circa 1374; Utrecht Archbishops' Museum, embroidery, circa 1510; Echternach, stained glass, by A. Wendling 1937–39.

Winefride of Holywell

(Wenefreda, Wenefred, Winifred, Gwenfrewi) Welsh virgin, martyr, saint

Feast-day: 3rd November

Life: W. was born in North Wales of a noble family and, according to a later Life, became a nun and the abbess of the nunnery at Holywell. D. circa 650.

Legends: At her prayers as a child, W. is carried to Christ by angels. – Her father, Theudith, gives W. into the care of monk Beuno. – W. refuses the attentions of Prince Caradoc, the son of King Alane. – Caradoc strikes off W's head. – Beuno takes Caradoc to task, who is struck dead. – Beuno raises W. from the dead by joining her head and body. – Witnesses to the miracle are converted and baptized. – A fountain springs up where W's head touches the ground. – Beuno sails to Ireland leaving his chasuble behind, which is thrown into the fountain by W. and follows Beuno across the sea. – On the death of Beuno, abbot Eleri takes W. to the cloister at Gwytherin founded by his mother, Theonia. – W. becomes its abbess.

Veneration and cult sites: W's grave is assumed to be in Gwytherin, Denbighshire (now Clwyd); relics translated to the abbey of SS Peter and Paul, Shrewsbury, in 1137/38.

Representation in Art: *Apparel:* as nun in the Benedictine habit (Oxford, St John's College MS 94, book illumination, circa 1420); as crowned nun (Warwick, Beauchamp chapel, stained glass, 1447); in contemporary, modern garments (Hampton Court chapel, stained glass, circa 1421/1429). *Attributes:*

sword (Oxford, St John's College MS 94, book illumination, circa 1420); crosier (Oxford, Bodleian Library MS Auct.D infra 2.II, book illumination, circa 1430/1440); palm branch (Cambridge, Fitzwilliam Museum MS J. 57, book illumination, circa 1490); block with severed head at feet (Westminster Abbey, Henry VII's chapel, figure, early 16th century). *Special scenes:* W. flies before Caradoc (New York, Pierpont Morgan Library MS M 105.m, book illumination). *Martyrdom:* Shrewsbury, abbey of SS Peter and Paul, seal relief, late 15th century. *Cycles:* Paris, Bibliothèque Nationale Lat 17294, book illumination, circa 1424/25.

Wolfgang of Regensburg

Benedictine, bishop, saint

Feast-day: 31st October

Life: * circa 924 in Pfullingen as son of free but not very prosperous parents; attended the monastery school in Reichenau, together with his schoolfriend Henry in the Cathedral School of Würzburg, where W.'s uncle Poppo was Bishop and Chancellor. From 956 teacher at the Cathedral School and deacon of the Cathedral in Trier, where his friend Henry was bishop. 964 called to the Imperial Chancellery in Cologne; declined a bishop's throne and 965 entered the Benedictine monastery at Einsiedeln. After being consecrated priest by Bishop Ulrich of Augsburg 971 attempt to carry out missionary work in Hungary. End of 972 appointed Bishop of Regensburg by Emperor Otto II; 973 W. gave the agreement for Prague to be raised to a Suffragen of Mainz; distributed the wealth between the monastery of St Emmeram and the Bishop's seat, by appointing Ramwold independent Abbot of St Emmeram; major reform of the monasteries, introduction of the Benedictine Rule to the Canon Convents of the Upper and Lower Minsters of Regens-

RITUALE
RATISBONENSE
ROMANO
ACCOMMODA
TUM.

ARMA EPISCOPATUS RATISBONENSIS

S.RUPERTUS   S.WULFGANGUS   S.EMERAMUS   S.ERHARDUS

burg, introduction of the rule of the "Chrodegang" for Cathedral Clergy. W. was the tutor of the children of the Bavarian Duke Henry the Quarrelsome. Because W. remained true to Emperor Otto at the rebellion of Henry, he had to leave Regensburg and flee to a private monastery of Regensburg at Mondsee, Upper Austria in 976/77. † 31st October 994 in Pupping near Eferding. Canonised 1052.

Legend: According to the Vitae of Arnold and Otlohs in 11th century: W.'s mother thought she was carrying a star in her body, when she conceived W. – When W. wanted to introduce a strict Rule into the Upper Minster, St Erhard appeared to support him in garments wet with in tears on account of the bad condition of the monastery. – During a Mass of W. the relics on the altar move around as a sign for stricter discipline in the Or-

der. – W. frees a lady from an evil spirit while he sings psalms. – W. calms a storm, which the Devil had raised to disturb the sermon. – W. heals a possessed woman in the church, while the chaplain secretly observes. – W. frees a man of anorexia through the Eucharist – W. revives his favourite pupil Tagino, when he had been hit by lightning. – W. heals a knight who had suddenly become infirm after defaming W. – W. frees a man from fetters on one hand, while St Adalbert does the same on the other hand at the request of W. – When the messenger, who is to announce W.'s confirmation journey, has his horse stolen, a replacement suddenly appears. – W. can see into the future, as he addresses the children of the Bavarian duke by their future titles. – W. lives the life of a hermit for one year in heat and cold, then settles at Abersee on the Falkenstein. – W. causes a spring to appear for thirsty Brothers. – When the devil tries to crush W. between two rocks W. leans with outstretched arms in the form of the cross on the mountain; the impression remains in the rock. – W. throws a hatchet from the peak of the mountain into the depths, so that he can build a chapel at the place where it lands, on the shore of the Abersee, from where W. can see the W. Lake. – the Devil must help W. as a horse and receives as wages the first pilgrim, a wolf, which the Devil in anger tears apart in the air. – When W. sleeps too long, he wants to hit his hands and feet against a stone as penitence, but they are soft as dough. – After 5 years in solitude W. is discovered by a hunter and brought back to Regensburg; when the small church wants to follow he commands it to stay in place. – St Otmar predicts his death 22 years after being raised to bishop. – W. informs Henry, later German Emperor, with the words "post sex" in a vision. While H. thinks he will die after six years, it really meant that he would be crowned German Emperor after six years.

Patronage: Bavaria, Hungary, Canton Zug, City and Bishopric of Regensburg; wood carvers, shepherds, wood cutters, colliers, sailors, carpenters; against gout, stomach ache, bleeding, lameness, dysentery, stroke, barrenness, miscarriages.

Veneration and cult sites: bones 1052 ceremonially raised by Pope Leo IX, laid in Regensburg St Emmeram, relics in Pupping (heart, intestines, since 1467); pilgrimages to St W. on Abersee (W. See), St W. am Stein (Upper Austria) Zelen Lhota (Bohemia), Chudenitz, Footprints Chapel; veneration with pilgrimage to Abersee from Sopron (Hungary).

Representation in Art: *Apparel:* as bishop in pontifical vestments with Mass chasuble (Regensburg, St Emmeram, grave, figure, 14th century); as bishop with pluvial (Kefermarkt, W. Altar, figure 1491/98); as bishop in non-liturgical dress with Cassock, rochett, mozetta and mitre (Jochberg, Tyrol, fresco, 18th century); as Benedictine in habit of the Order (Reichenau, parish manse, painting. 1729). *Attributes:* hatchet (Mondsee, Urbar, illumination, 1416); axe (Lautenbach, Baden, parish church, figure, 1510/20); model of church (St Wolfgang, figure, by M. Pacher, 1471/81); hatchet in roof of church (Eggenfelden, figure, end 15th century). *Special scenes:* W. crosses the Aisne (Düdingen, Switzerland, painting, 16th century); W. distributes corn to the poor (St Wolfgang am W. See, parish church, painting, by M. Pacher, 1471/81); the Devil holds the Mass book for W. (Munich, Alte Pinakothek, painting, by M. Pacher, 1475/80); the "Post Sex" vision of Henry by W. (Regensburg, St Emmeram, painting, by Selpelius, 1658); W. as helper of a wounded Bavarian duke (Munich, Bavarian National Museum, painting, end 15th century). *Cycles:* include St Wolfgang parish church, painting, by M. Pacher, 1471/81; St Wolfgang, painting, 18th century; Allersberg parish church, painting, circa 1730; Linz Upper Austrian Museum, Wolfgang box, painting, 18th century; Ochsenfurt, painting, 18th century.

Z

Zeno of Verona
Bishop, saint
Feast-day: 12th April
Life: presumably Z. came from Africa; was bishop in Verona from 362; † 12th April 371/72. Z.'s importance lay in his fight with Arianism and the return of paganism. – Z.'s writings, around 93 tracts, are mostly sketchy drafts for the exposition of the Holy Scriptures, baptism, the Doctrine of the Trinity and Mariology. The language is trained on the apologetic authors, such as Lactantius, Tertullian or Cyprian.
Legend: Messengers from the Emperor come to Z. while fishing. – Z. heals a possessed driver and brings the passing vehicle to a standstill. – Z. heals the daughter of Gallienus, for which Gallienus gives Z. a crown. – Z. frees Verona from danger of flood. – During a flood in Verona no water comes into the burial church.
Patronage: Verona, Pistoia, water patron.
Veneration and cult sites: a church stands over the grave in Verona; relics brought by Rhabanus Maurus to Fulda, Ulm, from there to Radolfszell. Centre of veneration the Zenoberg near Mais-Meran; the cult of Z. came to Isen through Corbinian; early attestation in the two Regensburg Sacraments.
Representation in Art: *Apparel:* as bishop in pontifical dress with chasuble (Reichenhall, St Z. relief, 13th century); as bishop in pontifical dress with pluvial (Schwaz, miner's Chapel, figure, 16th century). *Attributes:* fish on bishop's staff (Verona, St Z. figure, circa 1300); fish grommet (Munich, Georgianum, figure, 13th century); two fish on book (Reichenhall, St Z., choir stalls, figure, circa 1520); two fish on fish box (Schwaz, miner's Chapel, figure, 16th century); angling rod with fish (Milan, Brera, painting, by F. Morone, 1502). *Special scenes:* Z. heals the daughter of Gallienus (London, National Gallery, painting, by Peselino, 15th century); Z. gives the banner to riders and footmen of Verona (Verona, St Z. relief, by Master Nikolaus, circa 1135). *Cycles:* Verona St Z. main portal, reliefs, circa 1100.